THE CONTINENTAL LEGAL HISTORY SERIES

Published under the auspices of the

ASSOCIATION OF AMERICAN LAW SCHOOLS

A HISTORY OF CONTINENTAL CRIMINAL LAW

BY

CARL LUDWIG VON BAR

LATE PROFESSOR OF LAW IN THE UNIVERSITY OF GÖTTINGEN

AND OTHERS

TRANSLATED BY

THOMAS S. BELL

OF THE LOS ANGELES BAR

AND OTHERS

WITH AN EDITORIAL PREFACE BY

JOHN H. WIGMORE

PROFESSOR OF LAW IN NORTHWESTERN UNIVERSITY

AND INTRODUCTIONS BY

WILLIAM RENWICK RIDDELL

JUDGE OF THE HIGH COURT OF JUSTICE FOR ONTARIO

AND BY

EDWIN R. KEEDY

PROFESSOR OF LAW IN THE UNIVERSITY OF PENNSYLVANIA

THE LAWBOOK EXCHANGE, LTD.

Clark, New Jersey

ISBN 978-1-58477-013-8

Lawbook Exchange edition 1999, 2018

The quality of this reprint is equivalent to the quality of the original work.

THE LAWBOOK EXCHANGE, LTD.
33 Terminal Avenue
Clark, New Jersey 07066-1321

Please see our website for a selection of our other publications and fine facsimile reprints of classic works of legal history:
www.lawbookexchange.com

Library of Congress Cataloging-in-Publication Data

Bar, L. v. (Ludwig von), 1836-1913.
[Geschichte des deutschen strafrechts. English]
A history of continental criminal law / by Carl Ludwig von Bar and others ; translated by Thomas S. Bell and others ; with an editorial preface by John H. Wigmore ; and introductions by William Renwick Riddell and by Edwin R. Keedy.
p. cm.
Originally published: Boston : Little, Brown, 1916. (Continental legal history series ; v. 6).
Includes bibliographical references and index.
ISBN 1-58477-013-9 (cloth : acid-free paper)
1. Criminal law—History. 2. Criminal law—Europe— History. I. Title.
K5032 .B3713 1999
345'.009—dc21 99-32341
CIP

Printed in the United States of America on acid-free paper

THE CONTINENTAL LEGAL HISTORY SERIES

Published under the auspices of the

ASSOCIATION OF AMERICAN LAW SCHOOLS

A HISTORY OF CONTINENTAL CRIMINAL LAW

BY

CARL LUDWIG von BAR

LATE PROFESSOR OF LAW IN THE UNIVERSITY OF GÖTTINGEN

AND OTHERS

TRANSLATED BY

THOMAS S. BELL

OF THE LOS ANGELES BAR

AND OTHERS

WITH AN EDITORIAL PREFACE BY

JOHN H. WIGMORE

PROFESSOR OF LAW IN NORTHWESTERN UNIVERSITY

AND INTRODUCTIONS BY

WILLIAM RENWICK RIDDELL

JUDGE OF THE HIGH COURT OF JUSTICE FOR ONTARIO

AND BY

EDWIN R. KEEDY

PROFESSOR OF LAW IN THE UNIVERSITY OF PENNSYLVANIA

BOSTON

LITTLE, BROWN, AND COMPANY

1916

EDITORIAL COMMITTEE

OF THE

ASSOCIATION OF AMERICAN LAW SCHOOLS

JOSEPH H. DRAKE, Professor of Law in the University of Michigan.

ERNST FREUND, Professor of Law in the University of Chicago.

ERNEST G. LORENZEN, Professor of Law in the University of Minnesota.

WM. E. MIKELL, Professor of Law in the University of Pennsylvania.

JOHN H. WIGMORE, *Chairman*, Professor of Law in Northwestern University.

LIST OF TRANSLATORS

THOMAS S. BELL, of the Los Angeles Bar.

JAMES W. GARNER, Professor in the University of Illinois.

RAPELJE HOWELL, of the New York Bar.

JOHN LISLE, of the Philadelphia Bar.

ERNEST G. LORENZEN, of the Editorial Committee.

ROBERT W. MILLAR, of the Chicago Bar, Professor of Law in Northwestern University.

FRANCIS S. PHILBRICK, of the New York Bar.

LAYTON B. REGISTER, Lecturer on Law in the University of Pennsylvania.

JOHN SIMPSON, of New York.

JOHN WALGREN, of the Chicago Bar.

JOHN H. WIGMORE, of the Editorial Committee.

I might instance in other professions the obligation men lie under of applying themselves to certain parts of History; and I can hardly forbear doing it in that of the Law, — in its nature the noblest and most beneficial to mankind, in its abuse and debasement the most sordid and the most pernicious. A lawyer now is nothing more (I speak of ninety-nine in a hundred at least), to use some of Tully's words, "nisi leguleius quidem cautus, et acutus praeco actionum, cantor formularum, auceps syllabarum." But there have been lawyers that were orators, philosophers, historians: there have been Bacons and Clarendons. There will be none such any more, till in some better age true ambition, or the love of fame, prevails over avarice; and till men find leisure and encouragement to prepare themselves for the exercise of this profession, by climbing up to the vantage ground (so my Lord Bacon calls it) of Science, instead of grovelling all their lives below, in a mean but gainful application of all the little arts of chicane. Till this happen, the profession of the law will scarce deserve to be ranked among the learned professions. And whenever it happens, one of the vantage grounds to which men must climb, is Metaphysical, and the other, Historical Knowledge. HENRY ST. JOHN, Viscount BOLINGBROKE, *Letters on the Study of History* (1739).

Whoever brings a fruitful idea to any branch of knowledge, or rends the veil that seems to sever one portion from another, his name is written in the Book among the builders of the Temple. For an English lawyer it is hardly too much to say that the methods which Oxford invited Sir Henry Maine to demonstrate, in this chair of Historical and Comparative Jurisprudence, have revolutionised our legal history and largely transformed our current text-books. — Sir FREDERICK POLLOCK, Bart., *The History of Comparative Jurisprudence* (Farewell Lecture at the University of Oxford, 1903).

No piece of History is true when set apart to itself, divorced and isolated. It is part of an intricately pieced whole, and must needs be put in its place in the netted scheme of events, to receive its true color and estimation. We are all partners in a common undertaking, — the illumination of the thoughts and actions of men as associated in society, the life of the human spirit in this familiar theatre of coöperative effort in which we play, so changed from age to age, and yet so much the same throughout the hurrying centuries. The day for synthesis has come. No one of us can safely go forward without it. — WOODROW WILSON, *The Variety and Unity of History* (Address at the World's Congress of Arts and Science, St. Louis, 1904).

A lawyer without history or literature is a mechanic, a mere working mason; if he possesses some knowledge of these, he may venture to call himself an architect.—Sir WALTER SCOTT, "*Guy Mannering,*" c. XXXVII.

CONTINENTAL LEGAL HISTORY SERIES

GENERAL INTRODUCTION TO THE SERIES

"ALL history," said the lamented master Maitland, in a memorable epigram, "is but a seamless web; and he who endeavors to tell but a piece of it must feel that his first sentence tears the fabric."

This seamless web of our own legal history unites us inseparably to the history of Western and Southern Europe. Our main interest must naturally center on deciphering the pattern which lies directly before us, — that of the Anglo-American law. But in tracing the warp and woof of its structure we are brought inevitably into a larger field of vision. The story of Western Continental Law is made up, in the last analysis, of two great movements, racial and intellectual. One is the Germanic migrations, planting a solid growth of Germanic custom everywhere, from Danzig to Sicily, from London to Vienna. The other is the posthumous power of Roman law, forever resisting, struggling, and coalescing with the other. A thousand detailed combinations, of varied types, are developed, and a dozen distinct systems now survive in independence. But the result is that no one of them can be fully understood without surveying and tracing the whole.

Even insular England cannot escape from the web. For, in the first place, all its racial threads — Saxons, Danes, Normans — were but extensions of the same Germanic warp and woof that was making the law in France, Germany, Scandinavia, Netherlands, Austria, Switzerland, Northern Italy, and Spain. And, in the next place, its legal culture was never without some of the same intellectual influence of Roman law which was so thoroughly overspreading the Continental peoples. There is thus, on the one hand, scarcely a doctrine or rule in our own system which cannot be definitely and profitably traced back, in comparison, till we come to the point of divergence, where we once shared it in common with them. And, on the other hand, there is, during all the intervening centuries, a more or less constant juristic sociability (if it may be so called) between Anglo-American and Continental Law; and its reciprocal influences make the story one and inseparable. In short, there is a tangled common ancestry, racial or intellectual, for the law of all Western Europe and ourselves.

For the sake of legal science, this story should now become a familiar one to all who are studious to know the history of our own law. The time is ripe. During the last thirty years European scholars have placed the history of their law on the footing of modern critical and philosophical research. And to-day, among ourselves, we find a marked widening of view and a vigorous interest in the comparison of other peoples' legal institutions. To the satisfying of that interest in the present field, the only obstacle is the lack of adequate materials in the English language.

That the spirit of the times encourages and demands the study of Continental Legal History and all useful aids to it was pointed out in a memorial presented at the annual meeting of the Association of American Law Schools in August, 1909:

> "The recent spread of interest in Comparative Law in general is notable. The Comparative Law Bureau of the American Bar Association; the Pan-American Scientific Congress; the American Institute of Criminal Law and Criminology; the Civic Federation Conference on Uniform Legislation; the International Congress of History; the libraries' accessions in foreign law, — the work of these and other movements touches at various points the bodies of Continental law. Such activities serve to remind us constantly that we have in English no histories of Continental law. To pay any attention at all to Continental law means that its history must be more or less considered. Each of these countries has its own legal system and its own legal history. Yet the law of the Continent was never so foreign to English as the English law was foreign to Continental jurisprudence. It is merely maintaining the best traditions of our own legal literature if we plead for a continued study of Continental legal history.
>
> "We believe that a better acquaintance with the results of modern scholarship in that field will bring out new points of contact and throw new light upon the development of our own law. Moreover, the present-day movements for codification, and for the reconstruction of many departments of the law, make it highly desirable that our profession should be well informed as to the history of the nineteenth century on the Continent in its great measures of law reform and codification.
>
> "For these reasons we believe that the thoughtful American lawyers and students should have at their disposal translations of some of the best works in Continental legal history."

And the following resolution was then adopted unanimously by the Association:

"That a committee of five be appointed, on Translations of Continental Legal History, with authority to arrange for the translation and publication of suitable works."

The Editorial Committee, then appointed, spent two years in studying the field, making selections, and arranging for translations. It resolved to treat the undertaking as a whole; and to co-ordinate the series as to (1) periods, (2) countries, and (3) topics, so as to give the most adequate survey within the space-limits available.

(1) As to *periods*, the Committee resolved to include modern times, as well as early and mediæval periods; for in usefulness and importance they were not less imperative in their claim upon our attention. Each volume, then, was not to be merely a valuable torso, lacking important epochs of development; but was to exhibit the history from early to modern times.

(2) As to *countries*, the Committee fixed upon France, Germany, and Italy as the central fields, leaving the history in other countries to be touched so far as might be incidentally possible. Spain would have been included as a fourth; but no suitable book was in existence; the unanimous opinion of competent scholars is that a suitable history of Spanish law has not yet been written.

(3) As to *topics*, the Committee accepted the usual Continental divisions of Civil (or Private), Commercial, Criminal, Procedural, and Public Law, and endeavored to include all five. But to represent these five fields under each principal country would not only exceed the inevitable space-limits, but would also duplicate much common ground. Hence, the grouping of the individual volumes was arranged partly by topics and partly by countries, as follows:

Commercial Law, Criminal Law, Civil Procedure, and Criminal Procedure, were allotted each a volume; in this volume the basis was to be the general European history of early and mediæval times, with special reference to one chief country (France or Germany) for the later periods, and with an excursus on another chief country. Then the Civil (or Private) Law of France and of Germany was given a volume each. To Italy was then given a volume covering all five parts of the field. For Public Law (the subject least related in history to our own), a volume was given to France, where the common starting point with England, and the later divergences, have unusual importance for the history of our courts and legal methods. Finally, two volumes were allotted to general surveys indispensable for viewing the connection of parts. Of these, an introductory volume deals with Sources, Literature, and General Movements, — in short, the external history of the law, as the Continentals call it (corresponding to the aspects covered by Book I of Sir F. Pollock and Professor F. W. Maitland's "History of the English Law before Edward I"); and a final volume analyzes the specific features, in the evolution of doctrine, common to all the modern systems.

Needless to say, a Series thus co-ordinated, and precisely suited for our own needs, was not easy to construct out of materials written by Continental scholars for Continental needs. The Committee hopes that due allowance will be made for the difficulties here encountered. But it is convinced that the ideal of a co-ordinated Series, which should collate and fairly cover the various fields as a connected whole, is a correct one; and the endeavor to achieve it will sufficiently explain the choice of the particular materials that have been used.

It remains to acknowledge the Committee's indebtedness to all those who have made this Series possible.

To numerous scholarly advisers in many European universities the Committee is indebted for valuable suggestions towards choice of the works to be translated. Fortified by this advice, the Committee is confident that the authors of these volumes represent the highest scholarship, the latest research, and the widest repute, among European legal historians. And here the Committee desires also to express its indebtedness to Elbert H. Gary, Esq., of New York City, for his ample provision of materials for legal science in the Gary Library of Continental Law (in Northwestern University). In the researches of preparation for this Series, those materials were found indispensable.

To the authors the Committee is grateful for their willing co-operation in allowing this use of their works. Without exception, their consent has been cheerfully accorded in the interest of legal science.

To the publishers the Committee expresses its appreciation for the cordial interest shown in a class of literature so important to the higher interests of the profession.

To the translators, the Committee acknowledges a particular gratitude. The accomplishments, legal and linguistic, needed for a task of this sort are indeed exacting; and suitable translators are here no less needful and no more numerous than suitable authors. The Committee, on behalf of our profession, acknowledges to them a special debt for their cordial services on behalf of legal science, and commends them to the readers of these volumes with the reminder that without their labors this Series would have been a fruitless dream.

So the Committee, satisfied with the privilege of having introduced these authors and their translators to the public, retires from the scene, bespeaking for the Series the interest of lawyers and historians alike.

THE EDITORIAL COMMITTEE.

A HISTORY OF CONTINENTAL CRIMINAL LAW

CONTENTS

PART I

GENERAL HISTORY OF THE CRIMINAL LAW

TITLE I

THE ROMAN AND THE GERMANIC ELEMENTS

CHAPTER I

THE ROMAN LAW

CHAPTER II

PRIMITIVE GERMANIC CRIMINAL LAW

TITLE II

THE MIDDLE AGES

CHAPTER III

THE CHRISTIAN CHURCH'S LAW

CHAPTER IV

MEDIEVAL GERMANIC LAW

CHAPTER V

SCANDINAVIA AND SWITZERLAND IN THE LATER MIDDLE AGES

A. Scandinavia

B. Switzerland

CHAPTER VI

FRANCE IN THE LATER MIDDLE AGES

TITLE III

THE RENASCENCE, THE REFORMATION, AND THE 1700 s

CHAPTER VII

GERMANY'S RECEPTION OF THE ROMAN LAW IN THE EARLY 1500 s

CHAPTER VIII

GERMANY IN THE LATE 1500 s AND THE 1600 s

CHAPTER IX

GERMANY IN THE 1700 s

CHAPTER X

FRANCE, FROM THE 1500 s TO THE REVOLUTION

CHAPTER XI

OTHER COUNTRIES IN THE 1500 s–1700 s

A. Scandinavia

B. SWITZERLAND

C. NETHERLANDS

TITLE IV

THE FRENCH REVOLUTIONARY PERIOD

CHAPTER XII

THE FRENCH REVOLUTIONARY REFORMS

CHAPTER XIII

THE GERMAN REFORMS OF THE FRENCH REVOLUTIONARY PERIOD

TITLE V

MODERN TIMES

CHAPTER XIV

THE FRENCH CODE OF 1810, AND FRANCE IN THE 1800 s

CHAPTER XV

GERMANY SINCE 1813

CHAPTER XVI

OTHER COUNTRIES SINCE 1800

A. Austria

B. Netherlands and Belgium

C. Scandinavia

D. Switzerland

PART II

HISTORY OF THE THEORIES OF CRIMINAL LAW

CHAPTER I

ANCIENT GREECE AND ROME

CHAPTER II

THE PHILOSOPHY OF CRIMINAL LAW IN THE MIDDLE AGES

CHAPTER III

CRIMINAL THEORIES FROM GROTIUS TO ROUSSEAU

CHAPTER IV

CRIMINAL THEORIES FROM BECCARÍA TO FEUERBACH

CHAPTER V

CRIMINAL THEORIES FROM BENTHAM TO HERBART

CHAPTER VI

CRIMINAL THEORIES IN GERMANY FROM HEGEL TO BINDING

APPENDIX

EDITORIAL PREFACE

By JOHN HENRY WIGMORE[1]

It is a little curious that the history of the criminal law has been so scantily expounded by scholars, — scantily, that is, in relation to the other parts of the law. Of public law in general, there are histories enough. Of the civil law, there is an abundance of histories, alike for the particular doctrines and for the entire system, in summary and in extended detail, and for almost every country of the Continent. And a history of the sources of the law is still more popular in its attraction; most of the so-called histories of Spanish law, for example, include nothing beyond this part of the field. But the criminal law has remained largely without patronage.

One might speculate over this lack. The field is vast; yet the others are vaster. The criminal law is younger, — that is, it separates distinctly from civil or private law at a period much less than a thousand years ago; yet this should only make it more tempting. There is in criminal law less of generic principle continuously developing in definite traceable changes, and thus less logical interest; yet this, while it may repel some minds, ought to attract others.

Perhaps it is the miscellaneous breadth of the subject which has warned off all but the most courageous. For the history of the criminal law is partly also the history of crime itself, *i.e.* the history of social conditions and habits infinitely changing; and is partly the history of certain large moral attitudes involving the traits of whole epochs, — intent, moral responsibility, family and feudal solidarity, pardon, purposes and modes of repression and

[1] Professor of the Law of Torts and of Evidence in Northwestern University; former President of the American Institute of Criminal Law and Criminology; Chairman of the Editorial Committee for this Series.

punishment, methods of trial. To disentangle and trace all the aspects and details of modern criminal law in their development amidst the congeries of law, morals, religion, and custom in successive past epochs, is a huge and delicate task, which might well make the boldest historian halt.

For an example, take the penalty of imprisonment. When there were no prisons, this mode of punishment or repression would of course be non-existent. And the prison as a mode of punishment is a fairly modern device. But how can we to-day conceive of penal law without prisons? And so here we are plunged at once into the history of ideas of penal law, of social conditions, of judicial methods, in different communities.

Take again, the crime of forgery. In the days before the rise of the seal — that is, before the 1200 s — the monkish forgeries of parchment title-deeds formed one of the most extensive of crimes. Upon the rise of the seal, this crime takes on a new aspect. Three centuries later, with the spread of printing and the familiarity with writing, the setting of the crime shifts again. And in the nineteenth century, in the United States, the universal upspringing of local banks and a private bank-note currency, brings into existence on a large scale a variety of forgery before unknown anywhere. And finally, with the suppression of State banks and the institution of a Federal detective force, this crime almost disappears from practice within two generations, while the law remains on the books as a dry enactment, signifying little in the development of ideas. And (to pursue another aspect of the same crime) the contrast between the notarial system of the Continent and its non-existence in England and America, and between the administrative systems of the same countries, has left its mark in radical differences of the legal definition of the crime of falsification of documents, — differences so important that in more than one modern instance the terms of extradition treaties have proved futile.

Take one more instance, the related crimes of robbery and larceny. Different systems and different epochs have varied widely in defining the legal scope of the Commandment. The Romans punished most rigorously open violence, and were lenient with surreptitious larceny; while the early Germans strictly penalized secret theft, but cared little or nothing to repress robbery. The explanation must be sought in the traditions and temper of these peoples.

Without such a background, the history of the criminal law may degenerate into a mere catalogue of penalties and definitions. And this simply antiquarian treatment of it characterizes the earlier historians. Only in very modern times — presumably as a part of the evolutionary view of history — has the method changed. Of the few histories, those worth reading to-day are fewer. Perhaps we do not realize as we should that in Sir James Fitzjames Stephen's "History of the English Criminal Law" and Mr. L. Owen Pike's "History of Crime in England", taken in combination, we possess an account such as no other single country possesses, — except perhaps Italy.

An ideal history of the criminal law should cover three fields: first, the history of *criminal law in general*, — its moral and political ideas, its legislative movements, its general legal doctrines, and its penal methods; secondly, the history of *specific crimes* as defined by the law; and thirdly, the history of *crime* itself, — its practices, methods, and causes. But no such ideal history exists in print, — nor in prospect for some time to come. What we do find is a very few good histories of the first sort, for the separate countries; a few inadequate accounts of the second sort; and a few good accounts of the third sort, — of which Mr. Pike's is the best and the only comprehensive and notable one.

Of the first sort, Professor von Bar's history, here translated, is perfect of its kind, and is the only one for Germany. Moreover, it supplies incidentally many details of the second and the third sort of histories. It has so large a scope, beginning with Roman criminal law, and tracing the amalgamation of Germanic and Roman law under successive influences to modern times — that it serves well, with supplementary chapters for other countries, as a history of Continental criminal law. — For France, there is no adequate modern volume. Du Boys' history (published in 1874), though sound in scholarship, is on the older lines. Glasson's chapters in his eight-volume "History of French Law and Institutions" (unfinished at his death in 1907) carry the story only to the 1500 s; Stein's "History of French Criminal Law" only to the 1700 s. None of the other general histories cover the criminal law. — For Italy, the splendid general histories of modern scholars give adequate space to criminal law. That of Calisse is translated as a part of Vol. VII of this Series, "History of Italian Law"; the plan of this Series required that alignment. Italy has been the home of most of the new movements in criminal law; and the history of its criminal law will serve as the proper prelude to the present volume. — For Spain, no history of the criminal law has been published, not even as a part of a work in general history; except Du Boys' "History of Criminal Law on Spain" (published in French in 1872, and later translated into Spanish in 1874), which is of the older type. — For Scandinavia, Denmark is well provided in the general histories by Stemann (here used) and Matzen; the former of these dates in 1871, the latter in 1893–7; but the late Professor Matzen's work, though a most distinguished piece of modern scholarship, is in its treatment unsuitable for the present purpose. Norway has no history of its own, on this subject, but is adequately covered by the Danish works. Sweden has no work of its own.[1] — For Switzerland, Pfenninger's "Swiss Criminal Law" is mainly historical, and its chapters have here been drawn upon. — For Austria, von Bar's treatise supplies a full understanding. — For the Netherlands, G. A. Van Hamel's "Introduction to the Dutch Criminal Law" contains a short history (here used); no other modern account has been published. — For the Continent as a whole, needless to say, no other history is in print.[2] But a brilliant beginning has been made in Makarewicz's "Introduction to the Philosophy of Criminal Law on Historical Principles" (1906). This work covers only the leading ideas of criminal law from its beginning in primitive communities, with some attention to modern survivals and to specific crimes; but does not follow out the successive stages of each one in completion, nor trace the general movements of legislation. It is an earnest of the great possibilities

[1] Jaakko Forsmann's "Föreläsningar (Anteckningar) öfver straffrättens allmänna läror" (Helsingfors, 1900), and "Föreläsningar öfver de särskilda brotten", parts I–III (left unfinished at the author's death) begins each chapter with a brief historical survey of the topic, but does not offer a connected systematic treatment; moreover, it deals primarily with Finland's law.

[2] Albert Du Boys had indeed planned the work on a large and worthy scale. His "Histoire du droit criminel des peuples anciens" (1845), stopping at the Christian era, was followed by his "Histoire du droit criminel des peuples modernes" (1854–1860); Volume I for the Teutonic period, Volume II for the feudal period, Volume III for England. Then came his "Histoire du droit criminel de l'Espagne" (1870), and "Histoire du droit criminel de la France, XVIme–XIXme siècle, comparé avec celui de l'Italie, de l'Allemagne, et de l'Angleterre" (1874, 2 vols.). But his method was behind the times, even then; and the undertaking was beyond his powers. The great conception and the forty years' toil were for us fruitless. And this futility of it gives us a sentiment of sadness as we read his farewell preface, in which he announces the termination of his task, "un plan si vaste, que parfois il nous a semblé être au dessus de nos forces."

of the subject when treated by a master hand; and we may hope that its author will end by producing a systematic treatise including all aspects of the subject.

Of histories of the second sort — specific crimes — no complete modern treatise exists for any country, much less for the whole of the western Continent; though each of the above-mentioned works contains naturally more or less of this material. There are, however, two works from which one may, if in need, piece together a fairly connected account of the history of specific criminal definitions: S. Mayer's "History of Criminal Law from the time of Moses, Solon, etc., to the Present Day",[1] and O. Q. Van Swinderen's "Summary of existing Penal Laws in Netherlands and other Countries."[2] The former work, full of varied learning, takes up the various crimes in order, and examines their definitions in Greek, Roman, Jewish, Canon, and medieval German law, with brief references to modern Continental legislation; but the treatment is that of the older school, and there is no background and no tracing of evolution. The latter work, a superb study of modern comparative criminal law in its definitions and policies, prefaces each chapter with a page or two of history for Roman and medieval German and French law; but these united pages would not suffice as a connected history. After Makarewicz as a basis, Mayer and Van Swinderen, perused together, would provide the student with an excellent makeshift, until an adequate history of this part of the field is written.

The foregoing summary will serve to show the scope of the available sources of knowledge for the history of Continental criminal law, and to explain why von Bar's work was selected by the Editorial Committee as the most serviceable. It may be noted that the plan of choosing a treatise centering on one country, and of supplementing it by chapters for other countries, was employed by the Committee (as stated in the General Introduction) for the three subjects of Criminal Law, Criminal Procedure and Civil Procedure.

It remains to cite the books and essays here translated, and to give an account of the collaborators.

THE WORKS TRANSLATED. Professor von Bar's work, forming the main part of this volume, is entitled "Geschichte des deutschen Strafrechts und der Strafrechtstheorien." It is here

[1] "Geschichte der Strafrechte, etc.", Trier, 1876.
[2] "Esquisse du droit pénal, etc.", 9 vols., Groningen, 1901–12.

translated in full, — with the exception of the section on the French Revolutionary and Napoleonic Codes, replaced by the preferable chapter of Professor Garraud. Von Bar's work appeared in 1882, and has remained authoritative. The distinguished author wrote to the Committee in 1911 that he was satisfied not to make any changes in the text: "the later investigations have not been such as to give me any reason to make any substantial changes in the text." Nevertheless, to bring down to date its account of the modern legislation, to add citations of later literature, and to supply brief accounts of the history in the countries not covered by his work, certain additions were necessary.

The legislation of the 1800s in Scandinavia and the Netherlands, and since 1877 in Germany and Austria, is described by Dr. von Thót, in sections written for the purpose. The same author has added citations of historical literature.

For the Netherlands, the section on the history to the 1800 s was taken from Professor G. A. Van Hamel's "Inleiding tot de studie van het Nederlandsche Strafrecht" (2d ed., 1907, § 6, pp. 54–77; the third edition, 1913, does not change the text).

For Scandinavia, the section on the Danish-Norwegian history to the 1800 s was taken from Chief Justice L. E. Stemann's "Den danske Retshistorie indtil Kristian V.'s Love" (1871, Part V, §§ 101–107, pp. 572–647), with amplifications from the well-known earlier works of J. L. A. Kolderup-Rosenvinge, "Grundrids af den danske Retshistorie" (3d ed., 1860, §§ 163–165) and of J. E. Larsen, "Forelaesninger over den danske Retshistorie" (1861, §§ 163–165, supplementing the former work).

For Switzerland, the sections consist of an abstract by the Editor based on Professor Heinrich Pfenninger's "Das Strafrecht der Schweiz" (1890).

For France, three works were drawn upon. For the period from the feudal system till the 1500 s was used the late Professor Glasson's "Histoire du droit et des institutions de la France" (1887–1903, Vol. VI, ch. XII, pp. 640–705). For the period from the 1500 s to the 1700 s was selected Professor L. von Stein's "Geschichte des französischen Strafrechts und des Processes" (2d ed., 1875, being Vol. III of Warnkönig and Stein's "Französische Staats- und Rechtsgeschichte", Part IV, Tit. IV, pp. 608–630). For the Revolutionary and modern period were taken some introductory pages of Professor Garraud's "Traité théorique et pratique du droit pénal" (6 vols., 1898–1902).

For Spain and Portugal, no suitable account seems anywhere to exist.

For Italy, the reader is referred to Professor Calisse's work, in Vol. VII of the present Series. The chapters of Professors von Bar, Van Hamel, and Glasson, here translated, point out the influence of Italian jurists on the law of the other countries.

THE AUTHORS. CARL LUDWIG VON BAR was born in 1836, at Hannover, and died August 20, 1913. After a few years' service on the Appellate Court at Göttingen, he became professor at Rostock, then at Breslau, and finally at Göttingen (1879), where he had taken his degree and where he remained till the end of his life. His early interest was in criminal law; and the long list of his published works in that field extended to his closing years.[1] But he was led also into the study of problems of international criminal law, and thence into international law at large, both public and private; and in this field he acquired an authority which led him to be known, in other countries, chiefly as an international jurist. His "Das Internationale Privat- und Strafrecht" (1862) was here his first work, later expanded as a "Lehrbuch des internationalen Privat- und Strafrecht" (1892); and his "Theorie und Praxis des internationalen Privatrechts" (2 vols., 2d. ed., 1889), translated into English (by G. R. Gillespie) as "The Theory and Practice of Private International Law" (2d ed., 1892; 1st Amer. ed. Boston, 1883), made his name familiar among English-speaking lawyers. Indeed, it was on English soil, at Oxford, that his sudden death took place, during the meeting of the Institute of International Law; of which he had been one of the founders, forty years before. He also possessed the distinction of being one of the members of the International Arbitration Court at the Hague, and had received numerous academic honors from the Universities of Bologna, Cambridge, Padua, and elsewhere.

[1] "Recht und Beweis im Geschwornengericht" (1865); "Die Grundlagen des Strafrechts" (1869); "Die Lehre von Causalzusammenhange im Rechte, besonders im Strafrecht" (1871); "Zur Frage des Geschwornen- und Schöffengerichte" (1873); "Kritik des Entwurfs der deutschen Strafprozessordnung" (1873); "Grundriss zu Vorlesungen über deutsches Strafrecht" (2d. ed., 1878); "Systematik des deutschen Strafprozessrechts" (1878); "Handbuch des deutschen Strafrechts" (of which the "Geschichte" here translated, was Vol. I, but the only one published); "Probleme des Strafrechts" (1896); "Die projektirte Reform des italienischen Strafprozesses" (1902); "Die Reform des Strafrechts" (1903); "Gesetz und Schuld im Strafrecht; Fragen des geltenden deutschen Strafrechts und seine Reform" (3 vols., 1906–09).

Von Bar was in politics a pronounced liberal, and for a few years held a seat in the Reichstag. But owing to his deep disaffection to the Bismarckian policies (dating from his early years, as a native of Hannover, where, before the German Empire was consolidated, political disagreements were marked), he never held any government office. In his later years, when his influence in the Institute of International Law had become so notable, he took a prominent part as a pacifist, and became a Councillor of the Interparliamentary Union and President of the International Union for Mutual Understanding. It was a symbol of his deep interest in these movements that his death came on the very eve of a journey to attend the dedication of the Peace Palace at the Hague.

Ladislas von Thót is a native of Hungary, and has been judge of the criminal court in Budapest. He is a Fellow of the Royal Academy of Spain, Corresponding Fellow of the Royal Academies of Italy and of Greece, of the Petrograd Imperial Society of Jurists, etc. His astonishing command of many foreign languages has enabled him to pursue comparative researches of wide scope. His lengthy essay in "Der Gerichtsaal" (1912, LXXIX, pp. 142–392) on "Die Geschichte der ausserdeutschen Strafrechtsliteratur", with its vast array of bibliography, is a sufficient evidence of his extraordinary mastery of the literature of the subject. The list of the titles of his published works exhibits an unequalled versatility.[1]

G. A. Van Hamel, the veteran professor (now retired) of the University of Amsterdam, has long been recognized as one of the great figures of modern times in criminal law. With Franz von Liszt, of Berlin, and Adolphe Prins, of Brussels, he founded the International Union of Criminal Law, — the body with which the American Institute of Criminal Law and Criminology is affiliated as a national group. His writings on criminal law have been prolific,[2] and his scholarly authority is unexcelled.

Kristian Ludwig Ernst Stemann (1802–1876) was one of

[1] "Storia del diritto penale europeo", in "Il progresso del diritto criminale", ed. Carnevale (Vols. I–IV, *passim*, 1909–1913); "Droit pénal oriental", in "Mittheilungen der internationalen kriminalistischen Vereinigung" (Vol. XIX, 1912, pp. 110–227); "Geschiedenis van het italiensche Strafregt", in "Proceedings of the Royal Flemish Academy"; etc.

[2] Besides the work here translated from may be mentioned: "De tegenwoordige Beweging van het Strafrecht" (1891), numerous reports in the "Mittheilungen der internationalen kriminalistischen Vereinigung" (above mentioned), and articles in the "Tijdschrift voor Strafrecht", of which he is an editor.

Denmark's notable jurists and legal historians, and President of the Schleswig Court of Appeal from 1852 to 1864.[1]

HEINRICH PFENNINGER (1846–1896) was associate professor in the Faculty of Law of the University of Zürich from 1891 till his death; his chosen field was that of criminal law.[2]

ERNEST DÉSIRÉ GLASSON (1837–1907) was professor of Civil Procedure in the Faculty of Law of the University of Paris from 1879 until his death in 1907. Besides his work in that field, he is best known for his "Histoire du droit et des institutions de la France" (1887–1903), which had proceeded to eight volumes at the time of his death, and had then reached only the period of the 1500 s (with some portions completed into the 1700 s).

LORENZ VON STEIN (1813–1890) pursued a long and distinguished career as economist, historian, and jurist, in professorates at Kiel (1846) and Vienna (1855). His contributions to law and political science were numerous.[3] His "Französische Rechtsgeschichte", written in collaboration with Warnkönig, and their other joint work, "Flandrische Rechtsgeschichte", remain as scholarly monuments, and are marked by a penetration and wisdom having an unusual flavor of modernity.

LEOPOLD AUGUST WARNKÖNIG (1794–1866) was professor of law at Liège, Louvain, Ghent, Freiburg, and Tübingen. His special field was legal history, and for some time he served on the Royal Belgian Commission for editing Belgian historical sources; one consequence of which is Belgium's possession to-day of a superb series of critically edited medieval legal sources.[4]

FRANÇOIS GARRAUD, professor in the Faculty of Law at Lyon, stands as the preëminent modern French author on criminal law

[1] His other principal works were: "Schleswig's Rechts- und Gerichtsfassung im 17ten Jahrhundert" (1855); "Geschichte des öffentlichen und Privatrecht des Herzogthums Schleswig" (1866–67).

[2] His other publications were: "Der Begriff des politischen Verbrechens" (Schweiz. Juristenvereins-Versammlung, XVIII, Bern, 1880); "Entwurf eines Strafgesetzbuch für den Canton Uri" (Frauenfeld, 1894); "Grenzbestimmungen zur Criminalistischen Imputationslehre" (Festschrift für Berner, Zürich, 1892).

[3] "Geschichte der socialen Bewegung in Frankreich von 1789 bis auf unsere Tage" (1850); "System der Staatswissenschaften" (1852–57); "Lehrbuch der Volkswirtschaft" (1858, 1878); "Die Verwaltungslehre" (1865–68, 7 vols.); "Gegenwart und Zukunft der Rechts- und Staatswissenschaft Deutschlands" (1876).

[4] Among his principal works may be named: "Commentarii juris romani privati" (1825–32); "Flandrische Staats- und Rechtsgeschichte bis 1305" (1834–42); "Histoire externe du droit romain" (1836); "Histoire du droit belgique" (1837); "Histoire des Carolingiens" (1862).

and procedure. In his works the French combination of solid scholarship, exegetic clarity, and philosophic breadth, is seen at its best. Chapters of his treatise on Criminal Procedure are also used to supplement the translated text of Professor Esmein's "History of Criminal Procedure", forming Vol. V of the present Series.

THE TRANSLATORS. For the main work, von Bar's "History", and von Thót's additions, the translator is THOMAS S. BELL, now of the Los Angeles Bar. Mr. Bell, after graduating from the University of Colorado, and going as Rhodes Scholar to Oxford University, completed there a course in law and jurisprudence and was later (1908) Fellow in Jurisprudence at Columbia University. He afterwards practised for a time at the Tacoma Bar, and was lecturer on International Law in the University of Washington.

For Stemann's chapter, the translator is JOHN WALGREN of the Chicago Bar, who is also the translator of the Scandinavian chapter in Vol. I of this Series, "General Survey of Continental Legal History"; a further statement of his attainments is there made.

For the chapters from Garraud and Glasson, the translator is ALFONSO DE SALVIO, assistant professor of Romance Languages in Northwestern University; he is also the translator of the treatise of De Quirós on "Modern Theories of Criminality" in the Modern Criminal Science Series (published under the auspices of the American Institute of Criminal Law and Criminology).

For the chapter from von Stein, the translator is ROBERT WYNESS MILLAR, professor of Criminal Law and Procedure and of Civil Procedure in Northwestern University, and translator also of Engelmann's "History of Continental Civil Procedure" in the present Series, and of Garofalo's "Criminology" in the Modern Criminal Science Series.

For Van Hamel's chapter, the translator is T. DE VRIES, lately professor of Modern Languages at Calvin College (Michigan), and also (on the Holland Society's foundation) of the Dutch Language and Literature at the University of Chicago; author of numerous valuable works in Dutch, including a history of Sunday Observance Legislation.

SCOPE OF THE STORY. Rome and the Germanic peoples furnished the elements which fused a thousand years later. Hence the story begins by portraying the criminal law of imperial Rome and that of the primitive Germanic tribes. At the beginning of our era the two lay totally apart, an older and a younger system, one in the South and one in the North. The migrations of the Germanic tribes lead up to their acceptance of Christianity; and the influence of Christian religion and church law form the next episode in the story, and a chapter on this subject brings us to the period of the early Middle Ages.

The stage of the later Middle Ages, under the kingdoms and principalities of feudalism and of the weak Germanic imperialism claims next attention. Here a chapter describes the criminal law in the central Germanic regions; another chapter describes it in Scandinavia, where primitive habits, uninfluenced from outside, persisted longer; another chapter is given to Switzerland, where mountainous isolation served also to preserve certain native traits, in spite of the central location near to regions of advanced culture. Another chapter for the same period is given to France, where the continuous Roman tradition in the South, the Germanic settlements in the North, and the early strength of national monarchy, served to make a complex growth having special features.

This completes the second period, the Middle Ages, and brings us to the third period, the Renascence of Roman law in the 1400 s–1500 s, the Reformation, and the ensuing century of the "Enlightenment." — In Germany, the Roman law was adopted from Italy in a peculiar artificial fashion. Italy had then for nearly three centuries been reviving, popularizing, and adapting the classical Roman law; and Italy became now the teacher of Western Europe (except England) for a recast Roman criminal law and procedure.[1] Three chapters describe the progress of the criminal law in Germany under the scientific Reception (the 1500 s), the religious Reformation (the 1600 s), and the intellectual Enlightenment (the 1700 s).

We then turn aside, for two chapters, to survey the corresponding development for the same period in Scandinavia, Switzerland, Netherlands, and France. Scandinavia, still outside the

[1] Italy's history of criminal law is fully told in Professor *Calisse's* volume (translated by Mr. *Lisle*), No. VIII of the present Series, "History of Italian Law, Public, Criminal, and Private."

direct current of new science, exhibits the almost pure development of Germanic ideas. Switzerland and Netherlands, fully within the influence, present only locally variant types of its effect. The later religious and intellectual movements are shared in all four regions, in differing degrees. France has a special development of its own, partly through its earlier cultivation of the revived Roman law, partly because of its well-formulated bodies of local written law, but chiefly through its centralized monarchy and its advanced methods of procedure. Later, France leads Europe in the humanization of the criminal law. —

This brings us to the fourth period, that of the French Revolution, which amidst the crash of governments rapidly focussed the reformative demands in criminal law and started its universal regeneration. Two chapters here describe the influences of the Revolution in its own country and in Germany.

The fifth and last period, that of Modern Criminal Law in the 1800 s, is thus ushered in. It is a period of determined and incessant efforts to reform the criminal law radically while rewriting it in codes. But the constant contemporary advance of science, political principle, and sympathetic thought has been so rapid, and the rooted mass of worn-out older principles has been so great, that no one advance in legislation has long sufficed to meet the demands. And so the history of the century has been, on its surface, little more than a catalogue of these successive legislative efforts.

Here the four chapters devoted to the codifications of this period, and ending Part I, prepare us for Part II, the history of the theories of criminal law. As a part of this vast activity in legislation, law-makers have been led to reconsider basic theories of criminal law. To study its progress on the subjective side we therefore retrace our steps, and examine the dominating theories, in their development since men began to reflect on the purpose of law. Through Greece and Rome, the Christians, the medieval philosophers, the religious and the intellectual reformers, we reach at last the scientific era of the nineteenth century; and the history of theories merges into the current disputations of our own times.[1]

[1] For a more elaborate account of current scientific theory in criminal law since the middle of the 1800 s, the reader may be referred to *C. Bernaldo De Quiros*' "Modern Theories of Criminality" (Vol. I of the Modern Criminal Science Series).

EDITORIAL NOTE

PURSUANT to the plan of the Editorial Committee to introduce each Volume of this Series with a word from both a British scholar and an American scholar, the Committee preferred a request, four years ago, to LUKE OWEN PIKE, Esq., barrister of Lincoln's Inn, and assistant Keeper of the Public Records. The request was cordially granted.. Mr. Pike's notable work, "The History of Crime in England," distinguished him as the natural speaker for the purpose. His sound scholarship in his edition of the Yearbooks of Edward III and in his "History of the House of Lords" placed him among the most eminent of England's historians.

In later correspondence, since the outbreak of the War, Mr. Pike indicated his intention (assented to by the Editor) "to write, as it were, a new chapter of the history of criminal law on the Continent, in accordance with the object-lessons which the Continent is now providing." This intended chapter, however, has been lost to the world. In October, 1915, the preliminary proofs of this book were forwarded to Mr. Pike; but before the end of that month he had passed away; and no manuscript draft of an Introduction could be found among his papers, other than some unfinished notes made in preparation. Instructions had been left by him to destroy all papers "except those relating to the Continental Legal History Series published under the auspices of the Association of American Law Schools." Evidently the fulfilment of his plan had been postponed until the expected arrival of the proofs; which came at last, but too late.

The editorial plan for an Introduction on behalf of British legal science has nevertheless been enabled to be fulfilled, by the courtesy of Mr. Justice WILLIAM RENWICK RIDDELL, of the Supreme Court of Ontario. His distinguished name and his charming personality are familiar to the Bar of the United States; and his scholarship is attested in a long list of essays, indicating the natural zest of the historian to be uniquely compatible with the wisdom and practical activities of the judge. His goodwill to the cause represented by the present Series had already been shown by his Introduction to Volume V ("History of Continental Criminal Procedure"), and this emboldened the Editor to solicit the renewal of the favor.

J. H. W.

February, 1916.

INTRODUCTION

BY WILLIAM RENWICK RIDDELL [1]

THIS work is of extreme value to those who desire a scientific and philosophical knowledge of the principles underlying the criminal law, punishment for crime, commutation and pardon; and sidelights are cast by it upon criminal procedure. Its chief value therefore will be to the legislator and to him who wishes to influence the legislator, to the Executive and those concerned in the execution of the judgment of the Courts. The difficulties experienced in other times and other countries, and the manner in which they have been met and in part overcome, are object lessons which the statesman and the reformer cannot afford to neglect.

We English-speaking peoples may not segregate ourselves from the rest of humanity — we have our own conceit in the superiority of our own "culture" [2] which we treasure in proud and for the most part harmless self-satisfaction. But if and when that self-complacency goes so far as to make us wholly regardless of what other peoples are and do, it ceases to be harmless — the harm being infinitely greater to ourselves than to the "foreigner."

One of the lessons here taught — indirectly indeed — is the essential and fundamental unity of mankind; "there is a great deal of human nature in man." With the Greek the blood of a man who had been slain cried aloud for vengeance, just as the Hebrew record represents Yahweh as saying to the first murderer, "The voice of thy brother's blood crieth unto me from out the ground": the Roman said "Natura partes habet duas, tuitionem sui et ulciscendi jus", and Breathitt County lives up to its natural rights so declared.

[1] LL.D., F. R. Historical Society, etc., Justice of the Supreme Court of Ontario.

[2] See an article by Dr. John H. Wigmore on "The International Assimilation of Law," 10 Illinois Law Review at p. 387 (January, 1916).

The Jew was ordered to stone to death all of his clan who sought after strange gods; and while in the Roman system there was in theory no regard to religious opinions, a way was found to deal with the Christians, "a pestilent and pernicious sect" who were chiefly characterized by minding their own business and securing their eternal welfare. The Church possessed means of punishing heretics in the Middle Ages and before and after; and the Mormons in our Canadian West are secure from persecution only because certain of their theological antagonists have not the power as they have the desire.

"Eppur si muove!" The conception of what constitutes crime changes from generation to generation. The Chorus in Euripides' "Bacchæ" who

> "*θοάζ(ουσα)*
> *Βρομίῳ πόνον ἡδὺν κάματόν τ' εὐ—*
> *κάματον, Βάκχιον εὐαζομένα* (vv. 65–67),

sings

> *ὦ μάκαρ, ὅστις εὐδαίμων*
> *τελετὰς θεῶν εἰδὼς*
> *βιοτὰν ἁγιστεύει*
> *καὶ θιασεύεται ψυχὰν*
> *ἐν ὄρεσσι βαγχεύων*
> *ὁσίοις καθαρμοῖσιν*
> *τά τε ματρὸς μεγάλας ὄρ-*
> *για Κυβέλας θεμιτεύων* (vv. 72–79),

undoubtedly expressed the opinion of the poet and of his hearers.[1]

But sacred as were the Bacchantes and their orgies to the Greek, the Roman took a different view of them. The Senate thought "ut omnia Bacchanalia Romæ primum, deinde per totam Italiam, diruerent", and decreed "Ne qua Bacchanalia Romæ neve in Italia essent" (Livy, xxxix, 18). This was no "brutum fulmen"; hundreds were executed in public or in private, more were imprisoned or banished. Nor do I find that the Bacchanalia of Rome were worse — they could not be worse — than the orgy of Agaue, when she slew and dismembered her son.

[1] I quote Beckwith's edition of Wecklein's version (Boston, Ginn & Co., 1886) — "*θοάζουσα*" substituted for *θοάζω* for grammatical reasons. The Chorus speeding on her glad toil, her happy task, raising the Bacchic shout, cries "O happy he who to his blessedness, knowing well the divine mysteries, sanctifies his life, and is in soul initiated into the orgiastic band with holy ceremonies solemnly performing Bacchic rites in the mountains — and celebrating the prescribed orgies of the mighty Cybele."

The Flagellantes of a few centuries ago were for a long time as holy as the Howling or the Whirling Dervishes; but this generation could not stand the Holy Rollers.

In the ninth century B.C., a certain highly-revered person, when he was guyed by a lot of half-grown lads, turned and cursed them, just as the town-drunkard would to-day; and it was accounted to him for glory that thereupon two she-bears came out of the wood and tore the youngsters. To-day, the prophet would find himself in the Police Court for cursing, and he would be sent to the Penitentiary by any people who believed in the efficacy of prayer.

In some cases it may be that the change is not wholly for the better; while no one unless he were unusually bloodthirsty would wish the death penalty restored for inventing and spreading satires, scurrilous stories and satirical songs of a political nature, as the XII Tables prescribed, something better is much to be desired than the civil suit to which an ex-President of the United States was driven to defend his reputation. Perhaps the recent attempt in Pennsylvania to deal with the matter had some merits, but it fell before the ridicule of the untouched. The fact is that we have lost the Middle Ages sense of the importance of the word, spoken or written: and now no one would think of nailing a reviler of the City authorities to a post by the tongue until he cut himself loose.

So, too, in the matter of punishment, death was for long the only effective deterrent; if we except what was almost an equivalent, banishment. When mankind was composed of septs, clans, tribes, which looked on each other with hatred and dread, which had no intercourse with each other, to be driven from one's own was almost as terrible as death. Cain, made a fugitive, cried, "My punishment is greater than I can bear"; and many felt the like when driven like the scape-goat into the wilderness. The theory grew up that the soil of the fatherland stained by the blood of the slain could not bear the presence of the red slayer; and Theoclumenos *ἄνδρα κατακτὰς ἔμφυλον*, the crazed Orestes and the thrice unhappy Adrastos must forth *ἐκ πατρίδος*, at least till they receive absolution and purification. But the thought was never far absent, "You have taken life, be therefore deprived of all that makes life worth living."

That conception of the necessity of living with one's own has long passed away; and none can convince the throngs of immigrants to this continent that banishment is a real punishment.

Even the sentence of transportation lost its terrors for the "Sympathizers" of 1837–8, who were transported to Van Diemen's Land, and the Fenian invaders of 1866 were sent to the Penitentiary.

Imprisonment could not be, when there were no prisons; but prisons would have been built if imprisonment had been a real punishment. Until comparatively recent times, the richest and most powerful lived of choice and of necessity in buildings not far removed from a gaol, with thick stone walls, small windows, execrable sanitary arrangements, without provision for what we now consider ordinary decency. As between Sing Sing Prison and Carnarvon Castle, give me the Prison. Only those who, like Robin Hood, lived under the green-wood tree felt it a deprivation to be shut up — the sequestration from the rest of the world bringing with it the incidental but invaluable advantage of security from enemies.

When man could walk about reasonably safe from danger of sudden assault, imprisonment became something to be dreaded and the gaol a means of punishment, so that now there is bitter complaint if "prison forte" if not "dure" be awarded even to keep an accused safe till his trial.

We may perhaps have become too uniform in our manner of punishing different forms of offense against the law. Bentham was not oblivious to the value of making the punishment fit the crime; but he would not have gone so far as to extract the intestines from one who wrongfully girdled his neighbour's trees, and wind them about the trees in lieu of the abstracted bark; nor would he give the shameless, the choice between a heavy fine and running naked through the town. In Canada, the authorities a few years ago had to interfere with the Doukhobors, who persisted in marching "in puris naturalibus"; and any one who should attempt anything of the kind anywhere in civilization would soon be laid by the heels.

It is interesting to find in these pages the origin of much "fireside law", which is often but a survival in popular belief of what was once a legal fact. For example, it is a matter of implicit belief amongst the lower classes in Britain that if the rope used in hanging a criminal should break, he would go free. That this was the case in early German law is certain and almost certain that it was the case at least locally in England — the breaking of the rope being a token of Divine forgiveness.

All such matters and many more of like nature are touched upon; most are exhaustively treated in this interesting and valuable work. More valuable and interesting to many will be the general observations of the author — I may be permitted to mention one or two.

In drawing the distinction between the Roman and the Germanic conception of the relation of the individual to the State, it is said that according to the Roman conception the individual has no rights which the State is bound to respect, and that laws for the protection of the individual are mere voluntary concessions by the State which at its discretion may be withdrawn, — while according to the early Germanic conception, the rights of the individual as against the State are not based upon some law liable to be modified or suspended at will, for personal rights follow the Germanic individual everywhere, and decrees derogatory thereof are null and void. This most pregnant observation will lead the philosophic student and lawyer to consider the far-reaching results of each principle, and still more to consider how far the peoples and their descendants on both sides of the Atlantic remained and remain true to these their ideals.

The author's statement that "it is difficult for a conquest-seeking military system which is naturally adverse to being governed by laws, to preserve free institutions" is much more than a mere truism.

I conclude by bearing tribute to the author's recognition of the wrong of punishing the innocent in order to inspire others with terror; and to the value of his discussion of the uselessness (and worse) of cruelty in dealing with the transgressor real or supposed.

Osgoode Hall, Toronto,
March 1st, 1916.

INTRODUCTION

By Edwin Roulette Keedy[1]

A recent writer epigrammatically defined law as "the point where life and logic meet." If this definition were substantially correct, legal history would be neither very interesting nor significant. It is the lack of logic in the origin and development of the law that provides the charm and importance of this branch of historical study.

The criminal law, by reason of the nature of crime and the relation of the law to it, is characterized by even less logic than the civil law. Crime is generally the failure to restrain an instinctive impulse. To satisfy sexual desire, to injure one who has angered us, to take what one wants even though it belongs to another, — all these are natural impulses. The impulse to retaliate is of the same character and in this retaliation, first by the individual and then by the group, we see the beginning of the criminal law. The heedless character of this impulse to retaliate is shown by the fact that the law for a long period wreaked its vengeance against animals and inanimate objects in the same way that a person kicks a chair over which he has stumbled.

Criminal law may, therefore, with a large measure of truth, be defined as the instinctive reaction of the group against the instinctive action of the individual. This view of the criminal law is supported by the large part which the primitive emotions have played in its development. Fear, avarice, superstition, and religion are emotional factors which have greatly influenced the law. For instance, fear of revolution produced the harsh laws against secret societies in Russia and Prussia. Fear engendered in England by the French Revolution produced much of the severity of the criminal law at the beginning of the nineteenth century. Avarice and superstition combined to produce the laws

[1] Professor of Law in the University of Pennsylvania.

against witchcraft and sorcery, and avarice alone was a strong incentive for imposing monetary penalties and for confiscating the property of convicted felons. Religion is responsible for two kinds of laws, — those to protect itself, such as the laws against blasphemy and heresy, and those against personal vices.

Not only has the development of the law been largely affected by constant emotional factors, but radical changes have been produced by the emotional reaction aroused by a particular incident. The conviction and execution of Jean Calas in 1762, coupled with the notoriety given this case by Voltaire, started the movement for the reformation of the criminal law throughout Europe. A notorious case of flogging gave the impetus to reform in Switzerland in the last century. Though twenty-five bills providing for an appeal in criminal cases were presented to the British Parliament in the nineteenth century it required the case of Adolf Beck to secure the enactment of such a measure.

In the character of its accomplishment the criminal law differs materially from the civil. The civil law gives a reparation and reproduces as far as possible the *status quo*. Its accomplishment may be described as salvage. What the criminal law accomplishes is waste, for in return for one injury it imposes another, and compensates the loss to itself by creating a further one, for most punishments are after all simply legalized crimes. Furthermore, there is no logical connection between punishment and crime. What principle of logic can determine whether the punishment for robbery shall be death, mutilation, or imprisonment? It is the temper of the times that determines the character and extent of punishment. A noteworthy feature of criminal law is the great variety of penalties provided at different times for the same offense. The punishment for adultery, for instance, has ranged from a small fine to death in horrible forms. It is not to be concluded from the foregoing that theory and logic were entirely absent in the development of the criminal law. Their influence, however, was qualifying and explanatory rather than creative. They generally followed rather than preceded action.

A survey of our criminal law to-day discloses many of the same defects which prevailed in the past. There is the same lack of definite theory as to its function, and the same haphazard method of determining the character and extent of punishment. Laws are still enacted to meet particular situations without regard to what their effect will be in the future. What is even more striking, our legislatures enact statutes without considering the question whether they can or will be enforced. A notable instance of this is found in the recent laws for the sterilization of defectives and criminals. A popular theory was seized upon by enthusiasts and made the basis for legislative proposals, which became law in many States. The theory is now to a large extent discredited and the laws are not being enforced. Many persons hold the view that all that is necessary to change a condition is to enact a law against it. Others believe that law should register a moral sentiment higher than that actually existing in the community. The result of both views is a mass of unenforceable legislation. Important innovations are frequently made without sufficient consideration being given to their relation to existing law or to the machinery for enforcing them. Thus the work of the recently established psychopathic laboratories is hampered by the fact that the relation of their findings to the established principles of criminal law was not previously determined. The effectiveness of parole and probation laws is often impaired by failure to provide for sufficient supervision over the persons released under them.

Much of the inconsistency and ineffectiveness of our present criminal law could have been avoided if the lessons of the past had been applied, for the history of the criminal law has its greatest significance for the codifier and legislator. They will discover there the illogical basis of many cherished doctrines. They will learn further the necessity for determining the purpose of the criminal law and for viewing it as a whole. But most important of all they will discover that there are limits to the effectiveness of the law, and thus be brought to realize that there are conditions in which a prohibitory law is a source of more evil than good.

There is need to-day for a complete code of criminal law — not such a codification of existing law as we have had in the past nor a body of statutory law based on a theoretical principle, but a code in the preparation of which the function of criminal law is determined and which is fitted to actual conditions of life. In drafting such a code the question of enforceability would have to be faced. This would include among other things a study of the extent to which it is possible to regulate business affairs by law and would involve the necessity of distinguishing between public wrongs and private vices. The difficult problem of responsibility would have to be solved and a new classification of crimes would be required. It would be necessary to study the whole question of punishment — to determine its purpose, and to establish some relation between it and crime. The mooted questions whether the criminal law shall afford any redress to the injured party, and whether a person wrongly convicted of crime shall be compensated by the State, would have to be settled. In the drafting of such a code as has been described, the present volume would be of great value.

University of Pennsylvania,
Philadelphia,
February 16, 1916.

AUTHOR'S PREFACE

By CARL LUDWIG VON BAR

It will be readily admitted that, immediately after the publication of a comprehensive code of general application, an opportune occasion arises for a treatment of the law in which its interpretation is undertaken in a *dialectical* method. Nevertheless, this treatise, the first volume of which I herewith submit to the public,[1] is of a different character, and deals with the law rather in a *historical* method. If at this time such a treatment of the subject is to be justified, it is requisite that it represent an endeavor to comprehend and portray the present German Criminal Code, in all its parts and subdivisions as well as in its entirety, as the product and result of preceding ages.

Such an endeavor permits of both a philosophical and a practical treatment of the subject. The former is necessary, unless we are prepared to accept history as an irrational conglomeration of isolated facts. The latter is desirable, since the real sense of a statutory provision is more readily ascertained from a glance at the long course of its previous development than from the dialectical method, which, while easier and more striking, is often prone to lead to misconception. Our method also enables us to surmise intelligently the future development of the law. At least, we shall be in a position to avoid the mistake of regarding as new truths those old errors, which persist in coming to life in modern disguises and confuse us in our efforts to make true and permanent progress. We shall also be able to distinguish between actual knowledge and that dilettantism which so often accompanies movements of reform. This is a wisdom which can hardly be acquired from the latest periodicals or from an observation of current events.

[1] [No other volume was published. The author planned a General Handbook, of which the first volume was to be this history. — Ed.]

In order to attain our purpose — to obtain really practical results — it has seemed necessary to precede the historical treatment of particular legal principles with a general history of German criminal law. I do not, however, mean a history in the sense that one may expect to find therein a compendium of all the rules of criminal law which have ever existed, but rather a history in which an endeavor is made to present in a manner, clear but sufficiently concrete, the essential elements of each period treated in conjunction with the history of general progress. Moreover, not only a history of the *law* is necessary; there must be also a history of the philosophy of criminal law — a history of the *theories* of criminal law. For philosophy is part of history; in a certain sense it is as a mirror, reflecting in general conclusions the activities of the times and their causes, and shedding light upon the future. Philosophy has exercised a remarkable influence upon the field of criminal law, and this will be even more so in the future. Moreover, such a historical treatment should criticise the value of the individual theories, not only according to the criterion of their abstract correctness, but also in the light of their relation to the practical exigencies of that stage of progress of which they were a part.

The question may certainly be raised, in view of that investigation of details which is constantly going on, whether it is permissible for one to announce an intention of writing a *general* history of German criminal law. Undoubtedly in such a history there will be numerous gaps and deficiencies. Yet, in our estimation, it is desirable that there be undertaken, from time to time, such a general history of a branch of our law; since otherwise the results of the minute investigation of historical details would upon the whole remain inaccessible for the solution of single points of the law, and for the general comprehension of the practitioner and those who are influential in legislation.

As to the treatment of specific points in such a general history, there will necessarily be differences of opinion. Completeness is impossible, if the leading and essential features are not to be lost sight of in the mass of several details. The author must exercise considerable tact in regard to those matters as to which there is dispute, and he must bear up as best he can, if he is so unfortunate as to displease many and satisfy only a few. It can be hoped only that the author should have knowledge of the individual details in sufficient measure, and especially that he should not merely

rely upon works which have been written concerning the history of his subject, but that he should avail himself of the best original sources.

This last, and in my opinion indispensable, requirement placed a limitation upon my activity, — *i.e.* to deal only with the history of the German criminal law and to exclude the history of the law of other peoples whose progress is closely related, and to exclude also the history of the Norse criminal law. However, an occasional reference may be made to foreign law and foreign legal development.[1]

A short history of the Roman criminal law (which to a very considerable extent was "received" by us) is necessary. Following established custom, I have dealt with it from the beginning — notwithstanding the fact that, theoretically speaking, a history of the German criminal law should begin with German law, and the "received" foreign law should constitute only an incidental element. I have done this for the reason that the "reception" of the Roman law — at least, the indirect influence of the same — began at a very early period, — so early indeed that, with the sources at our command, a history of pure German law would cover a period, the limits of which could hardly be established with any degree of certainty.

Everywhere, as an ideal in my work, I have had before me a "liebevolle Hingabe", and so it will be in the future. It was not my purpose to create, to achieve new and brilliant results. I considered it well worth the while in this work to take the results achieved by others, and, in a general, accessible treatise which should not appear so learned and abstract as to be deterrent, to make them useful to a wider circle of readers. Possibly the history of criminal law will appeal to a considerable number of laymen, and perhaps also to many of the profession. However this does not preclude me from occasionally arriving at a new conception.

I have always been of the opinion that those new ideas which are permanent in the theory of law are only developments of that which has gone before, and not absolutely new and startling. It is from this point of view that I regard my own conception of the fundamental principle of criminal law. Perhaps it contains only

[1] In the history of the theories of criminal law, attention is given only to those foreign writers who can be shown to have had an actual influence upon the German literature.

that which seems of permanent value in the earlier theories, and regarded in this way it is not original. But originality can not well exist in a work whose purpose it is to collect divergent materials, and in which the individual feels that his share in the great sum total of scientific development is exceedingly small. Such is the character of this work; and, in accordance with my purpose as before stated, an attempt is made merely to recognize as far as possible the relative truth, the permanent elements in the divergent views.

This standpoint of *relative correctness* (*i.e.* of all theories) may be announced as the ideal of this entire work, in which the author gladly recognizes the special merits of other comprehensive works upon the subject of criminal law, and especially the "Handbuch" of Holtzendorff, consisting of individual contributions, and also Halschner's new "System." The existing treatises by Berner, Schütze, Hugo Meyer, and Von Liszt are directed towards other purposes, and consequently do not render superfluous the work here undertaken.

PART I

GENERAL HISTORY OF CRIMINAL LAW

TITLE I. THE ROMAN AND GERMANIC ELEMENTS

CHAPTER I. THE ROMAN LAW.

CHAPTER II. PRIMITIVE GERMANIC LAW.

HISTORY OF CONTINENTAL CRIMINAL LAW

CHAPTER I

THE ROMAN LAW

§ 1. Various Origins of Criminal Law. Vengeance. Influence of the Priesthood.
§ 2. Rome. Prominence of Religious Element. Roman Law not a Theocratic System. Early Suppression of Vengeance.
§ 3. Suppression of Vengeance in Cases of Homicide. Influence of the Principle of Vengeance in the Treatment of Other Crimes.
§ 4. "Perduellio." "Multæ Irrogatio."
§ 5. Roman Conception of the Relation of the Individual to the State. Germanic Conception of the Relation of the Individual to the State. Contribution of Roman Criminal Law to the Establishment of Individual Rights.
§ 6. The Judicial Law of the Empire. Real Explanation of Arbitrary Character of Roman Criminal Law.
§ 7. The Law of the Twelve Tables.
§ 8. Power of "Paterfamilias" as Supplement to Criminal Law. The Censorship. Infamy. "Actiones Populares."
§ 9. Other Criminal Legislation of the Republic. Statutes of Later Republic.
§ 10. Punishment in Statutes of Later Republic. Opposition to Death Penalty.
§ 11. Gradual Change in Character of the Criminal Law.
§ 12. Change in the Character of Exile as a Punishment. Increased Use of Capital Punishment. Corporal Punishment. Imprisonment. Hard Labor. Other Methods of Punishment.
§ 13. Infamy and Confiscation of Property.
§ 14. The Range of Criminal Law.
§ 15. The Crime of "Lèse Majesté."
§ 16. Persecution of the Christians.
§ 17. Sorcery and Soothsaying.
§ 18. General Circumstances Affecting Imperial Criminal Law. (1) Class Privilege. (2) Administration of Justice by State Officials. (3) Continued Disregard for the Criminal. (4) Reversion to more Primitive Conditions.
§ 19. Influence of the Jurists.
§ 20. Influence of Christianity in the Later Empire. Protection of State Sought by Numerous Penal Statutes. Other Effects of the Influence of the Church. Last Stages of the Roman Criminal Law.

§ 1. **Various Sources of Criminal Law. Vengeance.**[1] — The existence of two modern doctrines, concerning the nature of criminal law, — one of which regards punishment as a necessary consequence of crime, and the other would justify punishment as

[1] In regard to the matter contained in this chapter, the following writers may be consulted. *Invernizzi*, "De publicis et criminalibus judiciis Romanorum" (1787. Leipzig edition, 1846); *Welcker*, "Die letzten Gründe von Recht, Staat und Strafe" (1813), pp. 535 *et seq.; Abegg*, "De antiquissimo Romanorum jure criminali" (1823); *Jarcke*, "Versuch einer Darstellung des censorischen Strafrechts" (1824); *Köstlin*, "Die Lehre von Mord und Todtschlag" (Part I, 1838, "Das altrömische Parricidium"); *Osenbrüggen*, "Das altrömische Parricidium" (1840); "Geschichte des römischen Criminalprocesses" (1842); *Platner*, "Quæstiones de jure criminum Romano, præsertim de criminibus extraordinariis" (1842); *Rein*, "Das Criminalrecht der Römer von Romulus bis auf Justinian" (1844); *Laboulaye*, "Essai sur les lois criminelles des Romains concernant la responsabilité des magistrats" (Paris, 1845); *Du Boys*, "Histoire du droit criminel des peuples anciens" (Paris, 1845), pp. 237 *et seq.; Walter*, "Geschichte des römischen Rechts" (2 vols., 3d ed., 1860); *Rudorff*, "Römische Rechtsgeschichte" (2 vols., 1857, 1859); *Von Holtzendorff*, "Die Deportationsstrafe im römischen Alterthume" (1859. Part of larger work by same author in regard to the punishment of deportation); *Köstlin*, "Geschichte des deutschen Strafrechts im Umriss, herausgegeben von Gessler" (1859), pp. 1–47; *Geib*, "Lehrbuch des deutschen Strafrechts" (1861), Vol. I, pp. 7–123; *Henriot*, "Mœurs juridiques et judiciaires de l'ancienne Rome" (3 vols., Paris, 1863–1865); *Von Ihering*, "Geist des römischen Rechts" (citations to 3d edition), Vol. I, pp. 252 *et seq.; Von Holtzendorff*, "Handbuch des deutschen Strafrechts" (I, 1871), pp. 16–39; *Mommsen*, "Römische Geschichte"; *Mommsen*, "Römisches Staatsrecht" (2 vols., citations to 2d edition, 1876, 1877); *Von Wächter*, "Beilagen zu Vorlesungen über das deutsche Strafrecht" (1, 1877), pp. 56–77; *A. Pernice*, "Antistius Labeo, das röm. Privatrecht im 1. Jahrhundert der Kaiserzeit" (II, 1878); *Padeletti*, "Lehrbuch der römischen Rechtsgeschichte" (German edition by *Von Holtzendorff*, 1879); *Zumpft*, "Das Criminalrecht der römischen Republik" (2 vols. in four divisions, 1865 and later, deals essentially with procedure). Compare also: *Thonissen*, "Etudes sur l'histoire de droit criminel des peuples anciens" (2 vols., Paris, 1869), and *Thonissen*, "Le droit pénal de la république Athénienne précédé d'un étude sur le droit criminel de la Grèce légendaire" (Bruxelles and Paris, 1875).

[For more recent literature, see: *Accarias*, "Précis de droit romain" (Paris, 1886–1892); *Cornil*, "Droit romain" (Bruxelles, 1885); *Ferrini*, "Diritto penale romano" (Milano, 1898); *Brunnenmeister*, "Die Tödtungsverbrechen im altrömischen Recht" (Leipzig, 1887); *Mommsen*, "Römisches Strafrecht" (Berlin, 1888, 1899); *Zaumar de la Carrera*, "Derecho Romano" (Barcelona, 1883); *May*, "Eléments de droit romain" (Paris, 1891); *Rada y Delgado*, "Elementos de derecho romano" (Madrid, 1887); *Ronga*, "Instituzioni di diritto romano" (Torino, 1889–1890); *Mommsen* (with *Brunner, Goldziher, et al.*), "Zum aeltesten Strafrecht der Kulturvölker; Fragen zur Rechtsvergleichung" (1905); *v. Ihering*, "Das Schuldmoment im römischen Recht" (in his "Vermischte Schriften", 1879); *Hepp*, "Die Zurechnung auf dem Gebiete des Civilrechts" (1838); *Strachan-Davidson*, "Problems of Roman Civil Law" (2 vols., 1912); *Ferrini*, "Diritto penale romano" (Milano, 1899). — VON THÓT.]

[Both in the text and in the notes the German method of referring to the Corpus Juris has been followed. An explanation of this method of quotation can be found, *e.g.*, in *Sohm's* "Institutes of Roman Law" (English translation by *Ledlie*, p. 17). — TRANSL.]

a means of attaining a future end, — bears a certain analogy to the origin of criminal law, which may itself be traced to two sources. One of these sources is the principle of *vengeance* as a retaliation for a wrong.[2] The other source lies in the *subordination of the individual to some higher authority;* this authority, whether it be the family, the clan, the community, or even the State, is one which strives to maintain a certain degree of order, for purposes more or less clearly defined and understood.

In the history of different peoples, these two principles are mingled and confused in various combinations. Vengeance exercised by the individual is not readily subject to restraint, and tends to undermine the established authority, and for this reason the latter seeks to limit its exercise. But the only way in which the established authority can do this is, within certain limits, to take charge of the vengeance of the individual and exercise it in his behalf; for the essential nature of the spirit of vengeance is such that it will not submit to being arbitrarily set aside. There are also times when the established authority deems itself to be directly attacked; on these occasions it too — like any other avowed enemy seeking revenge — proceeds against the individual and proclaims him as its foe. The execution of such a criminal law, wherein the established authority is directly concerned, can be assigned to any individual among the people who volunteers his service. The public authority is as yet too weak to proceed independently to inflict punishment through its own agencies; or perhaps it is obliged to consider the indignation of the people because of the wrongful act, and perceives that it can make this public indignation especially effective to accomplish its own purposes. In such cases, as a matter of course, whosoever volunteers to act as the punishing agent in behalf of the community is obliged upon demand to justify his act, in like manner as he who exercises vengeance in his own behalf.[3]

[2] There can be no dispute as to the fact that the principle of vengeance is a root from which the criminal law has sprung, — although it is less in evidence in cases where there has been an advance in culture. *Cf. Thonissen*, II, pp. 66 *et seq.* and p. 258, in regard to blood revenge ("Blutrache") among the Hebrews. Among the Arabians there are three cardinal virtues: valor, hospitality, and zeal for vengeance. According to the Greek conception, the blood of a man who has been slain cried out for vengeance, until his relatives wreaked vengeance upon the slayer. If they failed to act, there fell upon them a severe curse. *Cf. Meier und Schömann*, "Der attische Process", p. 280; *Cicero*, "Topica", c. 23. "Natura partes habet duas, tuitionem sui et ulciscendi jus;" [*Kohler*, "Zur Lehre von der Blutrache" (1885).]

[3] *Cf.* especially as to the relationship of the "coercitio" and the "judi-

Influence of the Priesthood. — Thus it comes to pass that vengeance is exercised, not so much as the expression of an individual instinct, but rather as the servant of a higher ideal,[4] and that herein it often stands in conjunction with the precepts of religion. The crime offends the gods — the guardians of justice and morality; and the punishment which destroys the wrongdoer, purifies the sacred soil of the fatherland, which has been polluted by the commission of the crime,[5] and appeases the anger of the gods. Thus, punishment acquires to some extent a religious significance and coloring, and comes under the influence of the priesthood. It is safe to assume, moreover, that, if the priesthood is inclined to be lenient in its judgment of the act that has been committed, a way will be found by which the anger of the gods can be appeased in some manner other than the destruction of the criminal;[6] and on the other hand, the party seeking revenge finds moral support, and in some cases real assistance, if the agents of the deity have proclaimed the act as one entailing the curse of the deity. There are also acts which are in the nature of direct attacks upon the sanctity of the gods — upon the duty of allegiance owed to them. In such cases, the priesthood itself often exercises vengeance. Where the priesthood comes to be the predominating influence in the community, it is easy to understand that such duty of allegiance to the gods becomes one of first magnitude, and moreover that there come to be regarded as breaches of this duty many acts which by other peoples are considered merely violations of natural or civil law and not deserving punishment at all.[7]

catio" of the Roman magistrate and the origin of the "judicatio" in the "coercitio", *Mommsen*, "Römisches Staatsrecht", I, pp. 133 *et seq.*, 153 *et seq.* "The 'judicatur' is nothing other than a regulated and restricted form of the 'coercitio.'"

[4] As to the ideas of the inhabitants of India, *cf.* the "Laws of Manu," edited and translated by *Thonissen*, I, pp. 9, 10; [*Kohler*, "Das Indische Strafrecht" ("Zeitschr. für vergl. Rechtswissenschaft," 1903, XVI, 179.] As to these ideas, among the Israelites, see the Bible, Numbers, xxxiii and xxxv.

[5] According to the Greek and Oriental conceptions, the slayer must at least be driven from the country, the soil of which has been moistened by the blood of the slain. *Cf.* Odyssey, XV, 272: "*οὕτω τοι καὶ ἐγὼν ἐκ πατρίδος, ἄνδρα κατακτὰς ἔμφυλον* . . ."

[6] As to the cities of refuge ("Asylstädte") among the Hebrews, which furnished a protection to the slayer against the avenger of blood ("Goël"), when the killing was not premeditated, see the Bible, Exodus, xxi, 12, 13; *Thonissen*, II, pp. 264 *et seq.*

[7] [*Note by* L. VON THÓT. — Since the criminal law of Greece had much in common with the primitive criminal law of Rome, a brief description of the former will be of interest.

Modern accounts may be found in the following treatises: *Leist*,

§ 2. **Rome. Prominence of Religious Element.** — In the history of Rome, from the most remote periods of which we have

"Græco-Italische Rechtsgeschichte" (1884); *Glotz*, "La Solidarité de la famille dans le droit criminel en Grèce" (1904), and "L'ordalie dans la Grèce primitive" (1904); *Mommsen*, "Zum aeltesten Strafrecht" (cited in Note 1 above; article by *Hitzig*); *Loening*, "Geschichte der strafrechtlichen Zurechnungslehre, Vol. I: Die Zurechnungslehre des Aristoteles" (1905); *Kraus*, "Die Zurechnungslehre des Aristoteles" ("Der Gerichtssaal", 1904, LXV, 153, 172; a critique of Loening's volume); *Tesar*, "Staatsidee und Strafrecht; das griechische Recht ...bis Aristoteles" (1914); Abh. des krim. Inst. Univ. Berlin, III ser., I, 3].

In the *Epic Period*, *e.g.* in Homer, we find traces of blood vengeance. However, as Leist says: "It is certain that in the time of Homer, the system of blood vengeance was not in complete operation. The '*κασίγνητοί τε ἔταιτε*' are those from whom the slayer has to fear death. It was a sacred duty to punish the murder of '*παῖδες*' and '*κασίγνητοι*'" (*Leist*, "Graeco-italische Rechtsgeschichte", Book II, Part III, § 46). In the Odyssey, we read that Minerva praised Orestes because he had slain Ægisthus, the murderer of his father (Odyssey, I, 298). Theoclymenus tells Telemachus that he is a fugitive from his fatherland, because of the slaying of a fellow citizen, and that the man who was slain had many relatives and comrades, who have power to kill him (Odyssey, XV, 272–278). Moreover, Odysseus says that he who has slain one of his own countrymen who has only a few to avenge him, must, nevertheless, leave his parents and his fatherland (Odyssey, XXIII, 118–120).

For the *period succeeding the Epic period*, the laws of Draco may be mentioned. These made a distinction between homicide '*ἐκ προνοίας*', and '*μὴ ἐκ προνοίας*' (*i.e.* homicide with and without malice aforethought).

The Athenian state, in the period of its ascendancy, had a special and highly developed system of criminal law, which has been partially preserved in the works of the historical and philosophical writers.

The old criminal law of Attica contained the following punishments: capital punishment, imprisonment, banishment, public dishonor ("infamia"), money fines, and branding. Capital punishment was inflicted in the following methods. Criminals of the common class were put to death by hanging, but slaves or those whose home was without the State might be slain with a heavy club. Other methods were those of burning alive, strangulation, and beheading with a sword. Often the condemned was given a cup of poison to drink. Other methods were suffocation and the casting of the condemned from a high rock. Stoning, empalement and crucifixion were also employed.

The Athenian criminal law made use also of punishments by mutilation — the putting out of one or both eyes, the cutting off of the right hand, and the tearing out of the tongue. Flogging was employed as a means of corporal punishment. Imprisonment was but little used in Athens as a punishment. It was employed, however, when one had not paid a debt or had been convicted of theft. In such cases the condemned was obliged to spend five days and nights in jail, where he was chained and exposed to the derision and abuse of the multitude. Imprisonment on a ship was also practiced. Banishment was either for life or temporary. One method was that of ostracism, which was as a rule limited to cases of a political significance or in which the public order was concerned. However, it was seldom resorted to.

We obtain many references to punishment from the writings of various authors. It was a fundamental principle that the punishment of a slave should be corporal (*Demosthenes*, "Androtion", 610). Confiscation of property was incident to banishment (*Schol.* in *Aristophanes*, "Vesp.", 947). The names of those who were condemned to death were erased

knowledge, we find the above-mentioned elements of criminal law.

from the record of citizens (*Dio Chrysostom*, "Rhodiaca" 31). If a woman condemned to death was *enceinte*, the execution was postponed (*Plutarch*, "de sera num. vind.", 7). Those condemned to death were for three days before the execution of the sentence permitted to enjoy food and wine (*Zenobius*, III, 100). A man who had been sentenced to capital punishment was permitted to choose between the sword and the rope (Suidas). Where several were sentenced to die, the various executions took place on consecutive days, the order being determined by lot (*Schol.* in *Aristophanes*, "Pac.", 364). There was, for murderers, no right of refuge (asylum) (*Lycurg.* c. *Leverat.* § 93).

As to the fundamental principles of criminal law, the following points may be noticed. All accessories to a crime were punished alike, whether they be instigators, originators, or participants. Where the act was intentional the penalties fixed by law were inflicted, but where the act resulted from carelessness, there was an acquittal. In crimes of a serious character, there were no periods of limitation in favor of the criminal.

Taking up the crimes specifically, — high treason, ordinary treason, rebellion directed towards the overthrow of the democratic form of constitution, and sedition were punishable with the death penalty and confiscation of property. Counterfeiting and perjury were treated in the same way. Any one who, in a temple, before a court, before a magistrate, at the public games, or in an assembly, used offensive language towards another was sentenced to pay a fine of five drachmas. Attempts against life were punished with very severe penalties. Incitement to murder was also regarded as a crime — the instigator being subjected to the same penalty as the actual perpetrator. Attempt at murder was regarded in the same light as the consummated act. The penalty for murder was death or banishment for life and confiscation of property. Murderers were deprived of all public and private rights and forbidden to take part in all religious ceremonies, and if they refused to leave the country of their own accord, were put to death.

The elements essential to constitute the crime of murder were intention, absence of legal justification and the Athenian citizenship of the man who was slain. Assassination and poisoning constituted a special type of murder and both were punished with death. He who killed another through accident or negligence was obliged to at once leave the State, and remain in foreign parts until permitted by the relatives of the deceased to return. This crime also entailed religious penalties. Parricide was punished with the death penalty. The junior Archons ("θεσμοθέται") might kill those who were banished on account of murder. In fact, anyone was allowed to kill them, but the law forbade that they should be tortured or that a composition be required of them. If anyone killed in a sacred place a man who had been condemned to death, he was made to suffer the same punishment as was to have been inflicted upon the man whom he killed. He who plundered the property of a murderer who had not been sentenced to lose his property, was punished with a money fine.

The law regarded self-defense as a justification. No punishment was inflicted upon a man who slew another whom he found in an actual illicit relation with his wife, mother, sister, daughter, or concubine. The right hand of a man who took his own life was cut off and buried apart from the body. If any one died as a result of a fault of a physician, the physician was not regarded as a murderer. Assault and battery of a man, woman, or child was punished by a fine not exceeding 1000 drachmas. In later times this offense was punished more severely, *i.e.* with death. Capital punishment was inflicted upon the highwayman and upon one who had carnal knowledge of a girl against her will. If a man seduced a girl, and was himself unmarried, he was compelled to marry her. Severe

The religious element is especially prominent. Thus the word "supplicium", meaning punishment, and particularly capital punishment, is of religious origin. It signified, at first, a sin offering — a sacrifice with prayers for mercy — and is derived from "sub" and "placare" (to appease).[1] Often, when a crime[2] had been committed, special sacrifices were performed to appease the anger of the gods; the criminal was declared to be "sacer",[3] and, as an outlaw, cast forth from the communion of gods and men. Any one who killed him performed a task pleasing to the gods.[4] "Leges sacratæ" was the name later given to certain laws, which

penalties were inflicted for depriving a Greek citizen of his liberty without just cause. As other punishable acts, Plato mentions: offenses against religion, battery, the tearing down of walls, robbery, and theft. He who had stolen an object that was sacred, was punished by a confiscation of all his property, and his corpse could not be buried in Attica.

The criminal law of Sparta was of a different nature. It was distinguished by its extraordinary severity. Thus we know that a young Spartan, who had sewn a purple stripe on his tunic, was punished with death (*Plutarch*, "Instit. Laced."). We know also that the Spartans had stringent laws against refusal to enter into the marriage relation. The young people were punished with loss of honor and property, and were stripped of their clothing in the market place in the winter, while the people sang derisive songs (*Plutarch*, "Lyc.", 27). There is record of a judgment in the time of Lycurgus, by which a youth was subjected to a fine, because he had placed upon some goods a selling price which exceeded the real value, and thereby gave evidence of his own avarice. A king was compelled to pay a fine because he had won the hearts of all the people, although their admiration was justifiable (*Plut.*, "Agesilaos", 6). These examples sufficiently reveal the severity of the Spartan system.

A detailed examination would reveal many features in the Spartan legislation, distinguishing it from that of the rest of Greece. Thus we know that in Sparta theft was permissible. The vital matter was that the thief should not be caught. If he was caught, he was whipped for his lack of skill. It was not until a comparatively late period that the embezzlement of public funds was punished by banishment.

Offenses against morality were punished in Sparta by death. Theft in places that were sacred entailed the same penalty; as did also bribery of a priest or priestess, treason, rebellion, or infidelity in military affairs. The usual method of capital punishment was strangulation. But the Spartan criminal law also availed itself of decapitation, casting from a high rock, and the cup of poison. Among other methods of punishment, mention may be made of deprivation of honor and civil rights, banishment, and money fines.]

[1] *Rein*, p. 29. Also the words "castigare" (*i.e.* "castum agere") and "luere" (*i.e.* "pœnam luere") refer to purification.

[2] [The Roman law used various expressions to designate a crime, *e.g.* "fraus", "scelus", "maleficium", "flagitium", "peccatum", "delictum", "crimen", "probum", etc. All these expressions are used interchangeably. However, "maleficium" appears to have been more appropriately applied to a crime committed by a slave, and "scelus" to an offense against religion: *Ferrini*, "Diritto penale Romano", p. 36. — VON THÓT.]

[3] Deprivation of property as a punishment was in ancient times called "consecratio bonorum."

[4] I agree entirely with *von Ihering*, I, pp. 281, 282, who calls attention to the analogy of the Norse "Wargus", "Waldgängers." *Mommsen*,

in an emphatic manner prescribed the death penalty for any one who dared to violate the sacred rights of the Plebs (which were relatively the rights of the individual citizen), and such a one was called "sacer" ("quem populus judicavit").[5] Moreover, the capital punishments inflicted by the State were executed with customs which strongly remind one of the offering of victims as a sacrifice to the gods.[6]

Roman Law not a Theocratic System. — However, the old Roman criminal law did not, primarily, rest upon a theocratic foundation. The punishment was merely *increased* because of the curse of the gods. Because of their curse the individual was required to destroy the criminal, or at least to break off all relationship with him.[7] But the determination of the elements which constituted a crime was little influenced by a regard for the gods. We find nothing corresponding to the death penalties inflicted in the theocratic community of the Hebrews,[8] for a departure from the faith, nonobservance of holidays, and blasphemy. The acts which placed the accused in the position of "sacer" were more essentially those pertaining to the interests of the family and of the civil community.[9] The patron who violated his duty of good faith toward his client;[10] the son who wronged his father;[11] the daughter-in-law who repudiated the sacred duty of allegiance to the family — each of these became "sacer." An old law, dating back to the time of Numa, proclaimed as "sacer" the destroyer of boundary marks.[12] By

"Römische Geschichte", (6th Ed.), I, p. 175, is incorrect in his statement that such a slaying without judicial procedure is contrary to all civic systems of law.

[5] *Cf. Festus,* "De verb. significatu" under "Sacer Mons", and *Huschke,* p. 197, note; also Bible, Deuteronomy, xiii, 6–11; xvii, 2–5. Those who came to have knowledge of the forbidden departure from the Jewish faith were required forthwith to stone the guilty, although it is certainly possible that there could also be a judicial conviction. In Rome, also, a denunciation and public execution of the "sacer" was possible: *Rein,* pp. 32, 33.

[6] *Mommsen,* "Staatsrecht", II, p. 49, says that every death penalty was originally, in Rome, the offering up of a victim as a sacrifice.

[7] *Thonissen,* II, p. 313.

[8] *Plinius,* "Hist. nat.", 18, 3. *Cf. Gellius,* 11, 18.

[9] *Platner,* p. 26, is quite correct in the statement: "Civitate potius religio quam religione civitas continebatur."

[10] *Diongsius H.,* II, 10, states that the client also who violated his duties was declared "sacer."

[11] *Festus,* "Verb. Sig.", under "plorare" gives as a statute of Servius Tullius: "Si parentem puer verberit, aste olle plorassit, puer divis parentum sacer esto."

[12] *Ibid.,* under "termino," "Numam statuisse accepimus: eum qui terminum exarasset, et ipsum et boves sacros esse."

the Twelve Tables the thief stealing grain in the night was threatened with death. In like manner, by the maxim, "Suspensumque Cereri necari jubebant", [13] it is evident that a law affording so effective a protection to property was certainly not of a religious nature.[14] There appears to be only the intention, on one hand, to arouse a special feeling of repulsion towards the crime, and, on the other, to make the prosecution — probably rather lax in the case of many crimes, because *e.g.* of the existence of family relations — an especially vigorous one, by an appeal to religious sentiment and by granting the right of immediate execution. The only crimes which bore an essentially religious character were those acts which were directly detrimental to the sacred cults of the State; and these were few.[15] Apart from the disciplinary punishment against insubordinate priests, the only crimes clearly of this nature were violations of the chastity of the Vestal Virgins; these, for the priestess, entailed the penalty of being buried alive; [16] for her admirer, death by flogging.[17]

Early Suppression of Vengeance. — It is a peculiar characteristic of the Roman criminal law, that private vengeance was suppressed at a very early period. We find it, in a pure form, in none of the legal provisions which have survived, and from these provisions we are justified in drawing certain wider conclusions as to its non-existence.

§ 3. **Suppression of Vengeance in Cases of Homicide.** — Power to deal with cases of murder ("dolose Tödtung") [1] was acquired

[13] As to all these cases, *cf. Abegg*, pp. 45 *et seq.*

[14] There is nothing inconsistent with the denial of the theocratic character of the early Roman criminal law in the acceptance of the fact that the priests exercised a considerable influence upon the law and especially upon the criminal law. The Roman priests were State officials and this influence was a logical consequence of the fact that originally the temporal and spiritual powers were in the same hands: *Mommsen*, "Röm. Staatsrecht", II, p. 49.

[15] *Festus*, "Verb. Sig." under "pellices" states: "Pellex aram Junonis ne tangito; si tanget, Junoni crinibus demissis agnum feminam cædito."

[16] In the earliest periods the Vestal also was flogged to death.

[17] *Platner*, p. 27, is of the opinion that only slaves of the priesthood were dealt with under this criminal power of the priests. In that case the criminal power of the latter could be regarded as purely a disciplinary one. It is a fact, that there could be an investigation by State authorities of those who have been absolved, as it were, by the priests.

[1] [There are differences of opinion as to whether the element in murder spoken of as "dolus" corresponds to malice aforethought. According to *Leist*, "Gräco-Italische Rechtsgeschichte", p. 370, the conception of "dolus" combines legal conception of intention and also of premeditation. *Ferrini*, "Diritto penale romano", p. 86, on the contrary, asserts that the Roman "dolus", especially "*dolus malus*" signifies the "animus occidendi." In his opinion this is evident from the "Lex Cornelia", in which

by the public criminal authorities at an early date. "Quæstores parricidii",[2] and a sentence of death because of a slaying done intentionally and in the heat of passion, are to be found in the well known story of the Horatii.[3] There is record of a provision in the laws of Numa Pompilius, reading as follows: "Si quis hominem liberum dolo sciens morti duit, parricida esto."[4] By these same laws, in cases of homicide resulting from negligence ("culpose Tödtung"), vengeance could be avoided by the sacrifice of a goat as a sin offering. Since the State was concerned in the killing of one of its citizens, this sacrifice must be made "in concione", *i.e.* in the public assembly.

On the other hand, it is certain that the right of the husband or father to take immediate vengeance upon an adulterer, when found "in flagrante", long continued in existence. The "Lex Julia de adulteriis", enacted in the time of Augustus, in addition to enabling a complaint on the grounds of adultery to be brought

"dolus" signifies "animus occidendi", and certainly in the sense that if the "animus" exists, it is immaterial whether the killing be public or secret, done with violence or with cunning. One may imply in the word "dolus" a certain intention to injure. This appears from *Cicero*, who says: "Quod ergo es animo factum est, ut homines eadem facerent, id si *voluerunt* et perfecérunt, potestis eam voluntatem, id consilium, id factum, *a dolo malo sejungere?*" ("Pro Tullio", c. 10, 13, 14). There are also often found the expressions, "consulto", "sponte", "sciens et prudens", which, according to *Ferrini*, proves that the Roman criminal law made distinctions between different kinds of homicide. This differentiation was clear, since these various expressions were different designations of one and the same conception, *i.e.* "dolus." *Vogt* is of an opposite opinion ("Römische Rechtsgeschichte", p. 39). He says that the word "consulto", to which *Ferrini* refers, is equivalent to the word "premeditamente", and thus when a statute in dealing with homicide uses the word "consulto", it has reference to homicide done with premeditation, *i.e.* one finds in Roman law a correct conception of *murder*.

We prefer the opinion which justifies *Ferrini's* viewpoint; yet his conclusions seem incorrect and even daring. The meanings of "consulto", "sponte" and "sciens et prudens" etc. are identical, but are not the same as "dolus." This certainly is true of "consulto." The idea originally contained in "consulto" was that of meditation, of deliberation, taking one's own counsel. The conception is rather of the *result* of the meditation and deliberation; the determination upon the realization or non-realization of the purpose, *i.e.* malice aforethought. These ideas make the opinion of *Vogt* appear preferable. — VON THÓT.]

[2] There are differences of opinion as to the derivation and original meaning of the word "parricidium", which later signified the murder of near relations. *Rein*, p. 450, adheres to the derivation from "pater" and "cædere." Others prefer the derivation from "parens" and "cædere." *Osenbrüggen* cleverly proposes that it meant merely a wicked ("dolose") slaying, the word being derived from "para" which is equivalent to "per", with the same meaning as in "perjurus" or "perfidia." *Huschke*, p. 183, says it is derived from "parem cædere" and refers to the killing of an equal, a fellow comrade from among the people.

[3] *Livy*, I, 23.

[4] *Festus*, "Verb. sig." under "Parici Quæstores."

in a "judicium publicum", also contained detailed provisions calculated to restrict, as far as possible, the exercise of vengeance in such cases. From Gellius (N. A., X, 23) "in adulterio uxorem tuam si prehendisses, impune sine judicio necares", it may be inferred that theretofore the right had been given a wider range, and especially that the husband might instantly slay the wife apprehended in the commission of the guilty act.[5]

Influence of the Principle of Vengeance in the Treatment of Other Crimes. — Prior to the Twelve Tables recourse to vengeance was often taken in cases of personal injury.[6] The Twelve Tables established the "talio" as the limit to which vengeance might be exercised,[7] in case the offender was not able in some other way to settle with the injured party.[8] In the case of lesser injuries —

[5] *Cf. Abegg*, "Untersuchungen aus dem Gebiete der Strafrechtswissenschaft" (1830), p. 166. The husband could slay the adulterer, but not the wife, and could only slay the former if he belonged to the "viliores personæ." The father was permitted to slay the adulterer, provided, at the same time, he slew his own daughter.

[6] [The statutes prior to the Twelve Tables constitute the so-called "Jus Papirianum." These contain the "Leges regiæ", and were compiled by the Jurist Caius Papirianus. These statutes forbade the killing of children over three years of age under penalty of confiscation of property. But if the child was disobedient or a cripple then the act was unpunished. The daughter-in-law who mistreated her father-in-law became "exsecrata" and could be slain with impunity by any one. Intentional slaying was punished as "parricidium." He who killed another unintentionally was obliged to give "aries" to the relatives of the slain. The son who killed his father became "sacer" and anyone had the right to kill him. *Cf. Dionigi in Capuano*, "Dottrina e storia del diritto romano" (Napoli, 1864); *Sigonius*, "De antiquo jure civili Romano", lib. I, c. 5; *Capobianco*, "Il diritto penale di Roma" (Firenze, 1894), pp. 19–22; *Bruns*, "Fontes juris romani antiqui" (Tübingen, 1860). — VON THÓT.]

[7] The familiar provision in the Mosaic Law (*cf.* especially, Exodus, xxi, 24: "Eye for an eye, tooth for a tooth" (Do unto others what they do unto you), and other numerous and important examples of "talio" (*cf.* as to Greece, *Hermann*, "Lehrbuch", note 9 *et seq.*; "*εἴ κε πάθοι τά κ' ἔρεξε, δίκη κ'ὶ θεῖα γένοιτο*"), are not direct commands but rather limitations upon the right of vengeance, which the legislator was able to limit before he was able completely to suppress. *Cf.* especially, *Thonissen*, II, p. 66.

[8] That only bodily injuries done intentionally are referred to, may be inferred, on one hand, from the inclusion by *Gaius*, under the delict of "injuria", only acts done "dolo", and, on the other, from the abovementioned provision relative to a negligent ("culpose") slaying. If in the latter case the relatives of the slain man were obliged to be satisfied with the offering of a victim in expiation, in the case of bodily injuries they would not have a more extensive right of revenge. *Köstlin*, "Mord und Todtschlag", p. 44, and *Von Ihering*, "Das Schuldmoment in röm. Privatrecht" (1867), p. 11, are of another opinion because of the passage of *Gellius*, XX, 1, § 34. But the words "decemviri — neque ejus qui membrum alteri rupisset — tantam esse habendam rationem, ut an prudens imprudensve rupisset, spectandum putarent" refer (according to a more correct interpretation) to a case where the blow was given

"os fractum aut collisum" as distinguished from "membrum raptum" — the "talio" was completely excluded, and the injured party was granted a definite compensation.[9]

The method of dealing with theft was more closely related to the principle of private vengeance. The Twelve Tables permitted the killing of the "fur nocturnus"[10] and the armed thief (carrying weapons for his own protection). But in the later law this was allowed only as an artificial extension of the right of self-defense; and still later it was limited to actual self-defense,[11] since the man whose property was being stolen had the right to seize the thief whom he caught in the act. Moreover, the punishment provided for "furtum manifestum" was undoubtedly influenced by a regard for private vengeance.[12] "Pœna manifesti furti ex lege XII tabularum capitalis erat; nam liber verberatus addicebatur ei cui furtum fecerat" (*Gaius*, IV, 189). Here the "addictio" was a substitute for the ancient right to kill.

"dolo", and the special kind of injury was intended, as we to-day, in the classification of bodily injuries as "grave" and "minor", make a distinction in the consequence of the act. For of a "Violentia pulsandi atque lædendi", which as *Gellius*, *loc. cit.*, says should be restrained, there can be a doubt only in case of an intentional ill-treatment, and not in case of merely negligent ("culpose") injury in the doing of a thing that is legally permissible, and only with the former is the conclusion of the passage consistent — "quoniam modus voluntatis præstari posset, casus ictus non posset." One has it in his power to determine whether he will give a blow or a kick, but it is not in his power to injure according as the blow or kick happen to reach their mark.

[9] The most important passage is *Gaius*, III, 223, — "Pœna autem injuriarum ex lege XII tabularum propter membrum quidem ruptum talio erat, propter os vero fractum aut collisum trecentorum assium pœna erat veluti si libero os fractum erat; at si servo CL: propter ceteras vero injurias XXV assium pœna erat constituta." As observed by *Gaius*, in accordance with the value of money in the early periods ("in magna paupertate"), these fines were by no means as insignificant as they appear.

[10] "Decemviri in XII Tabulis — dixerunt — Si nox furtum factum sit, si im occisit, jure cæsus esto." *Macrob.* Saturn. I, c. 4.

Cf. Gellius, VIII, 1. XI, 18: "furem qui manifesto furto prensus esset, tum demum occidi permiserunt (XII Tab.), si aut cum faceret furtum, nox esset, aut interdiu telo se quum prenderetur, defenderet." *Cicero*, "Pro mil." c. 3. "Collatio leg. Mosaic." VII, pr. L. 9 D. Ad leg. Aqu. 9, 2. *Cf. Abegg*, "Untersuchungen", p. 142.

[11] "Collatio", VII, 2: "Paullus, Libro V ad legem Corneliam de sicariis et veneficis. Si quis furem nocturnum vel diurnum, cum se telo defenderet acciderit, hac quidem lege non tenetur: sed melius fecerit qui eum comprehensum transmittendum ad præsidem magistratibus optulerit." *Idem* c. 3, § 1: "Pomponius dubitat, num hæc lex sit in usu." *Paulus*, in L. 9 D. ad leg. Corn. de sicariis 48, 8: "Furem nocturnum si quis occiderit, ita demum impune feret, si parcere ei sine periculo suo non potuit."

[12] For the definition of "furtum manifestum" see especially *Gaius*, III, 184.

In order to prevent the party whose property was stolen from taking immediate vengeance [13] — a difficult thing to prevent when the thief was caught in the act — his rights were extended as far as possible.[14] Consequently, "furtum manifestum" at a later time was a basis for the prætorian action for a fourfold penalty,[15] while in "fur nec manifestum" only a twofold penalty could be claimed.[16] It is easy to understand why in a case of theft (except theft of field-produce, as above mentioned), there is nothing said as to the thief becoming "sacer." The law proclaimed as "sacer" the man against whom it required vengeance. But the legislator, in view of the attitude which exists everywhere in uncivilized times (one need only consider

[13] A slave, according to the Twelve Tables, forfeited his life; he was flogged and then cast from a high rock: *Gellius*, N. A. XI, 18.

[14] *Cf. Hepp*, "Versuche über einzelne Lehren der Strafrechtswissenschaft" (1827), pp. 132 *et seq.*

[15] Other explanations are not satisfactory, *cf. Hepp*, pp. 110 *et seq.; Rein*, p. 298, note; *Zumpft*, I, p. 376. That the thief caught in the act is always a very daring and dangerous person, is certainly not true; on the contrary he is just as likely to be a cowardly person. The proposition, that some special favor should be shown to the man who is vigilant as to his property, is too artificial for acceptance. His vigilance is certainly rewarded in any case, since he retains his possessions, and rewards and inducements for guarding one's property against unlawful acts are generally superfluous. The explanation that one who, because of fear, is not in a position to judge fairly, will inflict, upon the thief, who is caught in the act or who confesses, only the extreme penalty, is not satisfactory, in that it does not apply to a confession. Moreover, there is nothing to be said relative to the greater offense to the man whose goods are stolen by a "furtum manifestum." The fact that he is caught in the act is for the most part merely a consequence of a lack of skill on the part of the thief. The view taken in the text is also in accord with the early Roman conception, in L. 7. § 1 D. "De furtis," 47, 2, which required for a "furtum manifestum" the actual apprehension of the thief, and was not satisfied with the immediate knowledge that the act had been committed. In the time of Justinian (*cf.* § 3 J. 4, 1), the origin of the special legal rules in regard to "furtum manifestum" were no longer understood, — hence the wider extension of the conception. It was an artificial extension of "furtum manifestum," as *Gaius* himself says (III, 194), that according to the Twelve Tables he was considered a "fur manifestus" in whose home the stolen goods were found by means of a formal search ("lance et licio"). The individual with whom the stolen property was found without such a formal search had to pay three times their value because of "furtum conceptum" (not however if he could immediately show he had acquired the goods lawfully). This provision punished the receiver of stolen property. For the protection of the formal searching of a house there existed the "actio furti prohibiti" for fourfold the value of the stolen article, against him who did not permit a searching of the house when demanded in the proper manner. *Cf. Rudorff*, II, p. 352.

[16] A private settlement with money was frequently made, even before the Twelve Tables, as indicated by the old form of complaint: "pro fure damnum decidere opportere." The Prætor merely adopted an established custom. *Cf. Rudorff*, II, p. 350.

our own peasants), had little occasion to provide rigorous and summary punishment for injuries to property rights. The one exception, having to do with theft from the fields, may readily be explained as a concession to established custom and considerations of public policy.

§ 4. "**Perduellio.**" — In cases of homicide, private vengeance and private compensation disappeared at an early date, and were replaced by public punishment. The small Roman community, surrounded as it was by many enemies, regarded the murder ("dolose Tödtung") of one of its citizens as an attack upon its own strength and prosperity, and as a breach of the duties owed to it by the individual. This circumstance had a significant bearing upon the Roman criminal law.

Originally, the only crime against the State, as such, was "perduellio", *i.e.* the individual assuming as towards the State the relation of war ("duellum" = "bellum"; "perduellis" = base or evil enemy). It included, primarily, betrayal of the country to a foreign enemy, desertion to the enemy in time of war, and attacks upon the institutions of the country by the undertaking of acts which could be regarded as encroachments upon the supreme rights of the State. There were included among such acts, in the time of the Republic, attempts to establish a despotism, and attacks upon the magistrate of the Plebs, who was declared to be especially sacred, and in the time of the Empire, attempts against the person of the emperor.

According to the Roman conception, any act, in consequence of special circumstances, could be regarded as criminally prejudical to the interests of the State and be dealt with as such. Judgment in such cases was passed by the holder of the sovereign power, — in the early periods, by the king; later, in accordance with the "Lex Valeria", by the people, when appeal was taken to them as a tribunal of last resort; and, in accordance with the Twelve Tables, by the people as a court of first instance, in the "comitia centuriata." "Perduellio", as shown by the form of the complaint: "Tibi perduellionem iudico",[1] was not so much the criminal act as rather the position in which the offender was placed as a punishment — the treatment of him as an enemy of the State.[2] Under such conditions, it was also possible to regard

[1] *Livy*, I, 26, 7; *cf.* XXVI, 3.

[2] Correct view, *Rudorff*, II, p. 365, note 1, and *Huschke*, p. 185, note 109. To the contrary *Rein*, pp. 466 *et seq.*

as "perduellio" the murder of a citizen,[3] *e.g.* the murder of the sister in the story of the Horatii. On the same ground the Senate was able later, without further authority, to prosecute as State criminals the Bacchantes (a corrupting influence among the Roman women), since they appeared to have attributes prejudicial to the public welfare. The further criminal character of either the act or its author was of no consequence.

"**Multæ Irrogatio.**" — This indefinite character of "perduellio" is especially noticeable in its plebeian counterpart, the "multæ irrogatio" on the part of the plebeian magistrate.[4] Since the laws declared that violations of the sacred rights of the Plebs were acts reducing their author to a relation of war toward the Plebs, it was possible for the Tribunes of the Plebs (or perhaps the Ædiles) to levy upon the offender heavy fines, the amount of which would be arbitrarily fixed by the Plebs ("multæ irrogatio"). As acts entailing such a penalty, there appear (in addition to *e.g.* attempts to establish a despotism, retention of an office beyond its term, engaging in war without the order of the Senate, abuse of official power, and offending the people by vain display) also acts such as partiality in the distribution of booty of war, appropriation of public money to one's own use, employment of the army for private enterprises, abuse of the censorship, offenses against religion, sorcery, usury, and even lewdness and other offenses against morality in its narrower sense.

§ 5. **Roman Conception of the Relation of the Individual to the State.** — The exceedingly indefinite character of the old State crime — which originally was the only *public* crime — rests, in our opinion, not upon the nature of the crime itself,[1] but rather upon the peculiar Roman conception of the relation of the individual to the State. According to the Roman conception the individual has no rights which the State is bound to respect. This is forcibly illustrated by the well-known absolutism of the magis-

[3] *Cf. Nissen*, "Das Justitium, eine Studie aus der römischen Rechtsgeschichte" (1877), pp. 24 *et seq.*

[4] *Cf.* especially the excellent investigations of *Huschke*, pp. 145 *et seq.*, and particularly the remarks on p. 179.

[1] Herein we differ from the opinion of Huschke, "Crime as such is a mere ethical negation; it has in itself no valid distinction, since 'non entis nulla sunt prædicata'" (*Huschke*, p. 211). I believe that wrong ("Rechtsverletzung") and punishment are here interchanged. Crime, as a wrong, must have definite limits, just as it is necessary that there be a definitive establishment of the right that has been violated. However, punishment was originally of but one kind — banishment from the community or death.

trate in the time of the Republic, who, during his term of office, was regarded as directly representing the "populus." It appears also in the absence of any means by which an official act of a magistrate could be treated as null and void.[2] Furthermore, it is shown by the fact that the State treasury ("fiscus") could not be made a party to an action,[3] and also, later, by the absolute power of the emperor. There were, to be sure, some laws which sought to guarantee to the citizen, as against the State, a definite range of legal rights (and all laws relating to the "judicia publica" were such), and sought to place definite limitations upon the originally unrestricted criminal law of the State,[4] and thereby render it more certain in its operation. But according to the Roman conception these were only voluntary concessions on the part of the State, which at its discretion might be withdrawn, and are not consequences of an adherence to a uniform legal ideal. Consequently any such concession could be withdrawn, *e.g.* by the appointment of a dictator, if the Senate declared the State to be in danger.[5] Thus it is easily explainable why the right to liberty of the citizen as against the magistrate, since it was merely the result of a positive concession, was limited to the city of Rome and its immediate vicinity.[6]

Germanic Conception of the Relation of the Individual to the State. — According to the Germanic conception — and this comparison seems to us to be especially appropriate as an illustration — there obtain quite different conditions. The rights of the individual as against the State are not based upon some positive law, liable to be modified at discretion or suspended in its operation by the enactment of some other law, but are based upon that ideal of law of which contract and statute are merely the expression. Even the king, according to the Germanic conception of law, must submit to the jurisdiction of the court. Against the State treasury ("fiscus"), and against the State as a legal entity, "jura quæsita" in the fullest sense may be obtained.

[2] Against this there was effective only the intercession of a "par majorve potestas."

[3] Cases in which the "fiscus" was concerned were later decided by the "procurator fisci" and not by the court.

[4] As to this point, see the above cited work of *Nissen*.

[5] This also explains the fact that the Romans, especially in the time of the Republic, often gave to their criminal statutes an "ex post facto" effect — "qui fecit, fecerit" — without considering it as anything out of the ordinary. *Cf. Seeger*, "Abhandlungen aus dem Strafrecht" (II, 1862), p. 1 *et seq.*

[6] *Cf. Puchta*, "Institutionen", I, § 51, note 6.

Personal rights follow the Germanic individual everywhere, and decrees derogatory thereof are null and void.

Contribution of Roman Criminal Law to the Establishment of Individual Rights. — The significant bearing upon the world's history, customarily ascribed to the Roman Law [7] as a factor in assisting the individual human being to assume a position of importance "per se", and to acquire, to a certain extent, a position of independence towards the State, is contrary to fact. These results were obtained only when the Germanic ideal of law had impressed itself upon the progress of humanity.

Moreover, it is not true that in these respects the Romans were clearly in advance of the Greeks. The much greater strictness shown in limiting the jurisdiction of the Athenian magistrate, the actual and careful protection in Athens of the rights of the individual [8] as against the State, speak to the contrary. At any rate there did not prevail in Athens the Roman conception that the rights of the State are unlimited; that the individual should be fashioned after an ideal model; and that he could, arbitrarily, be reared as a component unit of the State. We do not find in Rome statutes enacted with a primary regard for the welfare of the individual, such as those of Zaleukos and Charondas penalizing evil association, or those of the Locrians penalizing the drinking of unmixed wine, or even those of Solon, which punished the lack of a business or trade,[9] and endeavored to prevent suicide.[10] While it, indeed, may be said that the Roman State made a sharper distinction than the Greek, between law and morality, yet it gave to the individual no rights inviolable as against the State.

This accounts for the many respects in which the Roman criminal law occupies an unfortunate position for comparison with the private law. It also explains the brutal (it may well be called) manner in which the statutes, the imperial constitutions, and the "senatus consulta" penalized acts which, in themselves, did not in any way violate a right — and perhaps could be regarded only as remotely prejudicial to a right. It also explains that element of indefiniteness and of analogy to regulations laid down by the police power, which characterizes the most comprehensive

[7] *Cf. e.g. Hildenbrand,* "Geschichte und System der Rechts- und Staatsphilosophie", I, p. 524.

[8] Especially in criminal procedure.

[9] *Hermann,* "Lehrbuch der griechischen Privatalterthümer", § 60, note 4, *seq.*

[10] *Hermann,* § 62, note 27. In Athens, the hand of one who had committed suicide was cut off.

of the Roman criminal statutes,[11] which, in order surely to reach preliminary acts, gave to them the same legal effect as the crimes to which they might refer. It also explains the fact that judicial practice in the field of criminal law, at least in its operation in the Roman State, has in part performed only a labor of Sisyphus, which did not produce real results until our own time. The theory of the Roman private complaint, in which legal principle obtained in a purer form, is often of more importance for us than the utterances of the Roman jurists concerning the "crimina publica." At least these utterances need to be supplemented or modified by reference to the private complaint before they become useful for our purposes.[12]

[11] *Laboulaye*, p. 265, explains this peculiar character of the composition of the criminal statutes by the statement that they were statutes whose purpose was to confer jurisdiction, and were of the same nature as statutes assigning to one and the same "quæstio" power to deal with different delicts. But jurisdiction was not the only matter with which the criminal statutes of the Republic were concerned. They also fixed punishments. Moreover the fact that more attention was given to the matter of jurisdiction than to an exact definition of the crime (*cf. Laboulaye*, p. 304) is further evidence of the arbitrary manner in which the Romans dealt with the substantive criminal law.

[12] The "Lex Cornelia de sicariis", a statute which governed the entire later development of the law relating to homicide, is an illuminating example of the method of procedure of the Roman criminal legislation. Carrying weapons with the intention of killing some one or merely with the intention to accomplish a theft, the manufacture or purchase of poison which was eventually to be given to some one, the starting of fires in the city of Rome and its immediate vicinity, the bearing of false witness with the purpose of causing capital punishment to be inflicted upon another, the bribery or the unfairness of a magistrate or "judex quæstionis" with the same end in view, the illegal condemnation of a Roman citizen by a magistrate or the Senate without a "judicium publicum" (*cf. Cicero*, "Pro Cluentio", c. 54), — these were all included under one and the same statute, a statute which forbade intentional homicide. By imperial constitutions and decrees of the Senate there were also added the crime of castration and even the holding of "mala sacrificia" (*cf.* L. 1, 4, 13 D. "Ad leg. Corneliam de sic.", 48, 8). The "Lex Cornelia de falsis" furnishes another example. By an extension of this statute (by decree of the Senate) anyone was punished for "falsum" who took money for suppressing evidence, and also, according to the "Senatusconsultum Claudianum", he who, in writing the testament of another, wrote out a disposition in his own favor, even at the request of the testator and perhaps "optima fide" (L. 15 pr. D. eod.; L. 3 C. "De his qui sibi", 9, 23). Here the mere *possibility* of a forgery sufficed to entail a criminal punishment. The "Lex Julia de adulteriis" without further enquiry punished as a procurer the husband who did not disown a wife whom he had apprehended in an act of adultery (L. 2 § 2 D. 48, 5). The "Lex Julia de vi" punished those who possessed an unusual quantity of weapons, nor were they allowed to prove that they had these weapons for a special purpose which, in itself, was legal. Also those were punished "qui pubes cum telo in publico fuit." All these cases were grouped with cases of actual violent attacks upon villages, of "stuprum violentum", and of theft with force of arms during a conflagration.

It might be argued in reply, that only statutes designed to serve a temporary end are being considered. But the description as a statute designed to serve a temporary end can not be applied to *e.g.* the "Lex Julia de adulteriis", enacted in the time of Augustus. Also the fact that laws, which if they were partly of a temporary nature could for centuries form, as it were, the skeleton of the public criminal law, and the fact that no later attempt was made to replace these laws by others of more definite legal principles, but that the further development of the criminal law in the imperial constitutions and the "Senatus consulta" followed the same arbitrary method is a sufficient revelation of the character of the Roman criminal legislation.

§ 6. **The Jurisprudence of the Empire.** — The legal science of the jurists of the time of the Empire [1] represents in many respects the reaction of the ideal of law against arbitrary methods of legislation. We notice that there was an endeavor to separate more strictly the various kinds of crime, which in the earlier statutes were grouped together at random. An attempt was also made to introduce more proper distinctions of the degrees of guilt. But for the most part it was impossible to remedy the statutes' lack of an exact statement of the acts constituting the crime. The interposition of legislation which was not supported by fixed principles and traditions (*i.e.* in this later period, the imperial constitutions and the "Senatus consulta") made the task more difficult. The ultimate result is that, in the public criminal law, arbitrary and accidental rules are far less widely separated from that which is of permanent value, than in the private law.

Real Explanation of Arbitrary Nature of Roman Criminal Law. — The final and real explanation of the peculiarly arbitrary character of the Roman criminal law is to be found in the fact that the constant wars in which, from the very beginning, the small Roman State was obliged to struggle for its existence, precluded, from the outset, the idea of a fixed and rigid boundary between acts which were essentially criminal and morally culpable, and those which merely were likely to prove dangerous. An act which, at other times, has no special significance, may in times of danger, assume a very different character. There is a tendency, for the

[1] *Cf.* also *Padeletti*, pp. 258 *et seq.* *Pernice*, pp. 1 *et seq.*, is of the opinion that to a great extent the treatment by the Roman jurists of the criminal law can be shown to be without principles and superficial. I doubt if his criticism and conception in this respect are correct.

sake of a prompt and vigorous repression and to avoid the difficulty of proof, to apply the full statutory penalty to cases in which a more exact and proper consideration would reveal a substantial defect in the facts necessary to constitute the crime. "In bello (populus) sic paret ut regi: valet enim salus plus quam libido." [2]

Since such times of danger were of frequent occurrence, and since, as was doubtless the case, the military training to which the citizens were subjected for the greater part of their lives made such a method of dealing with criminal law appear natural, and since, as already remarked, the freedom of the Roman citizen counted for little (outside of the immediate vicinity of the city), it was natural that the permanent legislation came to show no understanding of the difference between acts which are really criminal and acts which are merely dangerous. In addition to this there is the fact that, immediately after the time of the kings, the entire criminal jurisdiction (primarily as a result of the "provocatio" against the decrees of a magistrate) devolved upon the popular assembly which also possessed the legislative power, and were not strictly bound by statute; it passed judgment upon the person — the character of the accused — more frequently than upon the facts which constituted the basis of the complaint.

There is connected herewith that paramount consideration which was always given to "dolus" in the "judicia publica", and that neglect of the issues of fact relating to the crime. Even to-day, in State crimes, there is a tendency to give especial weight to (as the Romans would say) the "animus hostilis" against the "res publica."

§ 7. **The Law of the Twelve Tables.** — The law of the Twelve Tables is somewhat opposite in character to the other criminal legislation of the Republic. Its purpose, as already noticed, was clearly and firmly to set forth, as a protection of the Plebs against arbitrary treatment, the law which actually prevailed; to be a codification — in which, however, development along certain lines was not precluded. The provisions of the Twelve Tables are not of that indefinite character, analogous to the regulations by the police, which is later so often met with.

In addition to the rules, already mentioned, relating to murder (and possibly to manslaughter resulting from negligence), to theft, and to bodily injuries, the Twelve Tables also contained

[2] *Cicero*, "De rep.", I, c. 40, § 63.

provisions prescribing the death penalty for treason,[1] for (intentionally) setting fire to a house or to a supply of grain lying near a house,[2] for bearing false witness, for corruption when acting as a "judex" or "arbiter",[3] and for inventing and spreading satires and scurrilous stories.[4] It is recorded that the Twelve Tables punished (presumably with death) the utterance of magic formulas [5] to the detriment of another's person or another's crops.[6] Possibly they also contained other criminal provisions,[7] and also provisions in the nature of police regulations and against extravagance (*e.g.* prohibition of burial within the city) [8] and limitations upon expenditure in funeral processions and burials.[9]

§ 8. **Power of the "Paterfamilias" as Supplement to Criminal Law.** — Because of the simple conditions of life in the early periods of Rome, a great number of public criminal laws was not necessary.

In the first place, the criminal law was supplemented by the very extensive criminal and disciplinary power of the head of a household over the children, married women, and slaves under his control. Since this authority in no way precluded the exercise of the public criminal power, it was often optional with the accuser whether or not to invoke the public power, and it often depended upon the discretion of the magistrate whether or not he would interpose his authority. There were also subjected to the disciplinary power of the head of the household [1] many acts

[1] "Qui hostem concitaverit quive civem hosti tradiderit." L. 3 pr. D. "Ad leg. Jul. maj.", 48, 4.

[2] L. 9. D. "De incendio ruina", 47, 9.

[3] *Gellius*, XX, 1, §§ 7, 53. The false witness was to be thrown from the Tarpeian Rock.

[4] *Zumpft*, I, p. 482 refers this provision to satirical songs of a political nature.

[5] "Qui fruges excantasset . . . neve alienam segetem pellexeris." *Cf. Bruns*, "Fontes juri Rom. antiqui" (3d ed.), p. 28.

[6] The holding of assemblies by night in the city was also punished. "Primum XII tab. cautum esse cognoscimus, ne quis in urbe cœtus nocturnos agitaret." *Bruns*, *loc. cit.* p. 31.

[7] Concerning poisoning. *Cf.* also L. 236 D. "De V. S.", 50, 16.

[8] "Hominem mortuum in urbe ne sepelito neve urito." *Bruns*, p. 33.

[9] *Cf. Bruns*, pp. 33, 34.

[1] A complaint could also be lodged against slaves by virtue of the "Leges." In this case the usual punishments (*e.g.* fines), since they had no property, were inapplicable. *Cf.* L. 12 § 4 D. "De accusat.", 48, 2. As to "filii familias" *i.e.* the agnate descendants of a "pater familias", *cf.* L. 6 § 2 D. "Ad leg. Jul. de adulter." 48, 5. Perhaps the relation of the jurisdiction of the State to that of the "familia" was that "de facto" the judgment of the head of the household was respected. Undue severity of the head of the family gradually came into disfavor. Prominent women were spared the shame of a public execution, since when sentence had been passed they were turned over to their family for execution. *Livy*, XXXIX, 13. *Zumpft*, I, p. 358.

of those under his control, which if done by a person "sui juris" would come under the jurisdiction exercised by the Censor in matters of morality and custom.

The Censorship. — The Censors had no power of punishment as such. But they possessed the right to draw up the list of citizens liable to taxation and entitled to vote. Since every official act of a magistrate was valid and effective, regardless of its fundamental character, they did not consider themselves governed strictly (*i.e.* in matters of taxation) by the relative amount of the taxable property; they also regarded themselves as authorized to prejudice and "pro tanto" take away the political rights of an individual[2] for the duration of the census,[3] by transferring him to another "tribus" (by the "inter ærarios referre")[4] and by the omission of his name from the list of members of the Senate. In this manner he could be directly exposed to the disrespect and contempt of the multitude.[5] The Censors exercised their power in this same way in cases of perjury — which was not a criminal act by the civic law[6] — and also in cases of undue desire shown for innovation in proposing legislation, of lack of respect for the old statutes, of violation of the duty of respect due to authority, of extreme although not criminal cruelty, of neglect of discipline and morality in marriage, of celibacy, of undue luxury, and of bad management of household affairs.

Infamy. — The provisions of the civil law relative to infamy ("infamia") can also be regarded as supplementary to the criminal law. He, against whom judgment was passed as defendant in certain civil complaints based upon either a tort ("delict") or a breach of trust, became "infamis." This entailed the loss of the capacity of holding offices of honor and the right to vote in the public assembly, and also brought certain disadvantages in

[2] For personal unworthiness. Juristically speaking, the "Nota censoria" was *not* a punishment; it could result from a punishment: *Cicero*, "Pro Cluentio", c. 42 *et seq.* *Cf. Platner*, p. 13.

[3] The new Censors could with the new "lustrum" revoke the official acts of their predecessors by simply changing the lists. Thus there was often "ipso facto" a "rehabilitation." Loss of honor as a result of a "judicium" had a more lasting character.

[4] Later "ærarii" ceased to exist, and the power of the Censors was limited to the right to transfer from one of the honored rural "tribus" to one of the four "tribus" of the city: *Mommsen*, II, p. 384.

[5] According to the Ovinian "Plebiscitum" (442 A.U.) the power of the Censors was extended to drawing up the list of members of the Senate. *Mommsen*, "Staatsrecht", II, p. 397.

[6] For an ample statement of the different cases, see *Jarcke*, pp. 16 *et seq.*, and *Mommsen*, II, pp. 364 *et seq.*

legal proceedings,[7] which we at the present time would consider as not entirely unimportant. A man also became "infamis" when judgment was passed against him as defendant, in an "actio furti", "actio injuriarum", "actio fiduciaria", or any of the following "actiones", viz., "pro socio", "tutelæ", "mandati", and "depositi" ("directa").[8] An insolvent whose goods were seized and sold by his creditors by virtue of a "missio in bona" became "infamis." Infamy also resulted from actions in tort, in which the defendant avoided the passing of judgment against him by the payment of money. There were also a few cases, which we would treat as crimes, to which infamy [9] was the immediate and unfortunate, but only consequence.[10]

"**Actiones Populares.**" — The "actiones populares" [11] also constituted a later supplement to the criminal law. In these actions, a private person, by means of a civil procedure, laid claim to a money penalty which he received if the action was successful.[12] These cases,[13] as far as we have record of them, were founded, for the most part, upon the Edict of the Prætor; they generally dealt with matters which in modern times are subject to the police jurisdiction, or else had to do with injuries caused by negligence.[14]

Thus, liability to an "actio popularis" was incurred by mutilation of the Edict of the Praetor which was posted in a public place, by the killing or injuring of a man with something thrown out of a building, by the unauthorized erection of structures in a public place or way. Violation of graves, etc. was also thus penalized.

In a certain sense, the severe civil law obligation to make compensation *e.g.* for injury to another's slave, in accordance with the

[7] In respect to the capacity to be represented by others before a court or to represent others before a court. In certain cases incapacity to be a witness also resulted. L. 21 pr. D. "De testibus", 22, 5.

[8] L. 6 § 7. D. "De his qui notantur infamia", 3, 2. "Contrario judicio damnatus non erit infamis: nec immerito, nam in contrariis non de perfidia agitus, sed de calculo qui fere judicio solet dirimi."

[9] If one appointed an agent, the effects of infamy were avoided: L. 6 § 2. D. 3, 2. For this reason it was impractical under the later law: *cf. Savigny*, "System des röm. Rechts", II, p. 175.

[10] He also became "infamis", "qui bina sponsalia, binasve nuptias in eodem tempore habuerit."

[11] The time when the "Actiones populares" originated is not exactly known.

[12] [*Cf.* the "Penal Actions" of the English Law which were so popular with Parliament in the early 1800 s. — TRANSL.]

[13] As to the individual cases, *cf. Walter*, II, § 802; *Rudorff*, II, § 46.

[14] *Cf. e.g.* concerning injury by wild animals which were kept near the public highways, L. 40–42 D. "De ædil. edicto", 21, 1.

Lex Aquilia, and, generally, the large number of private penalties of the civil law, may be regarded as supplementary to the criminal law.

§ 9. **Other Criminal Legislation of the Republic.** — The other criminal legislation of the Republic — except that of the last period — has for us little of interest. During the aristocratic period of the Republic, crimes against private persons — "quum et res et cupiditates minores", as Cicero says,[1] were seldom committed by persons who were "sui juris."[2] As a result, substantially the only penal provisions were those against infringement of the rights of the Plebs, violation of the right of appeal to the people ("provocatio"),[3] hindering the election of the Tribunes of the people,[4] and the infliction of corporal punishment upon Roman citizens by a magistrate.[5] There were also statutes for the protection of public and political rights, and further laws against luxury ("leges sumptuariæ")[6] as continuations of the provisions laid down by the Twelve Tables.

The Statutes of the Later Republic. — The series of later statutes, which for us are of more importance, begins with the criminal statutes against the abuses ("excess")[7] of the magistrates in the provinces. The "Lex Calpurnia repetundarum" (605 A.U.) established a commission to investigate and decide complaints relating to these abuses and became the model for a whole series of such statutes; which, after Sulla, began also to deal with other

[1] *Cicero*, "Fragm. pro Tullio, § 9."

[2] *Cicero*, l. c. "ut perraro fieret, ut homo occideretur, idque nefarium ac singulare facinus putaretur, nihil opus fuisse judicio de vi coactis armatisque hominibus."

[3] Thus, soon after the overthrow of the Decemviri, the "Lex Duilia ne quis ullum magistratum sine provocatione crearet; qui creasset eum jus fasque occidi, neve ea cædes capitalis noxæ haberetur." *Livy*, III, 54, 55.

[4] "Qui plebem sine tribunis reliquisset." *Livy*, III, 55 ("Lex Duilia").

[5] The "Leges Porciæ" (as to which, see *Walter*, I, § 104). *Livy*, X, 9. "Porcia tamen lex sola pro tergo civium lata videtur quod gravi pœna, si quis verberasset necassetve civem Romanum, sanxit." *Laboulaye*, p. 94, sees in the "Lex Porcia" an extension of the "Lex Valeria", for the protection of citizens against the power of the magistrates in the Provinces (except as to soldiers). *Cf. Cicero*, II, "In Verrem", V. c. 55.

[6] Frequent mention is made of the "Lex Oppia" against extravagance in the clothing of women (539 A.U.) and the "Leges Orchia, Dedia" ("cibaria") against extravagance in banquets (*cf. Walter*, I, §. 256; *Rudorff*, I, § 14 [p. 37]).

[7] Abuse (Excesse) also in the sense of the dishonorable treatment of a Roman citizen. Thus a "Lex Sempronia" ("Ne de capite civium injussu populi quæreretur. — Si quis magistratus judicio quem circumvenerit, de ejus capite populi esse animadversionem"); *Cicero*, "Catilina", IV, 5; *Laboulaye*, p. 213.

than political crimes. The immediate practical consequence of most of these statutes was felt in matters of *procedure* rather than in the substantive law. This was the more so, since the judges, adhering to the traditions of the sovereign assembly in whose place they sat in judgment, often rested their decision not so much upon the specific act as upon the character and disposition of the accused.

That extortions [8] of the officials in the provinces should require a vigorous suppression at the hands of the Senate, that the guilty should be compelled to return the extorted sums, and that the tribunes of the people should propose to the people the infliction of a fine ("multa"), were nothing new.[9] But, hitherto, an investigation would ensue only upon a special petition, or when a tribune might feel himself called upon to intervene. Now the new statute granted the right to proceedings upon the complaint of an accuser, and created for such cases a strictly regulated procedure before a special tribunal of judges, an expedient which to some extent guaranteed a stricter observance of law than in the sovereign assembly itself.

This, of itself, led indirectly to an enumeration and definition of the acts liable to this procedure. Since the procedure proved satisfactory, this class of statutes began, little by little,[10] to include (at least in part) criminal acts which were directed against the rights of individuals.[11] The constantly sinking level of morality

[8] In close relation to laws against extortion are the laws against fraudulently obtaining office ("leges ambitus"), sale and purchase of votes in an election to a public office which in turn was used for extortion in the provinces. (Concerning the earlier laws see *Rudorff*, I, p. 80.) Concerning the "Lex Julia peculatus" (appropriation to one's own use of public property) enacted presumably by Cæsar, *cf. Rudorff*, I, p. 91.

[9] *Cf. Laboulaye*, p. 192, and *Mommsen*, II, pp. 289 *et seq.*

[10] The important "Leges majestatis" ("Lex Appuleja de majestate minuta" enacted about the middle of the seventh century of the city; "Lex Cornelia majestatis", 673 A.U.C.; "Lex Julia maj.", 708 A.U.C.) referred originally only to acts of the magistrates which were prejudicial to the honor or paramount rights of the "Populus Romanus." *Cf.* particularly *Cicero*, "In Pisonem", 21 (50): "Exire de provincia, educere exercitum, bellum sua sponte gerere, in regnum injussu populi ac senatus accedere, quum plurimæ leges veteres, tum lex Cornelia majestatis, Julia de pecuniis repetundis vetant." *Cf. Laboulaye*, p. 267. "Est majestas, ut Sulla voluit, ne in quemvis impune declamare liceret." *Cicero*, "Ep. ad div", 3, 11, 2. The "Lex Julia Cæsaris" laid the foundation for the later law; it is commented upon and continued in the Corpus Juris.

[11] Thus the "Lex Cornelia testamentaria" ("numaria", "de falsis") a general statute by Sulla dealing with forgery (the bribery of judges was also punished thereunder: *Paull.* Rec. S. V, 25 § 2); the "Lex Cornelia de sicariis et veneficis" (691 A.U.C.); the "Lex Pompeja de vi" (702

made necessary a more vigorous suppression of crime. Since the later judicial practice treated the cases subjected to punishment by these statutes only as examples, and imposed its own punishment "ad exemplum legis",[12] one may see in these statutes, to a certain extent (as already remarked), the skeleton of the later criminal law.

§ 10. **Punishment in Statutes of Later Republic. Opposition to Death Penalty.** — The nature of the system of punishment in these statutes is peculiar.

The old punishment of "sacer esse", although reverenced because of its antiquity and entitled to moral respect, had, from the juristic viewpoint, come to be a meaningless formula. Some exception may be made for those cases in which it was considered justifiable to proclaim one as the enemy of the country, and as such to kill him, — especially cases of conspiring or attempting to gain the power of king. Judging from facts that are extremely uncertain, a similar and meaningless formula was contained in the above mentioned provisions of the Twelve Tables, prescribing the death penalty for the disloyal behavior of a patron toward his clients.[1] In an advanced state of culture, not as yet given over to corruption, the permission granted to the general public to kill some one as a punishment was quite ineffective.

But against the introduction of the death penalty into the statutes there struggled the pride of the "Civis Romanus." Foreign kings often received their orders from the Roman magistrate and senator, and the plain citizen who cast his vote in the assembly for the magistrates and whose vote was solicited by the most distinguished, felt himself in turn a ruler, and a participant in the "Majestas populi Romani." Yet, as is well known, on extraordinary occasions the blood of citizens was shed freely. The disturbances of the Gracchi and the proscriptions in the civil wars were outside the domain of the criminal law. Also, in the provinces, Roman citizens were "de facto" deprived of their goods and lives by violent and wicked magistrates in the most shameful manner. One has only to think of the atrocities which Cicero (with good reason) attributed to Verres. Numerous

A.U.C.) and the "Lex Julia de vi" (708 A.U.C.) continued in the "de vi privata" under Augustus.

[12] *Cf. e.g.* L. 7, §. 3 D. "Ad leg. Jul. maj.", 48, 4: "si non tale sit delictum quod vel ex scriptura legis descendit, vel ad exemplum legis vindicandum est." L. 3 D. "Ad leg. Pomp. de parricidiis", 48, 9.

[1] *Cf.* also, *Padeletti*, p. 77, who infers an express prohibition in the Twelve Tables against the killing of a man without trial and judgment.

executions resulted from the proceedings of the Senate against the Bacchantes [2] and against the practice of poisoning which was prevalent among the Roman women.[3] Even the killing of the followers of Catiline at the command of the Senate could be regarded as a deed not entirely without color of law.[4] But the thought of the death penalty and the executioner seemed unworthy of the name of Roman. In extraordinary cases these things might be, but their mention in a statute of the later Republic was an impossibility. "Carnifex et obductio capitis et nomen ipsum crucis abest non modo a corpore civium Romanorum, sed etiam a cogitatione, oculis, auribus. Harum enim omnium rerum . . . etiam exspectatio, mentio ipsa . . . indigna cive Romano atque homine libero est." [5] For purely political offenses, and for abuse of public office, deprivation of political rights,[6] *e.g.* deprivation of the right to vote, was very effective. The "Aquæ et ignis interdictio", the prohibition of the use of fire or water upon his native soil, *i.e.* exile,[7] could destroy the political existence of the accused,[8] while the infliction of exorbitant fines [9] could destroy his economic existence. But one wonders how such punishments could be deemed sufficient in the case of ordinary (*i.e.* other than political) crimes.[10] In the later Republic, murder for hire and poisoning were practised almost as regular professions.[11] Even the killing of parents was not unusual.[12] Since the accused had

[2] *Livy*, XXXIX, 18.

[3] *Livy*, VIII, 18 and XL, 37.

[4] *Cf. Nissen*, pp. 32 *et seq.*

[5] *Cicero*, "Pro Rabirio", c. 5 (§ 16).

[6] *Cf. e.g. Diocass.*, XXXVI, 21, concerning the punishment of "ambitus."

[7] "Exilium hoc est aquæ et ignis interdictio." L. 2 D. "de publ. jud." 48, 1. According to the "Lex Tullia", ten years exile was fixed as a punishment for "ambitus." *Cicero*, "Pro Murena," c. 41 (§ 89).

[8] Since it was only in Rome that political life existed.

[9] *Cf.* relative to the gradually increased penalties for extortion in the Provinces, *Laboulaye*, p. 239.

[10] The punishment provided in the "Lex Cornelia de sicariis" was originally merely banishment. *Cicero*, "Pro Cluentio," c. 71.

[11] *Cf. Gengler*, "Die strafrechtliche Lehre des Verbrechens der Vergiftung", I (1842), pp. 40 *et seq.* *Henriot*, II, pp. 164 *et seq.* *Cicero*, "De nat. D.", III, c. 30 (§ 74) "— hæc *quotidianæ*, sicæ, veneni, peculatus, testamentorum etiam lege nova quæstiones."

[12] *Henriot*, II, p. 179. This may be inferred from the frequent mention by the poets of the killing of fathers and the motive of desire to obtain the paternal possessions. However this may have been furthered by the extreme extent of the "patria potestas." The "Lex Pompeja de parricidiis" subjected "parricidium" to the penalties of the "Lex Cornelia de sicariis." L. 1 D. 48, 9. The ancient "pœna culei," which was reëstablished in the Empire, stood in the way of a sentence in the Later Republic.

the right to avoid the passing of any sentence by voluntary exile,[13] and since this in no way prevented him from living in the place of his choice and there enjoying in safety and comfort the fruits of his crime,[14] it was, as if, in the case of the common class of criminals, who did not place a high value on residence at Rome and political rights, special care had been taken to secure their immunity from punishment. More than a sentence to any definite punishment, the accused had often to fear the enmity of the multitude, or the political opponent who, arousing that enmity by an accusation, used it for purposes of violence. It was thus, for example, that Clodius brought about the plundering and burning of Cicero's home. Consequently, it often happened that the actual facts causing the conviction were considered, rather than its technical basis. Thus, for example, the complaint against Verres, who caused innocent Roman citizens to be executed in the place of captured pirates, so as to make a good profit from the latter's ransom, was instituted, not on the grounds of this revolting murder, but rather on the technical grounds of extortion — the revolting facts of the case serving only, as we would say, "pro-coloranda causa." [15]

§ 11. **Gradual Change in the Character of the Criminal Law.** — In spite of this mild and aristocratic character of the criminal law which favored the criminal at the expense of public safety, we already find unmistakable evidence of those elements which characterized the sudden reversal in the character of the criminal law which came with the beginning of the Empire.

[13] Exile originally was not a punishment, but rather a means to escape punishment. *Cicero*, "Pro Cæcina", c. 34 (§ 100). However, voluntary exile could take place in accordance with the expression "Ei justum esse exilium", and therewith interdiction from fire and water and loss of all legal rights in the native country. *Livy*, XXV, 4; XXVI, 3. *Cf.* as to voluntary exile, *Geib*, "Geschichte des röm. Criminal processes", pp. 120 *et seq.*, p. 304. In Greece, also, there was originally a voluntary departure of the worst criminals. The individual could sever the tie which united him to the community, and thereupon the rights of the latter in regard to him came to an end. In other ways, in ancient times, the effects of exile were often quite severe.

[14] *Juvenal*, "Sat." I, 1, 48.

"— et his damnatus inani
judicio — quid enim salvis infamia numis? —
exul ab octava Marius bibit et fruitur dis
iratis —"

Cf. also *Suetonius*, "Div. Jul.", c. 42: "Pœnas facinorum (Julius Cæsar) auxit; et quum locupletes eo facilius scelere se obligarent, quod integris patrimoniis exulabant, parricidas, ut Cicero scribit, bonis omnibus, reliquos dimidia parte multabat."

[15] *Cicero*, "In Verrem" (A. II) V, c. 27 (§ 69).

In the first place, the Roman citizen, who, at home, enjoyed such extensive protection against arbitrary action of the magistrate, as a soldier in the field was subject, in matters of discipline, to the discretion of the commander or his lieutenant, which was *legally* without restraint. At such times there could be inflicted upon him the severest penalties of life and limb.[1] Until the Sempronian Statutes (631 A.U.), there could be no appeal against the official act of a magistrate "militiae" even by those who were not soldiers.[2] It is always difficult for a conquest-seeking military system, which is naturally adverse to being governed by laws, to preserve free institutions. In Rome the de facto committal to the emperor of the powers of commander-in-chief carried a grant of that convenient form of absolute criminal power (within the city) which had already come into existence during the civil wars.[3]

In the next place, another analogy already existed. At an earlier period, while slaves were, as a matter of fact, leniently treated, it had not only become customary for their masters to torture and kill them for offenses, but they were also liable to a particularly atrocious court procedure, in which, presumably, a leading part was played by the accusation of the master.[4] Such an inequality in the treatment of human beings must also in the long run work to the prejudice of the privileged class. As a result of the daily spectacle of public flogging and of cruel executions (by crucifixion, for which there was an especial place by the Esquiline Gate)[5] the idea gradually became familiar that in place of the ordinary penal method, which, in the later Republic, was bound to hold itself passive as against the person of a citizen and could only indirectly compel him to go into exile, it was feasible to proceed actively and directly against the person of the offender.[6]

As a matter of fact, the ancient exile, by which one could avoid further punishment, ceased in the time of the Empire to be really a punishment for the great majority of people ("inane judicium",

[1] Cutting off of the hand (*Val. Max.* II. 7–11); crucifixion (*Livy*, XXX, 43). *Cf. Du Boys*, p. 449.

[2] *Mommsen*, "Staatsrecht", I, pp. 65 *et seq.* II, p. 110.

[3] *Cf. Nissen*, pp. 140 *et seq.* Respect for the city boundary did not last long in the Empire.

[4] *Cf. Du Boys*, pp. 456 *et seq.*

[5] *Val. Max.* VIII, 4, 2.

[6] This difference is correctly pointed out in *Von Holtzendorff*, "Deportationstrafe", p. 60.

Juvenal calls it).[7] Under the all-embracing power of the emperor, political rights and political activity were no longer objects of consideration, and had come to be merely things to be played with or else were completely abandoned. At the most one was merely deprived of the special pleasures of Rome (which to be sure was a real grief for those of a sensitive disposition and those who loved the atmosphere of the capital).

In the cases of grave crimes, which were becoming more frequent even among the highest classes,[8] the emperors increased the penalties.[9] In this, they were acting in accord with popular sentiment. One can understand the indifference of the people to the shameful acts of murder by tyrants such as Tiberius, Caligula, and Nero. For it is difficult for those who stand at a distance to distinguish between guilt and innocence; and the people had become accustomed to feel that there was nothing extraordinary in the commission of crimes by members of the highest class.[10]

§ 12. **Change in the Character of Exile as a Punishment.** — The first punishment which underwent a legal change was that of *exile*. (The numerous death penalties inflicted by the emperors are often difficult to distinguish from plain murder; they could at least be condoned as the slaying of an enemy of the country, since the emperor might be regarded as the personification of the "Populus Romanus.")

Exile, in the time of Augustus, might be *relegation* ("relegatio"),[1] *i.e.* either banishment to a certain place or banishment with the prohibition to come within a certain radius.[2] Exile also, in so

[7] "Sat.", I, 1, 47, 48.

[8] Murder by poisoning was prevalent, *e.g.* the manner in which the notorious Lucusta, the helpmate of Nero, was able to openly engage in the business (*Suetonius*, "Nero," 33).

[9] *Cf.* note 14, § 10, *ante.*

[10] Women of the upper classes systematically practised abortion so as to retain their attractiveness and beauty (*Juvenal*, "Sat." VI, 594, 595). Ordinary theft appears to have been not uncommon among the higher classes ("honestiores," when stealing as common thieves in the public baths are called "fures balnearii" in L. 1 D. "de fur. baln.", 47, 17. "Principales civitatis" are mentioned as the originators or participators in "latrocinium" in L. 27 § 2 D. 48, 19). L. 1 D. (Ulpian) "De effractoribus", 47, 18 speaks of the punishment imposed upon certain "honestiores" who were "expilatores." § 2 of the same speaks of a Roman Knight as "effractor" (under Marcus Aurelius) and L. 10 § 1 D. "Ad leg. Jul. pec.", 48, 13 speaks of the robbery of a temple with great temerity and cunning by a "juvenis clarissimus." Hadrian provided a special punishment for "splendidiores" for interference with boundaries, L. 2 D. 47, 21.

[1] *Cf. Von Holtzendorff*, pp. 28 *et seq.*

[2] No one who was interdicted from fire and water was permitted to

far as the imperial power itself undertook the compulsory transportation of the accused, might be *deportation* ("deportatio"),[3] — a term which in the beginning meant merely the fact of the compulsory transportation, but later assumed the technical meaning of a form of relegation for life[4] to some fixed locality, and with more serious consequences. These consequences were, at first, fixed at the discretion of the emperor, who sentenced to deportation and relegation political criminals and those who figured as such. Not until later were they more definitely fixed by the jurists. The individual who underwent relegation did not lose his citizenship ("civitas") or right of making a will or being a beneficiary under a will ("testamenti factio"). Also, if he was banished only for a certain period,[5] he did not have to suffer even a partial loss of his property. But the individual undergoing deportation[6] lost his citizenship ("civitas") and all rights therewith connected,[7] and his property was confiscated.[8] In both punishments the place of banishment[9] was determined by the discretion or despotism of the emperor.

Deportation might be made to places where life was quite tolerable; but use was also made of desert islands, where the offender had in prospect a speedy death.[10] There were also those

betake himself to the continent nor to any island which was less than 50000 paces from the mainland (Cos, Rhodes, Sardinia, and Lesbos excepted). *Cf. Von Holtzendorff*, p. 31, Note 5.

[3] *Von Holtzendorff*, pp. 40 *et seq.*

[4] Only imperial favor could grant a "restitution." Sometimes hope of this was expressly taken away ("Irrevocabile exilium"; *cf. e.g.* L. 14 § 3 D. "de sacros. ecclesiis", 1, 2). *Cf. Von Holtzendorff*, p. 28. The practical importance of this addition, which Von Holtzendorff seems to have missed, was that the local governor was instructed not to forward the convict's requests for pardon and the like. *Cf.* L. un. C. "De Nili aggeribus", I, 9, 38.

[5] L. 7 §§ 3 4 D. "De interdictis", 48, 22.

[6] The dishonorable element of the punishment of deportation is apparent, since it was contrary to the viewpoint of the Republic, that there should be no direct personal coercion in punishment. *Cf. Von Holtzendorff*, p. 60.

[7] He who had been deported, retained the rights of the "Jus gentium."

[8] They allowed to the condemned only the so-called "Pannicularia", certain trinkets and articles of clothing (*cf.* the Rescript of Hadrian in L. 6 D. "De bonis damnatorem", 48, 20), his children (except in "lèse majesté"), and a portion of the property. For particulars, *cf. Von Holtzendorff*, pp. 79 *et seq.*

[9] In Egypt, deportation was to an oasis in the desert: L. 7 § 5 "De interdictis et relegatis", 48, 22.

[10] The island rock of Gyaros, one of the Cyclades in the Ægean Sea, was used for this purpose, as it was lacking in water: *Tacitus*, "Annals", IV, 30. *Cf.* also *Juvenal*, "Sat.", XIII, 246.

secret orders to kill, to which, under despotic emperors, the banished often fell a victim.[11]

Increased Use of Capital Punishment. — In the frequent *death penalties* (primarily for actual or alleged cases of "lèse majesté"), the despotism of the emperors[12] again asserted itself. In opposition to the old Roman view, which regarded capital punishment merely as the necessary destruction of the offender, and did not regard the pains of death as essential, there began under Tiberius (Suetonius points this out as something remarkable) efforts to prevent those sentenced to death from suicide.[13] Soon simple and specially devised forms of capital punishment[14] were extended to the field of crimes that were not of a political nature. The ancient punishment of "culeus", for the murder of parents, was reëstablished under the early Empire, or its place taken by "damnatio ad bestias."[15] In other cases of the murder of near relatives, the simple death penalty (decapitation) was used,[16] and later, this was also applied to persons of the lower class,[17] in the graver cases dealt with by the "Lex Cornelia de sicariis." The peculiar manner in which the Roman criminal law grouped at random heterogeneous cases under one and the same statute, (notably where later by "Senatus consulta" and imperial constitutions new cases were brought under rules of criminal law already existing)[18] necessarily made capital punishment more frequent. The fact that crimes often required a vigorous suppression because

[11] The soldiers entrusted with the escort often received this order *e.g.* under Tiberius and Caligula. *Cf. Von Holtzendorff*, p. 49.

[12] *Cf.* the fearful description of the reign of terror under Tiberius in *Suetonius*, "Tib.", 61.

[13] *Suetonius*, l. c. "Mori volentibus vis adhibita est vivendi." Later, choice of a special kind of death was a favor granted by the emperor. L. 8 § 1 D. "De pœnis", 48, 19.

[14] Crucifixion and burning alive, sentence to gladiatorial combat or to be torn to pieces by wild beasts in the public theatres (methods employed for persons of the lower class as well as slaves).

[15] L. 9 De. "D lege Pompeja de parricid.", 48, 9. The punishment of "culeus" was used if the sea was near; "alioquin bestiis objicitur secundum Divi Hadriani Constitutionem." "Culeus" was a leathern bag.

[16] Casting off of high rocks or drowning in the Tiber were also favorite methods (*cf. Suetonius, loc. cit.*), but were later forbidden (L. 25 D. "De pœnis" 48, 19). Strangling in prison was also abolished. Later they sought to regulate better the execution of the death penalty.

[17] L. 16 D. "Ad leg. Corn. de sic.", 48, 8 (Modestinus). It may perhaps be inferred from L. 4 D. eod. that as early as Hadrian, murder by persons of lower rank entailed the death penalty.

[18] Thus, by a Rescript of Hadrian, castration of a man, or allowing one's self to be castrated, and by a Rescript of Antoninus Pius, circumcision of one who was not a Jew, were subjected to the penalties of the "Lex Cornelia de sicariis." L. 4 § 2 D. 48, 8. L. 11 D. eod.

of the boldness[19] with which they were perpetrated has already been mentioned.[20] It is possible that the death penalty was compulsory in other cases, *e.g.* in the graver cases of counterfeiting.[21]

Corporal Punishment. — More remarkable than the death penalty was *corporal punishment*,[22] which, in the Republic, was never applied to a Roman citizen, and in the Empire was established only for persons of lower rank ("humiliores"). But, legally, these punishments were justifiable by the universal nature of the military power ("imperium") of the emperor. As a matter of fact, they were almost indispensable[23] in dealing with the pauper rabble who at that time swarmed to the great cities and especially to Rome. Otherwise, since the prevailing system of punishment by imprisonment was inadequate, it would have been necessary to resort to mutilation as a penalty.

Imprisonment. — The Romans also made use of *imprisonment* as a punishment. But it was not based upon the principle which alone is productive of results — the thought that, by a temporary deprivation of freedom as a punishment, the offender may be influenced to a more sensible use of his freedom when again attained. This idea had, indeed, been expressed by Plato,[24]

[19] Armed "Grassatores" (robbers) were upon a repetition of the offense punished with death. *Cf.* L. 28 § 10 D. 48, 19. Malicious incendiarism was frequent, *e.g.* in Rome, often to make an effective appeal to charity (somewhat as to-day it is done to get fire-insurance money). *Cf. Henriot*, II, p. 156. Concerning shameless and fraudulent bankruptcies, see *Henriot*, II, pp. 150 *et seq.*

[20] "Famosos latrones — furca figendos, compluribus placuit." L. 28 § 15 D. "De pœnis," 48, 19. Malicious setting of fires "in civitate" by a "humilior" was subject to the punishment of "bestiis objici." L. 12 § 1 D. "De incendio", 47, 9. According to L. 28 § 12 D. "De pœnis" (Callistratus) it was punished by burning alive. Concerning man-stealers, who made a business of stealing children and selling them into slavery, *cf.* L. 7 C. "Ad leg. Fabian." 9, 20, (Diocletian) and L. un. C. 9, 18 (Constantine).

[21] Counterfeiting of gold money (L. 8 D. "De lege Corn. de falsis", 48, 10, Ulpian). As is well known, counterfeiting was later treated in conjunction with "lèse majesté." L. 2 C. "De falsa moneta", 9, 24 (Constantine).

[22] This, consisting at the most in whipping with a cane ("fustigatio") is frequently mentioned. *Cf.* especially L. 8 §§ 3–5 D. "De pœnis", 48, 19. In addition to whipping with a cane, there were, under the later emperors, whipping with birches ("virgæ"), with lashes and knouts ("flagellum"). Balls of lead were later also woven into the knout ("plumba") (*cf. e.g.* L. 1 C. "De his qui potentiorum nomine", 2, 15) (Arcadius and Honorius) and thorns ("scorpio"). *Cf. Invernizzi*, p. 173. *Pauly*, "Realencyklopädie," VI, p. 2466.

[23] Concerning corporal punishment as an additional punishment in cases of "Relegatio", sentence to "Opus publicum", and "ad metalla", *cf.* L. 4 § 1 D. "De incendio", 47, 9.

[24] His "Sophronisterion" ("Legg.", IX, 908) is in its fundamental

who in this respect was in advance of his time. However, generally speaking it remained unknown to the prevailing opinions of ancient times. Ulpian did not regard imprisonment primarily as a means of punishment. Thus in L. 8 § 9 D. "De pœnis", 48, 19, he says: "Carcer ad continendos homines, non puniendos haberi debet." The rescript of the emperor Antoninus in L. 6 C. "De pœnis", 9, 47, reads as follows: "Incredibile est quod allegas, liberum hominem, ut vinculis perpetuo contineretur, esse damnatum."[26] But in the Empire imprisonment sometimes served as a punishment of short duration[27] for petty offenses, and also for cases in which, for the sake of the public peace, the temporary absence and safe keeping of the offender[28] was desirable.[29]

Hard Labor. — Moreover, since it was customary to punish slaves by *hard labor*, and since the lowest class of freemen were in reality little more respected than were slaves, by the all-powerful imperial officials, the idea easily arose of making use of the toil of convicted persons in the great works which were being undertaken by the State. This idea was perhaps furthered by an acquaintance with the custom of States annexed to Rome.[30] Thus even Pliny the Younger[31] speaks of the employment of convicts in public work ("opus publicum"), such as cleaning sewers, mending the highways, and working in the public baths. A severer type of this kind of punishment was a sentence "ad metalla" — labor in the mines — and "in opus metalli." The convicts in each of these instances wore chains, and, as "servi pœnæ" lost their freedom. For this reason the punishment was always for life.[32] Heavier chains were worn by those sentenced "ad metalla" than by those sentenced "in opus metalli."[33] These

ideal the theory of reformation of the 1800s. *Cf. Thonissen*, "Droit pénal de la république Athénienne", pp. 439 *et seq.*

[26] However the passage speaks of the use by the governors of chains in the prisons, of which the jurists approved.

[27] As appears at the conclusion of the passage, this was not unheard of in the case of slaves. Slaves and persons of the lower class were often actually (though perhaps not legally) treated alike. *Cf.* also: *Invernizzi*, pp. 173 *et seq.*, and *Henriot*, II, pp. 361 *et seq.*

[28] Imprisonment as a means of prevention was originally limited by statute to the term of office of the magistrate who inflicted it. *Cf. Mommsen*, "Röm. Staatr.", II, pp. 149, 529, 530.

[29] *Cf.* L. 8 § 9 D. "De pœnis", 48, 19. As to the use of imprisonment in Athens, see *Thonissen*, "Le droit pénal." p. 114.

[30] We also find among the Egyptians sentences to labor in the mines. *Thonissen*, "Etudes sur l'histoire du droit criminel des peuples anciens" (Paris, 1869), I, pp. 157 *et seq.*

[31] Ep. ad Traj. X, 41.

[32] *Cf.* Rescript of Hadrian in L. 28 § 6 D. "De pœnis", 48, 19.

[33] L. 8 § 6 D. "De pœnis", 48, 19.

punishments were popularly regarded as sentences to a slow and painful death.[34] The treatment of these prisoners must have been very severe;[35] according to the rescript of Hadrian, sentence to gladiatorial combat ("ad ludum"), where, if the chance so turned, a man might become free, was regarded as a lighter penalty.[36] Mention is also made of another kind of penal labor; younger persons were used *e.g.* in the hunting sports in the circus or as dancers, especially as sword dancers in the public theatres.[37] Often some temporary need was served; thus, Constantine, in the year A.D. 319, ordered the governor of Sardinia to cause to be sent to Rome those convicted for minor offenses; there they were employed in the grist mills. The "constitutio" which originated this "damnatio in pistrinam urbis Romæ" was often renewed.[38]

Other Methods of Punishment. — The other principal methods of punishment of the time consisted of denial of the right to carry on a trade,[39] declaration of incapacity for holding public office[40] (or perhaps only some public offices), degradation from a higher rank,[41] and money fines; these, in the Republic might be imposed *e.g.* on the complaint "de residuis" (failure to account for, and especially misapplication of public funds), and also under some circumstances in cases of peculation.[42]

§ 13. **Infamy and Confiscation of Property.** — *Infamy* ("infamia") and *confiscation of property* were in the nature of *supplementary punishments.* The former, even in the Empire, continued to be of considerable significance. The "infamis" could not (or to speak more accurately, was not entitled to) be appointed

[34] *Cf. Henriot,* II, p. 357.

[35] Women, who were considered unsuited for this severe labor, were sentenced in like cases to "ministerium metallicorum", *i.e.* to serve those sentenced to work in the mines. Such a sentence could also be limited in regard to its duration. L. 8 § 8 D. "De pœnis." If anyone was ill or weak and had undergone ten years of his sentence, it was provided that he could be turned over to his relatives for care. L. 22 D. "De pœnis."

[36] "Collatio legum Mosaic." XI, 7 §§ 3, 4 (Ulpian).

[37] L. 8 § 11 D. "De pœnis." The condemned were also in these cases "Servi Pœnæ."

[38] L. 3, 5, 6 C. Theodos. "De pœnis", 9, 40.

[39] L. 8 pr.; L. 9 § 10; L. 43 pr. D. "De pœnis", 48, 19.

[40] L. 5 § 2 D. "De extraord. cogn.", 50, 13. L. 7 §§ 21, 22 D. "De interdictis et releg.", 48, 22. There is also mention of a temporary suspension of such rights (*cf.* L. 7 § 20 D. "De interd. et releg."). This doubtless was the case, since even according to our modern conception such punishments are regarded as disciplinary.

[41] Concerning loss of rank of Decurian, *cf.* L. 43 § 1 D. "De pœnis." In other respects distinctions in rank were very important in criminal law and procedure.

[42] *Cf. Walter,* II, § 813.

to a public office.[1] Confiscation of property, either of all property, as incidental to every death sentence,[2] or of a portion only, as often incidental [3] to *e.g.* relegation for life, had, at Rome, under despotic emperors attained to a considerable importance. It differed however, from the custom of confiscating property at Athens [4] under the power of the people dominated by demagogues. In addition to the desire for personal revenge and the gratification of tyrannical whims, there was also, under bad emperors, the additional temptation to enrich the imperial treasury ("fiscus"), if the prosecution of a man of means was in question. Moreover, not to mention the numerous profits accruing to self-seeking officials from the sale of confiscated property, the bounties [5] awarded for incriminating information ("denunciatio") produced the well-known pest of the spy-system. Relations of confidence and trust, made sacred by custom and religion, were dissolved by the influence of this poison. The severity with which it was found necessary to prosecute the making of unfounded informations and complaints, and the extortions thereby made possible, were prejudicial to legal procedure. The higher the stakes for which the accuser or informer played, the less scrupulous would be his choice of the means to carry the case to a successful conclusion, and the more prone would he be to attempt to bribe witnesses and judges.[6] The fact that the profession of informer soon came to be regarded as actually infamous (*i.e.* causing "infamia"),[7] and that accusations [8] of slaves and freedmen against patrons were not tolerated,[9] together with the fact that the

[1] Thus *Savigny*, "System des röm. R.", II, pp. 201, 202 in relation to L. 2 C. "De dign." 12, 1. *Cf.* however, L. 2 D. "De off. assessorum", 1, 22. It is doubtful if infamy "ipso jure" entailed the loss of an office already acquired. This was not the case in the Empire, since the emperor and his legal representatives could deprive one of an office as a matter of discipline. The additional effect of infamy relative to appearance before a court need not here be considered.

[2] *Cf. Geib*, I, p. 115. L. 8 §§ 1–4 D. "Qui testamenta", 28, 1.

[3] *Cf. e.g. Paulus*, "Sententiæ Receptæ", II, 26, § 14; V, 25, § 8.

[4] *Cf. Thonissen*, "Droit pénal", p. 123. If the State treasury was empty or in need, prosecutions were instituted.

[5] *Cf. e.g.* L. 1, "De his quæ ut indignis", 34, 9.

[6] It would also happen that the accused would bribe the accuser. As to such a bribery see L. 29 pr. D. "De jure fisci", 49, 14.

[7] L. 1 D. 34, 9; L. 2 pr.; L. 44 D. "De jure fisci", 49, 14. An accusation which was not made for the sake of gain was not a cause of "infamia."

[8] Concerning such accusers ("delatores") *cf.* especially *Platner*, pp. 170 *et seq.*; *Rein*, p. 814; *Rudorff*, II, p. 460.

[9] Such accusers became liable to punishment under a "Constitutio" of Severus. L. 2 § 6 D. "De jure fisci." Some of the reasons for re-

good emperors, especially Titus, Trajan, and Hadrian, proceeded with the greatest severity against the "humani generis inimici", the "execranda delatorum pernicies", tended to the suppression of the evil. Nevertheless, in the case of the accusations most dangerous in these respects, viz. accusations of the crime of "lèse majesté",[10] the regard for the sacred person of the "princeps" and emperor easily outweighed all other considerations and prevented the evil from being plucked up by the root.

§ 14. **The Range of Criminal Law.** — Concerning the range of the acts for which punishment was inflicted, there can, however, be no question but that prior to the end of the classical jurists' period (except in the case of the crime of "lèse majesté" and the persecution of Christians) the criminal law itself did not go beyond the limits of real necessity,[1] even though these limits were often transgressed by imperial despotism. Law tended to develop more along the line of the protection of private rights and morality.

The "Lex Julia de adulteriis" in the time of Augustus (A.U. 736) was in these respects an interesting innovation. Its purpose was, by means of severe penalties, to check the increasing prevalence of immorality, — adultery (of which the husband as such could not be guilty), illicit relations of men with married women and with their own sex, pandering, and marriage and concubinage among near relations. This statute was peculiar, in that the general public was made the guardian of the morality and honor of the family. As opposed to the police power of the State, injury to individual rights and the interest of the family stepped into the background. While the right of the husband and father of the married woman to bring this complaint was favored, it was not exclusive.[2] After a certain lapse of time, a complaint could

jecting such accusations rested partly upon the grounds that the persons accused, if members of a high rank, should not be brought to a trial, and partly upon the grounds that the accusers had shown themselves especially dangerous, *e.g.* accusations by one condemned "ad metalla", "ne desperati ad delationem facile possint sine causa confugere." L. 18 § 3 D. "De jure fisci."

[10] In these cases, a slave was permitted to accuse his master. *Cf.* L. 6; L. 8 § 6 C. "De delat.", 10, 11.

[1] In this respect, there may be considered the weakening of the family tie, and the granting of Roman citizenship to a poverty-stricken multitude. The criminal power of the State was obliged to take the place of the disciplinary power of the head of the household and the "nota censoria" which being no longer of importance soon died out in the Empire. However the power of the head of the household was yet often exercised in respect to married women in the early Empire.

[2] L. 4 D. "De adulteriis", 48, 5.

be brought by any third party.[3] Moreover, the husband was punishable as a panderer ("lenocinium") if he failed to bring a charge against his wife if apprehended "in flagrante." It was only in a depraved state of society that provisions such as these, prejudicial to the peace of the family and conducive to extortions,[4] could be considered advantageous. The possibility of punishment for "lenocinium" (as appears from L. 8 and 9, D. "De adulteriis") goes far beyond the limits within which, at the present time, the interference of the criminal law or of the police is deemed justifiable.

The later extensions by imperial constitutions, senatusconsulta, and judicial practice,[5] of the "Leges Juliæ de vi" are more directly intended for the protection of private rights.[6] The same is true of the punishment for swindling ("stellionatus").[7] It is also important to notice that by this time theft ("furtum") in many cases was subjected to a public punishment, unconditionally, in the interest of public security.[8] In all cases in which there was a theft of a thing itself ("furtum rei"), and not merely a theft of its use ("furtum usus") or its possession ("furtum possessionis"), public punishment could ensue upon motion of the party injured;[9] and this was generally the practice. "Meminisse oportebat, nunc furti plerumque criminaliter agi." This was the only means by which theft could be held in check, "quia visum est

[3] Nevertheless it is conceivable that there frequently were no accusers. *Suetonius*, "Tiberius", 35.

[4] Concerning abuse of the right of accusation, *cf.* L. 18 (17) a. E. D. "De adulteriis", 48, 5.

[5] *Cf. e.g.* L. 1 § 2 D. "De vi privata", 48, 7; L. 6 D. eod.; L. 5 § 2; L. 6 D. "De vi publica", 48, 6; L. 152 D. "De R. J.", 50, 17: "Hoc jure utimur, ut quicquid omnino per vim fit aut in vis publicæ aut in vis privatæ crimen invidat."

[6] The above-mentioned provision against castration was rather in the nature of legislation for purposes of morality. Concerning the punishment of abortion by a married woman, *cf.* L. 4 D. "De extraord. crimin.", 47, 11.

[7] Peculiar cases of fraud were: the so-called "Venditio fumi", swindling through a pretense to be able to procure for the defrauded party a position of honor (*cf. Rein*, p. 723); also the case where a free man fraudulently allowed himself to be sold as a slave. (L. 7 § 1; L. 14, 18 D. "De lib. causa", 40, 12; L. 5 § 1 D. "De statu hom.", 1, 5. In this latter case the party who permitted himself to be sold lost his freedom as a punishment, if he was over twenty-five years of age.

[8] Thus "furtum" of "abactores", "directarii", "effractores" and "saccularii"; also "fures nocturni", "fures balnearii." Receipt of stolen goods was punished as a special offense; *cf.* Tit. D. "De receptat.", 47, 16.

[9] The injured party could choose between a civil action and punishment of the theft "extra ordinem": L. 93 D. "De furtis"; L. 3 § 1 D. "De off. præf. vigilum", 1, 15; L. 15 D. 12, 4.

temeritatem agentium etiam extraordinaria cognitione coercendam."[10] The general tendency of legal development was as follows: Torts and wrongs which merely rendered their author liable to an accusation in a popular assembly tended to become crimes, and, as such, to be subject to criminal punishments, or, at any rate, might be treated as crimes at the discretion of the magistrate or of the injured party.[11] This tendency was in part based upon the natural order of development of criminal law. In Rome it was also furthered by the sovereign power of the officials and by the prevalence of a poverty-stricken proletariat.

Attempt at a crime was punished by some special method of procedure or under the head of some other crime, rather than by virtue of a general statutory provision or in pursuance of some definitely expressed principle. *Accessories* to a crime were punished in about the same extent as at the present time. Bearing these two facts in mind, it can perhaps be said that, at the time of the classical jurists, the range of criminal law covered very nearly (but not exactly)[12] the field of wrongs punishable criminally under the early German common law.

Little by little, *negligence* ("culpa") (regard for which was originally foreign to the public penal law) also became liable to punishment, particularly in cases of homicide and starting of fires.[13]

§ 15. **The Crime of "Lèse Majesté."** — The crime of "lèse majesté" proved very important in the practical administration of criminal law. The interests of the State are naturally susceptible to injuries in many ways. These injuries may have a very considerable influence upon the fate of the State; for the State is not a thing definite and well defined, but to a certain extent may be conceived as existing at the same moment everywhere and nowhere. Therefore laws in regard to high treason and State treason easily assume an indefinite character. There is in such

[10] L. 93 D. "De furtis" (Ulpian).

[11] Concerning insult ("injuriæ"), *cf.* L. ult. D. "De injur.", 47, 10 (Hermogenian); also *e.g.* L. 3 § 7 D. "De sepulcro viol." 47, 12; L. 1 pr. § 1 L. 5 D. "De extraord. crim." 47, 11; L. 35 D. "De injuriis."

[12] Some differences are: *e.g.* according to the "Lex Cornelia de sicariis", many acts are punishable which are not punishable even as preparatory acts; violations of the person were punishable according to Roman law only when they were "injuriæ" and only when done with malice ("dolose"); offenses against morality were not identical with those of the present time.

[13] L. 3 § 1 D. 1, 15; L. 4 § 1 D. "Ad leg. Corn. de sic." 48, 8; L. 6 § 7 D. "De off. præs." 1, 18.

cases much that is less capable of being expressed by words than determined by the exercise of rational discretion. In a State in which the ruler is absolute, there is always a tendency to identify the interests of the rulers with the interest of the State. It becomes easy to ascribe to any act, which in fact is contrary to the real or presumed interests of the ruler,[1] the character of harmfulness to the State.[2] When we consider the absolute power of the emperor; his constant use of it to interfere in the administration of law; more important still, the time-serving attitude which, in every absolute government, grows with overwhelming vigor; the temptation held out by the power of confiscation for treason; and the procedure which, in the interest of the State against these presumed enemies, permits the important guarantees affording protection to the accused to be set aside,[3] — when we consider these things, we need no further explanation of those murders committed by Tiberius, Caligula, Nero, and Domitian and concealed under accusations of "lèse majesté." Later, in the compilations of Justinian, we find that these abuses are no longer given legal recognition.[4] But the utterances of the jurists, as well as the imperial rescripts (directed as they were against a body of citizens presumably timid and peace-loving), reveal what must have been the practice of those despots[5] and of their over-zealous officials.[6]

[1] Thus "lèse majesté" came to be "omnium actionum complementum" (*Tacitus*, "Annals", III, 38), the crime of the innocent "crimen illorum qui crimine vacarent." (*Pliny*, "Paneg.", 42.)

[2] Under Tiberius the slander of the emperor began to be treated as "lèse majesté." Previously Augustus, under the term "Crimen majestatis", had caused to be prosecuted "libelli famosi" which made accusations against eminent persons: *Tacitus*, "Annals", I, 72. *Cf.* *Paulus*, "Sententiæ Receptæ", V, 29, § 1.

[3] Persons were permitted to bring the charge, whose accusation, bearing no weight, in other cases, had ceased to be given consideration. No attention was paid to relations of trust, etc. (L. 7 pr. § 2, D. "Ad leg. Jul. maj." 48, 4). They tortured all or any of the witnesses whenever they thought any purpose would be served thereby (L. 10, § 1, D. "De quæst." 48, 18; *Paulus*, "Sententiæ Receptæ", V, 29, 2).

[4] Thus Marcian feels constrained to observe that the repair or the unintentional injury of the statues of the emperor did not constitute "lèse majesté." The law had once punished as "lèse majesté" even the removal of one's clothes or the chastisement of one's slave in the vicinity of a statue of the Emperor: *Rein*, pp. 533, 544.

[5] *Cf.* L. 2, C. "Ad leg. Jul. maj." 9, 8. The individual presenting the matter for decision had sworn by the spirit of the emperor that he would deal harshly with his own slave, but had not kept his oath. *Cf.* concerning the punishment of false oaths in which an appeal was made to the spirit of the emperor, *Rein*, pp. 533, 534.

[6] Modestinus in L. 7 § 3 D. 48, 4, gives a warning to over-zealous officials.

§ 16. **Persecution of the Christians.** — The persecution of the Christians bore a certain relation to the punishment of the crime of "lèse majesté." This persecution can be explained as follows. A State which makes religion an instrument to accomplish its own ends, as Rome had done from the beginning, can not remain indifferent to the intrusion of a new religion. However, it does not persecute a new cult merely as such, as is done in States dominated by a priestcraft. But it persecutes the new cult as soon as its own interest seems to demand. Thus the Roman State had always exercised its right to proceed against any cult which seemed especially destructive of morality or generally dangerous.[1] An example is furnished by the decree of the Senate against the fanatical cult of the Bacchantes (A.U.C. 547). There is recorded a large number of laws against the cult of Isis and Serapis and the suppression of the cult fostered in Gaul by the Druids. As appears from the general sense of the decree against the Bacchantes, it was not only those cults which manifested themselves publicly that were persecuted; Cicero says, expressing the spirit of the Roman State: "Separatim nemo habessit deos; neve novos, sive advenas, nisi publice adscitos, privatim colunto." Every new cult required, as it were, a definite license from the State.

Now the Christians, prima facie, provoked the suspicion and hatred of other people who judged by what they saw. They separated themselves from their fellow citizens; they refused to attend the public festivals; they offered no sacrifices to the local deities, and refused divine homage to the statues of the emperors. Thus they exposed themselves to blame for any public calamity; for the people were accustomed to attribute such calamity to the wrath of the neglected local deities. It was also alleged that the Christians, like the adherents and participants in other objectionable cults and mysteries, in their secret celebrations revelled in blood and sensuality. Thus they came to be regarded as guilty of "lèse majesté", and, finally, even as "publici hostes."[2]

The withdrawal of the Christians from all participation in the affairs of the heathen State, their prophecies concerning the judgment of God which should overwhelm all heathendom and the wickedness of the age, made them hated by many leaders in politi-

[1] *Cf. Platner*, p. 46 *et seq.*

[2] *Cf.* especially *Ebert*, "Tertullian's Verhältniss zu Minutius Felix" in the "Historish-philolog. Classe der Königl. sächs. Gesellschaft der Wissenschaften", Vol. V, N. 5, pp. 19 *et seq.* (pp. 337 *et seq.*); *Hausrath*, "Neutestamentliche Zeitgeschichte", III (1874), pp. 297 *et seq.*

cal affairs. These leaders, although they might have found that Christianity had much in common with their own ideals of morality, were unable to contemplate a State other than the heathen State as it then existed. To such men, since they placed their reliance in the old virtues of the Republic and the maxims of philosophy, a foreign sect flocking into Rome, behaving in an extraordinary manner, and yet reaching such a position as to win adherents even in court circles, necessarily appeared dangerous. So, from the very first, they from time to time punished the Christians as "rei superstitionis externæ." Thus Suetonius briefly and without a trace of pity, says: "Afflicti suppliciis Christiani genus hominum superstitionis novæ et maleficæ." Tacitus also, while telling of the Christians burnt at Nero's command as living torches in his garden, was of the opinion that they deserved the severest death penalties. He found fault merely with the fact that their death appeared to be inflicted at the caprice of an individual,[3] rather than as a public punishment inflicted for the well-being of the State. When Pliny the Younger, who was unable to attribute any special crimes to the Christians but nevertheless considered them dangerous, wrote to Trajan for his opinion, the emperor, desiring no doubt to act in accord with public sentiment, replied in those well-known and significant words: "Conquirendi non sunt; si deferantur et arguantur, puniendi sunt." Their prosecution was to depend upon whether or not anyone pressed a charge against them. The persecution of Christians was thereby made legal, whenever demanded by public sentiment. This also explains the peculiar fact that, at times, protection was afforded the Christians and their doctrines were allowed to spread, while, at other times, when the interest of the State seemed to demand it, they were suddenly proceeded against with frightful severity.

Undoubtedly a doctrine such as that of the Christians could not spread without arousing hate and persecution. But the fact that this persecution took, at times, so systematic a form and emanated from the State, was only possible because, first, of inherent faults from which the Roman criminal law had suffered from the beginning, and because, secondly, of its political character, which, without regard to the injury of specific rights, derived its conception of offenses from what it conceived to be the real or

[3] "Quamquam adversus sontes et novissima exempla meritos miseratio oriebatur, tanquam non utilitate publica, sed in sævitiam unius absumerentur": *Tacitus*, "Annals", XV, 44.

presumed interests of the State. Defects in the fundamental conception of law, which to the laity are difficult of comprehension, have, in stormy periods, exercised an influence upon the fate of a people.

§ 17. **Sorcery and Soothsaying.** — The crime of sorcery and soothsaying[1] is also closely related to the crime of belonging to a forbidden cult. Belief in the power of special incantations together with the sacrifice of victims was an ancient one with the Romans. During the Republic, public calamities were attributed to such causes. An extraordinary number of laws were enacted against them, *e.g.* in the case of the pestilence occurring in the city (320 A.U.C.), and during the Second Punic War (541 A.U.C.). During the Empire there was an invasion of superstitions from the Orient. Mention is often made of the "Chaldæi", "Arioli", "Astrologi", "Mathematici", and "Magi." There was a constant belief in the power of witchcraft. It was suspected that Germanicus lost his life from this cause.[2] There is also frequent mention of love potions and magic formulas. Sorcery and the mixing of poisons[3] were frequently associated.[4] Mere soothsaying was not severely punished. But the utterance of incantations concerning the life of the emperor and the consultation of a soothsayer by slaves "de salute domini" were punished with death. Not to mention the frauds which were frequently perpetrated through the medium of magic,[5] it was regarded as dangerous in itself, and prophecies concerning the approaching death of the emperor might cause public tumult. But, since even the emperors from time to time concerned themselves with magic,[6] and among the mass of the people these superstitions gradually supplanted the old State religion, it was impossible to actually curb the evil.

§ 18. **General Circumstances Affecting Imperial Criminal Law; (1) Class Privilege.** — In order to gain a proper conception of the practical operation of the criminal law of this imperial period, the following circumstances must be borne in mind. Against the

[1] *Cf. Rein*, pp. 901 *et seq.*; *Platner*, pp. 234 *et seq.*

[2] *Tacitus*, "Annals", II, 69.

[3] *Paulus*, "Sententiæ Receptæ", V, 23, 15; L. 13, D. "Ad leg. Corn. de sic.", 48, 8. Sorcery for good purposes was permitted. Charms for good purposes were much used.

[4] *Paulus*, "Sententiæ Receptæ", V, 23, 15.

[5] Swindling done by jugglers who went about with snakes is perhaps referred to in L. 11, D. "De extraord. crim." 47, 11.

[6] *Cf. Platner*, p. 237; *Rein*, p. 905.

powerful influences of the commerce of the world pouring into Rome, the large property interests owned by freedmen and persons occupied in ignoble callings, and the absolute power of the emperor, the old Roman freedom, once the pride of the citizen, could no longer prevail. But the emperors felt the necessity either of preserving established legal privileges or of creating new ones in their stead. Since, in reality, it was only the Senate who retained a semblance of political rights, these privileges must be made to reveal themselves in the criminal law.[1] They cost the emperor nothing, and they also enabled him to interfere constantly in the administration of the law by the governors of the provinces, and to remind them and their underlings of their subjection to the superior power of their emperor.[2] Thus, in the Digest, under the title "De pœnis", the first place is given to a passage from Ulpian, in which, before everything else, attention is called to distinctions of rank in the determination of punishments. For the higher classes,[3] relegation and deportation were the regular penalties. The former applied to substantially the same classes of cases punishable under the old "Leges judiciorum publicorum"; the latter was for cases covered by the "extraordinaria coercitio." But a desire to aggravate or mitigate the penalty would cause individual cases to be shifted from one group to another.[4] The punishments for the lower classes ("humiliores") were the death penalty, condemnation "ad metalla" or to "opus publicum", or corporal punishment.[5] However, in the case of crimes against

[1] This tendency did not cease completely until the time of Marcus Aurelius and Alexander Severus. Under despotic emperors such as Nero, Caligula, and Domitian, capital punishment of prominent men was very frequent, and the most distinguished men of the State might be seen laboring in penal servitude on building streets: *Von Holtzendorff*, p. 110.

[2] This is very apparent in the punishment of deportation, which was employed against those of higher rank. This could take place only by virtue of an imperial confirmation of the decree of the governor of the province. The "præfectus urbi", who was in Rome and passed judgment as it were, under the eyes of the emperor, had authority to sentence to deportation: L. 2, §§ 1, 2, "De pœnis", 48, 19.

[3] Senators, Knights, Decurions. Apparently other persons could at judicial discretion be treated as "honestiores." Concerning the special privileges of veterans and their children, *cf.* L. 3, D. "De veteranis", 49, 18; *cf.* especially *Von Holtzendorff*, p. 111.

[4] According to Hadrian's regulation, apart from cases of "lèse majesté", there could only be capital punishment in cases of murder of parents: L. 15, D. "De pœnis."

[5] L. 28, §§ 2, 9, D. "De pœnis." It is natural that many errors were committed in making such distinctions. According to L. 10, § 2, D. "De pœnis", corporal punishment unjustly undergone precluded the statutory "Infamia", which would otherwise ensue.

the emperor, all these distinctions vanished. In the graver cases of "lèse majesté", individuals of any rank were liable to the death penalty;[6] generally, deportation was deemed a sufficient punishment for those of the highest rank; but upon those of a lower rank ("humiliores"), the death penalty in the terrible form of "bestiis objici" was inflicted.

(2) **Administration of Justice by State Officials.** — Justice administered by officials, which, as early as the first century after Christ had completely crowded out and replaced the old adjudications of the people, reminds one in many of its external features of criminal justice as it is to-day administered in the larger cities. We find, as shown under the title in the Digest, "De custodia et exhibitione reorum", an extensive and precise system of imprisonment, with rules for the transportation of prisoners,[7] a register of previous convictions,[8] a record of prisons, and regulations to secure the humane treatment of prisoners held pending trial. The accusatory principle of procedure, although not directly abolished, tended more and more to become less important and to lose its real significance.[9] It was the duty of the numerous police officials to investigate crimes, and in their official capacity to institute criminal proceedings; the officers acting as magistrates were, as a matter of fact, the absolute masters of the procedure.

This manner of administering justice under the absolute power of officials, while in many respects preferable to the old adjudications of the sworn jurors, which were liable to be influenced by corruption, furthered informal and arbitrary methods,[10] and also gave rise to a variety of abuses on the part of the superior officials and their subordinates.[11]

[6] *Paulus*, "Sententiæ Receptæ", V, 29, § 1.

[7] L. 2, C. "De exhibendis et transmittendis reis", 9, 3; L. 5, C. "De custodia reorum", 9, 4.

[8] L. 11, § 1, D. 48, 3; L. 7, D. eod.

[9] [On this subject of procedure, see *Mittermaier's* chapter on Roman procedure, in *Esmein's* "History of Continental Criminal Procedure" (1913, transl. *Simpson*, in the present Series). — Ed.]

[10] As shown, *e.g.* in L. 18 §§ 9, 10 D. "De quæstionibus", 48, 18. The "Præses provinciæ" would cause the prisoners to be brought before him in large numbers from the prisons, and judgment could be passed immediately upon the event. The passages provide that the "Præses" should give notice of the days of visitation and hearing, so that the accused could prepare their defense and not be completely taken unaware in the matter of proof. *Cf.* also L. 12 D. "De publ. jud.", 48, 1.

[11] Against the scandalous abuses of the subordinate officials and their attempts at extortion L. 1 C. 9, 4 (A.D. 320) was directed. Concerning wrongful judgments and corrupted witnesses, *cf.* L. 18 § 6 D. "De adulteriis", 48, 5.

Continued Disregard for the Criminal. — In its changed form, the Roman criminal law remained true to its old attitude of disregard for the party who was sentenced. As in ancient Greece,[12] so in Rome it was not considered worth the trouble to give emphasis to a proper relation between the punishment and the crime, or to give much thought to such matters. There is here, as it were, a trace of the old manner of regarding the criminal as an enemy of the State, against whom one may resort to any expedient. There is not the faintest trace of the idea that after all the community must share the blame for the crime. Yet the Roman criminal law of the classical period is far removed from that attitude of grim self-satisfaction which is encountered in the deliberate aggravation of the offender's suffering, which later prevailed, under the influence of theological ideas, from the latter part of the Middle Ages until the 1700 s.[13] But identical severe penalties were applied to crimes of a very different nature; and if the time or the circumstances made it necessary, the most terrible sufferings of the condemned seemed a matter of small moment. Thus we find the same punishment of deportation inflicted for an act of violence whereby no injury was wrought, for the seduction of a virgin,[14] and also for a murder perpetrated by use of poison.[15] Anyone, who, without authority, *e.g.* to satisfy his curiosity, opened or read the testament of another person during his lifetime was sentenced to deportation,[16] probably "ad metalla." With disregard for the natural instinct of liberty, they did not hesitate to penalize with atrocious additional punishments attempts of prisoners to escape.[17] If a crime was being frequently committed in a certain locality, the punishment could

[12] *Cf. Thonissen's* comments on Plato's philosophy of criminal law: "Le droit pénal de la république Athénienne", pp. 445 *et seq.* Concerning the expressions of the Greek orators, see *Thonissen*, p. 73.

[13] *Cf. e.g.* 8, § 3, D. "De pœnis", 48, 19: "Nec ea quidem pœna damnari quem oportet, ut verberibus necetur vel virgis interimatur nec tormentis." Moreover, the barbarous methods of capital punishment which were used, insofar as they were not prescribed by the arbitrary despotism of individual emperors (see *Invernizzi*, p. 177, and *e.g. Suetonius*, as to such cases of atrocious punishment), were not founded so much upon an attempt to give pain to the criminal as upon religious and other motives, *e.g.* upon the ideal of a certain "talio" or retribution, — *e.g.* the punishment of being burnt alive for arson.

[14] According to L. 1 § 2 D. "De extraord. crim." 47, 11, there could under some circumstances be capital punishment in such cases, even of the "comites" of the chief offender.

[15] *Cf. Von Holtzendorff*, p. 130.

[16] L. 38 § 7 D. "De pœnis", 48, 19.

[17] L. 8 § 7 D. "De pœnis", 48, 19.

be increased,[18] according to Saturninus, to make a public example. As appears from the persecution of the Christians and especially from the famous rescript of Trajan above mentioned, when the interests of the State were in question, there was no very exact discrimination between guilt and innocence. Thus a decree of the Senate passed in the time of Nero provided that if anyone suffered a violent death at the hands of his own slaves, even those slaves should be executed who were freed by his testament[19] and who were kept at his home; and Tacitus,[20] while he makes mention of this, sees herein nothing out of the ordinary. "Factum est senatus consultum ultioni juxta et securitati." Condemnation to death in the gladiatorial sports or by exposure to wild beasts in the public theatres, in which case the prisoner was often long in anguish under the prospect of this terrible death,[21] are other examples of this same attitude of indifference.

Reversion to More Primitive Conditions. — A system of law, possessed of these characteristics, was always in danger of reverting to its condition in much earlier periods. The abnormal development, which we have noticed (*e.g.* in the crime of "lèse majesté"), the prosecution of crimes after the death of their author, the "damnatio memoriæ", and the punishment inflicted upon even the descendants of those guilty of "lèse majesté", — all these are not to be attributed solely to the despotism of

[18] L. 8 § 10 D. "De pœnis", 48, 19.

[19] The large numbers of slaves in Rome must often have appeared dangerous enough; that the slaves, in such cases as the above, should all be put to death was an old custom: *Tacitus*, "Annals", XIV, 42. *Cf.* tit. D. "De SCo. Silaniano et Claudiano" 29, 5. Those slaves only were spared who could prove that they hastened to the assistance of their master. Even Hadrian, who was usually mild of disposition, gave a rescript to the effect that a female slave, who (perhaps from astonishment or fear) had not called for help, should be put to death: L. 1, § 28, D. 29, 5.

[20] Annals, XIII, 32.

[21] Colattio Leg. Mosaic. XI. c. 7 § 4: "Ad gladium damnati confestim consumuntur vel certe intra annun debent consumi." There is no doubt that the provincial magistrates often sought to add lustre to the theatre by bringing large numbers of condemned persons into combat with lions, tigers, etc. It was against this abuse that the prohibition contained in L. 31, § 1, D. "De pœnis", 48, 19, was directed; in accordance with which, criminals were not to be transported from one province to another. Indeed, it is stated in the same passage, concerning convicts who have distinguished themselves in such combats and have for the time being escaped with their lives, that word be sent to the Emperor, if there can be this delay, that these convicts are worthy to be presented before the people of the City of Rome! Sometimes the spectators desired the release of the combatants because of their bravery and recklessness of life. But the provincial magistrates were not to comply with such desires.

the emperors. As has been shown by Mommsen, there were revived during the Empire many of the fundamentals of the old Roman constitutional law; and the same result could well take place in the field of criminal law.

§ 19. **Influence of the Jurists.** — This method of administration of justice through State officials made possible another and an entirely distinct influence, exercised by judicial practice. Even the imperial officers ought not in theory to allow themselves to pass their own judgment either upon the deed or upon the personal merit of the accused. Neither were they to frame the penalties according to the exigencies of general public policy.[1] In theory they appeared only as administrators of the statutory law, or of the will of the emperor or of the Senate, which had the same force and effect as a statute.[2] Nevertheless, viewed from another angle, the jurisdiction of these officials did go further. They were not (as were the "quæstiones" of the old popular courts) limited in such manner that they could only take cognizance of one certain offense and decide the guilt or innocence of its alleged author.[3] They investigated, at least as far as could be done by official proceedings, the facts of the case in every conceivable juristic aspect, and their authority in the fixing of penalties was very extensive.[4] Penalties were sometimes left entirely to their discretion. In some cases they could, of their own authority, even impose the death penalty; and Ulpian in the Digest, under the title "De pœnis", makes the general statement: "Hodie licet ei qui extra ordinem de crimine cognoscit quam vult senten-

[1] "Semper graves et sapientes judices in rebus judicandis, quid utilitas civitatis, quid communis salus, quid reipublicæ tempora poscerent, cogitaverunt": *Cicero*, "Pro Flacco", c. 39. *Cf.* herewith *Geib*, "Geschichte", p. 301. The latter, however, goes too far in speaking of the freedom of the lay judges (jurymen) from being bound by the law, and one must not forget that very often Cicero expresses a partizan point of view. To the contrary, *cf. Seeger*, "Ueber das Verhältniss der Strafrechtspflege zum Gesetz in Zeitalter Cicero's" (1869).

[2] But the emperor himself and the senate, when passing judgment as magistrates, did indeed consider themselves justified in exceeding existing laws (*cf. Geib*, p. 657), and the jurists and the courts constantly assumed rather a wider latitude for them than would be conceded in our times (*cf. Savigny*, "System des röm. Rechts", I, p. 300). The judges could not remit a sentence when once it had been passed. The right to remit sentences remained the exclusive prerogative of the emperor (L. 27 pr., D. 48, 19).

[3] [On all these terms of Roman procedure, consult *Mittermaier's* chapter in *Esmein's* "History of Continental Criminal Procedure" (1913, in this Series). — ED.]

[4] *Cf. Geib*, "Geschichte des röm. Criminalprocess", p. 660, and the authorities there given.

tiam ferre vel graviorem vel leviorem, ita tamen ut in utroque modo rationem non excedat." Now this "ratio" in the infliction of punishment was supplied by the judicial law embodied in the opinions ("consilium") emanating from the learned jurists. In spite of the interference of the absolute power of the emperor, in spite of the corrupt fibre of the officials and the corrupt human elements with which it had to deal, the jurists' learning performed its task. There can be no doubt that the science of law was at this time a real force, and that it performed its labors with no low degree of moral sensibility. "Quæ facta lædunt pietatem, existimationem, verecundiam nostram et ut generaliter dicam contra bonos mores fiunt nec facere nos posse credendum est"[5] is the well known utterance of the most famous of all the Roman jurists, a man who was himself executed by Caracalla (more correctly, murdered) as guilty of high treason.

The truth is that the ancient world, which regarded criminal statutes merely as a means to insure the punishment of an act deserving punishment, did not realize that the imposition of a penalty in excess of the plain meaning of the statute was not compatible with the security of the rights of the individual.[6] The Roman lawyers felt themselves justified not only in imposing penalties "ex sententia" and "ad exemplum legis",[7] but also in inflicting punishments, whenever the exigencies of life seemed to require it, for acts which previously had not been the occasion for punishment.[8]

But even here, as remarked, practice did not go beyond the limits of actual necessity. Roman jurists, even in the case of the crime of "lèse majesté", contending successfully against imperial despotism, introduced a distinction between "perduellio" and the other cases of "lèse majesté", and limited to the former the severe penalties which were indiscriminately imposed by the emperors.[9] They succeeded in getting the emperors to

[5] L. 15, D. "De conditionibus", 28, 7.

[6] *Cf.* as to Athens, *Thonissen*, "Droit pénal de la république Athénienne etc.", pp. 66, 140 *et seq.* *Cf.* as to Rome, *Henriot*, "Mœurs juridiques", etc., II, p. 106.

[7] *Cf. e.g.* L. 6, § 1, D. "De V. S." Also L. 22, §§ 8, 9, D. 48, 10, "De lege corn. de falsis." Also L. 7, § 3, D. 48, 4, and *Rein*, pp. 225, 226.

[8] *Cf.* Tit. D. "De extraord. crim." 47, 11, and in reference thereto, *Geib*, "Geschichte", p. 661. In the later empire, when the jurists' learning was in its decadence, the emperors sought again to restrict the authority of the judges. The prohibition freely to construe a statute, which was repeated by Justinian, had been enacted a century before his time. *Cf. Geib*, "Geschichte", p. 663.

[9] L. 11, D. 48, 4 (Ulpian).

give their sanction to the notable expressions of L. 7, § 3, D. 48, 4 concerning "lèse majesté." In addition to all this, we owe them our thanks for those two fundamental maxims, so far reaching in their consequences, which to-day dominate the criminal law and procedure of all civilized nations: "Interpretatione legum pœnæ potius molliendæ sunt quam exasperandæ",[10] and "Satius esse impunitum relinqui facinus nocentis quam innocentem damnare."[11] We also owe our thanks for the notable utterance of Marcian[12] concerning the imposition of penalties.[13] Again, we are indebted to Roman criminal lawyers for a correct theory of responsibility, and for those titles of the Digest which to-day are often too little appreciated, viz., "De furtis", "De injurias", and "De falsis"; as also for the title "Ad legem Aquiliam", so important for that cardinal point in criminal law, the relation between cause and effect. The last-mentioned title, as a result of the slight regard of their law for the consequence of an act, had influence only in private law, and was not made applicable to criminal law until the Middle Ages. However, since Roman criminal law from the beginning paid too little attention to the protection of private rights, and assumed, as it were, the character of police regulations, Roman juristic practice did not attain that high degree of development in the criminal field which we so much admire in Roman private law. This is shown by the history of the theory of "dolus", which, though the Roman criminal law laid so much stress on "dolus", was left only partially developed; the ultimate result of an act was in general given little consideration, and "dolus" can be accurately comprehended only when it is considered in relation to a specific result. But, perhaps it is on account of this very thing that the Roman criminal law had so stimulating an influence upon the German Law.

§ 20. **Influence of Christianity in the Later Empire.** — In the later Empire, the criminal law, upon the whole, tended to deteriorate. Just as the Christians had previously been persecuted, so now the power of the State, since the conversion of the emperors, was directed against the heathen, whose practices were

[10] L. 42, D. "De poenis", 48, 19.

[11] L. 5 pr., D. "De pœnis", 48, 19. The passage is taken from a rescript of Trajan.

[12] L. 11 pr., D. "De pœnis", 48, 19.

[13] Other maxims are: "In maleficiis voluntas spectatur, non exitus." Rescript of Hadrian in L. 14, D. 48, 9. "Cogitationis pœnam nemo patitur": L. 18, D. 48, 19. "Nec consilium habuisse nocet nisi et factum secutum fuerit": L. 53, § 2, D. "De V. S." (Paulus).

forbidden by stringent laws,[1] and soon, also, against heretics, *i.e.* those who rejected the beliefs declared by the State to be orthodox. It was now the heretics who were regarded as offenders and enemies of the Christian State. But the right of prosecution was by no means delegated to the Church; nor were individuals put on trial for their personal beliefs. This frightful calamity did not come to pass until the domination of theology in the Middle Ages. As yet, only the adherents of certain sects,[2] were persecuted, under special penal statutes of varying stringency, or were in some other way placed at a legal disadvantage.[3] Considering the hostility of parties within the Church towards each other at that time, there were among these sects many which could not well be tolerated without danger to the peace and the public safety.[4]

At this time, new and stringent penalties were laid down for the protection of the Church and the clergy. Laws were enacted against the disturbance of worship and against acts of violence toward members of the clergy when performing their duties, against seduction of nuns,[5] interference with the right of asylum afforded by the Church, and the violation of its privileges by public officials.[6] But the State, as it gradually became weaker, felt itself constrained to restrict with penal laws the extreme power of the clergy and its followers, although it made use of the Clergy in the supervision of the officers of criminal justice.[7] Thus, *e.g.*, "conventicula" in private houses, which often occasioned disturbances, was stringently prohibited. Against the abuses of the "parabolani" (the caretakers of the sick and needy of the Church), who were often at the absolute disposal of a bishop and constituted a powerful body-guard,[8] there were directed such provisions as L. 17, C. 1, 3 (417 A.D.).[9]

[1] *Platner*, pp. 248 *et seq.*

[2] Christians going over to the beliefs of Heathendom or of the Jews were also punished; *cf. Platner*, pp. 264 *et seq.* To offer circumcision to a Christian was later a capital offense.

[3] *Platner*, pp. 252 *et seq.*

[4] *Cf. e.g.* L. 2 and 3, C. Theodos. 16, 4 (A.D. 388, 392). These statutes forbade unauthorized disputations concerning religion. L. 5 C. ("De his qui ad ecclesiam") 1, 12 (A.D. 450, Marcian) threatened such cases with "ultimum supplicium."

[5] L. 5, C. "De episcopis et clericis", 1, 3.

[6] As to all these matters, *cf. Platner*, pp. 269 *et seq.*

[7] The bishops *e.g.* inspected the prison. L. 9 C. "De episcopali audientia", 1, 4 (A.D. 409, by Theodosius).

[8] L. 15, C. 1, 3 (A.D. 404, by Arcadius and Honorius). As to the interference of the Clergy with executions, *cf.* L. 6, C. 1, 4.

[9] Concerning acts of violence by the "Monachi", *cf.* L. 6, C. 1, 4 and L. 16, C. Theodos. 9, 40 (A.D. 398).

The importance which the clergy gradually acquired in the State is shown by the inclusion, in the imperial legislation, of even such provisions dealing with matters of discipline; as, L. 19, C. 1, 3, which forbade priests to live with women other than near relations, and Novel 123, c. 11, which forbade them to play the game of draughts.

Protection of State Sought by Numerous Penal Statutes. — The State now endeavored by means of countless penal statutes to protect itself against enemies of every character. Thus it sought to protect itself against the increasing inroads of the Barbarians by prohibiting, under penalties, the instruction of Barbarians in the art of ship-building,[10] and also the trade in weapons and articles the possession of which aided the Barbarians in war.[11] Against powerful landowners who began here and there, as it were, to play the part of sovereign, it protected itself by criminal provisions forbidding private prisons[12] and armed bodyguards ("isauri").[13] There were also statutes against persons who usurped property belonging to the State treasury ("fiscus") or rights therewith connected, and against misuse of the imperial mails,[14] interference with commercial intercourse with the metropolis, and arbitrarily raising the price of grain.[15] The State also protected itself against the faithlessness or negligence of its own officials by the imposition of heavy fines.[16]

Other Effects of the Influence of the Church. — Apart from the persecution of heathen and heretics and the above-mentioned offenses against the Church, the influence of Christianity is seen in the different manner in which adultery was treated. The

[10] L. 25, C. 9, 47 (A.D. 419).

[11] *Cf.* L. 11 pr., D. "De publicanis", 39, 4. Also L. 2, C. "quæ res exportari non debeant", 4, 41 (Marcian). The exportation of gold also was forbidden in L. 2 C. "De commerciis" 4, 63 (by Valentinian and Valens).

[12] *Cf.* L. 28, § 7, D. "De pœnis", 48, 19; also L. 1, C. "De privatis carceribus", 9, 5.

[13] *Cf.* L. 10, C. "Ad leg. Jul. de vi publ. s. priv.", 9, 12 (A.D. 468, by Leo and Anthemius).

[14] As to all these matters, *cf. Platner*, pp. 306 *et seq.*

[15] Attention was given to foodstuffs ("annona") as early as the Republic. Originally offenses of the kind mentioned were punished by the ædiles with a fine or were arbitrarily punished upon a complaint brought before the people. Later the "Lex Julia de annona" was in force. *Cf.* as to speculation in grain especially L. 6, D. "De extraord. crim.", 47, 11. As to illegal monopolies, *cf.* L. un. C. "De monop.", 4, 59. *Cf. Rein*, pp. 829, 830.

[16] Generally expressed in pounds of gold: *cf. Von Holtzendorff*, pp. 134 *et seq.*

right of filing an accusation is limited to the married parties themselves and their nearest male relatives. Thus adultery appears more as an offense against the family, and the relation of marriage is no longer ruthlessly sacrificed to the interests of the police power of the State.[17] This same influence also appears in an extensive political protection of slaves,[18] in whom Christianity saw primarily the friend and brother. It is also shown in the severer penalties now inflicted for a great number of crimes.[19] As appears in the so-called "Collatio Legum Mosaicarum et Romanarum" (composed presumably during the 300 s), there can be no doubt that the Church, regarding divine and human justice as identical, began to lay claim to the right to legislation in temporal matters, and to act in accordance with the Mosaic legislation (as at that time understood). Making appeal to certain familiar passages in the Scriptures, the Church began to demand the death penalty in a number of cases in which it had not been used by the Roman law, or, if used, had been applied with certain reservations or to only the lower classes of the people. Thus, there may be attributed to the influence of Christianity the infliction of the death penalty for adultery, enacted by Constantine but later repealed. The death penalty was also introduced by Justinian for cases of incestuous marriage. Moreover, in the words of L. 3, C. "De episcopali audientia" 1, 4 (by Valentinian, Theodosius, and Arcadius) "Homicida et parricida quod fecit semper expectet", we encounter significant thoughts of obligatory retaliation in kind ("talio") which are foreign to the Roman Law.

Last Stages of the Roman Criminal Law. — The chief cause, however, of the death penalties, which were so frequently enacted in the later Empire, was the caprice of the emperors and a system of legislation which was calculated to serve temporary purposes and had lost all sense of the distinction between punishment for crime and punishment for police pur-

[17] This change was introduced by Constantine. *Cf.* particularly *Von Wächter*, "Abhandlungen a. d. Strafrechts", pp. 118 *et seq.* and L. 2, C. Theodos. 9, 7 (L. 29 [30] C. J. 9. 9): "ne volentibus temere liceat fœdare connubia."

[18] *Cf. e.g.* L. 6, C. 11, 41 "De spectaculis" (A.D. 428) which forbade masters to place female slaves in brothels. Constantine had previously forbidden (*cf.* L. 1, C. "De emendatione servorum", 9, 14) the existing custom of inhumanly flogging slaves as a punishment for homicide.

[19] The counterfeiting of a "solidus" was punished by burning alive by L. 5, C. Theodos. 9, 21. Peculation entailed the death penalty (L. 1, C. Theodos. 9, 28), as did also the origination and circulation of "libelli famosi" (L. 10, C. Theodos. 9, 34).

poses. Reckless experiments were made with a crude theory of deterrence, without knowledge of the effect which excessive and varying penal provisions have upon the morals of a people. In this respect, it is sufficient to recall the barbarous penal provisions of the despotic Constantine against the crime of abduction,[20] and the provisions of the Code of Theodosius which threatened with severe criminal penalties the wearing of trousers in Rome or the wearing of long hair; to recall also the passage which provided deprivation of all honors and possibly deportation for those who ventured to use a thorn stick in urging horses of the imperial posts.[21]

Many of those deformities of the law were indeed repealed by the better emperors, among whom Justinian may be included. However, on the whole, the principles of the Roman criminal law, excellent in many respects, had only an uncertain and precarious application. They were known to the jurists but were never the absolute property of the people. On the other hand, it may be regarded as fortunate that these principles were preserved in the compilation of Justinian along with the numerous arbitrary features belonging to Roman State crimes and probably inseparable therefrom. The genius of the Germanic peoples was able to reject the irrational elements and at the same time to make the fundamental principles the permanent property of the entire civilized world.[22]

[20] Molten lead was poured into the mouth of the nurses (or governesses) who had loaned their assistance: L. 1, C. Theodos. 9, 24.

[21] As to this and similar matters, *cf. Von Holtzendorff*, p. 146.

[22] There is little of immediate interest for the history of German criminal law in the history of Roman criminal law after Justinian. It is deserving of notice, but not readily explainable, that the later Greek law had much in common with the German criminal law of the Middle Ages. Thus there was to be found composition and settlement with the injured party. *Cf. E. Zachariä v. Lingenthal*, "Geschichte des griechish-römischen Rechts" (2d ed. 1877), pp. 303 *et seq.*

CHAPTER II

PRIMITIVE GERMANIC CRIMINAL LAW

§ 21. **Prominence of the Element of Vengeance.** — The primitive Germanic criminal law,[1] far more distinctly than that of the

[1] In regard to the matter contained in this chapter the following writers may be consulted: *Wiarda*, "Geschichte und Auslegung des Salischen Gesetzes" (1808); *Henke*, "Grundriss einer Geschichte des deutschen peinlichen Rechts" (2 vols. 1809), *cf.* Vol. I, pp. 1–108; *Eichhorn*, "Deutsche Staats- und Rechtsgeschichte" (5th ed.), Vol. I, §§ 71, 206; *Rogge*, "Ueber das Gerichtswesen der Germanen" (1820); *Jarcke*, "Handbuch des deutschen Strafrechts" (Vol. I, 1827), pp. 10 *et seq.;* *Grimm*, "Deutsche Rechtsalterthümer" (2d ed. 1854); *Abegg*, "Untersuchungen aus dem Gebiete der Rechtswissenschaft" (1830); *Warnkönig*, "Flandrische Rechtsgeschichte" (3 vols. 1838–39); *Von Woringen*, "Beiträge zur Geschichte des deutschen Strafrechts", I, "Erläuterungen über das Compositionenwesen" (1836); *Wilda*, "Das Strafrecht der Germanen" (1842); *Von Wächter*, "Beiträge zur deutschen Geschichte, insbesonderer des deutschen Strafrechts" (1845), II, "Das Faust- und Fehderecht des Mittelalters"; *Walter*, "Deutsche Rechtsgeschichte" (2d ed., 1857), Vol. 2, pp. 319–417 *et seq.;* *Du Boys*, "Histoire du droit criminel des peuples modernes" (4 vols. Paris, 1854 *et seq.*); *Waitz*, "Deutsche Verfassungsgeschichte" (3d ed. 1880), I, especially pp. 418–442; *Köstlin*, "Geschichte des deutschen Strafsrechts im Umriss, herausgegeben von Gessler" (1859), pp. 58 *et seq.;* *Geib*, "Lehrbuch des deutschen Strafrechts", I (1861), pp. 152–196; *Osenbrüggen*, "Das alamannische Strafrecht im Mittelalter" (1860); *Osenbrüggen*, "Das Strafrecht der Langobarden" (1863); *Von Holtzendorff*, "Handbuch des deutschen Strafrechts", I, pp. 57–67; *Dahn*, "Westgothische Studien" (1874), pp. 140–242; *Pasquale del Giudice*, "La vendetta nel diritto Langobardo" (Milano, 1876); *R. Löning*, "Der Vertragsbruch im deutschen Recht" (1876); *Dahn*, "Fehdegang und Rechtsgang der Germanen" (1877);

Romans, is based upon the principles of vengeance [2] and self-defense. This criminal law, when it assumed the form of vengeance, belonged only to the party injured or his kinsmen ("sippe").[3] However, the party injured might be the community at large, if the offender made a direct attack upon the community, or fell short in the performance of duties owed to it.

The criminal, then, is the *enemy* of either the individual or the community. But it is only in the latter case (since it is only in his relation to the community that the early German appears as subject to authority) that the idea of *public* or State punishment acquires prominence. Thus, in the "Germania" of Tacitus,[4] the expression "discrimen capitis intendere" refers only to direct offenses against the community, such as treason, going over to the enemy, and disgraceful retreat [5] in battle; while the worst

Von Wächter, "Beilagen zu Vorlesungen über das deutsche Strafrecht", I (1877), pp. 77 *et seq.*; *Jastrow*, "Zur strafrechtlichen Stellung der Sclaven bei Deutschen und Angelsachsen" (1878); *Sickel*, "Geschichte der deutschen Staatsverfassung", Division I, "Der deutsche Freistaat" (1879). [*Cohn*, "Die Verbrechen im öffentlichen Dienst, nach altdeutschem Recht" (Karlsruhe, 1876); *Bennecke*, "Geschichte des deutschen Strafprozesses" (Marburg, 1886); *Budde*, "Ueber Rechtlosigkeit, Ehrlosigkeit und Echtlosigkeit" (Bonn, 1882); *Kohler*, "Studien aus dem Strafrecht" (Berlin, 1895); *Beschütz*, "Die Fahrlässigkeit innerhalb der geschichtlichen Entwickelung der Schuldlehre: Theil I: Vom primitiven Strafrecht bis zur peinlichen Gerichtsordnung Karls V"; *Brunner*, "Deutsche Rechtsgeschichte", 1st ed., Leipzig, 1887–1892; 2d ed., Vol. I, 1906; *Hoegel*, "Geschichte des österreichischen Strafrechts in Verbindung mit einer Erläuterung seiner grundsätzlichen Bestimmungen", 1904–5; *K. Maurer*, "Vorlesungen über altnordische Rechtsgeschichte"; Vol. 5, "Altisländisches Strafrecht und Gerichtswesen", 1910; *Heusler*, "Das Strafrecht der Isländersagas", 1911; *Gierke*, "Schuld und Haftung im alteren deutschen Recht", 1909; *Heusler*, "Institutionen des deutschen Privatrechts", 1883–5; *Schröder*, "Lehrbuch der deutschen Rechtsgeschichte", 5th ed., 1912.]

[2] "Lex Bajuv." VIII, c. 8 "secundum legem *vindicta* subjaceant."

[3] *Tacitus*, "Germania", c. 21: "Suscipere tam inimicitias seu patris seu propinqui quam amicitias necesse est." As in the early stages of legal development with other peoples, vengeance appears as a moral duty. As proof of this, it is only necessary to recall the Nibelungensage. As to the Norse Sagas, in which vengeance is enjoined upon near blood relatives as a moral duty, see *Wilda*, pp. 172, 177.

[4] "Germania", c. 12.

[5] "Licet apud consilium accusare quoque et discrimen capitis intendere. Distinctio pœnarum ex delicto. Proditores et transfugas arboribus suspendunt; ignavos et imbelles et corpore infames cæno ac palude, iniecta insuper crate mergunt." The much disputed "corpore infamis" certainly has reference to unnatural lewdness (*cf. Tacitus*, "Annals", I, 13). However this, according to the most primitive German law, was criminally punishable only when it occurred at encampments of the army, — just as, in Tacitus, mention is made only of crimes which took place during a military expedition. In the army, discipline was more strictly exercised than under the ordinary criminal law, and in the army the tempta-

offense against the individual, homicide, merely brought about, according to Tacitus,[6] a condition of hostility from which the payment of some composition would procure release. "Luitur enim et homicidium certo armentorum ac pecorum numero, recipitque satisfactionem universa domus." As has been correctly stated by Eichhorn,[7] it was only in cases of crime against the nation itself that the nation acquired power over the life or body of a free man. The "Lex Bajuvariorum" declares:[8] "Ut nullus liber Bajuvarius alodem aut vitam sine capitali crimine perdat; id ist si in necem ducis consiliatus fuerit, aut inimicos in provinciam invitaverit aut civitatem capere ab extraneis machinaverit. . . . Tunc in ducis sit potestate vita ipsius et omnes res ejus in patrimonium."[9] This, however, did not preclude the party

tion and inducement to the above-mentioned offense were especially great. *Cf. Arnobius*, "Adv. nationes", 4, 7 p. 146, 19 R: "Etiamne militaris Venus castrensibus flagitiis præsidet et puerorum stupris." For other explanations, *cf. Waitz*, I, p. 396 (2d ed.), p. 425 (3d ed.). *Henke*, I, p. 4, believes that "corpore infames" has reference *e.g.* to voluntary mutilation with the view to avoid military service. Also *Pasquale del Giudice*, p. 5, believes the passage of Tacitus has reference only to the exercise of disciplinary power in the army, and correctly calls attention to the fact that c. 11 of *Tacitus* says: "Silentium per sacerdotes quibus tum et coercendi jus est imperatur." The priests have the "jus coercendi" only during the public assembly.

[6] "Germania," c. 21.

[7] *Eichhorn*, I, p. 387.

[8] "Lex Bajuv.", tit. 2, c. 1.

[9] Where penalties of life and limb on account of private crimes occur in the Germanic folk-laws, they are in my opinion to be attributed to some foreign influence, — to the Roman law or to the ordinances of the kings. There is perhaps an exception for the numerous death-penalties on account of theft, which was considered dishonorable for a free man. On the other hand, *Von Amira*, "Ueber Zweck und Mittel der germanischen Rechtsgeschichte" (1876), pp. 57–59, reasserts the essentially religious character of early Germanic criminal law. I am unable, however, upon the whole to find justification for ascribing this character to the Germanic law, either in the Norse sources, in the relation between capital punishment and the sacrifice of human victims among the heathen Frisians, or in the above-mentioned passage from Tacitus (G. C. 7) concerning the criminal power of the priests. The idea that among the primitive Germans, in the case of crimes against the *community*, the gods who protected the same must also be reconciled is not to be rejected. But this religious flavor, as it were, is not to be taken as definitive of the character of the criminal law. The passage of Tacitus speaks only of crimes committed on military expeditions; the Germans, as Tacitus expressly states, believed in the *special* presence of their gods, and only during the military expedition, as Tacitus states, did the Germans submit to a certain criminal power in matters of discipline which was exercised by the priests and for this reason was held in greater respect.

Von Amira asserts that a larger part of the base acts which in heathen times were punished with death (sacrifice as a victim) were by Christianity made expiable or merely to entail outlawry. Yet although this may be correct in regard to the Scandinavians, it has not been proven true in regard to the territory of the Frankish realm, and in my opinion is

injured, in extreme cases, from his right to slay the criminal if the latter was not able to pay the composition levied by the community or fixed by mutual agreement. "Et si eum in conpositione nullus ad fidem tullerunt hoc est ut redimant, de quo domino non persolvit, tunc de sua vita conponat."[10] The criminal would be delivered by the judicial power to the family of the man slain by him, for the exercise of private vengeance, — as we find occasionally happening even in the later Middle Ages.[11]

The community appears to have been concerned in the crime only in so far as it arranged the peace between the hostile parties,

not the case. It is certainly correct, as *Richthofen*, "Zur Lex Saxonum" (Berlin, 1868), pp. 218 *et seq.*, has shown (Von Amira also refers to this) that the heathen Saxons inflicted capital punishment for murder, adultery, and certain other offenses not directly prejudicial to the community, and that most of those cases in which capital punishment was inflicted, found in the Lex Saxonum and the Saxon Capitularies of Charles the Great, which differ from those of the other German folk-laws, are received from and modelled after the more primitive law (*e.g.* burning of a church, homicide in a church). But it is not to be assumed from this, that the Saxon law, as it existed immediately before the statutes of Charles the Great or even a century earlier, is an example of the oldest Saxon law or the law of the race in the time of Tacitus. Private vengeance can be supplanted by public punishment without the intervening steps of composition, and this could readily occur in cases where the previous similarity between members of the same race vanished under the domination of an individual or of a powerful aristocracy comparatively few in number. This last was undoubtedly the case with the Saxons, among whom the "nobiles", who constituted, as it were, a caste from which the ordinary free men were excluded (*cf. Richthofen*, "Zur Lex Saxonum", pp. 223 *et seq.*) and who inflicted death upon the ordinary free man who married one of their number, and were even able to impose for themselves six (!) times the "wergeld" of an ordinary freeman. Such a condition did not exist among the other German tribes. Perhaps such a penalty as the above was applied only against those who were not nobles, and against nobles there was only the right of feud. This would explain the special protection of the "faidosus" in certain cases. (*Cf. Richthofen*, p. 231, as to provisions of this character in the "Lex Frisionum" which cast light upon the "Lex Saxonum.") This also explains why, after Charles the Great, the domination of the nobles being broken, there revived in most cases the old law of composition, which was so long retained as the most ancient law of North Germany. *Cf.* the comments of Sickel, pp. 72 *et seq.* and especially pp. 76, 77: "If one considers more closely the conditions under which the German priesthood lived, it will be seen that often the priesthood had conditions unfavorable for its development."

[10] "Les Salica", LVIII, 2 a. E. (ed. *Behrend*); *cf. Wiarda*, p. 272; *Pardessus*, "Loi salique", p. 664. *Abegg*, p. 319, also explains the passage in this way. In the supplements of Count Baldwin to the decrees of Ghent, in the last of the 1100s, it is said that for a case where an "extraneus" had wronged an "oppidanus" (citizen), and had not rendered him satisfaction within the fixed time ("quod si nondum satisfecerit reus), "licebit male tractato, sine omni forisfacto . . . qualemcunque potuerit vindictam sumere": *Warnkönig*, "Flandrische Staats- und Rechtsgeschichte", II, 1, note vii (p. 18).

[11] *Cf. Warnkönig*, "Flandrische Rechtsgeschichte", III, p. 160.

i.e. the offender and the party injured.[12] Then,[13] if the party injured announced that he would be satisfied with the payment of a composition, which in the most primitive times consisted of a number of cattle, the community received from the criminal (*i.e.* for the arrangement of the peace)[14] the "peace money" ("fredus" or "fredum").

[12] "Germania", c. 12: "Sed et levioribus delictis pro modo pœna: equorum pecorumque numero convicti multantur. Pars multæ regi vel civitati, pars ipsi qui vindicatur, vel propinquis ejus exsolvitur."

[13] It must have been realized that open hostility between numerous citizens was injurious to the community, "quia periculosiores sunt inimicitiæ juxta libertatem." Apparently the chiefs arranged the peace at the gathering of the army, and the "fredus" was originally a present *voluntarily* given by the offender.

[14] The more generally accepted view is (*cf. Waitz*, "Deutsche Verfassungsgeschichte", I, p. 440; *Gierke*, "Das deutsche Genossenschaftsrecht", I, p. 31) that the "fredus" was a *penalty* paid because of the breach of the peace, and not a *price* paid for the peace that was reëstablished (between the offender and the injured party); *cf. Walter*, "Rechtsgeschichte", II, §. 714; *Waitz*, 3d ed., I, p. 440. It is left undetermined which of these two was the case. To me, this distinction is unclear. Waitz rejects the idea of payment to the one who arranged the peace; but would he sooner admit payment for judicial activity? There is no special evidence for this, but rather there is only the general but incorrect impression (see *infra*) that the crime is a breach of the general peace. *Cf.* the contradictory position taken by *Kemble*, "The Saxons in England", I, p. 290; also the comments of *Moser*, "Patriot. Phantasien" (Abeken), IV, pp. 126 *et seq.*; *Von Wächter*, "Beiträge", p. 42; *Von Siegel*, p. 29. It can be positively proven that according to the "Capitularies" ("Cap. Karoli M. Ticinense", A.D. 801, n. 24 *Pertz*, p. 86) the "fredus" was not paid to the judge of the district in which the crime took place (*i.e.* where the peace was broken), but rather to the judge who arranged the composition; that the payment of the same was received for the injured party; and further that, according to the ancient rules of law and those obtaining until nearly the end of the Middle Ages (*cf. e.g.* "Lex Rib." LXXXIX; "Cap. Karoli M." A.D. 801; "Brünner Stadtr. a. d. Mitte des XIV Jahrhunderts", § 41 (in *Rössler*), p. 358; *Von Maurer*, "Geschichte der Städteverfassung in Deutschland", III, p. 658; "Brünner Schöffenbuch", n. 245) the judge might only receive this payment for negotiating the peace ("esmenda" or "wette") if the "satisfactio" or "compositio" had *previously* been paid to the injured party; and finally that the "fredus" or later the "wette" was *not* paid, if there had been *public* punishment ("Sachs. Landrecht", III, 50; "Schwabenspiegel", 176, ed. *Lassberg*).

Public punishment is a substitute for vengeance, and also the opposite of the arrangement of a peace. If it was (as corresponds with the modern but not the medieval view) a reëstablishment of peace between the community, the injured party, and the offender, then the "fredus" would be paid *both* in addition to "compositio" and to public punishment. It was not until the rise of a procedure under the direction of public officials that the "fredus" assumed the character of a public punishment (*Von Maurer, ante*). There is also connected herewith the fact that, until late in the Middle Ages, a far-reaching distinction was made between the criminal who voluntarily appeared and him who was captured. The former, according to the Bamberg law, even if he was convicted by witnesses, would be again set free; capital punishment was not permissible: *Brunnenmeister*, "Die Quellen der Bambergensis, ein Beitrag zur Geschichte des deutschen Strafrechts" (1879), pp. 44, 45.

Outlawry not the Most Primitive Form of Punishment. — The view of Wilda and others that the earliest punishment of the criminal, even in offenses against the individual, was a general outlawry, in the sense that the criminal was at once cast out among the wild animals of the forest, thus becoming a "forest rover" ("wargus") who could be killed by anyone with impunity, is not correct. Under these circumstances, as Von Amira points out, a contract with the party injured would be legally ineffective, and the outlawry would at once become public punishment in its strict sense. That outlawry of this character appears in the Norse sources is admitted.[15] But the Norse

Von Woringen, pp. 105 *et seq.*, is correct in his view that a crime did not originally cause general outlawry, but he incorrectly concludes that the "fredus" would have to be paid for the breach of the peace. Since peace had not been lost for the criminal, it could not well be repurchased. But what is the distinction between a broken peace and a lost peace? I am unable to see the difference. It is, however, proper to make a distinction between peace with the injured party and peace with the community. The fact that the amount of "fredus" was graded in accordance with the person who was injured is capable of a ready explanation by the view here accepted. Can not the price for negotiating the peace be varied in accordance with the importance of the controversy, and is not this what would naturally happen?

Sickel, p. 154, would maintain that the "fredus" was originally not a court fee, especially for the reason that the "collegium" of judges were too numerous to derive benefit from it. But could there not be certain favored ones, who *e.g.* made the proposal for the peace? The narrative of Gregory of Tours (Hist. Franc., c. 47) given by *Rogge* (p. 15, note 25), is in accord with the view that the "compositio" rested originally merely upon a compromise, which the leaders of the nation negotiated with a view to the advantage of the general public. The judges considered themselves justified in order to perfect a settlement someway or other, in conceding to some powerful party an amount as a "compositio" to which, according to strict justice, he had no claim. In no way did the later public punishment supplant the money paid for the peace, but rather it supplanted the exercise of vengeance, of private satisfaction. Consequently it is stated in the "Sächsisches Landrecht", III, 50, that if a German had incurred as a penalty the loss of life or hand, he should pay neither "wette" nor compensation; and the Kursaxon law even in the 1600 s did not recognize "wergeld", if the individual who was sentenced underwent the death penalty; while the Italians, proceeding from the independence of the civil claim in respect to the claim for punishment, allowed claims for damages to the descendants of the slain man in a judgment pronouncing the death penalty against a murderer or generally one who had slain another: *Berlich*, "Conclusiones practicabiles" (1615–1619), IV, 19, n. 15 *et seq.* and especially n. 24.

Confiscation of property, but not a definite amount of money as a penalty or as a compensation, is related to the idea of vengeance; since confiscation of property amounted to the economic destruction of the offender, while a definite measure of damages according to the old German viewpoint presupposed an agreement. Consequently, along with punishment by death or mutilation, there were numerous confiscations of property. The distinction between confiscation of property and "wette", "busse", is overlooked by *Köstlin*, "Krit. Ueberschau," Vol. 3, p. 183.

[15] *Cf.* in opposition to the opinions herein contested, the correct obser-

sources,[16] which are later than the time of the origin of the folk-laws, by no means exemplify the Germanic criminal law in its earliest form, and certainly it is not justifiable to maintain that all the legal institutions of the Norse people were those of the Germanic peoples generally. In the Germanic sources, the nearest approach to outlawry as a consequence resulting directly from the act (and not as something inflicted by the royal or judicial power as a punishment for refusal to submit to the law, or as a form of attainder) [17] is to be seen only in the fact that, in the earliest periods, the party injured was permitted to wreak vengeance upon the criminal,[18] to treat

vations of *Von Woringen*, pp. 103, 104, and *Hugo Meyer*, "Das Strafverfahren gegen Abwesende" (1869), pp. 48 *et seq.*

[16] *Von Amira*, "Das altnorwegische Vollstreckungsverfahren" (1874), pp. 1–78, especially pp. 18 *et seq.* *Cf.* the comments of *K. Von Maurer* in the "Münchener kritische Vierteljahrschrift", 16 (1874), p. 83 *et seq.;* [and Chap. VI, *post*].

[17] *Cf. Rogge*, pp. 19 *et seq.* Loss of the general peace did not occur until the offender had ignored the intervention of the community, and did not heed the summons of the complainant to appear before the assembly. But even this was not until the acceptance of this intervention had come to be regarded as a legal duty. This loss of the general peace in the French and German sources because of the existence of a strong kingly power appeared as a form of *proscription*. *Cf.* "Lex Salica" 56, 1 (Ed. *Behrend*): "Si quis ad mallum venire contempserit . . . si nec de compositione nec ineo nec de ulla legem fidem facere voluerit, tunc ad regis præsentia ipso mannire debet . . . § 2 . . . tunc rex . . . extra sermonem suum ponat eum." Rogge, however, is mistaken in his view that *at this time* the offender had the right to choose between "compositio" and feud. The offender appears to have been absolutely bound to pay the "compositio" if the injured party so desired. *Cf.* as opposed to Rogge, *Eichhorn*, I, § 18, note 6; *Von Woringen*, p. 38.

The development of the law in Italy as it appeared in the law of the Lombards is in conformance herewith. The so-called public ("städtische") ban which was so important in the later Middle Ages, and to which so much attention is given by both the statutes and the jurists was, in grave criminal cases, primarily a result of disobedience. However, it became a punishment in so far as, on failure of an accused, whose guilt was known, to present himself in the proper manner, the thought of compelling him to appear became subsidiary to the idea of making the ban (a partial or complete deprivation of legal protection) so severe that it took the place of the appropriate punishment. *Cf. Ficker*, "Forschungen zur Reichs- und Rechtsgeschichte Italiens" (I, 1868), pp. 92 *et seq.*, especially 97. The statement that under some circumstances the mere ban creating banishment was the equivalent of an independent punishment is not prejudiced but is rather supported by two arguments — on one hand, that if there was fear that disturbance and feud would result from the continued residence of the accused in the city, this punishment was suggested by reasons of expediency, and, on the other, that if the offender was not able to pay, banishment must have been regarded as of less severity than the punishment of mutilation which would otherwise be inflicted. The German "Reichsacht" or "Reichsaberacht" (*i.e.* ban of the empire) is, according to a correct conception, a ban because of disobedience and not "per se" a punishment of certain crimes: *Ficker*, pp. 174 *et seq.*

[18] *Cf. Eichhorn*, I, § 18; *Von Woringen*, pp. 32 *et seq.; Pardessus*, pp.

him as " faidosus ", and that possibly some of his comrades would take it upon themselves to support the party injured in his actions. There may also have been something of this character when the criminal rejected or paid no attention to the proposition of settlement offered to him by the injured party through the public assembly, or, at a later period, when the criminal ignored the summons of the king (or court) issued upon motion of the injured party.[19]

Possibly the development of the law in France may have been the same as that shown in the Norse sources; an indication[20] of this may be found in the passage of the " Lex Salica "[21] quoted by Wilda and in the " Lex Ribuariorum ", LXXXV.

Apart from those acts which were especially directed against the king or the community, a crime is not so much a breach of the *general peace* as it is a breach of peace[22] with the *party injured*.[23]

653 *et seq.*; *Von Wächter*, "Beiträge zur deutschen Geschichte", pp. 43 and 249. At a later period; indeed, the injured party was obliged to be content with a "compositio." However I do not agree with Von Amira in his view that this was the most primitive law. Rather does this exhibit a very early trace of the Germanic character which still appears in our modern duels, and which prefers to take the law in its own hands rather than assign it to a judge. However, Tacitus states that the immediate consequence of a wrong was the "inimicitiæ", which could be appeased by the payment of compensation.

[19] Moreover, vengeance was to be exercised with observance of certain formalities, — was public as it were, so that it could itself be distinguished from crime. Thus, among the Salian Franks the head of a man who had been slain in the exercise of vengeance was placed upon a stake, and a third party was not permitted to remove it: "Lex Sal.", XLI, 8, 2. Vengeance here appeared as a formal institution of law. *Cf. Wiarda*, p. 283. By the setting up of the head, the slayer as it were offered a public justification of his act: *Pardessus*, p. 658.

[20] The "Lex Salica" provided that anyone who should dig up and rob a buried body "wargus sit usque in die illa quam ille cum parentibus ipsius defuncti conveniat et ipsi pro eum rogare debent, ut illi inter homines liceat accedere. Et qui ei antequam parentibus conponat, aut panem dederit aut hospitalitatem dederit, seu parentes seu uxor proxima, DC dinarios qui faciunt solidos XV culpabilis judicetur." However, the offense here referred to has a distinct religious significance and for this reason the method in which it is dealt with may be explained as being exceptional.

[21] LV, 2 ed. *Behrend*.

[22] As stated by *Waitz* (3d ed.), I, p. 436, agreeing with *Walter*, § 705: "It may be said that in respect to the individual (*i.e.* the injured party and his family) the offender was without peace; he had destroyed the existing peace." *Cf.* also *Sickel*, who (correctly in my opinion) concludes, from the isolated lives of the individual families, that the community was not concerned with injuries to individuals.

[23] The acceptance of the view that crime originally among the Germans was a breach of the general peace is nothing other than the acceptance of the view that there was a public criminal law for what we to-day call crimes against individuals (*i.e.* as contrasted with crimes against the State as such). Such is the view of *Waitz*, I, pp. 427 *et seq.*, who here

According to the Germanic conception, the essence of a crime is not the breach of formal law and order, but rather the *violation of a substantive right.*[24] This is an idea which should be constantly held in mind if one would hope to gain a proper conception of the German criminal law and its historical development. In the Germanic conception of law, the so-called "formal crime",[25] *i.e.* a crime that does not violate a concrete right, is regarded as a special exception.[26] In the Norse sources it is most probable that this same condition obtained, *i.e.* the general outlawry resulted only because of regard for the party injured. The crime in itself is not a breach of the peace with the community at large, — although such may easily be its result. The classification of offenses

follows the (unclear in other respects) conception of Wilda. But if, as Waitz maintains, there was such an extensive criminal power as early as the time of Tacitus, how is the fact to be reconciled that in spite of a royal power that was increasing and becoming more vigorous, the public criminal power was less in extent and weaker even under kings such as Charles the Great? How is it to be reconciled with this view that, as even Waitz says (3d ed. p. 439), it was only the complaint of the injured party that brought about a prosecution of the wrongdoer?

[24] Herein I am completely in accord with *Löning*, "Der Vertragsbruch im deutschen Rechte", p. 48, who states that the feud was the *only* legal consequence of a wrong in the earliest Germanic law. The feud was, according to the "Lex Salica", ended by a pledge to render a composition, and the judgment is directed towards the performance of this pledge.

[25] It should be noted in connection herewith that, in the primitive Germanic law, the sacred or religious aspect of law is not very prominent. Crimes against individuals are not regarded as offenses against the Gods. Tacitus was of the opinion that it was only in case of offenses against the army that the priests had a criminal power, and thus explains it: "deum adesse bellantibus credunt." The special punishment of a violation of a place sacred to the Gods among the Frisians ("Lex Fris." Add. 11) can readily be explained by the idea that in this case the deity was wronged just as the individual whose home was wrongfully broken into.

[26] The punishment of unchastity as such, *i.e.* not merely as a wrong or injury to another person, *e.g.* the head of the household, was originally unknown to the Germanic law. The well-known passage of *Tacitus* ("Germania", c. 12) concerning the "corpore infames" probably refers to the punishment of sodomy. But from the general position of the passage, since Tacitus speaks only of the punishment of acts prejudicial to the army, it appears that it refers only to sodomy committed during a military encampment. *Cf.* note 5 *ante.* Also in "Cap. Ansegisi" c. 48 (*Pertz*, "Legg." I, p. 278) mention is made only of penalties enforced by the church for unnatural lewdness. Is it permissible to assume that the early punishment of unnatural lewdness was later discontinued? From the North German sources, it appears that offenses against morality were treated with extraordinary leniency until the 1200 s. Bigamy *e.g.* was punished in Lübeck with quite moderate fines. *Cf. Frendorff*, in the "Hansische Geschichtblättern" (1874), I, pp. 36, 37; *Rive*, "Zeitschrift für Rechtsgeschichte", III, p. 210 *et seq.* Moreover, in the later South German and Swiss sources unnatural lewdness is frequently referred to as "Ketzerei" ("heresy") and "Unchristliches" (*cf. Osenbrüggen*, "Das Alamannische Strafrecht", p. 289), a positive evidence of the origin of the legal rules dealing herewith in the influence of the Church.

as those which are and those which are not breaches of the peace was, in its original sense, based neither upon the elements constituting the offense, nor upon its object, but rather upon its legal consequences.

§ 22. **Special Relations of Peace.** — There were, as appears from the early German sources, certain special relations of peace in connection with certain persons, assemblies, places, times, and things. Thus there were such relations of peace in respect to assemblies of the people, also of the courts ("Dingfrieden"), and of the Church (including also persons attending the popular or court assemblies or the army or the Church). Other examples of a "peace" applied to the home, the mill, the royal palace or generally the place of residence of the king (or duke), or else have to do with the clergy or travelers. Now a breach of such a special relation of peace did not constitute a special kind of crime. It was merely a fact affecting an act of violence which would in any case have been a wrong, and deprived it of the possibility of justification on the ground that it had been done in pursuance of a lawful feud. The language of the ancient sources referring to this is unequivocal. Mention is always made of an act which would, in any case, be an offense; [1] nothing is said relating to an abstract breach of the peace, *e.g.* the peace of the court ("Dingfrieden") or the peace of the home.[2]

"**Breach of the Peace of the Land.**" — It was not until later that a special offense was constituted by the so-called "breach of the peace of the land" ("Landfriedensbruch"). This referred

[1] *Cf. e.g.* "Lex Salica" (ed. *Behrend*), LXIII. § 1: "Si quis hominem ingenuum in *oste occiderit* . . ."; "Lex Sax.", XXI, "Qui in ecclesia hominem occiderit vel aliquid furaverit vel eam effregerit . . ."; XXIII, "Qui homini ad ecclesiam vel de ecclesia die festo pergenti . . . insidias posuerit eumque occiderit"; XXVII: "Qui hominem *propter faidam* in propria domu occiderit capite puniatur." Here the home and the peace of the home does not constitute an exception. It was originally regarded as a violation of the peace of the home only if one entered a house *with violence* with a view of committing an act which was of a criminal nature apart from this special circumstance, *e.g.* to kill, to steal or to commit an act in pursuance of a feud. Entrance *with arms* (with or without the consent of the person dwelling in the house) was deemed the equivalent of entering with violence. *Cf.* "Lex Rib.", 64 (66); "Lex Burgund.", XV; "Lex Bajuv." (Textus I), XI, "De violentia." In "Ed. Rothari", 278 it is even stated: "Mulier curtis rupturam facere non potest, . . . absurdum videtur esse, ut mulier libera aut ancilla quasi *vir* cum armis *vim* facere possit." However, this rule was abolished in the law of the Lombards.

[2] If as *e.g.* in the "Cap. Karoli M." a. 803 (*Pertz*, "Legg", p. 126 it is said: "Ut ecclesia, viduæ, orfani, vel minus potentes pacem rectam habeant. Et ubicumque fuerit infractum sexaginta solidis componatur", yet it is only meant by this that violence under the justification of self-redress is not to be exercised against the parties named.

to private war between members of the higher classes, the tenants "in capite" of the crown, the barons, and the cities; such private wars continued long after the time when other acts of violence done by individuals had lost the justification of self-redress or feud, and also long after the time when a feud could be begun because of a breach of a promise specially given by an individual in respect to some definite point in dispute [3] settled through compromise or agreement.

§ 23. **Composition of Offenses.** — The offenses which in those times were the most important and with which the folk-laws were mostly concerned were homicide, personal injuries, and certain injuries to property. The folk-laws contain provisions fixing in very exact detail the amount of the damages ("compositio"). This latter, in cases of homicide, was called "weregildum", "werigilt" (meaning "man money" or "man price") and also "leudus" or "leudis." The damages were calculated with a regard to the importance of the part of the body injured or lost to the party injured, and also with regard to his rank.[1] In the gradation of the damages, attention was also paid to the violation of honor which accompanied the offense,[2] certain provisions

[3] *Cf. Löning,* "Vertragsbruch", I, p. 133, who correctly is opposed to the position taken by Wilda and also by Köstlin and Geib, who would exalt the pledged peace into being a higher variety of the general peace. It was not until later that a breach of a pledged peace constituted the special offense of "Urfehdebruch" (*i.e.* breach of oath to keep the peace): *Löning,* p. 500. This appears in "Ed. Rothari", 143 as a circumstance specially aggravating an act which would be an offense regardless of this circumstance. Such an act could be regarded as especially disgraceful, and came close to a suggestion of the idea that by its commission its author declared himself no longer governed by any rules of law (*cf.* the formula of outlawry in such cases, given by *Grimm,* p. 39). Legislation had every reason to deal very vigorously with such cases. The discussions of the Post-Glossators concerning the effect of a "pax facta" are in accord herewith. An offense was not regarded as a violation of the "pax" because the offender had previously made an agreement with the injured party, but only if the act was done "animo vindicandi" with a view to reviving the controversy which had been put aside. *Cf. e.g. Bartolus,* on "L. Verum est" n. 3–5 D. "De furtis"; the same on § Causa D. "De pœnis."

[1] Higher penalties were required for the injury or killing of an "ingenuus" than for the injury or killing of a serf ("litus") or "slave" ("servus"). According to the law of many of the peoples, a higher value was placed upon a noble (*cf. Grimm,* "Deutsche Rechtsalterthümer", pp. 272 *et seq.*); also upon one who was an associate of the king ("in truste dominica esse"). According to some laws, a higher "wergeld" was paid for women (if they were capable of bearing children), but according to others and more generally a lesser "wergeld." Lesser amounts were exacted for injuries done by a person who was unfree. (Regard was given however to the master who was liable for the acts of his "servus" if he did not deliver him for vengeance or later for the infliction of public punishment.) *Grimm,* p. 658.

[2] Thus according to the "Lex Sal.", XVII, 8, a larger satisfaction was

punish injuries to honor that were merely verbal.[3] As to violations of property, special consideration is given to the killing or injury of domestic animals, the destruction of houses by burning or in some other manner, mischief done to the fields, and theft.

§ 24. **Little Consideration Given to the Element of Intention.** — The primitive Germanic law has often been criticized on the ground that it paid attention only to the external injury and took no notice of the accompanying intention. It is a fact that it made no difference in the "compositio", as a rule, whether the injury was intentional or unintentional, whether it was done with or without premeditation. The lord, for example, who instigated his serf ("litus") to kill another,[1] acting intentionally and deliberately, paid no more as a "compositio" than he who caused the death of another by a degree of negligence so slight that perhaps it was scarcely distinguishable from mere chance.[2] Provisions punishing attempts at a crime[3] are very few; and the treatment of accessories to a crime[4] does not accord with the fundamental principles of a system of criminal law administered for public purposes.[5]

required for a blow with the fist than for a blow with a club. For injuries to the person, *e.g.* the cutting of the hair or beard against one's will, *cf.* "Lex Alam. Hloth." LX, n. 23, 24. As to pulling the beard, see the statutes of Æthelbirht Kap. I, n. 23 ("feaxfang"), *Schmid*, "Ges. d. Angelsachsen" (2d ed.), pp. 6 & 7; "Ed. Roth.", 383. As to closing of a road, "Lex Sal.", XXXI ("De via lacina"). As to the improper or lewd grasping of a woman (even the simple touching of an arm or finger), there was imposed by the "Lex Sal.", XX, a penalty of 15 "solidi." Rape is mentioned often and as one of the graver crimes (*cf.* "Lex Sal.", XXV, 1, "Ed. Roth.", 186).

[3] *Cf.* "Lex Sal.", XXX; reproach of cowardice: "Si quis alterum leborem (leporem) si clamaverit." "Lex Sal.", XXX, 5: "Si quis alium arga per furorem clamaverit." ("Ed. Roth.", 381.) It was considered even more serious if one accused another of having cast away his shield in battle: *Grimm*, p. 644 *et seq.*

[1] *Cf.* "Lex Sal." VIII ("Lex Fris.", I, 14).

[2] "Lex Sax.", LIII: "Si arbor ab alio præcisa casu quemlibet oppresserit, conponatur multa pleno weregildo a quo arbor præcisa est." *Ib.*, LIX: "Si ferrum manu elapsum hominem percusserit, ab eo cujus manum fugerit, conponatur excepta faida."

[3] *Cf. post*, § 36, the theory of attempt.

[4] Thus, as a rule, instigation was not treated as participation in crime: "Lex Fris.", II, 2, "Ed. Rothari" 10, 11. However the "Lex Visig." (*cf. e.g.* VI, 5, 12) often punished the instigator the same as the actual perpetrator, and caused public punishment to be inflicted upon all the perpetrators of a homicide where there were more than one.

[5] The "Lex Fris." (II, 2) is also interesting as to this matter. If one free man had instigated a second free man to kill a third, and he who did the killing had not escaped, but the relatives of the slain were able to make a demand upon him, then the law did not concern itself with the instigation but regarded merely the manifest act of the actual perpetrator. But the instigator must see to it how he may appease the rela-

Explanation of Lack of Consideration of Element of Intention. — This paramount consideration paid to the objective side of crime should not, however, be taken merely as an evidence of the barbarity of the Germanic tribes, nor should it be absolutely assumed that the Germans had no conception of guilt in its ethical aspect. In the first place, custom here to a certain extent represented the law. In the second place, a regard for the mental attitude and intention of the offender does appear from the character of those crimes which were regarded as especially serious. When legal development is in its infancy, the need for fixed rules, easy to handle, is greater than the need for a complete substantive justice which leaves more room for the exercise of discretion (and also at the same time more room for arbitrary action). Attempting to deal with individual cases at too early a stage of legal development is dangerous to freedom; for it would require a very extensive judicial power. Thus, under some circumstances, it is appropriate for the law, at a time when its administration of justice is as yet incomplete, to treat with equal leniency cases of either intentional or negligent injury, and also for it to presume [6] that an injury is due to negligence where we, upon a more exact examination, would consider it as merely a result of chance. Furthermore, it must be remembered that, where legal protection is inadequate, it is easily possible that there obtains for intentional injury the justification of self-redress and feud, or at least that such a justification exists in the minds of those who do the injury. There is no doubt that the customs made an early distinction between intentional and unintentional injuries. While the injured party, in case of grave injuries, and especially in case of the killing of a relative, could originally choose between resorting to

tives of the slain, — "nihil solvat, sed inimicitias propinquorum hominis occisi patiatur, donec quo modo potuerit eorum amicitiam adipiscatur." The "Lex Sax." (XVIII) in the case of intentional homicide (by instigation of a "servus") gave the relatives the choice between "compositio" and "faida" (feud). If the homicide merely resulted from negligence, a "compositio" was to be paid and accepted, "excepta faida." *Cf.* also "Ed. Roth." 75, 138 (147) showing a greater progress in legal development; "cessante faida, quia nolendo fecit."

[6] I have endeavored to give a more exact statement of these ideas in my work, "Das Beweisurtheil des germanischen Processes" (Hannover, 1866) especially pp. 41 *et seq.* *Cf.* also *Dahn* ("Westgothische Studien", 1874, p. 273), who says it is the characteristic of the German law of proof that it "primarily is founded upon presumptions."

[On this subject, see the citations at the beginning of this chapter, which point out that the Germanic failure to distinguish radically between intentional and unintentional harms is a characteristic of all primitive legal systems. — ED.]

feud or demanding a "compositio",[7] yet, where the act was unintentional,[8] he should at least be satisfied with the "compositio."[9] First by custom, and later by law he was bound so to do, since a feud was permissible only in cases of a public and intentional injury.[10]

Secrecy. — The element of *secrecy*[11] obtained an early prominence in the conception of crimes. By secrecy the offender fixed upon his act the character of unlawfulness, not capable of justification. Thus the satisfaction required for murder ("Mord"), *i.e.* a slaying followed by a concealment of the corpse,[12] was especially severe. Moreover, the conception of theft, at the time of the early law-books, and even later, involved the idea of a secret carrying away.[13] It was not the idea of the cowardice of

[7] As *Dahn* ("Fehdegang und Rechtsgang", pp. 34 *et seq.*) correctly shows, in the earliest period, the offender also could allow a feud to ensue and the penal provisions in the time of the Merovingians practically signified nothing further than that, if both parties chose the method of court procedure, the court would award to the party injured the amount therein specified. But the knowledge of what in a certain event one might pay and the other might receive made easier the way for an amicable compromise. The narrative of Gregory of Tours (*ante*) shows that often only the Church by special sacrifices was able to make a settlement possible.

[8] The provision that those of tender years were not obliged to pay "Friedensgeld" (*i.e.* peace money; *cf.* "Lex Sal.", XXIV, 5, "Si vero puer infra XII annos aliqua culpa committat, fretus ei nullatenus requiratur") shows that, just as in the Norse law, those of tender years were not subjected to outlawry: *Wilda*, pp. 640 *et seq.*

[9] The division of offenses into those which entail a breach of the peace and those lesser offenses which do not, although this can also be found in the Scandinavian sources (*cf. Wilda*, pp. 268 *et seq.*), belongs, however, to a later stage of development, which placed greater limits upon the province of breaches of the peace, *i.e.* cases which entailed vengeance and outlawry.

[10] *Cf. e.g.* "Lex Sax.", LIX. No "faida" (feud) could ensue "si ferrum manu elapsum hominem percusserit."

[11] *Cf.* also *Osenbrüggen*, "Der ethische Factor im altdeutschen Rechte" in his "Studien zur deutschen und schweizerischen Rechtsgeschichte" (1868), pp. 1–18.

[12] *Cf. e.g.* "Lex Rib.", XV. "De homine mordrido. Si quis ingenuus Ribuarium interfecerit et eum cum ramo cooperuerit vel in puteo seu in quocumque libet loco celare voluerit quod dicitur mordridus, sexcentis solidis culpabilis judicetur" (*i.e.* threefold "Wergeld"). "Ed. Roth." 14: "Si quis homicidium in absconso penetraverit . . . noningentos solidos conponat . . . ." According to "Lex Sax.", XVIII (ed. *Merkel*), a ninefold "wergeld" was paid.

[13] "Lex Sal.", XXXIII, 1: "Si quis de diversis venationibus furtum fecerit el *celaverit* . . . ." "Lex Bajuv." (Textus I), IX, 9: "Si quis *occulte* in nocte vel die alienum cavallum aut bovem aut aliquod animal *occiderit* et negaverit et postea exinde probatus fuerit tanquam furtivum conponat." *Cf.* also *post*, § 35, under the theory of theft. Among the Lombards and Alamanni the penalty for theft was ninefold ("Ed. Roth.", 253 *et seq.*). Furthermore, at an early date the death penalty for many cases of theft is to be found in some folk-laws ("Lex Sax.", XXVIII–XXX, XXXII,

a secret act that induced this distinction. That would be assuming an artificial moral conception, and is not in accord with the ideals of a system of law which was contending, first and foremost, with violence. This distinction was rather due to the fact that where the killing of a man or the taking away of a thing was public, the excuse was possible, in times when violent revenge and self-redress were prevalent, that the act was done in pursuance of a real or believed right; whereas a secret act would in general not admit of this justification.

§ 25. **Influence of the Early Kings.** — A strong kingly power, such as we find under the early Merovingians, which under the influence of Christian ideals [1] regards itself as the supreme guardian of justice, necessarily feels that offenses, even if primarily directed against individuals and not against the king or the community, are nevertheless violations of its own authority.[2] As early as the Merovingians we find the enactment of the death penalty for robbery [3] and for theft,[4] and the prohibition of private settlement in cases of theft.[5] We find also that the death penalty was prescribed for certain cases of incestuous marriage,[6] and that perjury was punished by the cutting off of a hand (the offender, however, being able to save his hand by a payment of money).[7] These public punishments seem however to have not long continued in use; although the kings,[8] especially the early Merovingians, often

et seq.). There is also the provision that the thief should pay his "wergeld" as a "fredus" ("Lex Fris." III, 1, 4). This also explains the unlimited right of vengeance in such cases, according to some passages. This right was supplanted by public punishment (see *post*).

[1] "Regum officium est proprium facere judicium et justitiam" says *Hieronymus* c. 23 C. XXIII. qu. 5. *Cyprianus* in c. 40 of the same: "Rex debet furta cohibere, adulteria punire, impios de terra perdere, parricidas et pejerantes vivere non sinere." *Cf.* also *Jarcke*, "Handbuch", I, pp. 21, 22 note. *Waitz*, II (2d ed.) pp. 155 *et seq.*, IV, p. 447. "Cap. Aquisgran." c. 32, 33 (*Pertz*, "Legg.", I, p. 95).

[2] The indefinite conception of "fidelitas", fidelity to the ruler and also to the law enacted and administered by him (to which conception it often appeared that no limits were set), undoubtedly furthered the development of the public law. *Cf. Waitz*, III, p. 296.

[3] *Cf.* "Childeberti const." A.D. (ca.) 554 (*Pertz*, "Legg.", I, p. 1).

[4] "Childeberti II et Chlotarii II Pactum" A.D. 593 n. 1 (*Pertz*, "Legg.", I, p. 3).

[5] *Cf.* the "Pactum" (n. 3) cited in the preceding note. "Qui furtum vult celare et sine judice compositionem acceperit, latroni similis est."

[6] "Childeberti II decr.", a. 596. n. 7.

[7] "Childeberti II decr.", a. 596. n. 2 and 5. This latter provision points to a theological origin.

[8] In the law of the Lombards there was, in certain cases, allowed to her relatives a right to punish a woman criminally; but the criminal law of the king had a subsidiary jurisdiction. *Cf.* "Ed. Roth." c. 221, also *Pasquale del Giudice*, p. 23.

acted quite arbitrarily [9] in the enactment and infliction of punishments, and especially under the Carolingians certain humiliating penalties known as "harmiscara" were inflicted, along with the royal ban.

Capitularies of the Carolingians. — In the Capitularies of the Carolingians, just as in the so-called "folk-laws", [10] intentional homicide was again as a rule punished by the exaction of a "compositio." [11] Most of all, the royal power was interested in the suppression of feuds,[12] and was well satisfied if the party injured would be content with merely a "compositio." It made use of outlawry to compel the parties to make an amicable settlement. We find that public punishment was inflicted only for robbery,[13] a crime dangerous to the community at large, for counterfeiting, false witness [14] (falsification of documents), and perjury.[15] But even in these cases, the penalty of cutting off the hand (the member with which the crime had been committed) could be avoided by a payment of money.[16]

[9] *Waitz*, II, pp. 151 *et seq.* As to "harmiscara", *cf.* the same, IV, p. 445.

[10] With the exception of the "Lex Visigothorum", in which there was a significant union of the principles of the Roman and Germanic law.

[11] In exceptional cases, the death penalty. "Cap. Aquisgran.", a. 817, c. 1 (*Pertz*, "Legg." I, p. 210): "Si quis aut ex levi causa aut sine causa hominem in *ecclesia* interfecerit, de vita conponat." (*Cf. Waitz*, IV, p. 231.) Furthermore, in other especially grave cases recourse might be had to the Constitution of Childebert, which had not been formally repealed. Thus it is stated in Cap. A.D. 779 ("Francicum") c. 8: "Ut homicidas aut ceteros reos, qui legibus mori debent, si ad ecclesiam confugeruit, non excusentur." *Cf.* also c. 8 of "Cap. Langob." Punishment of murder of *relatives* in Cap. a. 803 in "Lex Sal.", n. 5 (*Pertz*, "Leges", I, p. 113): "Si quis de libertate sua fuerit interpellatus, et timens ne in servitutem cadat aliquem de propinquis suis, per quem se in servitium casurum timens occiderit, id est patrem, matrem, patruelem, avunculum vel quemlibet hujusmodi propinquitatis personam, ipse qui hoc perpetraverit, *moriatur* . . . ."

[12] Thus King Rothari ("Ed. Roth." 74) stated that he had raised the amounts of the compositions for the purpose of thereby restraining feuds. *Cf.* also the memorial of the bishops to the king in the year 829 (*Pertz*, "Leges", I, p. 340).

[13] "Cap.", a. 779 ("Francicum") c. 23; "Cap. Tic.", a. 801 n. 4 (*Pertz*, "Leges", I, p. 84); According to the earlier Capitulary (c. 10) the death penalty was provided for theft in a church by means of burglary. As to the execution of the death penalty, *cf.* "Cap. Tic.", a. 801 c. 4 (*Pertz*, p. 84); "Cap. Aquisgran.", 813 c. 11: "Judices atque vicarii patibulos habeant."

[14] "Cap. Hlotharii", I, a. 832, c. 10 (*Pertz*, p. 361): "manus ei amputetur."

[15] The writer of false documents originally lost his thumb; later, his right hand.

[16] As to the ransom of the hand, see *Waitz*, IV, pp. 435, 436. Perjury was very prevalent under the later Carolingians.

The Royal Ban. — Criminal law received an addition that was very important, displaying more of the characteristics of a public punishment, in the royal ban, "bannus regius."[17] Since crimes against the person of the king were regarded as crimes against the community itself, and were already being punished according to the Roman law of "lèse majesté",[18] the disobedience of a royal command also had the appearance of a direct offense or injury to the king. The guilty party was obliged to pay the king the sum of sixty "solidi." His failure to make this payment constituted a separate offense, entailing severer penalties.[19] The penalty of the ban covered essentially those offenses which we to-day would consider within the domain of the police jurisdiction, the martial law, and the laws pertaining to the State treasury. However, its application was not limited to those matters. It also served the purpose of suppressing violent feuds; in many cases it imposed a public punishment[20] in addition to the "compositio"; in contrast to the feud, it extended a legal protection to persons and things which previously had enjoyed no such protection but nevertheless seemed to require it.[21]

§ 26. **Other Forms of Criminal Punishment.** — A certain penal power was also possessed by the husband over his wife,[1] and by the head of the household over the children under his control (*i.e.* in his house). Moreover, the master had, in respect to his slave,[2]

[17] As to the royal ban, *cf.* especially *Waitz*, II (2d ed.), pp. 589 *et seq.*; III, pp. 271 *et seq.*

[18] *Cf. Waitz*, II, pp. 149, 150 and for the later period, VI, p. 472.

[19] For illustration of the acts punishable by the royal ban, *cf. e.g.* Cap. A.D. 811. "de exercitalibus", c. 2–4 (*Pertz*, p. 169, 170).

[20] One may compare the eight early cases where the ban was used, mentioned in "Cap. de dominico" (*Pertz*, pp. 34, 35). In cases two, three, and four, — "Qui injuste agit contra viduas", "De orfanis", "Contra pauperinos qui se ipsos defendere non possunt", feud and self-redress against the persons mentioned was prohibited. (Possibly they apply also against unjust complaints, because of the danger of trial by battle.) In cases five, six, and seven: "Qui raptum facit, hoc est qui feminam ingenuam trahit contra voluntatem parentum suorum", "Qui incendium facit infra patriam, hoc est qui incendit alterius casam aut scuriam", "Qui harizhut facit, id est qui frangit alterius sepem aut portam aut casam cum virtute", acts which had previously been unlawful are subjected to *public* punishment. Case eight: "Qui in hoste non vadit" has reference to the military system. Case one: "Dishonoratio sanctæ ecclesiæ" has to do with the protection of the legal institution of the Church. *Cf.* "Cap. Saxon. Aquisgran." a. 797 pr. (*Pertz*, p. 75); Add. VII. to "Lex Bajuv.", 1 (ed. *Merkel, Pertz*, "Legg.", III, p. 477).

[21] Thus the King took *foreigners* also under his protection. *Cf.* "Epist. Karoli M. ad Offam regem Marciorum" a. 796 (*Walter*, "Corp. J. Germ.", II, p. 125).

[1] *Cf. Tacitus*, "Germania", c. 19.

[2] *Jastrow*, "Zur strafrechtlichen Stellung der Sclaven"; *Georg Meyer* in

a power of criminal punishment [3] which was unlimited [4] and doubtless was often exercised with great severity. The folk-laws, moreover, provided a public punishment for a slave who wronged a third party; this was either absolute, or modified [5] to suit the case where the master would not surrender the slave.[6]

Influence of the Punishment of Slaves. — The fact that punishments of life and limb were often employed against slaves by the injured party or his relatives, although this was gradually prohibited by the royal authority, undoubtedly had great influence upon the conception of the nature of criminal law. This influence became apparent later when, in times of political confusion, the number of persons who were absolutely free was much lessened by the oppression of officials and great magnates. Punishments which were daily inflicted upon slaves would soon come to be regarded as not absolutely improper for free men.[7] This was furthered by the fact that there was little apparent difference between the condition of the oppressed freemen or serfs, and that of the slaves.[8]

Effect of Loss of Freedom by Mass of the People. — The exor-

"Zeitschrift für Rechtsgeschichte, germanistische Abtheilung" (1881), p. 85 *et seq.*

[3] *Cf. Walter*, II, § 388; *Waitz*, I, p. 183; *Tacitus*, "Germania", c. 25: "Verberare servum ac vinculis et opere cœrcere rarum: occidere solent, non disciplina et severitate, sed impetu et ira, nisi quod impune sit." *Pasquale del Giudice*, p. 24, 25, believes that, according to the Lombard law, the master exercised a despotism over his slaves that was subject to no legal restrictions. "An. Liutpr." (*Neigebaur*) 56: "Ipsi vero domini distringant et inquirant servos sicut ipsi amant" ("Cap. Pip" a. 802, c. 16, *Pertz*, "Leges", I, p. 105). The criminal power of the master was originally merely an incident to his right of dealing with his slaves in any way he wished.

[4] *Cf.* concerning the punishments used against those who were not free; whipping, castration, cutting off of the hand, putting out of the eyes, capital punishment, — *G. L. Von Maurer*, "Geschichte der Fronhöfe in Deutschland" (4 vols. 1862, 1863), I, p. 533, 534. In the beginning there was a sharp distinction between those who were not free and the "liti" (*i.e.* serfs), although the latter could also be subjected to punishments of life and limb, while free men were penalized with money (*Maurer*, p. 535). However, a master could in many cases ransom his slave.

[5] "Lex Sal.", 12; "Lex Ribuar.", 58, 17 and 18; "Lex Alam. Hloth.", 38, 2.

[6] The master who would neither assume or excuse the act of his slave surrendered the offender to the mercy of the parties injured, *i.e.* the kinsmen of the slain. "Ed. Roth.", c. 152: "sic tamen ut servus vel ancilla ad occidendum tradatur ut *nulla sit* redemptio aut excusatio mortis servi vel ancillæ." *Cf. Pasquale del Giudice*, p. 29.

[7] Whipping as a punishment of free men of lower rank is often mentioned in the time of the Carolingians (*cf. Waitz*, IV, p. 436); *e.g.* if anyone without sufficient grounds appealed to the judgment of the king (came to the palace of the king). "Pippini cap." 7 (*Pertz*, p. 31) ("Si major persona fuerit, in regis arbitrio erit").

[8] *Cf.* the especially important development in these matters in the Anglo-Saxon law, in *Jastrow*, pp. 43 *et seq.*

bitant amount of the damages was far-reaching in its effect. Thirty, forty or fifty "solidi" were often exacted for injuries, and in cases of homicide these amounts were greatly exceeded. Thus the "wergeld" for killing a free Frank was two hundred "solidi." These sums were equivalent to the value of hundreds of cattle.[9] He who could not pay these amounts was reduced to a condition of bondage for debt,[10] a condition which often resulted in permanent slavery (even if it were not such from the beginning). He also often became a victim of the unrestrained vengeance of the injured family. "Quod si raptor (one who carried away a woman) solutionem . . . unde solvere non habuerit, puellæ parentibus adsignetur, ut faciendi de eo quod ipsi maluerint, habeant potestatem." [11] This vengeance (slaying) had to be exercised publicly in order to be legally justifiable. Among the Franks, for example, the corpse was placed upon a "bargus", a "clida", a structure similar to a gallows.[12] Thus the manner of putting to death did not differ so very much from the later executions by the public authorities. This was especially the case when the executions were arranged and carried out with great display by some individual possessed of great power and prominence. Thus private compensation often passed into public punishment.

Furthermore, in those frequent cases in which unimportant freemen (*e.g.* those who did not possess others as serfs or slaves) were unable to pay the large amounts exacted as damages, some form of public punishment, *e.g.* corporal punishment or even mutilation, would readily seem to be appropriate.[13] This was furthered by the fact that these punishments [14] would appear less severe [15] than being reduced to a condition of bondage for debt.[16]

[9] *Waitz*, II, p. 614. *Cf.* also *Roth*, "Geschichte d. Forst- u. Jagdwesens in Deutschland", 1879, pp. 21 *et seq.*

[10] *Grimm*, pp. 329 *et seq.*

[11] "Lex Burg.", 12, 3.

[12] *Cf. Sohm*, "Process der Lex Salica", pp. 178, 179, and *Pasquale del Giudice*, p. 56. The "Lex Salica" protected the guilty, before the execution took place, by a number of formalities calculated to induce the relatives to accept a payment and to bring about a ransom by any third party who was willing. The famous title of "Lex Sal.", "De chrene cruda" has reference to this.

[13] *Dahn*, "Westgothische Studien", p. 156.

[14] *Waitz*, III, p. 265.

[15] We also find that, in the criminal *procedure*, legal rules which earlier were only applied to the disadvantage of the unfavored classes were later applied to the privileged classes. Thus, according to the earlier Bamberg code, only a non-citizen could be restrained and imprisoned. In the course of the 1400 s this distinction ceased to exist: *Brunnenmeister*, "Die Quellen der Bambergensis" (1879), p. 44.

[16] The criminal law of the West Goths was to a certain extent typical

Under the Carolingians the idea of *public* punishment was clearly apparent only in cases of offenses against the king. In such cases we find capital punishment, mutilation, and confiscation of property. But, as the great mass of the people lost more or less of their freedom and were reduced to a condition of poverty, this idea continued to gain in prominence. Moreover, it found a real ally in a power which knew but one distinction of rank — the Church.

of the criminal law of the later Middle Ages, however with certain despotic additions. Punishments which elsewhere were applied only to slaves, especially flogging, were (although many distinctions of rank were made) also applied largely to free men. The law of the West Goths sought a better conception of the subjective side of crime. But herein it often lapsed into provisions of a false moralizing or theological nature and also an erratic zeal for deterrence and punishment. It combined in a peculiar manner the Roman and German law. *Cf.* also *Dahn*, pp. 141 *et seq.*

TITLE II. THE MIDDLE AGES

CHAPTER III

THE CHRISTIAN CHURCH'S LAW

§ 27. **Excommunication as the Foundation of the Criminal Law of the Church.** — Every association has the natural right to expel those of its members who will not conform to its general rules.[1] If denied this right, it is either forced to endure every

[1] Concerning the matter contained in this chapter the following writers may be consulted: *Eichhorn*, "Grundsätze des Kirchenrechts" (2 vols. 1831) (*cf.* also *Eichhorn*, "Deutsche Staats- und Rechtsgeschichte" (5th ed.), I, §§ 105, 106, 108 *et seq.*); *Du Boys*, "Histoire du droit criminel des peuples anciens" (1845); *Du Boys*, "Histoire du droit criminel des peuples modernes"; *Faustin Hélie*, "Traité de l'instruction criminelle" (I, 1866, 2d ed.); *Dove*, "Untersuchungen über die Sendgerichte", in the "Zeitschrift für deutsches Recht" (Vol. 19, pp. 321 *et seq.*); (*cf.* also *Dove* in the "Zeitschrift für Kirchenrecht," IV, pp. 1 *et seq.*, pp. 157 *et seq.*, V (1865) pp. 1 *et seq.*); *Eck*, "De natura pœnarum secundum jus canonicum" (1860); *Nic. München*, "Das kanonische Gerichtsverfahren und Strafrecht" (2 vols. 1865, 1866); *Waitz*, "Deutsche Verfassungsgeschichte" (2d ed., Vols. III and IV); *Sohm*, in the "Zeitschrift für Kirchensrecht" (1870), pp. 248 *et seq.*; *Richter*, "Lehrbuch des katholischen und evangelischen Kirchenrechts" (7th ed. prepared by *Dove*, 1874); *Edgar Löning*, "Geschichte d. deutschen Kirchenrechts" (Vols. 1 and 2, 1878); *Edw. Katz*, "Ein Grundriss des kanonischen Strafrechts" (1881); *Von Holtzendorff*, in his "Handbuch des deutschen Strafrechts", I, pp. 40–50. [For

variety of disorder, or else it must be given the right of direct coercion, or there must be placed at its disposal, for the compulsory enforcement of its orders, the power of the State.

The Christian Church, in its early periods, was constantly defending itself against the State. It tolerated the State only as a necessary evil. To avoid subjecting itself to further persecution, it forbade its adherents to litigate before the civil authorities.[2] It is self-evident [3] that the only weapon and defense against refractory members possessed by such an organization was expulsion. To this fact there may be attributed the essential characteristics of the criminal law of the Church.[4]

The oldest punishment of the Church is merely excommunication, which when applied to the Clergy necessarily amounted to dismissal; since expulsion from the association carried with it removal from offices held in the association. The association in question was, or appeared to be, of vital importance for the welfare or woe of the individual. Consequently, instead of permitting himself to be expelled from the association, he would prefer to subject himself voluntarily to certain disadvantages and sacrifices, if, in this way, he could undo the effects of his disobedience. Moreover, the association, since its value depended upon its numbers, would avail itself of expulsion — at least final and permanent expulsion — only in extreme cases. Thus the oldest punishments of the Church came to consist of either a complete or a partial exclusion from the Church itself, or, in a milder form, only from the sacrament or from office. There were also other punishments, the so-called penance, the fasts, self-scourging and allowing oneself to be scourged, the wearing of a penitential garment, pilgrimages, etc. Moreover the gifts of money and valuables, which later were given to good works and to the purposes of the Church, were originally voluntary gifts by which the giver

additional and later literature, see: *Aichner*, "Compendium juris ecclesiastici" (Brixen, 1890); *Bouix*, "Tractatus de principiis juris canonici" (Paris, 1882); *Brosy*, "Kirchenrecht" (Berlin, 1890); *Cavagnis*, "Institutiones juris publici ecclesiastici" (Roma, 1912); *Phillips*, "Lehrbuch des Kirchenrechts" (Regensburg, 1872–1889); *Sant*, "Prælectiones juris canonici" (Regensburg, 1886); *Albrecht*, "Verbrechen und Strafen, als Scheidungsgrund nach evangelischen Kirchenrecht" (Berlin, 1903); *L. Kahn*, "Étude sur le délit et la peine en droit canon" (Paris, 1898); *Silbernagl*, "Lehrbuch des katholischen Kirchenrechts" (Berlin, 1913); *Hinschius*, "Kirchenrecht" (1869–1897). (VON THÓT)].

[2] N. T., I. Corinthians, VI, 1 and 2 *et seq.* *Cf. Du Boys*, "Histoire du dr. crim. des peuples anciens", pp. 610 *et seq.*

[3] N. T., Matthew, XVIII, 15–17.

[4] *Cf.* also *Edg. Löning*, I, pp. 252 *et seq.*

forestalled his expulsion from the Church or secured his reïnstatement.

Comprehensive Nature of the Law "of Penance." Other Characteristics. — The duties of the Church theoretically embraced the entire life of the individual. Not only belief but also morals were subject to the authority of the Church; under minute inspection, every act or omission acquired a moral significance. Thus the criminal law of the Church was unlimited in its scope. And so it actually appeared in the penal provisions in use in the Middle Ages.[5] Their rules extended to excesses of every character, to passions such as greed, pride, envy, and even to uncleanliness. It was, however, only a system of moral law, a law aiming to bring about a reconciliation of the guilty with God and the Church, that assumed this wide jurisdiction. *This* law could be applied only in cases of grave and notorious offenses, or by virtue of the voluntary confession of the guilty; which might be procured through the confessional. The characteristics, therefore, of the so-called "law of penance", the churchly penalties which were to ensure the repentance and reformation of the offender were: *first*, a lack of definiteness in the acts which incurred these penalties, and definiteness only in that practically they were limited to the most important and frequent offenses, in any epoch or locality; *secondly*, limitations due to the lack of an effective criminal procedure.[6]

Influence upon the Criminal Law of the State. — This portion of the criminal law of the Church, founded as it was directly upon morality, had only a limited influence upon the law of the State relative to crimes. In the first place, the different penalties applicable to acts also forbidden by the temporal law expressed the views of the Church as to the varying importance of these acts. In the next place, an act for which the Church did not inflict a penalty at all was given the character (in the view of the Church) of not being generally reprehensible. These moral valuations of acts, and especially the latter (by which certain acts were

[5] *Cf. Wasserschleben*, "Die Bussordnungen der abendländischen Kirche nebst rechtsgeschichtlicher Einleitung" (1851); "Pœnitentiale Remense" in *Katz*, pp. 161–202 (from the 700 s).

[6] However, the Church, in the so-called "Sendgerichte" in the Carolingian period, and also later, as a matter of fact exceeded the principle of inflicting penance only for those sins which were either notorious or freely acknowledged. It bound by oath a number of the members of the congregation to lay information of sins or offenses which might be known to them, and it compelled the accused either to free himself upon oath or to undergo penance or punishment; *cf. Dove*, "Untersuchungen", p. 356.

regarded as not deserving punishment), potentially exerted an influence upon the temporal law. But this portion of the criminal law of the Church was naturally widely separated from the temporal law. Penance was inflicted by the Church without regard to whether or not temporal punishments were inflicted upon the offender; the essential purpose of penance was the offender's reformation.

§ 28. **The Disciplinary Law of the Church.** — The requirements of so extensive an organization as the Christian Church could not be met by a criminal law applicable only in cases where there was a voluntary confession of guilt or where the offense chanced to be notorious. The inadequacy of such a law was especially evident in its bearing on the non-performance of their duties by servants of the Church.[1] Thus, in addition to that indefinite system of penance above mentioned, there grew up in the Church a system of criminal law, which was based upon definite ideas of the various offenses, and also reached, by a special criminal procedure, acts that were neither notorious nor voluntarily admitted.

Its Similarity to the Criminal Law of the State. — In these offenses punishment assumed a totally different character. It was not limited in its application to offenders whom it might hope to lead to repentance, conversion, and submission to the Church; it could also operate against others — in extreme cases even by deterrence.[2] Here the criminal law of the Church is

[1] Herein it really acted in coöperation with the exemption of the clergy from the jurisdiction of the courts (see *post*). The disciplinary punishments of the clergy took the place of State punishment, since also in extreme cases the Church would expel the guilty from the clergy (to degrade him), and deliver him to the civic power for punishment. *Cf.* Innocent III in Cap. 17, X "De judiciis", 2, 1: "Præcipiatis exparte nostra Prælatis, ut laicis de clericis conquerentibus plenam faciant justitiam exhiberi . . . ne pro defectu justitiæ clerici trahantur a laicis ad judicium seculare . . ." The civic power had no reason to take offense at the extreme mildness of the punishments of the clergy. *Cf. Eichhorn*, "Grundsätze", I, p. 153. C. 3 X, "De crim. falsi", 5, 20 (by Urban III, 1186) even provided branding in one case as a punishment for the clergy.

[2] *Cf. e.g.* c. 1, X, 5, 26 ". . . ut pœna illius aliis terrorem injiciat, ne de cetero contra Romanam Ecclesiam in talia verba prorumpat." The purpose of deterrence is very apparent in the well-known provision that heretics who again became such, even if they later renounced their error, should irrevocably be turned over to the civic power for punishment, although "si postmodum pœniteant, ut pœnitentiæ signa in eis apparuerint manifesta", the sacrament of the Last Supper was not denied them. The Church however at this time did not require a judgment against heretics. But the judgment of the civic courts against those whom the Church had adjudged as heretics was a mere formality. The Church absolutely demanded and obtained execution or the infliction of a punish-

closely allied to the criminal law laid down by the civic community. The culpable act was judged not only according to its moral significance, but also according to certain external characteristics and effects. Since, in fact, the Church had means at its disposal [3] to carry out its will and commands, it was even able, to a certain extent, to take the place of the then somewhat defective political administration of criminal justice. Since morality was also the ultimate basis of the State's criminal law, the Church could take the standpoint that, if the State was lax in the punishment of certain acts in which the Church was especially interested, although they in no way constituted violations of the commands of the Church, it would itself undertake the punishment of these acts. Moreover, the influence of a powerful religious organization which has a firm hold upon the entire people is such that it can easily cause the civic community to punish acts which it has heretofore left unpunished. The Church then turned over to the civic power many cases formerly punished by itself, since the civic community now punished them adequately.[4]

§ 29. **Growth of Criminal Power of the Church. Privilege of Clergy.** — Though the Church's criminal law thenceforth was still essentially only that of a tribunal dealing with moral conduct,

ment of a permanent nature, without allowing a new examination of the judgment of guilt. *Cf.* c. 2, 4, 18 in VI. "De hæreticis", 5, 2; *Ægidius Bossius*, "Pract crim.", Tit. "De hæreticis", n. 35, and *Du Boys*, "Histoire de dr. cr. des peuples modernes", V, pp. 95, 96. The view that "pœnæ vindicativæ" might be applied and were applied only to the Clergy cannot be accepted (*Katz*, pp. 33 *et seq.*).

[3] As is well known, the chief sanction used by the Church was excommunication. The Church even prohibited business transactions with the excommunicated, although in the beginning this was so only where the punishment was "excommunicatio major." *Cf. Richter* (*Dove*), "Lehrbuch" § 214, note 13. Excommunication carried with it incapacity to bring a suit or to act as a witness, and incapacity to fill the office of judge even of a civic tribunal. Cap. 5 X. 2, 25, — c. 7 X. 2, 1; c. 38 X, 2, 20. According to the ordinance of Emperor Frederick II. (A.D. 1220 c. 7, *Pertz*, "Monum." IV, p. 236), civil attainder attached to those remaining in "greater" excommunication for a year, "non revocanda, nisi prius excommunicatio revocetur." A French judgment of the 1300s ordered that anyone who should see the party who had been excommunicated "crachât contre lui" (*Faustin Helie*, I, N. 199).

[4] This explains the fact that those cases in which mention is made of a "delictum mixti fori" do not form a separate class, and also the fact that sometimes, when the punishments of the Church were rather in the nature of mere penance, and for this reason did not seem to the civic criminal authorities to be sufficient, the latter paid no attention to the punishments which had already been inflicted by the Church; *cf. Richter* (*Dove*), "Lehrbuch", § 222. Moreover (except in case of a "delictum mixtum"), where the punishment seemed to the Church to be insufficient, the Church appealed to the civil authorities for a sharper punishment of the offender; *cf.* c. 8, X, "De foro comp.", 2, 2.

yet the Church in the Middle Ages went far beyond the bounds appropriate for a religious organization. This requires for its explanation a review of its historical relation to the State.

In the Roman Empire, as soon as the predominance of the Christian religion was definitely established, the Church began its efforts to make the clergy independent of the civic authorities by means of jurisdictional exemption. But against the firmly established and fully developed judicial system of the Roman State, it failed to make headway. An enactment [1] of Valens, Gratian, and Valentinian (A.D. 376) expressly specified that every criminal action involving a civil crime should be tried, not by the synod, but by the civic judge. The same rule obtained in the law of Justinian,[2] although certain imperial enactments during the intervening period manifested apparently a greater compliance with the claims of the Church.[3]

Union of the Criminal Laws of the Church and State under the Frankish Kings. — Under the Frankish monarchy, however, the Church obtained a complete jurisdictional exemption for all cases essentially criminal. As early as the 500 s, the chief authorities of the Church [4] were practically exempt from the civil jurisdiction. In cases of high treason, in which the death penalty would ordinarily be inflicted, there were applied to bishops [5] only the Church penalties (deprivation of office, excommunication, banish-

[1] L. 23, "Cod. Theodos.", 16, 2.

[2] Nov. 83 pr., §§ 1 and 2. Where a member of the clergy was pronounced guilty by the judge of a civic tribunal, he was merely deprived of his clerical character by the bishop before the execution of the sentence. A tribunal of the Church took cognizance only of "crimina ecclesiastica." Concerning the bishops, it was merely decreed by Nov. 123 c. 8, that no proceedings should be taken against them by the civil judge except by special order of the Emperor.

[3] *Cf.* L. 12, L. 41, L. 47; C. Theodos. 16, 2. Perhaps (as suggested by *Gothofredus* and *Eck*, p. 5, note 4) these passages merely have reference to insignificant offenses, in which a disciplinary punishment seemed to be sufficient. In L. 23, eod., the jurisdiction of the Church seems to extend only to offenses against discipline.

[4] *Cf. Du Boys*, I, pp. 404 *et seq.* and especially *Sohm* in *Dove's* "Zeitschrift für Kirchenrecht", IX, pp. 248 *et seq.*

[5] However, the royal despotism was at times not hindered in the use of other measures of violence. *Löning*, II, pp. 516 *et seq.*, is of the opinion that the Church did not possess an actual jurisdictional exemption, and that rather it was only a custom (and indeed one not always observed) to bring a complaint and secure a judgment against bishops in the Council before subjecting them to the judgment of the civic courts. But as a matter of fact the judgment of the Council would be really the determining factor. The cases in which the royal authorities made a direct prosecution (*i.e.* without first bringing a complaint before the Council) seem to be invariably cases of "lèse majesté", and in such cases, exceptional measures are often applied.

ment to a cloister). The kings appeared before the councils as accusers of the bishops.[6] Chlothar II, by an enactment [7] of A. D. 614, rendered all the lower clergy exempt from civic punishment.[8] In its place there was applied to clericals the Church's disciplinary powers. Thus in the "Edictum Pistense" (A.D. 864) [9] it is stated: [10] "Et de tali causa unde seculares homines vitam per-

[6] *Cf.* "L. Bajuv.", I, 10: ". . . episcopus si convictus crimine negare non possit, tunc *secundum canones* ei judicetur, si talis culpa sit, ut deponatur aut exilietur . . ."; I, 12: "De ceteris causis, diaconus vel clericus ab episcopis secundum illorum canones judicentur."

[7] *Pertz*, "Leges", I, p. 14.

[8] "Ut nullus judicum de quolibet ordine clericos de civilibus causis præter criminalia, per se distringere aut damnare præsumat, nisi eo convincitur manifestus, excepto presbytero et diacono. Qui vero convicti fuerint de crimine capitali, juxta canones distringantur et cum pontificibus examinentur." *Sohm* explains this provision correctly. All Clergy were punished by the disciplinary criminal law of the Church ("secundum canones" since the *civic* law of the Church was the constitutions of the Roman emperors) by their authorities ("cum pontificibus" = "a pontificibus"). It was only in respect to the lower class of the Clergy (including the "deacon" and those beneath) that the civic judge had the right of first trial ("districtio"). The well-known "Constitution" of Emperor Frederick II. (Auth. "Statuimus" Cod., 1, 3, "De episcopis et clericis") merely enforced anew a right which had long existed previously. The exponents of the Roman-Canon Law often denied (although on the whole without practical results) that the clergy were subjects of the rulers of the country, and denied therefore that they could commit the crime of "lèse majesté" against them. In this light the clergy became in fact a State within the State. *Cf.* (later) *Jul. Clarus*, § "Læsæ majestatis crimen", n. 7.

[9] c. 20 (*Pertz*, p. 497).

[10] The mild punishment of the clergy (*cf.* the so-called "Const. pacis Dei" Heinrich IV, A.D. 1085, *Pertz*, "Leges", II, p. 58: "Unde laici decollentur, inde clerici degradentur; unde laici detruncantur, inde clerici ab officio suspendantur et consensu laicorum crebris ieiuniis et verberibus usque ad satisfactionem affligantur"); the provisions exempting the clergy from the criminal jurisdiction of the civic authorities (in the "Sententia Henrici regis" A.D. 1234, *Pertz*, "Leges", II, p. 302); the fact that the tonsure was often conclusively accepted as proof of being one of the clergy (*cf.* concerning this and concerning the claim of the Church to base its own jurisdiction hereon, c. 12 in Sexto. "De sent. excomm.", 5, 11); and the fact that this jurisdictional exemption was frequently conferred (the bishops gladly conferred it since their power was thereby increased) — all these circumstances were the causes of numerous abuses. Chief among these abuses was the fact that many, in order to render themselves secure from civic punishment on some one occasion, received the tonsure and thereafter led worldly lives. On the other hand, even the Popes were obliged to maintain the civic jurisdiction. *Cf.* c. 27 (Honorius III) X, 5, 33. Also *cf.* "Schwabenspiegel" (L.) 225. *R. von Freising*, "Landrechtsbuch", c. 168: "Pfaffenn dye nicht beschornn sein vnnd nicht pfäfflich gewantt an yn tragenn, vnd fürentt sy messer oder swert oder annder waffenn oder vindet man sy in dem frauenhaus oder in ainem leuthaus, dye sol man richten als ainem andernn layenn. . . ." There is a somewhat different provision in *R. von Freising*, "Stadtrechtsbuch", c.16. Concerning the later custom in Italy, *cf.* especially *Decianus*, "Practica crim.", IV, c. 9 n. 106: "Ut clericus possit a laico detineri et puniri sex requiruntur. Primum quod non incedat in habitu et tónsura. Secundum quod

dunt, inde clerici ecclesiasticum gradum amittunt."[11] Moreover, as is well known, with the Frankish kings began a far-reaching union, or, one may even say, an amalgamation, of the temporal and spiritual powers. As a supplement[12] to the duty of the Church to care for the souls of men, the Church felt constrained, if the State did not perform its duty, to undertake in some matters a kind of temporal justice, *e.g.* illgotten gain must be returned, and compensation made for unlawful injury. Moreover, the kings realized the service rendered to the security of their rule by a religion which preached as its precept[13] obedience to the authorities and especially to the king. They also perceived the extent to which the ready and compact organization of the Clergy, supported by historical tradition and remarkable for its training, could be of service to the State. The great men of the Empire, who, strong in their own considerable resources, could often successfully dispute the jurisdiction of the king, and need not fear revenge or punishment, were thus compellable to submit to a public punishment, often humiliating.[14] And this was generally true, even though the Church was governed by motives of prudence in lending its services. The kings therefore accorded to the criminal power of the Church the most thoroughgoing support of the temporal courts and officers,[15] for the enforcement of every

ingerat se enormibus. Tertium quod frequens fuerit in illis. Quartum quod in eis deprehendatur. Quintum quod fuerit ter monitus. Sextum quod post monitionem fuerit incorrigibiles"! (Here at any rate there is a long tolerance of abuses.) *Cf.* also *Gandinus*, "De malef. Rubr. de pœnis", n. 34.

[11] In England the so-called "benefit of clergy", which in the course of time was also extended to other persons (*e.g.* to those who were able to write), gradually led to a lessening of many of the punishments, until in later times it was abolished as incongruous, and at the same time superfluous because of the more lenient character of modern law. *Cf. Stephen*, "Hist. of the Crim. Law", pp. 4, 532.

[12] Concerning the task of supplying the defects in the civil jurisdiction, assumed by the Church, and its results, *cf.* for later period, especially *Tib. Decianus*, "Practica crim.", IV, c. 10.

[13] *Waitz*, III, p. 271.

[14] Everyone, even the most prominent, were under the jurisdiction of the "Sendgerichte" of the Church. *Dove*, p. 355.

[15] "Cap. Mant." (A.D. 781), c. 6 (*Pertz*, p. 41): "comite vel sculdaz adiutorium præveat." "Cap. Missorum" (A.D. 853), c. 10 (*Pertz*, p. 420): "Ut missi nostri omnibus reipublicæ ministeriis denuntient, ut comites vel reipublicæ ministri . . . quando episcopus eis notum fecerit et quos per excommunicationem episcopus adducere non potuerit, ipsi regia auctoritate et potestate ad pœnitentiam vel rationem atque satisfactionem adducant." In the compact entered into by the sons of Louis the Pious, Lothair, Louis, and Charles (A.D. 851, "Conventus apud Marsnam", II, c. 5, *Pertz*, "Leges", I, p. 408), the Bishops were granted international legal privileges in the enforcement of penance. Thus arose the familiar maxim of the Middle Ages that the spiritual and temporal powers mutually

penance.[16] They even made use of the spiritual authorities for the better and more certain punishment of the persons liable to punishment under the civil laws,[17] and also for the suppression of feuds and blood revenge. On the other hand, the bishops appear as officials of the king; for the king claimed and exercised, in respect to their judgments (at least where the laity were involved) a supreme power of review.[18] Thus by virtue of the coercive coöperation of the civil officials, the Church was able to inflict degrading punishments upon even the most prominent individuals, or, instead or in addition, to compel the payment of considerable sums for pious purposes. Unfree persons it could thus punish, even peremptorily and to the last extremity.[19] Consequently

support each other, that the civil judge can have recourse to the bann of the Church, and "vice versa" the spiritual tribunal, if it fails to accomplish its purpose by excommunication, can resort to civil outlawry, and even that this punishment last mentioned atttaches itself "ipso jure" to excommunication of long standing. *Cf.* "Friederici II. imp. confœderatio cum principibus ecclesiasticis", A.D.1220 (*Pertz*, "Leges", II, p. 236): "Et quia gladius materialis constitutus est in subsidium gladii spiritualis, si excommunicatus in ea ultra sex septimanas perstitisse . . . nobis constiterit, nostra proscriptio subsequatur, non revocanda nisi prius excommunicatio revocetur." The "Sachsenspiegel", III, 63, § 2, however, denies direct effect to the ban of the Church; *cf.* "Schwabenspiegel Vorw." In England there was a special warrant of arrest, the writ "De excommunicato capiendo"; the excommunicated was placed in the county prison until he relieved himself of the excommunication; *cf. Folkard*, "The Law of Libel and Slander" (London, 1876), 4th ed. p. 77.

[16] *Cf.* the questions in *Regino*, "De syn. causis libr.", II, c. 2 (in the early 900 s).

[17] "Cap. Karol. M. Paderb." (A.D. 785) "De partibus Saxoniæ", c. 14 (*Pertz*, "Leges", I, p. 49; *Merkel*, "Lex Saxonum", p. 17): "Si vero pro his mortalibus criminibus latenter commissis aliquis sponte ad sacerdotem confugerit, et confessione data agere pœnitentiam voluerit, testimonio sacerdotis de morte excusetur" (this has to do with high treason and homicide connected with treason). "Cap. Aquisgran." (A.D. 813), c. 1 (*Pertz*, p. 188): "Ut episcopi circumeant parochias sibi commissas et ibi *inquirendi stadium* habeant de incestu, de *parricidiis*, adulteriis, cenodoxiis et alia mala quae contraria sunt Deo . . . Et . . . emendandi curam habeant." Thus in the Middle Ages the gravest crimes were often punished only with the penalties of the Church, pilgrimages, and erection of a cross. As to the criminal justice of the cities, in this regard, during the 1300 s and 1400 s, *cf. Von Maurer*, "Geschichte der Städteverfassung in Deutschland", III, p. 633.

[18] "Karoli II. Ed. Pistense" (A.D. 869), c. 7 (*Pertz*, p. 510): "Ut si episcopi suis laicis injuste fecerint, et ipsi laici se ad nos inde reclamaverint, nostræ regiæ potestati secundum nostrum et suum ministerium ipsi archiepiscopi et episcopi obediant, ut secundum sanctos canones et juxta leges quas ecclesia catholica probat et servat, et secundum capitula avi et patris nostri hoc emendare curent." However, complaints of the clergy against their superiors were not entertained by the King; *cf. Du Boys*, I, pp. 418 *et seq.*

[19] By the later Canonists, according to c. 10, Caus. 26, qu. 5, imprisonment by the Church in exceptional cases was deemed applicable even against laymen: *Eichhorn*, II, p. 80.

the Church exercised a criminal power that was secular as well as spiritual. It is thus easily explicable that the State recognized the jurisdiction of the Church in respect to the so-called "delicta mixta" by omitting to punish these crimes if they had been already punished by the Church.[20] Moreover the laity, at least the lower and poorer classes, often had sufficient reason for gladly subjecting themselves to the milder criminal justice of the Church.[21]

§ 30. **Influence of the Church's Right of Asylum.** — The right of asylum [1] belonging to the Church was yet a third means by which its criminal jurisdiction was indirectly extended. The hard-pressed criminal who was able to reach a church [2] was safe, at least for the time being.[3] It rested with the discretion of the spiritual

[20] *Prevention* of crime appears also to have been undertaken by both civic and spiritual powers; *cf.* c. 2 in Sexto "De exc.", 2, 12. *Katz*, pp. 40 *et seq.* denies the so-called "delicta mixti fori." This intermediate field of jurisdiction was the necessary result of the new life acquired by the State and Church under the Carolingians. c. 8 X, "De foro competente", 2, 2 is also of interest. However, the spiritual judge was able to inflict only the punishments of the Church. But it is not to be inferred from this that the punishments of the Church might not be supplanted by the punishments of the State.

[21] In the statutes of the cities it was sought later to limit the excessive subordination of the citizen to the spiritual jurisdiction. Thus, in the law of the city of Augsburg (A.D. 1276, ed. *Meyer*), Art. 22, it is stated: "Ez sol ein burger antworten in dem capitel umbe vier dinch umbe niht anders . . . ." Any one prosecuting a cause other than one of these four before the spiritual court was obliged to pay to the people a money fine. *Cf.* also "Sächsisches Weichbild", Art. 25.

[1] Concerning the history of the right of asylum, *cf. Richter*, "Kirchenrecht" (*Dove*), § 212. It was completely abolished in Germany during the 1700s, and in Protestant regions at an earlier date. *Decianus*, "Practica crim.", VI, 31, remarks: "Hoc vero cum lacrymis memorandum non silebo, quod apud Germanos Lutherana hæresi infectos nullus habetur locus sacer . . . et ideo nullus in his (templis) tutus est, quum ecclesias, id est templa habeant loco platearum"; *Löning*, I, pp. 317 *et seq.*, II, pp. 536 *et seq.* The right of asylum had its origin under the Christian emperors of Rome, but it was only a sort of foothold for intercession. In the Frankish empire, where criminal prosecution was generally a private proceeding, the right of asylum attained greater importance. As the idea lying at the basis of the right of asylum (which was also important in heathen times and among the Jews) it may be stated that, so far as the right of asylum has encroached upon the public procedure, the state criminal power, when it lacked confidence in itself (occasionally in ancient times the death penalty was inflicted in such a manner that it might be possible for the condemned to be saved by a special intervention of fate or the gods), obtained from the deity a ratification of its punishments, or if the condemned came in touch with the deity the punishment was forthwith mitigated or abandoned (as in Rome when the condemned on his way to the place of execution met a Vestal Virgin).

[2] "Schwabenspiegel", 329 (*Lassberg*), regards as already within the peace of the church those who have grasped the ring on the door of the church, and also attributed the right of asylum to the sacred courtyards of the church.

[3] *Cf.* c. 1, 2, 3, Can. 23, qu. 5, and "Lex Bajuv." 1, 7 (ed. *Merkel* T. 1): "Si quis culpabilis . . . confugium ad ecclesiam fecerit, nullus eum vim

power whether or not to give him up; and he was given up only after a preliminary mediation between the pursuer and the criminal. The latter, if the spiritual authorities deemed him guilty, was obliged to bind himself, in consideration of the former's foregoing all claim for slaying or mutilation,[4] to furnish satisfaction and damages.[5] "Ecclesia abhorret a sanguine." Thus the Church, in a certain sense, performed the function of an arbitrator between private revenge or the public criminal authority, on one hand, and the criminal on the other. A substantial restriction was hereby placed upon private vengeance, and the State's criminal power was rendered more lenient. The latter, to be sure, was thus often weakened and hindered, to the sacrifice of the public safety.[6]

Acquisition by Church of Temporal Jurisdiction. — Yet another indirect influence of the Church upon criminal law deserves consideration. In the Middle Ages, the Church came into possession of a great number of the civic tribunals. Thus it was enabled to administer justice (*i.e.* civic justice) through the civic officials and in accordance with the civil methods. It was only natural that civic officials in the employment of the Church should yield to the principles of the Church and its criminal law.[7] Moreover,

abstrahere ausus sit, postquam januam ecclesiæ intraverit, donec interpellat presbyterium ecclesiae vel episcopum. Si presbyter repræsentare ausus fuerit et si talis culpa est, ut dignus sit disciplina cum consilio sacerdotis hoc faciat, quare ad ecclesiam confugium fecit. Nulla sit culpa tam gravis ut vita non concedatur propter timorem Dei et reverentiam sanctorum, quia Dominus dixit: Qui dimiserit, dimittetur ei; qui non dimiserit nec ei demittetur." *Cf.* concerning the later treatment of the right of asylum, the (exceedingly canonistic) description of *Tiberius Decianus*, "Practica cr.", VI, c. 25 *et seq.*

[4] The right of asylum of the Church contributed much towards the substitution of composition for private vengeance. The kings, looking at the matter from their own point of view, had sufficient reason to sanction this right of asylum and to extend to it their protection: *Pardessus*, "Loi Salique", p. 656.

[5] The ban of the Church was the penalty attached to a violation of the right of asylum. However, in those times of violence there were frequent violations of the right of asylum, as also of the oath whereby the pursuer bound himself to be satisfied with the penalties levied by the Church.

[6] Abuses of the right of asylum in the case of grave crimes must have soon arisen. *Cf.* Cap. A.D. 779 (Francicum), c. 8 (*Pertz*, "Leges", I, p. 36). Necessities of life were not to be furnished the criminal ("homicidas aut ceteros qui legibus mori debent" runs the passage), and he could also be compelled by hunger to leave the place of refuge. *Cf.* also "Lex Sax.", XXVIII (ed. *Merkel*): "Capitis damnatus nusquam habeat pacem. Si in ecclesiam confugerit, reddatur." Concerning such exceptions (murder and dishonorable offenses) in other free States at a later period, see *von Maurer*, "Geschichte der Fronhöfe in Deutschland", IV, p. 250.

[7] For example, fundamental rules and customs of which the Church distinctly disapproved could hardly maintain themselves in such courts. For a case of this kind, *cf.* c. 2 X. "De delictis puerorum", 5, 23; an abbot acting as judge of a court inflicted a money fine upon a boy not

the Church must have been at this period extremely popular, as several circumstances allow us to infer. In a time when the criminal law of the State was weak and uncertain, the Church had at its disposal its own system of law, both comprehensive and powerful because of the learning bestowed upon its preparation. The Church was in exclusive possession of a higher state of culture. Furthermore it passed judgment (at least as a general rule) with no discrimination of person, and from the beginning regarded as its own the cause of the helpless and poor. Finally, in short, its justice was contrasted with that of the civic authorities, often exercised in the interest of petty fiscal exactions and marked by frequent oppression of the poor and humble.

§ 31. **Variation in Extent of the Church's Jurisdiction at Different Periods.** — These circumstances readily explain the variation in the jurisdiction of the Church at different periods. To punish crime was a concern of the Church; since all true crimes are also violations of morality and imperil the soul of the criminal, it was not difficult to discover that the Church also was concerned in punishing many crimes which were already punished by the State, and to lay a basis for using the criminal power of the Church. Thus there were included, under "delicta mixta" or "mixti fori", offenses against morality in the narrower sense, especially adultery, sacrilege, sorcery, and usury, in so far as Christians were guilty of the same. Blasphemy, forgery of papal documents, perjury, and breach of contract were also included.[1] This also readily explains the frequent controversies with the civic authorities,[2] the disputes among the learned jurists, and their subtle distinctions.[3]

considered old enough to be responsible, "secundum consuetudinem illius terræ"; the Pope forbade the enforcement "pro temporali pœna." *Aug. Aretinus*, "De malef. Rubr. Comparuerunt dicti inquisiti", n. 14, notes the different treatment of the testimony of women in "terris ecclesiæ subjectis" and in "terris imperii." At any rate, in "terris imperii" the "jus canonicum" did not "de jure" have precedence of the "jus civile." *Cf.* "Bajardi Addit. in Jul. Clarum" § "Raptus", n. 38.

[1] "Ratione pacti et voti fracti, item ratione juramenti vel fidei dationis" say the statutes of the Würzburg Synod 1407, 1446 A.D., has the Church her jurisdiction. *Cf.* the interesting references in *Sickel*, "Die Bestrafung des Vertragsbruches u. analoger Rechtsverletzen in Deutschland." (Halle, 1876), pp. 46 *et seq.*, especially 49–51.

[2] In some territories (those of princes who were clericals) the Church also had before its tribunals complaints and accusations of the Clergy against laymen: "Privileg. Carl IV für Würzburg", "Monum. Boica", XLI, pp. 307, 308. This reads: "Super publicis ac privatis injuriis" the Clergy and the judges of the tribunals of the Church may bring charges against laymen "coram judice ecclesiastico", "quemadmodum etiam in plerisque partibus Germaniæ ac præcipue in provincia Moguntina."

[3] *Cf. Tib. Decianus*, "Tract. crim.", IV, 27, 6.

"Pœnæ Medicinales" and "Pœnæ Vindicativæ." — The fundamental ideal of the punishment of the Church was the restoration of the guilty to the Church and to obedience to God. Hence the punishments of the Church were chiefly "pœnæ medicinales", — punishments calculated to cure the guilty of his faults. For this purpose, use was especially made of excommunication in both of its grades[4] ("excommunicatio major" and "minor"), the interdict,[5] and, in the case of priests, suspension. But the Church was not barred from using other punishments, and its doctrine mentions also "pœnæ vindicativæ" inflicted by the Church.

This distinction, however, had little real influence upon the actual operation of the criminal law of the Church. Those penalties which were designated as "medicinales" were also used by the Church as "pœnæ vindicativæ."[6] Moreover, the effect of many of the "pœnæ medicinales" was exactly the same as that of punishment inflicted by the civic authorities. This appears from the fact that, in the earlier periods, public penance of a humiliating nature, and later, severe fines and imprisonment, were inflicted. The penalty of imprisonment for life, though theoretically (as maintained by the Church) justified by the enormity of the offense, was a matter of fact substantially equivalent to the extermination of the offender.

Defects of Criminal Law of the Church. — Thus, one defect of the system lay in the uncertainty of its scope, due to the fact that the Church did not confine itself to the disciplinary offenses of the clergy nor to voluntary penances or ultimate expulsion. But this was not the only defect in the character of the Church's criminal law. Inevitably there was also a fluctuation between the punishment of external misdeeds and that of mere immorality or the mere possession of an opinion not in accord with the views

[4] Cap. 20, X. "De V.", p. 5, 40 (Innocent III).

[5] The interdict was nothing other than a modified application of excommunication to all places and regions.

[6] *Eck*, "De natura pœnarum secundum jus canonicum" (1860), p. 30. Theoretically these two varieties of punishment are very different. The "pœna medicinæ" has regard only for the intention which is deemed equivalent to the manifested act ("in maleficiis voluntas pro opere reputatur" is written before C. 25, D. I. "De pœnitentia", and in C. 29, *id.*, it says: "Si propterea non facis furtum quia times, ne videaris, intus fecisti . . . furti teneris, et (si) nihil tulisti"), and repentenace may at least remove a portion of the culpability. The "pœnæ vindicativæ" have as their purpose the separation of the guilty, as a corrupt part of the body, from the Church, c. 18, C. XXIV, qu. 3, or else have the purpose of deterring others, c. 1, X, 5, 26.

of the Church; and also a fluctuation between a concern for real penitence and a satisfaction with its external manifestations. The danger to its criminal law from this source is apparent in its older penal provisions which, in analogy to the early folk-laws, contained an exact calculation of penalties for each individual sin or transgression. And it is even more evident in the later system of indulgences, which permitted forgiveness of sins to be purchased outright by the payment of money.

Thus the history of the criminal law of the Church offers an illustration of the truth that only by adherence to an objective or outward standard can a steady development of criminal law be obtained. By taking the external standard, it is possible to reach gradually a juster valuation of inward or personal guilt. If we are to hope to detect inward guilt by human agencies, we must resort exclusively to external manifestations. Apart from the fact that, under a system of criminal law based on that theory, the inward guilt of malice and passion, of ambition and greed, are sure to receive their just deserts, there is, at any rate, no other means available to attain the end desired. Exclusive regard for the moral element leads endlessly nowhere.

§ 32. **Heresy.** — The crime of heresy was also based upon a theoretical and abstract standard of guilt.

How far the error involved in heresy is to be attributed to personal guilt is a problem which never has been and never will be solved. The Church, however, believed that it could solve this problem. It proclaimed as guilty those who held views contrary to its own and lapsed from the faith, if they could not be convinced of their error.[1] This attitude the Church adopted at a very early period. Even in the days of Rome,[2] it demanded and obtained from the State the most severe and terrible punishments of the State for those guilty of this offense.[3] Once it had thus

[1] *Tib. Decianus*, "Practica crim.", V, 8, n. 2: "Vere dicitur hæreticus qui errat circa fidem Christianum per intellectum et pertinaciter hæret errori per voluntatem."

[2] L. 1, C. J., 1, 5 "De hæreticis": "Hæreticos non solum his privilegiis alienos esse volumus, sed adversis muneribus constringi et subjici" (Constantine, A.D. 326). L. 4, § 1, C. eod. (Theodosius, A.D. 407): "Ac primum quidem volumus esse publicum crimen quia quod in religionem divinam committitur, in omnium fertur injuriam." The confiscation of property ordered by the last mentioned "constitutio" made the punishment of this offense by the secular authorities one to be feared. *Cf.* the later decrees, relating to heresy, of the German emperors. Const. Friederici II, A.D. 1220, § 6 (Statuimus), *Pertz*, "Leges," II, p. 244; Henrici reg. const., A.D. 1232, *Pertz*, p. 287.

[3] The heretic was not formally sentenced to death by the spiritual

induced the State to take such measures, it found later no difficulty, when its interests seemed to demand, in demonstrating its sympathy with harsh penalties in other cases. To this attitude the Church steadfastly adhered. And this was in spite of the fact that (as already remarked) it had in the beginning announced its abhorrence of punishments of life or blood, and that it also later exemplified this principle in the exercise of its right of asylum.

Ideal of Divine Justice and the Mosaic Law. — Naturally, then, the belief arose that, since all these punishments were not opposed by the Church and were indeed favored, their infliction was in furtherance of divine justice. And here, significantly, the Mosaic criminal law, which frequently is based on the "talio", or rule of like for like, began to be regarded under the influence of the Church as a direct divine command. It was looked upon, to be sure, as directed to the secular authorities and not to the Church itself; consequently, justice administered by the secular authorities was relieved of every doubt as to its own infallibility. Thus is explained that fanatical tenacity with which, even after the Reformation, criminal justice allowed itself to revel in blood and

authorities. But the death of one declared guilty of the "phaffen" followed as a matter of course (*cf.* c. 18, in VI. "De hæret.", 5, 2). Theoretically the secular jurists maintained the right of the civic judge to make an investigation of the verdict of the spiritual tribunal (*cf. e.g. Bartolus* in "Leg. Div. Hadrianus", [7] n. 3, D. "De custodia reorum", 48, 3); but as a matter of practice this was not done, or else it was expressly rejected in the statutes (*cf.* "Augsburger Stadtr." 1276, ed. *Meyer* p. 106, Art. 32; "Schwabenspiegel", ed. *Lassberg*, 313, "Bambergensis", 130: "Item wer durch den ördentlichen geystlichen richter für einen Ketzer erkant und dafur dem weltlichen Richter geantwort wurde, der soll mit dem fewer vom leben zum todt gestrafft weden"). *Cf.* also *Osenbrüggen*, "Das Alamannische Strafrecht", p. 375. Also *Clarus*, § fin., qu. 96, n. 7, denies that the civic judge has the right of examination, although the judges had usurped this right in certain cases, so that recently Philip II at the Senate of Milan had made unconditional execution of the sentence a duty. — There was a direct coercion to remain in the Church. If a Jew once converted to Christianity again became a Jew, he was put to death by burning. "Schwabenspiegel" (ed. *Lassberg*), 262. — The extent to which the Church lost all sense of justice towards real or alleged heresy is shown *e.g.* in the collection of extravagant principles of *persecution* (for one should not call them principles of *law*) found in *Tib. Decianus*, V, c. 20 ("Hæresis specialia"). The heretic *e.g.* lost "ipso jure" the ownership of all his property, his descendants to the second degree had no legal rights, he became "infamis." His sons lost their fiefs. Mere "cogitatio" was subject to punishment. There were also rules of procedure that were monstrosities. — Even apart from cases of heresy, the Popes at times favored provisions that were clearly unjust. *Cf. e.g.* c. 4 in VI, "De pœnis", 5, 9, directed against those who injure a cardinal, and (in analogy to the statutes of the Roman despots also) visiting the penalties even upon sons and grandsons. The significant analogy of heresy to "lèse majesté" appears in L. 4, § 4, c. 1, 5 (by Theodosius).

grewsome penalties, with an almost universal approval. Amidst an increasing progress and culture, the law remained, till well into the 1700 s, the bulwark, as it were, of cruelty and barbarity. So, too, the influence of the Church is responsible for that dominant aim (often extravagant) in later practice and legislation to make men moral, resulting in measures of moral police grossly overstepping the appropriate limitations of State interference. The idea of an external power, like the Church, intruding upon the moral life of the individual, observing, protecting, and punishing, had become familiar. What had earlier been done by the Church became later the province of the police power of the city or State.[4] Thus the Church laid the foundations for the later omnipotence of the State.

Ultimate Effect of the Criminal Law of the Church. — A long period was to elapse, and arduous effort was to be expended, before the criminal law freed itself from these untoward effects of the Church's influence. The weakness of the medieval State made their long continuance inevitable. This weakness itself had its origin (paradoxically enough) in the rugged natural strength of the Germanic race and its almost unlimited sense of personal individual liberty. This trait vested the individual with a liberty to barter away his liberty, and gave to the king the freedom to dismember the State, and parcel it out piece by piece. In other words, this weakness was due to the subordination of general public law and order to subjective or personal right.[5] Nevertheless, one permanent service to the Germanic peoples was rendered; for the Church represented and emphatically upheld the idea of an absolute objective law and order superior to all individual rights. In one aspect, this signified the equality of all before the law. In another aspect, it signified a better valuation of the subjective side of crime, of individual guilt, — the idea of reformation, implying that the punishment should benefit the offender.[6] To the Church, in the main, we owe our thanks for these contributions, — elements which, although only secondary, are nevertheless very important.

[4] Thus many acts punished by the Church later became punishable by the police authorities, *e.g.* unchastity.

[5] In the German kingdom, which at times (*e.g.* under Charles the Great) was so powerful, the personal (subjective) element was very prominent (*cf.* *Waitz*, "Verfassungsgeschichte", IV, p. 427.

[6] c. 63, 84, D. 1 "De pœnitentia."

Chapter IV

MEDIEVAL GERMANIC LAW

§ 33. **Result of the Degradation of the Mass of the People.** — Even in that stormy and restless period[1] ushered in with the

[1] In regard to the matter contained in this chapter the following writers may be consulted: *Henke*, "Grundriss einer Geschichte des deutschen peinlichen Rechts" (2 vols. 1809), Vol. I, pp. 109 *et seq.; Jarcke*, "Handbuch des deutschen Strafrechts", Vol. I (1827), pp. 21 *et seq.; Grimm*, "Deutsche Rechtsalterthümer" (2d ed. 1854); *Donandt*, "Geschichte des Bremer Stadtrechts" (2 parts, 1830); *Warnkönig*, "Flandrische Staats- und Rechtsgeschichte"; *Rosshirt*, "Geschichte und System des deutschen Strafrechts" (3 vols. 1838–1839); *Warnkönig* and *L. Stein*, "Französische Staats- und Rechtsgeschichte", Vol. 3, pp. 168 *et seq.*, 272 *et seq.*, 489 *et seq.; Von Wächter*, "Abhandlungen a. d. Strafrecht"; *Walter*, "Deutsche Rechtsgeschichte" (2d ed. 1857), II, §§ 701 *et seq.; Waitz*, "Deutsche Verfassungsgeschichte" (3d ed. 1880), Vols. III–VI; *Hälschner*, "Geschichte des Brandenburgisch-Preussischen Strafrechts" (1855); *Köstlin*, "Geschichte des deutschen Strafrechts im Umriss", pp. 114–207; *Kluckhohn*, "Geschichte des Gottesfriedens" (1857); *John*, "Das Strafrecht in Norddeutschland zur Zeit der Rechtsbücher", I (1858); *Du Boys*, "Histoire du droit criminel des peuples modernes" (4 vols., Paris, 1854 *et seq.*); *Osenbrüggen*, "Das Alamannische Strafrecht"; *Osenbrüggen*, "Das Langobard. Strafrecht"; *Geib*, "Lehrbuch des deutschen Strafrechts", Vol. I (1861), pp. 198–240; *Stobbe*, "Geschichte der deutschen Rechtsquellen" (Part II, 1860, 1864); *Osenbrüggen*, "Studien zur deutschen und schweizerischen Rechtsgeschichte" (1868); *G. L. Von Maurer*, "Geschichte der Fronhöfe in Deutschland" (4 vols., 1862, 1863); *Von Maurer*, "Geschichte der Städteverfassung in Deutschland" (4 vols.,

reign of the last of the Carolingians and often described as the period of " club law ", those foundations of a *public* criminal law which were previously laid in Germany and defended by the power and ability of the earlier Carolingians were not completely destroyed. However, they were buried, as it were, beneath the surface.

It must be here remembered that a large part of the people had been reduced to the position of bondsmen and serfs. This did not, indeed, take place in the manner and sense which one ordinarily ascribes to a change of status.[2] At any rate it must not be assumed that in the subjection of serfs and bondsmen under a feudal lord, criminal law became substantially changed from what it had been under the folk-laws and the royal statutes. These latter had also to do with the crimes of those who were not free. Nothing is more misleading than the conception that either in Germany or France, and especially in the former, the criminal law (except in those primitive times when some of those who were not free were legally treated as chattels) was one in which the rank of the accused made a fundamental difference.[3] The same forms of procedure obtain and substantially the same legal principles, and it is only a non-legal circumstance that a man who is not free and therefore possesses nothing, or at any rate is unable to pay the fine, is peremptorily subjected to a punishment of life or limb, which a free man possessed of property would avoid. Even where later in the records of the village communities we find penal rules of an autonomous nature, the distinction between the free and the unfree is not of especial importance.[4] It

1869–1871); *Von Holtzendorff*, "Handbuch des deutschen Strafrechts", I, pp. 57–65; *Frensdorff*, Introduction to *O. Francke*, "Verfestungsbuch der Stadt Stralsund" (1875); *R. Löning*, "Der Vertragsbruch im deutschen Recht" (1876); *Allfeld*, "Die Entwicklung des Begriffs von Mord bis zur Carolina" (1877); *Von Wächter*, "Beilagen zu Vorlesungen über das deutschen Strafrecht", pp. 84–100; *Frauenstädt*, "Blutrache und Todtschlagsühne im deutschen Mittelalter" (1881). [Later writers are: *Steffenhagen*, "Entwicklung der Landrechtsglosse des Sachenspiegels" (Wien, 1887); *Caspar*, "Darstellung des strafrechtlichen Inhaltes des Schwabenspiegels" (Berlin, 1892).]

[2] Such an over-estimation of the *legal* effect of change of status can be found *e.g.* in *Köstlin*, pp. 156 *et seq.*

[3] *Cf.* also *Du Boys*, II, p. 230. For example, the "Constitutio Friederici I." "Contra incendiarios" applied to persons of every rank (*Pertz*, "Mon. Legg." p. 183). In France, at a later date, a nobleman was compelled to pay a higher money fine than an ordinary citizen ("roturier") for the same act, — "Noblesse oblige."

[4] It is not maintained, however, that the old idea that a free man could lose his life or limb only for crimes directed against the community was without any actual influence. In the laws of those towns whose citizens

is only a non-legal circumstance that, owing to the very dependent position of the serfs, the verdict of the lord or his officials, the "Schöffen" (who, as in the local courts of the counts, were the parties rendering judgment), was often biased by arbitrary motives. And, finally, it is a non-legal circumstance, if one considers it closely, that the lords and princes were at the most obliged only to pay a money fine for a breach of the peace of the land, while for other persons this entailed criminal punishment. Since the lord was possessed of the power of acting as magistrate and was the head of a smaller State within the greater State, *i.e.* the empire, it was not difficult for him to commit any offense he might wish under the guise of a feud or even in the exercise of magisterial power. It is therefore incorrect (as *e.g.* Köstlin has done) to maintain, that in the case of those of high rank, criminal law legally lost its true character and became merely a feudal criminal law. Sentences to death of persons of the rank of count or prince are quite frequent in German history, although in the post-Carolingian period such sentences could be executed with difficulty.

There can however be no question but that harm resulted from the splitting up of the Empire into a countless number of small principalities. In a certain sense, use was still made of the idea of public punishment. The injury or slaying of a person subject to one's own feudal lord could also be conceived as the doing of an injury to the lord, the infliction upon him of a loss, and also as an injury to a higher power. This in part explains those confiscations of property to the lord's advantage which were so frequent during this period and which are also found among the charters of the cities.

§ 34. **Feuds and Self-Redress.** — The most important hindrance to the development as well as to the administration of criminal law lay in the difficulty of distinguishing a crime from a permissible form of self-defense or self-redress. It was an ancient right that, in case the courts refused or were unable to give assistance, a free man might procure redress by the exercise of his own strength.[1] This right now became especially the privilege of all

were vassals of some feudal lord, punishments of life and limb were in wider use than where the population was made up of a group of free men.

[1] Here I agree with the conclusions of *von Wächter* ("Abhandlungen", p. 251). He who raised a feud staked everything on his sword, and if necessary the other party could rely on his own sword. There is nothing to indicate that it was the duty of the individual against whom a feud was raised to offer himself with tied hands as a defenseless victim for vengeance. Such an obligation would be nugatory.

those belonging to the knighthood. In those times when the power of the courts was feeble, it was difficult to enforce an absolute denial of this right. It was natural that under the pretext of self-redress — or self-defense against another's self-redress, since this also was not amenable to punishment [2] — violent crimes were committed. This was furthered by the fact that, among the Germanic peoples, it was a widespread custom to ignore the courts and simply proclaim a feud against the individual against whom one believed he had a complaint. In the exercise of this feud, acts of robbery, waylaying, capture, killing, and the destruction of property by fire seem to have been permissible.

The "Landfrieden." — Those statutes [3] known as "Landfrieden" [4] (regional peace-compacts) were enacted for the empire by the kings and emperors, and for the provinces by the princes with the approbation of the imperial officials and (where appropriate) of the prominent persons of the province. They had for their primary purpose the settlement beyond all doubt of the distinction between crimes and permissible feuds.[5] Certain methods were prescribed for the carrying on of feuds (formal

[2] *Cf. Warnkönig*, III, 1, pp. 160 *et seq.*

[3] Concerning other criminal statutes of the 1000 s and 1100 s, *cf. Stobbe*, I, p. 475. Henry II, in 1019, enacted a statute dealing with "parricidium" and murder. Henry III, in 1054, enacted for Lombardy a statute concerning poisoning. Frederick II and his successor enacted numerous statutes against heresy. Henry VII enacted in Italy a statute concerning "lèse majesté."

[4] The "Landfrieden" contained not only provisions concerning the breach of the peace, but also criminal rules of any nature whatsoever, such as proof (especially by oath), duelling, and police regulations. They covered the entire kingdom, or a great part of it, and applied to *all* inhabitants and *all* classes in so far as the degree and kind was not expressly fixed in accordance with the rank of the offender. The "Landfrieden" of the Empire served as a model for the "Landfrieden" of the provinces, and to a certain extent for the statutes of the cities. The princes might, if they chose, cause the "Landfrieden" to be supplemented (*cf.* "Landfrieden" of 1287, § 44, *Pertz*, "Mon. Legg." II, p. 452). As to the significance of the "Landfrieden", *cf.* notably *Waitz*, VI, pp. 419 *et seq.* As to individual "Landfrieden", *cf. von Schulte*, "Lehrbuch der D. Reichs- u. Rechtsgeschichte", 3d ed., § 73. Also *cf. Gierke*, "Das deutsche Genossenschaftsrecht", I (1868), pp. 501 *et seq.*

[5] The "Landfrieden" should not be confused with the "Gottesfrieden" ("Treuga Dei", Truce of God) introduced by the efforts of the clergy (first in France, but also in Germany). This provided for a cessation of feuds on certain days of the week and certain seasons of the year, and also that certain classes of persons should have a continuous peace (*i.e.* should not be subjected to acts of violence done in pursuance of feuds). *Cf.* the so-called "Constitutio pacis Henrici IV. Imp." A.D. 1085. *Pertz*, "Mon. Legg." II, pp. 55 *et seq.* "Sachsenspiegel", II, 66. The only penalties for breach of the "Gottesfrieden" were those of the Church (excommunication).

preliminary challenge [6]), and it was requisite that one should first have unavailingly prosecuted his complaint before a judge. In addition to this, a certain immunity from breach of the peace was declared to protect certain persons and places,[7] *e.g.* the clergy, travellers, merchants, country folk in the fields, the churches, the highways, and the inhabitants of a village when within its walls.[8] Obviously, this was in essence only a new assertion and extension of the old law. The fact that these "Landfrieden" were decreed and confirmed by oath for only certain fixed periods is to be explained by the idea that, for this fixed period, there was established, as it were, a presumption of an established law and order, so that anyone who fictitiously alleged a legally justifiable feud was obliged to bring formal proof of the existence of those conditions without which the act of violence was regarded as a crime.

As a consequence of a crime now being deemed a violation of the "Landfrieden", there also arose the conception that a crime was essentially a breach of the peace, and hence in the first instance was to be regarded not as the violation of an individual right, but rather as a rebellion against the general law and order. Thus also there arose that special conception of a breach of the "Landfrieden" as the unlawful exercise of a feud, which moreover was in itself an offense without the commission of any other crime; for, if anyone with an armed force merely entered the territory of another, the elements essential to the crime existed.[9] Hence also arose that conception of a breach of a "hand peace" ("Handfrieden") or "pledged peace", which later disappeared and is not

[6] "Const. Friederici I. de incendiariis", A.D. 1187 (*Pertz*, "Legg." II, p. 185): "Statuimus etiam ... ut quicumque alii dampnum facere aut ipsum ledere intendat, tribus at minus ante diebus per certum nuntiam suum diffiduciet eum ...." *Cf.* "Const. Henrici regis", A.D. 1234 (*Pertz*, "Legg." II, p. 314).

[7] "Sächs. Landr." II, 66, § 1.

[8] Furthermore, a distinction was made between feuds against persons and feuds against things ("res"). (*Cf.* "Henrici I. treuga" presumably of A.D. 1224, *Pertz*, "Legg." pp. 266 *et seq.*) Violence (for the most part) was to be directed against persons and not against things. Consequently setting anything on fire was (as a rule) unpermissible. *Cf. Kluckhohn*, p. 144.

[9] *Cf.* the general and indefinite provision in the "Landfrieden" of Rudolph I of 1287 (*Pertz*, "Legg." II, p. 449, n. 10): "An sweme der lantfriede gebrochen wirt, beziuget er daz ... daz der einen zu ahte tun der den lantfrieden gebrochen hat." Perpetual "Landfrieden" of 1495, § 1 ("Neue Samml. der Reichabschiede" II, p. 4): "Also dass von Zeyt dieser Verkündung niemand ... den andern bevehden ... überziehen ... noch auch eynich Schloss, Stett, Märckt, Bevestigung, Dörffer, Höff oder Weyler *absteygen*, oder on des andern Willen mit gewaltiger That freventlich einnemen . . . sölle."

mentioned in the Bambergensis or Carolina. This however did not constitute a special crime, but rather affected the character of a crime that had been committed, or established beyond dispute a breach of a "Landfrieden." If, for example, a special peace was pledged between two contending parties — and this often came about as a result of the mediation or compulsory intervention of the authorities — an offense committed in violation of this special duty of keeping the peace was liable to special punishment as a breach of a "pledged peace." — In general, the "Landfrieden" also furthered the idea of public punishment, since their observance was bound by oath and therefore acts violating the "Landfrieden" appear as breaches of an oath of fealty. Thus manslaughter in violation of a special "pledged peace" was (by a constitution of Henry II)[10] peremptorily punished as perjury with the loss of a hand.[11]

Among those smaller groups of unfree persons, subject to a lord and not belonging to the knighthood, or united in a city, the reasons for peace in the sense that one could not by violence procure redress against his fellows, were self-evident.[12] The small group, standing apart from those outside, could permit no private war

[10] A.D. 1019, c. 3 (*Pertz*, "Mon. Legg." II), p. 38.

[11] "Henrici regis Constitutio generalis" A.D. 1234 (*Pertz*, "Legg." II, p. 301): "Si quis treugas datas violaverit; si cum ipso in cujus manum treuge fuerant compromisse . . . *violator manum perdat.*" *Cf.* also "Mainzer Landfrieden" A.D. 1235, c. 3 (*Pertz*, "Legg." II, p. 314). "Rudolfi I, Const. pacis gener." A.D. 1281, n. 30 (*Pertz*, II, p. 428), "Hantfrid"; "Swer zwischen zwein veinden einen hantfriede machet." According to the "Sächs. Landr." the breach of a pledged peace cost a man his head. Under Charles the Great, such an offense was punished as perjury. *Cf.* "Cap." A.D. 805 (in villa Theod. promulgatum) c. 5 (*Pertz*, I, p. 133): "manum quam perjuravit perdat." *Löning*, "Vertragsbruch," I, p. 133, correctly shows that the "handfriede" was not (as *e.g. Wilda*, "Das Strafrecht der Germanen," pp. 229 *et seq.*, and *Geib*, "Geschichte das römischen Criminal process" (1842), I, p. 171 infer) a *superior* variety of the ordinary "Frieden", but rather that it signified nothing more than that prior quarrels should be abated. On the other hand, I am unable to agree with *Löning*, pp. 488 *et seq.*, that any act which even if it was not unlawful "per se", yet as soon as it endangered a pledged peace or otherwise appeared prejudicial to the same, was considered as a breach. In my opinion the passages quoted by Löning do not bear him out. In any case, according to the early Germanic view-point, the raising of an ill-founded complaint, if one be convicted of the same, constituted a wrong in itself, and therefore if any one raised a complaint on account of an act which had already been settled by a "pledged peace", he always committed a wrong. Concerning "Handfrieden" in Switzerland, *cf.* especially *Osenbrüggen*, "Studien", pp. 382 *et seq.*, and *Schlierlinger*, "Die Friedenbürgschaft" (1877), especially pp. 11 *et seq.*; *Frauenstädt*, "Blutrache, 39."

[12] *Gaupp*, "Deutsche Stadtrechte des Mittelalters", II, p. 50. *Cf.* also the "Rechtsbrief für Medebach", A.D. 1165, § 5. He who killed another "infra fossam" forfeited his life. He who killed "extra fossam" any one who was under the protection of the lord merely made payment.

within. Thus, for example, in the " Berner Handfeste " of 1218,[13] it is stated: " Qui infra terminos et pacem vobis aliquem occiderit sine omni contradictione decollari debet." Here the punishment appears as based upon a " Dorffrieden " (village-peace) or "Stadtfrieden " (town-peace), and since the entry or residence in the cities rested upon the free will of the citizen, there were in the cities more grounds for giving play to reasons of expediency; and the development of the criminal law in accordance with the ideals of deterrence became very manifest. However, efforts along these same lines are not totally lacking in the " Landfrieden " and the royal ordinances dealing with individual crimes.

§ 35. **Changes in the Theory of Specific Crimes.** — During this period and prior to the reception of the Roman Law the conception of specific crimes [1] underwent several material changes and developments.

Treason, which originally was a crime only against the community or the army to which the offender belonged, came to be applied also to private relations. During the period of which we speak, it is often difficult to mark the distinction between private and public law, and the policy of self-defense, of which the smaller communities were obliged to be constantly thinking, rendered necessary the observance by their members of the strictest fidelity towards their rulers. The violation of this duty of fidelity, even by merely harboring hostile sentiments, came naturally to incur death and other severe penalties.[2] A crime was spoken of as

[13] The extent to which the idea of a *justifiable* feud continued to prevail, even after it had been substantially suppressed by the public law, is shown by the discussion of *Bonifacius de Vitalinis*, "De maleficiis", "Rubr. de incendiariis", n. 2. He discusses carefully and answers affirmatively the question whether if someone has set fire to the house of A "inimicitiarum causa", and from this origin the house of B is also burned, A is bound to render compensation to B? This discussion has a meaning only in the light of the notion that A might have furnished ground for a well-founded "inimicitia." The same notion appears also in the city-statute provisions that if anyone in the city took part in a feud, he must suffer the consequences. Here one may note a remarkable provision in the statutes of the city of Casale in Italy ("Monumenta Patriæ jussu Regis Caroli Alberti ed. Legg. Municipales", col. 1031, 1032): those who had an "inimicitia" with a citizen of Casale could impute it to their own fault if they came into the province of Casale and were injured; he who injured them was not punished; but the citizen of Casale must have caused the "inimicitia" to be entered in a public book designated for that purpose, otherwise the "inimicitia" was not regarded. *Cf.* also the statute of Dinkelsbühl (*Gengler*, "Deutsche Stadtrechte", p. 85); here the fact of the ill-will was reported to the burgomaster.

[1] This is treated in fuller detail in the discussion of the appropriate theories.

[2] "Verrath" (high treason), *i.e.* "Perfidia enormis" ("Recht von Winterthur", § 12, *Gaupp*, I, p. 137).

"traditio" or as having been committed "cum tradicione", if it were done under circumstances which indicated a conscienceless treatment of the party injured, especially where he was slain, or which had placed him helpless and defenseless in the power of the criminal. Thus, for example, the slaying of one while he was asleep, the seduction of a married woman, and adultery were all spoken of as "treason."

The earlier distinction between *murder* and manslaughter no longer obtained. Murder no longer is a slaying, followed by a concealment of the corpse. It is rather a slaying in violation of some special relation of confidence,[3] in contravention of some special (*e.g.* "pledged") peace, or a slaying induced by a base motive (especially desire for gain).[4] Manslaughter included every other intentional wrong dangerous "per se" to life and actually producing death. It especially included cases of homicide in which the man slain had, *e.g.* by his effrontery, given a certain degree of exculpation.

The infliction of bodily injuries underwent in the local laws a more complete development. A distinction was often based upon the nature of the instrument with which the wound was inflicted, and upon the circumstances, whether or not the wound was inflicted with premeditation.[5] The drawing of a sword or knife was punished both as an attempt and as a jeopardizing of the public peace.

In the statutes of the cities special attention was given to the offense of breach of the "Hausfrieden" (*i.e.* peace of the house or home).[6] Attention was also given (apart from numerous police regulations[7] touching the markets and trade in general) to individual varieties of fraud, falsification of goods, weights, and measures. Bigamy[8] now more often appeared as an offense

[3] "Mort" (murder), *i.e.* "Perfidia" ("Recht von Winterthur" cited above).

[4] *Ph. Allfeld*, "Die Entwicklung des Begriffs von Mord bis zur Carolina", pp. 62 *et seq.* *Cf. Frensdorff*, p. lxi.

[5] In the North German sources: "Vorsate."

[6] *Cf.* also "Lex Sax.", XXVII. The slaying of a "faidosus" (*i.e.* outlaw) in his own house was punishable with death. *Cf.* also "Lex Rib.", LXIV.

[7] Concerning the police ordinances of Nürnberg, *cf. Siebenkees*, "Materialien zur Nürnberger Geschichte", pp. 676 *et seq.* *Cf.* "Brünner Schöffenbuch", N. 221. Mention is also made of "gemachte wandel." We find in Italy very comprehensive police ordinances, often enacted with a view to hinder traffic in necessities of life that were dangerous to health, fraudulent, or spoiled. *Cf. e.g.* "Statuta Taurini", "Monumenta Patriæ", "Legg. Munic.", col. 678 *et seq.*

[8] *Cf. e.g.* concerning the earlier law in the "Hansischen Recesse",

entailing secular penalties, and in the South German sources mention is also made of offenses contrary to nature. On the other hand, no change in the old conception of adultery (regarded merely as a wrong to the husband) was apparent until towards the end of the Middle Ages.

§ 36. **Equality before the Law.** — As far as the general fundamental principles of criminal law are concerned, during the later Middle Ages, the life of the unfree was legally protected just as the life of freemen; their death at the hands of their master was punishable by the State as manslaughter.[1] Although, *e.g.* as in the Italian statutes, severe punishments were sometimes provided for "forenses" in contrast with "cives",[2] and in the cities a distinguished citizen was given a certain right to chastise unimportant persons and those of the rabble,[3] and consideration was given "de facto" to the person in the application of the law, yet in legal theory, the equality of all persons before the law was a recognized principle.

Instigation, Attempts, Negligence, and Premeditation. — Instigation to crime (which was not distinguished from moral assistance and thus was frequently called "counsel to crime")[4] was generally punished in the same manner as the physical commission of the offense. However, in many cases other methods of rendering assistance were not uniformly treated as equally important. A general conception of attempt was not reached.[5] Acts which we to-day would punish as attempts, were punished as acts dangerous "per se" and even as acts which pave the way for the commission of a wrong. In many sources[6] the distinction between acts committed "culpa" (*i.e.* by negligence) and those committed "dolo" (*i.e.* with malice) is correctly made.[7] Only the latter

Frensdorff, in the "Hansischen Geschichtsblättern", I, pp. 17, 36; "Hamburger Recht von 1270", X, 6.

[1] "Schwabenspiegel", 73 (Ed. *Lassberg*).

[2] The Jurists raised the question whether such statutes were permissible. *Cf. Angelus Aretinus*, Rubr. "De Bononia homicidium", n. 2.

[3] Sometimes the rabble, public porters, and people of such type were even excluded from the "Stadtfrieden." In such a case one could abuse such persons with impunity, so long as the Council of the City did not exercise its discretion and interfere. *Cf. von Maurer*, "Geschichte", III, p. 161.

[4] *Cf. John*, pp. 215 *et seq.*, 231 *et seq.*

[5] *Cf.* as to the theories of attempt, *John*, pp. 141 *et seq.*

[6] On the other hand, in the "Schwabenspiegel", 182–184 (*Lassberg*) we find unfortunate perversions of the correct theory. Here homicide done "culpa" (*i.e.* with negligence) is treated, through a misconception of the Roman-Canon law and a perversion of the theory of the "Talio", as a crime deserving the death penalty.

[7] *Cf. e.g.* "Sachsenspiegel", II, 38. According to the "Sachsenspiegel"

entail physical punishment. We often find a special rule for crimes committed with "vorsate" (*i.e.*[8] with special deliberation and premeditation — especially in cases of bodily injuries, etc.

Moralizing Tendencies. — The effort to determine more exactly the element of inner guilt, the subjective side of the crime, led to many futilities. To reach right solutions was impossible without a more complete juristic development. In the latter Middle Ages the number of the judgments by the "Schöffen" (lay-judges) moralizing on a false basis is by no means inconsiderable. The "Schöffen" of Brunn inflicted the death sentence sometimes "ob malam voluntatem", and they banished from the city those who in despair over losses at dice had cut off their own thumbs.[9] Such a tendency is especially evident in the treatment of suicide[10] which was regarded as punishable by the secular law.

Herein may doubtless be traced the influence of the Church, and indeed the Mosaic law was regarded as divine law of complete and existing efficacy.[11]

§ 37. **Effects of Changes in the Law of Proof.** — A quite peculiar effect was brought about by the change in the old Germanic law of proof. Except in cases where the accused was apprehended in the act or was under some existing legal disability, the ancient law set him free if he took oath to his innocence. Although other elements enter into the origin of these rules,[1] their practical effect was, in the one case, to establish a presumption of innocence and in the other, *i.e.* where the accused was apprehended in the act or was under some legal disability, to establish a presumption of guilt.

only "wergeld" was paid in cases of homicide resulting from negligence. Corporal punishment was prohibited.

[8] The meaning of "vorsate" has been pointed out by *John*, pp. 64 *et seq.*

[9] "Brünner Schöffenbuch", N. 539, 270. In the first case the offender was guilty of a bodily injury very reprehensible from the moral standpoint, but there was no possibility to surmise an intention to kill.

[10] As to the treatment of suicide in South Germany, *cf. Osenbrüggen*, "Studien", p. 337. To the early Germans suicide by an aged man weary of life seemed honorable. Later it was regarded as a relapse into heathendom, the realm of Satan.

[11] *Cf. e.g.* "Schwabenspiegel", 201.

[1] The law of proof, in cases where the offender was caught in the act, was originally nothing other than a justification of private vengeance against the offender who was in one's power. *Cf. Dahn*, "Fehdegang und Rechtsgang der Germanen" (1877), and especially *R. Löning*, "Der Reinigungseid bei Ungerechtsklagen im deutschen Mittelalter" (1880), pp. 97, 98.

This presumption of guilt was now given extended application, and even became a " præsumptio juris et de jure ", *i.e.* amounted to an incontrovertible finding of the fact of guilt. Thus a man suspected of counterfeiting was convicted without further proof, if a certain amount of false money was found on his person,[2] or a man was hung for theft if the article missed by another was found on his person and he could not prove purchase from a third party in public market.[3] Thus, especially in Southern Germany, the law of self-defense came to be particularly deformed as a result of such a presumption being raised to a rule of law. From the standpoint of proof, if a distinction is sought between self-defense and chance-medley, it is not improper to ask if he who alleges self-defense has himself received any wounds[4] or if he endeavored to avoid the aggressor.[5] But as rules of substantive law such presumptions are improper. There may well be cases of self-defense in which wounds have not been received by the accused, nor three steps taken in retreat.[6] So long as in cases of homicide it was only a matter of adjusting the payment of the " wergeld ", such presumptions could be endured and something could be said in their favor. But it was altogether a different matter if the false presumptions had as their result the beheading of the accused.[7] It became still worse as the system gradually grew up of public prosecution of offenses by State officials, for a private accuser was at least obliged to lay an information charging the offense, and often was placed upon oath. But a crude method of considering expediency in matters of police control resulted in the establishment of such presumptions,[8] and led even to the

[2] "Sächs. Landr." II, 26 § 2; "Stadtrechtsbuch", *Ruprecht von Freysing*, c. 57.

[3] "Brünner Schöffenbuch", N. 545. *Cf.* "Stadtrechtsbuch", *Ruprecht von Freysing*, c. 21. If the town beadles slew anyone who went without a light in the night and did not allow himself to be taken, they could free themselves by oath from the charge of manslaughter, saying they had done the deed "frid willen." But if they had a standing grudge against the slain man, then they were forthwith obliged to suffer for it. Yet it might well be that one might slay for a justifiable reason another against whom one happened to have a standing grudge. *Cf.* also *id.*, c. 38. If two were taken having upon them stolen goods of a certain value, both were hanged, — although one asserted his innocence.

[4] "Bamberger Recht" (ed. *Zöpfl*), § 158.

[5] "Schwabenspiegel" (*Lassberg*), c. 79.

[6] *Cf.* *Osenbrüggen*, "Das Alamannische Strafrecht", pp. 151 *et seq.*; *von Bar*, "Das Beweisurtheil des germanischen Processes" (Hannover, 1866), pp. 86, 87.

[7] In Constance in 1443, any one would be beheaded who could not positively prove that he had retreated three steps. *Osenbrüggen*, p. 153.

[8] It was provided by a statute of Strassburg, of 1322, § 175, that if

practice of capital punishment for acts that were merely dangerous, *e.g.* the carrying of a knife forbidden by law.[9]

Arbitrary Character of the Law. — To make up for the deficiencies of the procedural law, thus ensued an increase in the severity of the substantive law. And this substantive law itself acquired a certain discretionary or arbitrary character. As a result of the instability of the legal system of the entire empire, the law had to be periodically, not exactly created anew, but at least again put in force and declared as effective for the smaller groups and communities. It might almost be said that the existence of the criminal law was merely a matter of contract [10] or rested upon the will of the ruler. In the Middle Ages there are even cases of voluntary submission to public punishment as a penalty for mere breach of contract. At times no hesitancy was shown in punishing with cruel penalties even the most insignificant offenses when they were opposed to the interests of the landowner or might derogate from the respect due to the city. That penalties were imposed by a village court for the girdling of trees is well known and has been a subject of frequent comment.[11] But it is not the only example. According to another custumal, a cruel death (to be inflicted with a plow) was the punishment for a destroyer of boundary stones;[12] while by a third custumal [13] the burning of the soles of the feet was prescribed for one who had damaged trees in the forest. According to the "Schöffenbuch" [14] of Brunn any one who reviled the "Schöffen", because of a decision he believed to be unjust, was to be nailed to a stake by the tongue until he cut himself loose. In the Freiburg "Stadtrechte", [15] the death penalty was prescribed both for polluting

any one wounded or slew another, then the penalty of loss of head or hand was inflicted upon all who had followed him bearing drawn swords, pikes or halberds, just as upon him who actually inflicted the wound or dealt the death blow. *Osenbrüggen*, p. 169.

[9] Even the carrying of a knife of forbidden length entailed the loss of a hand. "Wiener Stadtr.", 1221, § 39. "Rudolph I Landfrieden of 1281", § 55 (*Pertz*, "Legg.", II, p. 430). Unauthorized manufacture of skeleton keys for another was punishable with the loss of a hand. "Brünner Schöffenbuch", N. 548. *Cf.* also "Prager Stadtrechtb.", N. 57.

[10] The "Landfrieden" must also have been sworn to by individuals. "Const. Henrici IV", A.D. 1103 (*Pertz*, "Legg." II, 61); "Rudolph I Const. pacis", A.D. 1287, c. 39 (*Pertz*, "Legg." II. p. 451).

[11] Custumal of Oberursel of 1401 (*Grimm*, "Weisthümer", III, p. 489). The intestines were to be drawn from the offender and wound around the tree. *Cf.* concerning offenses against the laws of the forest and chase, during this period, *Roth*, "Geschichte des Forst- u. Jagdwesens in Deutschland", pp. 131 *et seq.*

[12] *Grimm*, III, p. 590. [13] *Ibid*, I, p. 490. [14] N. 536.

[15] 1520, Fol. 95, 97.

the springs of the city and for laying violent hands upon the night watchmen. It is conceivable that the first-mentioned refined and barbarous punishments were not actually carried out. But they were not mere jests,[16] and they reveal that such penalties for such cases were deemed justifiable.

§ 38. **Confusion resulting from the Term "Frieden."** — As is often the case with mere words, the use of the word "Frieden" was of far-reaching importance. Since from early times grave crimes had been called "Friedbrüche" (breaches of the peace) and now their punishment was no longer based upon some especially agreed or pledged peace, it was an easy step to place on an equality [1] with these grave crimes, in respect to punishment, minor offenses which were forbidden by the "Landfrieden" or "Stadtfrieden." Thus, even in the Saxon "Landrecht" [2] (which upon the whole is free from extravagances) the death penalty is prescribed for the litigant who, after being enjoined by a judge from the use of a piece of land, nevertheless in spite of the "Frieden" as to the same declared by the judge, again undertakes its cultivation. Although it may of course be argued that in those times disobedience towards a judge or lack of respect for judicial decrees were not things to be tolerated, yet such abnormal severity can be explained only from the association of this "Friedbruch" with a "Friedbruch" in the early sense. As is also shown by the Goslar "Statuten",[3] the conception of a "Friedbruch" was by no means limited to grave crimes; as a result of this, attainder ("Verfestung") might ensue for lesser acts which also were called "Friedbruch", and where attainder attached to an individual, his life was forfeited, no matter how insignificant may have been the "Friedbruch" of which he was guilty.[4]

[16] In the Middle Ages great importance was often attached to the spoken word. *Cf.* the case in Constance cited in note 7 *ante.*

[1] Thus *e.g.* by "Rudolph I Landfrieden" of 1281, § 8 (*Pertz,* "Legg." II, p. 427) the unauthorized keeping for sale of wines and liquors was regarded as a "Friedbruch." In connection herewith it may be noted that where the offense consisted of the breach of a specially "pledged peace" (or of a peace enjoined by the state authorities), it was, according to many sources, rather the formal conception of a violated utterance that formed the essence of the offense, *e.g.* the violated command of the authorities. *Cf. Schlierlinger,* "Die Friedensbürgschaft", pp. 12 *et seq.*, p. 59, and especially "Sächs. Landr.", III, 9, § 2: "Brict en man den vrede, den he vor sic selven lovet, it gat ime an den hals."

[2] III. 20 § 3.

[3] *Göschen,* "Goslar'sche Statuten", p. 291.

[4] "Vestinge nimt den manne sin lif, of he begrepen wirt dar binnen." "Sächs. Landr.", III, 63, § 3. *Göschen,* p. 477. *Cf.* p. 56, line 55; p. 57, lines 12–14; p. 59, line 10: "Wert en in der veste begripen, de vestinghe

Reversion to Primitive Conceptions. — The idea that legal protection depended upon one's belonging to some association or group, together with the fact that even within as well as outside the walls of the cities there was but little actual protection afforded to life or property because of the constant feuds and the continual increase of professional rascality,[5] resulted in a revival of the most primitive and harsh conceptions of criminal law. The criminal if he was not a member of the small local group was again regarded as an enemy against whom the doing of any act was permissible. Thus *e.g.* the "Stadtrecht" of Augsburg,[6] while men of means residing in the city were treated with great consideration in respect to arrest or conviction, provided that if a stranger scoffed at a citizen of Augsburg, everyone should run to the spot and that thereupon any wounding or even slaying of the stranger was permissible. We find in the Laws of the Cities ("Stadtrechte"), provisions that a stranger who outside of the city is mistreated or wounded by a citizen can obtain no satisfaction within the city before its courts.[7]

Severity of the Law. — Thus criminal justice, especially in the States of the South of Germany, gradually became extremely harsh and cruel. The Statutes of Augsburg of 1276 were written in blood. The hard-hearted citizen-body,[8] proud of their wealth, caring everything for property and little or nothing for the life or misery of the poor man, were willing to inflict the loss of a hand as a penalty for merely entering an orchard or grass plot with intent to steal, while prostitutes (who, as is well known, were numerous in even the respectable cities of the Middle Ages) were for the simple violation of a police regulation punished by slicing off the nose.[9]

Application of Mosaic Law. — In addition, the application of the Mosaic Law and the theological idea of the "talio" (eye for

nimt ime dat lif." *Cf.* especially *Planck*, "Das deutsche Gerichtsverfahren im Mittelalter", II (1879), p. 300.

[5] Concerning this *cf.* Cap. A.D. 789, c. 78 (*Pertz*, "Legg. I", p. 65), and especially *Avé-Lallemant*, "Das deutsche Gaunerthum" (1858), I, pp. 43 *et seq.*

[6] Supplement to Art. XXXV, ed. *Meyer*, p. 105.

[7] *Gaupp*, "Deutsche Stadtrechte des Mittelalters", II, p. xv.

[8] Also in North Germany outside of the cities there were death penalties for certain cases of theft, *e.g.* serious thefts in the night ("Sächs. Landr." II, 28), theft of plows from the fields ("Sächs. Landr." II, 13, § 4). *Cf.* also *Osenbrüggen,*" Der Nachtschach" in his "Studien", pp. 241 *et seq.*

[9] The order to leave the city within the sacred forty days. "Augsburger Stadtrecht", 113 (ed. *Meyer*, p. 190).

an eye, etc.), became predominant, especially in South Germany. It is true that the Mosaic criminal law [10] by no means appears so harsh as may be inferred from a mere literal interpretation of single passages; and the "cutting off", so frequently mentioned, refers merely to an avoidance of divine wrath and not to an actual punishment; often the "talio" is merely the basis for compensation or a means of compelling compensation. But in the Middle Ages the expressions of the Mosaic Law were construed singly and literally, and where offenses against religion and morality are concerned it is in many respects harsh and cruel. The idea of the "talio" (originally unknown to the Germanic law) [11] often reappears exactly in its well-known Mosaic form in the South German statutes.[12] This contributed not a little towards making the criminal law harsh and cruel, and the more so since its alleged divine origin seemed to preclude any compromise or mitigation.[13]

Cruelty of the Punishments. — Because of all this, cruelty [14] and studied aggravation [15] of punishment towards the end of the Middle Ages reached the last extremity, — while at the same time it was generally believed that this was but the performance of a task pleasing to God. The concisely stated system of capital punishment in the "Sachsenspiegel" (II, 13) [16] the severity of which is shown by the inclusion in theft of anything of three shill-

[10] *Cf. Saalschütz*, "Das mosaische Recht", II (1853), pp. 437 *et seq.*; *Saalschütz*, "Archäologie der Hebräer", II (1856), pp. 271 *et seq.*

[11] *Grimm*, "Deutsche Rechtsalterthümer", p. 647; *Osenbrüggen*, "Studien", pp. 151 *et seq.* It was only in case of false complaint and in a few related cases that the principle of "talio" was applied in the old Germanic law. In such a case it seems especially natural. The wrongful attack was turned against its author.

[12] *Cf. Osenbrüggen*, p. 153. As to the principle of "talio" in bodily injuries, *cf. e.g.* "Stadtrechte" of Vienna in 1221 (*Gaupp*, "Deutsche Stadtrechte des Mittelalters", II, p. 241). Here the "talio" was applied only in case the wrongdoer was unable to pay the amount of the composition. In the "Stadtrecht für die Wiener Neustadt", it is called "secundum legem institutam a Domino."

[13] Concerning the opinions prevailing until well into the 1700s and their effects continuing to the present time, see below.

[14] For a long time in Nürnberg women were buried alive for simple theft. *Siebenkees*, "Materialen zur Nürnberger Geschichte", II, p. 539.

[15] If *e.g.* a Jew was being executed, a cap of glowing pitch was placed on his head.

[16] "Alle mordere, unde die den plug rovet oder molen oder kerken oder kerchof, unde vorredere unde mortbernere, oder die ire bodescap wervet to irme vromen, die sal man alle radebreken. Die den man slat oder vat oder rovet, oder bernet sunder mortbrand, oder wif oder maget nodeget, unde den vrede breket, unde die in overhure begrepen werdet: den sal man dat hovet afslan. Die düve hudet oder rof oder emanne mit helpe dar to sterket, werdet sie des verwunnen man sal over sie richten als over jene."

ings of value, contains frequent penalties of death and breaking on the wheel. An enumeration of the forms of mutilation used as punishments in the south of Germany (branding, cutting off the hand, the ears, the tongue, putting out the eyes) is revolting, and the modes of death varied between breaking on the wheel, quartering in the cruelest manner, pinching with red-hot tongs, burying alive, and burning. Even the executioners complained about the cruelty in the infliction of the punishments required of them.[17] Gallows covered and surrounded by corpses, which rotted as they were devoured by birds of prey, were a plain mark of the neighborhood of an important court, especially a city court.[18]

Failure of the Law. — Yet the cruelty of these punishments in no way served the purpose of lessening crime.[19] "Nec his tormentis et cruciatibus arceri potest quin semper scelus sceleri accumulent," says Celtes. Professional swindling (reference to which can be found as early as in the Capitularies) increased as a result of the numerous feuds, and developed into a well-banded organization.[20] The smallness of the judicial districts, the limitations upon the jurisdiction of many of the courts,[21] and the defective legal machinery, impaired the power of justice and favored the escape of criminals. At the same time the rabid pitiless hostility, especially to offenses against property, of a criminal law

[17] In Nürnberg, in 1513, the executioners complained about the cruelty of burying alive. *Siebenkees*, p. 599.

[18] "Qui delicta committunt levi etiam aliquando causa diversis pœnis et generibus tormentorum exquisitis afficiunt" are the words of a contemporary, *Conrad Celtes* ("De origine, situ, moribus Germaniæ, Norimbergæ") in giving a horrifying description of criminal justice at the end of the 1400 s. (The passage from this book, which is now rather rare, is given in *Malblank*, pp. 37 *et seq.*, and *Henke*, I, pp. 290–292.)

[19] In the sources for the law of the Middle Ages, frequent mention is made of imprisonment ("Cippus"), but uniformly only as imprisonment preliminary to trial, and generally of a revolting nature. *Cf.* also *Streng*, "Das Zellengefängniss" (Nürnberg, 1879). Imprisonment as a punishment occurred only occasionally, in cases of money fines for breach of police regulations where the offender was unable to pay the fine, and its duration in such cases was short. *Cf. e.g.* "Prager Statutarrecht", N. 20, 21.

[20] *Cf.* concerning *Sebastian Brandt's* "Narrenschiff", and the "Liber Vagatorum", with its clarion warning, published by *Luther* with a preface, *Avé-Lallemant*, I, pp. 137 *et seq.*

[21] The baronial courts, which could not use the blood ban, had the right only to take preliminary cognizance of graver crimes and were obliged to deliver the criminal to the public courts of the lord. If the judge did not appear, to receive the criminal, at the place fixed by custom for the delivery, the criminal was bound (symbolically) with a straw band, *i.e.* he was allowed to flee after he had been stripped to the waist. *Cf. Grimm*, "Weisthümer", III, p. 640, N. 6; p. 685 and *Maurer*, "Geschichte der Fronhöfe in Deutschland", IV, p. 406.

enacted and administered by the wealthier class had, as its consequence, a similar hostility on the part of the offenders and their following. Add to this that, through the dishonorable punishment of exposure on a pillory (for lesser offenses, especially the first theft), and through the public floggings, the sense of honor and self-respect was lamentably destroyed.[22] The punishment of infamy (which was at this time markedly developed) closed the doors to most of the honest occupations, and the frequent banishments from the cities and the country districts[23] made the offenders homeless and deprived them of means of livelihood. In addition to this a deplorable part was played by the frequent confiscations (partial or total) of property; this penalty applied not only to treason against the community, but also very often to homicide and even to severe wounding, and to heresy.[24] It

[22] The Middle Ages developed a considerable number of dishonorable and degrading punishments, which in part had a humorous aspect, but which if they did not render the offender infamous (permanently), nevertheless could operate to his disadvantage. Among these we find the punishments of "Schandkorbes" (literally "disgrace basket"), the "Schnelle" (*infra*), the "Badekorbes" (literally "bathbasket"), the "Wippe" ("strappado"), ducking into water, ridicule by children, riding on a donkey, carrying a plow-wheel with dogs or saddles, etc. *Cf. Grimm*, "Deutsche Rechtsalterthümer", pp. 725, 726; *Von Maurer*, "Geschichte", IV, pp. 269 *et seq.*, pp. 378, 379. Where the degrading punishment consisted in the carrying of an object — a mild form of this sort of punishment — an object was chosen in accordance with the calling and rank of the offender. Thus, *e.g.* a bishop was obliged to carry some paper with writing. The "Schnelle" or "Schuppe", a basket out of which the offender was obliged to jump into a puddle or into a horse-trough, was much used in the case of bakers who did not bake bread of the proper weight. *Cf. Osenbrüggen*, "Studien", p. 364; *Gierke*, "Der Humor in deutschen Rechte" (1871), pp. 48 *et seq.* Concerning the "Schuppenstuhl", a punishment much in use, *cf.* especially *Frensdorff*, in the "Hansische Geschichtsblättern" (1874), pp. 30 *et seq.*

[23] As to this, *cf. Walchner*, "Geschichte der Stadt Radolphzell" (1825), p. 70; *Avé-Lallemant*, I, p. 87; "Brünner Schöffenbuch", N. 540. "Ab antiquo consuetum est, quod quicumque pro maleficio flagelletur membris mutiletur vel aliter secundum justitiam corpore vitiatur, illi civitas est interdicta." As to banishment in Flanders, *cf. Warnkönig*, "Flandrische Rechtsgeschichte", III, 1, pp. 173 *et seq.* In Flanders regular circuits were made to look for banished persons.

[24] *Cf. e.g.* City law of Hagenau, of 1164, §§ 12–15 (*Gaupp*, "Deutsche Stadtrechte des Mittelalters", I, p. 98); City law of Innsbruck, of 1239, § 7 (*Gaupp*, II, p. 254). The grounds for these extensive confiscations of property are not sufficiently ascertained. In the time of the Carolingians we find them in connection with exile and capital punishment (*Waitz*, "Deutsche Verfassungsgeschichte", IV, p. 439), and generally for breach of faith (*Waitz*, III, p. 265) and also in graver crimes such as parricide and incest. Partial confiscation was threatened as a supplementary punishment *e.g.* in the "Constitutio Henrici III. Langobardica über den Giftmord" (*Pertz*, "Legg." II, p. 42). (As to the gradual mitigation of this punishment, *cf. Osenbrüggen*, "Studien", pp. 185 *et seq.*) In my view, the confiscations of property in the Middle Ages were connected in one

became much restricted in the later enactments; and an argument against it was doubtless found in the maxim that a man pays for everything with his head. But even as late as the Carolina (Art. 218) it was found necessary to limit the frequent and often quite illegal confiscations of property, whereby "wife and children are reduced to beggary."

§ 39. **Incidental Circumstances having a Demoralizing Influence.** — There were, moreover, a number of incidental circumstances by which the demoralizing influences resulting from so crude a system of criminal justice were greatly increased.

In the first place, in the case of many crimes and especially in manslaughter, it was of vital importance whether judgment was rendered immediately after the act (or what amounted to the same thing, the offender was caught while under that form of conditional outlawry known as "Verfestung"), or whether the offender was able to achieve for himself temporary safety and then to negotiate a settlement in money. It was only in the former case that the death penalty prescribed for manslaughter was applied, and there were sometimes even express provisions to this effect.[1] Because of the inadequate legal machinery of the various territories and judicial districts, and because of the numerous free States[2] which furnished temporary protection to fugitives,

aspect with the unfree status; since originally they were to the advantage of the lord of the city, and according to the French feudal law the commission of certain crimes by the feudal tenant caused him to forfeit his movables to his lord; *cf. Du Boys*, II, p. 221 *et seq.* In another aspect, they were connected with the fact that a breach of the peace entailed outlawry, *i.e.* the loss of all the offender possessed within the community, as confiscation very frequently occurs during the 900 s, 1000 s, and 1100 s.

[1] *Cf. e.g.* "Rechtsbr. von Passau" of 1225, § 24; "Eisenacher Statut" of 1283; "Rechtbuch" of Duke Albrecht for Klagenfurt of 1338, § 8 (*Gengler*, "Deutsche Stadtrechte", p. 291). As to Bremen also, it is stated by *Donandt*, "Versuch einer Geschichte des Bremer Stadtrechts", II, p. 289, that a captured slayer was beheaded; but it was possible for one to free himself from outlawry by the payment of money. The "Constitutio Friderici I de incendiariis" of 1187 fixed the punishment of decapitation only for the incendiary who was captured. On the other hand, he who gave himself up of his own free will, or relieved himself of the attainder, was to undergo only the penance (going on a pilgrimage) inflicted by the Church, pay compensation, and suffer banishment for a year and a day.

[2] Every courtyard of a lord, and later every place of residence of one of his officers, was a "free place", whence one could negotiate for a money settlement of a case ("Freihöfe"). Customarily the fugitive had six weeks and three days for this purpose; even at its expiry he was not required to be delivered up, but he could be brought to a place (*e.g.* in a forest) from which further flight was easily possible. There were penalties of considerable severity for the violation of this right of asylum, which originally belonged to the courtyard of anyone who was entirely free.

wealthy offenders who had numerous friends and relatives must often have been able to attain temporary safety and negotiate a settlement. On the other hand, every crime, for which conditional outlawry (*i.e.* "Verfestung") was pronounced against the fugitive offender, entailed the death penalty in case the offender was captured.[3] This conditional outlawry, in case the offender

Cf. Von Maurer, "Geschichte", IV, pp. 246 *et seq.*, and also *Frauenstädt*, "Blutrache und Todtschlagsühne im deutschen Mittelalter" (1881), pp. 56 *et seq.* Frequently this right of the "free places" was based upon a privilege granted by the emperor or prince. Later, privileges of this character, because of the evil conditions to which they gave rise, were only granted under limitations. — In this connection belong the provisions of the statutes of cities relating to the peace of the home ("hausfriede"). Anyone who fled to the house of another, if the judge himself did not demand him, was temporarily secure from arrest. He who was able to reach his own home, had there a definite period of peace, within which he was often able to make good his escape. *Cf. Osenbrüggen*, "Der Hausfrieden" (1851), pp. 26 *et seq.*, pp. 40 *et seq.*

[3] "Sächs. Landrecht", III, 63, § 3. "Vestinge nimt dem manne sin lif, of he begrepen wert dar binnen." "Augsburger Stadtrecht" of 1276, Art. XXXVIII. "Swer in der aht ist, wert über den gerichtet, den sol man ouch das haupt abslahen. . . ." *Cf. Göschen*, "Goslar'sche Statuten", p. 477. However, this severity could not always be kept up, when in the cities the punishment of "Verfestung" began to be extended to less important cases, as *e.g.* in the law of Lübeck. Although originally the distinction between "Verfestung" and "Stadtverweisung" was clearly marked, — the latter being a punishment inflicted upon one who was absent, and the former being a penalty for contumacy on the part of one who was absent (*Frensdorff*, p. xxiv) — "Verfestung" often resulted in "Stadtverweisung" and involved complete or partial confiscation of property. *Cf. Frensdorff*, p. lii. It had also many varieties (*Frensdorff*, pp. xx, xxi). "Acht" ("āhta" or "ahtunga" *i.e.* "persecutio") or "Verfestung" ("proscriptio") is not a punishment of a crime, although many have so regarded it (*e.g. Hälschner*, p. 31; *Waitz*, VI, p. 492; *Hugo Meyer*, "Das Strafverfahren gegen Abwesende", pp. 68 *et seq.*). It is rather (as has been correctly pointed out by *R. Löning*, "Der Vertragsbruch und seine Rechtsfolgen", I, p. 219) an incident of procedure resulting from the refusal, in a serious case, to appear before the court. It was only when this refusal, by persons of certain ranks and classes (especially those who could avail themselves of a feud), came to be customary and regular, that "Acht" actually assumed the character of punishment. The practical effect of "Verfestung" was that, as a result of the contumacious behavior, the punishments provided for the offense became increased to capital punishments (thus *Frensdorff*, p. xviii). "Verfestung" (or "Acht" as it was generally called when declared by the kings) is simply a milder form of outlawry. No one was allowed to furnish food or roof to one against whom "Verfestung" or "Acht" had been pronounced. Yet such a one was not entirely bereft of all rights. The accuser however gained the privilege of making proof, and according to the law of Lübeck he was required to prove merely the "Verfestung," and not the charge as a result of which the "Verfestung" had arisen (*Frensdorff*, p. xxix).

It is peculiar to the "bannitio" of the Italian statutes, to which the Italian jurists gave so much attention, that the "bannitus" could be attacked with impunity by anyone. (*Clarus*, § "Homicidium" n. 71, even raises the question whether the "bannitus" could avail himself of the plea of self-defense against a person who attacked him relying upon

did not relieve himself thereof within a year and a day, became a complete and absolute attainder within the district whose judge had pronounced the sentence.[4]

Private Settlement in Cases of Crime. — In spite of the punishments of life and limb so often categorically expressed, there obtained as a matter of fact, not only in cases of manslaughter[5] and wounding, but often in cases even of robbery and theft,[6] the so-called "Taidigung", *i.e.* private settlement with the injured or possibly with his relatives. The authorities of a city were often in need of preserving the peace between two of its powerful families,[7] and for a long time, in cases of manslaughter, the inter-

this impunity provided by statute.) Herein is seen the influence of the numerous factional strifes of the Italian cities.

[4] In order to make the "Verfestung" more extended in its application, it could be brought up before a higher judge and ultimately before the court of the king. In such case it came to be imperial outlawry, applicable to the entire empire. "Verfestung" pronounced in certain courts was "ipso facto" applicable to the entire territory. Frequently agreements were made between the cities for the mutual observance of sentences of proscription pronounced by any of them. As to this, *cf. H. Meyer* (cited above), pp. 86 *et seq.*, and *Frensdorff*, pp. xxiv *et seq.* According to the "Brünner Schöffenbuch", n. 482, anyone proscribed for theft was hanged, upon a mere written request certifying that he had been justly proscribed. According to the "Schleswig-Holstein'schen Landtheilung" of 1490, banishment was to apply to the whole country. *Cf. von Warnstedt*, "Zur Lehre von den Gemeinde-Verbänden, kritische Beleuchtung des Rechtsstreits, betr. die Glückstädter Strafanstalten" (1878), p. 34. We find in the cities and also in the royal courts certain lists of those who had incurred "Verfestung" and "Acht" ("Liber proscriptorum"). *Cf.* "Alberti I Const. pacis", 1303 § 37. *Pertz*, "Legg.", II, p. 483.

[5] Moreover, in many places intentional manslaughter not involving high treason was not punished with capital punishment until the Carolina came into effect. According to the "Braunschweigische Echteding" of 1532, n. XXIX (*Hänselmann*, "Urkundenbuch der Stadt Braunschweig", p. 342) it entailed banishment from the city for fifty years, a money fine of thirty guilder payable to the council, and settlement with the blood relatives of the party slain. Concerning the securing of immunity by the payment of money even in cases of murder, in Flanders, *cf. Warnkönig*, "Flandrische Rechtsgeschichte", III, 1, p. 160.

[6] *Cf.* "Klagspiegel", Title "de pœnis" (fol. 31b of the Strassburg edition, 1533). "Item Du solt mercken, das vmb ein yegklich, darumb dann über das blutgericht möcht werden, getaidingt vnd übereinkommen mag werden on pen." Until 1527 the nobility in the Mark of Brandenburg claimed the unlimited right to make a settlement with "Wergeld" and "Gewette" for even malicious manslaughter. *Cf. Hälschner*, "Geschichte", p. 117, and for remarkable illustrations in the 1600 s in Hannover (Vogtei Celle), *cf. Bülow und Hagemann*, "Practische Erörterungen" II, p. 260.

[7] Concerning peaces proclaimed by the authorities, which not only the families but also their "famuli" and "servi" were bound to observe, *cf. e.g.* "Brünner Schöffenbuch", n. 530, 534 and also "Wormser Reformation", VI, 2. tit. 23. (*Cf.* also *Osenbrüggen*, "Studien", p. 483.) It frequently happened that a pledged peace was declared void by the interested parties. This liberty in turn came to be restricted by the statutes.

vention of a criminal judge was regarded only as a last resort in case the families concerned could come to no agreement.[8] In order to prevent private feud-vengeance they often compelled the relatives of a man who had been slain to accept compensation.

When once a complaint had been lodged, there could be a settlement only with the approval of the judge,[9] and, if the accuser without such approval discontinued the prosecution, he was himself subject to fine.[10] However, this approval of the judge, who received the fee which was paid (the ancient "Fredum") and often something besides, was not difficult to obtain, and thus the right of administering justice (which was granted as a piece of property, as appurtenant to a fief), was always regarded as a source of revenue.[11]

The "Grace" of the Rulers. — Here one can observe the working out of the old conception, viz. that since the king has the authority to protect the peace, a violation of the peace is, as it were, a wrong done to the king or ruler and that in the settlement

[8] In Italy, it was for a long time a matter of controversy whether or not a "pax" concluded with the party injured precluded the criminal prosecution. As to this, *cf. Bonifacius de Vitalinis*, "Rubr. de pœnis", n. 4 *et seq.* This writer also discusses with great clearness many dubious points therewith connected, *e.g.* whether compromise is permissible where there are many heirs. As to the extraordinary favor shown to atonement for manslaughter in northern Germany, even late in the Middle Ages, *cf.* notably *Frauenstädt*, pp. 136 *et seq.* Frequently the relatives of the slain forbore bringing a complaint because of fear for themselves. *Frauenstädt*, p. 169.

[9] The "pax" or "remissio" required in Italy also the "approbatio" of the court. (*Cf.* the very clear description in *Clarus*, § fin. qu. 58.) Even in the middle of the 1500s the "pax" played an important part.

[10] "Sächs. Landr.", I, 53, § 1, II, 8; "Stadtr. von Ens von 1212", § 21 (*Gaupp*, II, p. 222); "Wiener Stadtr. von 1221", § 31; "Brünner Schöffenbuch", n. 52; "Klagspiegel", Tit. "de pœnis", Fol. 131b.

[11] *Cf.* concerning such "Taidigungen", especially, *Zöpfl*, "Das alte Bamberger Recht, als Quelle der Carolina", p. 114. The obligations assumed in such cases were very exactly observed. In the year 1328 a man killed another in Bamberg, and in expiation pledged himself to perform church penance together with his relations. If he did not fulfill this obligation he was, without possibility of pardon, to be immediately put to death. It was as if he had upon oath offered himself for execution in case he did not fulfill his pledge, and apparently even if his relatives refused to join him in the church penance. *Cf.* supplement V, n. CIV to the "Bamberger Recht" in *Zöpfl*, p. 164 of the "Urkundenbuch", and *Zöpfl* (cited above), p. 115. The importance of the element of voluntary subjection appears in the instance cited by *Cantzow*, "Pomerania", II, p. 448 (*cf. Jarcke*, "Handbuch", I, p. 32) in the '70s of the 1400s. A young man of good family had unintentionally in a jest killed his friend. His friend's relatives allowed him to be sentenced to death, intending to later set him free, and having in mind to gain credit for themselves for having given him his life. The condemned man, however, was too proud to accept this, and permitted himself to be executed at the churchyard, and refused all consolation from the executioner.

of this wrong he may act in his discretion and pleasure just as a wronged private citizen might act in regard to feud and composition. Both in the royal ordinances [12] and in the statute books of the local lords [13] there is often to be found the indefinite threat that the individual violating a certain order or prohibition shall forfeit the "*grace*" or "mercy" ("Gnade", "misericordia") of his king or lord. This "grace" [14] had to be regained by the payment of a sum sometimes fixed, but more often determined at the discretion of the king or lord. The offender was often allowed peace for a certain time until he could collect this sum.

It was understood that this "grace" was to be interposed where a definite punishment was threatened, and that this right belonged not only to the lord but also to his officials. Yet, where it was a wrong against a private person that constituted the offense, this "grace" could be interposed only with the consent of the party injured,[15] or where he did not insist upon the extreme letter of the law. Where a man had been slain, this consent had to be given by his relatives. All this shows how deeply-rooted was the old idea that a crime was primarily a violation of a specific individual right and only incidentally a wrong to the established law and order. When not influenced by some base motive, it was frequently the intercessions of the Clergy or the prayers of the relatives (or friends) [16] of the offender which caused the judge, instead of giving the regular sentence (some penalty of life or limb), to sentence the offender to pay a money fine, or to go upon a pilgrimage, or perform some other pious work. It is, however, very apparent that although no legal distinction was herein made between the poor and humble and the rich and prominent yet there was a great practical distinction. The former did not have those

[12] *Cf. Waitz*, VI, pp. 450 *et seq.*

[13] *Cf. e.g.* "Freiburger Stiftungsbrief" of 1120 § 14 (*Gaupp*, II, p. 21): "gratiam Domini ducis amisit." "Stadtrecht" of Dattenried of 1358 § 26 (*Gaupp*, II, p. 180). Death sentences were often worded: "sit in potestate" (or "in gratia", or "in misericordia") "domini." *Cf. Warnkönig*, III, p. 162.

[14] *Cf.* the oldest statute of Soest, § 6 (*Gengler*, p. 441): "Causa quæ . . . mota fuerit et terminata vel per justitiam vel per misericordiam . . ." Kaiser Sigmund in 1433 granted the city of Luzern a special privilege in respect to judgments subject to "grace."

[15] *Hälschner*, "Geschichte", p. 45.

[16] According to "Peinliche Halsgerichtordnung von Davos" in Switzerland in the year 1650, on the last day of the session of court, the question was to be asked, "If any man or woman spiritual or secular would intercede for the pardon or mitigation of punishment of the poor persons." In this it was sought to secure a scrutiny, by the moral sentiment of the people, of the severity of the judgment.

influential mediators upon whom the latter could rely. Hence, sometimes, the judges would not dare to inflict a well-deserved death sentence upon a prominent person; in so doing, they deemed that they were but acting in accordance with custom.

Other Peculiar Customs. — Often, according to an old custom (surviving even until the end of the 1600 s), the condemned was permitted to live, if some woman (originally only a virgin) desired him for a husband. Later this peculiar law also found application where a condemned woman was desired by some man as a wife.[17]

Influence of Accidental Circumstances. — An influence was accorded also to accidental circumstances. Thus the executioner had the right to free for a money payment every tenth man who was delivered to him for execution.[18] As in the primitive periods, the criminal was not executed outright but rather offered as a victim to the elements,[19] so later mere chance was often allowed to prevail as a sign of forgiveness manifested by God, and thus to preclude the carrying out of the sentence.[20]

Uncertainty of the Court Procedure. — Most important of all, the *uncertainty* of the *court procedure* should be considered, especially the law of proof in the later Middle Ages. A description of this must be left to the historian of criminal procedure.[21] We find strange combinations of the Germanic and Roman rules of proof, — oath of purgation, proof by compurgators and witnesses, "ex parte" proof, and confrontative proof (wherein a hearing is given to both sides). There was also often torture.

[17] *Cf. Osenbrüggen*, pp. 377 *et seq.*

[18] "Sachsenspiegel", III, 56 § 3. "Schwabenspiegel", 126 (*Lassberg*). "Landrechtsbuch Ruprechts von Freysing", Cap. 88. As to this *cf.* especially *Abegg*, "Zeitschrift für Deutsches Recht", vol. 15, p. 76. On the other hand the executioner often decided the method of death punishment. *Abegg*, p. 58, etc.

[19] Placing in a boat without helm or rudder is mentioned in the Sagas. *Grimm*, p. 721. *Cf.* also record of the Cloister Frauen-Chiemsee (*Grimm*, "Weisthümer", III, p. 671), where a proceeding of this sort was ordered, in a case where the judge before whom the offender was triable was not on hand. As to this, *cf. Osenbrüggen*, p. 341.

[20] As *e.g.* in capital punishment by hanging, if the rope used in hanging the accused broke. *Abegg*, "Zeitschrift für Deutsches Rechts", vol. 16, pp. 317 *et seq.* In Zürich in the 1500 s and 1600 s the punishment of drowning for the killing of children was so done that to be saved was not impossible, and thus the punishment assumed the form of a judgment of God, *Osenbrüggen*, p. 348. At times some influence may have resulted from the idea that the execution as a judicial act had come to a formal end. *Cf.* the case in Basel given by *Osenbrüggen*, p. 353.

[21] [Consult Vol. V of the present Series, *Esmein's* "History of Continental Criminal Procedure." — ED.]

The old accusatorial procedure[22] is still found, but of a kind so deformed by a preliminary official investigation based on torture that it contained only a shadow of its former character. There was also a number of popular turbulent methods of procedure for cases where the offender was apprehended in the act and for cases having to do with persons of bad reputation.[23] Moreover, it was not with injustice that the author of the "Klagspiegel"[24] speaks of "the foolish old hen judges in the villages", better qualified to sit in judgment on the cases of "knavish chickens" and "other rascally cattle", than cases of offenses under the criminal law. In the year 1496,[25] almost immediately after its organization, the Imperial Supreme Court, having reference to the complaints coming almost daily from all parts of Germany about the injustice and arbitrary actions of the criminal courts, addressed itself to the imperial assembly sitting at Lindau in the following significant words:[26] "Item so teglich wider Fürsten, Reichsstet vnd ander aberkeit in klagweis in einem gericht anbracht wird, das sy leute unverschuldet an Recht vnd redlich Ursach zum tode verutheilen vnd richten lassen haben sollen vnd durch die Fründt rechts wider dieselben begert . . . ist bescheids not, wie es . . . am Cammergericht gehalten werden sol." The Reichstag of Freiburg in Breisgau in 1498 thereupon passed the following decree:[27] "Auf den artickel, dass viele zu dem tode one recht vnd unverschuldt verurteylt werden . . . wirdet not seyn, deshalb ein gemein Reformation und Ordenung in dem Reich fürzunemen, wie man in criminalibus procediren soll."

[22] As appears in the "Nürnberger Halsgerichtsordnung."

[23] The so-called "Leumundsverfahren."

[24] Rubric "Quando judex per se inquirere potest", fol. 113*a* of ed. 1533, Strassburg.

[25] *Müller*, "Reichstheatrum", II, 78, 446. *Cf. Brünnenmeister*, "Die Quellen der Bambergensis" (1879), p. 1.

[26] "Insomuch as complaints are daily brought in court against princes, states of the realm, and other authorities, that they cause people who are innocent under the law and against whom there is no genuine case, to be sentenced and condemned to death, and whose friends demand that justice be done . . . there is need for instructions as to what course shall be taken by the court."

[27] "Neue Sammlung der Reichsabschiede", II, p. 46, "Reichsabschied zu Freiburg", § 34. "As to the claim that many who are innocent are sentenced to death in contravention of the law . . . it is necessary to undertake a general reform and regulation in the empire as to procedure in criminal matters."

Chapter V

SCANDINAVIA AND SWITZERLAND IN THE LATER MIDDLE AGES

A. Scandinavia[1]

§ 39*a*. **Early Customary Law. Primitive Feuds and Kin Vengeance.** — There is perhaps no other branch of law in the history of which the progressive development of the social state and public authority, and the reconstruction of society, are so plainly traceable, as in criminal law. Here individual independence is perceived to yield and gradually become subjected to State control. Public right presses forward alongside of private right until it takes the lead and dominates. This development takes place mostly by way of customary law. Its course can not be positively assigned to definite periods, but is nevertheless clearly evidenced both by historical testimony and also in the sources of the law. For ancient times, the Sagas and the Icelandic Grágas, with the earliest sources of Norwegian law, reveal much to us; and in the later provincial codes are found many traces which markedly refer

[1] [§§ 39 *a, b, c*, are from Stemann's "Den Danske Retshistorie," and auxiliary sources, named in detail in the Editorial Preface. The portion from Stemann is translated in full, omitting only the footnote quotations there given from the Scandinavian texts, and an occasional passage of detailed illustration; from the other sources a few gaps have been supplied by the Translator's condensation and insertion. — Ed.]

to the early conditions no longer prevalent; the new order of things forms in its turn a transition to the system of later legislation.

A leading work on the history of criminal law, including the nations of the North, and largely utilized in later treatises on this subject, Wilda's "Strafrecht der Germanen",[2] emphatically disputes the assertion, advanced especially by Rogge in "Das Gerichtwesen der Germanen",[3] that a real law of crimes and punishments was almost unknown in primitive ages. But the conflict between these views is not so great as it appears to be. Only the entire absence of such a law in early times is by the one view denied, while by the other only a relatively small importance and a limited sphere are ascribed to it. It must be acknowledged that, when the historic age commences, faint traces are already found of a law for the punishment of crimes in its modern sense.

Crime in modern penal justice is considered chiefly as an infraction of the law in its objective sense, and punishment as a means of restoring public law and order. But the sole concern in the early ages was the individual's injury; it was left to the injured party himself to procure reparation, both for the outward material damage inflicted and for the personal contumely. This authority to wreak vengeance ("Hævn") on the offender, by the aid of his kin if needed, was limited only by public opinion, founded on the natural sense of right and custom and usage. A feud, or relation of hostility, arose between the wrongdoer and the sufferer, and their respective blood-kindred; this could be settled by reconciliation alone, which frequently was attainable only after a feud ("Feide") of long duration. Such a pact was generally conditioned on the payment of a fine ("Bøde"); this was deemed to be not only reparation for the physical damage, but also satisfaction for the impeached honor.

The narratives of various events, found in the Sagas (especially from the close of the 800 s to the commencement of the 1100 s), which undoubtedly have a historical basis, describe almost exclusively gross acts of violence and wrong, mayhem and murder. In the latter case it behooved the kin of the slain to wreak blood vengeance (Sagas of Niala, Viga Styrs, Heidaviga, Grettis, and Vatnsdæla). While it was held to be a sacred duty not to leave unavenged the slaying of kin, and hence the acceptance of a money satisfaction was deemed dishonorable, nevertheless, the circumstances were taken into consideration, especially the provoca-

[2] Halle, 1842. [3] *Ibid.*, 1820.

tion and the mode (whether the crime was committed in the heat of passion or deliberately), and also the conduct of the wrongdoer subsequently. On this latter point the early law-texts of Sweden and Norway contain extensive provisions. Thus, under the Gotland law-text,[4] the slayer could tender reparation for the life only after a year had elapsed; during this period he, with his nearest relatives, must at first abide in hallowed places of refuge, or sanctuaries, and thereafter in distant and unfrequented localities, in order to escape the "Hævn", or exaction of the toll of blood for blood. Should the tender not be accepted at the expiration of that period, he must resume such a mode of life for the two following years; but the law expressly declares that the acceptance of the "Bøde" (or, amount of penalty and satisfaction) after the lapse of the first year should not disgrace the family kin. By the Östgöta law-text [5] the tender could be made only after three years; and similar requirements are contained in the early Gula-thing law-text.[6] Until expiation is made (according to Andreas Suneson) [7] the murderer must absent himself from the sight of his opponent, lest he offend him by his presence.

Private Fines. — Reconciliation was made either at the "Thing" or in front of the court ("Retten"), and the amount depended on the parties' negotiations. Instances are noted where this determination was left to the party wronged or to the kin entitled to prosecute the cause; and in some isolated cases the amount was fixed by the guilty one himself ("Sjælfdæmi"). As a rule, however, settlement was negotiated by agents appointed by both sides ("Voldgiftsmænd", the men of the violence-gift), who were chosen by the relatives or chieftains. In order that the offender might present himself in safety at the peace parleys, proclamation was made for his immunity from attack, confirmed by a solemn oath from the hostile party ("Grid," "Gruth"), for his journey forth and back, and for the entire time until the affair should be decided. For such guaranties there occur formulas ("Gridamal") in the Sagas and the Grágas; and even as late as the provincial Codes this warrant of security is referred to; its breach being termed a "deed of infamous treachery." [8]

[4] [Circa A.D. 1300 — TRANSL.]
[5] [Circa A.D. 1300 — TRANSL.]
[6] [Circa A.D. 1200 — TRANSL.]
[7] [Archbishop Suneson, whose writings (A.D. 1206–1215) are noted as one of the sources of Scandinavian law, in Professor Hertzberg's account, in Vol. I of the present Series (Ch. I, Part VII, § 14, p. 545). — TRANSL.]
[8] "Heres occisi . . . debet adversariis suis interim pacem promittere

After reconciliation made and the mulct paid over, it was incumbent upon the transgressor and his kin to make the "oath of equality" ("Ligheds-Eed"). This declared that if he himself had suffered the wrong, he would have entered into accord on the same conditions; the intent being to grant to the wronged kin a bill of honor, by the offender's express declaration that there was no disgrace in accepting the mulct instead of demanding revenge. Thereupon, the treaty was affirmed by the surviving kin with another oath ("Trygdeed"), securing for the guilty party and his kin full peace and safety for the future. This oath, for which a very solemn formula is prescribed in the Grágas, was given by the law-text of Skaane,[9] only in cases of murder, while the oath of equality was also given in cases of reparation for wounds and blows.

The community's public authority interfered only where the crimes were directed not against individuals but against all the people, or where, by reason of the perfidy or treachery of their commission, they were deemed extremely vile and heinous. Otherwise, the community's only concern was that the cause was conducted in accordance with custom and usage. It may be assumed, however, that the members of the "Thing," in some instances, when the proceedings were held there, brought some influence to bear on the accord and reconciliation.

Limitation of Private Vengeance. — At an early period, notably after the introduction of Christianity and under the influence of the priesthood, bounds were placed on the practice of exacting personal revenge, — partly as to its extent (permitting it only for deliberate and grave crimes), and partly as to the time, place, and manner. Thus, it was authorized by the Grágas, in certain instances, only at the very time and place of the offense ("a vighvalli"); in others, at the next general assembly ("Al-thing"). But in all cases it was incumbent upon the avenger, after slaying the offender, immediately to announce his act to his neighbors and witnesses, who were thereafter to testify at the "Thing"; for he was bound to enter the cause at the next "Al-thing" and make complaint against the deceased, in order to have judgment whether he was to

et eandem in signum indissolubilis firmitatis contingendo manu sua manum alterius alicuius roborare, et hoc facto ad maiorem securitatem aliquis de prudentioribus debet, pacis illius deum custodem et factorem cum sanctis omnibus, cum apostolico, cum rege, cum pontifice, cum iustis omnibus invocare, execrari vero quemlibet et anathematizare, qui promisse paci presumpserit obviare" (*Suneson*, V, 6).

[9] [The modern province of Skåne, in southern Sweden. — TRANSL.]

be proscribed and outlawed for his deed. Another cause contributing to limitations of the "Hævn" (or revenge) was the development of the principle of "peace", or "fred", — already known even in the mythological age. This signified an inviolate peace proclaimed over certain places and periods. The practice was gradually extended, so that every man was immune and enjoyed in his home and premises the rights of a sanctuary ("Huusfred"); or in his ship ("bunkæ brut"), or at the customary public meeting-places (including the Eyre and the journey thither and back), viz. the market, the church and churchyard (and going to and fro), as well as the "asylum courtyard", annexed to the churches and monasteries. During "hallowed" periods of the year, also, the "peace of God" prevailed ("pax ecclesiastica"). Even as early as the reign of Canute the Great his Church law mentions, in connection with the Church peace, the king's peace. Valdemar II promulgated an order for a special peace, to prevail everywhere in the presence or vicinity of the monarch; and this also appears in the law of Skåne.

While the right of "Hævn" (vengeance) was thus gradually confined in divers modes, and the wrongdoer on the other hand was afforded the opportunity to ward off retribution by negotiating for reconciliation, there came about eventually a customary law regulating the amounts of the fines and damages in cases of various offenses, until a definite "Bøde"-system was developed. In cases of grave wrongs the injured party was still generally permitted to choose between accepting the tender and wreaking vengeance. But even here curtailments were made. Self-redress more and more ceased to be viewed as a right or even as permissible, as the conception and treatment of crime and its logical consequences gradually changed. Such heinous crimes came already at a very early period to be considered not only as private offenses but also as breaches of public peace and order. Fines must be paid not only to the offended individual but also to the king. Thus the "bøde" was no longer merely a reparation and satisfaction for the injured party, but also a penalty for the breach of the general peace. When the offender failed to pay the amount of the penalty, or when his guilt was so great as not to be redeemable, he was placed under ban and doomed to be an outlaw, or punished by death or by corporal suffering. These public retributions, which for a long time figured as exceptions to the general practice of "bøde"-payments, became in the course of time constantly more frequent.

Church Mulcts. — In these changes (as already noted) the ecclesiastics exercised considerable influence. This was partly due to the social influence of the teachings of the Roman Church, in which crime and punishment were conceived as offense and atonement before God; and partly to the special ecclesiastical penal code, which in the course of time more and more extended its sway. Canute the Holy (so Saxo relates) bestowed upon the bishops and priests exclusive jurisdiction over misdemeanors committed directly against religion and the Church. Under this class of offenses, the Church laws of Skåne and Sjælland[10] enumerate offenses against the peace of the Church or of God ("Hælghæbrut"), against the person of the priest and church property, and other direct infractions of the Church canons. The priest also exercised co-ordinate jurisdiction with the regular authority in other grave penal causes.

The ordinances referred to provide that for breaches of the peace of the Church the mulct should be three marks; and if the offender did not possess that amount, it behooved the parish, in Skaane, to pay the priest for him, while in Sjælland he was subjected to a severe fast. Other misdeeds calling for Church mulcts were church robbery, incest, adultery, manslaughter, maltreatment of church officials and their near relatives and homicide generally. In most cases, money penalties were exacted. Heinous crimes were punished with excommunication and anathemas; these being of two degrees, one excluding the offender from all intercourse without the church as well as within, and the other only from the actual church and its ministrations. This ecclesiastical jurisdiction was generally exercised by the bishop on his regular circuit through his district; the matter being brought to his attention upon complaint or by general rumor. For secret crimes, the Church law provided that where the criminal, before being accused, had admitted the crime in the sacrament of confession, and received a certificate of the priest, he should be exempt from further punishment; indicating that by such confession, and the penance therein imposed, he was deemed to be restored to grace with God and the Church; so that even where the crime later became revealed, he was not amenable to punishment at the hands of the prelates, and the latter sought to extend this immunity so as to bar the secular power from action.

[10] [Circa A.D. 1170. — TRANSL.]

§ 39*b*. **The Provincial Codes.**[1] **Growth of Public Authority.** — In the provincial Codes not only do numerous traces remain of the "Hævn," and especially the blood vengeance, as an important factor in the system of retribution, but it is also frequently referred to as the very reason for some of the new provisions. It is apparent from the context that private revenge, while no longer deemed compatible with the social order, was nevertheless still so deeply rooted in the common conscience that the taking of a life on that ground was not classed with other offenses of the same order, — at least where the deed was not so done as to bar it from condonation.

This conception appears in the procedure and oaths required of the guilty party in negotiating for reconciliation, in order to escape the retaliation, and also in the determination and division of the fines and damages. The laws expressly refused the excuse of "Hævn", where the slaying was a breach of a pledge of peace during pending negotiations, or where reconciliation had been made and satisfaction accepted; in such cases the deed was punished as one without provocation. But under the prevailing general rule, though a fine was incurred by blood vengeance, the ordinary punishment for slaying a man, viz. outlawry, was not inflicted. The Jydske Code,[2] distinguishes such homicides and those done in perilous necessity or self-defense, from those committed on an inoffensive victim or "causeless man." Though self-defense thus relieved from punishment, it did not excuse the payment of reparation; it was sometimes a matter of doubt whether an act done in an affray was one of defense or of revenge. Indeed, some expressions in these laws seem to assume that the injured party had the right of choice between prosecuting the offender or practising vengeance, which right the law aimed to restrict. Only in one case do any of the provincial Codes expressly authorize a deed of vengeance on the spot, — the wronged husband had the right to kill or wound the adulterer while in the bed itself.

This limitation of the practice of private revenge may be considered as the first important step in the transition from the conception of crime as an affair of purely private right to that of the later penal system. Similar marks of transition are also found in other provisions of the provincial Codes. The basic principle

[1] [These codifications date during the 1200 s in Denmark, Norway, and Iceland, and during the 1300 s in Sweden. See Chap. II, Part VII, pp. 547–555, Vol. I of this Series, "General Survey." — TRANSL.]

[2] [A.D. 1241. — TRANSL.]

advanced by Archbishop Andreas Suneson, that the power of the State inflicts punishment in order to correct the evil will and intimidate from offenses is recognized in some passages of the preface of the Jydske Code, unmistakably of canonical origin, yet this doctrine is not practically carried out in the Code, for the reason that the view-point of private right still appears as mainly predominant. Public authority, nevertheless, asserted itself in various directions; its right and duty is recognized not only to procure reparation for the injured party, but also to punish the wrongdoer, in order to effect a restoration of the peace and an atonement for the offense itself.

System of Public and Private Fines. — Under the provincial Codes, an offense may ordinarily be discharged by "Bøde", signifying both fine and reparation; outlawry or other punishment is inflicted only for heinous crimes. Distinction is made between three classes of infractions: the first including all wrongs for which satisfaction is paid to the party injured, only; the second, all acts for which is incurred a fine payable to public authority; the third, such breaches of right as are not atonable with money payments. These differences, which also determined the mode of accusation and prosecution, depended on the subjective nature of the act and other circumstances.

Public penalties were imposed only where there was deliberation and guilty intent; for these alone made the act a breach of public order. Under the general rule, therefore, fines were not payable to the king or the bishop for accidental harms; but here the injured party, as a rule, could demand the "Bøde"; this reparation being due for the harm done him, whether with or without intent, by the person causing it. Thus, though a fine might be required in addition to the damages, and though the law of many localities made no distinction in this respect between intentional and unintentional acts, it is nevertheless apparent that the relation between the act and its effects, as well as the nature of the omission or carelessness, were taken into consideration.

Hence the distinction between the "act of hand" and the "handless risk" ("Handagærning" and "handløs wathæ"). The latter included primarily such injuries as were not caused by any one's personal activity, but by cattle or inanimate things which were chargeable to some one's safe custody (in which cases a small penalty was payable); it also included other harms attributable to some prior personal act having a consequence not anticipated.

This difference of degree of negligence is not expressed in general rules, but it is nevertheless noticeable in specific provisions. Thus, in a case mentioned in the earlier law-texts, where several men are cutting down a tree and its fall causes the loss of a life, the other laborers must pay three marks to the nearest relative of the deceased; this provision, however, being limited, (according to Erik's Law of Sjælland,[3]) to cases where the accused had ceased to take part in the task and left the spot. Where the tree slips from the hands of any one, the latter pays the total fine. For death or wounds caused by a weapon not owned by the user, the owner is fined three marks if he loaned it for that purpose, or a smaller amount if it was taken without his knowledge or against his will. A fine is likewise imposed upon one who so negligently places his weapon that it falls and wounds or kills another; the Jydske Law extending this rule to chance injuries from a weapon held in the owner's hand. For death or personal injuries suffered from the overturning of a wagon or the stroke of a rider on the road, the driver or rider is compelled to pay either the full "Bøde" for a deliberate act, or a less amount according to the degree of his carelessness or the contributory negligence, if any, of the victim. Similar rules came into vogue for injuries to cattle.

The fine ("Bøde") paid to the injured party being regarded as reparation for harm, and that paid to public authority as a penalty for the act itself, the former was incurred by parents for offenses committed by children, but not the latter, except in later legislation for manslaughter.

Procedure. — In all cases where the offended party alone was entitled to exact "Bøde", it was left wholly to him whether he should accuse and prosecute, or negotiate for reconciliation, or waive his rights and pardon the wrong. Where public penalties of punishment were ordained, in addition to private damages, the injured party was primarily entitled to institute the charge; but his right to settle or abandon the case was limited in various ways, in the interest of public authority. The rule is accordingly laid down in the law of Skåne, King Erik's Law of Sjælland, and other Northern legislation, that after reconciliation made for a wrongful act as being accidental, the royal official was empowered to require verification by oath that the act was not wilful; the injured party to be the first of the defendant's witnesses. Moreover, the authority of the official to prosecute immediately after an offense

[3] [About A.D. 1250. — TRANSL.]

or to carry on a cause instituted by a private person, is recognized, by the law of Sjælland especially, in several provisions; evidencing that this power could be exercised to a considerable extent. And if, in general, the right of accusation belonged to the private party, and that of the king's representative was only subsidiary and exceptional, yet it appears from specific provisions that the latter could commence or intervene in the proceedings on almost any occasion, wherever there was reason to fear that the jurisdiction of the king would be lost because of the unwillingness or inability of the private prosecutor to institute or proceed with the action.

This privilege applied to all cases of murder and "forty mark" offenses, wherein the complainant either sought to wreak personal vengeance or was unable to start or follow up the prosecution. So also, in cases of wounds, for which the victim had failed to accuse or proceed in the cause, the official could prosecute the offender, and in addition the injured party was fined three marks for his laxness. In all these instances, however, official complaint was conditioned upon the wrongful act being an undoubted fact and notorious throughout the "Herred" or district. Larceny and robbery were subject to official prosecution only when suit was instituted but not followed up by the victim; the latter then being also subject to fine. While the object of such public action in the foregoing cases was solely that of enforcing the king's prerogative to exact fines, without controlling the relation between the parties committing and suffering the offense, other cases are enumerated in the laws in which it was the duty of the public official to assist the complainant, when a helpless widow or minor, or a person sojourning abroad without relations able to prosecute his claim. Then (as well as in all cases where the offended person had not forfeited his right by laches), it was the duty of the official to secure satisfaction for the private party first and then for the king.

Crimes subject to outlawry and not atonable by money fines, were to be prosecuted by the king's official; and for these the private victim was permitted neither to accept damages or renounce his right of vengeance, without the consent of the king. In the region of the Jydske law, a pact between the inhabitants and their bishop, made with royal sanction, in 1228, indicates that a rule here prevailed, similar to that of Sjælland, that official prosecution could be made for wounds only when the victim had made a complaint, or where the misdeed was open and notorious; for the bishop in this agreement surrendered the power theretofore exercised by him, of instituting, by his delegate, but without such condition precedent, a proceeding against such an assailant for infraction of church rules; this prerogative evidently having been considered an exception. In the Jydske Code, however, this canonical prerogative was later restored, in disregard of the pact, while the right, conferred by the latter, to summon into court both the offender and the injured party if they had made a reconciliation outside of the bishop's court, was retained. In the Articles of Thord Degn and in Erik's Code of Sjælland a provision appears, imposing a fine of three marks to the king on the party wounded for failing to proceed with his cause, and further authorizing the "Fogede" (the royal bailiff) to vindicate the right of the crown where the injured party fails to enter complaint. A party robbed who failed to pursue his action before the twelve true men, after having instituted it, was amenable under the Jydske Code to a fine of three marks to the king and the accused. Public accusations for this crime seem to have been as rare as for larceny. Even in manslaughter this seems to have been the case, notwithstanding the kin of the deceased had failed to proceed with their cause; but here, also, a larger fine for the king became due where reconciliation was made outside of court. In the Jydske Code there is in fact nothing indicating certainly that the public authority was to institute proceedings even for felonies beyond the degree expiable by fine ("Ubødemaal"); and it is very doubtful whether the Code, in its provisions for the infliction of punishments, does not assume either that a previous private complaint was made or that the offender was apprehended in the act and brought to the "Thing." This Code, which is more harsh than Erik's Code of Sjælland in its punitive measures, would seem thus not to authorize public and official accusations to the same extent as the Code of Sjælland.

Accessories. — Where several persons had together committed an offense, they could clear themselves with a single fine by holding together in declaring that they had been "equally good", where it was only an issue whether the act was an accident ("um the wiliæ samæn wære, tha bøtæ ikky mære æn enæ bøtær"). Otherwise, the general rule was enforced that every participant in the act, including mere accessories, should pay the full fine. For grave crimes punishment was meted out even to a companion of the wrongdoer, who had taken no part in the commission of the offense ("in comitatu"; "i færth oc i fylgi"), — a fine of three marks to the private complainant and a like amount to the king. This provision was inserted in the proclamation for Skåne of Canute VI, December 28, 1200, for cases of murder, and became thereafter part of the Code of that province; and a similar rule was applied, under the Sjælland Codes, in all cases too grave for mere fines and in all "forty-mark suits." The reason for this provision was undoubtedly the not infrequent practice of those times for a bandit to sally forth with a large retinue of his kin and allies, generally armed, to commit the plotted deed (especially to fulfil a feud of vengeance), when the mere presence of his companions served as his support. An example of this doctrine of punishing an accessory before the fact is presented in the case (referred to already) of one person lending another a weapon for the purpose of murder; by all the provincial Codes he was amenable to a fine of three marks. Counseling and abetting misdemeanors was penalized only exceptionally; Erik's Code of Sjælland mentions only the taking of life, when the instigator was fined nine marks; but the Code of Skåne exacted this penalty, to the extent of three marks, when any one by his advice brought about the imprisonment of another or influenced a magnate to do violence to another's property. — The responsibility of the master of the house ("Husbonde") for the acts of those under him was recognized. For misdeeds done by his serfs ("Traelle") or free servants by his direction, and in the case of the former, by his suggestion, he was adjudged the transgressor. Furthermore Valdemar's Code of Sjælland exempts from fine one commanding his thrall, or free follower, to assault another, where the command is not carried out. This is not inconsistent with the Skåne rule, holding that he who by force is prevented from striking another is as guilty as if he had carried out his intent; nor with that of the Jydske Code, which likewise condemns an assailant whose blow misses and reaches only his victim's garb or horse. The mere attempt was, at this stage of the law, not punished, unless it had got as far as an actual attack, as in the last-mentioned cases. This doctrine on the whole represents the general tenor of the various provisions on this point in medieval Germanic and Northern law.

Elements of the Money Forfeitures. — The essential distinction made between private and public fines, the former being regarded as restitution and damages for the subjective injuries of rights, and the latter as reparation for the objective infraction of justice, is pointed out by Archbishop Anders Suneson. He also clearly separates the satisfaction obtained by the offended party for the personal affront, with the indeterminate compensation incident thereto, from the reparation for the actual material loss sustained, both of which elements enter into the private "Bøde" ("duplicata quadraginta marcarum satisfactione, una regi pro violatione iusticie alteraque pro irrogatione iniurie"). This difference is also evidenced throughout the Codes, so that the term "at bøtæ" (to atone; to forfeit money as punishment) implies paying the debt for the dishonored right, as opposed to the phrase "at gjælde" (to give equivalent), signifying a making good of the property loss. Both terms, however, are used for each conception, whence doubt often arises as to what is included in the action.

In determining the amount of the fine, the basis of calculation was one silver mark (eight ounces of silver), which was of equal value to eight "Øre," a coin exchangeable for three "Ørtuger," and the latter in turn being ten "Penninge" (money; pennies). In course of time, however, as the weight of minted coins was decreased, this relative value changed, and in the period of the provincial Codes one silver mark equaled three marks in pennies. Unless the term "silver mark" was expressly used in provisions as to fines, one mark signified the minor coin standard. Some exceptions to this are noted; but it would appear that the king's fine was not affected by fluctuations in the relative values of coins, except by the king's grace. The more ancient practice of making restitution by goods instead of money, such as cloth or cattle, regarding which the earliest legal sources of Norway and Iceland contain extensive regulations, was still largely retained. Where the amount of physical damages sustained was easily ascertainable, the legal private fine could be demanded aside from such compensation; but where the loss was irreparable, as in cases of injury to limb or affront to personal honor, the pecuniary forfeiture included also satisfaction for this element, and the amount consequently varied considerably according to the nature and extent of the wrong. Instances appear of fines from one "Øre" to six marks, and by cumulative fines for several injuries there was sometimes paid a sum of five silver marks or fifteen penny marks. This latter combination, however, according to Suneson, was made only where charges of manslaughter and robbery were joined, or several injuries to limbs; the complainant in other cases having to choose a particular charge, thereby excluding claim for other fines, yet still being entitled to be reimbursed for his actual loss sustained.

Forty-Mark and Three-Mark Causes. — Distinguished from these purely private mulcts, there are found in all the provincial Codes two fines, of forty and of three marks respectively, which were more in the nature of punishment, offenses being thus divided into "forty-mark" and "three-mark" causes.

The first class included breaches of a special peace, that is, misdemeanors which were not of the degree of felonies beyond expiation by pecuniary forfeitures. Among these are mentioned the following in Erik's Code of Sjælland, (whose provisions are in part similar to those of the other Codes of the period): (1) manslaughter, wounds and other mayhem, in fulfilling a feud of vengeance on one to whom the assailant had made a guaranty of peace and immunity, or who had promised to pay fines and damages; the acceptance of such a promise and the reconciliation thereby presumed operating as an implied warrant of safety; (2) breaches of the peace of the church and eyre or "Thing" by wounds or blows, and murder on the road to the assizes; the Jydske Code, however, declaring the latter crime, as well as murder committed in the presence of the "Thing," to be too grave for pecuniary amends; (3) breach of the peace of the market by manslaughter, wounds, or blows; (4) breach of the peace of the home and hearth by violence and ravage, including, in this class, similar havoc wrought in any one's ship, and the taking of a person's life while in his shore booth; (5) imprisonment, kidnapping, and rape; the latter, however, being declared by the Jydske Code too grave an offense for ransom by fine; and (6) willful arson of the house, mill, or other structure of another, except where attended with loss of life. The Jydske and Skåne Codes also assign to this degree of felonies a breach of the king's peace by wounding or maltreating another while the king was in the same "Herred," or district, according to the former Code, or in the same province, according to the latter. Robbery of corpses was also included in the former Code, while the latter provided a penalty of three marks, and Erik's Law of Sjælland one of nine marks for this offense. These forty-mark mulcts were regarded as an expiation for the breach of the public peace, and the offender must also pay the private damages for affronts and losses, varying according to the nature of the act; this principle also being applied to his companions, who were subject to the public fine of three marks. There was furthermore a general rule that where the injured party was entitled to these forty and three marks, similar amounts were also to be forfeited to the king by the chief aggressor and his accessories. All forty-mark prosecutions were disposed of at the "Land-thing", which referred them for investigation to a body of its members, resembling a jury, termed in Sjælland "Nævninger" and in Jylland "Sandemænd" (true men).

The only public fines accruing to the "king's right," other than the above forty-mark cases, were the three-mark penalties, except cases of self-redress, where the amounts varied. These three-mark fines, which are frequently inserted in the Grágas and the Codes of Norway (the latter terming them "full right"), are imposed not only for crimes but also in certain civil cases. A peculiar feature is that they were at times both a private and a public penalty and in other cases only one of the two. In the first instance, the payment was generally three marks to the complainant and a similar amount to the royal exchequer; the latter fine always being fixed at such amount, while the former occasionally varied between smaller and larger amounts. The double penalty was inflicted chiefly in the following cases: (1) robbery and trespass (with some exceptions); (2) accessories, presumed from companionship (already explained); (3) wounds; the payment to the injured party here varying from six marks (when the weapon entered the body or limb or penetrated it completely), to three marks (for lesser injuries). Under Canute VI's Ordinance for Skåne and the Skåne Code, one guilty of inflicting wounds incurred always a royal penalty of three marks; whereas in Sjælland the public fine was imposed only where the wounds were so serious as to necessitate the calling of the surgeon. The Jydske Code, while silent on this subject, declares that for wounds inflicted by chance no fines are payable to the king. (4) For the slaying of cattle, there was a double fine of three marks, one for the king and the other for the owner. (5) In Sjælland and Jylland, for theft of articles worth less than half a mark, where the thief was caught in the act or with the stolen goods in his possession, three marks went to the king. (6) In all provincial Codes there were several provisions for this double fine for "impeding right" (contempt of court), — where a person legally summoned absented himself without sufficient cause from the "Thing", or in other mode displayed arrogance or refused to fulfil a duty imposed by law; where a person removed timber which he had cut on another's premises, after prohibition by the owner; where an oath-bound promise was not performed. So, too, the grantor of land, unable to deliver good title, in Jylland had to pay the double three-mark fine, but in other districts only to the buyer; on the other hand this fine was to be claimed by the king alone when the "old men" (witnesses to title) would not make oath.

In contrast to the finable misdeeds stand those heinous crimes, which could not be atoned for by money, but involved outlawry or some other public punishment. These are termed in the provincial Codes, both of Sweden and of Norway, unfinable cases ("Orbøtæmal"). Being generally heinous breaches of peace and faith, or vilely treacherous in their manner of commission, they are termed "infamous deeds" ("Nithingsværk"). On the question which transgressions were to be classed of this degree, there was more or less conflict between the various Codes; and this fact is certainly responsible largely for the gradual change in the penal system.

Outlawry. — The term "peace", in legal phraseology, like the term "right", has both a subjective and an objective meaning. It signifies in part the position of the individual, as entitled to the recognition by others of certain rights, which society has undertaken to protect against unjustifiable infractions, and in part the general public system of law and order. Every violation of a right thus imports theoretically a breach of the peace in this double sense. But in a less developed notion were included in this double sense only gross violations of right and such acts as involved the breach of some specially important class of peace. The offender who by his act had forfeited that status in society which entitled him to its protection was declared "without peace" ("fredløs", "utlagar"). The basic principle therefore in the early Northern legal system was that whoever would not recognize the rights of others, should not himself enjoy any. So long as self-redress was regarded as permissible for the injured party, the offender's "peacelessness", at least in relation to the injured party, ensued as an immediate consequence of the misdeed, without any necessity for bringing the cause before the "Thing" or obtaining judgment.

But the gradual limitation and restraints imposed on private vengeance, as already described, show that quite early the rule came into vogue that outlawry should be incurred only upon a decree of the men convoked in the "Thing." Furthermore, the outlawed offender was allowed a certain period for escaping from the revenge thus sanctioned; being immune from attack for the entire day when the decree was promulgated and the succeeding night, in Skåne and Sjælland, for a day and a month in Jylland, where the period was later shortened to three days and nights. At the expiration of this respite, his deprivation of the peace became effective with all its strictness; he was in total outlawry. While a price was not placed on his head (as in the Icelandic Grágas), he was exposed to the feud of his opponent or the blood vengeance of the latter's kin; and according to the general rule (as Archbishop Suneson records it) his life could be taken by any one. He was further ostracized from all intercourse with the members of the community; every one was prohibited, under the three-mark penalty, from harboring him or in any way dealing with him; even the monastery sanctuary was barred to him as an asylum. His possessions escheated to the king, after his victim or the heirs and relatives of the latter had received satisfaction; and it would appear, from the ancient Danish sources, as well as the earlier Swedish and Norwegian codes and the municipal Ordinance of Slesvig, that this forfeiture for what were classed as "heinous crimes" extended both to real and personal property. The later provincial Codes, however, limited this forfeiture to personalty only, on the principle that none can forfeit his landed estate, or more than his personal effects; the only exception (named by Anders Suneson and the Code of Sjælland) being the crime of treason, and this provision was adopted in the Ordinance of Erik Glipping for Nyborg, in 1282, and in King Oluf's Charter.

On comparing the later provincial Codes with the earlier Ordinances of Canute VI and Valdemar II for Skåne, distinctions and changes will be noted, in that certain offenses, which had previously been adjudged causes of outlawry, might now be cleared by fines (outlawry resulting only when these were not paid), while other crimes, once subject to fines only, were given heavier punishment than fines. The following is a list of the later outlawry crimes, according to Suneson: (1) murder or wounding in vengeance of one who already had paid fines, or who had been acquitted; (2) murder at the "Thing" or (according to the Code of Jylland), on the road to the "Thing"; (3) murder in the church or the churchyard; (4) murder combined with ravage or breach of hearth and home; the Ordinance of Canute VI and the Code of Skåne, however, classing this crime as finable, and Suneson limiting outlawry to murder committed by a guest on his host, or vice versa, — here altering the earlier rule; (5) murder during the presence of the king in the same province, in the Ordinance of Valdemar II and of Skåne, the Jylland law limiting the territory to the same "Herred", and the Code of Sjælland being silent on the subject; (6) for kidnapping the betrothed, wife, mother, sister, or daughter of another, there is a contradiction in Suneson; in one place he classes this crime as subject to outlawry, and in another place states that rape is a forty-mark offense (as also appears in the Skåne, Sjælland, and the old Slesvig town laws); from a fragment of an earlier code of Skåne, and the Code of Jylland, terming such crimes "heinous", these changes would appear to have been made during the reign of Valdemar II; (7) arson likewise is declared by Suneson to be punishable by outlawry, but in another place (agreeing with the Code of Skåne), by death, the latter being inflicted in Sjælland and Jylland only where loss of life resulted from arson and the miscreant was caught in the act, — otherwise he could become a fugitive, losing the "peace", while proved arson alone was a forty-mark case; (8) failure to pay fines for manslaughter rendered the defendant an outlaw under the ordinances of Skåne and Valdemar II, as well as in Suneson's account; Valdemar's Code of Sjælland also provides that the manslaughterer, after having bought his peace from the king, should tender damages to the relatives of the deceased; if the latter did not venture to insist that the crime was unfinable, he should be notified of the terms of his peace, outlawry attaching only upon his failure to pay his fines; Erik's Code for the same province also imposed outlawry for failure to pay fines for manslaughter (though manslaughter was not in itself subject to outlawry) or for other forty-mark crimes.

The distinction is here to be noted between two kinds of peace-purchase, — the one affording the offender a means of escaping outlawry in the first instance, and the other restoring him into peace after the latter had been lost, this being possible only by the consent of the king and of the offended party or his kin. Thus, the Jydske Code provided that where the murderer promptly tendered the lawful fines, the cause would not go to the "true men" (or jurors at the "Thing"); while if no tender was made, he was either outlawed or ordered to pay fines, according as the court found that he had taken the life of an offenseless man or had acted in self-defense or in justifiable feud; but if he became "peaceless" or was found by the verdict to merit outlawry, he could regain his peace only by the consent of the king and the injured party.

Where the three-mark penalty (imposed in various civil and misdemeanor cases for contempt and disobedience of the legal authorities) was not paid, outlawry was also applicable; but gradually for this default there came into vogue a minor degree of outlawry. This is found in the Code of Skåne for theft only, where the defendant has first been outlawed at the "Thing of the Herred" ("Madband"); he was excluded from all intercourse with the inhabitants of the "Hundred", and later was declared "without peace" at the "Thing of the Land" by reason of defaulting before that assembly. This case is likewise dealt with in Valdemar's Code of Sjælland, the expression here used being "loss of personal security" ("Manhælg"); the same sentence also being imposed upon one charged with assault or robbery who fails to clear himself in some mode; there is no mention, however, of proceedings at the "Land-thing." A similar "loss of personal security" is provided for in Erik's Code of Sjælland for those guilty of assault, who, when persisting in contempt, are finally declared outlaws by the "Land-thing." So the Jydske Code imposes a like penalty where amends are not made for wounds or claims for wages not satisfied. This judgment was thus evidently not intended as a punishment for the crime, but for the failure to submit to authority and as a pressure to enforce payment of the fines which would absolve the fugitive from the judgment. The outlawry had effect only within the jurisdiction of the "Thing", whether "Herred" or "Land", but the extent of the loss of security differed, in that under Valdemar's Code of Sjælland a general loss of legal protection seems to have resulted, whereas Erik's Code for that province and the Jydske Code limited the right of injuring him to the accuser only, who could strike and wound him, yet not deprive him of life or limb nor attack him in a sanctuary.

Other Public Punishments. — Thus, in the provincial Codes the general rule was that offenses could be atoned for by fines and damages, but that where these were not forthcoming, or where the crime itself was so heinous as not to be atonable by fine, outlawry ensued. The outlawed person, in either case, if he neither availed himself of the legal period of flight, nor purchased his peace, became completely "rightless." He might be slain by any one with impunity. The king could have him chastised and corrected, as appears in various laws. Until a free man had thus been outlawed, however, the public authority had no power to inflict punishment on him.

The only exception to this rule in the provincial Codes was for theft. This offense was deemed in the earlier ages the vilest of crimes, and the thief did not share the privileges preserved for those accused of other crimes previous to outlawry. Some of the punishments inflicted for theft were unknown for other offenses, *e.g.* serfdom and maiming. In determining the punishment the judges must have regard to the value of the stolen goods, and to whether or not the defendant had been caught in the act or the missing property been found in his possession. The boundary between grand and petty larceny in all the Danish provinces was three penny-marks; capital punishment was inflicted only where the value of the goods stolen was not less than this amount and where in addition the thief had been caught in the act and brought to the "Thing." By the Code of Skåne, a thief might be hung; but the penalty for petty larceny varied from the whipping post to loss of limb or serfdom to the king. For church theft, or robbery combined with murder, he was broken on the wheel, or (according to Suneson) stoned or burned to death. To these provisions Valdemar's Code of Sjælland adds that the "men of the Thing" shall decide upon the nature of the punishment for grand larceny, with the approval of the complainant. The Jydske Code names capital punishment as the regular penalty for grand larceny where the thief has been caught in the act, or been found with the stolen goods in his possession, or confessed the crime. It also contains a notable reference to the injured person's right (formerly conceded, and still retained in the town Code of Slesvig) to slay the thief when caught in the act; this being now a prohibited form of self-vengeance, but the king's bailiff having the power to hang him without hearing and judgment. For petty larceny, the thief was branded with the thief-mark, and for a second offense he was hung, regardless of the value of the stolen goods.

The crime of arson carried the death penalty in all the provinces. By the Code of Skåne, whoever by the ordeal of hot iron was found guilty of deliberate arson and was arrested after the lapse of the period allowed for his escape, was to be hung. According to Suneson, the death penalty applied where arson was committed for the purpose of theft; while, by Erik's Code of Sjælland and by that of Jylland, this was done only where arson was combined with murder and the miscreant caught in the act; here the mode prescribed by the Sjælland Code was specifically burning at the stake or breaking on the wheel or casting down from a cliff. Where not caught in the act, but convicted by law, he was accorded the customary period of escape; at its expiration the same penalties applied, unless he was pardoned by the king's grace. — Capital punishment is also decreed by the Jydske Code for counterfeiting and robbery.

Wherever life was forfeited, the movable property of the culprit, remaining after satisfaction made to the victim, escheated to the king.

§ 39*c*. **Penal Legislation A.D. 1300–1500.** — The foregoing account of the provincial Codes shows that the penal law was still generally considered as having chiefly a private character, both as to the specific crimes, the penalties imposed, and the mode of prosecution. For most offenses amends could be made by fines to the injured party and to the ruler. Were these not forthcoming, the accused could be forced into outlawry; outlawry, furthermore, ensued directly as the penalty for the graver crimes; capital punishment was inflicted only for a few offenses deemed especially treacherous and vile. The right of complaint for wrongs amenable to fine inhered primarily in the offended party, public prosecution being here only subsidiary, and usually only where the crime was notorious; but for crimes not atonable by fine, especially when notorious, public prosecution was the regular mode.

In the sources and authorities of the succeeding centuries up to the 1500 s, no general or radical alterations in this system are apparent, other than that the punishments for certain crimes were made more severe, and that certain of the earlier provisions were not always enforced. Thus the older rules are repeated almost without change in the Ordinances of Erik Glipping of 1282, 1283, and 1284. So, too, is reënacted in the Ordinances for Vordingborg and Nyborg, of 1282, the rule of the provincial Codes applicable to theft, that no one shall be imprisoned unless caught in the act or legally convicted of a crime punishable by forfeiture of life or limb; to this provision the Vording law adds murder, rape, or mayhem done in a village where the king is present; and the Nyborg law adds that one not caught in the act, nor proved guilty in other manner, shall have the legal time for making his escape, and that no punishments shall be inflicted other than such as are described in the law nor unless the accused is legally proved guilty. These regulations were almost literally repeated in the later Charters (" Haandfæstninger ").

Was the feud-revenge on kindred still countenanced? The Helsingborg Ordinance of 1283, after reënacting the provisions of Valdemar's Code for Skåne, that the relatives of the murderer are not in duty bound to contribute to the "man-fine", unless he had become an outlawed fugitive, expressly prohibits the victim's kin from taking vengeance on the guilty one's kin while he was yet alive, classing such revenge as unprovoked murder. A similar rule is also laid down in the Articles of Thord Degn, which also penalize violent acts of vengeance with a royal fine of forty marks and outlawry; such self-redress being declared to be a contempt of the king's judicial authority. This Ordinance of Helsingborg, in 1283, also accords with the earlier Provincial Codes in penalizing acts of violence ("Hærvaerk") with fines of forty marks, and murder in church or in the home of the slain with outlawry. The Ordinances of 1284, however, are more severe, decreeing outlawry also for mayhem inflicted at such places, also applying this penalty to the companions of the wrongdoer, and including such offenses when done against a guest in the house of a third party. The Jydske Code provides death for such crimes, where the offender is caught in the act; and it adds an express provision for public prosecution in such cases, this being prescribed by the Articles of Thord Degn only where a fine was due to the king. These ordinances also reproduced the provision of the provincial Codes that one sentenced to pay fines for a grave offense who failed within the time allowed to render satisfaction or produce a bondsman should be outlawed.

Market-Town Laws. — The "peace of the village" is referred to as early as the Jydske Code. A crime committed within the boundaries of the village was subject to an additional and special fine; so that murder or injury to limb involved a penalty of forty marks, — the amount in some cases going to the village exclusively, in addition to that due the king, and in other cases being divided between the local and the general government. In the "Market Towns" ("Kjøbstaederne"), the claims of the offended party were generally satisfied first, before the public fines were exacted; one exception is found, however, in the general Town Code of Queen Margaret (1294), in which the royal claim came first, that of the offended party next, and then the claim of the town. That these Town Ordinances contemplated general public indictments is indicated by various passages, — as where it is said that public prosecutions are not proper for acts of chance or accident or in self-defense, nor during "holy time"; that they shall be made at the village "Thing"; and also that the king's officer shall not be limited to notorious crimes in filing charges. Other provisions aimed at preserving the peace of the village, preventing offenses, and insuring the punishment of offenders. Such are the oft recurring rules that all burghers are in duty bound to come to the rescue of one attacked, and to apprehend a fugitive offender and deliver him to the bailiff; the apprehender being entitled to share in the fine. Carrying weapons in public places was likewise prohibited. Fugitive offenders were to be listed, and their names were later announced yearly at the "Thing."

Besides the general "peace of the village", the city and provincial Codes also name a "peace of the market", the day and hour for holding the market being specified; and in the town Code of Kopenhagen (1294) the king's peace is specially mentioned. Outlawry is the penalty for certain crimes; for failure to pay fines and damages, outlawry could be inflicted, as also imprisonment or loss of life or limb. In these town codes and charters (A.D. 1294, 1485, 1507, etc.) it was furthermore expressly stated that outlawry there inflicted was effective throughout the realm, and vice versa; that the outlaw could regain his peace only by making amends to all concerned, and should forfeit his life otherwise on returning. In the earlier town Codes of Kopenhagen (dating from the time when the city was under the bishop's rule), life-imprisonment was provided for several crimes which in later laws entailed death in that town (and in other towns at an earlier date).

The increasing severity of punishment in the later town Codes is especially noticeable in the general Town Code of Queen Margaret; but there is considerable variance in this respect. The earlier town Law of Skåne allowed manslaughter to be atoned with fines, while in the charters granted to several market towns in Skåne by Valdemar Atterdag (A.D. 1361, 1415) outlawry was imposed. Manslaughter, in the town Code of Roskilde (A.D. 1268), was fined, the amount varying according to whether the offender was a burgher or a stranger; and the Kopenhagen Code of 1294 imposed imprisonment for life; while that of Queen Margaret (1387–1412) prescribed capital punishment for every murder; as also the later Kopenhagen Code and the general Town Code of King Hans (1481–1513).

B. SWITZERLAND [1]

§ 39*d*. **The Common Law of the Later Middle Ages (Peace; Pledged and Commanded Peace; Crimes; Penalties).** — In the Germanic districts which now form Switzerland, there were many local variances of detail. But the general features of the common law were substantially the same in all the cantons, even in those using what is now the French language. The South German law-book, the "Schwabenspiegel", did not possess any general authority, nor was it even a general model. Each canton had some special enactments of its own. The Bern "Gerichtssatzung" (Judiciary Act) of 1593 is the most representative source for the body of later medieval tradition. The old Swiss common law was markedly the product of local ideas and needs. In form, its features were simplicity and a concreteness of detail.

In substance, it was the old Germanic *peace-law*, but based on a special sense of personal "honor" most marked in the sturdy free communities of these uplands. The basis of the respect for the peace-command was the honor of the participants. The peace-breaker was honor-less, a breaker of faith; this was the basic principle. "The peace-breaker", said the Zug Book of Laws, "shall for two years be deemed a perjurer and honor-less; his word shall neither hurt nor help any one. He shall bear no other weapon than a broken sickle, and shall for one half-year drink no wine outside of his own house."

The more modern notion of "peace" as public and general law and order is alien to the medieval idea. In the earlier thought there were only specific "peaces" ("Friede"). The most general forms were of course the peace of the land and the peace of God. But there was also the peace of the town, of the army, of the market, of the church, of the court, of the home.

An important part is played by the "pledged peace" and the "commanded peace", *i.e.* a peace specially supervening between individuals. The pledged peace takes the form of a voluntary settlement of a quarrel by the parties. The commanded peace is a higher form, imposed on them by authority. Every member of the community has a right and a duty to command the peace, to part the combatants, and to pursue the wrongdoer. When a quarrel arises, any citizen may and must command the peace of

[1] [This section is by the Editor; its authority is the treatise of Dr. PFENNINGER; for this Author and work, see the Editorial Preface. — ED.]

the land (or of the lord). The parties must be separated (and the details of the proceeding were carefully regulated), and must then clasp hands in peace. Thenceforth they are under a special responsibility; and a curse, an insult, or even a contemptuous word will be a breach of this peace. To evade this more serious responsibility was naturally a frequent object of the parties — by refusal and flight, for example — and the law took note of this in some of its measures. The special peace was limited in its duration, — sometimes, by order of the judge, until the next market day or like term; but often, by custom, till the parties next ate and drank together, and the evasion of this, by a feigned friendly act, was also struck at by law.

The importance of the peace as a basis of the criminal law is seen in the numerous prohibitions of conduct likely to lead to a breach of the peace, — placing hand on sword, lifting a stone, lying in wait, insults, etc. These have sometimes been construed as early recognitions of the doctrine of *attempt*. But the emphasis was not so much on the intent or preparation as on the prevention of a breach of the peace. It cannot be conceded that there was as yet any distinct recognition of attempt as an independent offense, nor of criminal intent in the modern sense.

Another aspect of the peace-law is seen in its reliance upon the *citizen's duty to interfere* to keep the peace. No public police existed. Only gradually and later was there a magistracy with "ex officio" powers and duties to arrest. The medieval principle of the individual citizen's duty to help is in strong contrast with the later attitude (bred by generations of strong magisterial authority) which finds the citizen cautious about meddling and ready enough to leave all such matters to the official police.

Still another aspect is the important distinctions based on *personal honor*. Offenses as well as punishments were classified by their relation to this sense of honor. Murder and stealing are honor-losing; manslaughter and robbery are honor-keeping. Breach of faith and fraud are honor-losing; an open act of anger is honor-keeping. Injury done in mutual combat with weapons is honor-keeping; injury to a weaponless man is honor-losing.

And finally, as another aspect of the peace-system, is to be noted the persistence of the *self-help* principle for the victim of a wrong. The blood-feud is still found, especially in the primitive cantons, at the close of the Middle Ages. The right of every free man to bear and use arms and to vindicate his family and personal honor is seen in this long survival. Its spirit appears in the formula of the Bern Judiciary Act (1593) for delivering the body of the fleeing homicide to his victim's family: "If after summons in open meeting he does not appear, let him be known as gone out of peace to no-peace, out of safety to un-safety, and let the killer's body be delivered to the friends of the lifeless one to do as they think fit."

Crimes.—No complete emuneration of offenses is given in the statutes. Custom and discretion controlled more or less. Murder was the killing of one with whom there was a pledged peace, — punished by death on the wheel; for manslaughter, the penalty was beheading. Bodily injuries were still classified in detail, — wounding, bloodletting, mayhem, blows with and without weapons, hand-laying, and so on. How far was *self-defense* and *self-redress* ("Nothwehr", necessity) recognized? In early Germanic law, this principle of excuse or extenuation is given a very broad scope; it could be used even for stealing and other property wrongs, and it justified death done upon the wrongdoer. But gradually it became restricted; "lawful necessity" ("rechte Nothwehr"), a phrase of the "Schwabenspiegel", represents this restricted principle. In Swiss law its gradual limitations did not so much go to the kinds of wrongs for which it was available, as to the kinds of harm permissible; to inflict death was allowable only in the extremest cases. Here the judge's discretion played a large part.

Penalties. — *Fines* in the nature of private settlements still persisted long after State authority was well organized. Then these were replaced by a judge-imposed fine, divided between the court and the injured person. Finally, the court takes the whole fine, leaving the injured person to his private suit for compensation. Both stages are seen in the Bern Judiciary Act of 1593.

Meanwhile, *corporal penalties* come into use, as a part of the growing system of repression by political authority. Town government becomes more powerful. The burghers' tradal prosperity asserts itself, alike against robber barons and the lower vagabond and criminal classes. Deterrence by fear is the dominant spirit of this system. There was no organized preventive repression by police methods. Imprisonment as a punishment is scarcely known. Cruel modes of the death penalty are devised; along with hanging and beheading are found wheel-breaking, boiling, burning, burying alive, empaling, and immuring. Mutilation is a frequent mode, — tongue-slicing, ear-clipping, hand-hewing, eye-scooping, hot-iron-searing, and scalping (in three cantons). The notion of "lex talionis" — an eye for an eye, a tooth for a tooth — is constantly apparent. The occasional penalties of loss of freedom were the prison, the galleys, house-detention, and restriction to a specified locality. Banishment was the chief penalty of this sort; it varied much in the periods of time and the district of expulsion. Confiscation of property usually attended it.

The *honor-penalties* were elaborated. They involved a loss of honor and of weapon for a greater or less time, usually with some ignoble incident, such as carrying a broken weapon, dragging a stone, standing at the church-door, wearing an unseemly garment.

The application of the severest penalties was, to be sure, more or less rare; commutation of a cruel death to simple death, or of death to banishment, is frequently recorded. The lay-judge of the popular governments tended to milder penalties than the official judge of the imperial and royal regions.

Chapter VI

FRANCE IN THE LATER MIDDLE AGES[1]

§ 39e. **General Features of Medieval Criminal Law in France.** — The Custumals of the Middle Ages contain no account of what we call to-day the theory of criminal law. No endeavor was made in those days to determine carefully what constitutes the true basis of the right to punish, the desirable qualities of a punishment, and the defects to be avoided. Our ancient authors accept without inquiry the very simple, but often altogether false, ideas which were current in their time. The Italian jurisconsults of the 1300 s were in advance of our own; for Gandinus, Bartolus, and Baldus in their writings allotted a relatively important part to criminal law; yet even they, in spite of the early Renascence of law in their country, did not study the problem of the right to punish, — did not even seem to suspect its existence. We find in their works numerous details concerning judiciary organization, the procedure of penal tribunals, and punishments, but no thought concerning the nature and extent of the right to punish. All, however, strive to give greater prominence to inquisitorial procedure, that is, to the procedure initiated by the judge.[2] Baldus advocates this procedure as soon as a criminal act is publicly known; but, while trying by this means to assure a more general and efficacious repression, he carefully avoids the subtleties of scholasticism; unlike other jurisconsults of his time, he condemns torture, and

[1] [This chapter = Glasson, "Histoire du droit et des institutions de la France", Part IV, Chapter xii, Vol. VI, pp. 640–705. For this author and work, see the Editorial Preface. — Ed.]

[2] [On these points of procedure, see *Esmein's* "History of Continental Criminal Procedure", Vol. V of the present Series. — Ed.]

claims even that the judge ought to incur the death penalty if the accused when subjected to torture dies from the effect of the suffering.[3] As for French practitioners, sometimes they followed Germanic or Roman traditions, sometimes they were prompted by the opinions of the Church; but never did they attempt to construct a purely rational penal system. This question did not yet even exist for them. Certain crimes, such as homicide [" meurtre "], arson, battery, wounding, and insult, were punished according to the old Germanic traditions. Other crimes, such as heresy and usury, had a clearly canonical origin.

Not infrequently, too, through the influence of the Church, we find the punishments of conscience mingled with those of society. Many penalties, such as penance, " l'amende honorable," pilgrimage, and especially excommunication, which ought to have preserved a purely religious character, found their way more or less into the law; though this did not extend beyond an imitation of practices common in the previous period, especially under the Carolingians. The secular criminal judge, moreover, often took into consideration the confession and the repentance of the culprit, and on these grounds diminished the punishment to a marked and even excessive extent. That the judge should proceed thus in the tribunal of conscience we can easily understand; but it was dangerous to follow the same method in secular justice.

Though some of the punishments inflicted in the Middle Ages originated in the old Germanic regional Customs (chief among these is the fine, certain forms of mutilation, and perhaps even hanging), yet certain offenses are borrowed from Roman law. This, however, was at the end rather than at the beginning of the Middle Ages. In the earlier days, criminal justice had been exercised chiefly by the courts of the feudal lords and even by those of

[3] See on these various points: *Savigny*, "Histoire du droit au moyen âge", trans. *Guénoux*, Vol. IV, especially pp. 184, 201, 203, 227; *Du Boys*, "Histoire du droit criminel de la France, depuis le XVIe jusqu'au XIXe siècle", Vol. V, p. 271, *et seq.;* Bethmann-Hollweg gives a list of the jurisconsults of the epoch who treated the question of criminal procedure and incidentally touched upon certain questions of penal law. The most famous in the 1100s and 1200s are Bulgarus, Placentinus, Albertus Galeotus, Hubertus de Bonacurso, Hubertus de Bobio, Rolandinus de Romanciis, Giovanni Andrea, Albertus de Gandino, and Jacobus de Belvisio. Most notable is the name of Guillaume Durant (or, Durandus), born in 1237, the author of "Speculum juris". See *Bethmann-Hollweg*, "Der Civilprocess des gemeinen Rechts," Vol. VI, §§ 129, *et seq.*, p. 197, where considerable information concerning these jurisconsults and their work will be found. On this same subject see also *Savigny*, "Histoire du droit romain au moyen âge."

certain cities. The assiduous efforts put forth by royalty to regain the right of jurisdiction over feudalism are well known. Royalty was stoutly seconded in this task by the legists (or secular jurists), who labored at transforming feudal criminal law into royal criminal law. It was in this period that they revived a large number of the old Roman laws. Even the 1300 s and 1400 s saw the law-makers reëstablish the crime of "lèse majesté", as it had been understood by the Roman jurisconsults of the imperial epoch, with the sole aim of consolidating the authority of the king and of raising his person still higher in the social hierarchy.

But if it is only incidentally and, as it were, casually that the jurisconsults give any hints as to the nature and the basis of the right to punish, they try very early, nevertheless, to classify both crimes and punishments. Most of the old Custumals strive to group the violations of the law and even set down for each of them the punishment which is ordinarily its recompense. It was seen that each Custumal should include a kind of summarized penal code, to enable every man to know the law both for crimes and for punishments.[4] Logically, there is among crimes an obvious distinction which lies in the very nature of things; *i.e.* some are specially serious, others are ordinary. One may, no doubt, lay down further distinctions; for example, among crimes some are heinous; but that would be entering prematurely into the details of the subject, and we shall see that all Custumals did not go so far.[5]

Beaumanoir classifies crimes under three headings:[6] there are great crimes, such as homicide ("meurtre"), treason, rape, suicide, arson, theft, heresy, and counterfeiting, — all, in general, punishable by death. Medium crimes and petty misdemeanors are

[4] See, for example, *Beaumanoir*, chapters 30, 31, 32, 33. Chapter 30 is devoted to offenses ["*meffès*"] in general; chap. 31 treats chiefly of larceny; chap. 32 refers to disseizins, violence and disturbances; chap. 33 deals with fraud. Further on, chap. 69 deals with accidental injuries. By bringing together all these chapters we can form a clear idea of Beaumanoir's entire system of criminal law. The "Livre de jostice et de plet" also treats of crimes and punishments, beginning with book XVII, tit. 11, p. 275 *et seq.*, to the end. See also "Anciennes coutumes d'Anjou et du Maine", F, no. 1255, Vol. II, p. 467, Vol. IV, pp. 264 *et seq.; Bouteiller*, "Sommė rural", book I, tit. 28, p. 287; tit. 29, p. 304; tit. 35, p. 418. This last title is devoted to larceny; the preceding titles deal in general with all crimes and all punishments. One may also consult the "Grand coutumier de Normandie", chaps. 67 *et seq.*

[5] Nevertheless, heinous crimes were more than once set apart. Thus, Philip III obtained from the papacy the concession that the crusaders should be deprived of the privilege of the clergy and be responsible to secular tribunals for such crimes; *cf. Langlois*, "Le règne de Philippe III le Hardi", p. 271.

[6] *Beaumanoir*, chap. 30, vol. I, p. 410.

equally numerous, and each of them presents often a great variety as to details; there are insults of all kinds, damage to property or its possession, offenses against procedure, etc. These offenses are generally punished by fine; but if the judge finds this insufficient he has the right to add a prison penalty, and when the culprit is unable to pay the fine he is arrested for the debt.[7]

The " grand Coutumier de Normandie " distinguishes two kinds of charges, some are " simple ", and end " per simplicem legem ", others are criminal, and are known as " querelæ per legem apparentem." They are called criminal because they charge a crime which may involve loss of life or limb, and they are said to " end by means of visible law ", *i.e.* by the duel or by some other form of the judgment of God.[8] The " Anciennes coutumes d'Anjou et du Maine " make no distinction between great and medium crimes; but it is plain that their authors are acquainted with this division, for they make use of it in their account of crimes and punishments.[9] In the " Grand Coutumier de France ", the division is better accentuated, and its author even is careful to reserve the term " crime " for the most serious infractions; he calls " misdemeanor " (" délit ") what Beaumanoir before him had designated under the name of " lesser offense." Bouteiller, on the other hand, continues to say that crimes are either capital or non-capital, according to whether they deserve death or some other penalty.[10]

Throughout the early Germanic period in France the conception of the feud, or right of personal vengeance, had persisted, undergoing some modifications in the course of centuries.[11] And

[7] *Beaumanoir*, chap. 30, no. 19, Vol. I, p. 416. — Bouteiller was thus to express the same idea later: "En delit ne chet point de cession"; that is to say, the debtor cannot transfer property in order to avoid arrest for debt, and if he cannot atone for his crime with money, then he must pay "by bodily punishment and imprisonment; for it would be too great an inducement to evildoing if a poor man were acquitted of his crime because of his poverty." *Bouteiller*, "Somme rural", book II, tit. 20, p. 801.

[8] "Grand coutumier de Normandie", chap. 67, *Gruchy*, p. 61. — This Custumal continues the enumeration of the chief crimes as follows: "There are different kinds of criminal complaints according to the different consequences of the various crimes. There are complaints for murder, homicide, wounding, broken truces, rape, theft, robbing of a plough, plundering a house or personal property, and treason."

[9] See "Ancienne coutume d'Anjou et du Maine", F, no. 1255, Vol. II, p. 467 *et seq.*

[10] See book I, tit. 28, p. 170. It will be noticed, however, that certain punishments were classed with the death penalty, and from that time the crime became, under such circumstances, a capital one.

[11] In certain regions we find traces of the right of vengeance down to

it is still this same basis on which the jurists of the Middle Ages placed the right to punish. But instead of a private vengeance it is now a matter of public vengeance: it is society, and no longer the individual, that demands reparation for the wrong done by the criminal. Beaumanoir declares explicitly that criminals must be taught that there is a right to vengeance for all offenses.[12] He does not even incline toward lenity, and his habits as a magistrate accustomed to repress crimes lead him to say that in case of doubt one must punish severely in order to give an example to others.[13] Bartolus has no different doctrine. "There are", he says, "two legal ways of avenging crimes; the accusation by a private party and the procedure initiated by the judge. The judge initiates his procedure, 1st, when he is called upon to make an investigation as a result of an accusation; 2d, when he begins an investigation of his own accord." [14]

But during the latter part of the Middle Ages the idea of the right to punish shows a marked decrease of rigor. The "Anciennes coutumes de l'Anjou et du Maine" speak no longer of the brutal right to vengeance; they still lay weight on the example afforded by punishment, but the latter is also considered as a means imposed upon the criminal of paying his debt to society, and at times of making it impossible for him to disturb the public peace. We see also the beginning of the idea of social self-defense.[15] Bouteiller

the end of the Middle Ages, and even during the first part of the following epoch. See, for example, *Guyot*, "Un nouvel exemple d'urfehde", Nancy, 1892, and the critical study of this memoir which I published in the "Bulletin du Comité des travaux historiques et scientifiques, Section des sciences économiques et sociales", 1892.

[12] *Beaumanoir*, chap. 30, no. 1, Vol. I, p. 410, where the word vengeance is met at every instant. It is also stated that the lord takes vengeance on the criminal, but in so doing he appears as the representative of society and not as a private individual.

[13] *Beaumanoir*, chap. 30, no. 61, Vol. I, p. 429. "It is an excellent thing to anticipate criminals, and to punish them so severely, according to their crimes, that through fear of justice others will take warning and abstain from offending."

[14] "Jus, ex quo sumitur vindicta, est duplex, scilicet accusatio et officium judicis. Officium exercitur, quando per inquisitionem ad alterius denuntiationem proceditur quandoque per inquisitionem factam proprio motu judicis." See *Du Boys*, "Histoire du droit criminel de la France", Vol. V, p. 280.

[15] "Anciennes coutumes d'Anjou et du Maine", L, no. 404, Vol. IV, p. 308: "The judge ought to know that a criminal must be punished for four reasons: 1st, for his crimes; 2d, in order to frighten and give an example to others against evil-doing; 3d, in order to remove the said malefactors from the community of good people and thus avoid their exercising an evil influence over them; 4th, to prevent the evils which they might still commit if they escaped. The judge must exercise impartiality in judgment between the parties with no regard to persons."

does not attempt, any more than others, to specify the cause of punishment, but he advises the judges to be indulgent and to take into account a host of circumstances in its application; — the character of the victim, the condition of the criminal, the time and the place where the crime was committed, and the previous habits of the culprit.[16]

These are only the observations of a jurist inclined toward indulgence. Society's right to vengeance, and the necessity of intimidating through the dread of corporal punishments, are the two bases of the right to punish in the Middle Ages. With such principles they could have devised punishments more or less fixed, more or less uniform for all, and of a severity commensurate with the gravity of the crime; yet nothing of the kind was done.

Under the influence of old Germanic regional Customs certain offenses continued to be punished with extreme leniency; they were repressed only by means of simple fines. Beaumanoir allowed himself to add imprisonment whenever the fine seemed to him clearly insufficient. On the other hand, under the influence of Roman law, and even of old Germanic regional Customs, extremely severe punishments were inflicted at times. This severity astonishes us to-day, especially when we consider the cases where the Church succeeded in making people consider simple sins of conscience as real crimes.

However, there did not exist, properly speaking, a punishment directly and necessarily attached to a certain crime. To be sure, the Custumals point out the punishment with which the culprit is ordinarily threatened; but they give us only hints. Generally, the judge enjoys the most absolute power; he can strike as he pleases. In short, punishments are arbitrary. A certain offense is sometimes punished with extreme severity, sometimes with reprehensible indulgence. In 1330, at Chambéry, a man guilty of arson is led to the stake; while another, guilty of the same crime, is punished with only a ridiculous fine of ten deniers. A little later, of two men accused of sodomy, one is burned alive, the other makes a composition with the count for eighteen gold florins, and

[16] *Bouteiller*, "Somme rural", book I, tit. 29, p. 180: "It can and ought to be known that the punishment of the law was regarded by the ancients as a means of curbing the evil intention of criminals, those who wish to injure and wrong others, and oppress them by their demands; nevertheless, the judge must always understand punishment in its milder form; for as the wise man says, justice without mercy is too hard and mercy without justice is too lax; and therefore there ought to be moderation and a middle course for the wise discretion of the judge."

the count even remits him the amount.[17] At times the most severe punishments were inflicted without the formality of a trial. On June 30, 1278, Pierre de la Broce was, without trial, hanged at the gallows for common thieves,[18] probably by virtue of the then asserted right over life and death attributed to the king as the symbol of justice. To be sure, such irregularities were not common, and the necessity of a legal procedure was recognized; but the procedure tended to become more and more secret, and thus to deprive the accused of guarantees of fair treatment.

Side by side with these serious defects — a continual cause of injustice and inequality — two essential and very just principles had, however, been proclaimed at a very early date, namely: every crime implies volition and freedom on the part of the one who has committed it; and every crime is essentially its author's personal act.

Beaumanoir gives numerous applications of the principle that crime implies intent and freedom in evil-doing. Thus, he who kills in war commits no offense, not even if by mistake he has taken his friend for an enemy.[19] No more is a man responsible for the accidental homicide committed in a tournament or a joust.[20] Nor are parents responsible for the death of one of their children through mere chance.[21] One is not answerable for a death or wounds of which he has been the involuntary cause, if he had used care to prevent such a misfortune.[22] In this respect, as can be seen, the law had far advanced from the Germanic primitive law which did not distinguish clearly the crime of murder from the involuntary act which caused death or wounds.[23] From this point of view considerable change and progress had been achieved.

Since crime implied evil intent, the man who kills or wounds in self-defense is not guilty.[24] This principle of the right to self-

[17] *Chapperon*, "Chambéry à la fin du XIVe siècle", pp. 182 and 183.

[18] See *Langlois*, "Le règne de Phillippe III le Hardi", p. 30.

[19] *Beaumanoir*, chap. 69, no. 2, Vol. II, p. 489.

[20] *Beaumanoir*, chap. 69, no. 17, Vol. II, p. 492. The following number gives other examples of homicides committed by mere chance and which entail no punishment.

[21] *Beaumanoir*, chap. 69, no. 5, Vol. II, p. 485.

[22] *Beaumanoir*, chap. 63, nos. 3 *et seq.*, Vol. II, p. 419.

[23] See, for instance, law of the Visigoths, X, 8; law of the Saxons, tit. XII. — *Nani*, "Studii di diritto Longobardo", p. 38; *Viollet*, "Etablissements de Saint Louis", Vol. I, p. 232. Bouteiller tells us that homicide is considered lawful in war or in a judicial duel; also if one kills a man who, having been outlawed the pale of the law, breaks the ban. This last case is a relic of the primitive system which it would have been better to suppress.

[24] *Beaumanoir*, chap. 30, nos. 65 *et seq.*, Vol. I, p. 432.

defense was invoked in certain Royal Letters of January 28, 1368 (concerning the parish of Péronne), which made a notable extension of the principle; according to Article 8 of these Letters, whenever, in self-defense, one kills a man who wishes to enter a house without right, one is not liable to any punishment.[25]

Beaumanoir is not alone in proclaiming the principle of the necessity of a criminal intent; we find it also in almost all the other custumals which touched upon this question. The "Grand Coutumier de Normandie" deals with the case of a lunatic killing or wounding another man; he must be put in prison, but through mere precaution, without trial, and without infliction of any punishment, and while there he must be cared for at his own expense, if he is well-to-do, and by charity, if he is poor.[26] One of the Custumals of Anjou remarks that the intent is one of the essential elements of the crime.[27] According to the "Livre des droiz et des commandemens" lawful defense of one's self, or of those who are closely related, excludes criminality, if the defense is proportional to the attack.[28] Bouteiller notes that, according to the Custumals, the death penalty is incurred even when the homicide is the result of a simple imprudence, unless the prince grants a pardon; but he clearly prefers the Roman doctrine which exempts from all punishment.[29] Suicide is no crime if it is the act of an insane person, or if it is induced by poverty.[30]

But from the moment that criminal intent is found, there is a crime, regardless of sex or age. Women are punished like men, with only rare exceptions. They incur the death penalty, except that it is inflicted in a special manner; they are burned or buried alive instead of being hanged. However, Bouteiller advises that,

[25] Letters of Charles V, January 28, 1368, *Isambert*, Vol. V, p. 320.

[26] This Custumal adds that it is even prudent, before the lunatic has disturbed the public peace, to have him guarded by his own family, or, if there be no relatives, by neighbors. See "Grand coutumier de Normandie", chap. 79, edition *Gruchy*, p. 184; "Livre de jostice et de plet", p. 73.

[27] "Anciennes coutumes d'Anjou et du Maine", L, no. 409, Vol. IV, p. 310.

[28] Thus it is not permissible to employ weapons against one who threatens only with the fist and the stick, unless one is feeble or sick; thus it depends on the circumstances. See "Livre des droiz et des commandemens", nos. 500 and 997.

[29] *Bouteiller*, "Somme rural", book II, tit. 40, edition of 1621, p. 1493.

[30] "Registre criminel de Saint-Martin-des-Champs de Paris", pp. 196 and 299; *Bouteiller*, "Somme rural", book I, chap. 39.

while in prison, they be treated more gently than men, and he adds that in civil cases they incur only a half fine.[31] Minors are punished like adults as soon as they have reached the age of discernment;[32] minority in itself is no ground for excuse. But it was decided at an early date that there was no crime before the age of fourteen or fifteen, according to the regional Customs; except, as Bouteiller adds, that corrective measures should be applied to wards who have offended.[33]

In view of the Custumals so clearly admitting the principle of responsibility and making such varied applications of it, it is curious that they should have committed the solecism of allowing criminal prosecutions against animals. This procedure was used, not only when the animals figured as the accomplices in certain crimes committed by men, but also when they were charged as the only guilty parties. We find many examples of such trials in the Middle Ages, and they are not uncommon even in the following period. These prosecutions of animals are too well known to need here any special account of this judicial curiosity. An actual mock trial was held when the animal had (for instance) killed a woman or a child; the death penalty was inflicted, with all formality at the usual place of execution. The Church has often been reproached with favoring these trials; but there is no serious proof to support this accusation. The truth is that jurists and the Custumals conceded something to popular beliefs; moreover, another motive was the general one of deterring from crime by inspiring fear. Upon the revival of Roman law (A.D. 1200–1300), it was possible to invoke certain texts of the Digest which seem to concede intelligence to animals and hence a capacity for crime.[34] But the jurist Ayrault, in a later century, remarked that if these trials were conducted for the purpose of intimidation, they completely missed the aim in view; for in his day they had ended by causing ridicule rather than the desired effect. Long before then, Beaumanoir had expressed disapproval of these trials of animals; he found it absurd to condemn an animal devoid of intelligence; at the same time, he hinted that the feudal lords had some interest

[31] *Bouteiller*, "Somme rural", book II, tit. 40, ed. 1621, p. 1495.

[32] "Anciennes coutumes d'Anjou et du Maine", F, no. 253, Vol. II, p. 115.

[33] *Beaumanoir*, chap. 31, no. 12, Vol. I, p. 462; "Livre des droiz et des commandemens", Vol. II, no. 463; *Bouteiller*, "Somme rural", book II, tit. 40.

[34] See, for instance, l. 1, § 11, "Si quadrupes pauperiem fecisse dicatur", IX, 1.

in preserving these trials, and that also is perhaps one of the reasons which explain their frequency in the Middle Ages.[35]

The owner, indeed, without being chargeable strictly with a crime, might be held responsible for the act of his animal, and might be liable, not for the appropriate punishment, but for damages and even some penalty; the master's liability is not that of the author of the crime, but merely that of one responsible for the animal.[36] And it is here worth noting that the old regional Customs often preserved the enormous fines imposed in the preceding period in such cases. In the Germanic laws it was natural to find that, in case the death of a man was occasioned by an animal, its owner was to pay composition as if he were the author of the homicide.[37] This was explainable in an epoch when no distinction was made between willful and accidental homicide. But by the Middle Ages new principles had evolved; it was conceded that there is no crime without evil intent. Henceforth, as Beaumanoir pointed

[35] It is curious that this passage is not known to or, at least, has not been cited by the authors who have devoted monographs to trials against animals; *Beaumanoir*, chap. 69, no. 6, Vol. II, p. 485: "Those who administer justice in their lands put animals to trial when they kill a person; so, if a sow or some other animal kills a child, they hang the animal and drag around the body; but this should not be done, for dumb beasts do not know what is right and what is wrong, and therefore it is justice lost. For justice should be done to avenge the offense, and in order that the author of the crime may know and understand that he suffers for this offense a certain punishment; but this understanding is not to be found in dumb beasts. This consideration is denied them by those who try in court and put to death dumb beasts for crimes; the lords do this for their own profit, as a thing to which they are lawfully entitled." Bouteiller also devotes a paragraph to trials of animals in title 38 of book I, of his "Somme rural", ed. 1621, p. 267. For the details concerning these trials and examples of them which have been noted, one may consult, among other works, the following: *Louandre*, "Epopée des animaux", in the "Revue des Deux Mondes" of January 15, 1854; *Ménabréa*, "De l'origine, de la forme et de l'esprit des jugements rendus au moyen âge contre les animaux", Chambéry, 1846–1847; a report made before the "Académie Delphinale", August 6, 1847, by Canon Chambon, on the preceding work of M. Ménabréa; *Berriat Saint-Prix*, "Recherches sur les procès fait dans le moyen âge aux animaux." This author notes more than eighty death penalties or excommunications pronounced between 1120 and 1741 upon all sorts of animals, from the donkey and the sow to the grasshopper. See also *Du Boys*, on the proceedings against animals during the Middle Ages, appendix to Vol. V of the "Histoire du droit criminel de la France", p. 656; *Tanon*, "Le registre criminel de Saint-Martin-des-Champs", p. cxiv; [*Evans*, "The Criminal Prosecution and Capital Punishment of Animals", New York, 1907; *von Amira*, "Thierstrafen und Thierprozesse", Innsbrück, 1892. — ED.]

[36] *Beaumanoir*, chap. 69, no. 6, Vol. II, p. 486.

[37] See, for example, Law of the Saxons, tit. XIII, § 1; Edict of Rotharis, chap. 14; *Pertz*, "Leges", Vol. IV, p. 15; *cf.* Salic Law, tit. XLI, § 6.

out, the master could no longer be considered as the author of the offense committed by his animal, not even as its representative; for him it could be only a matter of liability to damages for the harm done. But as punishments had become, in general, much more severe than in the previous period, and in many instances the death penalty had even replaced heavy fines, these penalties did not seem too rigorous when applied to the present class of cases. This would explain the maintenance and even the new imposition of very heavy fines. For example, the Custom of Touraine-Anjou imposes a fine of a hundred sous and one denier, called "relief d'homme", upon the owner of a domestic animal which has caused the death of a person;[38] and the same Custom of Touraine-Anjou even pronounces the death-penalty against the owner if he knew the vicious trait of his beast. These are evidently measures borrowed from the law of the preceding epoch. Beaumanoir likewise imposes the enormous fine of sixty sous upon the owner of an animal doing damage to the fields.

Roman law had allowed the owner to avoid prosecution by making a noxal surrender of the animal. But, with the Romans, the owner was prosecuted rather as the person necessarily liable for the animal's act than by virtue of his personal responsibility. Our old Custumals did not grasp this distinction. In general, they do not speak of noxal surrender, and their silence impliedly excludes it. Under the influence of Roman law, certain Custumals indeed admitted it, but with a notion of responsibility which was foreign to Roman law. Thus, according to Liger, the owner can make a noxal surrender if he has been careful and has taken all needful precautions to prevent the animal from doing harm; if not, the noxal surrender is not allowable, and the person injured must be recompensed. Thus, in the first alternative they admit a responsibility limited by the value of the animal; in the second, the responsibility is unlimited, or rather, there is a true personal fault on the part of the owner.[39]

Evil intent alone does not constitute a crime; the crime must

[38] "Coutume de Touraine-Anjou", § 114; *cf.* "Etablissements de Saint Louis", book I, chap. 125, ed. *Viollet*, Vol. II, p. 233.

[39] "Anciennes coutumes d'Anjou et du Maine", F, no. 421, Vol. II, p. 163. *Cf.* "Livre des droiz et des commandemens", Vol. I, nos. 119 and 228. We note that the Salic Law had already allowed in one case a kind of noxal surrender. "Loi salique", tit. XXXVI. *Viollet*, "Etablissements de Saint Louis", Vol. I, p. 234, believes that noxal surrender did not find a place in the law of Anjou. He is right for the first part of our period, but not for the second, as we have just seen; for the noxal surrender entered it under the influence of Roman law.

be committed or at least attempted. But one may search in vain in the Custumals of the Middle Ages for a theory of attempt; the texts of this period have no definite conception of the attempt; they dwell only on the accomplished act, without inquiring whether the offender had purposed to commit a greater offense. For instance, one who purposed to commit murder but succeeded only in wounding his victim without endangering his life, is prosecuted for blows and wounds, but not for attempted murder. With greater reason, the mere planning of a crime is held not equivalent to committing it; one who admits in court that he was going to find a man in order to kill him will not be punished for murder; for "the intent to kill, without the accomplished fact", is not a crime.[40] Such, indeed, had been the principle of the Germanic folk-laws.[41]

No one could be put to trial a second time for the same offense; in this respect Roman law had exercised a beneficial influence, and had helped to fix clearly principles which had remained rather obscure during the preceding period.[42]

There were numerous precautions to prevent ill-founded criminal prosecutions; a severe penalty threatened the one who falsely lodged a criminal charge.[43] A crime must be fully proved; in case of doubt, the accused was to be acquitted. Confession seemed to be the best proof. The rule finally evolved was, that a confession was necessary, before the court might lawfully pronounce the death penalty.[44] But this principle led finally to disastrous results; for, as is well known, it developed the free use of torture. In some instances, when the rule forbad torture, because the accused had consented to submit to interrogation, and this did not sufficiently prove the crime, they nevertheless pronounced a provisional and fictitious sentence against the accused (though he should have been acquitted), and he was taken to the place of execution, in the hope that this sham proceeding would lead him to a confession; they must after all release him, if he still persisted in his denials.[45]

[40] "Etablissements de Saint Louis", book I, chap. 40, Vol. II, p. 55.

[41] See *Wilda*, "Das Strafrecht der Germanen." But the criminal attempt seems to have been classed with the accomplished crime.

[42] See, for example, "Anciennes coutumes d'Anjou et du Maine", F, no. 898, Vol. II, p. 319, where Roman law is explicitly cited; "Livre des droiz et des commandemens", Vol. I, no. 225, and vol. II, no. 366.

[43] See, for example, "Livre des droiz et des commandemens", Vol. II, no. 322.

[44] "Livre des droiz et des commandemens", Vol. II, nos. 322, 323, 644.

[45] Sometimes, however, it was permitted to banish him from the territory which came under the jurisdiction of the court where he had

The act and the evil intent together made crime; yet the guilt was not the same in all cases; it varied widely according to the circumstances. Our modern codes recognize excuses, extenuating circumstances, and aggravating circumstances. The Custumals mention certain excuses. But we do not find in them any really logical and scientific theory for extenuating and aggravating circumstances. One can scarcely detect even a rough outline of such a theory in Bouteiller; and he is influenced by Roman law, more or less modified. Thus, he says, the crime will be more serious, sometimes because of the status of the victim, for example, a churchman, an officer of the king, a woman, or a girl; sometimes on account of the place, as when committed in a church, in a hall of justice, in the lord's castle, at the fair or in the market place; and again by reason of the time, for example, when committed on a great Church festival, such as Easter, Pentecost, Christmas; still farther by reason of the rank of the criminal, when in a high station of life, or by reason of the importance of the harm done; and, finally, premeditation and habitual wrongdoing are also aggravating circumstances. As the most extenuating circumstance for homicide, Bouteiller ranks the heedlessness of the offender; in this case the punishment ought to be more lenient, though there should be no acquittal.[46] The truth is that judges enjoyed an absolutely discretionary power in the application of punishments; and under such a system, it was unnecessary to indicate in precise and fixed terms the aggravating or the extenuating circumstances.

There were, however, certain excuses which bound the judge to acquit, or at least to inflict a less severe punishment. Beaumanoir conceded that children may rightfully rob their parents to get sustenance, *i.e.*, to buy food, though for no other reason; in that case, therefore, there was no crime.[47] Likewise the texts allowed the inmates of a house to kill with impunity the night thief,[48] and the husband to put to death his wife and her accomplice caught in the act of adultery.[49] Beaumanoir justifies a homicide done

been arraigned. See *Tanon*, "Registre criminel de Saint Martin-des-Champs", pp. xcix and 228; [and *Esmein*, "History of Continental Criminal Procedure", Vol. V of the present Series. — ED.].

[46] *Bouteiller*, "Somme rural", book I, tit. 29, p. 182. According to an ordinance of 1356, the city of Tournai had the privilege of asylums for involuntary murderers; *Isambert*, Vol. IV, p. 795.

[47] *Beaumanoir*, chap. 31, no. 12, Vol. I, p. 462. At this point Beaumanoir (no. 13) remarks that theft implies criminal intent.

[48] "Anciennes coutumes d'Anjou et du Maine", F, no. 393, Vol. II, p. 155; "Livre des droiz et des commandemens", Vol. II, no. 903.

[49] *Beaumanoir*, chap. 30, nos. 102 to 104, Vol. I, p. 455; "Anciennes

by a man who has been insulted with violence and extreme outrage.[50]

Crimes being personal (as the old Custumals say), they must, from the point of view of penal justice, bring punishment against their authors only. Suppose that a band of criminals has been caught, says Beaumanoir; the law must punish only those against whom there is good proof.[51] An old Norman treatise tells us that a certain bailiff of the Duke, as soon as he learned of a crime, used to arrest the parents of the suspect; but the seneschal of Normandy suppressed this abuse, and warned the bailiff that he could use such harshness only against the offender and his accomplices, that is, his partners in the crime.[52] It followed, still more plainly, that the heirs of the offender were not to be prosecuted in his stead.[53] No clear distinction, however, is made at this epoch between joint principal and accomplices. In general, they are all placed on the same level and subjected to the same punishment, as if each had himself alone committed the crime.[54] This principle is applied even in the case where the penalty incurred is a fine; in other words, each guilty party in the same crime must be condemned to pay the whole fine.[55] But when it is a matter of corporal punishment, it is easy to see that the judge's power to inflict a discretionary punishment would allow him to punish very differently according as the participants played a more or less important part, principal or accessory. Still, there are cases where the Custumals class with the author of the crime persons who to-day would no longer be treated with that rigorous severity; and thus it is natural to find the Custumals placing on

coutumes d'Anjou et du Maine", F, no. 1317, Vol. II, p. 488; "Livre des droiz et des commandemens", Vol. II, no. 820.

[50] *Beaumanoir*, chap. 30, no. 101, Vol. I, p. 454.

[51] See in Beaumanoir the curious story of the pilgrim, chap. 69, no. 21, Vol. II, p. 494.

[52] "Etablissements, coutumes, assises et arrêt de l'Echiquier de Normandie", ed. *Marnier*, pp. 44 and 45.

[53] "Anciennes coutumes d'Anjou et du Maine", F, no. 519, Vol. II, p. 198.

[54] *Bouteiller* seems to lay down a certain theory of complicity, but it is only in appearance, for he limits himself to saying that one must distinguish those who have participated in the crime with full knowledge of the fact, from those who were ignorant of the plan or the doing of the crime, although the latter have taken a certain part in it; as, for example, if when a theft was being committed they were on the watch believing in good faith that they were merely waiting for some one; in the former case alone are they guilty. However, even this jurist makes no distinction between joint principals and accomplices: see "Somme rural", book I, tit. 29, and book II, tit. 40, edition of 1621, pp. 310 and 1490.

[55] *Beaumanoir*, chap. 30, no. 92, Vol. I, p. 447.

the same level the author of the crime and one who has planned or instigated, or ordered it.[56] But to hold guilty of homicide one who, when able to rescue another from danger, failed to go to his aid,[57] seems pressing this principle rather far.

In general, the Custumals are apt to class with the author of the crime its concealer, especially in case of theft. This may be accounted for by the reprobation always attached to receivers of stolen goods; there is good sense in the old saying: "the receiver is worse than the thief." [58] Innkeepers, though not actually classed with thieves, were naturally held responsible for the thefts committed on their premises, or by their servants and their lodgers. But that was a matter wholly within their personal control and they could, in certain cases, avoid liability.[59]

Apart from theft, connivance by concealment could hardly be a crime, unless it involved concealing the criminal's person. But no one ever thought of classing with the criminal the man who received him under his roof. It is true, some texts punish with death the person who, with full knowledge of the crime, gives shelter to a murderer, unless he be a relative.[60] But this principle does not seem to have been generally accepted; in most cases a separate penalty was applicable to him who sheltered a criminal.[61]

[56] *Beaumanoir*, chap. 31, nos. 9 and 11, Vol. I, p. 461; "Livre des droiz et des commandemens", Vol. II, no. 229.

[57] "Livre des droiz et des commandemens", Vol. II, no. 362. Likewise we read in the "Livre de jostice et de plet", p. 307: "And if one sees another commit murder, kill, desert, betray, rob and maim, and does not raise a hue and cry, or does not do his best to capture him, what will be the result? It is said that he must seek pardon of the king. For it is evident that when he does not do his best to capture or to raise a hue and cry, he consents to the deed. Now if one asks: Am I bound to capture or to raise a hue and cry in case of other offenses, the answer is yes, in case of highway robbery, demolishing a house, and similar serious cases, or cases where loss of life or limb is entailed. In other cases one is not so bound, except in case of injury to himself or to his people; for these one must help in good faith."

[58] "Capitulaire d'Ansegise", book III, chap. 23; *Pertz*, "Leges", Vol. I, p. 303; "Livre de jostice et de plet", p. 281; *cf. Viollet*, "Établissements de Saint Louis", Vol. I, p. 251; *Beaumanoir*, chap. 31, nos. 7 and 8, Vol. I, p. 460 and chap. 69, no. 19, Vol. II, p. 493; "Anciennes coutumes d'Anjou et du Maine", B, no. 35, Vol. I, p. 83; C, no. 29, Vol. I, p. 219; F, nos. 1354 and 1355, Vol. II, p. 499.

[59] See in this respect, "Anciennes coutumes d'Anjou et du Maine", F, nos. 602 to 615, Vol. II, p. 222; K, nos. 217 to 219, Vol. IV, p. 108; N, nos. 39, 40, 42, Vol. IV, p. 528.

[60] "Livre des droiz et des commandemens", no. 348, Vol. II, p. 20.

[61] Some Letters of Louis VIII, of April, 1226, hold that he who gives refuge to a heretic is deprived of the right to be a witness before the law, to receive honors, to make his will, and to inherit property. See also Articles 2 and 3 of the April Ordinance of 1228 in *Isambert*, Vol. I, pp. 227 and 230.

The principle that crime was essentially personal had some limitations. Whenever a criminal committed suicide to escape prosecution, they tried him and inflicted the penalty on his corpse; so too, when the culprit had been killed while trying to escape justice. Even in the 1500 s, Ayrault in his book, "De l'ordre, formalité et instruction judiciare", still maintained these doctrines; sanctioning the prosecution of the corpse (even though not dying by his own hand), for those guilty of treason, parricide, or other heinous crime. The crime of treason was visited even on the traitor's posterity; the penalty of confiscation for treason was a serious injustice to the common welfare, in that it was frequently imposed, and fell upon the family of the offender. But these were the only exceptions to the principle of personal guilt; public disapproval checked the occasional attempts to extend them.[62]

§ 39f. **Specific Crimes.** — In primitive legal systems a crime is regarded as more serious when the offender is taken in the act than when he is not; it provokes in the victim a keener wrath and hence a more lawful one. The right of vengenance, too, is often found persisting for a longer period under these circumstances; when it disappeared it was replaced at first by a particularly heavy pecuniary composition, then by a severer punishment than the usual one. These peculiarities of the Frankish epoch had generally disappeared by the time of the Middle Ages; but there still remained a few traces, especially in theft. Taking a man in the act of stealing or of committing adultery permits the killing of the offender.[1] Any one has the right to arrest an offender, and to bring him before the court, when caught in the commission of any crime whatsoever.[2] At times, this right even becomes a duty. In Paris, an ordinance of Philip the Bold, of 1273, enjoined upon the neighbors, for certain kinds of offenders taken in the act, to ar-

[62] On March 2, 1326, Charles II, King of Navarre, was accused, before Parliament in the presence of the king and the peers, of the crime of "lèse majesté", although he had been dead since the first of January of the same year. During the trial the court affected to be ignorant of this circumstance; and when the case was put to the judges, the king's lawyer maintained with faltering words that according to feudal law it was permissible to continue proceedings in case of felony even after the death of the vassal. But finally, in spite of their desire to confiscate the lands of the deceased, the charge was allowed to lapse. See *Isambert*, Vol. VI, p. 620.

[1] *Beaumanoir*, chap. 30, nos. 102 *et seq.*, Vol. I, p. 455; "Livre des droiz et des commandemens", Vol. II, no. 580.

[2] *Glasson*, "Clameur de haro", may be referred to; here it is enough to mention the point.

rest them or at least to raise a hue and cry.[3] To do speedy justice, jurisdiction was given not only to the judge of the lord under whom the offender lived, but also to the judge of the place where the crime had been committed, as well as to the one upon whose territory the offender had been arrested.[4] Moreover, since the offender was taken in the act, the crime was by that very fact sufficiently proved.[5] But, save these differences, the distinction between crimes when the offender is or is not taken in the act, had at this period lost all practical usefulness; the jurists prefer a different point of view.

Beaumanoir tells us that crimes are great, medium, or small, according to their gravity.[6] Among the first he puts expecially murder, homicide, treason, poisoning, suicide, rape, arson, certain thefts, heresy, and counterfeiting. Batteries and wounds of all kinds, false witness, petty thefts, insults, contempt of court, displacement of land-marks, violation of seizin, disobedience of police measures taken by the lord, violence against the property or possession of another, and delayed payment of certain rents, — these were medium or even petty crimes. The other Custumals contain analogous distinctions, except for some differences in details. There is, however, a great difference between the classification of Beaumanoir and that of Bouteiller. The former does not lay any stress on the kind of punishment; he classifies crimes from the point of view of their gravity in themselves. The latter terms capital crimes those punishable by death or some other punishment classed with death, such as banishment, and non-capital crimes those for which the regional Custom inflicts a less severe punishment, such as pillory, brand, or fine. Thus, for Bouteiller, capital crimes include "lèse majesté" and other treason, murder and homicide, rape and abduction, certain forms of violence, sacrilege, heresy, sedition, conspiracies, insults to the king, witchcraft, corruption in magistrates, sodomy, blasphemy, brigandage, and the

[3] *Isambert*, Vol. II, p. 650.

[4] *Beaumanoir*, chap. 30, nos. 84 and 85, Vol. I, p. 442. Later, they extended these rules of jurisdiction even in cases when the criminal was not taken in the act.

[5] *Beaumanoir*, chap. 39, no. 10 and chap. 61, no. 2, Vol. II, pp. 95 and 376; "Assises de Jérusalem, cour des Bourgeois", chapters 203, 208, 209, 251; *Charondas*, "Notes sur le Grand Coutumier", p. 117. In Beaumanoir's time, whenever the judge could not satisfy himself that the person charged was either a notorious offender or taken in the act, he was obliged, if no one appeared and complained, to release the accused at the end of the customary period allowed for freemen to appear in court. See *Beaumanoir*, chap. 30, no. 90, Vol. I, p. 446.

[6] *Beaumanoir*, chap. 30, Vol. I, pp. 410 *et seq.*

more serious forms of larceny; among non-capital crimes he places insults, batteries and wounds, carrying of weapons, violations of the game and fish laws, etc.

Of all crimes the gravest of course is "lèse majesté." It is not found in the early Custumals. It appears only at the end of the period, as an effect of the revival of Roman law. Bouteiller defines "lèse majesté" as meaning all attempts against "the noble majesty of the king." No one but the king himself can sit in judgment on it within the kingdom, — whatever be the station of the accused, even a churchman of the highest rank. The trial never begins by inquest of the country; a special procedure is required; if the proof is not clear, torture may be used upon the accuser as well as the accused; if the former is convicted of false complaint, he incurs the penalty that the accused would have suffered. He who advises only is equally guilty with him who acts overtly in such a design. Whoever has knowledge of the design must immediately reveal it, on pain of sharing in the guilt. There is no appeal. The culprit is quartered or flayed alive; all his goods are forfeited to the lord or the king. The offender's children are to be "exiled, there to suffer a merited death; and the reason is that the crime of treason is so horrible and detestable that by its very nature it contaminates the offspring of the offender; and therefore the roots and the trunk must be destroyed." If the prince spares the lives of the children, the latter are none the less branded with infamy for the rest of their lives, stricken with civil death; the sole exception is that daughters are entitled to a fourth of their mother's fortune. All these rules were borrowed from the imperial Roman law; a glance at the title of the Code "Ad legem Juliam majestatis" (IX, 8, 1) will show its origin.[7]

The crime of "prodition", or "treason", is related to that of "lèse majesté"; it includes disloyalty to the feudal lord, or to some other person. In the former case, it is always a capital crime; in the latter, only when death results.[8] In Beaumanoir's time, conspiracies and plots, it seems, were frequent, especially by townspeople against their overlords. If the lord learns of it before the plot is carried out, he may have the leaders hanged,

[7] *Bouteiller*, "Somme rural", book I, tit. 39, pp. 478 and 479. The "Livre des droiz et des commandemens", no. 762, Vol. II, p. 195, informs us that the man guilty of "lèse majesté" can never lodge an appeal.

[8] *Bouteiller*, "Somme rural", book I, tit. 39.

and may imprison for a long term the other participants. Beaumanoir speaks of a long term of imprisonment as the penalty for those who make combinations and declare strikes.[9] Bouteiller also deals with crime of combination which he calls " monopoly " and considers as a case of " lèse majesté."[10] In this class he puts also sedition, which consists in revolting against one's lord, conspiring against the prince's ordinance and edict to overthrow the government, and dealing with enemies and infidels.[11] With this crime of treason against the king or the lord, some Custumals class highway robbery and the abduction of girls; so that in these cases the offender has no appeal from the death penalty.[12]

The foregoing may be classed as crimes against society or its representatives. Passing to crimes against individuals, we find them of variant degrees, but alike resulting in some injury to a person, to a family, or to property.

Of course the most serious offense against the person is *murder* (" assassinat "), that is, homicide (" meurtre ") with premeditation, in whatever manner, by blows causing death, by poisoning, etc. The Germanic folk-laws had not distinguished clearly murder from involuntary homicide; their distinction was rather between the killing done in public or in secret. In the former case they inflicted the ordinary punishments, whether the killing were voluntary or not. The main concern was to give some satisfaction to the family's demand for vengeance; and as secret homicide rendered this vengeance more difficult, it was considered a crime especially grave.[13] During the later Middle Ages these old notions survive in the writings of some of the jurists.[14] But gradually there develops a clearer idea of the nature of the crime. The term " guet-apens " indicates murder, that is, killing with premeditation, rather than secret homicide. But since these two circumstances are most often found together, *i.e.* since murder takes place almost always in secret, there is still, for a while, some difficulty in distinguishing one from the other. They finally succeed in defining homicide (" meurtre ") as the act of killing one's fellow-

[9] *Beaumanoir*, chap. 30, nos. 62 and 63, Vol. I, p. 430.

[10] *Bouteiller*, "Somme rural", book I, tit. 28, p. 290.

[11] *Bouteiller*, *ibid.* Jacques Cœur (as is well known) was prosecuted, tortured, and sentenced for having dealings with infidels. See *Clément*, "Histoire de Jacques Cœur", p. 279.

[12] "Livre des droiz et des commandemens", no. 762, Vol. II, p. 195.

[13] See our Vol. III, p. 560.

[14] See, for example, *Glanvill*, book XIV, chap. 3; "Livre de jostice et de plet", p. 290.

man in ambush (" guet-apens "), that is, with premeditation. This crime corresponds with what we call to-day murder.[15] Even Bouteiller does not yet distinguish clearly murder from unpremeditated homicide. He recognizes that homicide by carelessness ought not to be punished, but adds immediately that even in that case the death penalty is incurred unless the prince grants pardon.[16] Beaumanoir terms it a homicide when mere blows and wounds result in death within forty days.[17] Usually, homicide is the term applicable to any killing which becomes notable because of the means employed or of the rank of the victim. Poisoning, for example, was always and rightly considered an especially odious crime.[18] Murder is especially heinous if committed by a woman against her husband,[19] by a son against his father, or by a father against his son. The old Custumals remind us of the well-known Roman punishment, which consisted in putting the parricide into a leather sack with a rooster, a dog, a monkey, and a serpent, to be thus thrown into the sea or into a river, so that he might lose at the same time the sky, the air, and the earth.[20]

Mere batteries and wounds did not fall within the category of capital crimes. But one who assaulted a pregnant woman was condemned to be hanged. If the *infant* died *in its mother's womb* as a result of this ill-treatment (and of course, if the mother was killed outright), the crime was termed " encis." [21] This crime of

[15] "Livre de jostice et de plet", pp. 288 and 289; "Anciennes coutumes d'Anjou et du Maine", E, nos. 76 and 77, Vol. I, p. 429; F, nos. 1321 *et seq.*, Vol. II, p. 489; F, no. 1369, Vol. II, p. 503; I, no. 96, Vol. III, p. 258; L, no. 288, Vol. IV, p. 264.

[16] *Bouteiller*, "Somme rural", ed. 1621, book II, tit. 40, pp. 1488 and 1493.

[17] *Beaumanoir*, chap. 69, no. 22, Vol. II, p. 95. Notice this period of forty days, which is certainly of very old Germanic origin.

[18] "Livre de jostice et de plet", p. 284. On this point one sometimes finds cited the "Livre des droiz et des commandemens", no. 823; but this text deals with enchanters' philters rather than with poisonings properly speaking; the offender must nevertheless pay with his life if the philter has caused death; otherwise, the judge may mitigate the penalty. On the poisoning of wells, see "Anciennes coutumes d'Anjou et du Maine", E, no. 87, Vol. I, p. 435.

[19] *Beaumanoir*, chap. 69, no. 16, Vol. II, p. 491.

[20] L. 9, "De lege Pompeia de parricidiis", 48, 9. Enlarging on this text, a decree of Hadrian had ordained that if the sea was not near the place where the crime had been committed, the offender was to be thrown to the wild beasts. But the latter form of punishment no longer existed in the Middle Ages, and in such case the guilty man was thrown into the river. *Cf.* "Livre de jostice et de plet", p. 284; *Bouteiller*, "Somme rural", ed. 1621, book II, tit. 40, p. 1492.

[21] See "Etablissements de Saint Louis", book I, chap. 27; "Livre de jostice et de plet", p. 279; *Bouteiller*, "Somme rural", ed. 1621, book II, tit. 40, p. 1488; "Livre des droiz et des commandemens", no. 251.

"encis" has by some writers been positively traced back to the Salic Law, which in the title "De via lacina" awards a pecuniary composition three times heavier for a blow inflicted on a woman than on a man.[22] But this text does not even mention a pregnant woman, and this interpretation seems questionable; it is simpler to believe that, probably through traditional usages, a special protection was accorded to the unborn child. This protection, however, was accorded only as against a third party, and not as against its parents. It is indeed astonishing, at first impression, to find the regional Customs of that period repressing with severity the crime "encis" and yet relatively indulgent toward the crimes of infanticide and abortion. Yet there is here an apparent contradiction only. According to early usage, against which the Church struggled with difficulty, the father and the mother were conceded a kind of right of life and death over the child just born. Amidst such traditions, infanticide could not constitute a crime. The tradition was no longer in force, it is true, in the Middle Ages, but the influence of old Germanic regional customs prevailed. Roman law, to be sure, decreed the death penalty for infanticide;[23] but here it was not followed, and ancient usage prevailed. Strange to say, the Church contributed in some measure to the survival; it did indeed condemn infanticide energetically; but as it never pronounced the death penalty for any crime, the result was that, whenever a woman was brought before a church court for this offense, the sentence was only a short imprisonment or even a less severe penalty.[24]

Furthermore, in certain regional Customs which had remained entirely untouched by Roman law and under the influence of the primitive tradition allowing parents the right of life or death, the killing of a child by the father or the mother was always more or less excused, whatever the age of the child.[25] Naturally, the

[22] "Loi salique", tit. 31.

[23] Const. I, "De his qui parentes vel liberos occidunt", 9, 17.

[24] See *Bernard of Pavia*, "Summa decretum", V, 9, ed. *Laspeyres*, p. 219; *Viollet*, "Etablissements de Saint Louis", Vol. I, p. 250.

[25] See, in this respect, the curious text of chapter 35 of the "Très ancien coutumier de Normandie" (ed. *Tardif*, p. 29; ed. *Warnkönig and Stein*, p. 15): "Si pater per infortunium suum filium occiderit, pœnitenciam agat ab ecclesia sumptam, et si inique eum occiderit, exul ibit a tota potestate ducis. Uxor ejus sequatur eum; post vero decessum sponsi sui redire poterit ad hereditatem suam. Et quoniam filius de sanguine et visceribus patris exivit, pater pro homicidio filii morte non punietur. Et, si inique filium murdrierit, igne comburatur." It is curious that this last clause, awarding the penalty of death by fire, is not found in the French manuscript. It was probably added of special

Customs were extremely lenient in case of infanticide. The "Etablissements de Saint Louis", under the influence of the Church, inflict no criminal penalty on the woman guilty of a first infanticide (though probably they required her detention in a monastery designated by the Church), but in case of a second offense the guilty mother was to be burned alive.[26] This rule is still recognized, at a later date, by the "Livre des droiz et des commandemens", which requires that the mother guilty of a first infanticide be delivered up to the Church, but for a second offense be condemned in the secular tribunals to be burned.[27] Certain custumals of the end of this period show a greater severity; the woman is punished with death even for a first infanticide; so also the woman guilty of abortion,—an offense which does not seem to be noticed by earlier Custumals.[28]

The least serious offenses against the person are *batteries, wounds, insults*, and the like. Legal writers on the customary law, notably Beaumanoir among the earliest, and Bouteiller among the latest of our period, class these offenses as medium or non-capital crimes. We find in certain texts of the Middle Ages, especially the oldest, some traces of the old classifications of the Germanic folk-laws, which distinguish between different kinds of blows and wounds and punish them according to their gravity. Thus, in the Custom of Orléans they distinguish as many as three kinds of blows: one which causes a wound on the head, without, however, resulting in death; one which produces a sore or causes the flowing of blood, punishable by a fine of sixty sous; and one which results in no sore and no flowing of blood, punishable by a fine of only five sous.[29] The same distinctions are found later in Bouteiller; blows and wounds are punished by a fine of sixty or of five sous according to whether they cause blood to flow or not.[30] However, some woundings were punished more severely, because of their nature and the circumstances. For example, instead of the usual simple fine,[31]

purpose, at the period when, under the influence of Roman law, the murder of the child by burning began to be considered as a horrible crime.

[26] "Etablissements de Saint Louis", book I, tit. 39, ed. *Viollet*, p. 55.

[27] "Livre des droiz et des commandemens", no. 349.

[28] "Anciennes coutumes d'Anjou et du Maine", F, no. 1368, Vol. II, p. 503.

[29] "Livre de jostice et de plet", p. 279; "Etablissements de Saint Louis", book II, chapters 23 and 24.

[30] *Bouteiller*, "Somme rural", book II, tit. 40, edition of 1621, p. 1474.

[31] "Registre criminel de Saint-Martin-des-Champs", p. cvii; "Anciennes coutumes d'Anjou et du Maine", F, nos. 370, 1370, 1398, 1400, Vol. II, pp. 148, 504, 508, 509, and I, no. 120, Vol. III, p. 277; L, nos. 319, 322, Vol. IV, pp. 27 and 275.

the death penalty or some other discretionary punishment was inflicted if the victim died later or suffered any mutilation;[32] whenever the wound caused the loss of a limb, the offender incurred the penalty of like for like, even in Bouteiller's time;[33] in other cases the circumstances would attenuate or even remove the guilt. Beaumanoir puts the case of a person killing or maiming another in a scuffle; he is guilty, if the victim belongs to the party against which he was fighting; but it is no crime if the person belongs to his own band; the latter case being evidently considered as a mere accident.[34] Any other use of force against the person was punished in various ways, generally (being non-capital) by fines; *e.g.* force used to prevent a person from making his will.[35]

Insults were ordinarily treated like blows and wounds, — non-capital crimes punishable by fines. The various custumals, however, differ as to details. Some distinguish two kinds of insults, treacherous and ordinary; the former are classed with blows causing sores, the latter with blows not causing blood to flow; respectively punished by a heavy fine and a fine of five sous.[36] The "Grand Coutumier de Normandie" distinguishes according to whether or not the insult consists in charging an offense which, if true, would threaten a penalty of life or limb; here the insult is criminal, and is punishable by a heavy fine of chattels; in the other cases the offense is a minor one.[37] An insult to a son or to a wife is deemed to have been offered at the same time to the father or to the husband; so that the offender commits two offenses and incurs two fines.[38] Finally, certain insults are of special gravity on account of the status of the persons addressed, and are

[32] "Registre criminel de Saint-Martin-des-Champs", p. 35; "Anciennes coutumes d'Anjou et du Maine", E, no. 80, Vol. I, p. 432; I, no. 99, Vol. III, p. 261; "Grand coutumier de Normandie", chap. 74, ed. *Gruchy*, p. 175. The term "méhaing" applied specifically to a wound causing mutilation.

[33] *Bouteiller*, "Somme rural", ed. 1621, book II, tit. 40, p. 1492.

[34] *Beaumanoir*, chap. 69, no. 8, Vol. II, p. 487.

[35] *Bouteiller*, "Somme rural", ed. 1621, book II, tit. 40, p. 1490.

[36] "Etablissements de Saint Louis", book I, chap. 154 and book II, chap. 25. — "Coutume de Touraine-Anjou", no. 143. — "Anciennes coutumes d'Anjou et du Maine", F, nos. 1336 to 1337, 1342, 1349, 1399, 1422, Vol. II, p. 495; I, nos. 121 and 122, Vol. III, p. 278; L, no. 322, Vol. IV, p. 275.

[37] "Grand Coutumier de Normandie", chap. 86, ed. *Gruchy*, p. 196. Moreover, one who orders an insult is punished as well as the one who uttered it: "Anciennes coutumes d'Anjou et du Maine", F, nos. 1345 and 1350, Vol. II, pp. 497 and 498; "Livre des droiz et des commandemens", nos. 287, 506, 592.

[38] "Livre des droiz et des commandemens", nos. 608 and 648.

punished by a fine of sixty sous or more in discretion.[39] According to Bouteiller, one who insults the king, his feudal lord, or his mother, is to be exposed on the gibbet for three days, branded, and banished from the province.[40] This jurist is the first to distinguish insult from defamation; but of the latter, however, he makes virtually a serious insult entailing a fine of sixty sous; this rule is found also in most of the other custumals.[41]

Though blows, insults, and wounds are (as already remarked) in general punished by more or less heavy fines, yet if the offender cannot pay he is imprisoned for the debt.

Most crimes against the *family* consist in offenses against women. There are, however, some which might be committed against men. Thus the crime of castration is punished like homicide.[42] Bestiality is classed with rape, and is punishable by burning, both for men and for women.[43] In Beaumanoir's time, the crime of "rapt", or the abduction of women, was very frequent; the great jurist gives us on this topic some curious information. First he observes that one must be cautious in lodging an accusation of this crime; for often girls or women falsify when they assert that they have been carried off by force and violence. It seems, moreover, that abduction was practised, not only to seduce or to marry an unmarried female, but also upon married women in order to get possession of the valuables which the women might take with them.[44] This offense of abduction incurred the death penalty; but the offender could avoid it by marrying his victim, with her consent; marriage then stopped the judicial proceedings.[45]

Rape is no less grave a crime than abduction, and is also punishable by death; but the victim must make speedy complaint and exhibit visible signs of the violence.[46] If the rape was followed

[39] "Livre des droiz et des commandemens", no. 651.

[40] *Bouteiller*, "Somme rural", ed. 1621, book II, tit. 40, pp. 1477 and 1486.

[41] *Bouteiller*, "Somme rural", ed. 1621, book II, tit. 40, p. 1478.

[42] "Livre des droiz et des commandemens", no. 362.

[43] "Registre criminel du Châtelet", Vol. I, pp. 225 and 567; "Registre criminel de Saint-Martin-des-Champs", p. xcix.

[44] *Beaumanoir*, chap. 30, nos. 95 *et seq.*, Vol. I, p. 449.

[45] "Anciennes coutumes d'Anjou et du Maine", F, no. 1328, Vol. II, p. 492; L, no. 288, Vol. IV, p. 264; "Livre des droiz et des commandemens", nos. 202, 762; *Bouteiller*, "Somme rural", ed. 1621, book I, tit. 39, p. 477; book II, tit. 40, p. 1489. The punishment would have been the same if a man or a child had been carried off. See the text first cited.

[46] On this subject one will find in the Custumals numerous details: see *Marnier*, "Etablissements de Normandie", p. 34 *et seq.*; "Livre des droiz et des commandemens", nos. 335, 345, 902; "Anciennes coutumes d'Anjou et du Maine", A, no. 9, Vol. I, p. 45; F, no. 1320, Vol. II, p. 489;

by marriage, it was not punished, — as in the case of abduction. If both crimes were committed, subsequent marriage excused both.[47] Carnal intercourse by consent with an unmarried female was no crime; but she must be taken as wife, or given a dowry according to her condition in life.[48] But a guardian who takes advantage of his ward is punished by confiscation of all his goods, banishment, and even by death penalty if he returns from banishment.[49]

The most serious crimes against *marriage* are, naturally, bigamy, adultery, and marriages between persons prohibited by the Church. Bigamy included, not only the marrying of two living wives, but also the marrying a widow.[50] The punishment for adultery varied greatly, according to locality; sometimes it was severe, and sometimes altogether ridiculous. Mostly no punishment needed to be inflicted; for the regional Customs gave the husband the right to kill his wife when she was caught in the act.[51] According to the "Livre de jostice et de plet" adulterers might crave pardon of the king for the first two offenses; the third time they incurred the penalty of exile and of general confiscation.[52] At Villefranche, in Périgord, adulterers had the choice between a fine of a hundred sous or running naked through the town;[53] according to the Custom of Prissey, near Mâcon, adulterers paid a fine of sixty sous or were whipped through the town.[54] This alternative penalty, shameful and contrary to public decency, was widely spread in the Middle Ages, especially in the South, though finally its objectionable character was recognized; in Bouteiller's time it seems to have disappeared in the North, where

L, no. 288, vol. IV, p. 264. See also "Livre de jostice et de plet", pp. 282, 285, 290.

[47] "Anciennes coutumes d'Anjou et du Maine", F, no. 1367, Vol. II, p. 503.

[48] "Anciennes coutumes d'Anjou et du Maine", F, no. 1319, Vol. II, p. 488.

[49] *Bouteiller*, "Somme rural", ed. 1621, book I, tit. 39, p. 479.

[50] They had wished also to maintain that the husband became bigamous when he had relation with a woman knowing that she was an adulteress. See on these different points, "Anciennes coutumes d'Anjou et du Maine", K, nos. 13 *et seq.*, Vol. IV, p. 50; L, nos. 441 and 442, Vol. IV, 326. — See also "Livre des droiz et des commandemens", no. 836, which does not admit bigamy on the part of the cleric in a particular case.

[51] *Beaumanoir*, chap. 30, nos. 102, 103, 104, Vol. I, pp. 455 and 456.

[52] "Livre de jostice et de plet", p. 280.

[53] Royal Letters of October, 1357, in the "Recueil du Louvre", Vol. III, pp. 201 and 210.

[54] Royal Letters of October, 1362, in the "Recueil du Louvre", Vol. III, p. 597.

the penalty of the fine only was inflicted.[55] Occasionally, the judicial duel was ordered in litigations of this kind, *e.g.*, by a judgment of the Paris Parliament in 1386, as related by Jean Le Coq, who was counsel for one of the accused and a witness of the combat.[56] Those who, without papal dispensation, contracted marriages forbidden by law suffered a general confiscation of all their possessions, in favor of the lord high justiciar; this penalty was clearly borrowed from the Roman law.[57]

Of crimes against *property*, arson is the gravest and theft the most frequent. Most custumals punish the crime of arson by death; others are less severe, but perhaps more cruel, for they speak of loss of the eyes or of some other inhuman punishment.[58]

The medieval jurists are usually severe against theft, or larceny, which they class in most cases as a capital crime. The Custumals distinguish several kinds of theft. Thus theft with violence is termed " violerie ", " eschapelie ", " force "; it is virtually a distinct crime, punished with particular severity, almost always by death.[59] Whether the stolen property was taken from an owner, a borrower, or a pledgee, was immaterial; either might bring the charge, if within a year from the crime.[60] Although the medieval law had generally outgrown the principle of primitive law, which deemed the crime more serious when the offender was taken in the

[55] *Bouteiller*, "Somme rural", edition of 1621, book II, tit. 8, p. 1257.

[56] Jean Le Coq entertained the belief (still surviving in his day) that God intervened in these ordeals, and yet the man who was killed at the duel in question was innocent, as was proved by the testimony of the guilty person himself, who confessed it on his deathbed. See *Isambert*, Vol. VI, p. 619.

[57] *Cf.* Const. 6, "De incestis nuptiis", VI, 6; and "Livre des droiz et des commandemens", no. 837, Vol. II, p. 232.

[58] "Livre de jostice et de plet", pp. 279, 305; "Livre des droiz et des commandemens", no. 347. See also the ordinance of Philip V, November 16 to 19, 1319, an ordinance ratified by the queen, Countess of Bourgogne, against incendiaries and those who, under pretext of private war, disturbed public peace in the earldom of Bourgogne: *Isambert*, Vol. III, p. 231.

[59] "Etablissements de Saint Louis", book I, chap. 82; "Grand Coutumier de Normandie", chap. 71; "Livre de jostice et de plet", 280, 285, 300.—"Anciennes coutumes d'Anjou et du Maine", B, no. 22, Vol. I, p. 78; F, no. 1334, Vol. II, p. 493; "Coutume de Bayonne", chap. 114, no. 9.

[60] "Assises de Jérusalem", chap. 58; *Jean d'Ibelin*, chap. 119; *Pierre de Fontaines*, "Conseil", chap. 20, no. 10; "Ancien coutumier de Bourgogne", chap. 18; *Beaumanoir*, chap. 31, no. 15, Vol. I, p. 464. This jurist does not, however, allow the bailor to recover possession of the property unless the bailee is insolvent, chap. 31, no. 16. See also in respect to theft, "Livre de jostice et de plet", pp. 279, 281, 292.

act (because the victim then feels more keenly the violation of his right), yet in the case of theft we find the law still directly influenced by the early Germanic traditions, for the thief taken in the act is punished with great severity. The notion of taking in the act was fulfilled if the owner pursues without delay or relenting and succeeds in catching him while still in possession of the stolen goods.[61] The offender is then brought before the court of the place where he has been caught, and is not allowed to purge himself; while if not taken in the act, he must have been brought before the judge of the lord on whose land he resided, and would have been allowed to defend himself.[62]

At the period when the Salic Law treated theft as a private wrong only liable to a fine, the imperial Capitularies were already making it a genuine violation of the public peace, severely punished; the thief was to have his eye put out; for a second offense his nose was cut off; for a third, he was condemned to death.[63] The medieval Custumals preserved, in general, this system, introducing no change except as to the manner of mutilation;[64] thus Liger requires that, according to the kind of animal stolen, the thief be condemned to death, have his eyes put out, or his nose cut off.[65] But furthermore, the Custumals punished certain thefts (even when the offender was not taken in the act) with particular severity; they imposed the death penalty, with confiscation of property, according to the circumstances of the crime or the rank of the persons, for a theft by night, or with violence, or by a servant from his master, or by a vassal from his lord.[66] Conversely, thefts

[61] "Très ancienne coutume de Bretagne", chap. 101; "Grand Coutumier de Normandie", chap. 71, which requires, however, that the victim of the theft should raise a hue and cry. According to the Custom of Bayonne (chap. 67) if one night has elapsed since the theft, the offender is not taken in the act.

[62] "Assises de la cour des bourgeois", chap. 241; "Etablissements de Saint Louis", book II, chap. 2. — *Beaumanoir*, chap. 30, no. 93 and chap. 31, nos. 1 *et seq.*, no. 14; "Grand Coutumier de Normandie", chap. 23. For the curious particulars of the procedure for theft, see *Jobbé-Duval*, "Etude historique sur la revendication des meubles en droit français."

[63] Capit. of 779, *Pertz*, "Leges", I, 38.

[64] "Coutume de Touraine-Anjou", no. 22; "Etablissements de Saint Louis", book I, chap. 32.

[65] "Anciennes coutumes d'Anjou et du Maine", F, no. 1379, Vol. II, p. 505.

[66] "Assises de la cour des bourgeois", chap. 232; "Charte communale d'Abbeville", Art. 2; "Olim", Vol. I, pp. 240 and 328; "Livre des droiz et des commandemens", nos. 347 and 580; "Anciennes coutumes d'Anjou et du Maine", B, no. 28, Vol. I, p. 81; C, no. 26, Vol. I, p. 217; D, nos. 33, 81, 82, Vol. I, pp. 406, 432; F, nos. 796, 797, 1371, 1373, 1382, Vol. II, pp. 288, 504, 505; I, no. 101, Vol. III, p. 262.

of least importance, involving objects of little value, were punishable only by banishment or by fine.[67]

This general system is still found in Bouteiller. He considers larceny, when the offender is taken in the act, as a capital crime, if the stolen object is worth more than five sous; below this sum, it is punishable the first time by the loss of the ear, the second time, by death. Theft not taken in the act is punishable only by a fine of fourfold value in favor of the lord, or by the lash if the offender is insolvent. Bouteiller is, however, more severe for certain thefts, such as robbing of graves, children, and cattle; but, on the other hand, he recommends the judges to be indulgent toward the man who has stolen through necessity. Finally, he classes with theft (but not confusing them) certain acts which to-day would constitute breach of trust, cheating, or other forms of dishonesty; thus he inflicts a fine of fourfold upon the man who, knowingly, sells the same object to several persons.[68]

The crime of *forgery* (falsification) is also a property offense, and has numerous varieties: false money, false merchandise, false measure, false writing, false complaint, false witness, false oath, etc. All these offenses are, in general, capital, and are severely penalized.

Counterfeiters are punished by death or by the loss of the eyes; quite often they are condemned to be thrown into a boiling caldron.[69] Bouteiller regards counterfeiters guilty of "lèse majesté"; coinage was, according to him, a royal prerogative, and he demands that they be boiled; but he warns us against confusing with buyers of false money.[70] He who counterfeits merchandise must have his hand cut off and the merchandise destroyed; if he has merely sold false merchandise without manufacturing it, he incurs a fine of sixty sous.[71] He who uses false measures is quite often condemned to the loss of the thumb.[72]

[67] "Registre criminel de Saint-Martin-des-Champs", pp. 94, 104, 111.

[68] See on this last point "Somme rural", ed. 1621, book II, tit. 40, p. 1480, also p. 1471; "Livre de jostice et de plet", pp. 104 and 280. For the general theory of theft or larceny, see book I, tit. 35, p. 318.

[69] "Livre de jostice et de plet", p. 281; "Registre criminel de Saint-Martin-des-Champs", p. 97; "Anciennes coutumes d'Anjou et du Maine", C, no. 25, Vol. I, p. 215; F, no. 1364, Vol. II, p. 502; L, no. 289, vol. IV, p. 265; "Livre des droiz et des commandemens", no. 347. See also *Boutaric*, "La France sous Philippe le Bel", p. 321.

[70] *Bouteiller*, "Somme rural", book I, tit. 39, p. 481, where interesting details can be found on the various crimes whose object may be money.

[71] "Livre des droiz et des commandemens", no. 260, Vol. I, p. 411; "Anciennes coutumes d'Anjou et du Maine", B, no. 158, Vol. I, p. 163; C, no. 144, Vol. I, p. 345; D, no. 115, Vol. I, p. 445; F, nos. 1393 and 1420, Vol. II, p. 507 and 513; L, no. 325, Vol. IV, p. 280.

[72] "Anciennes coutumes d'Anjou et du Maine", B, nos. 154 and 157

Forgery, properly speaking (consisting of forging or altering a document) is, in general, punishable by the pillory; but if the offender is an officer or a notary, then by death.[73]

The *false witness* is threatened with the pillory, a long imprisonment, or a discretionary fine;[74] he who brings false complaint is threatened with banishment or fine.[75] But they are less severe against false oath, which is only punishable by a fine of sixty sous, except in serious cases when this pecuniary penalty then becomes discretionary.[76]

With offenses against property can be classed those against the *game* and *fish* laws. Although the day of exaggerated penalties for such cases had not yet come, the hunting or the fishing rights of the feudal lords or the king were already protected by severe measures. The law finally reached the general principle that hunting was to be reserved for certain persons. An ordinance of January 10, 1396, proclaimed that nobody had the right to hunt unless he were a noble or a townsman living on his property; hunting implements found in the houses of plebeians were to be confiscated; peasants were allowed only to keep watch-dogs, to scare away wild animals from the crops.[77] Some time earlier, the right to hunt in the royal forests had been regulated by special ordinances; royal Letters of September 7, 1393, forbade the hunting of wild animals in the royal forests unless by royal Letters signed by the Duke of Burgundy as general master of the hunt; and an ordinance of March 29, 1396, required besides, that these Letters should be verified by the master-general of waters and forests.[78] Violations of game and fish laws were still classed in Bouteiller's time among non-capital crimes. He who hunted or fished at the expense of his lord forfeited his personal property; in other cases a mere fine, usually sixty sous.[79] He who stole game

Vol. I, pp. 162 and 163; C, nos. 142 and 144, Vol. I, p. 344; D, no. 115, Vol. I, p. 445; F, nos. 1392 and 1409, Vol. II, pp. 507 and 510; I, no. 137, Vol. III, p. 288; L, nos. 322 and 325, Vol. IV, pp. 275 and 280.

[73] "Livre de jostice et de plet", p. 284; "Registre criminel de Saint-Martin-des-Champs", p. cii; "Livre des droiz et des commandemens", no. 285; "Anciennes coutumes d'Anjou et du Maine", F, no. 1331 and 1332, Vol. II, p. 493.

[74] *Beaumanoir*, chap. 30, nos. 45 *et seq.*, Vol. I, p. 424. *Cf.* Vol. II, pp. 118, 396, 398.

[75] *Bouteiller*, "Somme rural", book II, tit. 40, edition of 1621, p. 1491.

[76] *Beaumanoir*, chap. 30, nos. 87 *et seq.*, Vol. I, p. 433.

[77] Ord. of January 10, 1396, *Isambert*, Vol. VI, p. 772.

[78] *Isambert*, Vol. VI, pp. 756 and 770.

[79] "Anciennes coutumes d'Anjou et du Maine", D, nos. 113 and 127, Vol. I, pp. 444 and 451; I, nos. 135 and 154, Vol. III, pp. 287 and 300.—

or fish incurred usually a similar fine; if by night, he incurred death.[80]

There were also numerous minor *police measures,* usually inflicting only fines, although at times very heavy ones. At this period the issuance of royal ordinances had not become frequent, as it did in the following period; but there was a legislative activity in the interest of public peace and order, and, where royal ordinances are lacking, we find measures of this kind in the regional Customs and in the town statutes. Gambling is what the royal power chiefly endeavors to repress; the very multiplicity of ordinances seems to prove their inefficiency.[81] Possibly these prohibitions were prompted, rather by the desire of preventing men from amusing themselves at the expense of military service, than of protecting them from pecuniary ruin. In Paris, an ordinance of the provost forbade card playing, tennis, bowling, dice, and nine-pins in the taverns;[82] this was indeed a police measure intended to prevent quarrels. Bouteiller recommends that keepers of gambling houses be condemned to a fine of sixty sous.[83]

It was forbidden to maintain *houses of ill-fame;* mostly local customs regulated sexual morals. At times the penalty was very severe; according to the "Livre de jostice et de plet," the keeper of a house of ill-fame is to be whipped and banished from the city, and his property confiscated to the king.[84] Other police measures prohibited the wearing of masks in the street; going about with weapons or armor; pasturing animals in the wheat at certain times of the year.[85]

Vagrancy is a plague of all epochs; but in the Middle Ages it seems to have been less serious than is generally believed; for abbeys and monasteries were always ready to shelter indigent

"Livre des droiz et des commandemens", no 437. — *Bouteiller*, "Somme rural", book II, tit. 40, edition of 1621, p. 1476.

[80] *Beaumanoir*, chap. 30, no. 105, Vol. I, p. 456. — Ord. of Philip the Fair of 1299, *Isambert*, Vol. II, p. 724.

[81] Ordinance of Philip the Fair of 1319 forbidding, under penalty of a fine, the playing of dice, backgammon or trick-track, quoits, nine-pins, billiards, bowling and other similar games which divert men from military drills: *Isambert*, Vol. III, p. 242; Ordinance of Charles V of April 3, 1369, which forbids, under penalty of a fine, the participation in games of chance and enjoins the practice of the bow and cross-bow: *Isambert*, Vol. III, p. 352.

[82] January 22, 1397, *Isambert*, Vol VI, p. 782.

[83] "Somme rural", book II, tit. 40, ed. 1621, p. 1473.

[84] "Livre de jostice et de plet", p. 282.

[85] Ord. of Charles VI of March 9, 1399, *Isambert*, Vol. VI, p. 844: *Bouteiller*, "Somme rural", book II, tit. 40, ed. 1621, pp. 1474 and 1483.

persons. Still, we find at times in the old regional Customs measures against vagrants; magistrates may arrest them, imprison them temporarily, examine them, and if no crime can be charged against them, may expel them.[86]

Naturally there were also at this period fiscal offenses, — nonpayment of fees or tolls for crossing fields, indirect taxes on wines, salt, and other articles; [87] but they offer nothing exceptional, and are common to all times. What is more curious, and peculiar to the period, are certain offenses, half civil, half feudal, which concern the property-system, — for instance, taking possession without the seisin of the lord; delay in paying quit-rents, taxes on sales, or similar dues; all of them misdemeanors, generally punishable by fine.[88] We note, also, that Beaumanoir considers disseizin and disturbance of possession as genuine offenses, and therefore he treats of them after the other misdemeanors.[89]

Certain offenses, equally characteristic of the time, may be designated *offenses of procedure*. The extreme rigor of the formalities of judicial procedure in the Middle Ages is well known. The observance of the strictest formalities was sought by severe methods; a violation resulted not only in the loss of the case, but very often also in a fine, at times even very heavy; and the men of law were the more insistent on this respect for formalities as the fines benefited the lords. These penalties imposed by the sheriff for errors of procedure were an important time of revenue for the lords. For ample proof of this, one may consult the old accounts of the Exchequer of Normandy.[90] Sometimes the regional Customs, showing pity on the poor plaintiffs, exposed as they were every instant to a great variety of fines, conceded the right to ask permission to speak without incurring the dangers of technical errors; the lord or his representative could grant them this favor, or, at any rate, up to a certain sum.[91] A defendant especially ran

[86] "Anciennes coutumes d'Anjou et du Maine", D, no. 84, Vol. I, p. 434; F, no. 43, Vol. II, p. 48; I, no. 103, Vol. III, p. 264; L, no. 294, Vol. IV, p. 267.

[87] *Bouteiller*, "Somme rural", book II, tit. 40, ed. of 1621, p. 1484.

[88] *Beaumanoir*, chap. 30, nos. 38 to 45. He who is accused of not paying his quit-rent, his field-rent in kind or similar dues, import duties or town duties, may, however, clear himself by oath: *Beaumanoir*, chap. 30, nos. 68, 70, 71, Vol. I, p. 434.

[89] *Beaumanoir*, chap. 32, Vol. I, p. 465.

[90] *Cf. Delisle*, "Des revenus publics en Normandie au XIIe siècle", in the "Bibliothèque de l'Ecole des Chartes", 3d series, Vol. III, pp. 105 *et seq.* *Cf.* "Great Roll of the Pipe", I, Richard I, 71.

[91] *Roisin*, "Franchises de Lille", p. 29, no. 6. *Cf. Brunner*, "La parole et la forme dans l'ancienne procédure française", in the "Revue

great risk, from the very beginning of the trial; in fact, he was obliged, under pain of a fine, if ordered by the judge, to answer word by word the charge formulated against him;[92] he even risked falling "in misericordiam curiæ", which gave ground for a discretionary fine, so that, in strictness, the lord would have the right to seize all his personal property. If the defendant wished to plead an excuse, he could do so only after making answer, or, at least, together with his answer.[93] With his proof especially the law was severe; any technical fault in furnishing it forfeited the right to furnish it, and brought on also the fine which would have been inflicted in case the proof, if properly made, had not been complete. In taking an oath, the formula, the utterance, the attitude of the swearer, the manner of placing his hand, were all strictly prescribed. "Très ancien Coutumier de Normandie" gives curious details on this subject. The inexperienced plaintiff (it tells us) will fall on his knees to take oath, without awaiting the judge's order; for this alone he is "in misericordiam ducis", and the clerk records the fine in his register; whereupon, the party rashly rises, to retrieve his error, but this time commits another, for he should have awaited the order of the judge, and for this second error he incurs a new fine.[94] One might multiply examples, but they are too well known to need dwelling upon.[95] The counsel ("for-speaker", "prolocutor") ran less danger than the client himself; nevertheless, he must take care not to go beyond his powers, for later his client might disavow his acts, and if the client was successful in this, the counsel incurred, in his turn, a fine in favor of the lord.[96] Once sentence was passed, the appeal must

critique de législation et de jurisprudence", nouv. sér. I, 1871–1872, pp. 22, 480, [reprinted in his "Forschungen", 1894; originally published in "K. K. Wiener Akademie der Wissenschaften", Vol. 77, p. 655. — ED.].

[91] See "Olim", Vol. II, p. 744, no. 56 and p. 774, no. 114.

[93] See for example *Beaumanoir*, chap. 19, no. 11. *Cf. Brunner, loc. cit.*, pp. 34, 237, 240, 241.

[94] "Três ancien Coutumier de Normandie", ed. *Tardif*, chap. 65, p. 56: "1o, Placitatores vero ponebant in misericordia simplicem populum, quoniam absque precepto justicie genua sua flectebant venientes ad juramenta sua. Cum igitur, genua flectentes, se audissent accusari de afflexione genuum, surgebant; placitatores vero eos accusabant, quoniam surrexerant absque precepto justicie, et ita clericus justicie eos in pellicula sua scribebat in misericordia. 2o, De hoc dixit Normannus d'Orgieville quod ipse tantum vixerat ut videret ludere in curia domini. Regis ad Bernardum Beccantem, sicut pueri ludentes dicunt: 'Bernarde, surge'; qui, nisi cito surrexerit, in facie intingetur. Eodem modo scribit clericus in pellicula intingit populum simplicem injuste in misericordia."

[95] See in this respect *Brunner, op. cit.*, pp. 246, 250, 254, 256.

[96] *Beaumanoir*, chap. 5, nos. 7 and 14; *Desmares*, "Décisions", 412. *Cf. Brunner, op.* and *loc. cit.*, p. 553.

be taken on the spot and according to formula, under pain of losing the right of appeal and being fined. There was also a fine against the appellant if defeated on the main point; and a fine against the judges of the previous trial if he wins.[97]

After the formalism disappeared, the procedural fines were preserved, but with a different aim, to punish the bad faith of plaintiffs. Thus, there were fines, more or less heavy, reaching at times the sum of sixty sous, against one who failed to present himself on continuance of a civil case; [98] against one who wrongly opposed an attachment; against one who lost in an action for novel disseizin, or of breach of peace, of truce, or of faith (as formerly against one who lost his appeal); against the debtor who denied his debt or his written agreement; against the creditor if he claimed twice what was due him, or if he arrested his debtor without right; against one who bought property in dispute; and against a plaintiff who summoned the defendant before the wrong judge.[99] Judges and lawyers were equally punished when they failed in their duty. If the judge took a bribe, he incurred a discretionary fine, the loss of his office, and damages.[100] The lawyer guilty of the same offense suffered the same penalties. A discretionary fine and the loss of office were the penalties for the counsel or the attorney who made with a client the agreement of "quota litis." [101] The counsel whose acts were disavowed for excess of authority also incurred a fine; as also one who insulted a client.[102] It seems that the mere act of pleading without power of attorney was a misdemeanor, although no disavowal followed; the offender must pay the judge two capons.[103] The clerk or the bailiff also, who drew up a document and forgot to date it, incurred a fine of two capons to the judge.[104]

Besides crimes and misdemeanors of types common to all ages,

[97] *Beaumanoir*, chap. 61, nos. 44 and 51, Vol. II, pp. 391 and 395; "Anciens coutumiers de Picardie", ed. *Marnier*, pp. 38, 58, 61, 72, 84.

[98] *Bouteiller*, "Somme rural", book II, tit. 40, ed. 1621, p. 1467. According to the "Registre criminel de Saint-Martin-des-Champs", he who failed to present himself in a criminal case was to be banished; see pp. cv and cvi.

[99] *Bouteiller*, "Somme rural", book II, tit. 40, pp. 1467 to 1472, 1479, 1480, 1483.

[100] *Bouteiller*, book II, tit. 40, p. 1481.

[101] *Bouteiller*, book II, tit. 40, p. 1482.

[102] *Bouteiller*, book II, tit. 40, p. 1482.

[103] [For the narrow limits of the attorney's authority at this period, see *Brunner's* essay, translated in III "Illinois Law Review" 257 (1908), "The Early History of the Attorney." — ED.]

[104] *Bouteiller*, book II, tit. 40, p. 1470.

the feudal State, with its special social relations, developed what may be termed *feudal offenses;* they formed the sanction for the duties of fealty, faith, and homage imposed on the vassal toward his lord, and the duty of protection imposed on the lord toward his vassal. The vassal guilty of treason forfeited his fief, which returned to his lord; on the other hand, the guilty lord lost the vassalage due him.[105] If the vassal commits at the same time, a treason and a common law offense, as, if he makes an attempt on his lord's life, or on the honor of his lord's daughter, both the feudal forfeiture and the ordinary penalties are inflicted.[106] The violation of sworn faith must not be confused with the neglect of faith and homage; the latter offense, during the early Middle Ages, also entailed absolute forfeiture, but later it was punishable only by conditional forfeiture.[107] Less serious feudal offenses were in general punishable only by fines. Thus, in the earlier period, according to the "Assises de Jérusalem," the vassal owed a subsidy or "aid" (on penalty of a felony) only when needed to ransom his lord from the enemy; in later times, the failure to pay any sort of subsidy or "aid" led only to a suit by the lord against the vassal.[108] In Germany and in Lombardy neglect of military service led to confiscation of the fief; in France it was early conceded that a mere fine was imposed for refusal to enter the army or to pay for exemption in time of war.[109]

As feudalism had led to the creation of offenses peculiar to that social status, so also the influence of the Church, extending over the secular life, had led to the recognition of certain offenses special to this period. The most serious of these special crimes, repressed

[105] *Beaumanoir*, chap. 45, Vol. II, p. 214. — *Jean d'Ibelin*, pp. 190 *et seq.*, Vol. I, p. 303.

[106] "Anciennes coutumes d'Anjou et du Maine", C, no. 48, Vol. I, p. 244. So also, if the offense had been committed by the lord toward his vassal; see "Etablissements de Saint Louis", book II, chap. 38, ed. *Viollet*, Vol. II, p. 463; "Anciennes coutumes d'Anjou et du Maine", B, no. 55, Vol. I, p. 93; C, no. 49, Vol. I, p. 245; E, no. 129, Vol. I, p. 452; F, no. 940, Vol. II, p. 336. — Without directly offending his lord, the vassal might commit an infamous deed, for instance, abjure the Christian religion; in this case also there ensued dissolution of the feudal lien.

[107] *Jean Le Coq*, "Question 172", cites a decree of 1388 which refuses to the lords the right of confiscating the fief, but he remarks that this is a new rule.

[108] "Assises de Jérusalem", *Jean d'Ibelin*, chap. 269, Vol. I, p. 397; "Etablissements, coutumes, assises et arrêts de l'Echiquier de Normandie", ed. *Marnier*, pp. 33 and 101.

[109] *Brussel*, "Nouvel examen de l'usage général des fiefs", Vol. I, p. 167. As for Germany and Lombardy, see "Libri feudorum", II, 24, 6; "Constitutio de expeditione romana", § 2, *Pertz*, "Leges", Vol. II, p. 3.

with the greatest rigor, was naturally the crime of *heresy*. In Gaul, under the Merovingians, and in Italy, under the Lombards, a certain régime of tolerance had been established between Catholicism and Arianism. Under the Carolingians we still find no systematic legislation against heretics; at that epoch heresy was rare and created little apprehension. But the appearance of Catharism, toward the year 1000, gave rise to a radical change in the law. Catharism — the heresy of the Albigenses — spread with alarming rapidity through Italy, Spain, France, and Germany. In a society like feudalism both civil and religious, it constituted one of the gravest dangers. Thus, as soon as heretics became numerous, the Church and royalty stopped at no measure to eradicate them. The Church no longer contented itself with sending heretics before the ordinary tribunals; it created the tribunal of the Inquisition, or the Holy Office, having a special jurisdiction over offenses against the faith. It deprived heretics of the benefit of the ordinary canonical procedure, which conceded important guarantees to the accused: in particular, the accused could not obtain the names of the witnesses and of the informers; the disqualifications of witnesses disappeared in all trials of heretics; the accused was refused the assistance of a lawyer; and, finally, torture is introduced, following the Roman law. The repression of heresy led to the reappearance of this cruel expedient; for apparently torture was applied but little by the judges of the Church, apart from trials against heretics. But unfortunately, it now came into general use in secular courts.

Following the Northern practices, the regions of the South came to adopt the punishment of burning alive, as the usual one for heretics; although this practice had no justification either in statute or in tradition. As early as the 1000 s, this terrible penalty had been employed with extreme rigor in Germanic countries and in the North of France. But in the regions of Southern France the treatment of the Albigenses at the same period was markedly different; during the first part of the century, they incurred spiritual penalties and were rarely put to death; during the second part of that century, and even to the end of the 1100 s, Catharism was even tolerated. Several Councils undoubtedly ordained measures against the heretics, but it does not seem that they were seriously applied, and at all events they resulted only in the confiscation of property and imprisonment, not the death penalty. The pontificate of Innocent III (1198) marked a new phase in the history of the movement against heresy, and inspired the crusade against the Albigenses. Without enacting new penalties, it strove to enforce existing laws, by stimulating the zeal of princes, and by causing most of these Church laws to be adopted also by the cities in their statutes. Finally, in 1209, the crusaders of the North, invading the southern provinces, began to burn all heretics. To this invasion we owe the introduction of the penalty of burning in these countries. From that time on, burning became the common punishment of heretics throughout France.[110] Aubry de Trois Fontaines gives us the account of the punishment of 183 heretics who were burned at Mont Aimé in the presence of a large number of priests and an immense concourse of people.[111] As is well known, Jeanne d'Arc was also burned for heresy, on the 29th of May, 1431. At times a different penalty was used; thus, in 1381, Hugues Aubriot was condemned for heresy to spend his life in a pit subsisting on bread and water.[112] But these cases were exceptions.

In the 1200 s the climax of severity was reached in punishing the heretics of the South, — the Albigenses. The Church displayed a great activity, and at its instigation royalty also adopted the severest measures. The Lateran Council had already ordered, at the beginning of this century, the extermination of heretics; their personalty was confiscated to the civic authorities (except in case of clerical heretics, when it reverted to the Church).[113] In France a royal ordinance was issued in 1228 against the heretics of Languedoc.[114] The following year the Council of Narbonne excommunicated the Albigenses, required the presence of a priest when a will was executed, and appointed inquisitors in all parishes; another Council held at Toulouse in the same year confirmed the Inquisition and enacted the most severe measures against heretics.[115]

[110] *Julien Havet* has well shown this in his memoir entitled: "L'hérésie et le bras seculier au moyen âge jusqu'au XIIIe siècle", Paris, 1881. However, he has not perhaps given enough weight to Roman influence, which, in time of danger, suggested to the Church the idea of more severe repression, extending the death penalty, and resulting in the adoption of torture against the heretics. See on this question an article by *Ficher*, in the "Mittheilungen des Instituts für österreischischen Geschichtsforschungen", 1880, pp. 177–226, 430; also *Paul Meyer*, "La chanson de la croisade contre les Albigeois"; *Viollet*, "Etablissements de Saint Louis", Vol. I, p. 252.

[111] *Pertz*, "Scriptores", Vol. XXIII, p. 944, quoted by *Viollet*, *loc. cit.*

[112] *Isambert*, Vol. VI, p. 561.

[113] "Lateran Council of 1215", chap. 3, in *Hefele*, "Conciliengeschichte" (French translation), Vol. VIII, p. 123; *Labbe*, Vol. XI, p. 74, col. 148.

[114] *Isambert*, Vol. I, p. 230.

[115] *Isambert*, Vol. I, p. 234. See also an ordinance of April, 1250, addressed to the inquisitors: *ibid.*, Vol. I, p. 254.

Under pretext of heresy, all kinds of abuses seem to have got a footing,—especially arbitrary arrests; thus, Letters of April 27, 1287, enjoined upon the seneschal of Carcassonne to resist arrests made under pretext of heresy, unless the crime were first proved. Beginning in the following century, these severe measures revive in force. No appeal is allowed from the sentences of bishops and inquisitors, either by heretics, or by their abettors or accomplices or their defenders.[116] The magistrates must, under pain of the loss of their offices, swear to expel heretics from their jurisdiction; the lords are also under obligation to rid their lands within a year of these criminals, under pain of confiscation in favor of the Catholics.[117]

The "Etablissements de Saint Louis" show us the procedure employed and the penalty usually pronounced against heretics. Every person suspected of heresy was to be arrested by the secular authorities and delivered to the bishop; the latter examined him as to his faith; if the accused was convicted of heresy, the bishop delivered him to the civil power, which condemned him to death, ordinarily by fire, declared him infamous, and pronounced the confiscation of his personalty in favor of the lord; his real estate was respected, probably under the influence of old Germanic regional Customs.[118] Finally, the houses serving as meeting places for heretics were to be razed; though this practice was abolished by Letters of October 19, 1378.[119] These proceedings exhibit the allotment of jurisdiction prevailing between the spiritual and the secular authorities. The Church claimed the right to prosecute heresy and apostasy, as well as witchcraft, adultery, and usury;[120] but since, on principle, it could not pronounce the death penalty and yet heresy merited it, it avoided the difficulty by delivering the offender to the secular authority. The Church tried him and declared whether he was guilty of heresy, then it turned him to the secular authority, which undertook to sentence him to death and execute him.[121]

[116] Year 1298, *Isambert*, Vol. II, p. 718.

[117] Letter of December 15, 1315, in *Isambert*, Vol. III, p. 126.

[118] "Etablissements de Saint Louis", book I, chapters 90 and 127, ed. *Viollet*, Vol. II, pp. 147 and 240; "Livre de jostice et de plet", p. 12; "Anciennes coutumes d'Anjou et du Maine", B, no. 94, Vol. I, p. 120; C, no. 87, Vol. I, p. 304; E, nos. 77 and 87, Vol. I, pp. 430 and 435; F, no. 1365, Vol. II, p. 502; I, nos. 96 and 106, Vol. III, pp. 258 and 267; "Livre des droiz et des commandemens", Vol. I, no. 255; *Bouteiller*, "Somme rural", book I, tit. 28, ed. of 1621, p. 290.

[119] *Isambert*, Vol. V, p. 491.

[120] *Beaumanoir*, chap. 11, nos. 2 and 25, vol. I, pp. 157 and 167.

[121] "Etablissements de Saint Louis", *loc. cit.*; *Beaumanoir*, chap. 11, nos. 2, 12, 25, Vol. I, pp. 157, 162, 167.

Sorcery, witchraft, incantation, and other more or less similar acts, were considered as the next most serious crimes against the Church. During the period in question royal ordinances had not yet dealt with these crimes.[122] Moreover, there was no accord, regarding these offenses, between the civil and the spiritual authorities, as in the case of heresy. The Church claimed the prosecution of sorcery; [123] but we see, from certain cases tried before the secular courts, that the latter claimed to take cognizance whenever the sorcery or incantation had caused death or sickness; [124] under the influence of Roman law they had come, in certain cases, to consider sorcerers and soothsayers as guilty of homicide.[125] Bouteiller shows unheard-of severity against those convicted of this crime; they are to be exposed on the gibbet, branded with hot iron, and even burned, according to the heinousness of the case.[126] He pronounces the same penalty against enchanters and those whom he calls the invokers of devils; interpreters of dreams he would subject to the torture with iron broaches. But all these crimes he places under the jurisdiction of the secular authority, not under that of the Church.[127]

Through the Church's influence, also, *sodomy* continued to be a crime; this was borrowed from Roman law, which, according to certain writers, had been influenced by Hebrew law; [128] that Roman law borrowed this crime from Hebrew legislation, we do not believe has been proved; but undoubtedly the Church borrowed it from Roman law, and brought about its acceptance in the Middle Ages. Here, as with heresy, the Church finds the person guilty; then the secular authority pronounces the penalty and enforces it. This penalty consists, for the first two offenses, in a mutilation; but on a further offense the offender is burned alive.[129]

[122] The first ordinance known against enchanters, sorcerers, and soothsayers is that of October 9, 1490; *Isambert*, Vol. XI, p. 190, also p. 252.

[123] *Beaumanoir*, chap. 11, no. 25, Vol. I, p. 167.

[124] "Registre du Châtelet", Vol. II, pp. 312 *et seq.*

[125] "Anciennes coutumes d'Anjou et du Maine", F, no. 1327, Vol. II, p. 491.

[126] *Bouteiller*, "Somme rural", book II, tit. 40, ed. 1621, p. 1486.

[127] *Bouteiller*, "Somme rural", book I, tit. 39, ed. 1621, p. 486.

[128] Leviticus, xx, 13. *Cf.* "Collatio legum mosaicarum et romanarum", in *Giraud*, "Novum Enchiridion", p. 293.

[129] "Etablissements de Saint Louis", book I, chap. 127, where the word "hérité" does not seem to be taken in its ordinary sense and to signify heretic, but designates rather a person guilty of sodomy. See *Viollet*, "Etablissements de Saint Louis", book I, p. 254, "Livre de jostice et de plet", pp. 279 and 280; "Anciennes coutumes d'Anjou et due Maine", F, no. 1365, Vol. II, p. 502; *Bouteiller*, "Somme rural", book I, tit. 28, ed. 1621, p. 292 and the remarks of *Charondas*, p. 302.

The other and less heinous crimes claimed for the Church's jurisdiction, *blasphemy*, adultery, and usury, are not all necessarily religious. But, in view of the numerous ordinances enacted against blasphemy during the later Middle Ages, it may be asserted that this crime was of daily occurrence, and yet that neither the secular authority nor the Church were after all able to repress it.[130] The treatises of the time tell us that blasphemy is punished with less severity than heresy; but its punishment is severe enough: he who has indecently blasphemed against God or the Virgin Mary is to be fined, put in the pillory for three days, with a placard on which his crime is named in large characters, so that every one may know of it, and then he is banished from the country.[131]

There remains one offense which was unquestionably introduced by the Church, by a false interpretation of a passage from the Gospels, — the crime of *usury*.[132] Jurisdiction was here conceded to both secular and Church courts, — at least, according to Beaumanoir;[133] but it may be supposed that this double jurisdiction came about only slowly, and that the Church at one period had claimed for its sole perquisite the prosecution of this crime, but merely failed to gain its point;[134] The kings in the Middle Ages issued many ordinances against usury;[135] but this crime has had a

[130] We note especially the following ordinances against blasphemers: Ord. of Philip the Fair of 1293, *Isambert*, Vol. II, p. 692; ord. of Charles VI of May 7, 1397, *Isambert*, Vol. VI, p. 777; Letters of the Dauphin of January 8, 1409, *Isambert*, Vol. VII, p. 228; Letters of King Charles VI of September 7, 1415, *Isambert*, Vol. VIII, p. 424; Letters of the Dauphin Regent of October 8, 1420, *Isambert*, Vol. VIII, p. 648; ordinance of Charles VII of December 1, 1437, *Isambert*, Vol. VIII, p. 852.

[131] "Registre criminel de Saint-Martin-des-Champs", p. 102; *Bouteiller*, "Somme rural", book II, tit. 40, ed. of 1621, p. 1486. The royal ordinances more than once enacted different punishments; see the ordinances already cited.

[132] See what is said in the writer's "Eléments de droit français", Vol. I, p. 167. The Church no longer holds to-day that lending on interest is an offense.

[133] *Beaumanoir*, chap. 68, no. 5, Vol. II, p. 477.

[134] In the 1000s there was in Anjou a mixed tribunal for the repression of the crime of usury; see *Viollet*, "Etablissements de Saint Louis", Vol. I, p. 255.

[135] Ordinance of 1268, *Isambert*, Vol. I, p. 338; ordinance of 1274, *Langlois*, "Regne de Philippe III le Hardi", p. 299; ordinance of 1311, *Isambert*, Vol. III, p. 11; declaration of December 8, 1312, *Isambert*, Vol. III, p. 27; ordinance of July 28, 1315, *Isambert*, Vol. III, p. 116; ordinance of February 1318, *Isambert*, Vol. III, p. 201; ordinance of January 12, 1330, *Isambert*, Vol. IV, p. 377; ordinance of March 25, 1312, *Isambert*, Vol. III, p. 404; ordinance of May 19, 1337, *Isambert*, Vol. III, p. 428; ordinance of February 13, 1345, *Isambert*, Vol. IV, p. 517; ordinance of September 18, 1350, *Isambert*, Vol. III, p. 573; ordinance of July 18, 1353, *Isambert*, Vol. III, p. 679; ordinance of March 1360,

checkered career, and the very variability of legislation on this subject is a proof of the mistake involved in penalizing a transaction perfectly lawful in itself. Thus, in certain cities (perhaps by virtue of local charter) lending at interest was permitted to all.[136] The ordinance of Philip the Fair, of 1311, while forbidding usury, permits, however, the lending on interest at the fairs of Champagne and of Brie.[137] Some Letters of June 2, 1380, grant to five financiers of the city of Troyes, the exclusive right to lend on usury.[138] Later, in December 1392, the same privilege is accorded for money to three Lombards of the same city for fifteen years.[139] Again, an ordinance of March 6, 1466, authorizes all inhabitants of Tournai to practice usury.[140] But on the whole the status of usurers was always precarious in the Middle Ages. Jews and Lombards were often enough authorized to lend with interest; and it is curious that lending at interest, though forbidden to the Jews among themselves, by the Old Testament, and also to the Christians, according to a false interpretation of the Gospel,[141] was thus authorized as between Jews and Christians. One may, to be sure, explain this by the circumstance that from the religious point of view they were considered as strangers to one another; but the permission given to the Lombards is more difficult to explain, and can only be attributed to the exigencies of commerce. However, both Jews and Lombards were continually subjected to the most arbitrary measures. In 1270, they were expelled from the kingdom; [142] though presumably they soon returned, for ordinances were issued against usury in 1311, 1312, 1315, and 1318.[143] In 1330, debts due to usurers were reduced by one third. This was evidently a measure destined to prevent the ruin of debtors, on the theory that nothing is more ruinous than the compounding of interest; but, the higher the interest the more rapidly it compounds, and the more danger a money-lender runs the higher is the interest, so that, in reality, this protection turned against the debtors.[144] In 1332, the king took a wiser step, by fixing the rate of interest.[145] But soon there is a return to even more radical prescriptions: in

Isambert, Vol. V, p. 114; ordinance of December 5, 1363, *Isambert*, Vol. V, p. 157; ordinance of March 3, 1402, *Isambert*, Vol. VII, p. 46, etc.

[136] See *Giry*, "Histoire de la ville et des institutions de Saint-Omer", p. 296.

[137] *Isambert*, Vol. III, p. 11.

[138] *Ibid.*, Vol. V, p. 530.

[139] *Ibid.*, Vol. VI, p. 715.

[140] *Ibid.*, Vol. X, p. 574.

[141] Luke, vi, 34 and 35.

[142] *Isambert*, Vol. II, p. 651.

[143] *Ibid.*, Vol. III, pp. 11, 27, 116, 221.

[144] Ordinance of January 12, 1330, *Isambert*, Vol. IV, p. 377.

[145] *Isambert*, Vol. IV, p. 404.

1337, debtors are forbidden to pay what they owe to Lombard usurers, and are enjoined to record the amount of their debts;[146] in 1350, the debts due to the Lombards are confiscated in favor of the king, the latter to collect the capital, but to remit to the debtors the accumulated interest;[147] in 1363, is proclaimed a confiscation of the property of Italians, Lombards, ultramontanes, and other usurers;[148] in 1356, the right of the Lombards to prosecute their debtors is suspended;[149] in 1363, debts due to the Lombards are annulled, except those already protected by final judgments;[150] in 1402, a commission is appointed to discover, try, and punish usurers.[151]

With the progress of commerce, the authorities came to be less severe; the right to lend on usury was more easily and more widely granted. But usury continued, nevertheless, to be considered as a crime. The Custumals mention the penalties for those who practiced it. According to the "Etablissements de l'Echiquier de Normandie", whoever was convicted, after his death, on the oath of twelve neighbors, of having lent money with interest during the year and day before his death, suffered confiscation of his chattels.[152] The confiscation of personal property was indeed the penalty generally incurred by the usurer, but as it was inflicted only after his death, it was in reality the heirs that were punished; at times, however, the penalty was pronounced while the offender was still living. His property went, traditionally, to the feudal lord; but the king laid claim to it, at an early period.[153] The secular authorities also claimed (as already noted) jurisdiction over trials for usury, even against clerics, in spite of the protestations of the Church; their claim was based on the ground that it was a matter of contract. Nevertheless, the penalties inflicted upon usurers were spiritual as well as temporal,—excommunication, exclusion from the cemetery, and consequently refusal of confession and the sacraments. In certain regions, custom imposed on the usurer, while alive, instead of the confiscation of personal property, a fine

[146] *Isambert*, Vol. IV, p. 428.
[147] *Ibid.*, Vol. IV, p. 573.
[148] *Ibid.*, Vol. IV, p. 679.
[149] *Ibid.*, Vol. IV, p. 841.
[150] *Ibid.*, Vol. V, p. 157.
[151] *Ibid.*, Vol. VII, p. 46.
[152] "Etablissements, coutumes, assises et arrêts de l'Echiquier de Normandie", ed. *Marnier*, p. 34.
[153] The definition of usury need not here be gone into; it belongs rather under the history of contract; *cf. Beaumanoir*, chap. 68, nos. 2 *et seq.*, Vol. II, p. 476; "Anciennes coutumes d'Anjou et du Maine", A, no. 21, Vol. I, p. 47; B, no. 95, Vol. I, p. 120; C, no. 88, Vol. I, p. 304; F, nos. 572, 583 to 587, Vol. II, pp. 212, 216; K, no. 212, Vol. IV, p. 106; L, no. 445, Vol. IV, p. 327.

in favor of the bishop, and in addition banishment by his feudal lord. This we learn from Bouteiller's "Somme rural" where he points out the advantages of forbidding usury, for otherwise the people would be encouraged to idleness.[154] But this view, by the time of Charondas, his annotator, ceased to commend itself; the latter points out that bankers are allowed to lend at interest, and that thus they render useful service and are even welcome in France.

Suicide was regarded (perhaps under the influence of the Church) as a crime. Self-killing had been punished in Greece, and at times in Rome, when done to escape criminal proceedings, was treated as an offense.[155] On the other hand, in early France, suicide was not included by the Church in its claim of jurisdiction, but was left to secular justice.[156] Proceedings were brought against the corpse of the suicide, whether his motive had been to escape criminal justice or any other reason. Suicide was excused only when committed in a moment of mental alienation, or as a result of intense sorrow; but in a doubtful case neither was presumed. On a verdict of guilty, the court pronounced confiscation of personal property in favor of the lord or of the king.[157] The custom long was to order the corpse of the suicide to be hanged and then destroyed. But the later treatises speak only of the confiscation of personal property; whence may be supposed that the hanging of the corpse, a practice both odious and absurd, had fallen gradually into desuetude.[158]

§ 39*g*. **Punishments.** — In the Middle Ages punishments are not inflicted to reform the offender, but rather to secure the community's vengeance, and, most of all, to intimidate evil-doers. The notion of satisfaction for injury, very general at the beginning of the Germanic folk-law period, had almost entirely disappeared. The leniency of the Frankish laws toward criminals — a leniency sometimes carried to excess — had ceased to play any appreciable

[154] *Bouteiller*, "Somme rural", book II, tit. 11, ed. 1621, p. 1295.

[155] See for example, *Titus Livy*, XVI, 1.

[156] "Anciens coutumiers de Picardie", ed. *Marnier*, p. 60.

[157] See on these various points *Beaumanoir*, chap. 69, nos. 9, 10, 12, 13, Vol. II, pp. 487 *et seq.;* "Registre de Saint-Martin-des-Champs", pp. 113, 193, 219; *Bouteiller*, "Somme rural", book I, tit. 39, p. 468. *Cf. Brégeault*, "Procès contre les cadavres dans l'ancien droit", in the "Nouvelle Revue historique de droit français et étranger", year 1879, Vol. III, p. 619.

[158] "Registre criminel de Saint-Martin-des-Champs", pp. 112 and 218; "Anciennes coutumes d'Anjou et du Maine", B, no. 97, Vol. I, p. 121; I, no. 94, Vol. III, p. 256; *Bouteiller*, "Somme rural", book II, tit. 40, ed. 1621, p. 1490.

part; punishments had become severe, at times even cruel. Certain jurists, indeed, while conceding that the punishment must be proportionate to the offense, deprecate an extreme severity; influenced by Roman law, they advise the judge to take into consideration the circumstances of the crime.[1] The judge did, indeed, enjoy apparently a very extensive power in the determination of the penalty. No maximum nor minimum hampered him. But in reality he had not a large range of discretion. The penalty of imprisonment was almost unknown; for the most serious crimes almost always the death penalty was prescribed; he had only a choice between the different kinds of painful punishments. Fines alone were often left entirely to his discretion. Whenever a royal ordinance, the regional Custom, or even a seigniorial regulation fixed a punishment for an offense, the judge was naturally bound to apply it,[2] without discretionary power.[3] All the jurisdictions could, in theory of law, make use of the punishments, even the seigniorial tribunals and the town courts.[4] The Custumals often carefully enumerated these punishments.[5]

Undoubtedly the most common punishment was *death*. It was used for almost all serious crimes, with remarkable prodigality. The Custumals do not complain of this; and if they sometimes refer to it, they rather approve of cruelties intended to intimidate the people. (It is notable however, that the " Livre de jostice et de plet ", evidently influenced by the Church, in a passage insisting that, before putting a man to death, every effort should be made to discover the truth, criticizes the death penalty as open to the charge of unmaking what God had made.)[6] This punishment was

[1] See, for example, "Livre de jostice et de plet", pp. 277 *et seq.; Bouteiller*, "Somme rural", book I, Vol. 29, ed. 1621, p. 305.

[2] It was conceded that the lord of the manor could fix punishments: "Anciennes coutumes d'Anjou et du Maine", I, no. 9, Vol. III, p. 390.

[3] "Livre des droiz et des commandemens", no. 787.

[4] "Registre criminel de Saint-Martin-des-Champs", p. 93. The aldermen of Saint-Omer could pronounce the penalties of death, mutilation, banishment, pilgrimage, burning of the hand, or the "amende honorable", not to speak of the less severe punishments, such as fines; see *Giry*, "Histoire de la ville de Saint-Omer", pp. 218 to 225.

[5] See, for example, "Livre de jostice et de plet", pp. 277 *et seq.; Beaumanoir*, chap. 30, Vol. I, pp. 410 *et seq.;* "Anciennes coutumes d'Anjou et du Maine", F, nos. 363 *et seq.*, Vol. II, p. 144; *Bouteiller*, "Somme rural", book I, Vol. 29, ed. 1621, p. 304; book II, Vol. 40, p. 1464.

[6] "Livre de jostice et de plet", p. 113: "And if any one offends before the people and absconds and through malice does not wish to come forward, he shall have no longer term than the time of his absence; but he shall have the term of the punishment, namely, of three assizes; for

imposed for murder, homicide, poisoning, rape, abduction, arson, and for the most serious thefts,[7] serious either because of the importance of the objects stolen or because committed by several persons.[8] The methods of putting to death varied; in general (probably under the influence of Germanic traditions), they hanged the men and burned or buried alive the women. But this distinction was customary only, not mandatory; there are instances of men being buried alive for the crime of theft,[9] and of men being burned for rape or bestiality.[10] Counterfeiters were thrown into boiling water.[11] In certain specially heinous cases, the death penalty was preceded by an ignominious torture or even a mutilation; thus, often for abduction, and for all the worst crimes, notably that of "lèse majesté", the offender was dragged around the locality before being hanged.[12] At times also, for heinous crimes, the offender, instead of being hanged, was decapitated or quartered.[13] The punishment of death by breaking on the wheel appeared very late in France; we do not find it in the early Custumals; Bouteiller tells us only that, in his time, in the region of Hainaut, the abducter, instead of being hanged, was burned alive.[14] Up to the end of the 1300 s, it was the cruel custom to refuse to the condemned the consolation of the last confession; but an ordinance of Charles VI of February 12, 1396, reformed this.[15]

Next to the penalty of death came that of *mutilation*. It varied infinitely in its application, but was always inconceivably cruel. This punishment had been borrowed, for the most part, from old Germanic usages. In theft, the system of Capitulary laws had in-

we must bear much and wait before putting a man to death; for it is a serious thing to unmake what God has made and to do what he does not wish done."

[7] "Etablissements de Saint Louis", book I, chap. 35; "Livre de jostice et de plet", p. 280; *Beaumanoir*, Chap. 30, nos. 2 to 13, Vol. I, pp. 410 *et seq.*; "Anciennes coutumes d'Anjou et du Maine", E, nos. 77, 80 to 82, 85 to 87, 91, 92, 95, 98, 99, 104, 105, Vol. I, pp. 430 *et seq.*; F, nos. 1363 to 1388, Vol. II, pp. 502 *et seq.*; "Livre des droiz et des commandemens", nos. 347 *et seq.*; "Registre criminel de Saint-Martin-des-Champs", pp. xcii *et seq.* *Cf. Wilda*, "Das Strafrecht der Germanen", p. 498. Beaumanoir cites the example of a woman who was burned for having murdered her husband, chap. 69, no. 16, Vol. II, p. 491.

[8] "Registre criminel de Saint-Martin-des-Champs", pp. xcvii, xcviii, cxi.

[9] *Ibid.*, pp. xciv and cxi.

[10] *Ibid.*, pp. xciv and cxi. [11] *Ibid.*, p. 226. [12] *Ibid.*, pp. 88 and 121.

[13] "Anciennes coutumes d'Anjou et du Maine", F, no. 1363 *et seq.*, Vol. II, pp. 502 *et seq.*, giving an enumeration of all the principal cases incurring the death penalty and its various modes of application.

[14] *Bouteiller*, "Somme rural", book I, Vol. 39, ed. 1621, p. 477.

[15] *Isambert*, Vol. VI, p. 775.

flicted for a first offense mutilation, the death penalty only in case of a third offense.[16] Sodomy also, for the two first offenses, was punished by mutilation.[17] By the law of the Custumals, one who laid hands on his lord had his hand cut off; [18] one who used false measures lost his thumb.[19]

The punishment of *whipping* was rarely applied. Most frequently reserved for children, it was inflicted occasionally upon adults, for example, for unlawful blows, or for false witness in minor matters.[20]

Among the other severe punishments occur the *pillory* and the *brand.* The pillory, or "carcan," consisted in exposing a man to the public in a more or less disgraceful position. This punishment was especially used for blasphemers, in certain cases for forgers. Beaumanoir tells us that the false witness is punished by a long imprisonment, by the pillory, and by a discretionary fine.[21] An edict of King Philip VI of 1347, required that the blasphemer be put in the pillory, and permitted any one to throw mud or other filth in his face.[22] For sundry crimes the offender was branded with hot iron on the cheek.[23]

Banishment and imprisonment were much less severe. Thus, banishment was applied in the least serious cases, such as petty theft, begging, and default in a criminal case. The banished party had only to leave the territory of the jurisdiction pronouncing the punishment. Nevertheless, it involved (like the preceding punishments) confiscation of the property to the lord. One who wilfully

[16] Capit. of 779, *Pertz,* "Leges", I, 38. *Cf.* "Etablissements de Saint Louis", book I, chap. 32; "Cartulaire de Notre-Dame de Paris", Vol. III, p. 274; "Registre criminel de Saint-Martin-des-Champs", pp. c, ci, 221; "Coutume de Touraine-Anjou", no. 22; "Anciennes coutumes d'Anjou et du Maine", E, no. 1379, Vol. II, p. 505.

[17] See, for example, "Livre de jostice et de plet", p. 279.

[18] "Anciennes coutumes d'Anjou et du Maine", F, no. 1372, Vol. II, p. 514.

[19] "Anciennes coutumes d'Anjou et du Maine", F, nos. 1392 and 1393, Vol. II, p. 507.

[20] "Registre criminel de Saint-Martin-des-Champs", p. ciii; "Anciennes coutumes d'Anjou et du Maine", F, no. 1386, Vol. II, p. 506. In serious cases false witnesses were hanged.

[21] *Beaumanoir,* chap. 30, nos. 45 *et seq.,* Vol. I, p. 424.

[22] We must not confuse with the pillory the forked gibbets, that is, posts or columns supporting blocks of wood, to which were bound the criminals who had just been hanged or strangled. These forked gibbets were a sign of "high justice", as a privilege of the lords or of the municipalities. See "Registre criminel de Saint-Martin-des-Champs", pp. cii, cxii *et seq.,* where will be found details on the gibbet of Paris. *Cf. Laurier,* "Fourches et pilori"; *Flammermont,* "Histoire des institutions municipales de Senlis", p. 25.

[23] *Bouteiller,* "Somme rural", book II, tit. 40, ed. 1621, p. 1494.

harbored under this roof an outlaw incurred a discretionary fine, and his house was demolished by order of court.[24]

Imprisonment was at this period not regarded as genuinely a punishment. Mostly it was a means of securing the accused's appearance in a criminal case; moreover, to the same end,[25] they put the plaintiff also in prison; and those also who could not pay fines imposed; but in this case it was rather an imprisonment for debt.[26] There was also, in England and in certain parts of France, notably in Normandy, an imprisonment "forte et dure", which was, however, more a means of indirect restraint than a punishment; it was inflicted pending trial, and never for one who had already been convicted.[27] The treatises also inform us that there were prisons for the confinement of prisoners of war.[28] And it is also true that in certain cases, very rare however, imprisonment appears to have been a real punishment. Beaumanoir says so plainly for false witness, adding that if a fine is inadequate imprisonment may be added.[29] Are we to infer that there were several kinds of prisons? One might think so, from a passage in the "Livre de jostice et de plet." [30] Undoubtedly whoever possessed the right to do justice had a prison. Even monasteries had them, not only for the exercise of their secular jurisdiction, but also by virtue of spiritual authority; monks sentenced to oblivion were confined in them till

[24] *Beaumanoir*, chap. 30, no. 36, Vol. I, p. 422; "Anciens coutumier de Picardie", ed. *Marnier*, pp. 46 and 51; "Registre criminel de Saints Martin-des-Champs", pp. civ *et seq.*; "Anciennes coutumes d'Anjou et du Maine", F, no. 1273, Vol. II, p. 474. *Cf.* F, no. 1438, Vol. II, p. 517, for cases where one's goods can be returned to him.

[25] See "Etablissements de Saint Louis", book I, chap. 104; "Livre des usaiges et anciennes coustumes de la conté de Guynes", no. 333, p. 169; "Livre des droiz et des commandemens", no. 257, Vol. I, p. 410; "Grand coutumier de Normandie", chap. 76, ed. *Gruchy*, p. 180.

[26] "Registre criminel de Saint-Martin-des-Champs", pp. cx, 130 and 199.

[27] In Normandy, imprisonment "forte et dure" implied that a person charged by public rumor was not also a defendant on a charge brought by an individual; he was none the less put in prison, and to make him consent to examination he was placed in close confinement ("dure prison"), "with little to eat and drink"; but this punishment could not last more than a year and a day. See what is said on this point in the writer's "Histoire du droit et des institutions de l'Angleterre", Vol. III, pp. 605 *et seq.* *Cf.* "Grand Coutumier de Normandie", chap. 68, ed. *Gruchy*, p. 167.

[28] "Livre de jostice et de plet", p. 119.

[29] *Beaumanoir*, chap. 30, nos. 19, 45 *et seq.*, Vol. I, pp. 416 and 424.

[30] "Livre de jostice et de plet", p. 119: "Thus the prisoner is helped: the name prison applied to the prison of a great lord, the prisons for thieves, the prison for enemies." For the privileges enjoyed by certain prisoners, especially as to prescription, See "Anciennes coutumes d'Anjou et du Maine", F, nos. 865, 1081, 1142, 1143, Vol. II, pp. 311, 409.

their death. But the royal power did not concern itself with prisons until a late period, and then at first only with certain ones, notably those of Paris. — The information that has come down to us justifies the assertion that prisons, even in the Middle Ages, were already places of debauchery and cruelty, whence the accused or the condemned came out more perverted than when they had entered.[31]

The *pecuniary penalties* of the Middle Ages consisted chiefly in total or partial confiscation and in various amounts of fines. *Confiscation* was sometimes a principal, sometimes a secondary penalty. In some cases it extended only to certain kinds of property, in others to the party's whole estate. A great diversity of practice appears in the regional Customs. But they commonly limited confiscation to personal property; this was the general system.[32] But this might be accompanied by various sorts of harm inflicted on landed property; houses were burned or demolished, meadows and fields upturned, vineyards uprooted, etc.; the land afterwards to be restored to the offender's family. — This confiscation of personal property, with devastation of landed property, was the regular accompaniment of a sentence to a capital punishment; for this involved the "putting outside the law", or what we would call today civil death.[33] It must be remembered, however, that confiscation of fiefs was subject to special rules of feudal law. A general confiscation of property, personal and real, is not prescribed in the regional Customs; it is found only for heresy or for "lèse majesté" in Anjou and Maine.[34] In the earldom of Flanders it was limited

[31] See, on the prisons of Saint-Martin-des-Champs, "Registre criminel de Saint-Martin-des-Champs", p. cxix. For the ordinances regulating prisons, see ordinance of December 24, 1398, *Isambert*, Vol. VI, p. 826; April 1410, *Isambert*, Vol. VII, p. 230; regulation of May 1425, *Isambert*, Vol. VIII, p. 698; ordinance on the police of the prisons of Paris, October 1485, *Isambert*, Vol. XI, p. 147. *Cf.* Letters of King John of 1351, declaring that the abbots and superiors shall visit and console twice a month in their prison the monks condemned to oblivion: *Isambert*, Vol. IV, p. 673. On the Châtelet prison, see *Fagniez*, "Fragment d'un répertoire de jurisprudence parisienne au XVe siècle."

[32] *Beaumanoir* devoted an entire chapter to this distinction; chap. 23, Vol. I, p. 332.

[33] *De Fontaines*, "Conseil", pp. 292 and 483; "Etablissements, coutumes, assises et arrêts de Normandie", ed. *Marnier*, p. 77; "Anciennes coutumes d'Anjou et du Maine", F, nos. 1307, 1364 *et seq.*, 1433 *et seq.*, Vol. II, pp. 484, 502, 515; L, nos. 116 *et seq.*, Vol. IV, p. 196. The aldermen of certain cities had the right to pronounce this penalty of devastation and house-burning on those who were "put outside the law"; see *Giry*, "Histoire de la ville et des institutions de Saint-Omer", pp. 218 to 225.

[34] "Anciennes coutumes d'Anjou et du Maine", F, no. 1433, Vol. II, p. 515.

to five crimes:[35] treason to the liege lord, flight in a battle against unbelievers, participation in an insurrection, heresy, and suicide;[36] and even in these cases, enough must be reserved to support the offender's wife and children and pay his debts; the remainder went to the lord.[37] Bouteiller tells us that in the territory of Mortagne, on the Escaut, confiscation had never been sanctioned, even for personal property, in the case of the death penalty; for then, indeed (he says), the punishment would fall on the heirs rather than on the criminal himself. In certain cases, very rare however, confiscation of personalty or demolition of the house was inflicted although there had been no capital crime committed. Thus, he who died while practicing usury incurred confiscation of personalty; and Beaumanoir informs us that if a person shelters an outlaw, he is punished by a discretionary fine and his house demolished.[38] — Finally, in many cases, there might be a mere partial confiscation, — usually of the subject of the offense, as, the merchandise sought to be smuggled without paying duty.[39]

On the other hand, the severity of the letter of the medieval law was often lessened in practice, and even by royal ordinances. The king, when he was the beneficiary of a general confiscation, often gave back a part of the estate to the deceased's relatives.[40] The practice of laying waste the fields and destroying or burning the houses of those "put outside the law" fell into desuetude in more than one locality. Letters of Charles V, of June, 1366, abolished in Saint-Amand-en-Puele the custom of burning the houses of capital offenders, by permitting the family to purchase immunity.[41]

Fines became less harsh, without the need of enactments to that end. For fixing the fines, the amounts used in earlier times had been preserved of record and were used as precedents; so that, as money diminished notably in value, this alone produced an appreciable diminution of the penalty. For example, in the Frankish

[35] *Bouteiller*, "Somme rurale", book II, Vol. 15, ed. 1621, p. 783.

[36] *Beaumanoir* speaks also of general confiscation in case of suicide, chap. 69, no. 9, Vol. II, p. 487.

[37] The early regional Customs of Anjou and of Maine prescribe, also, that he who profits by the confiscation shall pay the debts; that was evidently a principle of common law; see "Anciennes coutumes d'Anjou et du Maine", F, no. 1166, Vol. II, p. 442.

[38] *Beaumanoir*, chap. 30, no. 36, Vol. I, p. 422.

[39] "Livre des droiz et des commandemens", no. 259.

[40] See, for example, the measures taken in favor of certain relatives of Pierre de la Broce, in *Langlois*, "Le règne de Philippe III", p. 32, note 3.

[41] *Isambert*, Vol. V, 253.

epoch a penalty of sixty sous had been the typical royal fine incurred for violating the royal ban; there was also a minimum fine, also typical, but varying according to the regional or folk-law under which the offender lived.[42] Now we find also in the feudal period these two common fines, the one heavy, the other light; the first is still called "the fine of sixty sous," the second, which varies according to localities, is very often of five sous, and is called in the texts simply "fine" ("amende") or "gage de la loi," that is, security required by local custom. Numerous texts of the Custumals (too tedious to cite) speak of this "fine of sixty sous"; it continued to be a very frequent one, even in the latest Custumals of the Middle Ages, for example, in the "Somme rural" of Bouteiller, and it persisted to the end of the Old Régime in many regions.[43]

Independent of these two general fines (the one of sixty sous, or heavy fine, the other of five, six, or seven sous, according to the regional Customs and called "amende de loi"), there were other pecuniary penalties more or less severe, but varying greatly according to the regional Customs. In many cases the amount was purely in discretion; the guilty person was deemed to be "in misericordiam regis", and the fine could be more or less than sixty sous according to the pleasure of the judge. For instance, according to Beaumanoir, the amount was discretionary for the offender who used violence in court, or who escaped after arrest for debt, or who sheltered in his house a convict "put outside the law," or who bore false witness, etc.[44] According to the early regional Customs of Anjou and of Maine, the discretionary fine was applicable to the plaintiff in a personal property case who relinquished his suit,

[42] See, for example, *Boretius*, "Beiträge zur Capitularienkritik", pp. 159 and 167; *cf.* "Leges", I, 227.

[43] See, for example, *Beaumanoir*, chap. 30, nos. 78, 88 *et seq.*, Vol. I, pp. 432 and 444; according to the first of these texts, he who injures the grain is liable only to a fine of five sous. See also in regard to fines, "Livre de jostice et de plet", pp. 278 *et seq.;* on the fine of sixty sous, or heavy fine, "Anciennes coutumes d'Anjou et du Maine", F, nos. 1398, 1401 *et seq.*, 1412 *et seq.*, 1424, 1429, Vol. II, pp. 508, 509, 511, 513, 514. The early regional Customs of Anjou and of Maine speak also of the "amende de loi", which in these regional Customs was of seven sous and six deniers; it was imposed especially upon those who did not pay their quit-rents or other money dues, and in certain lawsuits upon the losing party, etc.; *ibid.*, B, no. 171, Vol. I, p. 172; C, no. 160, Vol. I, p. 352; E, nos. 108 *et seq.*, Vol. I, p. 442; F, nos. 1399, 1407, 1416, 1426 *et seq.*, 1431, 1432, 1487, 1498, Vol. II, p. 509 *et seq.;* I, nos. 130, 131, 133, 140, 141, Vol. III, p. 283; L, nos. 318 *et seq.*, Vol. IV, p. 273. See also "Livre des droiz et des commandements", in the alphabetical table, 5th fine.

[44] *Beaumanoir*, chap. 30, nos. 20, 35, 36, 45, Vol. I, pp. 417, 418, 422.

the merchant who sold imitation cloth, the party who wrongfully resisted the enforcement of a royal mandate, the landholder who executed a fraudulent deed to evade the relatives' right of re-purchase; and in other instances.[45] Sometimes the regional Custom itself fixed the amount, even in excess of sixty sous, keeping ordinarily to the tradition of the earlier law; thus the regional Custom of Anjou speaks in two cases of a fine of a hundred sous, called " relief d'homme ",[46] which was certainly borrowed from the Capitularies legislation or even from the earlier folk-laws (" Leges ").[47] — In other cases, the regional Custom fixed amounts between the fine of sixty sous and the " amende de loi." According to Beaumanoir, for insult the fine varies according to the station of the persons and the gravity of the case.[48] The " Etablissements de Saint Louis " speak of a fine of fifteen sous for assault. The same rule obtains in Vermandois, provided the victim is in no danger of death or maiming.[49] Other texts mention fines of ten and twenty sous for blows, violence, and mere insults. This was the most common punishment for lesser crimes; the rate alone varied according to the different regional Customs.[50] — Whenever a fine did not seem sufficient, the judge could add imprisonment.[51]

As already noted, the multiplicity of fines for errors in legal pro-

[45] See "Anciennes coutumes d'Anjou et du Maine", E, nos. 78, 109, 115, 257, Vol. I, pp. 431, 442, 445, 543; F, nos. 661, 684, 1396, 1397, Vol. II, pp. 242, 249, 508; I, nos. 97, 129, 137, 289, Vol. III, pp. 259, 283, 288, 413; L, no. 325, Vol. IV, p. 280.

[46] A fine paid by the vassal in order to redeem his fief. (Note of the TR.)

[47] "Etablissements de Saint Louis", book I, chapters 108 and 125. *Cf. Viollet*, "Etablissements de Saint Louis", Vol. I, p. 246. The first case of this fine of a hundred sous and one denier is where one's animal has killed a person, the owner being ignorant of its vice; for if he had known its vice, he would have been hanged: "Etablissements de Saint Louis", book I, p. 125, Vol. II, p. 236. The second case is that of a person who, accused of a capital crime, has furnished bail and then fled; the surety then in his place incurs the fine of a hundred sous and one denier. "Etablissements de Saint Louis", book I, chap. 108, Vol. II, p. 190. According to the "Livre des droiz et des commandemens", no. 344, the fine of a hundred sous and one denier is also applicable to an abandonment of a charge of crime. But it cannot be inflicted upon a boy less than fourteen years old for involuntary homicide. See *ibid.*, no. 346.

[48] *Beaumanoir*, chap. 30, nos. 21 *et seq.*

[49] "Etablissements de Saint Louis", book II, chap. 24. *Cf. Bordier*, "Philippe de Remi, sire de Beaumanoir", p. 389; *Viollet*, "Etablissements de Saint Louis", Vol. I, p. 246; *Tanon*, "Le registre criminel de Saint-Martin-des-Champs", p. 107.

[50] In the following texts it was of ten, twenty, or thirty sous in Anjou and Maine: "Anciennes coutumes d'Anjou et du Maine", E, nos. 100, 101, 106, Vol. I, p. 438; F, nos. 1400, 1411, 1415, 1427, 1430, 1431, Vol. II, pp. 509, 511, 514; I, nos. 120, 126, Vol. III, pp. 277, 280.

[51] *Beaumanoir*, chap. 30, no. 19, Vol. I, p. 416.

ceedings, — against the lawyers if they had faultily pleaded, and against the judges if they had given an erroneous judgment, at times very heavy, often led to the ruin of individuals and even of communities.[52] Whenever the king's court desired to protect the loser from a similar misfortune, it inserted in the decision a "retentum", which exempted from a portion of the fine; *e.g.*, in 1310, a judgment sentenced a party to pay a fine of two thousand francs to the king, but with a "retentum" that he need pay only one thousand.[53]

The king had always the power of making a total or partial *remission* of any punishment whatever, or of substituting one less severe; he had even the right of removing the criminality and of thus preventing or stopping prosecution. In the former case, he granted "Letters of Remission"; in the second, "Letters of Abolition." The former represented his power of pardon, the latter his power of amnesty. There are numerous examples of these. Amnesty was granted at times to one or more individuals, at other times to an entire city; thus the city of Paris obtained "letters of abolition" from the Regent during the captivity of King John, dated August 10, 1358.[54] During the first part of the period here treated the king apparently reserved as an essentially personal privilege the right of granting Letters of Abolition of of Remission; it did not belong to his officers or magistrates, unless he delegated it to them in due form. Thus Letters of Charles VI, of September, 1398, allowed the provost of Paris to remit fines of ten pounds and over, in civil cases, to persons imprisoned for non-payment.[55] Likewise, a mandate of Charles VI, of March 13, 1401, conferred upon the Chancellor of France the right to grant, in council, all the Letters of Abolition and of Remission.[56] The same privilege was possessed by the great vassals of the crown, and was also con-

[52] For the ruin of certain communities as a result of fines inflicted upon them by the court of Parliament, see *Flammermont*, "Histoire des institutions municipales de Senlis", pp. 23, 36, and 51.

[53] *Isambert*, Vol. III, p. 11.

[54] See, for example, Letters of King John of December 9, 1357, *Isambert*, Vol. IV, p. 862; Letters of the Regent, August 10, 1358, *Isambert*, Vol. V, p. 35; Letters of King John, May 22, 1369, *Isambert*, Vol. V, p. 94; Letters of Charles V, September 23, 1367, *Isambert*, Vol. V, p. 292. See also Letters of Discharge of Charles V of July 1373 in favor of the lord of Amboise, who had caused an officer of the king, while exercising his duties, to be carried off by force, kept in prison, and made to pay, granted on condition that the guilty man pay a fine to the king, remain a week in prison, and give satisfaction to the plaintiff. *Isambert*, Vol. V, p. 392. Amnesty could thus be granted on certain conditions. See also *Marnier*, "Anciens coutumiers de Picardie", p. 54.

[55] *Isambert*, Vol. VI, p. 826.

[56] *Ibid.*, Vol. VIII, p. 14.

ceded to counts and barons; but it was not conceded to the lords having " high justice " who were not also lords of manors, unless they had acquired the right, either by grant or by usage.[57] More than once such Letters became the subject of mercenary traffic by the possessors of this privilege or those through whose agency they were obtained.

[57] "Anciennes coutumes d'Anjou et du Maine", E, nos. 11 and 13, Vol. I, p. 391; I, nos. 15 and 17, Vol. III, p. 181; L, nos. 308 and 310, Vol. IV, p. 270.

TITLE III. THE RENASCENCE, THE REFORMATION, AND THE 1700 s

CHAPTER VII

GERMANY'S RECEPTION OF THE ROMAN LAW IN THE EARLY 1500s[1]

[1] For the matter contained in Chapters VII–IX, the following writers may be consulted: *Malblank*, "Geschichte der peinlichen Gerichtsordnung Kaiser Karl V." (1783); *Henke*, "Grundriss einer Geschichte des deutschen peinlichen Rechts" (2 vols. 1809), Vol. II; *Zöpfl*, "Das alte Bamberger Recht als Quelle der Carolina" (1839); *Herrmann*, "Freiherr Johann v. Schwarzenberg. Ein Beitrag zur Geschichte des Criminalrechts" (1841); *Von Wächter*, "Gemeines Recht Deutschlands, inbesondere gemeines deutsches Strafrecht" (1844); *Warnkönig und L. Stein*, "Französische Staats- und Rechtsgeschichte", III, pp. 611 *et seq.; Schäffner*, "Geschichte der Rechtsverfassung Frankreichs", III, pp. 427 *et seq.*, pp. 601 *et seq.*, IV, pp. 322 *et seq.; Köstlin*, "Geschichte des deutschen Strafrechts im Umriss, herausgegeben von Gessler" (1859), pp. 200 *et seq.; Geib*, "Lehrbuch des deutschen Strafrechts", I, pp. 240 *et seq.; Von Stintzing*, "Geschichte der populären Literatur des römisch-kanonischen Rechts in Deutschland" (1867); *Berner*, "Die Strafgesetzgebung in Deutschland vom Jahre 1751 bis zur Gegenwart" (1867); *Allard*, "Histoire du droit criminel au XVIème siècle" (Paris, Leipzig, 1868); *Von Holtzendorff*, "Handbuch des deutschen Strafrechts", I, pp. 67–143; (History of the criminal law of countries other than Germany, *Von Holtzendorff*, pp. 144–238); *Güterbock*, "Die Entstehungsgeschichte der Carolina auf Grund archivalischer Forschungen" (1876); *Von Wächter*, "Beilagen zu Vorlesungen über das deutsche Strafrecht" (1877), pp. 100 *et seq.; Brünnenmeister*, "Die Quellen der Bambergensis, ein Beitrag zur Geschichte des deutschen Strafrechts" (1879); *Von Stintzing*, "Geschichte der deutschen Rechtswissenschaft" (I, 1880).

Collections of the literature dealing with the matter contained in these chapters may be found especially in the following writers: *G. W. Böhmer*,

§ 40. **Reasons for Reception of the Roman Law.**—*Reception of the Roman Law.*—The reception of the Roman law,—or to speak more correctly, the combination of Roman and German legal principles, which, towards the end of the Middle Ages, came about in the other domains of the law—could not long be excluded from the province of criminal law. Here the change came about in a much more correct manner. It lacked those inconsistencies and incongruities which we so often find in the other branches of the law,—the ill effects of which are in part so numerous in our legal institutions, remaining even until the most modern times. In great part, criminal law is nothing other than an application of the generally prevalent philosophic truths and fundamental rules of morality. Assuming the existence of the methods of procedure requisite for the ascertainment of the facts involved in the concrete case, that treasure of wisdom acquired by one people may to a certain extent be transferred to the law of another, without rendering it incongruous. This is so, just as to-day the so-called general part of the criminal codes of the most highly civilized nations is (with the exception of the system of punishment) often transferred to nations that are less civilized. And where their civilization is similar in degree, different States feel the need of providing punishment for the same acts. To a less extent than the private law does the criminal law contain rules that are arbitrary or based upon expediency or merely relics of the past. Its purpose is to protect the general system of law,—that system from which it may at first glance appear very different. Yet the wall which is designed to protect this system may contain essentially the same construction, and under some circumstances must contain the same construction. But there was more in the reception of the Roman law by the criminal law than the mere absence of injury to either. The

"Handbuch der Literatur des Criminalrechts" (1816); *Von Wächter*, "Lehrbuch der römisch-deutschen Strafrechts" (2 vols. 1825, 1826); *Kappler*, "Handbuch der Literatur des Criminalrechts" (1838); *Geib*, "Lehrbuch", I; *Nypels*, "Le droit pénal français progressif et comparé" (Bruxelles, 1864); *Binding*, "Grundriss zu Vorlesungen über gemeines deutsches Strafrechts" (2d ed. 1877). [Later writers are: *Pfeilschifter*, "Das Bamberger Landrecht, systematisch dargestellt" (Erlangen, 1898); *Kohler* and *Scheel*, "Die Bambergische Halsgerichtsordnung" (Halle, 1902); *Zöpfl*, "Die peinliche Gerichtsordnung Kaiser Karl V." (Berlin, 1893); *Oppermann*, "Die Schuldlehre der Carolina" (Leipzig, 1904); *Christiani*, "Die Treuhand der frankischen Zeit" (Breslau, 1912); *Kantorowicz*, "Gobler's Karolinenkommentar und seine Nachfolger" (1904); *Kohler* and *Scheel*, "Die Karolina und ihre Vorgängerinnen" (3 vols. 1900–1904).—VON THÓT.]

was furthered by the fact that the Bambergensis, in dealing with points which did not seem to it to be sufficiently established in legal practice, had observed cautious limitations, and within certain bounds had preserved local custom. A short and popularly esteemed encyclopedia [21] of the secular law of the times, known as the "Layenspiegel", and composed by the secretary to the Nördlingen council, Ulrich Tengler,[22] reproduced in its third part, dealing with criminal procedure, substantially the contents of the Bambergensis. This was expressed, however, in a more theoretical form, in brief and general maxims. Through this book the courts were given an even greater familiarity with the Bambergensis and the Italian legal learning. In 1516, with only a few changes, the Bambergensis, reproduced in the "Brandenburgische Halsgerichtsordnung", was introduced into the Frankish territories of the margravate of Brandenburg.

§ 43. **The "Carolina."** — Thus the Bambergensis now presented itself as the natural foundation for a general statute regulating procedure in criminal courts (*i.e.* "peinliche Gerichtsordnung") and applying to the entire empire. In spite of the complaints [1] as to the shortcomings of the criminal law, repeatedly brought to the knowledge of the Reichstag, no action had yet been taken. But finally, at the Reichstag of Worms, in 1521, the reform of criminal justice was again taken up, and this time in earnest. The commission, for that purpose appointed, was able on the 21st of April, 1521, to submit a draft to the States for further action.[2] This draft was essentially a reproduction of the Bambergensis, but it also made use of the so-called "Correctorium Bambergensis", a collection of Bamberg decisions and ordinances of the years 1507 to 1515, which explained, supplemented, and changed particular points in the Bambergensis.[3]

communes, administrative councils, official classes, etc. *Cf. Stobbe*, "Geschichte der deutschen Rechtsquellen", p. 241. Concerning the separate editions, *cf. Rosshirt*, "Neues Archiv d. Criminalrechts", IX, pp. 245 *et seq.*; *Stobbe* (*ante*). The first edition, by *Hannsen Pfeyll*, appeared in Bamberg in 1507. The five following editions (*i.e.* until 1543) were printed in Mainz by Schöffer. An altered edition appeared again in Bamberg in 1580 (of this a second edition in 1738). As to the later editions, see *post*.

[21] *Cf. Stintzing*, "Geschichte der pop. Lit.", p. 446; "Geschichte der Rechtswissenschaft", pp. 85 *et seq.*

[22] Published first in 1509.

[1] *Cf. e.g.* the Mainz memorial of the States of the empire to the Kaiser in 1517. *Cf. Harpprecht*, "Staatsarchiv", III, p. 365; *Güterbock*, p. 25.

[2] *Güterbock*, p. 45.

[3] *Cf.* as to the so-called "Correctorium", *Hohbach*, in "Neues Archiv

This draft,[4] first submitted to the Administrative Council ("Reichsregiment"), did not become a law; nor did the second draft proposed by the Administrative Council at Nürnberg in 1524.[5] A third draft was submitted to the Reichstag at Spier in 1529. Finally, a fourth draft, submitted in 1530 to the Reichstag at Augsburg, was enacted as law by the Reichstag at Regensburg in July, 1532, under the name of "Kaiser Karls des funfften und des heyligen römischen Reichs peinlich gerichtsordnung."[6]

Local Opposition. The "Saving Clause." — The opposition which had to be overcome in the introduction of a criminal code of such a general nature consisted for the most part in the far-reaching demand for the preservation of specific local rules of law. Many States opposed the "Halsgerichtsordnung" because they regarded it as an attack on their hard-won autonomy, and as an encroachment upon the (extremely summary) method of criminal justice practised by them. On behalf of the City of Ulm, at the Town Assembly at Esslingen, in 1523, the following declaration was made:[7] "The 'Halsgerichtsordnung' tends solely to the disadvantage of the States of the realm, and can only be understood as encouraging and fostering all criminals." Electoral Saxony, with other States, *e.g.* Electoral Brandenburg, joined in opposing the "Halsgerichtsordnung", because its provisions appeared irreconcilable with the Saxon law and the right of "Taidigung" (private composition)[8] still in force there. The result of these circumstances is to be seen in the so-called "sal-

des Criminalrechts", 1844, pp. 233 *et seq.*, 1845, pp. 105 *et seq.*, 173 *et seq.* *Cf.* also *Güterbock*, pp. 61 *et seq.*; *Stintzing*, I, p. 514.

[4] Schwarzenberg, although a member of the Administrative Council ("Reichsregiment"), probably took no part in the composition of the first draft.

[5] This draft was in recent times accidentally re-discovered by Güterbock in the "Königsberger Provincialarchiv." (*Cf. Güterbock*, pp. 85 *et seq.*) The manuscript had been brought to Königsberg by Schwarzenberg, who in the years 1526 and 1527 resided at Königsberg with Duke Albrecht of Prussia. It may well be maintained that Schwarzenberg took part in the preparation of the Nürnberg draft. *Cf. Güterbock*, p. 93.

[6] Generally referred to by the abbreviation P.G.O. (*i.e.* "peinliche Gerichtsordnung") or C.C.C. (*i.e.* "Caroli constitutio criminalis"). As a matter of fact, Charles V had done very little towards this legislative work.

[7] "Die Halsgerichtsordnung sei niemandem mehr als den Reichsstäden zum Nachtheil erdacht und zu nichts fürständiger, als alle Uebelthäter zu harzen und zu pflanzen." *Cf. Abegg* in "Archiv des Criminalrechts" (N. F. 1854), pp. 441 *et seq.*

[8] *I.e.* "Wergeld" and "Busse." *Cf.* the declaration of the Saxon chancellor Christian Baier, quoted by *Güterbock*, pp. 136, 185.

vatorische Clausel"[9] (*i.e.* saving clause) of the preface to the Carolina: "Yet We, in gracious consideration of the electors, the princes and the States, desire in no way to detract from their ancient and well-established legal and customary usages."[10]

Nevertheless, the Carolina was not hereby (as is often incorrectly assumed)[11] reduced to the mere position of a code offered to the States for their acceptance.[12] Its provisions appear, indeed, as a rule, as compared to the well-established legal customs, to have only subsidiary validity.[13] But to some provisions, as exceptions, is attributed the force of absolutely binding rules.[14] The limitation contained in the wording of the clause that *new* laws in contravention to the Carolina were not to be introduced, was also later ignored by the States of the realm. However, other circumstances than the Saving Clause and the opposition in support of local rules, contributed to the peculiar fate of the Carolina.

§ 44. **Comparison of the Carolina and the Bambergensis.** — Both in its general plan and in by far the greater number of its individual provisions, the Carolina corresponds very closely[1] to the Bambergensis. Like the Bambergensis, it is primarily a system of procedure. Like the Bambergensis, it treats of the substantive criminal law incidentally, in dealing with sentences.[2] General theories are in part treated, along with the crimes in which they appear of especial importance, *e.g.* self-defense is treated along with homicide.

Yet it is by no means a mere copy of the Bambergensis with occasional changes in those designations of persons and things appropriate only to Bamberg. Apart from provisions relating to procedure, an essential improvement can be noted in Article 145, which places very substantial limitations upon confiscation

[9] We find a similar clause in the "Reichspolizeiordnungen" ("Imperial Police Regulations"). *Cf. Stobbe*, II, p. 186.

[10] "Doch wollen wir durch dise gnedige erinnerung Churfürsten, Fürsten vnnd Stenden, an jren alten wolhergebrachten rechtmessigen vnd billichen gebreuchen, nichts benommen haben."

[11] *E.g. Geib*, "Lehrbuch des deutschen Strafrechts", I, p. 276.

[12] This conclusion is thoroughly confuted by *Von Wächter*, "Gemeines Recht", pp. 31 *et seq.* *Cf.* also *Güterbock*, p. 194.

[13] *Cf. Stintzing*, "Geschichte der deutschen Rechtswissenschaft", p. 627.

[14] *Cf.* Arts. 61, 104, 105, 135, 140, 204, and also Art. 218 dealing especially with abuses.

[1] The number of Articles is different. The Bambergensis contains 278 Articles and the Carolina contains 219.

[2] Arts. 104–180.

of property, and also in Article 218, dealing with various abuses. The Carolina, since it sets forth the generally prevailing law, corresponds even more closely than the Bambergensis to the doctrines of the Italian legal practice. In various aspects may be noticed the assistance received from the jurists. Local law, as it was contained in the Bambergensis, is abandoned. The activities of the Reformation, which had now intervened, had led to changes in only a few passages, as, for example, the absence in certain places of mention of the clergy.[3] The omission of Article 130 of the Bambergensis, dealing with heresy, was occasioned not so much by the view that heresy was not a crime, but rather because spiritual jurisdiction was no longer recognized in the way it had been recognized in Article 130.[4]

Careless Manner of Publication. — The publication of this new and important imperial statute was made in a peculiarly careless manner. It was intended to be directly binding not only upon the States of the empire, but also upon all subjects and dependencies of the empire, and particularly upon all official authorities. Publication took place at the press of the Mainz printer, Ivo Schöffer, who was given a special privilege for this purpose. In this privilege it is declared: " es soll auch keynem andern gedruckten Abschiedt an eynichen ort inn oder ausserhalb gerichts oder rechts geglaubt werden." [5] And yet not a single copy of the original was retained by the imperial officials. Presumably the only original text was the one delivered to the printer. The principal edition of February, 1533 (there is a dispute as to the existence of an earlier edition), is not free from typographical errors, and there is also no lack of mistakes in the writing and editorial work of the original draft. Often these mistakes are such as to make it difficult to ascertain the meaning.[6] Because of these difficulties, an edition satisfying all critical requirements is not extant, and indeed only became possible after Güterbock's investigations of the original records.[7]

[3] *Cf. Stintzing*, "Geschichte", I, pp. 628, 629.
[4] *Güterbock*, pp. 260 *et seq.*
[5] *Güterbock*, p. 207. "No faith or credit shall be given to any copy printed in any other place within or without court or law."
[6] *Güterbock*, pp. 217 *et seq.*
[7] Later editions were prepared by *Koch*, *Reinhold Schmid*, and *Zöpfl*. The edition by *R. Schmid* also gives the text of the "Bambergensis." The edition by *Zöpfl* (1842) contains the "Bambergensis", the "Brandenburgica", also the draft (*i.e.* preliminary draft) of 1521 (Worms) and that of 1529 (Speier), here referred to as the first and second drafts. An edition by *Zöpfl* in 1876 gives in a synoptic form the Carolina, the Bam-

Varied Application of the Carolina. — The Saving Clause of the Carolina rendered possible a great diversity of conditions in the various States. If in a given jurisdiction the abuses so vigorously repudiated by the Carolina did not exist, one might even hold the opinion that all of the former law could be included under the "good customs theretofore in use", and that these therefore had not been altered by the Carolina, and that consequently the Carolina could be simply ignored. It was also possible to make a special edition of the Carolina with modifications and supplements, clearly showing, for the provincial courts, the rules which were valid along with the Carolina as "good" custom in variation therefrom. Or, again, Carolina might be adopted literally and completely, and published without local addenda, on the ground either that special customs in addition to the Carolina did not there exist, or that the courts would not be in doubt in respect to them.

All of these above-mentioned attitudes were taken. The "Rechtsbuch" of Rottweil, of 1546, and the statutes of the city of Frankenhausen of 1558, merely reproduced their earlier law, paying no attention to the Carolina. The new "Brandenburgica" of 1582 was a reproduction of the "Brandenburgica" of 1516, with a few supplements referring to the Carolina. The "Landesordnung" of Henneburg of 1539 was a new compilation, consisting of specific provisions of the Carolina and a reproduction of a "Landesordnung" of Tyrol of 1532.[8] Publications of the Carolina with no additions at all were made *e.g.* in Electoral Cologne in 1538, in the "Cölner Reformation" of the secular courts, by the Duke of Pomerania in 1566, and in 1564 by Duke Heinrich of Braunschweig-Wolfenbüttel. Simple instructions to the courts to be guided by the Carolina were given in Electoral Brandenburg in 1540,[9] and in the "Hofgerichtsordnung" of Celle in 1564.[10] Modifications of specific provisions only of the Carolina were made *e.g.* in the Frankfurt "Reformation" of 1578, and to a greater extent in the "Malefizprocessordnung" for Bavaria,

bergensis, the "Brandenburgica", and both the above-mentioned drafts. A small edition by *Zöpfl* of the text only of the Carolina appeared in 1870. *Cf.* also *G. W. Böhmer*, "Ueber die authentischen Ausgaben der Carolina" (Göttingen, 1837). [But now see the citations in note 1, § 40, *ante.* — ED.]

[8] This is based upon the "Malefizordnung" of 1499 and the "Freiburger Stadtrecht."

[9] *Halschner*, "Geschichte des Brandenburgisch-Preussischen Strafrechts" (1855), p. 113.

[10] *Cf. Von Wächter*, "Gemeines Recht", pp. 38 *et seq.*

which formed the last part of the Bavarian "Landrecht" of 1616.

General Effect of the Carolina. — As a matter of fact, the influence of the Carolina over the local laws was much stronger than might be inferred from the wording of the Saving Clause. Actually, it obtained general force, to the extent that deviations therefrom could not be justified by appeal to statute or special custom. The intrinsic merit of the work secured for its common law a predominance for a long period, in spite of the increasingly prevailing tendencies towards local autonomy.

Especially in the south of Germany, the services rendered by the Carolina to the legal conditions of the times were clearly manifest. The greater exactness and precision of definition which characterized the Carolina, as contrasted with earlier legislation, were important features. The same may be said of its suppression of numerous abuses, and of its elimination of provisions in the nature of rules of proof completely perverted or no longer suitable in the new state of legal knowledge. As already noted, the punishments of the Carolina, as contrasted with those of the south of Germany, may upon the whole be regarded as mild. The gradual elimination of "Taidigung" (*i.e.* private composition) and of judicial discretion in sentences, was a step in advance, even though individual cases thereby lost the benefit of judgments based upon humane considerations. But in the north of Germany the case was somewhat different. There the Carolina brought about an increase in the severity of penalties. Punishments by mutilation had previously been practised but little. The Carolina, by sanctioning the purely inquisitorial form of procedure, perhaps prevented the development of a form of procedure corresponding more nearly to the earlier German law.

CHAPTER VIII

GERMANY IN THE LATE 1500s AND THE 1600s

§ 45. **Relation of the Carolina to the Reformation.** — How the Carolina can be termed [1] "an achievement of the spirit of the Reformation" is certainly not clear. This would have the strange implication that the conscientiousness, with which the Carolina infuses the criminal law, was not a general characteristic of the Germanic spirit, but merely a special characteristic of the spirit of the Reformation. The prominent men of the times were indeed all under the influence of the Reformation; this sufficiently explains the large share taken in the production of the Carolina by men such as Schwarzenberg and Baier.

Religious Tolerance. — As a matter of fact, the position taken by the reformers was unfavorable, rather than favorable, to progress in the general conception of criminal law. Of course, since the adherents of the Confession of Augsburg and the reformed faith had obtained recognition from the Empire, there could be no call for a common law punishment of the adherents of this Confession; so too, in the Catholic States, the impropriety of proceeding against them under the criminal law as heretics was

[1] Thus *Güterbock*, p. 207.

gradually established. The logical consequence of the Reformation, since it demanded a free and open examination of religious dogmas, would have led to a declaration that the punishment of heresy was not permissible. But logic has not always been observed by religious organizations; and ultimately the persecution or tolerance of those of another faith came in the great majority of cases to be merely a question of power.

Luther, to be sure, had at first expressly denied the existence of the right to coerce another in a matter pertaining to faith;[2] it would be excellent to have faith and convictions entirely free. But like Augustine, when he acquired greater power,[3] he changed his opinions; moreover, the excesses of the Anabaptists and the Peasants' War warned him of the necessity of caution.[4] As is well known, he wrote against the "Meister Omnes" and the "false prophets", and advocated reform only through authority. When even the mild-hearted Melanchthon[5] found justification for the punishment of certain heretics on the grounds of blasphemy (a theory which for a long time afterwards permitted in Protestant countries a prosecution by criminal law of the various sects),[6] it is not to be wondered at[7] that Calvin and his followers preached and appear[8] to have practised the old persecutions of heresy in their harshest and most repellent form. As a matter of fact, the principle of freedom of religious faith was not achieved

[2] *Cf. Luther's* Works, published by *Jenischer*, Vol. 22, p. 85. As to the extent to which obedience is due to worldly authority, "Heresy can never be prevented by force", p. 90.

[3] *Cf.* the writing: "An den christlichen Adel deutscher Nation."

[4] *Cf.* also *Janet*, "Histoire de la philosophie morale et politique" (2 vols., Paris, 1868), II, pp. 38 *et seq.*

[5] Works, XII, pp. 696 *et seq.*

[6] *Brunnemann*, "Tractatus de inquisitionis processu", IX, n. 2, asserts that it is criminally punishable if any one denied the truth of the Ecumenical Council. Various punishments ("exilium", "deportatio") were inflicted by followers of the Evangelical churches, the death penalty was inflicted by the Catholics. Among the former the punishments were mitigated by appeal to Novel 129 ("Hæretici quiete viventes asperius tractandi non sunt"). The extent of the conception of blasphemy is evident from *Damhouder*, "Praxis rer. crim.", c. 60, n. 11. Hereunder is included, according to *Damhouder:* "negare Dei filium non esse verum hominem."

[7] *Cf. post,* Part II, under "History of the Theories of Criminal Law."

[8] *Cf.* notably the well-known and repulsive history of the condemnation and burning of Michael Servetus in 1553 at Calvin's instigation (*Gaberel*, "Histoire de l'église de Génève" (1855), II, pp. 226 *et seq.* A heresy trial of Valentin Gentilis was prevented in Geneva, — he was in 1566 executed at Berne. The esteemed work of the Geneva divine, *Theodor Beza*, "De hæreticis a civili magistratu puniendis" completely embraced the theories of the Papists in regard to prosecutions of heresy.

by the Reformers, and was not established until the period of Philosophy in the 1700 s.

Unfortunate Results of the Reformation. — The immediate result of the Reformation was a retrogression in the general conception of law.[9] While the antagonism between Church and State during the Middle Ages had often led to a thoroughgoing and critical examination of the doctrine of law and State, and the power of even the Pope himself was often substantially limited by appeal to the "Lex naturæ", the Reformers, in accordance with the doctrine of Paul, "All authority is from God", readily regarded divine and secular law as identical. Consequently their theory of criminal law was nothing other than a complete identification of secular and divine justice. It was simply a justification of the "status quo", based in one aspect upon the Bible and in another upon motives of temporary expediency, without an attempt to harmonize Christian love[10] and cruel penalties.[11] In this respect, on the whole, the discussions of Thomas Aquinas, not to mention many of a later date, had been of a somewhat higher character.

§ 46. **The Literature of the 1500 s and 1600 s.** — Powers of thought and action were absorbed by the theological controversies. This explains why, although the Carolina made some practical improvement in legal conditions, one cannot speak of a scientific administration of criminal law in Germany during the 1500 s. The work achieved during this time consisted simply in copying what the Italians had written on points not covered by the Carolina, and thus in supplementing the Carolina.[1] The German writers did not interpret the Carolina as a code; they did not develop the principles of the Carolina and draw logical conclusions therefrom, nor did they expound the statute primarily from the

[9] *Cf. Janet*, and especially the accurate proof in *Gierke*, "Johannes Althusius und die Entwicklung der naturrechtlichen Staatstheorien" (Breslau, 1880), pp. 64 *et seq.*, pp. 273, 275; *Gierke*, "Das deutsche Genossenschaftsrecht", Vol. III (1881), pp. 625 *et seq.*

[10] *Cf. Luther's* "Kirchenpostille, Predigten über die Evangelien", 4, n. "Trinitatis" (Works, edited by *Plochmann*, 13, p. 41): "Der Richter dienet Gott."

[11] *Cf. Calvini*, "Institutiones Relig. Christ.", Lib. IV, c. 20 n. 1: "... Deo jubente ab auctoritate omnia fieri ... Divinis mandatis ulcisci."

[1] Thus *Perneder* (died 1540) in his so-called "Halsgerichtsordnung" published often after his death ("Von Straf und Peen aller und ieder Malefizhandlungen in kurzen Bericht genommen ... "), says that his work, in its explaining and widening of the Carolina, consists of the common subsidiary law (*Wächter*, p. 77).

statute itself. Their work was rather in the nature of supplementary codification, by reference to the Roman law and the Italian literature. Reference to the former, in the absence of knowledge of legal history, was uncritical and often absurd; the best results were obtained when they simply copied the Italian jurists. The learning of the latter had reached its zenith[2] in Aegidius Bossius,[3] and above all in the lucid and learned treatise of Julius Clarus.[4] The German writers were, however, less tedious when (as often) they adhered to the superficial and commonplace "Praxis rerum criminalium" of the Hollander, Damhouder;[5] direct use of this was made in the practice, and it acquired a high reputation in Germany. To all works of this character there is more or less applicable the statement made by Wächter, in his masterly treatise on the literature of this period anent that especially lifeless and depressing book by Ludwig Gilhausen, "Arbor judiciaria criminalis"; he says: "The articles of the Carolina appear, so to speak, like great unmelted dumplings floating in a broth concocted from the Roman Law and the Italian authorities."[6]

[2] Along with these mention should be made of: *Hippolitus de Marsiliis* (died 1529), judge in many cities of Lombardy, professor in Bologna ("Practica causarum criminalium"); *Bonifacius de Vitalinis*, "Tractatus super maleficiis" (the characteristics of this writer are too unfavorably given by *Allard*, pp. 401, 402; he is not so entirely devoid of original ideas as Allard infers); *Tiberius Decianus* (died 1581), "Tractatus criminalis." This last-mentioned writer however does not merit the praise bestowed upon him by *Wächter*, p. 68. It is rather the fact that he apparently clearly marks the beginning of the decline of the Italian learning. It is worthy of notice that in Decianus a beginning is found of the arrangement of the so-called "general part" (now common to continental treatises on criminal law). His deductions, however, are often arbitrary (*e.g.* his discussion concerning the "pœna extraordinaria", IX, 36, n. 3) and contradictory; and as a zealous Papist, Decianus was too much under the influence of the Canon Law, *e.g.* cherished extreme views in regard to the prosecution of heretics.

The most famous of the later Italian jurists was *Prosper Farinacius* (died 1618). In his very voluminous writings he attempted to concentrate all that had been written. Remarkable for their erudition, but overwhelmed in a wilderness of citations, his writings are difficult to read, and often fail, amidst the mass of qualifications and distinctions, to reveal the principle upon which he proceeds in his decision of disputed questions; they are laborious and dry reading ("Opp. omnia", 9 vols. fol., Frankfurt, 1616, of which Vol. II contains the "Tractatus de testibus," Vols. IV and IX, "Decisiones Rotæ").

[3] A Senator of Milan, born 1486, died 1546. "Tractatus varii qui omnem fere criminum materiam complectuntur" (Venice, 1512).

[4] Born 1525 at Alexandria, died 1575 at Saragossa, as adviser of Philip II. "Sententiarum receptarum libri V. s. practica criminalis" (1560 first, with successive Commentators; notes of *Bajardus* are also important).

[5] As to Damhouder, *cf.* especially *Stintzing*, "Geschichte", I, pp. 604 *et seq.* The earliest well-known edition is that of 1554.

[6] The first work after the publication of the Carolina was a Latin

Yet this method of dealing with the Carolina is not as strange as it may seem. It was the intention of its authors that it should be supplemented, not directly from itself, but rather from the "kaiserliche beschriebene Recht", *i.e.* from the Italian legal practice, and from the local law. More accurately examined, the misconception of that purpose is found, not in the literature next following the Carolina but rather in that later literature which treated the Carolina as a genuine code, to be supplemented primarily from its own principles.

The Jurisconsults and the Law Faculties. — It is also quite possible that the really learned legal practice, which in that period was represented not so much by the treatises and text-books as by the "Consilia" (opinions furnished to clients),[7] always looked immediately for guidance to Italian legal science; and that the Carolina, during the period immediately following its first publication, merely had the effect of confirming opinions elsewhere acquired. This is seen in the works *e.g.* of Joh. Fichard,[8] Recorder of Frankfort-on-Main, and the most famous legal adviser of his times,[9] and also in the works of Mynsinger.[10] The Carolina was not intended for the really learned jurists. This explains why, even in those States where the Carolina had been specially promulgated, the jurists of high reputation continued to base their opinions, not on the Carolina, but on the Roman and Italian

translation of the same by *Gobler*, 1543. A later and better Latin paraphrase is that by *Remus* ("Nemesis Carolinæ") published in 1594. Both these were again edited in 1837 by *Abegg*. Other works completing the system of the Carolina are: *Gobler*, "Der Rechten Spiegel" (Frankfurt, 1550); *Heinrich Rauchdorn*, "Practica und Process peinlicher Halsgerichtsordnung" (1564); *Joh. Arn v. Dorneck*, "Practica und Process peinlicher Gerichtshandlung" (1576); *Abraham Sawr*, "Straffbuch" (first in 1577); *Vigel*, "Constitutiones Carolinæ publicorum judiciorum" (1583, in spite of the praise bestowed upon it by Wächter, this work is not much superior to the others mentioned above); *Harpprecht*, "Tractatus criminalis" (first in 1603). *Kilian König's* "Practica und Process der Gerichtsleufte, nach Sechsischem gebrauch" etc. (first in 1541) contains little concerning criminal law. (*Cf.* also *Hälschner*, p. 121, *note; Geib*, I, pp. 287 *et seq.; Stintzing*, "Geschichte", I, pp. 630 *et seq.*)

[7] In the beginning, they would have little to do with the seldom lucrative criminal cases; moreover the jurists were also often clerics, and therefore could refuse to take part in the "Blutgericht" ("Blood court", *i.e.* criminal court). *Cf. Stintzing*, I, p. 608.

[8] Concerning Fichard, *cf. Stintzing*, I, pp. 586 *et seq.*

[9] *Cf.* "Consilia" (1590 fol.) Cons. 61. Here, in dealing with a case coming before the court in 1549, the provisions of the Carolina concerning homicide resulting from chance medley were not observed.

[10] *Mynsinger*, "Observ.", III, 9, in discussing the punishment of attempt makes no mention of the Carolina. (As to Mynsinger, born 1514, died 1588, *cf. Stintzing*, I, pp. 485 *et seq.*)

authorities. Indeed, they invoked the Carolina for the most part only upon an appeal reviewing the proceedings in a lower court, to determine whether or not a lower court had erred.[11] Consequently the scientific and practical activities and abilities of the higher courts, and especially of the law faculties (who were constantly acquiring more and more of a dominating influence in practice), are not to be judged by the above-mentioned literature. The practical business of giving advice and rendering opinions was extraordinarily remunerative and held in much honor; it made such demands upon the time of jurists of reputation that they did not aspire to literary activity, but left this to those of more subordinate and mediocre abilities.[12] The " Consilia " of Fichard and of the Tübingen Faculty give evidence of a far superior grade of legal practice than one would surmise from the scientifically valueless literature. They reveal that moral earnestness and courage which defended the oppressed against the despotism of princes,[13] and brought the law faculties gradually to that high position which they maintained during the ensuing three centuries.[14]

§ 47. **Domination of Theology. Witchcraft. Blasphemy.** — There were two enemies against whom legal science was obliged to defend itself. These were the bigoted theology and the despotism of the princes. It is notable that the assistance of the power of the princes later served to overcome theology.

The domination of theology manifested itself in many particulars. The most important was the atrocities of the *witchcraft trials*, by which (far more than by war or plague) many regions during the 1500 s and 1600 s were periodically decimated.[1] At beginning, to be sure, the Church had vigorously condemned

[11] *Cf. Seeger*, "Die strafrechtlichen Consilia Tubingensia von der Gründung der Universität bis zum Jahre 1600" (Tübingen, 1877), p. 33.

[12] *Ibid.*, pp. 28 and 31 *et seq.*

[13] *Cf.* the "Consilium der Sichardt'schen Sammlung", cited by *Seeger*.

[14] In general, since the middle of the 1500 s, the activity of the learned jurists in criminal causes became more extensive (*cf. Stölzel*, "Die Entwicklung des gelehrten Richterthums in deutschen Territorien", I (1872), pp. 349 *et seq.*, and *Stintzing*, "Geschichte", I, p. 635). After the middle of the 1500 s, the criminal law was treated as a distinct and separate subject, *e.g.* in Tübingen, Jena, Rostock, Ingolstadt (*cf. Stintzing*, I, p. 635).

[1] *Cf.* especially *Soldan*, "Geschichte der Hexenprocesse", recently revised by *Heppe* (2 vols., 1880), and *Von Wächter*, "Beiträge zur deutschen Geschichte", pp. 81 *et seq.*, pp. 277 *et seq.*; *Stintzing*, "Geschichte", I, pp. 641 *et seq.* In the bishopric of Bamberg, *e.g.*, with a population of 100,000, there were executed, during the years 1627–1630, 285 persons. A witchcraft judge in Fulda in 18 years brought his number of death sentences up to a total of 700.

belief in the possibility of an alliance with the Devil.[2] But later it recognized it officially. There was no more effective way to arouse the people to fanaticism against heretics than to make it clear to them that the heretics were in league with the Devil.[3] Thus, in Arras, in 1459, a large number of the Waldenses were burned to death, on the ground of an alleged alliance with the Devil. In 1484, Innocent VIII ordered the judges commissioned to sit in heresy cases for Germany, Heinrich Institor (Krämer) and Jacob Sprenger (both of them professors of theology), to prosecute sorcerers also with the utmost zeal. With the approval of the Faculty of Theology of Cologne there was composed for these two heresy judges the so-called "Malleus maleficarum" ("Hammer of Witches"), a formal treatise on the belief in witches and their inquisition. The inquisition of witches, especially with the use of torture, now acquired truly revolting features.

The Bambergensis[4] and the Carolina[5] had proceeded with some moderation, since they made sorcery a crime punishable with death at the stake, only when it was injurious to others. In other cases the penalties were left to judicial discretion. Enlightened men, such as Fichard,[6] denounced the charges of nocturnal dances and intercourse with the Devil as products of the imagination. But judicial practice, inspired by theology and at the same time fearing it,[7] soon began to throw aside the limitations imposed by the Carolina.[8] Invoking the same principle as in other matters, it declared the Mosaic law to be a command unequivocally binding upon the authorities.[9] And so, with all seriousness, the judicial trials investigated the various kinds of alliances with the Devil.[10] Upon the whole the Protestant theol-

[2] Charles the Great in 785 had ratified a decree prepared by the Synod of Paderborn, by which expression of belief in witchcraft was forbidden. *Cf. Soldan-Heppe*, I, p. 128.

[3] *Von Wächter*, p. 89.

[4] Bambergensis, 131.

[5] Carolina, 109.

[6] "Teutsche Rathschläge", p. 112.

[7] Leyser, as is well-known, would not willingly take issue with the theologians. He twice changed his opinion in regard to incense, each time to bring himself into harmony with the theologians of the country in which he lectured. (*Cf.* Sp. 586, n. 1.)

[8] According to the "Constitutiones Saxonicae" of 1572, IV, 2, death by burning was the penalty even if no harm had been wrought. Soothsaying and magic also entailed the death penalty (by the sword).

[9] *Cf.* Exodus, xxii, 18: "Thou shalt not suffer a witch to live."

[10] *Cf. e.g. Carpzov*, "Practica nova Imperialis Saxonica rerum criminalium" (1635), qu. 49 n. 23 *et seq.*

ogy,[11] constantly more and more bigoted, was just as active as the Catholic theology in its incitement of the prosecution of witches. There may often be found in the libraries peacefully bound together in the same volume the products of this insane superstition of both Catholic and Protestant theologians, who in other matters were contending furiously.

Another evidence of this domination of theology is to be found in the fact that (by virtue of the above-mentioned opinion about the direct obligation of many expressions in the Bible) [12] the right of the magistrates and rulers to *remit death sentences* was successfully contested.[13] As against "Lex divina", that power of the "Princeps", to which the Italian writers had such frequent recourse, did not appear to obtain. In doubtful cases of this character the rulers even referred the matter to the clergy for their opinion; this was done even until the 1700 s.[14]

Still another example of the zeal of the bigoted clergy is seen in the severe punishment [15] of *blasphemy;* [16] so, too, in the punishment of *unchastity,* in many of the Protestant countries,[17] and especially in Electoral Saxony, where the power of orthodoxy was supreme. There we find death by the sword prescribed for adultery,[18] and unless special reasons for mitigation (and in prac-

[11] However, in some of the Protestant countries the rulers took a rational attitude (*e.g.* Mecklenburg, Würtemberg).

[12] In one of the opinions rendered by the Faculty of Tübingen in 1695, the view was sustained that the civil authority could straightway inflict a penalty valid under the Mosaic law (*Harpprecht,* "Consil.", 53, n. 17, 18.)

[13] *Cf.* concerning reference of cases to the theologians for their opinions, especially in reference to mitigation of punishment, *Leyser,* "Sp." 597, n. 28, 30. Leyser was of the opinion that in homicide there could be no period of limitation against the punishment, and no mitigation of the punishment (*e.g.* because of the youth of the offender), since the divine command was expressed without qualification. A Brandenburg case was referred to theologians for their opinion, whether the death penalty could be remitted in the case of persons seemingly not responsible.

[14] According to *Frölich v. Frölichburg's* "Commentar zur P.G.O." (1710), II, 211, the clergy in deciding the question whether a child was a human being or a monster considered whether or not it could have been baptized.

[15] In Saxony the more serious cases of sacrilege were punished by breaking on the wheel. *Carpzov,* II, qu. 89 n. 18 *et seq.*

[16] The generally lenient Tübingen Faculty (*Harpprecht,* "Consilia", 81) in 1680, in a not extreme case, imposed the death penalty, and in 1706 in a more serious case imposed the death penalty in an aggravated form. The bigotted *Brunnemann* ("Tractatus de inquisitionis processu", 9, n. 1) reports a case in which the Frankfort Faculty had imposed a sentence of cutting out the tongue, and adds "nec ejus me pœnitet."

[17] In 1681, the Faculty of Tübingen sentenced to death with the sword a boy of seventeen apparently physically and morally depraved, for sodomy with animals.

[18] The "Kursächsiche Constitution" of 1543 provided death by the

tice these were apparently quite liberal) could be invoked, this penalty was for a long time relentlessly carried out.[19]

The distinction between the provinces of the temporal and spiritual judges finally became so confused, that in Protestant countries where the clergy were more or less given "de facto" recognition as State officials, the Courts pronounced the regular punishments of the Church.[20]

§ 48. **Despotism of the Rulers.** — The Protestant theology also tended to strengthen the principle of the omnipotence of the sovereign, by casting upon it the lustre of divine authority. This power of the "Princeps", by application of the Roman maxim "Princeps legibus solutus",[1] had already been given a very questionable extension from the Italian jurists. The Reformers made direct use of the secular authorities, especially in the States of the empire, for the spreading of their doctrines. Consequently they often preached absolute submission to established authority,[2] even to a bad ruler. The established authority was to them the direct representative of God. The maxim of Theodor Beza:[3] "Rei publicæ quidem interest, non modo ne quis re sua . . . sed etiam se ipso . . . male utatur", laid the foundation for a power of the State in matters pertaining to police regulation that was absolutely despotic in character.

This absolute power was even considered a sufficient basis for the enactment of higher penalties than would otherwise have been justifiable, on the ground that the offender had transgressed a supreme command of the ruler and repudiated the ruler's authority.[4] For example, in contravention of the common law, it was

sword for adultery of the husband as well as the wife, and this punishment was to be inflicted upon the third party even in a case where there was forgiveness on the part of the injured spouse. *Carpzov*, II, qu. 54 n. 32 *et seq.*

[19] The influence of the clergy also led directly to judgments containing a false moralizing element. In Zofingen (Switzerland) in 1613, pursuant to a decision obtained after reference to the clergy, a man was beheaded because he had not saved his wife in an accident. *Osenbrüggen*, "Studien", pp. 2, 3.

[20] Thus, by a judgment given in *Carpzov*, II, qu. 92 n. 37, a usurer was sentenced to death, not only without honorable burial, but also without receiving the Sacrament.

[1] *Cf. Theod. Reinkingk*, "De regimine sæculari" (1613 ed. 1) 1, 2, c. 12, n. 8 *et seq.*, who, however, in accordance with the Middle Ages theory would hold the "princeps" bound by "leges divinæ" and "naturales."

[2] *Cf. Calvini*, "Institutiones Relig. Christ.", IV, 22 c. 2, 3, 27.

[3] "De hæreticis", p. 23 (ed. of 1555).

[4] *Cf.* the "kursächsisches Mandat" of 1584 concerning the punishment of poaching, "von Niemand uns trotzen lassen."

deemed justifiable to punish with heavy penalties the stealing of wild deer,[5] since this was prejudicial to the exercise by the prince of his noble passion for the chase. Where the property or any other special interest of the ruler seemed jeopardized, it was considered justifiable to ignore all ordinary limits in the fixing of penalties.[6]

§ 49. **The Crime of "Lèse Majesté."**—The crime of "lèse majesté", which was gradually made to cover attacks upon the States and their rulers, possessed often, as formerly in the time of the Roman Cæsars, a terrible significance. It was used even by the Protestant theologians and their zealots as a means to destroy their opponents and to prosecute heresy. As is well known, Craco, the Saxon privy councillor, suffered martrydom with slow torture at the command of the Electoral Prince August, because he was accused of a conspiracy to introduce Calvinism into Electoral Saxony.[1] As in the time of the Roman emperors, a political minister's failure, actual or apparent, in acts of State, was attributed to disloyalty; and the prince's prior sanction signified little if after the event his altered opinion condemned it. Moreover, no distinction was made between the private interests

[5] In Würtemberg, towards the end of the 1500s, the punishment of putting out of the eyes was inflicted for stealing deer. Emperor Ferdinand I interfered with this custom (*cf. Kress*, 159, § 5 n. 3). *Cf.* as to the punishment of poaching during this period, also *Roth*, "Geschichte des Forst- und Jagdwesens in Deutschland", pp. 468 *et seq.* In Tyrol, at the beginning of the 1700s, the extreme penalty was a sentence to the galleys: *Frölich v. Frölichburg*, "Commentar zur P.G.O." II, 4, 6.

[6] A royal decree ("constitution") of Braunschweig-Lüneburg of the 3d of January, 1593, against adultery and harlotry, made the latter punishable with the sword when committed in churches, cloisters, or "auf unseren Schlössern" (*Kress*, "Commentar", Supplement, p. 851). An Edict of Hannover of Sept. 12th, 1681, imposed death by hanging for theft of the royal silver plate, without distinction as to how much or how little was stolen (*Kress*, p. 851). *Cf.* also in the 1700 s, the Royal Prussian Edict of Jan. 4, 1736, against stealing within the royal palace ("Corpus Constitutionum Marchicarum", II, Abth. III, N. 75). As an example of legislation of this character is frequently cited a Prussian Edict of 1739. "If an advocate or attorney or any other such person shall have the presumption to cause a direct petition in a legal proceeding or plea for a pardon to be presented to his Royal Majesty by soldiers, or if any other of the people be prevailed upon by him to present to his Royal Majesty a direct petition in a settled and decided case, then shall his Royal Majesty such person . . . cause to be hung and cause a dog to be hung with him." *Cf.* also, *Berner*, "Lehrbuch des deutschen Strafrechts", § 54, and concerning this Brandenburg-Prussian legislation, *cf.* the exposition (somewhat too lenient however) of *Abegg* in *Hitzig's* "Zeitschrift für Criminalrechtspflege in den Preussischen Staaten" (1836, Supplement, pp. 129 *et seq*).

[1] *Cf. Kluckhohn*, "Der Sturz der Krytoclavinisten in Kursachsen" (1574) in *Von Sybel's* "Historischer Zeitschrift", Vol. 18 (1867), pp. 77–127.

of the princes and the interests of the country.[2] Thus, in the outrageous proceedings for treason against Crell, the Chancellor of Electoral Saxony, who after a ten-years' imprisonment was in 1601 brought to the scaffold, the charges were that this once powerful counselor of the electoral prince had asserted for the prince prerogatives which he did not possess, had aroused discord in the royal court, and had incited the prince to a hatred of his consort.[3] In the times from the 1700 s on, when ministers were all-powerful (and sufficient mischief may indeed be laid at their doors), their office was for these reasons not without its dangers.[4] Even to hold a high position might later become high treason on the part of the overthrown favorite. Leyser [5] even discusses in all seriousness whether "Ministrissimatus" (*i.e.* the preferred position of an all-powerful minister) does not in itself constitute a crime.

Other Illustrations of the Despotism of the Rulers. — Moreover, when they were not concerned in furthering some base interest, the rulers began to gratify their individual whims and caprices in defining offenses and in fixing the penalties. "Superiori nihil impossibile" is the statement of Brunnemann, when advising the utmost extremity in threatening punishments. The "Constitutiones Saxonicæ" (1572) [6] no longer regarded the limitation imposed by the Carolina upon the introduction of new crimes into the law. Blumlacher, in the preface to his commentary upon the Carolina, makes an express statement in regard to this: "Hodie quilibet Princeps in territorio dicitur esse Imperator." [7] In 1710, by an ordinance of the Elector of Hannover, mistakes of masons and carpenters whereby danger of fire could arise were punishable by imprisonment at hard labor in the galleys for life. By another of these ordinances in 1726 a negligent bankruptcy was punishable with the galleys, and a fraudulent bankruptcy with life imprisonment.[8] However, judicial practice

[2] *Cf. Leyser*, "Sp.", 575, n. 2, concerning the trial of the unfortunate Baron Görtz, executed in Sweden.

[3] *Leyser*, "Speculum", 571 n. 55, 56.

[4] *Ibid.*, 575, n. 5, speaks of the peculiar practice of questioning of the Faculties concerning the punishment of ministers.

[5] *Ibid.*, 570.

[6] For example, the old Saxon law in respect to rape was restored, and theft was punished by new rules. *Cf.* IV, 31, 33.

[7] This unlimited power of legislation was based upon the provisions of the Peace of Westphalia. *Cf.* J. R. A. § 171, Verb. "Demjenigen nachgelebt werden soll, was" etc.

[8] The edicts against the gypsies are also notable. They were by im-

soon began a successful opposition to ordinances of this character.

The power of the rulers manifested itself not only in autocratic legislation, but also by interfering in the trial and decision of individual cases. Already in the Italian jurists [9] was to be found the principle that the sovereign "ex plenitudine potestatis" not only can remit penalties but also can inflict penalties and correct errors in judicial decisions, and that in so doing he is not bound by the ordinary rules of procedure.[10] Thus, while increasing limitations were being placed upon the right of the judges and the lords of inferior courts to remit punishments, and the modern pardoning power of the rulers was being developed, there often came about in the several States an expansion of the power of the rulers in the matter of increasing punishments. In Brandenburg, and later in the Kingdom of Prussia, the ruler became the regular source to which appeal was taken for the review of criminal cases of a more serious character, and to which all the appropriate proceedings had always to be submitted.[11] It is easy to see how this often led to perverse, albeit well meant, decisions.[12] The judges, moreover, in accordance with the Roman traditions, gave broad support to the right of the "Princeps" to proceed of his own motion directly against those who were enemies of the country and therefore also against enemies of its rulers, — just as had been done by the possessor of the Roman sovereign power, against those guilty of "perduellio." [13]

§ 50. **Abuses of the Criminal Law.** — It is therefore not surprising that, in certain cases, the old idea of regarding the right

perial law declared to be without rights ("Polizeiord. 1577", tit. 28). According to an Edict of Frederick William I of Prussia, Oct. 5, 1725, gypsies who were found in the country and were over eighteen years of age were mercilessly punished on the gallows.

[9] *Cf. e.g. Bossius*, tit. "de homicidiis", n. 97 *et seq.* The maxim however is older. *Kress*, "Comment.", Art. 99, § 3, infers that where a judge has passed too lenient a sentence, he can apply to the "princeps" to have it corrected.

[10] Often during the 1700 s the judgments of the faculties were drawn in form of advices to the princes, especially if the statutory law seemed to the "Collegium" to be too severe.

[11] *Cf. Hälschner*, "Geschichte", p. 141.

[12] *Cf. Fichard*, "Teutsche Rathschläge", cons. 70, n. 11 *et seq.* "In consistorio principis non requiritur ordo processus"; a maxim which however here referred only to the emperor.

[13] *Reinkingk*, "De regimine sæc.", I, 2, c. 12, n. 35; *Pufendorf*, "De jure nat.", VIII, c. 3, § 33: "aliquando absque ambagibus processus ab executione fieri initium queat" (!). *Cf.* also *Leyser*, "Speculum", 641 n. 12, 646 n. 7, who relies upon L. 16, § 10, D. "de pœnis", and in extreme cases approved of putting to death with poison (!)

of administering justice as essentially a property right led to some infamous compromises for the suppression of justice. Thus, when von Hoym,[1] the President of the Exchequer of Electoral Saxony, who had been guilty of numerous briberies, embezzlements, instigation of money frauds and extraordinary extortions against his tenants, was prosecuted, with much display in 1693, he got off with paying to the Elector the sum of 200,000 thaler; the alleged offenses were as good as proven; an application of torture had procured from von Hoym a confession; but the poor tenants never got any redress and he was reinstated in all his old dignities.[2]

Carpzov[3] breaks out in complaints against the evil judges of the lower courts (and of the higher courts as well) who make a business out of inflicting fines and are not ashamed to say in public: "Well, God be praised, the ledger makes an excellent showing this year in offenses and fines." As late as the end of the 1700 s there was a small principality (which fortunately has long since been mediatized), in which a court commissioner travelled about for the purpose of extorting high money fines by instituting absurd prosecutions for adultery,[4] so that the homes and estates of many people were sold at auction to the court Jews. Ultimately this unbelievably scandalous practice was energetically suppressed by the Supreme Court of the Empire.[5]

§ 51. **Scantiness of Legislation. Evasion of the Carolina; Berlich and Carpzov.** — However, along with this insincere and despotic administration of the law,[1] here and there the opinions

[1] *Cf. Helbig*, "Die kursächsische Kammerpräsident von Hoym", in the periodical "Im neuen Reich" (1873), II, pp. 473 *et seq.*

[2] No form of underhand dealing, and no violation of law or contract, were disdained in getting their hands on anyone whose persecution was desired by the lord or his favorites. *Leyser*, "Speculum", 572, n. 6, speaking of a trick of this kind done in the vicinity of Hamburg 1664, calls it a "dolus bonus," and remarks "nec improbe actum."

[3] "Practica", III, qu. 116, n. 13 *et seq.*

[4] Thus, a man seventy-two years of age was fined 1200 guilder on account of two acts of adultery alleged to have been committed many years previously.

[5] "Bibliothek für peinl. Rechtswissenschaft" (1797, Vol. I), p. 2, pp. 278 *et seq.* The Rescript of the Imperial Supreme Court ("Reichskammergericht") was dated May 17th, 1793.

[1] Sometimes offenders were hung merely that the petty ruler might show that he possessed the privilege of "Blood ban." *Cf. Oldekop*, "Observ. crim." V, 19: "Vae tibi qui hoc modo jura jurisdictionemque tuam tueri desideres et actum peri imperii." *Gmelin* ("Grundsätze über Verbrechen und Strafen", 1785, p. 292) relates that it was reported to him that a nobleman in opposition to the opinion of a law faculty caused a prisoner to be hanged in order to demonstrate his possession of the "Blood ban."

of the Courts and law faculties were gradually acquiring an influence, in mitigating the cruel punishments [2] and in making criminal justice serviceable to the well-being of the public at large.[3] As

[2] In the 1600 s the administration of criminal law, reflecting the conditions of the times alternately varied between barbarous severity and an almost inconceivable leniency and a tacit immunity to the most notorious criminals when they later ceased their criminal activities. In this respect, see the information gathered by *Niemeyer*, from the acts of the Hannoverian court of Meinersen, "Ueber Criminalverbrechen, peinl Strafe und deren Vollziehung bes. aus alter Zeit" (Lüneburg, 1824), pp. 61, 62, 104. At the end of the 1500 s, justice was dealt out, in Meinersen and vicinity, with severity in accordance with the Carolina. During the period between 1618 and 1660 grave crimes such as theft and even murder were punished only with banishment, church penance, and money fines. On the other hand, little scruple was often shown in the sentence and execution of death penalties; *e.g.*, the officials in Meinersen considered it remarkable that a messenger who was to bring three death sentences from the Helmstädter Faculty was obliged to wait two days and brought back only two death sentences. Often the messenger on the same day on which he transmitted the record would return with the death sentence! (*Niemeyer*, p. 116.)

Concerning the revolting cruelty (occasionally shown in Hannover) inflicting death by flies, wasps, ants — cf. *Freudentheil*, "Beilageheft zum N. Archiv des Criminalrechts", 1838. On the other hand, humorous features were not entirely lacking. Occasionally, for the sake of a better admonition and education in the case of the execution of punishments, certain of the spectators were also, with the general approval of the public, cudgeled. Thus the officials in Meinersen, where a son had murdered his father, caused a number of grown up sons of peasants, after viewing the execution of the offender, to be themselves cudgeled. *Niemeyer*, p. 121.

[3] In the *mitigation of punishments* there long prevailed the influence of the ancient legal conceptions. *E.g.*, even in the 1600 s the request of a "puella" to marry the offender was recognized as a ground for not carrying out a death sentence and for commending the offender to the pardon of the lord of the land. In this way, especially in cases of adultery, death sentences were often avoided. *Cf. Carpzov*, II, qu. 88, n. 25. Many later writers, failing to recognize the original meaning of the term, limited this rule to the request of a "meretrix" (!) because she would thereby be enabled to live an honorable life. *Cf. contra, Carpzov*, II, qu. 88, n. 25. Mitigation might also be given for special ability of the offender in his art, trade, or profession (*cf. Carpzov*, 1. c. n. 62); the "Codex Max. Bavaricus" felt it necessary to specially repeal this as a mitigating circumstance. The *intercession* of others was also regarded as a ground for the interposition of the pardon of the ruler. *Fichard*, "Teutsche Rathschläge", cons. 121, because of the intercession of the entire community and because the offender was one "Ansehnlicher von Adel" (having the appearance of nobility), changed to banishment and damages a sentence to death by the sword. Use was also made of the provisions of the later Roman law, in individual cases, to exempt persons of the higher rank from punishments involving life or limb. Thus, in 1611, an academic Council set up the principle that a student, who had committed theft, should be spared, since he was "angesehener Leute Kind", from undergoing the death penalty otherwise entailed by theft. (*Cf. Leyser*, "Sp.", 532, n. 15.) The University of Leipzig in the 1600 s availed itself of a special papal privilege whereby students of Leipzig were liable, for "homicidium", only to life imprisonment and for theft, only to banishment. The electoral Saxon legislation felt it necessary to abolish this and especially that part referring to manslaughter, since it was contrary to

a matter of fact, the judicial assumption of such powers was forced upon the profession by the inactivity in legislation. The legislation of the various States merely furnished solutions of single points (at most of doubtful value), and the imperial legislation, after the enactment of the Carolina, almost completely abandoned the field of criminal law. We encounter nothing other than a few provisions relating to blasphemy, wanton oaths, and profanity,[4] and sundry police regulations having to do with the trades and professions, luxurious living, etc.[5] A draft was made of an imperial statute to check the increasing excesses of duelling;[6] this draft, which misguidedly treated the principals as guilty merely of ordinary manslaughter and their seconds as accessories, was not enacted as an imperial statute, but was given effect either by the local law in various States or by the so-called "Duellmandaten", which were based upon the same defective principle and were out of harmony with public sentiment.[7]

Absolutely nothing was done by imperial legislation, and extremely little by local legislation, towards substituting other penalties for the punishments by mutilation which were so much used in the Carolina and which gradually fell more and more into disfavor. Little was done by legislation towards lessening the number of the simple and aggravated forms of death penalties which were so frequent in the Carolina. The judges felt themselves obliged to evade the statute. This tendency undermined

divine command. *Cf. Ziegler*, "De juribus majestatis", Lib. I, c. 5, n. 26, 27. Presumably there was some connection between these privileges of the University and the old "benefit of clergy." *Carpzov*, II, qu. 62, n. 20 *et seq.*, was of the opinion that the benefit of clergy in Protestant countries could no longer be recognized because of the transfer of the jurisdiction to the civic authorities.

"Transactio" (*i.e.* settlement) with the party injured was also for a long time given force in mitigation. Even *Carpzov*, II, qu. 80 n. 11 *et seq.*, was of the opinion that "transactio" did not exclude prosecution by the authorities, but that it precluded the "pœna ordinaria." Later, "transactio" was regarded merely as a ground for mitigation of the punishment by commendation to the pardon of the ruler. The view that "transactio" does not preclude public punishment is to be found in *Oldekop*, II, qu. 1. Also *cf.* n. 23 *et seq.*, of the same in regard to the many abuses resulting from "transactio."

[4] R.P.O. of 1577, Tit. 1, § 2, Tit. 2 and 3.

[5] Concerning such matters, the Imperial police regulations contained quite extensive provisions. As to this and the particular provisions therewith concerned, *cf. Elben*, "Zur Lehre von der Waarenfälschung" (1881), pp. 52 *et seq.*

[6] Imperial opinions, July 1668, confirmed by imperial decree of same date.

[7] *Cf.* especially *Heffter*, "Lehrbuch des gemeinen deutschen Strafrechts", § 370. *E.g.* "Braunschweig-Lüneb. Duell-Edict" of 1687.

the respect for the statute and ultimately led to almost complete liberty of discretion in penalties. And it spread notably as soon as the Carolina began to be treated, not as a more or less popular abridgment of the Roman-Italian law, but rather as a code whose principles and their deductions were to prevail over those of the Roman-Italian practice in case of conflict.

Berlich and Carpzov. — This last-mentioned method of dealing with the Carolina is especially noticeable in the writings of the Saxon jurists, Matthias Berlich [8] and Benedict Carpzov.[9] These jurists first gave an independent position to German criminal doctrine and practice by the citation and discussion of the native German law and the numerous decisions of the Saxon courts, especially of the Leipzig Bench of "Schöffen." Carpzov's work, in spite of the attacks of his contemporary, Oldekop,[10] exer-

[8] *Berlich*, "Conclusiones practicabiles", I, qu. 20, n. 32: "Et certe in delictis atque pœnis dictandis magis ad Ordinationem Caroli crimin. quam ad definitionem juris civilis respiciendum est. *Prædicta enim ordinatio juris communi derogat.*" This work appeared first in the years 1615–1619. As to Berlich, *cf. Stintzing*, I, p. 736.

[9] It cannot be maintained that Carpzov, in respect to the general theory of criminal law, marks an advance in comparison with the Italian writers. He ranks rather lower than Bossius and Clarus. German legal doctrine is merely indebted to him and to his predecessor Berlich for a certain independence. ("Nisi Berlich berlichizasset Carpzov non carpzoviasset!") Carpzov's striving for candor and his love of justice are everywhere apparent; it is incorrect to charge him with extraordinary severity. (*Cf. e.g.* III, qu. 116, n. 11 *et seq.*, concerning the cruel, irrational system of justice and its greed for money; also III, qu. 123, n. 20 *et seq.*, concerning the judges' independence of the orders of the ruler.) But he is entirely lacking in the matter of form and arrangement. As a bigoted adherent of the theological legal traditions, he regarded the Mosaic law as "jus divinum", having precedence over the law of the land. (*Cf.* III, qu. 111, n. 59.) He also gave broad scope to the crime of heresy, and indulged in a most absurd discussion of sorcery. He also often confused proof with substantive law, and the legal with the moral valuation of an offense. His theory of "crimina excepta", *i.e.* certain very grave crimes in which the usual fundamental maxims concerning proof and justification should not be regarded, is very specious. It was however shared by many others.

(*Cf.* as to Carpzov, especially *J. S. F. Boehmer*, "Præfatio ad Bened. Carpzovii practicam.") Carpzov, born 1595, died 1666, was Professor and "Ordinarius" of the Leipzig Law Faculty and of the Bench of "Schöffen." It is said that he pronounced twenty thousand judgments of death. His famous "Practica nova Imperialis Saxonica rerum criminalium" first appeared in 1638.

[10] Oldekop, born 1597 at Hildesheim, had decidedly a subtler mind than Carpzov. As a free-thinker he had serious doubts about the justice of the witchcraft procedure; even at this early period, he offered the true explanation of the strange confessions made in such cases. He had a better knowledge of the Roman law, and had more respect for statute law, and he contended justly against the numerous arbitrary and ill-founded decisions appearing in Carpzov. However, he had less knowledge of and paid less attention to the native law, and for this reason he

cised a predominating influence over the German practice for nearly a century.[11]

§ 52. **Recognition of the Principle of Mitigating Circumstances.** — The evasion of the Carolina was first accomplished by the introduction of numerous grounds for mitigation of punishments. Already the later Italian practice[1] had permitted the judge to inquire whether the legislator, although the concrete case might fairly be within the general provisions of the act, had exactly such a case under contemplation. The more the harsh penalties of the Carolina, *e.g.*, death penalties inflicted for the violation of a mere property right, came to run contrary to public sentiment, the more these grounds for mitigation were recognized. To be sure, they often strike us as very strange, reminding us of the reasoning of the old judgments of guilty with recommendation to the grace of the ruler.[2]

Rise of Imprisonment as a Penalty. — In such deviations from the statutory penalties, the judge exercised a free hand. One consequence was (and here the maxim " Salus reipublicæ suprema lex esto " came more and more to be applied, especially after Pufendorf), that sentences of imprisonment in **penitentiaries** (workhouses) now came into vogue.[3] These institutions

does not have Carpzov's historical significance. ("Observationes crim. u. contra Carpzovium Tractatus.")

[11] In eastern Germany, *Brunnemann's* "Tractatus de inquisitionis processu" (first printed in 1648) was highly but undeservedly esteemed. He was Professor in Frankfort and died in 1072. There is absolutely nothing original in this bigoted Protestant jurist. In the crudest manner conceivable he continually confuses the functions of the judge and the legislator; and his juristic arguments are often simply nonsensical.

[1] *Cf. e.g. Decianus*, "Pr.", VIII, C. 14. Also *Mynsinger*, "Observ." II, 30, infers that the judge generally has the right to change the punishment, even if a "pœna certa" is fixed by the statute.

[2] In a judgment of the Faculty of Tübingen, a reason for mitigating the sentence was that the father of the offender, guilty of pillaging, through the punishment of his son "would be plunged into great tribulation." In *Carpzov*, II, qu. 80, n. 100 are mentioned, as reasons for mitigation, the plight of the offender's wife, and his young children still dependent, and his promise of compensation.

[3] A workhouse was erected in Berne in 1615, in Basel in 1667, and in Celle 1710–1731. *Cf. Wagnitz*, "Historische Nachrichten und Bemerkungen über die merkwürdigsten Zuchthäuser in Deutschland" (1792), II, pp. 143, 229. In Netherlands they had "ergastula nautica" which, as stated by Damhouder, were often far more feared than torture and the death penalty, and of which *Damhouder*, "Praxis rer. crim." C. 151, draws a terrible picture. Besides convicted criminals, there were sent here vagabonds, persistent beggars, and even reprobate sons at the instance of their parents. However, as Damhouder remarks, the people there confined for the most part became worse (n. 24). Great severity of treatment alternated with an easy-going regimen of pleasant ease (card-playing, etc.) in the "Popina." On the other hand, *Damhouder*, "Praxis", 110,

had been erected, since the beginning of the 1600 s (first in Lübeck in 1613, and in Hamburg in 1615), primarily as a police measure, for the reception of unemployed vagabonds. Originating in the cities of the Netherlands, they found increasing approval and wider imitation.[4] Sentences to "opus publicum"[5] were also imposed (for which authority could be found in the Roman law), *i.e.* to the building of roads, fortresses, castles and manor-houses, to military service against the Turks,[6] and even to labor on the Venetian galleys. The treatment of the prisoners in these institutions varied greatly, and the sentences of the judges were thus indefinite in their consequences. Originally, the rasping of foreign dyewoods was the most usual occupation for prisoners.[7]

On the other hand, the discretion of the judge might at any time resort again to the old punishments by mutilation.[8] These did not completely disappear until the beginning of the 1700 s. In the first third of the 1700 s, cutting off the hand (in certain cases) is the only remaining punishment of this character.[9] More-

n. 59 makes mention of a beneficent school in Bruges for beggars and other despised persons. Concerning the erection of penitentiaries and workhouses in the Duchy of Holstein during the period 1730–1740, *cf.* *Von Warnstedt*, "Zur Lehre von dem Gemeinde-Verbänden, kritische Beleuchtung eines Rechtsstreits" (1878), pp. 30 *et seq.*

[4] *Theod. Reinkingk*, "De regimine sæculari et ecclesiastico", II, 1, c. 7, n. 6 recommends the establishment in each province of workhouses for beggars, vagabonds, and idlers. *Cf.* also *Pufendorf*, "De jure naturæ et gentium", VIII, c. 3, § 4.

[5] Condemnation to "opus publicum" at the beginning of the 1600 s. *Cf. Sande*, "Decis. Fris.", 5, 9, dec. 3.

[6] *Cf. e.g. Reinkingk*, II, 1, c. 8, who describes this as the "optimus relegandi modus." Opinion of the law faculty of Tübingen in 1697 in *Harpprecht*, "Consilia", I, 1, n. 139; also condemnation to twelve years military service against the French, *Harpprecht*, 53, n. 64.

[7] *Cf.* concerning the workhouses in the 1600 s, especially *Krausold*, "Miracula S. Raspini", (Merseburg, 1698); who on the authority of Tabor draws a gloomy picture of the workings of the "Triga", *i.e.* the gallows, public flogging, and banishment ("indurati homines his . . . pœnis non emendantur, sed efferuntur potius ut excandescunt"), and complains that in spite of these cruel punishments, the country was infested with bands of robbers and life and property were not safe; as a substitute penalty he recommends rasping houses [*i.e.* where the prisoners were obliged to rasp wood used in dyes]. *Cf.* also *ibid.*, pp. 52 *et seq.*, and the "Ordnung" of the Hamburger House of 1686. Such pictures are instructive, in view of certain theories obtaining at the present time.

[8] *Lauterbach*, "Collegium theoretico-practicum", 48, 19, n. 10 (Tübingen 1690, *et seq.*) declares himself decidedly opposed to corporal and mutilating punishments. *Kress*, "Commentatio succincta in Constitutionem Criminalem Caroli V" (Hannoveræ, first ed., 1721), points out that the putting out of eyes was plainly no longer an effectual penalty. *Boehmer*, "Meditationes in Constitutionem Criminalem Carolinam" (1st ed. 1770), 112, § 1, observed that cutting off the ears was made use of only in the case of deserters.

[9] *Cf.* concerning a penalty of cutting off a hand inflicted in Oldenburg

over, after the end of the 1600 s, the punishment of banishment (for the State's own subjects) came more and more into disfavor.[10] Public flogging was gradually replaced by imprisonment [11] and by corporal punishment not public. The numerous forms of death penalty were slow to be repudiated.[12] Eminent jurists,[13] however, protested against the indignities which in earlier times were often inflicted upon the corpse of the offender; Carpżov relates that even in his time the death penalty had in many cases been supplanted by life imprisonment.

Change in Law of Proof. — Another field for unlimited judicial discretion was the *law of proof*. The Carolina [14] had provided that a conviction was not to be based merely upon circumstantial evidence. However, some Italian writers had advanced the opinion that since in the " extraordinaria cognitio ",[15] the judge was not bound by the rules of the " judicia publica "; and since in that " cognitio " he might inflict a " pœna extraordinaria ", so he was also permitted, in a case where the proof was not conclusive, to inflict a " pœna extraordinaria "; this, however, was less than the " pœna ordinaria " and could not consist of a death penalty.[16] To harmonize this view with the provision of the Carolina prohibiting the infliction of criminal punishment upon mere circumstantial evidence, that provision was deemed to apply only to graver offenses in which torture could be applied and thus sure proof by confession could be obtained.[17] But even this last

as late as 1714, *Leyser*, "Speculum", 604 n. 3, and concerning a Mecklenburg case of this character in 1731, *cf.* n. 22 of the same.

[10] As to the evils resulting from banishment, *cf. Reinkingk*, 1, c. II, c. 7.

[11] In *Berlich*, "Concl.", V, 57, n. 5, can be seen the more frequent use of "carceratio" in the less serious of the graver offenses, and as early as 1617 a Würtemburg ordinance substituted for corporal punishment the punishment of "opus publicum." In Hannover, public flogging and the pillory were abolished in 1727. *Kress*, Art. 198, § 4 n. 1.

[12] From the philosophical viewpoint attacks were made upon capital punishment as early as Carpzov. *Cf. Carpzov*, "Pr." III, qu. 101, n. 26 *et seq.*

[13] *Cf.* however, the hesitating arguments in *Carpzov*, "Pr.", III, qu. 131, n. 32, *et seq.*

[14] Carolina, 69, 22.

[15] [For these terms of criminal procedure, see *Esmein*, "History of Continental Criminal Procedure," transl. *Simpson*, in the present Series, *passim*. — ED.]

[16] *Cf. Julius Clarus*, § fin., qu. 20, n. 4, *et seq.* Another well-known application of the distinction between "pœna ordinaria" and "pœna extraordinaria" was made when the inquisitorial procedure was first introduced. At first this procedure was to result only in a "pœna extraordinaria." *Cf. Biener*, "Beiträge zur Geschichte des Inquisitionsprocesses", p. 51.

[17] *Cf. Berlich*, IV, 15 n. 8, IV, 16 n. 11, V, 46; *Carpzov*, III, qu. 116.

limitation was soon no longer observed. In all cases where the judge was "morally" (*i.e.* actually) convinced of the guilt of the offender, but there was an absence of the technical legal proof, *i.e.* a confession, or the testimony of eye-witnesses, he sentenced the offender to "extraordinary" punishment, or as it was later called, "suspicion" punishment ("Verdachtstrafe").[18] This measure was used in cases where, though the commission[19] of the act was proven, some one of the elements of the crime was not proven legally or even proven in any sense, *e.g.* the live birth of a new-born child said to have been killed by its mother.[20]

§ 53. **Doctrines as to Judicial Discretion in Defining Crimes.** — In the case just considered, an act was punished which the statute did not in any way make amenable to punishment. But, furthermore, in pursuance of this tendency, acts came to be punished which were not even reached by any specific definition of a crime, but were in the personal view of the court deemed to merit punishment; and this judicial extension of analogies was carried to a pitch nowadays incomprehensible. For example, Kress[1] (who more than any other of the writers on criminal law prior to Feuerbach was careful to abide within the statute), in classifying offenses into crimes against the law of nature and offenses which merely contravene positive law, proceeds to observe that for the former the criterion is the "sana ratio" rather than the "variantes formulæ juris civilis." And although Leyser[2] in one place complains about the arbitrary reasonings of the jurists who decide cases not according to the statute but according to their individual views as to the propriety of the statute for the case under consideration, yet, when he comes to other cases, he proceeds in the same manner as those whom he censures,[3] or else he concedes the author-

[18] *Cf.* "Codex Maxim. Bavaric Crim." I, C. 12, § 11. In Electoral Saxony the "Verdachtstrafe" had obtained statutory recognition at an early date. "Const. El. Saxon." 33, p. 4. *Cf. Carpzov*, II. qu. 81 n. 13. However, many had raised sound objections against the propriety of this "suspicion punishment." But practical need carried the day in spite of its incorrect theoretical basis. *Cf. Carpzov*, III. qu. 142, n. 3 *et seq.*, L. 6, D. "De accus." 48, 2 was also relied upon. *Cf. Carpzov*, III, qu. 116, n. 51; *Leyser*, "Speculum", 630, n. 11.

[19] *Sande*, "Decis. Fris." 5, 9, defin. 3.

[20] *Cf. Boehmer*, "Meditationes in C.C.C.", 131 § 55, who here punishes simply for "sævitia in cadaver commissa."

[1] *Kress*, "Commentatio succincta in Constitutionem Criminalem Caroli V" (Hannoveræ, 1721), 112, 113, n. 2.

[2] "Speculum", 537 n. 22.

[3] *Cf. Hälschner*, p. 163.

ity of custom (" usus ") to correct the shortcomings of the statute. Boehmer, who without doubt was the most important German writer on criminal law prior to Feuerbach, is of the opinion that, since " salus reipublicæ " is the supreme guiding principle for interpreting individual statutes, and is even, where the circumstances demand, superior to the statute, it is permissible to exemplify this doctrine with offenders.[4] He believes that no penalties are unconditionally prescribed by the statute. " Augent, secant, temperant jurisconsulti "; even death penalties may be imposed where the statute speaks only of a " pœna arbitraria."[5]

Consequently there is nothing surprising in a judgment rendered in 1721 by the Faculty of Helmstadt with Leyser's approval. A man charged with manslaughter pleaded self-defense, and the case involved considerable doubt because the records of the proceedings were in another State and could not be obtained; the decision was that " in order to protect the community from this dangerous individual ", he should be confined in a penitentiary or some other well-guarded place at moderate labor *for the rest of his natural life.* Nor are we astonished that Boehmer, even in cases of a complete acquittal after an inquisition (where the torture was successfully undergone or the accused was put to his oath of innocence), favored confinement in an " ergastulum probatorium." Analogies which from our viewpoint are simply impossible were resorted to in order to punish acts which seemed morally reprehensible or likely to be dangerous.[6]

Where the power of the judiciary was so absolute, partiality was sometimes shown in the judgments. Often persons of higher

[4] "Meditationes in C.C.C.", Art. 105 § 3. As to increasing the penalty, see *Ziegler*, "De juribus majestatis" (1681), I, c. 6, n. 13.

[5] *Berlich*, IV, 15, n. 6, was, however, of a different opinion in regard to "pœna arbitraria." In accordance with the common law he would recognize only "pœna pecuniaria" and banishment. According to *Clarus*, § fin., qu. 83, n. 11, a "pœna arbitraria" should at least never amount to capital punishment.

[6] Such decisions may be seen in *Berlich*, IV, 36, n. 30. A prison guard who had got with child an imprisoned maid-servant and fled with her after she had destroyed her child, was without hesitation sentenced to death by the sword; and the same sentence was imposed on the girl.

The "apponere scalas ad fenestras" was under certain circumstances to be punished with death, IV, n. 20. Improprieties were punished under the title of "Stellionatus" (*Carpzov*, III, qu. 133, n. 2, *et seq.*). Thus, in 1695, the Faculty at Tübingen unhesitatingly punished a man for mere failure to keep a promise. *Harpprecht*, "Consil." 47. *Leyser*, "Speculum", 581, n. 8, considers the death penalty as legally justifiable against one who seduced the daughter of his master.

rank received, on some pretext or other, light sentences for crimes that were really brutal. At times the judges seem to have absolutely lost all conception of the gravity of the crime.[7]

[7] *Cf. e.g. Harpprecht,* "Consil." I, n. 139, and see the same for a decision of August 19th, 1681, by which a bold highway robbery was punished with only a few months compulsory labor. In another passage the Faculty consoles itself with the reflection that divine justice must have overtaken the individual subjected to torture where he loses his life. In another case they regarded the death penalty as not unreasonable, because they did not perceive "how the young offender, who had neither father or mother, could have been saved from complete ruin of body and soul." *Harpprecht,* "Consilia", I, 100.

Chapter IX

GERMANY IN THE 1700 s

§ 54. **Beginnings of a Change. Gradual Suppression of Witchcraft Trials.** — But while at the end of the 1600 s the judicial power was continually encroaching upon the legislative, and the practice was becoming more arbitrary, yet on the other hand, during this period and at the beginning of the 1700 s, a distinct improvement in other features was noticeable. In the first place, enlightenment began to dawn in the views upon the prosecution of witchcraft; and when we contemplate the former monstrosities, this is a service to humanity that can not be too highly estimated. Special mention should here be made of the Jesuit Friedrich von Spee [1] and of the valiant efforts of the indefatigable jurist Thomasius.[2] Kress had already asserted, although rather guardedly, that it was difficult to accept witchcraft as possible.[3] Boehmer,

[1] "Cautio criminalis s. de processu contra sagas", first published in 1631.

[2] *Cf.* particularly, "Vom Verbrechen der Zauberei" (1701, 1702).

[3] "Casus si dabitur, respondebitur." "Comment.", Art. 44. Judicial practice came to be more exacting in the acceptance of proof, especially proof of the injury. *Cf. Wächter*, "Beiträge", p. 301. The cautious Leyser however would not absolutely disavow the possibility of magic ("Speculum", 608).

by the middle of the 1700 s, treated the entire proposition as a delusion.[4]

Emancipation from Theology and the Mosaic Law. — All through the criminal law we find the unwholesome influence of theology gradually eliminated; and here, too, we see the fearless Thomasius (the practical value of whose work is to-day entirely too little appreciated) effectively joining in the contest with his numerous minor writings. The separation by the legal philosophers of the Mosaic law into two parts, of which one was of universal obligation and the other of special application only to the Jewish peoples, was now also recognized by the writers on criminal law, in the sense that they referred the penal provisions to the category last mentioned and held that for the present times they had no application. Ultimately, legal theory no longer gave any attention to the Bible. The criminal law was rested simply upon the advantage or the necessity of punishing a wrongful act. These principles were finally made popular, and gradually brought into currency with practical writers on criminal law, by Beccaria's famous book, of which mention will be made later.[5]

This divorce of law from theology led to a recognition of the impropriety of the persecution of those of another religious faith.[6] A milder treatment ensued for offenses allied to religious belief, and also for unchastity, so far as the latter did not also constitute a violation of the rights of others. Another consequence was the attempt to draw a line between wrong in the legal sense and immorality, and to reserve the former alone for the criminal courts; though here it was often forgotten (as is natural in such revolu-

[4] "Meditationes in Constitutionem Criminalem Carolinam" (first published in 1770), 109.

[5] *Cf. e.g. Reinkingk*, "De reg. sæc.", II, 2, c. 2, especially § 5; *Sande*, "Decis. Fris.", 5, 9; *Leyser*, "Speculum", 577, n. 20, and as marking the conclusion of the development, *cf. Engau*, "Elementa juris crim." (5th. ed., 1760) § 3, who absolutely denies the juristic obligation of the Mosaic Law.

[6] As opposed to the punishment of heretics, *cf.* especially *Ziegler*, "De juribus majestatis" (1681), I, 16. Nevertheless, for the spreading of dangerous opinions "propter scandalum", he declared banishment was permissible (n. 10). *Cf.* also *Frölich v. Frölichslichsburg*, II, 1, tit. 4, § 4, who argues that the "flebile beneficium emigrationis", belonging to the adherents of the Augsburg Confession in accordance with the Augsburg decree § 24, belonged also to the Reformers after the Peace of Westphalia. *Leyser*, "Speculum", 566, in such a case limited the right of the authorities to banishment. However, he conceded the compulsory imposition of religious instruction, to the end that where possible the party in question might be rescued from his error. *Cf. ibid.*, a decision of the Wittenberg Consistorium, to which Leyser gave his approval.

tions of opinion) that law has its basis in morality and also that the violation of an individual right is not invariably an essential of a violation of State security in the objective sense.

Effect of Doctrine of Law of Nature. — Furthermore, as a consequence of the rise of the doctrine of a Law of Nature, human nature was now taken into consideration. An act which is merely the result of a strong natural impulse,[7] if not in direct violation of the rights of others, no longer appeared to be a crime. The psychological analysis of crime gradually began to be made, and offered a foundation for a general theory of responsibility; for it led to the reflection that the offender has not invariably enjoyed that freedom of action which a legal system permeated by the idea of eternal perdition had assumed to exist. The doctrine arose that unless the criminal had acted with moral freedom [8] he should not undergo the full penalty of the law. This led to numerous further inconsistencies (later criticized by Feuerbach), and another basis for discretionary variance of decision was thus created.

Signs of Progress. Kress and Boehmer. — Along with these elements, tending both towards a breaking down of the old law and a progress to a better system,[9] it is notable that legal science in Germany began to avail itself of more ample sources and methods. The Hollander, Antonius Matthæus,[10] in his Commentary upon Books 47 and 48 of the Pandects, had indeed successfully undertaken to interpret the Roman criminal law in its native spirit, without foreign mixture and under the guidance of the Roman literature. But, on the other hand, the knowledge of early German sources of law, which had been gradually accumulating since Conring, began to exercise an influence upon the method of dealing with the criminal law. This can be clearly seen in the excellent commentaries of both Kress [11] and Joh. Sam. Friedr. von Boehmer,[12] the latter marking the zenith of German

[7] *Cf. e.g. Kress*, "Commentatio succincta in Constitutionem Criminalem Caroli V" (Hannoveræ, first published 1721), Art. 180, § 3, n. 2; *Hommel*, "Rhapsodia quæstionum", 441: "Lenocinium, incestus, sodomia, stuprum sind letzerem nicht Verbrechen, sondern nur Unanständigkeiten, turpitudines."

[8] Concerning these theories, which later were held particularly by Kleinschrod and Klein, and which were undisputedly the dominant theories at the end of the 1700 s, *cf. Feuerbach;* "Revision der Grundsätze des peinlichen Rechts", I, pp. 274, *et seq.*, pp. 278, 279.

[9] This is to-day frequently overlooked.

[10] "De criminibus", first published in 1644.

[11] "Commentatio, etc."; see note 7, *ante.*

[12] "Meditationes, etc."; see note 4, *ante.*

criminal jurisprudence prior to Feuerbach. The difference between these writers and Carpzov and the Italians is clearly apparent. The position of Carpzov as an authority was completely destroyed by Boehmer's "Observationem zu Carpzov's Practica."[13]

§ 55. **The Universities.** — The Commentary form of exposition, hitherto employed, now fell into disuse among the jurists, and there began to appear systematic treatises on the criminal law. This was primarily due to the instruction now begun to be given in the universities. During the 1600 s specific courses on the criminal law were not given at the universities. Criminal law received attention only in lectures upon the Roman law, in comments on the text of the so-called "Libri terribiles" of Justinian.[1] In the first half of the 1700 s, however, criminal law began to be treated as a separate subject, or at any rate in conjunction with criminal procedure.[2]

The Early Treatises. — The first "compendia" of the criminal law did not indeed possess any special scientific value. Of these the one by Engau, "Elementa juris criminalis Germanico-Carolini", appearing first in 1738,[3] had perhaps the widest circulation. But the formulation of an independent system always sooner or later leads to an attempt to establish general fundamental principles under which the individual elements may be classified, and induces a deeper investigation of the subject-matter of the law. The arrangement of a so-called "general portion" in the early "compendi", although rather meagre, must in criminal law more than in any other legal study have been an important help and inspiration.

But the interest aroused was too little concerned with the positive (existing) law. It inquired rather, what the law should be. That compilation which was regarded as the foundation of the common law, *i.e.* the Carolina, was outgrown, as a penal system, by the advance in civilization and public opinion. The theological foundation of the Carolina and its now antiquated methods of expression were objects of ridicule. Leyser called it a "monumentum inscientiæ"; and Boehmer, in the preface to his "Medi-

[13] "Bened. Carpzovii Practica . . . variis observationibus aucta a J. Sam. Frid. Boehmer" (Francof. 1753).

[1] *Von Wächter*, "Gemeines Recht", p. 96.

[2] *Cf. Henke*, II, pp. 166, 306.

[3] As to other compendiums by Gärtner (1729), Kemmerich, Boehmer, *cf. Henke*, II, p. 306; *Meister*, "Princ. juris crim." (first published in 1755).

tationes ", said of the Bambergensis and the Carolina: "magnam spirant simplicitatem et ipsa compilatio parum salis in autore arguit."[4]

This explains the peculiar character of the textbooks of this period. Though the statutory law was set forth, it was briefly noted, and then was given no further attention. The writer's views were based usually on any sort of authority whatsoever, and always in accordance with the humane tendencies of the times, especially in the sense of placing the greatest possible limitations upon the power to punish;[5] as an occasional expedient, reference was made to the undefined power of police control.[6]

The New Theories of Criminal Law in Italy and France. — Yet judicial practice instinctively felt that by this emancipation from the positive law, it was working its own destruction. Hence arose the frequent and repeated complaints concerning the evasion of the statutes, made by eminent jurists such as Leyser, Kress, and Boehmer. But (as already remarked) they themselves in other places evaded statutes in the same way. This accounts for the interest displayed at this time in the establishment of a correct theory of the criminal law, which might serve as a basis for a new and comprehensive code suited to the times.

The new ideas, emanating from Italy through Beccaria and Filangieri,[7] and from France through Voltaire,[8] found in Germany a well-prepared and fruitful soil. Thus, at the end of the 1700 s, there began that conflict of criminal theories which has continued until the present time. The beginning of this conflict is marked by the essay of Globig and Huster, on "Criminal Legislation",

[4] In order to be correct in one's judgment of such statements, one must bear in mind that it is quite a different matter to treat the Carolina in a purely theoretical and historical manner, as we now do, and to speak of its law.

[5] Malblank's naïve remark concerning the (earlier) writer on criminal law, Meister, is well known: "The lamented Meister . . . revealed in his criminal judgments a heart friendly to humanity, and he possessed in a high degree the ability artfully to harmonize his kindly sentiments with the law so that one never perceived a marked deviation from the law and yet he always accomplished his purpose."

[6] *Cf. Hälschner*, p. 161.

[7] The Austrian Von Sonnenfels also joined vigorously in the movement, — especially in opposition to the too-frequent death sentences. *Cf.* his "Grundsätze der Polizei-, Finanz-, und Handlungs-Wissenschaft" (3d ed., 1777, 3 parts).

[8] Voltaire made it his especial task to set forth the injustice done by the inquisitorial procedure of his time; he also vigorously assailed the theological conception of law and the State. *Cf.* especially: "Le mépris d'Arras" (1771), and "Prix de la justice et de l'humanité" ("Œuvres", ed. Beuchot, Paris 1832, Vol. 40, pp. 540, *et seq.*, Vol. 50, pp. 254, *et seq.*).

which received the prize offered by the Society of Economics at Bern in 1783. The main thesis of this work was the need of a code which contained a complete and plain formulation of the criminal law, — although the authors (by one of those curious limitations of vision frequently recurring in history) maintained also that any doctrinal interpretation of the code by jurists would be superfluous and injurious.

§ 56. **Legislation of the 1700 s; the Bavarian Code of 1751.** — In the meantime, there had already been considerable legislative activity in three of the most important States. Bavaria and Austria had received comprehensive codes, — Bavaria, the "Codex Juris Bavarici criminalis" of 1751, and Austria, the "Constitutio criminalis Theresiana", of December 31st, 1769;[1] and Prussia had made reforms in several special statutes. Both of the Codes gave evidence of a considerable advance in juridical and technical aspects.

The Bavarian Code contained numerous definitions,[2] the work of an able jurist, Kreitmayr, which were in favorable contrast to the prior crude method of framing the laws. The introductory and final sections of the first part formed a so-called "general part" in the modern sense, although admittedly a defective one. Punishments by mutilations were abolished.[3] Witchcraft, however, was still copiously dealt with; notorious heretics, who "do knowingly utter, support, and stiff-neckedly maintain opinions contrary to the articles of the Christian Catholic faith" were to be punished, either by permanent banishment or by imprisonment on scanty rations, until such time as they acknowledged and abandoned their errors. Those who zealously spread heretical doctrines, or misled others, or incited them against the authorities, such seducers of the faithful were to be executed with the sword and their bodies burned upon a funeral pyre. The provisions against poaching were very severe. In several provisions the doctrine of the 1700 s, of the absolutism of the ruler, still receives emphasis; *e.g.* any contempt, actual or apparent, of the command of a ruler is in itself a capital offense.[4]

[1] Both deal also with criminal procedure. *Cf.* especially *Berner*, "Strafgesetzgebung", pp. 8, etc.

[2] *Cf.* the provisions as to attempt, I, 12 § 3; Instigation, I, 12 § 5; Abetment, I, 12 § 5.

[3] I, 1, § 8. Branding with a hot iron, the pillory, and flogging were retained.

[4] c. 11, § 1. Persons who had been banished from the country were threatened with death in case they returned. They were to be executed

The Austrian Theresiana. — The Austrian "Theresiana" of 1769 is a carefully elaborated statute, with a fairly comprehensive "general part." Everywhere it gives evidence of the endeavor to do injustice to none and conscientiously to balance guilt and punishment. The principle of the mitigation and aggravation of penalties is given special treatment, and is also carried out for the separate offenses. The preface states that a purpose of the Code is to eliminate the difficulties encountered by the officials and courts because of the dissimilarities in the criminal statutes of the separate crown territories; but this is not (as Berner would have it) [5] the only purpose of the statute; for the defects of the previous laws are also expressly emphasized in the preface. The Code renounces a theological basis (in principle, though not always in effect), and declares the purpose of punishment to be: the improvement of the offender, the satisfaction of the State, and the deterrence of the masses. In its treatment of punishments affecting the civil status of individuals, there appears a beginning of a clearer conception, which treated certain penalties as barring the way to special honors but not as affecting ordinary callings,[6] and at the same time tried to make them suitable to the nature of the particular crime and often even to the individual case. Sorcery was treated virtually as a deception and fraud.[7] The use of the pillory as a punishment was limited; exile of subjects of the crown territories was to be imposed only with the sanction of the authorities.

as "contemners of the command of the hereditary and electoral princes." Express denial of allegiance to the ruler was to be punished by quartering. II, 8, § 1.

[5] *Berner* (pp. 11 *et seq.*) is too harsh in his condemnation of the law, and gives his attention exclusively to its darker aspects, which will be next taken up and are indeed very conspicuous.

[6] As to loss of honorable position and rehabilitation, see I, 10. It is remarked that military service is in no way to be regarded as a punishment, but rather under some circumstances as a school for obedience.

[7] Conditional, however, in some cases upon the assent of the rulers. *Cf. Tr. v. Maasburg*, "Zur Entstehungsgeschichte der Theresianischen Halsgerichtsordnung mit besonderer Rücksicht auf das im Art. 58 derselben behandelte Crimen magiæ vel sacrilegii" (Wien, 1880). *Cf.* the same, pp. 59 and 60, for a remarkable opinion of the Imperial Chancellor Prince Kaunitz-Rietberg. Prince Kaunitz vigorously expresses his opposition to the "arbitrium judicis" in cases of capital punishment, to the severe use of corporal punishment, to torture (which was now abolished among other civilized peoples), to branding, and to the "Crimen magiæ" which was generally ridiculed. Also *cf. Wahlberg*, "Forschungen zu Geschichte der alt-österreichischen Strafgesetzgebung", in *Grünhut's* "Zeitschr. für das Privat- und öffentliches Recht" (VIII, 1881), pp. 254, *et seq.*

Nevertheless, the valuation of the specific crimes showed still a thorough spirit of bigotry. Blasphemy was treated as the "first and worst" offense. Perjury was classed as a kind of blasphemy. Apostacy from the Christian faith was a crime. That the offender was a Jew was sometimes treated by the lawgiver as a reason for increasing the penalties. Sexual relation between Jew and Christian was a crime, punished with flogging. Suicide, moreover, was ranked as a crime, — in keeping with the inherently theological and moralizing spirit of this Code. An attempt at suicide (in natural correspondence with the general attitude of the courts of those times) was punishable with discretionary penalties; and the body of the self-murderer was to be destroyed like that of a beast. Torture was expressly preserved in its most repulsive forms (fire, etc.). With a holy and well-meant zeal and a spirit of crude deterrence, the legislator extended the death penalties even beyond the scope of the now ancient Carolina — in some cases with a really barbarous intensity of suffering.[8] He even considers it necessary at times "for an example to the masses" to perform execution upon the corpse of one who had died before punishment.

The Theresiana is not a complete code in the modern sense. The legislator sometimes [9] refers to earlier statutes; and (as in the Codex Bavaricus) he still allows the judge to punish acts which are merely analogous to some defined crime,[10] — although only with the permission of the appellate court.

The Statutes of Frederick II of Prussia. — In like manner the separate statutes of Frederick II of Prussia show the impression of the movements for reform. One of the first acts of Frederick the Great had been to abolish torture completely.[11] In 1744, banishment was superseded by imprisonment in a fortress or penitentiary. The punishment of infamy was also substantially limited, in 1756, "because the offender who is subjected to infamy becomes a useless member of society, and if he obtains his release from the prison or workhouse, he finds himself without means to earn his bread in an honorable way." Capital punishment for several classes of theft (committed without violence) was abolished in 1743. In repealing the penalties for simple unchastity, the

[8] *E.g.* by first tearing open the breast; a frequent penalty is the burning and mutilation of the convict prior to his execution.

[9] *Cf. e.g.* II, 73.

[10] I, II, § 10; II, 104.

[11] *Cf. Hälschner*, pp. 174, 181.

king gave considerable attention to the prevention of child murder (a problem much discussed in the 1700 s). Here, however, he was only acting in accordance with the spirit of the times, *i.e.* the ideal of the absolute State, policing morals and seeking by severe penalties to check conduct which is contrary to the general sentiments of mankind but is after all not to be reached by coercive penalties; a policy which fritters itself away in a mass of details that now seem to us extraordinary.[12] By a rescript of December 6, 1751, the bodies of suicides were no longer to be turned over to the scavenger, but were to be buried, privately but honorably. Later, however, in the reign of Frederick the Great, certain of his ordinances show a reaction against too great lenity on the part of the courts. Thus the principle of the "talio" for cases of homicide in a personal encounter was réstored; for the aged king perhaps felt that he had been in advance of the spirit of the times; and another ordinance provided severer punishment for those who imperilled the safety of the highways.

§ 57. **The Austrian Code of Joseph II of 1787.** — The abolition of torture had been effected in the German Austrian crown lands and in Galicia and the Banat by an imperial decree of January 3, 1776. This was followed, on the 13th day of January, 1787, by the Austrian Code of Joseph II dealing with crimes and penalties, in which an attempt was made (although, on the whole, with little success or consistency) to realize the reformatory ideals of the age. The legislator, indeed, undertook his task with sufficient seriousness. It was his desire to eliminate all despotism from the administration of criminal justice, and to draw a proper distinction between offenses that are criminal and "political offenses" (*i.e.* police measures). An endeavor was also made to strike a proper balance between crimes and their punishments, and to adjust the latter so that their influence should not be merely ephemeral. This task the statute sought by means of short, concise statements, which stand in favorable contrast with the long-drawn-out expressions theretofore in use.

All previous penal statutes dealing with crimes were repealed,

[12] "Circulare . . . wegen Besichtigung der Schwangerschaft halben, solches aber leugnenden Weibspersonen" of Aug. 1, 1756 ("Nov. Corpus Constitutionum Marchic.", II, N. 74, p. 158). Ordinance of Feb. 8, 1765, against the murder of unborn illegitimate children, concealment of pregnancy and confinement ("N.C.C. March." III, pp. 585, *et seq.*) In § 2 of the same the disclosure of pregnancy is required on penalty of six years in prison, even if the child is born alive. It is further prescribed that the mother at the time of delivery shall summon assistance.

and in this respect the Code was designed to be comprehensive. For the first time, the judicial condemnation of an act by analogy to some other crime was now completely prohibited; [1] and thereby a sanction was in fact first given to one of the most important principles of modern criminal law. At the same time a limitation was placed upon judicial discretion in respect to punishments and their amount, by announcing the principle which we at the present time regard as self-evident,[2] viz. that there shall be no deviation from a statutory penalty except by special authority of law.[3]

Its System of Punishments. — In accordance with the tendencies of the time, the Code took the step (rather too venturesome) of abolishing [4] all capital punishments [5] (except those of martial law). In its treatment of punishments involving permanent or temporary loss of status and honorary rights,[6] and in its abolition of periods of limitation, the Code exhibits a high-minded idealism. But this aim was bound to suffer shipwreck among the conditions of real life. And indeed it seemed all the more out of place alongside of harsh penalties still retained, — punishments revolting in character and sometimes studiously aggravated [7] with a view to the greatest possible deterrence; for it prescribed three varieties of flogging (*i.e.* with canes, with

[1] Part I, § 1. Part II, § 3.

[2] The common law doctrine had regarded it as justifiable to change a penalty fixed by statute. In France, also, until the period of the Revolution the maxim prevailed: "Penalties lie in the court's discretion."

[3] I, 2, § 13.

[4] As a matter of fact, Joseph II favored the harshest theory of deterrence; capital punishment was abolished by him in this spirit only, and not (as in Tuscany) in the spirit of the reformatory theory. As to this, *cf.* *Wahlberg* in *Grünhut's* "Zeitschrift", VIII, pp. 274 *et seq.*

[5] I, 2, § 20. It is an evidence of the lofty sentiments of Joseph II that offenses of "lèse majesté" were to be mildly punished, and that there should be no death penalty for high treason directed against the person of the sovereign. *Cf.* *Wahlberg* in *Grünhut's* "Zeitschrift", VII, p. 573; VIII, p. 280. The Emperor regarded those guilty of "lèse majesté" as out of their right minds and proper subjects for reformation.

[6] According to I, 184, the offender, after undergoing his sentence or receiving pardon, was to be deemed completely rehabilitated, and no prejudice thereafter was incurred by him.

[7] As to the punishment of the galleys in Hungary, in cases of condemnation to severe imprisonment and public labor, *cf.* "Oesterreich. Criminalgerichtsordn." of 1787, § 188. *Hess*, "Durchflüge durch Deutschland, die Niederlande," etc. (Hamburg, 1800), Vol. 7, p. 117, says: "A Danube vessel towed by human beings is so repulsive a spectacle that even an executioner who has become familiar with breaking upon the wheel will turn his eyes away." *Henrici*, "Ueber die Unzulänglichkeit eines einfachen Strafrechtsprincips", pp. 94, 95.

leather whips, or with birch rods), and it made liberal use of the branding-iron.[8] Nevertheless, the central element of the system of penalties of this Code of Joseph II was imprisonment. The modes of imprisonment, to be sure, were sometimes such as rational good sense (of even the Romans, let us say) would never have approved.[9] For example, the punishment of "imprisonment in chains" consisted in chaining the criminal in a dungeon so closely as to allow only the necessary movements of his body; this penalty always included an annual flogging by way of public example. In the worst forms of imprisonment, the offender wore an iron ring about the middle of his body by which he was fastened night and day to his appointed spot, and, if the labor imposed upon him permitted, heavy irons were also placed upon him.

Its Classifications and Definitions. — The separation of offenses into those which were criminal and those which were merely contrary to police regulations[10] (a distinction which, indeed, formed a step of progress) was likewise marked by perversity in its application. All offenses of negligence, a number of offenses generally deemed dishonorable (such as theft up to 25 gulden, and cheating of a heinous sort), and many other serious forms of fraud, were treated as offenses against police regulations and withdrawn entirely from the jurisdiction of the ordinary courts; while, on the other hand, the penalty inflicted by the police authorities might be as harsh as severe flogging.[11] Though the standpoint of bigoted religion was abandoned, it was replaced by that of a rigid police morality. Blasphemy was no longer a crime; the blasphemer was merely treated as deranged, until his recovery was assured.[12] But freedom of religious faith did not really exist;[13] the legislator did not punish heretics as such, but he still exhibited his fear of their influence as disturbers of the traditional social order.[14] Withal, the common law conceptions of crime were in the Code warped beyond recognition and

[8] Sometimes of a revolting nature. Public branding signified that on both cheeks the figure of a gallows was indelibly branded; I, 24.

[9] A piece of perverted refinement, which could mostly hurt only the family of the convict, was that the income of his property was confiscated during the period he was undergoing sentence.

[10] I, 2, § 25. [11] I, 2, § 27. [12] II, 61.

[13] As to this, *cf.* especially *Wahlberg* in *Grünhut's* "Zeitschrift", VIII, pp. 281, *et seq.*

[14] II, 64, 65. By section 64, the pillory and strict imprisonment were prescribed for one who presumed to induce an adherent of the Christian religion to abjure that faith, to renounce all religion, or to accept a religion which rejected the Gospel.

broadened into vagueness; offenses were dealt with in the most heterogeneous and strange combinations. Apart from the more difficult questions (*e.g.* the relationship of falsification and fraud) the same category was made to include defamation, damage to property, and nuisances on the public highways. Pandering for immoral purposes, the offense against nature, and even adultery, were classed among the so-called "political offenses", along with incendiary negligence and unlawful disguising.[15] More attention was paid by the legislator to external incidents in the manner of commission of the act than to the relations of rights and wrong and the social interests which were endangered or injured by the act.[16] As a result, the existing and well-established distinctions in the definition of offenses in the common and especially in the German law were completely obscured, while at the same time an excessive part was allotted, in the definitions of the Code, to the questionable element of "malicious intent."

§ 58. **The Prussian Landrecht of 1794.** — The criminal portion of the "General Prussian Territorial Code" ("Landrecht"),[1] after long and thorough preparation,[2] was promulgated February 5th, 1794.[3] It may be justly described as the code of a State which undertook to be a moral policeman with solicitude and conscientiousness, cherishing the belief that in each and every particular it was able, by means of education and, when needful, by punishment, not only to prevent crimes but also to promote the welfare of its people. Its prison penalties were relatively mild.[4] But its commands and prohibitions intruded themselves into all the petty details of domestic life. Its constant preachment, "Beware!" sought to save its people from even the inducement to crime. The State was not at all disturbed over the fact that the precise acts for which it threatened its by no means trifling penalties were either left too little defined or were inherently incapable

[15] II, 46, 57, 59.

[16] Mendicancy and housebrawls are in II, 59, treated together.

[1] Title 20 of Part 2.

[2] Chiefly the composition of Klein, later made Councillor of the Supreme Court.

[3] As to the earlier drafts and preliminary work, see especially *Hälschner*, pp. 191 *et seq.* The above-mentioned prize essay of Globig and Huster exercised a considerable influence in the compilation of the Code.

[4] The statute provided for imprisonment both in a penitentiary (or fortress) and in an ordinary jail. No excessive measures aimed at deterrence were incidental to these penalties of imprisonment; except a flogging of the convicts at the beginning and the end of their period of confinement (the "welcome" and the "farewell"). *Cf. e.g.* 1197, 1227.

of being reached by the courts;[5] and this indifference is often from our modern viewpoint ludicrous enough.[6] The State proceeded upon the assumption that peaceableness and obedience are the foremost duties of its citizenry, and that therefore, where the State fears that its foundations (whose destruction would involve that of everything else) may be attacked or even disturbed or prejudiced, it may act without any regard for moderation[7] or the recognized limits of justice. Hence, its definitions of offenses were as elastic, to use a modern expression, as india-rubber.[8] It was willing to employ such rigorous measures, dominated as it was by the notion that the one important thing was to break any refractory self-will of its people.[9]

[5] *Cf.* especially §§ 888–932. § 906 merits special mention: "Any person to whom an unmarried pregnant woman communicates her secret must not reveal the same, under pain of discretionary but substantial penalties (§§ 34, 35) as long as there is no reason to anticipate an actual crime by the woman." § 929: "It is also incumbent even upon persons who do not occupy a special relation to said woman, if she has communicated to them her pregnancy or has confessed, to admonish her to observe the statutory provisions (§§ 901 *et seq.*)."

[6] *Cf. e.g.* §§ 1308, 1309: "Anyone who with a view to his own profit shall by means of slander promote discord among near relations or married couples shall suffer a substantial fine or corporal penalty proportionate to the malicious intent and the harm resulting therefrom." "Anyone who promotes this discord with a view to deprive the natural heirs of their inheritance or legacies and to direct such to himself or others, shall be punished as a swindler." § 933: "No one shall commit against or in the presence of a person, whose pregnancy is evident or known to him, acts which are likely to arouse violent emotions." (!)

[7] According to § 93, anyone guilty of high treason was to be executed, with the most severe and horrible punishments of life and limb, proportionate to his evil intention and the injury contemplated. § 95 says: "Persons guilty of high treason shall not only forfeit all property and civic honors, but also transmit the burden of their calamity to their children (!), if the State with a view to avoiding future danger shall find it necessary to banish them or to place them in permanent confinement (!)." In § 109 death by burning is imposed for the betrayal of one's country.

[8] § 151: "Anyone, who by impudent and insulting criticism or ridicule of the laws and ordinances in a State shall arouse dissatisfaction and restlessness of the citizens against their sovereign, incurs a penalty of imprisonment in a fortress or jail of from six months to two years duration."

Cf. also the perverse provision of § 157 for the punishment of injury inflicted in self-defense; and § 119: "Anyone who knowingly enters into relations whereby the State in any manner whatsoever *could* (!) become involved in external insecurity or dangerous complications, although he is not acting with evil motive and although no harm actually comes to the State, shall be punished by imprisonment in a jail or fortress for a period not less than six months or more than two years."

[9] Moreover, the State must be deprived of nothing useful, nor of any of its useful citizens; *cf.* § 148: "Anyone who induces a factory foreman, servant or workman to go abroad or assists him therein, or who reveals to foreigners secrets of manufacture or trade, and likewise anyone who

The legislator appears withal to have regarded his newly devised commands and prohibitions as hardly less important than the offenses enshrined in long-settled tradition. The regulation of masked balls and masquerades is united with the suppression of rebellion; and the petty police of the house and the hunt (on such matters as those contained in § 738 [10] and § 741 [11]) is given precedence over the punishment of assaults and homicides. Naturally enough, a code so characterized by its attention to moral policemanship introduced for all citizens a general duty of preventing almost every variety of crime. Every man became, as it were, a deputy of the police against all other men. Naturally, too, the offender's willingness to confess and to turn State's evidence was made a general reason for mitigating penalties [12]; for here the reprehensible nature of the offense was offset by the offender's obedience to authority. Moreover, the Code was designed to be a book of general influence on the people; by instructing them, it helped to prevent crimes. Thus it aimed to render superfluous and to supplant that mass of legal learning which the great Frederick in his day had so abominated (and not entirely without reason).[13]

In contrast with these cardinal defects, the Code possessed certain features of merit. It dealt with the principle of responsibility in a more systematic and correct manner than any of the other codes already mentioned.[14] Its treatment of offenses against religion was as a rule more correct than that of earlier legislation.[15]

intentionally deprives the fatherland of any other advantage of this character in favor of foreign States, incurs a penalty of from four to eight years, imprisonment in a fortress or penitentiary."

[10] "Mothers and nurses must not take children under two years of age into their beds and allow them to sleep with themselves or with others."

[11] "Travelers or hunters who carry loaded weapons must, if they enter a house or sojourn anywhere among people, either keep the same under their immediate care or remove the charge."

[12] §§ 58 *et seq.*

[13] The legislator did not limit himself to penal provisions; he intersperses a number of provisions having to do with discipline and compensation for damage.

[14] Negligence was no longer treated as a mitigating circumstance of offenses importing malicious intent. *Cf. Hälschner*, p. 210 *et seq.* The merit of the Code herein is not so important as Hälschner assumes, since the distinction between negligence and intent is not clearly stated and is marred by presumptions.

[15] These are classed under the heads of insult to religious companies, incitement of public tumult, incitement to disobedience of the laws, etc., and disturbance of the public peace (§§ 214–218). Nevertheless, one is reminded of the earlier notions by the prohibition to found a sect whose doctrines openly reject reverence of the Deity (§ 223).

The common law definitions of offenses (so rankly distorted in the Code of Joseph of Austria) were preserved, upon the whole, much more accurately.[16] And here was apparent that able technical equipment of the draftsman Klein, which Feuerbach later unjustly criticized.

Thus it was that Prussia after all attained a fair success with the criminal portion of its General Territorial Law; for in the definition of those offenses which are most important in the daily administration of the law no changes were made, and its own special additions were either ignored or not followed to their logical consequences.[17] It did, indeed, exhibit those shortcomings which a casuistic legislation always entails; and for Prussia it had the special disadvantage that it accustomed the Prussian practitioners to regard their law as something entirely apart, and thus effected a certain separation from the common judicial practice of Germany.[18]

§ 59. **The Austrian Code of 1803.** — The frightful severity of the Austrian Code of Joseph II brought about during the reign of Leopold II the mitigation of a number of its penalties. The penalties of imprisonment in chains, labor in the galleys, public flogging, branding, restriction to a diet of bread and water, and sleeping upon bare boards, were all discontinued. In the reign of Francis II, the work [1] of framing a new code reached its consummation [2] in the "Penal Statute for Crimes and Graver Police Offenses" of September 3, 1803.

[16] In this respect, indeed, there are some unfortunate deviations from the common law. *Cf.* §§ 1110, 1366, concerning "furtum usus", poaching (§ 1145) which is treated as theft (sometimes even more severely), forgery (§§ 1378, 1380).

[17] An example of such a perversion of definitions of offenses may be seen in § 1495: "Upon those who injure the country, who harm many citizens or the public at large, or place them in jeopardy, shall in every case be imposed a penalty of several years' imprisonment in a fortress."

[18] The literature of the Prussian criminal law was in substance a mere collection of the statutes. Klein, in the preface to his book, "Grundsätze des gemeinen deutschen und preussischen peinlichen Rechts" (1796, 2d ed. 1799), regarded as a part of the Prussian law the general maxims of the common law; and this was also frequently maintained by the best Prussian jurists.

[1] *Cf. Herbst,* "Handbuch des allgemeinen österr. Strafrechts", 1, (6th edition, 1878), pp. 9, 10. Also *Wahlberg,* in *Grünhut's* "Zeitschrift", VIII, pp. 283 *et seq.*, especially in regard to the opposition of Sonnenfels and Froidevo, to the reactionary principles.

[2] In 1797, a draft of the Code had already gone into effect in West Galicia. The Code applied to all the provinces of the Austrian crown, with the exception of Hungary, the district of Hermanstädt, and the military frontier.

In this Code the death penalty was retained for a few crimes besides high treason, viz. murder,[3] homicide incidental to robbery, forgery of commercial paper, and certain cases of incendiarism. An endeavor was made to give rational treatment to the penalty of imprisonment in its various aspects; although the spirit of the times rendered discrepancies inevitable. In the penalties affixed to crimes (in the stricter sense) the theory of deterrence clearly prevailed.[4] Even in the penalties for misdemeanors (" Vergehensstrafe ", *i.e.* punishment of the graver offenses against the police measures), while a distinction was made between imprisonment with and without hard labor,[5] there is no lack of measures which were ineffectual or were such as injure the self-respect of the offender and render difficult his reëstablishment in the civic community. Corporal punishment of persons of low rank was abundantly dispensed.[6] But, the judge was given an extensive power to mitigate the penalties; and (as observed by Herbst) the Austrian Code of 1803 became in practice one of the mildest of the modern codifications.

The " General Part " (as Berner correctly points out) was framed, in contrast to most of the later German codes, with wise reservations, and was so elastic that an ample field remained for adjustment between theory and practice. The definitions of the " Special Part " (like those of its forerunner, the Code of Joseph) were in many respects faulty; and the classification (as crimes, misdemeanors, or lesser offenses) was in many specific instances open to objection.

[3] Murder ("Mord"), according to the Code (*cf.* I, § 107), embraced also the manslaughter ("Todtschlag") of the German Code. "Todtschlag" according to § 123 is a "malicious act dangerous to life and resulting in death."

[4] I, § 14. "The worst punishment, *i.e.* 'Kerkerstrafe' of the third grade consists in this: The convict shall occupy a cell removed from all companions, in which however he shall have such light and air as is necessary for the preservation of health. He shall always wear heavy irons on his hands and feet, and there shall be placed around his body an iron ring, by which he shall be fastened during the time he is not engaged with his labors. On only two days of the week he shall have a warm but small meal of meat, on the others he shall be limited to bread and water. His bed shall be bare boards, and he shall be precluded from meeting or conversing with people."

[5] "Arrest" of the first and second grades.

[6] II, § 17: "The imprisonment may be made especially severe: (*a*) by corporal punishment, (*b*) by deprivation of food, (*c*) by public exhibition, (*d*) by hard labor, or (*e*) public common labor." II, § 15: "Corporal punishment shall be inflicted only on servants, laborers, and people of that class who earn their livelihood day by day and whose imprisonment for even a few days would injure them in their occupation and their support of their families."

Chapter X

FRANCE, FROM THE 1500 s TO THE REVOLUTION[1]

§ 59*a*. **General Features; Lack of a Criminal Code.** — The 1500 s find France virtually at the end of the internal struggle for domination between the royal power and the feudal estates. By the 1500 s the estates are organically united under the kingdom. By the 1600 s, under Louis XIII and Richelieu, the feudal system is completely absorbed in the sovereign royal power. In the 1700 s, under Louis XIV and his successors, royal absolutism reaches its height. And though the seigniorial jurisdictions still survive, and the royal jurisdiction is divided into the two classes of ordinary and extraordinary jurisdiction, yet the law both of crimes and of criminal procedure was substantially the same in all the courts of this period.[2]

Amidst this progress of political centralization, its accompanying activity in general legislation and legal science, and its thoroughgoing changes in private and public law, the notable fact is that the criminal law of France underwent no radical change. It may be asserted without exaggeration that the law of the 1200 s is that of the 1700 s.

[1] [This Chapter is taken from L. von Stein's "Geschichte des französischen Strafrechts und des Prozesses", 2d ed. 1875, pp. 586–620; the translator is Mr. Millar. For this author and work, and the translator, see the Editorial Preface.

§ 59*a* represents a condensation of the author's text; §§ 59*b*–*e* are a translation; slight liberties were taken with the text to adapt it to the purpose. — Ed.]

[2] [For the history of criminal procedure in France, see *Esmein's* "History of Continental Criminal Procedure," translated by *Simpson*, being Vol. V of the present Series. — Ed.]

The royal legislation, exhibiting the activity of the new royal power, fills the first half of the 1500 s, and includes the Ordinance of 1493 and Louis XII's Ordinance of Blois of 1498, dealing with courts and procedure. It culminates, for that century, with the Ordinance of Villers-Cotterets, in 1539, which became the foundation-stone of the judicial system for the whole ensuing period. A second great group of legislative achievements begins under Louis XIV, with the Civil Ordinance of 1667, regulating civil procedure;[3] followed by the Criminal Ordinance of 1670, regulating criminal procedure. In 1673 came the Ordinance of Commerce, and in 1681 the Ordinance of Marine, — two great monuments to the initiative genius of Colbert the statesman.[4] But amidst these varied legislative products, no code of criminal law was enacted. The Old Régime in France never had a Criminal Code.

The reason for this notable fact lay perhaps chiefly in the peculiar history of French criminal procedure. The great invention of France in this field was the public prosecutor.[5] This official, as a part of his function, was accustomed to make a motion (" conclusion ") specifying the penalty which he demanded to be imposed on the accused. In these " conclusions ", therefore, there was a wider range of variation than there would have been under the strict letter of a criminal code; and the power and authority of the official prosecutor was correspondingly enhanced. The infliction of some punishment, apart from the details of the specific penalty, was enough to satisfy the interests of the State. And thus the criminal law was content to be embodied in these " conclusions ", while at the same time it preserved the wide discretionary range which was regarded as essential. — This may explain the lack of any legislation during this period comparable to Charles V's German code.

Roman Principles in France. — The study of the Roman law in France culminates in the middle of the 1500 s. Alciat, the Humanist, Cujas, Baudouin, Doneau, Douaren, Hotman, — these were the notable names of the world in that epoch.[6] But the

[3] [The subject of French civil procedure is treated in *Engelmann's* "History of Continental Civil Procedure," translated by *Millar*, being Vol. VII of the present Series. — ED.]

[4] [The work of Colbert is described in Vol. II of the present Series, "Great Jurists of the World." — ED.]

[5] [For the history of the public prosecutor, see *Esmein's* "History of Continental Criminal Procedure," being Vol. V of the present Series. — ED.]

[6] [These jurists, and their work in making France the center of Roman

effects of this scientific activity were widely different in the fields of private law and of criminal law.

During the 1500 s the numerous bodies of local customary law were reduced to codes, pursuant to a system prescribed by royal ordinance. These customary codes, forming a native French common law, came into competition with the Roman legal science of the jurists. The task of the next two centuries was to reconcile these two bodies of legal principles. Gradually an amalgamation took place. The private law became a composite one, with the Germanic and the Roman elements varying in different regions.

But in the criminal law no such situation was presented. The codes of local customs contained nothing of criminal procedure, and little of criminal law. Hence no such contrast and competition here arose between the local native principles of customary law and the jurists' principles of Roman law. The Roman law movement of the times thus obtained sole and unobstructed domination. The private customary law, when codified, had become the subject of university study. But for the study of criminal law, there was little but Roman materials, including the works of the then modern Italian criminal jurists.[7]

Moreover, the tendency, above mentioned, to merge criminal law and procedure, and to regard the former solely from the latter standpoint, was thereby emphasized. Both were developed in the hands of royal judges, trained in the Roman law, who had no native criminal law principles to master. The judge's rooted tendency to merge substantive law in procedure was a feature which French criminal law never afterwards lost. A natural consequence was the subsidence of any systematic study of the substantive law. The "conclusions" of the public prosecutor contained all that was needed; and the procedure became and remained the principal object of attention. And thus it came about that, in the legal development of France, the lack of a science of criminal law was as notable as the lack of a criminal code.

Of the few and fruitless attempts of jurists to place the substantive criminal law on an independent footing, only the following

law study, are described in Vol. I of the present Series, "A General Survey of Events, Sources, Persons, and Movements in Continental Legal History." Alciat and Cujas are the subjects of special studies in Vol. II of the Series, "Great Jurists of the World." — ED.]

[7] [For the rise of criminal legal science in Italy, see *Calisse's* "History of Italian Law," being Vol. VIII of the present Series. — ED.]

need be noted: Jean Duret's "Traicté des peines et des amendes", of 1453, which shows the main outlines as they persisted until the 1800 s; Ayrault's "L'ordre, formalité et instruction judiciaire", of 1576; Soulatges' "Traité des crimes", of 1762; Jousse's "Traité de la justice criminelle", of 1771, which is the standard source of information for the 1700 s; and Muyart de Vouglans' "Institutes au droit criminel", 1747, "Lois criminelles de la France dans leur ordre naturel", 1780 (in which the author sought to do for criminal law what Domat had done for the Pandects of civil law).

§ 59*b*. **Discretionary Character of the Penal System.** — The criminal law of this whole period stands in a close and peculiar relation to procedure. While the latter, even as to matters of detail, came to be treated with the utmost clearness and precision, it was far otherwise with the former. Neither legislation nor legal science discloses anything like a systematic and well-defined body of criminal law. Positive enactments concerning crimes and punishments did not produce, as they did in Germany, a recognized subject-matter to which the functioning of procedure is restricted; in the field of repression, procedure holds absolute sway.

It was this situation, more than anything else, which, in the preceding period, had brought about the ascendancy of the royal judicial officers, — which had enabled them to make themselves both respected and feared, throughout the kingdom, as the relentless pursuers of crime and criminals, irrespective of kind or degree. The supplanting of earlier forms of criminal procedure by that of public prosecution,[1] which became an accomplished fact in the 1400 s, had placed what was left of the seigniorial power completely in their hands. Moreover, it seems to be true that crime, in its essence, consists in the idea of an injury sustained by the general personality through the injury to the individual. Now, when this general personality attains to supremacy, it is quick to feel injury, and encounters on every hand what it regards as occasions of offense. Thus occurs the phenomenon, of which we here meet an example, namely, that the punishing power increases in strength as the ruling organism advances toward absolute dominion. The magistrates of the King looked upon themselves as the State; it was therefore but natural that they

[1] [*I.e.* the form of procedure that came in with the public prosecutor. See *ante*, § 59*a*, note 5. — TRANSL.]

should undertake to determine what acts constituted crime, as well as to settle the punishment of these acts. This tendency of bureaucratic officials to force slight offenses into the category of serious ones and to heighten the severity of punishment, is something that the State can effectively counteract only by a system of penal legislation. For the latter has a twofold significance in the present regard. Not only does it create a definite sphere for the activities of procedure, but, at the same time, it marks out certain limits which the State, in its relation to the free action of the individual (and also, consequently, of the agents of the State), may in nowise transcend. By a step of this sort, the State voluntarily fixes the boundaries of its own jurisdiction in the domain of private freedom, and recognizes the liberty of the individual, as opposed to its own absolutism.

Such a system of legislation the French kingdom had never had, principally because, as we may well suppose, the monarchy had never been inclined to concede this much to the rights of its subjects. In any event, the result was that, down to the time of the Revolution, the official judge and the official prosecutor alone had the power to declare what was crime, and to say what penal consequences should follow the act so declared to be crime. In the absence of a general penal law, every criminal judgment came to be a law for its own case. This is the most notable characteristic of the repressive function during the period before us.

When some act had come to light which either the judge or the public prosecutor regarded as calling for punishment, the judicial investigation was set on foot. On its termination, the prosecutor formulated his complaint, specifying therein some particular punishment which he sought to have inflicted. That done, the court, after consideration of the complaint, decided the matter according to its individual discretion. And it was this individual discretion, and this alone, which determined the manner and measure of punishment. If a Regional Custom or an Ordinance had already prescribed a penalty for an act of the same description, it could not, of course, be ignored. But provisions of the sort were seldom closely observed; instead of the law controlling the judge, the judge controlled the law. The condition thus existing could not fail to give rise to abuse of power on the one hand, and insecurity of life and property on the other. And enduring as it did, almost without opposition, from the 1500 s on, it powerfully contributed to exasperate the people against their rulers, and to emphasize the need for a system of penal legislation resting upon entirely different principles.

Writing in the middle of the 1500 s, Imbert says: "In this kingdom, all punishments are discretionary." [2] And, in a note to the same passage, Automne concedes that "where a punishment is discretionary, and is left to be determined 'officio judicis,' the judge has power to sentence the offender to death", as, indeed, had been recognized by a Decree [3] of 1545. Only new punishments the judge is not allowed to invent or apply: he is restricted to those already in use. This fearful power is still unabated in the 1700 s. We find Jousse [4] using the identical words of Imbert: "In this kingdom, all punishments are discretionary." Criminal law is really nothing else than the unfettered will of the judges. Nowhere than in this field is more manifest the final and decisive triumph of the royal magistracy over the old law: here these agents of the monarchy reach the zenith of their dominion over public and private right.

Moreover, this state of things moulds all legal thought in penal matters. Because of the legislative authority of the judges and prosecutors, the writers, as early as the 1500 s, are compelled to devote their attention to cases, instead of to principles. They deal solely with individual crimes, and, even with these, in a fragmentary way. Although fuller and more orderly, Jousse's treatment is essentially but little different from that of Duret. Any science of criminal law that the present period possesses is in reality scarcely more than a guide to procedure. Positive enactments, at best, furnish mere examples for practical application. The whole penal law centers in the "conclusion" of the prosecutor and the judgment of the court. No doubt the legal profession thereby acquired an influence and standing unknown in countries having a real system of penal legislation; but, on the other hand, the same causes degraded the criminal law and made it the mere tool of police administration.

So much for the general character of the criminal law. Our task now divides into two branches. The first is to ascertain

[2] "Practique judiciaire tant civile que criminelle," Bk. III, c. XX, § 7 (1548). [This book first appeared in Latin under the title of "Institutiones forenses", soon after the Ordinance of 1539. *Stein*, p. 605. — TRANSL.]

[3] [For the nomenclature of French royal legislation, see Vol. I of the present series, "A General Survey of Events, Sources, Persons, and Movements in Continental Legal History," p. 249. — TRANSL.]

[4] "Traité de la justice criminelle de France," Pt. I, Tit. I, p. 4.

what, in the main, were the limits of the prevailing notions of crime and punishment; the second, briefly to survey the several crimes in so far as they came within the purview of definite legislation. From a practical standpoint, the first is the more important; and in dealing with it, we are not to lose sight of the fact that the courts were the principal instrument, not only in designating the manner and measure of punishment, but also in the development of the notions into which we are inquiring.

§ 59c. **Crime; General Notions and Classification.** — Under conditions such as those above outlined, the conception of crime must needs be far from scientific. In the older days, before the Criminal Ordinance of 1670, there had been no attempt whatever to attain any definiteness in this respect; the matter in all likelihood having been left entirely to the interpretation of the courts. Even in the 1700 s, the notion is still vague and sterile.[1] There was no less uncertainty as to the old distinction between "crime" and "délit." "Délit" and "crime" soon became convertible terms. Soon, too, and especially in practice, mere police offenses became classed as "délits."[2] Any clear-cut notion of crime was consequently out of the question. Crime was anything that could be made the subject of punishment; and anything could be made the subject of punishment that the judge regarded as punishable. This feature appears to have been most pronounced in the 1500 s — a time when the disturbed condition of the public peace both necessitated and excused resolute encroachments on the part of the judiciary. Thus Duret classes as punishable offenses such matters as the giving of "false directions as to the way",[3] the attempt to exact excessive dowries and marriage portions ("dots et douaires"),[4] failing in "submission or reverence to the great of the land",[5] and drunkenness (complaining that "over-indulgence in wine is not punished according to the equitable law of the Ocrenses whereby the drunkard is inexorably put to death").[6] Here too, he includes idleness, mendicancy, and vagabondage. Idleness and mendicancy, it is

[1] *Jousse*, "Justice criminelle", Pt. I.
Crime signifies any unjust act tending to injure society and disturb the public peace, which is forbidden by law and deserves to be punished with more or less severity. *Lange*, "Nouvelle pratique", Bk. I, c. I, pp. 2, 3.

[2] "According to the usage of the bar", "délits" are "the lesser 'crimes' and those which require a merely civil reparation or a pecuniary penalty." *Jousse, loc. cit.*

[3] "Traicté des peines et amendes", pp. 47, 48.

[4] *Ibid.*, pp. 56–58. [5] *Ibid.*, pp. 124, 125. [6] *Ibid.*, p. 97 b.

to be noted, were punished under Henry II, by consignment to the galleys. For vagabondage the penalty was ordinarily corporal chastisement, but, in case of repeated offenses, the offender was to be put to death (Ordinance of 21 October, 1561),[7] and every judge had jurisdiction to inflict the death penalty.

The first step out of this confusion was the Criminal Ordinance of 1670. By introducing a definite order and scale of punishments, it came to supply the division of crimes according to their penal consequences, and thus to pave the way for systematization of the criminal law, with the attendant limitation of the arbitrary powers of the courts. After its enactment, we begin to see attempts at classification. These, however, are wholly destitute of scientific value, being in part purely arbitrary, in part merely practical. Jousse has "eight ways of considering crime." [8] Of his arrangement we need only mention two features. One is the division of offenses into public and private, atrocious, aggravated ("qualifiés"), minor ("légers"), capital, and non-capital.[9] The other is the distribution of offenses committed by ecclesiastical persons, under the three heads of common offenses ("délits communs"), privileged offenses (or cases), and purely ecclesiastical offenses. Common offenses were those over which the secular courts had exclusive jurisdiction; privileged offenses (or cases) those over which the secular and ecclesiastical tribunals exercised jurisdiction in common for purposes of investigation, but whose punishment rested solely with the secular courts. The third class, purely ecclesiastical offenses, concerned only the ecclesiastical courts. But classifications of this description could lead to no system of criminal law. They represented no more than abstract standpoints from which individual crimes were regarded.

Equally unsatisfactory is the further treatment of crime in general. In dealing with this part of his subject, Jousse does not once touch upon the notions of plurality of offenses,[10] moral

[7] *Duret, op. cit.*, pp. 125, 126.
[8] *Loc. cit.*
[9] "How then", asks Lange (*op. cit.*, p. 3) can we support the distinction between capital and non-capital crimes, when "all punishments are discretionary in this kingdom?" "To be sure", he continues, "there is not a certain determinate punishment for every species of crime", but the distinction has nevertheless this advantage, that it prevents the judges "from turning minor offenses and those which are punished with least severity into offenses of a graver description." This passage gives us some idea of the fears with which men were still beset in the year 1755.
[10] ["Concurrenz" in the original = "concursus delictorum" (Fr. "con-

responsibility, criminal attempt, criminal intent, or the constituent elements of crime. The only thing taken into consideration is the impulse ("mouvement"), and it is this which determines the "quantum" of punishment. How Roman law conceptions had invaded this field is apparent from Duret. In his introduction,[11] he tells us that "there is ordinarily a presumption of malicious intent ('dol et fraude') in the case of crimes", and that punishment is to be increased or lessened according to the criminal impulse ("impétuosité"), the manner of the harm ("coustume de mal"), and the circumstances in general. The judge will weigh the criminal facts ("qualitez") on every hand, and thereupon decree "a more grievous penalty,"[12] — or else "the judge, after considering the cause, may limit, or altogether dispense with, the punishment, according to the personal condition of the offender, his ignorance, or unforeseen error."[13] Out of these disjointed dicta, Jousse constructs a kind of system in his chapter: "Concerning the Aggravation or Mitigation of Punishment." What we find here is in truth much the same as what Beaumanoir had said in the 1200 s: there is but little advance. Crimes are more or less serious according to the impulse "which brings about their commission", or according to "their attendant circumstances."[14] On the other hand, the subject of accomplices has a whole Title to itself, and is dealt with at considerable length.[15] Significant of the absence of scientific treatment is the fact that neither the name nor idea of *Principal* anywhere appears. And this, we take it, simply because, to Jousse's mind, the real question is that of the punishment of the participants, and, in the case of the principal, that question answered itself. It is settled by the rule now adopted from the Italians, Julius Clarus and Farinacius: all who join in the offense are to be punished alike, whether the case is that of conspiracy, joint principalship, aid by remaining on watch extended by one to the other, employment of one by the other to commit the crime, or instigation of one by the other to the same end. Where the offense is very serious, even guilty knowledge encounters punishment of an identical description

cours de plusieurs délits") which exists where "a plurality of yet unpunished offenses comes before a court as the subject-matter of a single judgment." *Geyer* in *von Holtzendorff's* "Rechtslexikon", *s.v.* "Konkurrenz." — TRANSL.]

[11] "Traicté des peines et amendes", p. 6 b.

[12] *Ibid.*, p. 8 b.

[13] *Ibid.*, p. 9 a.

[14] "Justice criminelle", pp. 9–17.

[15] *Ibid.*, Tit. II.

with that inflicted on the actual doer of the criminal act. In this regard, especially, Farinacius dominated the views of jurists in the 1700 s. But in case of a remote participation, where the accomplice is not the proximate cause of the crime, his punishment is always moderated according to circumstances. The same is true of assistance rendered after the fact — receiving stolen goods, concealing the offender, extending him mere advice and comfort. More exact determination is left for the individual case.

§ 59*d*. **Penalties in Use.** — In France, the history of punishment, as the means whereby the State bends to its own the will of the individual, reflects, even more faithfully than does that of crime, the several stages in the nation's political development. At first (according to the greater consensus of historical opinion), the infliction of punishments is a purely local matter and their form varies with locality; next, the system is thrown into confusion through the intrusion of Roman law and the usurpations of the royal magistrates; finally, in the period before us, there arises a general consciousness that, as all France is under the sway of one body of royal officials, so also it is due to have one system of punishments which shall prevail throughout the land.

At the outset, a certain element of uniformity was attained in this, that the magistrates, of their own accord, everywhere imposed the same sort of penalties. The underlying cause was the adherence to the old methods of punishment brought in from Germanic sources: the judges, as we have seen, were forbidden to invent new forms.[1] But the application of punitive measures was completely discretionary: even the provisions of positive enactments affecting the case seem to have been rather a guide than a rule. So far as legislation is concerned, there was no such thing as a system of punishments, and even the legal writers treat these in a cursory and merely illustrative fashion.[2]

The resulting absence of safeguards for life and property brought about the Criminal Ordinance (1670). In Title XXV, Article 13, this enactment specified certain punishments as forming a second class following the death penalty; and thus laid the foundation for a penal classification. Meagre as was the provision in

[1] See *Imbert, ut sup.*, and also *Jousse*, "Justice criminelle", I, III, p. 41.

[2] Although Duret follows his preface with the outlines of a scheme of punishment, he does not furnish any description of the punishments themselves. *Imbert* (Book III, c. XXI) speaks of some punishments, but without any intention of treating the subject exhaustively.

question,[3] the Ordinance was received with much satisfaction; for men felt that here was a return to the old order of things and the starting point of a complete penal system. Not before the 1700 s, however, does the latter become fixed. The best and most comprehensive exposition of it is that given by Jousse.[4] As this system had incorporated all the earlier punishments, a brief outline of it will be sufficient for our purpose.

Capital punishments [5] form the *first* class. These are:

(A) The *death penalty* (natural death): burning at the stake; breaking on the wheel; quartering; hanging; or beheading.[6]

(B) And further:

(*a*) Consignment to the *galleys for life*. The punishment of the galleys must have come into use in France at the beginning of the 1500 s, but definite historical proof as to its origin is lacking.[7] The earliest Ordinance which refers to the punishment is that of 15 March, 1548,[8] but Guyot [9] cites two Decrees of 1532 and 1535, respectively, in which mention of it is made. Before commencing his service the prisoner is branded; and, according to a Declaration of 1677, whoever maims himself to escape the punishment is

[3] The Article runs thus: "After the punishment of natural death, the most rigorous are those of torture with reservation of the proofs in their entirety ("question avec la réserve des preuves en leur entier"), consignment to the galleys for life, banishment for life, torture without reservation of the proofs ("sans réserve des preuves"), consignment to the galleys for a term of years, flogging, 'amende honorable', and banishment for a term of years." [The distinction between torture with and without reservation of the proofs was this: in the former case the prisoner was not released if he successfully withstood the torture: the proofs in hand could still be used against him and might result in his conviction (although not in a sentence of death); while, in the case of torture without reservation of the proofs, ability to withstand the torture resulted in the prisoner's acquittal: the proofs in hand were said to be "purged" and went for naught: *Stein*, pp. 687, 688; and see also *Esmein*, "History of Continental Criminal Procedure", transl. *Simpson*, being Vol. V of the present Series. — TRANSL.]

[4] "Justice criminelle", Pt. I, Tit. III, with which the same author's notes on the Criminal Ordinance may be profitably compared.

[5] *Op. cit.*, p. 42 *et seq.*

[6] The headman's block took the place of the gallows in the case of persons of noble birth.

[7] [A popular account ascribes the first employment of convict rowers in France to the 1400 s, when Jacques Cœur, the rich merchant of Bourges, put into service four galleys thus manned. Galley labor as an official institution is said to date from the seizure of these four vessels by Charles VII. *Alhoy*, "Les bagnes", pp. 2, 3 (Paris, 1845); *Quanter*, "Deutsches Zuchthaus und Gefängniswesen", p. 150 (Leipzig). — TRANSL.]

[8] "Recueil général des anciennes lois françaises", XIII, p. 70. It speaks only incidentally of convicts ("forçats") and galleys.

[9] "Répertoire de Jurisprudence", *s.v.* "Galères." This account does not refer to the Ordinance of 1548.

put to death. In the case of offenders not physically fit for labor in the galleys, the sentence is generally changed to that of banishment for life. Of earlier date is the rule by which convicts released from the galleys are forbidden to return to Paris under pain of renewed galley-service. For women, life-imprisonment, or whipping followed by banishment for life, takes the place of the galleys.[10]

(b) *Banishment for life.* — This punishment (as also banishment in general during the present period) is derived from the old law. The banishment may be either from a designated part of the country (" hors du ressort "), or else from the kingdom at large. It was much disputed whether there could be a banishment from the kingdom for a term of years,[11] and whether banishment for life from a given locality could be classed as a capital punishment.[12]

(c) In the case of extremely serious offenses, criminal proceedings may be brought against the *dead.*[13] Two punishments here come in question, namely: dragging the corpse on a hurdle (" sur la claie "), and judicial condemnation of the decedent's memory.[14] These are important on account of their consequences. Every capital punishment brings with it confiscation of the offender's property; pronounced against the living, it brings also civic death.

Confiscation (as it passed from the old law into the regional Customs, and thence into the newer criminal law) is in principle simply the reversion of the estate to the feudal superior, whose grant is regarded as revoked by the sentence of capital punishment. It therefore requires no special judgment, but follows

[10] Both Imbert and Duret are silent on the subject of the galleys. Their first mention appears in Note q to the second Book of Imbert's work. Jousse tells us nothing of their earlier history. (See *op. cit.*, p. 47, *et seq.*)

[11] Lamoignon decides in the negative, as do most of the other writers. *Guyot*, "Répertoire", *s.v.* "Bannissement."

[12] *Jousse*, "Justice criminelle", p. 50 *et seq.*

[13] [This "striking peculiarity of the Roman law of treason" appears also in Scottish legal history. "Several trials for treason after the death of the criminals took place in Scotland during the reign of James VI., who piqued himself on a strict adherence to the classical standards of antiquity, though he frequently selected the worst models for imitation." Lord *Mackenzie*, "Studies in Roman Law", pp. 410, 411 (Edinburgh, 1898). — TRANSL.]

[14] ["Condamnation de mémoire": the "damnatio memoriæ" of the Roman criminal law. "Damnatio memoriæ" ensued in cases of high treason ("perduellio") and, according to *Mommsen*, rested on the notion that in this instance the punishment took effect, not from the moment of the sentence, but from the moment of the crime, and that the proceeding against the dead offender was a declaratory one. "Römisches Strafrecht", p. 987 (Leipzig, 1899). — TRANSL.]

automatically upon the judgment of conviction. That it must have redounded to the decided benefit of the feudal lords and the judges goes without saying. The situation is clearly expressed by the maxim which forms Article 183 of the Custom of Paris: "He who confiscates the body confiscates the estate." [15] It is this close connection with the feudal relation (and consequently with the history of the transformation of the old allodial holdings into fiefs, which, in itself, assumed such manifold forms) that enables us to perceive how the right of confiscation came to exist. But confiscation was in nowise a general consequence of every capital punishment throughout France. For one thing, it was by many of the custumals confined to the single case of "lèse-majesté." Then, again, a variety of rules prevailed as to the kind of property subject to confiscation. And, finally, in the regions of written law, the right did not obtain at all. Soon, however, attempts to make it general began to appear. These were fostered by two things: the lack of definiteness as to what constituted "lèse majesté,[16] and the uniformity of procedure. The magistrates invented the rule that, in regions where confiscation was not recognized, the heirs were to be assessed a suitable fine. As early as 1588, we find the Parliament compelled to enact, by special Decree, that the fine in question "must not eat up the greater part of the convicted man's property." [17] By the Ordinance of July, 1685,[18] it was fixed at one-fourth of the estate.[19] As might be expected from the nature of the right, the confiscated property went to the local lord of the High Justice.[20] Naturally, too, these confiscations produced an important revenue. Like other matters of the sort, they were the subject of farming, and it was chiefly the existence of this practice which stood in the way of their abolition.

Closely akin to confiscation, is the other consequence of capital

[15] "Qui confisque le corps, il confisque le bien."

[16] Confiscation in cases of this character was first directed by the Ordinance of 1539, which provides for and regulates its application (Art. 1, 11). By Art. 13 of the Ordinance of 1679, the duel is put on the same footing as lèse majesté.

[17] See *Jousse, op. cit.*, p. 100.

[18] Art. 45.

[19] *Jousse, op. cit.*, p. 100.

[20] ["Seigneur Haut-Justicier du lieux." For the high, the low, and the middle justice, see *Brissaud*, "History of French Public Law", transl. *Garner*, being Vol. IX of the present Series. — TRANSL.] The rule stated in the text gave rise to a host of questions as to the persons thereby entitled. These questions are discussed by Jousse, *loc. cit.*, but need not be here entered into.

punishments, namely *civic death.* It is derived, in part, from the rules of the feudal law regarding the loss of "respons en cour",[21] in part, from the Roman law notions of "infamia" and "damnatio in metallum."[22] Civic death means the absolute loss of all civil rights; "it sunders completely every bond between society and the man who has incurred it; he has ceased to be a citizen, but cannot be looked upon as an alien, for he is without a country; he does not exist save as a human being, and this, by a sort of commiseration which has no source in the law."[23] Such a notion of civic death appears to have been too dreadful even for the legal writers of the period. Thus Jousse lays it down that civic death destroys only the civil rights, — the right to sue, to testify in a court of justice, to make a will or take under a will, to transfer or take by gift, — leaving intact such rights as appertain to the "jus gentium" — the capacity to contract, and even to enter into the marriage relation. But marriage, under these circumstances, is without civil consequences: the children are incapable of inheriting from either father or mother.[24] The effect of civic death dates from the publication of final judgment: from that instant, the man is as dead, and administration of his estate takes place. Nevertheless, the obligation to pay a life-rent remains unaffected; and he is equally liable for an unpaid marriage portion due to his wife, inasmuch as the matrimonial relation is still regarded as possible.[25]

No mention of this penal consequence is required in the judgment; it follows as a matter of course, and is effective (without exception) throughout the kingdom. In regions where the law permitted, civil death was accompanied by confiscation; elsewhere, by a fine assessed against the heirs. When confiscation first took its place as a specific and independent consequence of

[21] [One was said to have lost the "respons en cour", "when he has lost the right to testify in a court of justice or is no longer entitled to act as surety." *Ragueau and Laurière,* "Glossaire du droit françois", *s.v.* "Respons" (Niort, 1882). — TRANSL.]

[22] [Otherwise "metalli coercitio" or "damnatio ad metalla": condemnation to hard labor in the mines ("Digesto Italiano", XVIII; I, p. 1442). This under the Empire "was regarded as the heaviest punishment after that of death, and, as in the case of the latter, was preceded by scourging. It carried with it the loss of liberty and necessarily of property and other rights." (*Mommsen,* "Römisches Strafrecht", pp. 949, 950.) "Damnatio ad opus metalli" was a distinct punishment of a somewhat milder character. (*Ibid.*, p. 951.) — TRANSL.]

[23] *Guyot,* "Répertoire", *s.v.* "Mort civile."

[24] *Jousse,* "Justice criminelle", pp. 85 *et seq.*

[25] Numerous controversies, tending in effect to a mitigation of these rules, are here mentioned by Jousse.

capital punishment does not clearly appear. The earliest Ordinance, in which it is mentioned, couples it with transportation.[26] All persons sentenced to banishment from the kingdom and to civil death are to be transported to Corsica,[27] and there held in confinement.

To punishments of the second and third classes the term "afflictive"[28] is applied. The *second* class comprises punishments which are at once afflictive and corporal. It includes:

(a) *Maiming punishments:* slitting or piercing the tongue; cutting off the lips; cutting off the nose; cutting or burning[29] off the hand.

(b) *Non-maiming corporal punishments:* branding (scarcely ever imposed except in connection with flogging or consignment to the galleys); flogging (generally employed where the offender belonged to the lower classes and as an accompaniment of banishment for a term of years); the "carcan"[30] and the pillory (these

[26] Ordinance of December, 1556, "Recueil des anciennes lois françaises", XIII, p. 467. Confiscation is not referred to by either Imbert or Duret.

[27] Transportation later was to French Guiana: Ordinance of 1763, "Recueil général des anciennes lois françaises", XXII, p. 394.

[28] [In the period under discussion the term "afflictive" as applied to punishment appears to be without any very fixed meaning. Jousse's use of it differs widely from that of Muyart de Vouglans. The latter includes all the punishments specified in Tit. XXV, Art. 13, of the Criminal Ordinance (see *ante*, p. 9 *note* 3) in his first class, which he treats under the heading of "Corporal Punishments." "We shall call by this name," he says, "all those punishments which tend to destroy the body or to afflict it in some manner, whether by mutilation of its members, or on account of the physical suffering which they impose. For the same reason, they are called 'afflictive' punishments, although this latter term is ordinarily employed to designate such as tend merely to deprive the man of his liberty" ("Institutes au droit criminel", p. 398, Paris, 1757). By what a distinguished French author of our own day calls "an evil heritage from the old law", punishments under the present French penal code (apart from the case of police offenses, "contraventions") are either afflictive and infamous ("afflictives et infamantes") or infamous alone, or else correctional ("correctionnelle"). "If then," says this writer, "we seek a definition of 'afflictive' punishments" — a definition whose traces we have lost for want of historical data, and which is no longer capable of exact formulation, — "we can only say that afflictive punishments are those which are imposed on the offender with the purpose of 'afflicting' him, of making him suffer; while correctional punishments are those applied to the criminal with the object of reforming him. This is how we come to term 'detention' (imprisonment for political offenses), 'reclusion' (penitentiary imprisonment) as afflictive punishments, and 'emprisonnement' (ordinary imprisonment) as correctional, although each and all are merely punishments which deprive the man of liberty, too often, indeed, undergone in the same establishment." *Ortolan*, "Éléments du droit pénal", Vol. II, § 1610 (Paris, 1875). — TRANSL.]

[29] Burning, however, was resorted to only in cases of lèse majesté in the first degree.

[30] ["The "carcan" consisted of an iron collar which was clasped around

also being frequently recognized as proper in connection with other punishments).

In the *third* class (according to Jousse), that of **non-corporal afflictive punishments**, are comprised:

Consignment to the galleys for a term of years; imprisonment ("reclusion") for a term of years; exile ("exil"); servile labor (degrading labor performed in public); and "amende honorable."

Exile is almost always pronounced by "lettres de cachet" and is to be distinguished from banishment ("bannissement") in that it entails no infamy. *Servile labor* is mentioned in an Edict of 10 November, 1542, and is unquestionably taken from the Roman law. Allied punishments sometimes imposed are condemnation to the military service, and degradation from nobiliary rank,[31] the latter occurring only as a complement of other punishments.

The punishment of "*amende honorable*" deserves special notice. It dates from the 1100 s: the "Etablissements de Normandie" mention it in connection with parricide and infanticide; it lasts until the Revolution. As treated by Imbert, it is of but one sort, and is pronounced "in case of an offense against the honor and authority of God, of the King, of the public weal ('chose publique'), or of a private person."[32] Subsequently,[33] it is imposed in cases of "public scandal", and appears in two forms: simple or dry ("simple ou sèche") and "in figuris." *Simple "amende honorable"* requires the offender's presence "in the Chamber of Council, where, kneeling and with bared head, he craves pardon, but only of the persons injured by his act." This, therefore, is the most drastic form of personal apology that can be exacted. The "*amende honorable in figuris*" is the true "amende honorable" of an older period. It takes place in public, and is, in essence, an apology of the culprit before God and man for the offense which he has committed. Clad only in a shirt, with a torch or taper in his hand, and frequently with a halter about his neck, he appears before the door of the court house, or the church (sometimes before both), and there on bended knees,

the offender's neck and, by means of an attached chain, served to secure him to a wall or post. — TRANSL.]

[31] ["Degradation de noblesse." This is described by Muyart de Vouglans as a species of civic death, differing from civic death proper (see *supra*) in but one respect, namely, that it is not attended with confiscation of property. "Institutes au droit criminel", p. 414. — TRANSL.]

[32] *Imbert*, "Practique judiciaire", LIII, c. XXI.

[33] *Jousse*, "Justice criminelle", II, p. 64.

he declares that "falsely and in despite of truth, he has said or done such and such a thing, and that he craves pardon of God, of the King, of the officers of the law, and of the offended person." [34] At a later day, the expressions to be used are specified in the judgment.[35] The "amende honorable in figuris" was seldom imposed as an independent penalty; it was generally combined with a capital punishment, and took place before the execution of the latter. Women as well as men were subject to it, and it could even be pronounced in the case of an offending corporation.

With the single exception of exile, all these punishments entail the infamy of the offender, — a feature which they share with the fourth class, where infamy is really the punishment itself. In this *fourth* class — the **infamous** ("infamantes") **punishments** — are included:

Compelling the offender to wear a sort of foolscap,[36] and conveying him in this ignominious headdress through the streets;[37] public exposition on a scaffold or ladder; public reproof or reprimand ("blame") (in suffering which the offender is bareheaded and kneels); deprivation of public offices or privileges; the public burning of seditious writings; and fines ("amendes").

The burning of seditious writings takes place, without any preliminary judicial investigation, upon the simple requisition ("requête") of the public prosecutor. It is accompanied by prohibition of printing or sale, and the command to all and sundry to deliver up any copies of the objectionable writing that may be in their possession.

In the highest degree characteristic of the tendencies of the criminal law is the position to which the *fine* becomes relegated in this period. The fine rests upon the notion that reparation of the injury inflicted is an essential part of the punishment for every crime. Hence, as the State comes to regard the sheer criminal impulse as the chief element of crime, the fine, as a punishment, disappears, and true punishments take its place. While, in the period before this, the fine had been restricted to the case of mere

[34] *Imbert, loc. cit.*

[35] *Jousse, op. cit.*, p. 66.

[36] "Estre mitré", according to Imbert.

[37] ["Stow relates that, in the seventh of Edward IV, certain common jurors must (for their partial conduct) ride in paper mitres from Newgate to the Pillory in Cornhill, and there do penance for their fault. Again, in the first of Henry VIII (1509), Smith and Simpson, ringleaders of false inquests, rode the City (also in paper mitres) with their faces to the horse's tail; and they were set on the pillory in Cornhill." *Francis Watt*, "The Law's Lumber Room", 2d Series, p. 52 (London, 1898). — TRANSL.]

police offenses, a wide field had yet been left to its exclusive dominance. In the present period, however, the time of the absolute monarchy, it has wholly ceased to exist as a true punishment. Even the influence of such of the Custumals as still recognize it as such, has been unable to preserve for it the old significance; and it becomes nothing more than a mere appendage of the punishing power proper. How this evolution has been brought about best appears from an examination of the result — namely, the law of fines in the 1700 s. Here we find a distinction made between criminal fines, police fines ("amendes de contravention"), and civil fines. A civil fine is the judgment for damages awarded in favor of the civil party. Police fines ("amendes de contravention") are applicable in an extensive and well-defined category of offenses: injury to vert, felling timber, stealing wood, poaching ("amendes de chasse", "amendes de pêche"). They also include procedural fines[38] ("amendes de consignation et condamnation") and fines for violations of the regulations concerning the administration of tax-farming grants[39] ("droits des fermes"),[40] which last-mentioned class had its origin in the criminal law of the custumals.

Criminal fines, in short, represent merely the form under which the penal fines of the old law linger in this period. Only in the most exceptional way are they independent punishments: "The fine is scarcely ever imposed by itself: it is almost always combined with some other punishment."[41] In all cases where this occurs, its amount is discretionary, but must be at least equal to the costs of prosecution. In payment, it is postponed to the judgment in favor of the civil party, but takes precedence of all other pecuniary penal exactions, even that of confiscation, and can be enforced by execution against the body of the defendant, *i.e.*, the latter can be imprisoned until he pays. How this result had been worked out, it is difficult to say. It is not unlikely, however, that the fine-maxims of the old custumals had been the original basis for determining the amount. In any event, these fines formed the mainstay of the magisterial power

38 [For procedural fines, see *ante* § 39 *f*, *Glasson*. — TRANSL.]

39 [Under the monarchy, all revenues arising from indirect taxation came to be farmed, at first, by local contract, but later (in the 1600 s) by a general contract covering the whole of France, made with a single group, the farmers-general. See *Brissaud*, "History of French Public Law", transl. *Garner*, being Vol. IX of the present Series. — TRANSL.]

40 *Guyot*, "Répertoire", *s.v.* "Amende." Here the subject of police fines undergoes close examination.

41 *Jousse*, "Justice criminelle", pp. 69–72.

in its dealings with the lower classes of society, and could not be other than a grievous burden to the suffering masses.

Infamy, as has been said, was an essential feature of the foregoing punishments. The notion of infamy is plainly taken from the Roman law, and we find it here quite as loose as it was there. A distinction is made between infamy in law and infamy in fact. What their respective consequences were, does not distinctly appear: even Jousse is not entirely clear.[42] Infamy disqualifies one from taking office; the official who incurs it is compelled to relinquish his place; the infamous man cannot testify, or else his testimony is regarded as untrustworthy. An important question in this connection concerns the imposition of an unconditional fine. If this is not to be followed by infamy, the judgment must expressly so declare, by adding the words "without that the said fine carries any note of infamy."

The *fifth* class consists of the merely **civil punishments** ("peines non infamantes"), which are:

Admonition or warning (sometimes coupled with a fine); the "aumône",[43] (a pecuniary mulct distinguishes from the "amende" in being non-infamous); the "pœna dupli, tripli," etc. (applicable only in the case of embezzlement of public moneys and complicity in criminal bankruptcy); and some others of lesser moment.[44]

There remains to be mentioned the matter of **imprisonment.** Imprisonment is distinctive in its nature, in that, with its adoption as a punitive measure, there begins to arise the notion of an end in punishing, other than mere chastisement and intimidation. Where the necessity of attaining this end has not impressed itself upon the State, imprisonment, as a means of true punishment, is bound to fail. Hence, in France down to the Revolution, imprisonment was in theory a mere means of securing the execution of the sentence, — although, to be sure, it found at times practical employment as a real punishment. In this view, there was uniform reliance on the text of the Digest: "carcer ad continendos homines, non ad puniendos haberi debet." [45] The prisons are therefore to be used "for the safe-keeping of criminals during the judicial investigation of their causes", and

[42] "Justice criminelle", pp. 113–115.

[43] [So called from the fact that it was devoted as an *alms* to pious and charitable purposes. The particular objects are specified in *Muyart de Vouglans,* "Institutes au droit criminel", pp. 416, 417. — TRANSL.]

[44] See *Jousse,* "Justice criminelle", pp. 77–84.

[45] Lib. XLVIII, Tit. 19, "De pœnis."

cannot be treated as a means of "punishment to be inflicted by the judges." Only individual exceptions appear: the most important are the commutation of the punishment of death or that of the galleys into that of imprisonment for life, and the recognition of imprisonment ("reclusion") in a penitentiary establishment ("maison de force") in the case of women and minors. These, too, are the only instances in which imprisonment has infamy as a consequence. But a true system of punishment, based upon deprivation of liberty, did not exist.[46]

From among the punishments above enumerated the public prosecutor made his selection in the individual instance, when no penalty had been expressly appointed by Ordinance. Yet, even if it had been specified, the judge had the power to increase or diminish "the legal punishment according to circumstances." [47] To the system existing by virtue of such legislative provisions it now becomes necessary to turn.

§ 59e. **The Several Crimes and their Punishments.** — In this field the specific principles found application. Definitions, the constituent elements of crime, extenuating and aggravating circumstances, — these are all topics of discussion by the jurists of the period. The treatment often has a certain amount of historical background; with Ayrault and Duret, however, this is chiefly a matter of reference to the Roman law, feudal law being completely neglected. The authorities invoked were, first, the various Ordinances and the decrees of the courts, in particular those of the different Parliaments; secondly, the Roman law and the writings of the Italian practical jurists, Julius Clarus and Farinacius. The borrowing from the last is in part direct (this is especially the case with Jousse), and in part indirect, that is to say, from the commentators on the regional Customs, and through these from the French criminalists proper. Responsible as was the influence of Clarus and Farinacius for a great enhancement of severity in punitive measures, the French law nevertheless remains indebted to them in many particulars for perspicuity and comprehensiveness. Indeed, the learning devoted to this part of the subject attained a volume and precision which cannot even approximately be here reproduced.[1] All that we can do is to lay before

[46] *Jousse*, "Justice criminelle", p. 79; *Guyot*, "Répertoire", *s.v.* "Mort civile" and "Prison."

[47] *Jousse*, "Justice criminelle", Vol. II, p. 593.

[1] In Jousse's work the subject of the several crimes and their punish-

the reader a brief characterization of the several crimes, — requiring him to bear in mind that a systematic classification does not appear before the end of the 1700 s (when, indeed, it still falls short of being a general one), so that even Jousse follows the old plan of Duret and enumerates the different crimes alphabetically.

The *first* group, that of offenses against religion and the church, by Imbert, and even at a later day, termed "spiritual treason" ("lèse majesté divine"), consists of the several crimes now to be mentioned:

Sacrilege is "any profanation of sacred things." It thus embraces all offenses (whether by way of theft or not) against property dedicated to the service of God, and all crimes committed in "holy places." According to Jousse, the punishment is discretionary, yet under the Declaration of 1682 it is ordinarily death; all accomplices are to receive the same sentence.[2]

Heresy comprises a whole group of offenses which find separate treatment. Among these are the assembling for sectarian worships; the practice of baptismal rites by persons other than priests; every adoption or acceptance of the "pretended reformed" religion; every relapse to that religion; the lending of aid or countenance to Protestants in their beliefs; as well as failure to conform to the marriage observances of the Catholic Church. So, too, it was heresy for Protestants to emigrate from the Kingdom. By the Edicts of 31 May, 1685, and 13 September, 1699, such emigrants, together with all who aided in their attempt to escape, are to be sentenced to the galleys for life. Other instances of heresy are the refusal to receive spiritual succor, while in a state of illness; apostasy; adherence to any schism; and, finally, atheism. At first, the punishment was burning at the stake; later, it was varied "according to the character of the heresy and the accompanying circumstances," although for this there was a series [3] of legislative enactments [4].

Under **magic** and **sortilege**, four classes of offenses are recognized: witchcraft and sorcery; pretended foretelling of the future;

ments extends from Vol. III, p. 212 to Vol. IV, p. 322. Our references will be chiefly to this writer, inasmuch as he is the best known.

[2] *Jousse*, "Justice criminelle", pp. 95–106.

[3] These are assembled in "Code pénal, pp. 13 *et seq.* [The book thus entitled is a collection of the principal Ordinances, Edicts, and Declarations touching crimes and punishments. It was compiled by *Laverdy*, and appeared in 1752. *Stein*, p. 604. — TRANSL.]

[4] *Jousse*, "Justice criminelle", IV, pp. 465–480.

addiction to superstitious practices; and the combination of any of these with impiety and sacrilege. In the 1500 s and early 1600 s, belief in witchcraft and in "intercourse and communion with evil spirits" still found acceptance, as appears from the text of Duret.[5] But the Ordinance of July, 1682, openly declaring all such matters to be "illusions", legal opinion accordingly adopted the more reasonable view that, although there were no "real sorcerers or soothsayers", the practices of such persons are nevertheless the subject of punishment, "either because of their impiety or because of the harm that they work to others." [6] The punishment for this crime varied from burning at the stake to flogging.[7]

Simony is the buying or selling of "things spiritual." Grouped with this offense is "confidence", which exists where one enters upon the enjoyment of a spiritual or ecclesiastical right and the performance of the duties thereto appurtenant, with intent to make over this right to another at a later day.[8] The punishment of such offenses is loss of all benefices vested in the wrong-doer.[9] Here belongs, also, the taking possession of an ecclesiastical living by high-handed means, — which likewise brings about the forfeiture of all benefices.[10]

Next come **blasphemy** and **profanity**. Blasphemy may be committed either by writing or word of mouth. It occurs when a man ascribes false attributes to the Divinity, or denies the Divinity's true attributes, or whenever there is insult offered to God, the Virgin, or the Saints. The penalties prescribed by the Ordinances are of many different sorts. The upshot, however, is that simple blasphemy and profanity are punished with a discretionary fine, which is to be doubled in case of a second offense. By the Declaration of 30 July, 1666, the punishment is increased to such

[5] "Traicté des peines et amendes", p. 154 a, b.

[6] [*Cf.* the remark of Selden, quoted in *Professor Thayer's* "Trial by Jury of Things Supernatural" ("Legal Essays", p. 329, Boston, 1908): "The law against witches does not prove there be any, but it punishes the malice of those people who use such means to take away men's lives." — TRANSL.]

[7] *Jousse*, "Justice criminelle", Vol. III, pp. 752–767.

[8] [Specifically "a 'confidence' is a contract by which an ecclesiastic receives a benefice on condition of paying the emoluments, or a part of them, to a third person; or covenants to resign the preferment at a specified time. The person holding a benefice on such terms is called a 'confidentiaire.'" *W. H. P. Jervis*, "A History of the Church of France" etc., Vol. I, p. 212, *note* (London, 1872), citing *Héricourt*, "Lois ecclés. de France", F. c. XX, 28, 29; "Mémoires du clergé de France", Vol. VIII, p. 8. — TRANSL.]

[9] *Jousse*, "Justice criminelle", IV, pp. 110–118.

[10] *Laverdy*, "Code pénal", pp. 14, 15.

an extent that for the eighth repetition the offender suffers the loss of his tongue.[11]

Disorderly behavior during divine service receives discretionary punishment. At such a time, too, all taverns and shops must be kept closed, or the keeper will feel the hand of the law.[12]

A *second* principal group is formed by the crimes of **temporal treason** ("lèse majesté humaine"). The evolution of this notion of "lèse majesté", better than almost anything else, enables us to recognize the development which had been going on in the idea of the State. Since the 1500 s, it had become clear to legal science that, although the Prince represents the State, the State is in no sense merged in the Prince. Thus arose the new conception of temporal "lèse majesté" — a conception which, throughout this whole period, preserved the same character and became clearer only in respect of the systematization that it underwent. Duret placed under this head all evil-intentioned deeds which are directed against the Prince, his councillors, or his gendarmerie, or which create public disturbances, injure the State, betray it, or set on foot conspiracies.[13] The efforts of later writers bring order out of this notional chaos. A distinction is taken between temporal "lèse majesté" in the first and in the second degrees, — which is substantially that between "lèse majesté" proper and high treason. Temporal "lèse majesté" in the first degree embraces every attempt upon the person of the Prince, his children, or those in the line of succession to his throne, and every attack upon the State whether by overt act or by secret "leagues or associations." This offense is "one of the most atrocious that can be committed," because Sovereigns are "the images of God, representing in the governance of their several States that authority which is exercised by God in the governance of the Universe."[14] "Lèse majesté" in the second degree (or, as Jousse has it, in the lesser degrees) comprises all offenses "which cause prejudice or damage to the public weal", or "the King's authority", "interfere with the due execution of public justice", or injure the sovereign rights of the Kingdom, and all offenses directed against "the persons or the functions of magistrates or other persons who represent the Sovereign", such as foreign ambassadors. Thus,

[11] *Jousse*, "Justice criminelle", III, pp. 260–272.
[12] *Laverdy*, "Code pénal", pp. 12–14.
[13] "Traicté des peines et amendes", pp. 106 *et seq.*
[14] *Jousse*, "Justice criminelle", III, p. 681.

all officialdom is included in the notion of the State, and all crimes committed within this circle or against any member of it share the same common character. Specifically these crimes are:

"**Lèse majesté**" **proper**; that is to say, attempt upon the life of the Prince, or of any member of the princely house. Extraordinary punishment is provided for this crime by the Ordinance of 1539. The offender is to be plucked with red-hot pincers and, after boiling lead has been poured into his wounds, is to be torn asunder by horses;[15] his house is to be razed to the ground and his estate confiscated. Under the Criminal Ordinance of 1670,[16] there is even a criminal proceeding against his corpse.[17] All other species of "lèse majesté" in the first degree are followed by confiscation, the razing of the offender's dwelling, and death; even guilty knowledge is visited with the like punishment.[18] On a par with the offense in question, according to the view of Jousse, is every species of rebellion, but here the death penalty is inflicted in a less aggravated form.

High treason; which includes every resistance to the royal command, every insult to the King, every appeal from the King to the Emperor,[19] or to the Pope, the assembling with weapons or followers in derogation of the royal authority, the fortifying of castles, and a large number of kindred acts. In serious cases the punishment usually is "confiscation of the body and estate"; in other instances its extent depends upon the circumstances of the particular offense.[20]

Under this head of high treason, also fall, for the reason assigned, certain specific crimes of a different description, namely:

Counterfeiting of money. — Two principal species are recognized: counterfeiting of money, proper, and "billonage." The former consists of unauthorized coining, coining with false weight and standard, imitation or counterfeiting of inscriptions, clipping coin, or uttering false money. "Billonage" is the melting down of good coin or in any other manner converting it into bullion or, exporting coined money from the realm.[21] For any sort of coun-

[15] [This was the manner of death inflicted, in 1610, upon Ravaillac, who assassinated Henry IV, and, as late as 1757, upon Damiens for attempting the life of Louis XV. — TRANSL.]

[16] Tit. XXII, Art. 1.

[17] For examples, see *Jousse*, "Justice criminelle", p. 683.

[18] *Jousse*, *op. cit.*, III, pp. 674–705.

[19] Decree (2) of 1417, in Papon's collection, LXII, Vol. I.

[20] *Jousse*, *op. cit.*, pp. 689 *et seq.*, pp. 454–456.

[21] Declaration of 24 October, 1711; Edicts of May 1718 and February, 1726.

terfeiting of money, even for the act of uttering false coin, the penalty is death.[22]

Counterfeiting of the royal letters or seal.[23]

Peculation: that is to say, the embezzlement of royal or public moneys, or the use of such moneys for one's own benefit " through an infinity of evil artifices contrived by the financiers to enrich themselves at the expense of the King and the public." The punishment is consignment to the galleys for life, but, in the course of time, this has come to be seldom applied, and the court uses a discretionary power in fixing the penalty.[24]

Extortion and malversation in office. — In this case, likewise, the practice is to modify the punishment according to circumstances. By the Ordinances of Moulins [25] and of Blois,[26] extortion by officials was punishable with " confiscation of body and estate," yet the death penalty is scarcely ever inflicted, — giving way to banishment coupled with one of the infamous punishments.[27]

Duress of imprisonment (" chartre privée ") which exists where a private person, with strong hand, deprives another of liberty. It is numbered among attacks upon the sovereign rights of the State, under " lèse majesté." The principal doctrinal source is the Roman Code.[28] The punishment is a matter of judicial discretion, but based on Farinacius.[29]

Obstruction of public justice (" rebellion à justice "): This occurs through any resistance to the exercise of the judicial power, or concealment of criminals. An associated offense is that of prison breaking. In spite of the provisions of the Criminal Ordinance,[30] escape from prison is seldom punished except when accompanied by the use of violence or the commission of some other crime. The turnkey who affords a prisoner the means of escape incurs consignment to the galleys. In other cases there is a fine and, at times, heavier punishment.[31]

Duelling. — By the opening of the 1500 s, the duel had completely fallen into disuse as a procedural feature. In the period with which we are dealing, it is not only discountenanced, but for-

[22] *Jousse, op. cit.*, II, pp. 452–454.
[23] *Ibid.*, III, pp. 373, 374.
[24] *Ibid.*, IV, pp. 21–38.
[25] Art. 23.
[26] Art. 280.
[27] *Jousse, op. cit.*, III, pp. 767–810.
[28] Lib. IX, Tit. 5, "De privatis carceribus."
[29] Questio 27, n. 35: *Jousse, op. cit.*, III, pp. 283–286.
[30] Tit. XVII, Art. 25.
[31] *Jousse, op. cit.*, IV, p. 95.

bidden under rigorous penalties. Indeed, the hatred which the French kings displayed toward this one-time institution is quite remarkable. The last instance of a formally sanctioned duel was that between the Lords de Chataigneraie and de Jarnac, in the presence of Francis I.[32] In the combat, de Jarnac, a favorite of the then Dauphin (afterwards Henry II) lost his life; his death so affected the Dauphin that when the latter came to the throne he vowed that never again would a duel be permitted in his Kingdom. At a later day, Louis XIV swore by his kingly honor, and publicly declared in the two Edicts of 1651 [33] and 1679,[34] that the offense of duelling was beyond the hope of pardon — a declaration repeated by Louis XV in the Edict of February, 1723. The attitude thus adopted by the monarchs had necessarily a great influence upon legal opinion. Jousse says that duelling is " more criminal than homicide ", and the Ordinance of 1679 classed it as a species of " lèze majesté." For these reasons the details of the offense are a matter of close study. Distinction is made between challenge without combat and the consummated duel. Sending a challenge is punishable with two years' imprisonment, a heavy fine (to be paid to the nearest hospice), and suspension from all offices for a period of three years, — subject to increase according to circumstances. The same consequences attend acceptance of a challenge. In the case of a consummated duel, the punishment of both parties is death " without remission ", and this regardless of their wounds. Nor does death in the combat stay the action of the penal law. Here there is judicial condemnation of the decedent's memory, and confiscation of his estate, or, where that is not possible under the local rule, two-thirds of the estate is taken, by way of fine, for pious uses. All who participate are visited with severe punishment. He who delivers the challenge incurs flogging and branding, and, upon a second offense, consignment to the galleys for life; the mere looker-on loses all his offices and dignities, or else the fourth part of his property. One good effect of this unreasonable severity was that it occasioned the establishment of Courts of Honor. By the Edict of August, 1679,[35] as judges of honor were appointed the Marshals of France,

[32] [In his consummate study of the duel in France, *Alexander Coulin* makes it clear that the royally authorized duel of the 1400 s and early 1500 s, such as the one here mentioned, was quite other than the old trial by battle. "Verfall des offiziellen und Entstehung des privaten Zweikampfes in Frankreich", p. 138 (*Gierke's* "Untersuchungen zur deutschen Staats- und Rechtsgeschichte", 99 Heft). — TRANSL.]

[33] Art. 24. [34] Art. 36. [35] Art. 2.

the Governors-General and their Lieutenants. These, again, were authorized to appoint a certain number of nobles, in every province, as arbitrators, with jurisdiction to determine questions of personal honor and, incidentally, to cite before them the contending parties. From the decisions of such local tribunals, an appeal lay to the Marshals.[36]

The unlawful **carrying of arms** and the **wearing of masks** were forbidden by the Ordinance of 1487 — a prohibition which is often repeated. The Ordinance of 9 May, 1539, allowed the populace to overpower and kill (" courir sus ") the offender, but by that of 5 August, 1560, imprisonment and the loss of weapons were prescribed. Later, both cases are treated as mere police offenses.[37]

Crimes against the person constitute the *third* main class.

Homicide in general (" homicide ") is grouped under four heads: (*a*) justifiable homicide (" homicide par nécessité "); (*b*) accidental homicide; (*c*) homicide by negligence, and (*d*) murder (" homicide volontaire ", " meurtre ", " assassinat "). The killing of an adulterer is not punishable. Where there has been a wounding, the case is one of homicide if death ensues within forty days. Attempt to kill, in general, is not punished as severely as the consummated offense. It is only the proximate attempt, conspiracy to kill (" machination de tuer "), the hiring of an assassin, and instigation of another to commit homicide, which are visited with the death penalty. Self-defense is discussed quite fully. But the learning of homicide is without anything distinctive: on principle, it is based upon Farinacius. The punishment for murder is breaking on the wheel; more exact determination is left to the courts.[38]

Poisoning (" crime de poison ") is dealt with as a separate offense, and is more serious than ordinary murder. Its punishment is death in an aggravated form, varying with the circumstances of the case.[39]

Parricide is murder committed upon the person of a relative, — even upon that of a natural ascendant or descendant, or of a relative by marriage. In a wider sense, it includes infanticide, concealment of pregnancy, and exposure of children, as also the murder of the master of the house by his servant. The notions here involved are the common ones of the 1700 s, —

36 *Jousse, op. cit.*, III, pp. 320–328.
37 *Ibid.*, IV, pp. 56–67.
38 *Ibid.*, III, pp. 480–565.
39 *Ibid.*, IV, pp. 41–45.

based upon the Italian practical jurists, — and hence need not further detain us.[40]

Suicide is still a crime. The estate is to be confiscated and a criminal proceeding had against the corpse. These rules, however, become greatly modified in practice.[41]

Crimes against marriage, *i.e.* adultery and bigamy, likewise present a situation where the punishment is governed by a general practice. The chief doctrinal sources, as to adultery, are the 134th Novel, c. 10 and the Authentica "Sed hodie[42] Codicis ad legem Juliam de adulteriis." The woman who offends is "authenticated",[43] *i.e.* is immured in a cloister, and loses her property rights. The man is punished in different ways, — sometimes by death, but latterly at the discretion of the judge.[44] Similar considerations apply to bigamy and polygamy, in default of special laws.[45]

For the several forms of the **crime against nature** the punishment is burning at the stake.[46]

Of the offenses grouped under the designation of **carnality** ("luxure"), rape is punished with death, as is also carnal connection with a female child. In other cases, resort is had to some severe penalty of a different description, although death is usually specified in the prosecutor's demand.[47]

Pandering is attended with banishment, loss of the ears, whipping, and the like. Later, banishment comes into general use.[48]

Incest comprises every case of sexual intercourse between kindred, as far as the degree of aunt and nephew. It does not, however, cover commerce between persons who are akin only by

[40] *Jousse, op. cit.*, III, pp. 248–254; IV, pp. 1–26.

[41] *Ibid.*, IV, pp. 130–142.

[42] [In the first nine books of the Code, the Glossators inserted "extracts from the Novels which completed or modified a considerable number of constitutions. These extracts were called 'Authenticæ', in contradistinction to the collection of Novels in nine collations called 'Authenticum' or 'Corpus authenticorum.'" *Tardif*, "Histoire des sources du droit français", p. 121 (Paris, 1890); and see also Vol. I of the present Series: "A General Survey of Events, Sources, Persons, and Movements in Continental Legal History", p. 136.

The Authentica "Sed hodie" is so called from the opening words of the first sentence: "*Sed hodie* adultera verberata in monasterium mittatur; quam intra biennium viro recipere licet." Corp. Jur. Can., ed. *Beck*, Code, Lib. IX, Tit. 9, XXX (Leipzig, 1831). — TRANSL.]

[43] ["Authentiquée": signifying that there is applied to her the punishment of the "Authentica." *Dupin and Laboulaye*, "Glossaire de l'ancien droit français", *s.v.* "Authentique" (Paris, 1846). — TRANSL.]

[44] *Jousse, op. cit.*, III, pp. 212–248.

[45] *Ibid.*, IV, pp. 51–56.

[46] *Ibid.*, IV, pp. 118–125.

[47] *Ibid.*, III, pp. 705–752.

[48] *Ibid.*, III, pp. 810–817.

virtue of the sponsorship relation, as in the case of godfather and god-daughter. There is no express legislative provision as to the punishment; this is graduated to the closeness of the relationship, and is either death or one of the infamous punishments.[49]

Among **crimes against property**, we encounter, first of all, that of **arson** (" incendie "). Its punishment is arbitrary, and varies with the circumstances. Burning at the stake is the penalty where loss of life has been occasioned. Lesser punishments are employed where only property had been destroyed.[50]

Next follows **theft** (" vol "), which is " every fraudulent abstraction and carrying away of the goods of another, with intent to convert them to the taker's use." Differentiation as to kind is solely by reference to the " circumstances which render the theft more or less grave." These are (*a*) the character of the offender (*e.g.* theft by a domestic); (*b*) the place of commission (highway robbery; theft in a public place or during a conflagration); (*c*) the time of commission (theft in the night-time); (*d*) the manner of commission (theft by breaking and entering, by the display of weapons, or by violence); (*e*) the nature of the thing stolen (property dedicated to sacred uses, horses, cattle, and other grazing animals, wagons, etc.); (*f*) its quantity or amount (grand and petty larceny, the definition of which is different by different regional customs); and (*g*) repetition of theft. As to the last, it is to be observed that the rule making the third theft by the same individual a distinctive species has been naturalized from the Charles V's German " Constitutio Carolina " and from Farinacius. The punishment of theft is of many sorts. This is due to the lack of general legislation, and also to the fact that a number of the regional customs had their own provisions on the subject, which have become elaborated by the judicial law. With his practical bent, Jousse has thrown light upon almost all the possible cases.[51]

Quite as extensive a field is covered by **falsification** (" faux ") — a term used to designate both forgery and crimes of fraud. Falsification embraces " every act calculated to destroy, impair, or obscure the truth, to the prejudice of another and with intent to deceive him." A first class consists of falsification in the exercise of a public function, for which the punishment may be anything from the death penalty down, in the discretion of the court.

[49] *Jousse, op. cit.*, III, pp. 561–573.
[50] *Ibid.*, III, pp. 658–666.
[51] *Ibid.*, IV, pp. 166–267.

Private falsification includes the forgery of documents and falsification generally by word or act (wherein is embraced the giving of false weight or false measure). Its punishment is, in part, according to the customary law, in part, discretionary; and consists of fine, banishment, or corporal chastisement.[52]

Perjury (false witness) is the subject of especial punishment. According to the Ordinance of 1531, the death penalty is to be applied. In practice, however, a modification of this rule had come about, and the punishment was in the discretion of the court. False witness against the accused in a criminal proceeding called for a severer penalty, and was visited with the punishment to which the person falsely accused had become liable.[53]

Fraudulent bankruptcy is treated by Jousse as a species of theft. By the Ordinance of 10 October, 1536, bankruptcy, when accompanied by fraud and wrong-doing ("fraudes et abus"), was made punishable by "amende honorable", corporal chastisement, the "carcan", and the like, according to the nature of the offense. Severer measures were prescribed by the Ordinance of Orleans[54] and Blois;[55] and an Edict of 1609 appointed the death penalty. Although this last provision was repeated in the Ordinance of Commerce[56] (1673) and in a Declaration of 1716, it was not observed in practice; the provisions of the Ordinance of 1536, however, remained in force. Accomplices incurred a fine, in certain cases a corporal chastisement.[57]

Usury, *i.e.* "any illicit gain derived from money in virtue of a prior agreement," still remained a crime. Nevertheless, a distinction was made between usury and interest. The exaction of a lawful rate of interest was permitted; this, under the Ordinance of February, 1770, being fixed at 5 per cent. ("au denier vingt").[58] The various questions are dealt with by Jousse in considerable detail. By the Ordinance of Orleans, the

[52] For the particular cases, see *Jousse, op. cit.*, III, pp. 341–416, where they are exhaustively considered.

[53] *Jousse, op. cit.*, III, pp. 411–442.

[54] Art. 142.

[55] Art. 245.

[56] Tit. XI, Art. 12.

[57] *Jousse, op. cit.*, III, pp. 254–260.

[58] It is interesting to note the steady decline of this legal rate. By the Ordinance of 1254, it was fixed at 4 sols on the livre (20 per cent.); by that of July, 1315, at 15 per cent. It later became 10 per cent. ("au denier 10"), and so remained until 1507. Its subsequent course was as follows: 6¼ per cent. ("au denier 16") by the Edict of July, 1601; 5⅝ per cent ("au denier 18") by the Edict of March, 1634; 5 per cent. ("au denier 20") by the Edict of December, 1665; and 4 per cent. ("au denier 25") by the Edict of June, 1766. See *Jousse, op. cit.*, p. 269.

punishment of usury was corporal chastisement and confiscation of property — a provision frequently reënacted, but mitigated in practice.[59]

The last division (and one of a subsidiary character) is that of **insults**. Here was included every species of insulting language or conduct, in general, and, in particular, "every offense which a man occasions to his neighbor through a contumelious motive" ("motif de mépris"). The latter is of three sorts: insult by word of mouth, insult by writing, and insult by conduct. In the case of oral insults, a retraction is required, and the offender is often compelled formally and publicly to vindicate the honor of the insulted person, either by lodging a document in the judicial record-office, or by appearing in open court, with uncovered head, and there making oral acknowledgment of his wrong-doing. If the insult is offered by a person of low degree to one of higher, then, in addition, the culprit is condemned to imprisonment or such other punishment as the judge shall determine. In other instances, there is a fine in the nature of a judgment for civil damages in favor of the injured person; in others again, a penal fine; and, in very serious cases, even infamous punishments, such as "amende honorable" and banishment. As to insults by writing, the law is the same, except that the defamatory libel is suppressed, or is torn up in public. For every sort of insult by conduct ("real" insults) the penalty depends upon the circumstances, the extent of the injury, the person injured, the place, or the nature of the act, and varies from mere public censure ("blame") to "afflictive" and infamous punishments. There is, besides, an award of damages to the injured person. The different cases are gone into quite fully by Jousse.[60] It is to be noted that he includes arson and "violatio sepulchri" under the present head. Especial mention is deserved for **defamatory libels** and the enactments relating to **offenses of the press**. Printing, publication, or sale of matter amounting to a defamatory libel was forbidden by the Ordinance of 17 January, 1651, and many subsequent enactments, under penalty of whipping and, in case of repetition, death. For falsely stating the place of publication, as well as for printing in foreign countries, the Ordinance of 10 September, 1572,[61] prescribed confiscation of the book and a fine to be fixed at the court's

[59] *Jousse, op. cit.*, IV, pp. 267–284.
[60] *Op. cit.*, III, pp. 573–671.
[61] Art. 10.

discretion. The Ordinance of Moulins [62] prohibited the publication of any book without permission of the Crown ("sans privilège du Roi"), punishing infractions with confiscation of property and corporal chastisement; and, by the Ordinance of 11 December, 1547, no book dealing with religious matters could be printed or sold unless first examined and authorized by the doctors of theology, the punishment in this case being confiscation of "body and estate." The Press Law proper is the Edict of August, 1686, which consolidated all the preceding enactments. Later enactments merely carry out the plan there laid down. Thus, the Regulation of 28 February, 1723, provided that any one guilty of circulating writings against religion, the King's service, the good of the State, the purity of manners, or the honor and reputation of families or individuals should (in addition to the punishments prescribed by existing law) incur the forfeiture of all privileges, rights, and offices. So, too, the Declaration of 10 May, 1728, punished the same offense with the pillory, banishment, and severer punishments. Likewise, by a Declaration of 17 April, 1757, it was enacted that the author of any writing "tending to give offense to religion, to agitate the minds of the people, to assail the authority of the King, or to disturb the peace of the State will be punished with death"; [63] further, that all who take part in its printing, publishing, or dissemination are to undergo the like punishment; [64] and, finally, that failure to observe the formalities indicated in the Ordinances shall entail a punishment which may extend to consignment to the galleys for life.[65] And Jousse does not hesitate to add that all who have authorized or counselled the publication must be punished in the self-same manner.[66]

This concludes the list of crimes in the true sense of the word. There were many other offenses of a special nature such as those relating to the forests, to hunting, and to fishing, as well as an entire group of marine offenses which are dealt with in the Ordinance of the Marine. Examination of these, however, would throw but little light on the general features of the criminal law of this period, and, consequently, does not require us to prolong this survey.

[62] Art. 78. [63] Art. 1. [64] Art. 2. [65] Art. 3.
[66] *Op. cit.*, III, pp. 651, *et seq.*

Chapter XI

OTHER COUNTRIES IN THE 1500 s–1700 s

(Scandinavia, Switzerland, Netherlands)

A. Scandinavia

§ 59*f*. **Scandinavia during the period 1500 s–1700 s.** — *The 1500 s.* The legislation of the first half of the 1500 s exhibits an increasing progress in penal law to the conception that the end to be sought was not the securing of private redress and damages so much as the maintenance of public order and safety. The system, however, was not essentially changed. More severe penalties were prescribed for divers offenses with a view of enforcing more effectively the duty resting upon the public authorities. The reason set forth for these drastic enactments was the lawless conditions prevailing during the internal strifes and wars; and the crimes especially dealt with were murder and gross personal violence, which frequently passed unpunished.

Private Vengeance Prohibited. — It is apparent, however, that the basic principles of the earlier provincial Laws remain. The system of fines, which had grown out of the ancient custom of taking the law into one's own hands, was preserved. Personal feud and vengeance, while not allowed, still served to distinguish such an act from one committed on an offenseless man, and subjected the doer to outlawry or forfeiture of life in exceptional cases only.

[1] [The first four headings of this Section continue Stemann's "History," etc., already cited in note 1 to § 39*a*; for this author, see the Editorial Preface. — Ed.]

The Laws of Christian II penalized with death all cases of deliberate homicide; if the defendant escaped, he and his companions in the act were outlawed; any one of them, if apprehended, was to be executed by the royal official; but any one could slay him with impunity; to harbor him was cause for outlawry. For the taking of life by accident or in self-defense, peace must be bought by fines to the kin and the king; the amounts were to be determined by the "Land-judge" and were exacted from the defendant himself, his kindred not being bound to contribute; attacks upon the latter by the kinsfolk of the deceased were prohibited.

These general rules were followed by succeeding kings. No new penal principle developed; the chief aim being more effectually to enforce the rules of the earlier codes. This is seen in the Ordinance of Frederick I for Fyen, of May 18, 1523, and the Decree of Christian III for Kopenhagen, of 1537, which attribute the frequent cases of murder to the practice of private vengeance, as well as to the custom for the slayer to obtain release by paying fines to the kin of the deceased (to which his relations contributed) without the cause reaching the law's tribunal. The chief purpose of these enactments, as well as those of 1547, 1551, and 1558, was, therefore, the abolition of the "Haevn" (or feud) the coercion of a resort to court proceedings.

These laws also prescribe death for homicide (except where done by accident or in self-defense), whether the offender was caught in the act or declared outlawed and later apprehended; his personal estate was forfeited, half to the king and the other half to the heirs of the deceased; the offender's relations being declared exempt from contribution or vengeance. Where the fugitive made good his escape, or purchase of peace by money was offered him by the king and kin, his relatives were to produce two thirds of the legal "man-fine" to the victim's heirs, as provided in earlier legislation. Vengeance on kin was prohibited in all cases, and an old rule was revived prohibiting reconciliation without legal procedure. But these provisions were limited to manslaughter committed by yeomen ("Bonde") or burghers ("Kjøpstadmand") and not applicable to the nobility. The latter preserved the right of private vindication; and charges involving the life or honor of any of its members came only under the jurisdiction of the king and the high court of the realm (an exception being noted in the Kallundborg Decree of 1576, ch. 13, providing the death penalty for a nobleman who should deliberately kill his brothers).

Outlawry still ensued for unmulctable offenses, or on failure to produce legal or promised fines. The provision in the Ordinance of Erik Glipping of 1284, was reënacted in the Decrees of 1547 and 1558, outlawing any one who should fail to pay a forty-mark or other important fine or secure a bondsman therefor within six weeks after sentence. Outlawry, however, was put into practice chiefly for crimes subject (under the revised laws) to capital punishment where the felon was not caught in the act and escaped during the period of time allowed after sentence. This period, which had varied from a day and a month to three days and three nights, was now fixed at a day and a night; if caught thereafter, the death penalty was exacted. The second Ecclesiastical Law of Christian II authorized any one to kill a fugitive murderer; and while there is a decision of the House of the Lords, of 1537, acquitting the defendant from punishment for such an act, the Decrees are silent on the subject, and it is doubtful if outlawry operated to this extent any longer. By the Act of 1537, it behooved the royal bailiff to " mete out justice on his neck " where the murderer had not been seized in the act but was sworn to be outlawed, and he was later charged with the duty of pursuing and apprehending the fugitive. While these Decrees do not expressly authorize every person to seize the outlaw, there is recorded a judgment of the Viborg Land-Thing of 1570, according to which all present at a " Thing " where a murder was committed were in duty bound to seize the criminal; and this rule was later made general.

Where reconciliation was made and fines paid, the offended party delivered a " letter of release of feud " (like the earlier " Trygdeed," *ante*, § 39a) whereupon the royal official proclaimed " the peace of the king upon him." Where in particular cases there was a doubt as to the manner of punishment, or aggravating or extenuating circumstances appeared, the defendant was referred to the " king's favor or disfavor " and his case was decided directly by the ruler.

Penalties. — The ecclesiastical jurisdiction had been transferred, at the time of the Reformation, to the State; and this led to some changes in penalties. Thus, the Decree of 1537 prescribed death for a spouse guilty of adultery, and also for the paramour, this penalty being later limited by the statute of 1539 to a third offense, and later laws not mentioning the third party. For seduction, fines were imposed, payable to the offended party and the king (as theretofore to the bishop), and repeated offenses later involved the death penalty. In the Ordinances of Frederick II, of 1582, incest and bigamy are referred to in connection with adultery, but no special section covers these crimes, while the penalties were made the same as for adultery under Christian IV, viz., forfeiture of estate, exile, and in case of failure to depart, death. False swearers were deprived, under Christian II, of the two fingers raised for the oath; the later Act of 1537 termed this a mode of warding off the wrath of Deity; this punishment was reserved by later acts for repeated perjuries deliberately made. Witchcraft would seem, in the Ecclesiastical Law of Christian II, to have already involved the death penalty, if actual injury had been inflicted upon some one; it also punished with whipping a consultation with witches. While the Decrees generally do not expressly deal with this offense, the stake was in use, as is shown by divers judgments under Christian IV (1617); necromancy and superstitious practices were punished with forfeiture of goods and exile.

By sundry other amendments to the penal laws, public punishments were imposed for offenses which had previously been subject to fines only, as well as for misdemeanors which were not violations of any individual right but involved the moral and public order. There was a more general extension of public prosecution; and express declaration is made of the general duty of the public officials to watch over the enforcement of law.

Legislation in the 1600 s.[2] — The internal disorders which devastated Denmark after the death of King Frederick I led to the enactment of severer statutes for the punishment of crimes. With Christian III's ascent to the throne the government acquired increased authority and undertook to extend to the entire kingdom the operation of the penal laws in force in market towns. The crime of murder, hitherto relegated largely to the sphere of private vengeance, was now made subject to public prosecution. The chief obstacle was the insistence of the nobility on the preservation of its privilege to settle its feuds with the armed hand. A measure of considerable progress aimed against this privilege was the Proclamation of May 1, 1618, inhibiting generally duels with firearms. The privileged class, however, continued to exercise its

[2] [This paragraph sums up §§ 163–165 of J. L. A. KOLDERUP-ROSENVINGE's "Grundrids af den danske Retshistorie" (Copenhagen, 3d ed., 1860), together with the notes thereon by J. E. LARSEN in his "Forelæsninger over den danske Retshistorie", §§ 163–165 (Copenhagen, 1861). — ED.]

powerful influence in the government, as is evidenced by its issuance of "letters of release of feud", binding the kin of the person killed, without the cognizance of public authority, during the reign of Christian IV.

A notable feature in the criminal legislation of this period, is that, as a motive for ordaining punishment for crime, in addition to securing the order of the State and preventing crime, it professes to aim at diverting the wrath of God, and his punishment of the people.

Offenses penalized by capital punishment were: (1) deliberate murder, committed by those not of the nobility; (2) rape; and (3) adultery. Offenses against the administration of justice were heavily penalized — unrighteous judges, clerks forging the records of the "Thing", and perjurers. While accidental acts were no longer generally held criminal, there was nevertheless retained in the Manor Act of Frederick II the provision of the Law of Erik of Pomerania, prescribing a barbarous penalty for negligently causing a conflagration ("if damage result through the neglect of any one from fire and light, then he shall immediately be seized and thrown into the same fire, if he be caught in the act"). Imprisonment at hard labor at Bremerholm or in the House of Correction became frequent punishments under Christian IV.

The jurisdiction of the State authorities now embraced that of the former ecclesiastical courts, and was extended to include many acts not involving wrongs to individuals. Among the offenses now recognized were witchcraft, vagrancy and beggary, incest, concealment of child-birth, and relapse into the Catholic creed. Moral conditions during the 1500 s had been at a low ebb; the priesthood, monks, and nuns being especially depraved. At the Council of Constance it is recorded that over seven hundred "pleasure-maids" were present at the gathering. Even the Reformation effected little change, and improvement came only with the spread of knowledge. Gluttony, drunkenness, libertinism, and gross living were common. Private feuds and self-redress were frequent. A large number of persons were executed for witchcraft, towards the close of the 1600 s; and among these victims of superstitious creeds are found noble ladies, one of whom, Christence Kruckow, was charged with having instituted at the university a "Stipendium decollatæ virginis."

The dominant principles in the *Swedish-Finnish penal codes* during this period were the following:

(1) The " lex talionis " is the highest justice according to the Law of God, *i.e.*, the Mosaic Law; (2) The legislator shall endeavor to intimidate miscreants from criminal actions by the most severe penalties; (3) The legislator shall seek to soften the wrath of Deity and save the realm from his vengeance by the most severe punishments.

Regarding the first proposition, the Church rules were not only viewed as the sources of the national religion, but also, especially the principles of the Old Testament, were deemed positive legislation of Divine origin, binding on all nations in all ages.

The adherence to the second rule is amply evidenced in penal history, notable in the Manor Laws, the military law, and special ordinances. Thus, Gustavus Adolphus prescribed death for the killing of a stag or a swan.

The doctrine contained in the third principle was followed in many enactments, such as the patent regarding felonies of May 1, 1653, the royal statute regarding fines and breaches of the Sabbath (October 2, 1665), and the law of infanticide (March 1, 1681 and November 15, 1684). Likewise, it appears in the prosecutions for witchcraft during the close of the 1600 s, wherein the " law of God " was enforced without mercy and the witches burned, in order to secure immunity from " the rage of Satan and his cohorts " and to divert the wrath of the Lord from the realm. Nor was this idea confined to offenses against morals and religion; it is notable in the act regarding duels (August 22, 1682).

In course of time, however, the general conscience came to disapprove of these harsh punishments, and while the provisions still lingered in the books, milder penalties were employed in actual practice. The Penal Code of Queen Cristina introduced a system more in accord with this common sense of justice and actual practice. A thorough reform is visible in the Code of 1734 — the labor of a century. Nevertheless, the dominant principles remained unchanged, although the principle was now recognized that the penalty should aim to be only a just retribution. Draconic punishments still remained; capital punishment being prescribed in sixty-eight cases.

Marking an epoch in the development of penal law, is the act of the Swedish Parliament, January 20, 1779, expressing that new humane tendency which became dominant during the latter half of the 1700 s. Gustavus III was well versed in the "enlightened" philosophy of the 1700 s; and it had been his genuine desire to introduce an even more thorough reform than that which was embodied in the statute of 1779.

B. SWITZERLAND [1]

§ 59g. Switzerland in the 1500s and the 1600s; the Reformation Period.	§ 59h. The 1700s; the "Aufklärung" Period.

§ 59g. **The 1500 s and the 1600 s; The Reformation Period.** — Whether the Carolina ever had force in Switzerland, either formally or substantially, opinions have differed widely. Most of its provisions dealt with procedure, and therefore would not be applicable. No doubt it was more or less used by magistrates for their guidance. In matters directly involving the peace-law, the Carolina in Germany displaced the former rules; but in Switzerland the peace-law was little affected by it. For example, the law of self-defense and self-redress was restricted by the Carolina to cases of life and limb, but in Switzerland preserved its larger scope. Again, the attempt as an independent offense was broadly recognized in the Carolina, but was not recognized in Switzerland.

The Reformation, of course, affected the criminal law in Switzerland much as it did in Germany, even in the cantons which remained Catholic. This period of law shows a stern and even harsh spirit of repression, and is in many respects a retrogression. Religion, morality, and authority are its marked elements. Offenses against religion and creed become numerous, as in Germany, and are harshly punished. Blasphemy, adultery, incontinence, and sinful acts generally, become prominent in criminal justice. Church and State mutually assist in the zealous task.

There were, to be sure, differences observable due to local conditions and personalities. Calvin at Geneva, Zwingli at Zürich, Luther in Germany, had dominant influence, each in his own way. Calvin introduced a terrorist ecclesiastical administration, emphatic in its puritanism. Zwingli's nature was liberal and democratic; his heart was with the common people, and he led a struggle against the privileged aristocratic families. Luther was in the confidence of the German territorial princes, and their ambitions were closely related with the success of the Protestant faith. In

[1] [These two sections are by the Editor, using Dr. PFENNINGER's treatise as authority; for this author and work, see the Editorial Preface. — ED.]

Germany, but not in Switzerland, the Roman law was introduced bodily (partly by legislation, partly through the professionally educated judiciary). With it came the doctrine of the ruler's authority as the all-sufficient basis of law. This culminated in the exaltation of judicial discretion as the measure of crimes and penalties, and of governmental absolutism as representing divine authority in the repression of crime and sin. From the excesses of these doctrines the Swiss cantons were relatively exempt.

Nevertheless, Swiss criminal law exhibited the general features of the times, — a harshness and cruelty in the penalties, — an emphasis on the sinfulness of crime, the wrath of God for a people's offenses, and the God-commanded duty of obedience to authority. In Geneva, Calvin's censorial laws, Draconian in their strictness and arbitrariness, were so harshly enforced that at last the town rose and expelled him. But his spirit still dominated. Not until the all-European reaction of Rousseau's time did that community tear itself free from its intellectual slavery and recover its old Swiss spirit of freedom. In his "Lettres de la Montagne," Rousseau describes the abnormal authority of the Geneva Council in criminal matters: "Its power is absolute in every respect. It is prosecutor and judge. It sentences and it executes. It summons, arrests, imprisons, tries, judges, and punishes, — itself alone does all."

And yet this stern and intolerant system had its due place in the history of progress. It led in a great movement of regeneration in morals and the building up of State authority in criminal law. After the political anarchy and the riotous pleasure-loving excesses of the Middle Ages, it signalized a natural reaction towards orderly government and beneficent asceticism and self-castigation. One of the historians of Bern's laws thus sums up the period: "It was not a mere matter of new religious dogmas, but of the renovation of the moral life, personal and national."

§ 59*h*. **The 1700 s; the "Aufklärung" Period** — To reconstruct a picture of the criminal law of the 1700 s is not easy. The sources were multifarious; Roman law, Canon law, and the Carolina; practice-books, judiciary acts, local custumals, — all these were found more or less in every canton. Much of the medieval law persisted, in name at least. The Territorial Law-Book of Glarus, as late as the issues of 1807 and 1835, still preserved parts of the peace-law dating back to the 1400 s. In Schwyz as late as 1700 was found the custom of delivering over the homicide's body to the victim's family. In Glarus the last wager of battle and the last witch-trial took place only in 1707.

But the cruelest of the old penalties had fallen into disuse. In Zürich, empaling and immuring had not been inflicted since the 1400 s, nor drowning since 1615; and by the 1700 s beheading had become the usual mode of execution. The figures of executions in Zürich and Schwyz show plainly the diminishing harshness: in the 1500 s, 572 executions; in the 1600 s, 336; in the 1700 s, 149. The modes of execution are equally significant: in the 1500 s, by fire 61, by gallows 55, by drowning 53; in the 1600 s, by fire 14, by gallows 10, by drowning 9; in the 1700 s, by fire 2, by gallows 16, by the wheel 1, by the sword (beheading) 106.

Most of the changes towards progress came about by judicial practice; express legislation is found for only the extremest defects; in the Bern Law-Book revisions from 1753 to 1793 is almost nothing of importance. But though legislation was not active, public opinion, as reflected in the literature of the period, was fully responsive to the new thought of the times. The "Aufklärung" period, here as in Germany — that movement of the leaders of educated thought to banish popular error and superstition and to introduce liberal thinking and "enlightenment" — showed its influence in criminal justice. The all-European agitation against torture received a welcome here and showed early results. Montesquieu's influence was widely felt. The beneficent possibilities of education found some of their leading apostles in Switzerland.

And as the new period of the 1800 s arrived, ushered in by the French Revolution, what were some of the principal features in which the survival of the traditional ideas of Swiss criminal law might still be seen?

1. The old peace-law still preserved its rules for the citizen's duty to intervene by parting the combatants and giving information to the court. The principle of honor in word and act was still a living one. Stealing and fraud were still more heavily penalized than wounding or even manslaughter; in Schwyz two men were hung for stealing and fraud as late as 1822. The absconding debtor was regarded as a thief. Gambling, the squandering of family property, shirking of labor, and the like, were strictly reprehended. The modern point of view, which condones or admires smart dealing, tricky business methods, and clever evasion of obligations, so long as one keeps out of jail, was as yet nowhere

accepted in Switzerland. The primitive notions still prevailed that one's word should be as good as gold,—" honor with the word and with the sword." The Territorial Law-Book of Glarus declared that he who fails to pay his debts shall no longer be trusted in his word; the bankrupt was " honor-less "; and in this canton, it is recorded, so firm was the sense of honor that ordinarily neither note nor receipt was given when money passed.

2. In some of the cantons a mildness of penalties, remarkable for this period, is observable. In Uri, the death penalty was restricted to murder and arson. The wrongdoer is often described in the judgments as only a misguided man; the intercession of his family is given weight; the sentence is modified " in view of the circumstances of the case." No doubt this lenity may be attributed to the (nowadays often criticized) tendency of lay judges to undue weakness in imposing extreme penalties; and in these primitive cantons the tribunals were composed sometimes of as many as 200 or more citizens. But there is a general atmosphere of primitive patriarchalism,—benevolent, and yet crude in its methods. Flogging remained long in use as a judicial penalty; a notorious case of excess, in Uri, as late as 1865, aroused national resentment, and evoked even foreign comments on " the barbarous justice of Swiss democracy." Other penalties also serve to illustrate the simplicity of a primitive community,—confession, church-penance, listening to an appointed sermon, pilgrimage. And equally suggestive were the sentences to be imprisoned by one's father, to be watched over by one's friends, or to abstain from wine or social company.

3. Nevertheless, the path was already prepared in many ways for accepting the new ideas of Napoleon's and Feuerbach's criminal codes in the next century. The old classical Swiss principle of individual manhood as its own defense, " honor and the sword," had in many cantons gradually become an anachronism. Habitual weapon-bearing, as a general custom, had long disappeared. The traditional right of self-defense and self-redress was strictly limited. The individual had become overshadowed by official authority. The peace-law system was antiquated and inefficient; and with it would disappear the kernel of the old law. A killing while under a special peace might still be legally murder; but the community was ready to accept a new point of view as soon as the law should formally sweep away the relics of the old system. For most of its details were plainly relics of the past. Chiefly in form

only was the criminal law in contrast with the coming ideas; the community was substantially ready for them.

C. NETHERLANDS[1]

§ 59*i*. **Sources of Criminal Law in the Netherlands before the 1500 s.** — After the fall of the Carolingian monarchy, there succeeded an epoch about which little is known. In all probability, the common law together with the King's law, in altered and perfected form, still prevailed in every-day usage, and became predominant as active law through its administration by the justices' courts. With the exception of the written sources of law, in which the common law found sanction, the most important sources of the common law in the 1500 s were the collected customs and usages.

The written law began developing in some sections of Netherland in the 1000 s, in others later, in the shape of charters, privileges, liberties, patents granted by the counts or other territorial lords, as well as municipal and rural laws, decisions, ordinances, court regulations, market privileges, etc. In the field of criminal law, these written sources originally included, as a rule, the assessments of fines; furthermore, they corroborated the common law as regarded the ordinary crimes, or they fixed penalties for newly defined offenses, *e.g.*, the clipping of money, begging, cattle-stealing, etc. Some of these rural and municipal laws for that period even contain fairly complete codifications of criminal law. For information regarding the law in earlier or later times, the investigator should not overlook the law books, explanations, or compilations such as the invaluable "Law-book of Briel" by Jan Matthyssen, of about 1400, and the "Rural Law of Overyssel" by Melchior Wynhoff in 1559.

The Canon criminal law, although it did not prevail directly in the civil courts, became powerful in more ways than one. It influenced the people to regard crime as a sin (along with the "delicta ecclesiastica", the "delicta civilia" and especially the

[1] [The ensuing three sections are translated (with a few omissions) from §§ 3–11 of Professor G. A. VAN HAMEL'S "Netherlands Criminal Law." For this author and work, see the Editorial Preface. — ED.]

"mixta"), against which the Church threatened her penalties ("pœnitentiæ", "pœnæ medicinales", "pœnæ vindicativæ"). It colored the views of the law-givers, and especially of the writers of standing, who frequently cited ecclesiastical decisions; while judgments of courts were influenced, partly by the Canon law in a narrow sense, partly by the authority of Christianity, in general, — based upon biblical passages, particularly the Mosaic law. Meanwhile, however, with the coming of the Reformation, the Canon law proper gradually ceased to be of importance in the development of the law of crimes in these sections of the country.

§ 59j. **The Roman Law and the Carolina.** — The great event in the history of the law, known as the Reception of Roman Law, exercised in the Netherlands as elsewhere its powerful influence in the field of criminal law. An acquaintance with the Roman law undoubtedly began as early as the 1100 s and 1200 s, when the young men of the Netherlands began to visit the Italian law schools. The Roman law became further known through the development of legal procedure under the influence of those learned jurists who had already begun to exercise control over the government in the cities, but whose direct authority in the matter of the administration of justice assumed a decisive character during the rule of the Burgundian princes. The courts were then being composed of professionally trained jurists, and the Great Council had just been created (1473–1482) and permanently established at Mechelen in 1503.

Roman law had acquired, in the meantime, a positive legal status. The Instruction of Charles the Bold to the Council (1462) is the oldest known authority in which it is ordered to "proceed after the contents and the form of written laws"; while in Friesland, which first acknowledged the authority of the Roman law, the "imperial laws" were definitely adopted by the confirmation letter of Charles V, in 1524. Whether the Roman law carried equal weight in all the provinces depended very naturally upon whether the written criminal law was equally complete in all localities.

That division of classic Roman practice relating to criminal law was, without a doubt, very slow in developing as compared with private law, for no systematic treatment of the law of crimes is to be found in the Roman law-sources. Because of the imperfections and deficiencies of the national criminal law, and the growing need of a system of public law, the Roman criminal law found a fertile soil prepared for its growth and development. The criminal law of which we are speaking is that of the Corpus Juris (mostly contained in "Libri terribiles" XLVII and XLVIII of the Digest, and Liber IX of the Codex). It had developed, (*a*) from the old law of the "delicta privata", (*b*) from the continually expanding "leges publicorum judiciorum" ("crimina publica", "pœnæ legitimæ", "ordinariæ"), (*c*) from the penalizing by means of "Acta" and "Constitutiones" of various acts (more serious forms of the "delicta privata", or actis which could not be classified under any "lex publicorum judiciorum"), to which, as "crimina extraordinaria", with the "extraordinaria cognitio" of the imperial judges, a "pœna extraordinaria" or "arbitraria" was applied. An especially wide choice of penalties under the public law was given in this latter Roman law, *e.g.*, capital punishments of every description; corporal punishments which maimed the victim, and those which did not; confinement at hard labor; confiscation of property, etc. The various crimes were not clearly defined and distinguished, and there was no systematic development of general principles in the early sources. For instance, the definition of the several crimes was not sharply made; and though "dolus" was expressly required, attempt or participation was also included in the general idea of each crime. But the Roman law, including criminal law, as accepted in the 1500 s, was not the pure law of the classic sources. The Roman source law in its original form had been worked over by the Glossators and Postglossators; and the criminal law in particular had been to a certain degree systematized and scientifically treated by such Italian criminalists of the Middle Ages as Albertus Gandinus, Angelus Aretinus, and others. This legal system acquired an ever-increasing influence, as later writers, in the course of time, gradually worked out and applied its principles.[1]

It will thus be seen that there existed in the Netherlands provinces, since approximately the 1500 s, a system of public criminal law which continued in practice until the epoch of the first general codification of the 1800 s, and which, according to the writers of this epoch, was derived from the following sources: the common law, written law in general (imperial, provincial, and local enact-

[1] On the Reception of the Roman Law in the Dutch provinces: *W. Modderman*, "The Reception of the Roman Law" (1873), 63; *G. de Vries Az*, "Historia introducti in provincias, quas deinceps respublica Belgii uniti comprehendit, juris Romani" (1839); and other writings quoted by Modderman.

ments), Roman law, ecclesiastical law (partly canonical and Mosaic in character), and lastly, authoritative writers.

The Constitutio Criminalis Carolina, and the Criminal Ordinances. — Two general ordinances regarding the criminal law must be noted, the Constitution Criminalis Carolina (C.C.C.) of 1532, and the Criminal Ordinances of Philip II of 1570. It has been rightly remarked that " in judging of the authority of these ordinances in the several provinces, two questions in particular must be considered, *i.e.*, to what extent the legislative power of the one who gave the ordinances had developed in each province, and whether the formalities required to make the ordinances binding have everywhere been complied with " (Fockema Andreæ).

The Carolina (" Keyser Karls des fünfften und des heyligen Römischen Reichs peinlich Gerichtsordnung ") is one of the most remarkable of all the relics of historic German criminal law, on account of its origin, contents, and authority. Instituted in 1530 and 1532 by the German diets of Augsberg and Regensburg, it was the outcome of the necessity for combating the many abuses in administration of justice and the lack of knowledge of the prevailing law on the part of the unlearned judges of that period. The German Empire was already fortunate in the possession of the Bambergensis (1507, " mater Carolinæ "), an excellent model containing a systematic collection of Germanic and Roman-Canon criminal law, which had become established under the authority of the Italian criminalists. It was compiled, in part, by Johannes Freiherr of Schwartzenberg and Hohenlandsberg (1528), who also participated in the writing of the Carolina.

The Carolina is an ordinance of 219 Articles, providing for the administration of justice, and largely made up of rules of procedure. Certain provisions of the substantive law of crimes are included in Arts. 104–180, in which may be found not only definitions of various crimes and of a great variety of penalties, but also an elaboration of certain general doctrines, *e.g.*, self-defense, complicity, attempt, and extent of responsibility. While it creates little new law, it sets forth the existing law in intelligible language. It continually advises in doubtful cases the invoking of the " counsel of the jurisconsults ", thus leaving every opportunity for the continuing development of the practice. Though the ordinance (through the " Clausula salvatoria " of the Preface) contains a concession to particularism, and though it did not formally carry the weight of absolutely binding general law, yet, because of its own worth and the additional value which it acquired through use by authoritative writers, it remained the foundation of the general law of crimes in Germany. In certain German States it continued to prevail until 1871, when the code of criminal law for the North German Union was introduced.

It was a debatable question, even in the latter part of the 1700 s, whether this ordinance, intended for and prevailing in the Emperor's German States, had any effect in the Netherlands, particularly in the province of Holland. It is pretty generally understood, however, that not only was it never formally introduced, but that no attempt was made to do so. Nevertheless, it had considerable influence, — partly because some courts acknowledged its authority, and partly because some of the criminalists of the 1700 s (particularly J. S. F. Boehmer, author of the "Meditationes ad C. C. C.", 1770), who took it as the basis of their views, influenced the administration of justice in this country.

A similar controversy had been waged over the binding authority of the Criminal Ordinances of Philip II, of the 5th and 9th of July, 1570, the former treating of the measure, the latter of the method, of Criminal Justice, and both extensively commented on by the Dutch writer Wigele Van Aytta. The basis of the dispute, however, was not the same in the two cases. For these ordinances were instituted by the king as lord of the Netherlands, while they were also proclaimed in some provinces, particularly in Holland and Gelderland. By the Pacification of Ghent (Art. 5), they were "suspended", entirely, according to certain authorities, while according to others, only in regard to the provision concerning heresy; and the Union of Utrecht did not recede from this resolution. Moreover, as the ordinances came from Philip and the Duke of Alva, and were considered to be contrary to the old privileges and customs, their introduction met with continuous opposition on all sides; but they were nevertheless followed in very many provisions, particularly by the law courts of Holland. "During the period of the Republic, the ordinances retained a certain formal value, but they had no binding authority" (R. Fruin). Meanwhile, it should be noted that but few provisions of substantive criminal law are contained in these Ordinances, and these are found almost exclusively in the first-named Ordinance; among them being provisions in regard to crimes affecting the administration of justice, the prohibiting of private composition for offenses, principles regarding uniform rules of punishment, with certain discretionary penalties specified, and a provision that a person should be condemned only according to written laws, etc.[2]

Nothing came of the attempts of Charles V and Philip to collect the customs of the several parts of the country, and consolidate and unify the law; for the Revolution broke out, and the course then taken by political events frustrated this design. Consequently, the various inequalities and uncertainties of the law continued a part of the system until the codification of 1809. As late as the end of the 1700 s the question was officially mooted, in a case of murder, whether justice should be administered according to the Roman law, the Mosaic law, the Carolina, or an old charter of 1342.

§ 59*k*. **General Features of the Criminal Law from Later Medieval Times to the 1700 s.** — Amidst so much uncertainty in the law, with so many situations on which the laws were silent, it was not surprising that resort was had to the decisions and writings of famous jurists. The quotations found in the works of the different Dutch writers of both an earlier and a later period serve as proof of this condition of affairs. To be sure, the customs, some written laws, proclamations, ordinances, statutes, etc., selections from the Roman law sources, and from the Bible, are also quoted, but the principal reference is to the army of authorities, beginning with the Glossators, down to the immediate predecessors or contemporaries of the author. The Dutch writers of the different periods are therefore of great importance.

As representative of the 1500 s must be named Jodocus Damhouder of Bruges (1507–1581), a Fleming, whose "Praxis rerum criminalium" went through various editions in Latin, Dutch, and French, and became an authority in other countries also.[1] In the 1600 s

[2] As to the authority of the Carolina in the Netherlands, see *J. M. Kemper*, "Introduction to the Criminal Law", p. 160, and *J. A. Fruin*, "Vaderl. Letteroef.", 1867, p. 340.
As to the authority of Philip's Ordinances, see *Kemper*, *ib.* p. 168; *Fruin*, *ib.* p. 432; *A. Oudeman*, "Criminal Procedure and Criminal Law", 1873, p. 3; *B. Voorda*, "The Criminal Ordinances", 1792, Introd. §§ 4–6.

[1] Damhouder's treatise was published in three languages, first in Latin, then in Dutch, and finally in French; the Latin edition being the most ample. The first edition appeared in 1555, then numerous others in the 1500 s and the 1600 s; a German one appeared in 1565. It was afterwards discovered that Damhouder had plagiarized his book almost entirely from the "Criminal Practice" ("Practycke Crimineele") of *Philips Wielant* (1439–1519), a Ghent lawyer. The only known manuscript of Wielant's work, accidentally discovered, was edited in 1872 (Ghent) by *August Orts*, who writes: "Damhouder of Bruges adorned himself with the feathers of the peacock; the European fame enjoyed by

came Antonius Matthæus (1601–1654), professor at Hardewyk and Utrecht, who in his work "De Criminibus" (which also includes a treatise on the Utrecht municipal law) went back to the sources of the Roman law, as distinct from Germanic and Canon law acquiring, for this reason, a wide influence abroad in the field of scientific law. Belonging also in this century were Hugo Grotius, who wrote the "Introduction to Dutch Law"; S. van Groenewegen; Joh. Voet (1719), author of "Commentarii ad Pandectas"; F. Zypaeus; Pieter Bort, counsel for the courts of Holland and West Friesland, author of a "Treatise on Criminal Matters"; and Simon van Leeuwen, whose writings in the field of criminal law are indispensable guides to the administration of justice and the conceptions of law of this period. In the 1700 s, the principal writers were E. van Zurck, on the law of Holland, J. Schrassert, on the law of Gelderland, J. Moorman, and J. J. van Hasselt, J. L. Kersteman, and Prof. B. Voorda; and (during the latter part of the 1700 s and the early 1800 s) J. van der Linden, and others.

The writers outside the Netherlands, who were quoted as authoritative, include first, the great masters among the Glossators and Post-glossators who dealt with Roman law in general, particularly Bartolus (1357) and his pupil Baldus (1400); second, the writers on Italian criminal practice of the 1300 s and 1400 s (developed from Roman principles) such as Albertus Gandinus; Jacobus de Belvisio (died 1335); and Angelus Aretinus. The Italian criminalists of the 1500 s exerted still a strong influence: Hippolytus de Marsiliis (Bologna, died 1529), Aegidius Bossius (died 1546); and most important of all, Julius Clarus (member of the Supreme Court at Milan; died 1607), and Prosper Farinacius (Attorney-general at Rome; died 1618). Jurists of other countries were also cited, among them being the Frenchman Antonius Faber (died 1624); the Spaniard Antonio de Gomez, professor at Salamanca (1st half of the 1500 s); such German writers as Andreas Gail, "the German Papinian" (Chancellor of the Elector of Cologne; died 1587), and particularly the Saxons, Matthias Berlichius (professor at Leipzig; died 1638), and his still more famous and influential successor, the learned Benedictus Carpzovius (member of the Supreme Court and professor at Leipzig; died 1666). The most important work of Carpzovius was the "Practica nova Imperialis Saxonica rerum criminalium"; a Dutch translation of it,

him was fraudulently obtained, — stolen from its lawful owner, Wielant of Ghent."

made with some abridgments by Dr. Didarik van Hogendorf, a judge of Rotterdam, remained authoritative in the Netherlands even longer than in Germany, because of its intrinsic worth and the method of its presentation, which was both systematic and adapted to the needs of the practice. Finally, toward the end of the 1700 s, are to be noted as no less authoritative the "Meditationes ad Constitutionem Criminalem Carolinam" already mentioned, by J. S. F. Boehmer (1704–1772); the notes on the work of Carpzovius, by the same writer; the manuals of Boehmer and Meisler, recommended by van der Linden for university studies; and the work of Quistorp, and others, quoted by Meister, and after him referred to as authority in preference to his own work.

It must not be forgotten, with regard to this enumeration, that, with the growth of less drastic principles, and more reasonable scientific conceptions, many of the older writers were abandoned as authorities, and there arose representatives of the new order, who will be later mentioned.

Character of Criminal Law of this Period. — The character of the substantive criminal law (which, as derived from the various above-mentioned sources, prevailed until the first general codification) naturally resembled in many particulars the criminal law of other countries.

Viewed from the standpoint of form, the variety of sources and the independence of the numerous courts resulted in numerous striking inequalities in the law, which could be obviated only by a general codification. A phenomenon of much greater significance, and one which tended to become even more widespread, is the fact that, owing partly to the instability, incompleteness, and confusion of the sources, there was an ever-increasing arbitrariness in the administration of the criminal law, by virtue of which many decisive questions could be decided "at the discretion of the judge." This power of the court was exercised in changing and alleviating the ordinary fixed penalties of the common law, or written law, whenever there appeared "great and notable reasons." In some cases the judge might alter the method of capital punishment and increase its severity; in others, the written law or practice left the judge the choice of an exceptional penalty, *i.e.*, fine, imprisonment, lighter corporal punishment, or exile, in cases where the offense was not serious or "full proof" of the offense was lacking. In some instances, even the determination of an act's criminality was lodged in the court, when the act done was one for which no penalty had been provided in the written law. Now and then, contrary to the old but well-acknowledged rule, the infliction of capital punishment for acts never before expressly so penalized by any law, was left to the discretion of the judge. And besides this domination of the judge's discretion, another abuse of authority was not uncommon, in that parties accused of certain crimes either less serious in nature or difficult of proof (for instance, adultery) often compromised with the bailiffs and justices, by buying off the prosecution.

The main feature of the substantive criminal law of this period was its almost exclusive domination by the passion to deter from crime by severity and cruelty. Capital punishment was employed on a large scale and for all kinds of crime; and this penalty was inflicted in various cruel ways, — hanging, beheading, breaking on the wheel, drowning, burning, even quartering, — sometimes prescribed by written law, sometimes left to the judge's discretion. Corporal punishment — sometimes in the form simply of torture, though frequently carried to the extent of maiming members of the body or destroying the organs of senses — was frequently employed, either by way of increasing the severity of capital punishment or of accompanying the penalty of exile or of infamy. The complete or partial confiscation of property was also a frequent penalty. Confinement in prisons played a minor part; the rule ran that "the dungeon exists for detention, and not for punishment"; but one who suffered detention in the dungeons was often exposed to everything from which even a cruel man would protect his beasts (Dr. Schorer). In addition to all these penalties were the exquisite cruelties of the rack, *i.e.*, "the more thorough examination", the practice of questioning prisoners (in the so-called "extraordinary" procedure) for the purpose of inducing their confession. Through a misunderstanding (due to a printer's error in one of Philip's Ordinances), the rack was employed for this purpose, not only in cases of overwhelming evidence, but also (contrary to the original rule) in cases where the evidence was altogether insufficient. — Prosecutions for witchcraft, and the burning and banishing of witches, were another feature of the times — a terrible demonstration of the effect of superstition. And this entire system of cruelty and ignorance was upheld in subtle essays, supported by the most learned authorities, and administered by the most venerable and conscientious men.

Yet it must never be forgotten that in comparison with other countries the Netherlands led in the hope for better things. The first authoritative voice raised against prosecutions for witchcraft was that of the physician, Johannes Wier (1563) of Arnhem. The medical faculty of Leyden also took its stand against the practice. Although witches were burned in German towns until the middle of the 1700 s, the last one executed in the Netherlands was in 1597, the last one exiled in 1610. Shortly afterwards S. van Leeuwen publicly denounced prosecutions for witchcraft as a mark of superstition. The rack, it is true, was not formally abolished until 1798, and the authorities contrived to maintain it even later; in 1798, it was defended by one Voorda, as indispensable, "unless the common welfare was to be sacrified to rogues and villains"; but by that time the institution was already thoroughly discountenanced. Confiscation of property was abolished in Holland in 1732, in Zealand in 1735, and in Gelderland. As early as the end of the 1500 s and the early part of the 1600 s punishment by imprisonment was introduced; these "rasp-houses" and houses of correction, originally designed for youthful criminals, were later on used for adults also; and "steady labor" was made a part of the penalty, "as a means of bettering their lives." In general, however, the Netherlands during this period made a very poor showing in the field of criminal law.

The Reform Movement of the Later 1700 s. — In the second half of the 1700 s, a strong movement for reform developed throughout Europe. Before long, it led to the diminution of the worst abuses, and, toward the end of the century, destroyed them altogether. But its effect on criminal law and procedure was not completed until well on in the 1800 s. This reform movement started from below, in a suddenly-awakened popular opinion, and was directed against the unfair methods and the subtle learning of the authorities in the administration of criminal justice. It soon gained a foothold in all circles of thought and among all nationalities. Its origin may be ascribed primarily to two events, which made an overwhelming impression on public opinion. The first was the conviction and execution of Jean Calas, in the criminal court of Toulouse; falsely accused of the murder of his son, he was condemned to death and broken on the wheel; Voltaire, in 1752, exposed this case to the world in all its injustice.[2] The second event

[2] For the celebrated case of Calas, *Coquerel*, "Jean Calas et sa famille" (1858); *Hertz*, "Voltaire und der französische Strafrechtspflege im 18ten Jahrhundert" (1887), p. 157. In consequence of Voltaire's efforts, the judgment against Calas was afterwards (1765) set aside.

was the publication of Beccaria's treatise, "Dei delitti e delle pene," which protested against the death penalty, corporal punishments, the rack, and other iniquities of the old system of criminal justice. This work, though scientifically not well thought out, won a hearing by the fervor of its style. It demands were immediately echoed on all sides. It was "a cry of distress uttered from the conscience of mankind", and it was read in almost every European language.

This reform movement, however, was merely one of the phenomena of the so-called era of "Enlightenment" ("Aufklärung"), when the contest between freedom of thought, on the one hand, and tradition on the other, was being waged along so many different lines. The protest against cruelty of the criminal law found support in the spirit of the times. The reform movement was largely instituted and guided by the representatives of the philosophical school, then becoming active in the entire field of natural law. Chr. Thomasius (1665–1728), in particular, by his doctrine of discrimination between law and morality, and his dissertations against the practices of witchcraft, the rack, and degrading punishments, may be considered the direct forerunner of this entire period. In the second half of the 1700 s its leaders were Rousseau, Montesquieu, Voltaire, and their sympathizers, the encyclopædists and the humanists, in France, Wieland and the school of Wolff (Engelhard, 1750) in Germany, Filangieri in Italy. They arraigned the antiquated criminal law at the bar of Reason. Voltaire took personal interest in obtaining freedom for numerous innocent victims of the law, and his example was imitated. Criminal justice became a prominent topic of discussion in scientific and literary circles. A society of economists at Bern offered a prize for the best essay on the great subject (1783); the essay by Globig and Huster was the successful one among forty-four competitors. Enlightened princes, advised by wise statesmen, sought to embody the new ideas in laws and ordinances, — Catherine II of Russia, in her Instruction to the Commission on a Draft Penal Code (1768); Leopold II of Tuscany, in a Penal Code abolishing the death penalty (1786); Frederick II of Prussia, in several ordinances reforming criminal procedure (1780); Maria Theresa of Austria, whose efforts (advised by Sonnenfels) resulted, however, only in a new code (the Theresiana, 1768) imbued with the old spirit, and her son Joseph II, in a Penal Code (1787) which became the basis for future advances. But much of all this effort was only transitory and inadequate in its effects. Not until the tremendous political shock of the French Revolution was felt did the old criminal system begin really to crumble away.

The new thought penetrated but slowly in the Netherlands. It had its supporters (such as Schorer) and its prudent but sympathetic advocates (such as Calhoen). It had also its opponents (such as Barels and Voorda), warning all against "the errors of the new-fashioned philanthropy." But the spirit of the times had rendered the philosophy of the law attractive. Particularly after the rise of new scientific methods in law in Germany, criminal authorities of a very different quality from those of former times had become available. As J. M. Kemper expresses it, "the appeal to philosophical German and French writers was already being voiced before the courts almost as often as one had heard exclusively, in former years, the names of Damhouder, Matthæus, and Carpzovius." At first, the manuals by Quisdorp, Boehmer, and others, before mentioned, were cited. Later, the works of Klein, Kleinschrod, Grolman, and Feuerbach, the founders of the new German science of criminal law, replaced the former philosophers. But legislation and unity of legislation were chiefly necessary for the administration of justice and the advancement of legal science. These were made possible by the Dutch revolution of 1795.

TITLE IV. THE FRENCH REVOLUTIONARY PERIOD

Chapter XII

THE FRENCH REVOLUTIONARY REFORMS[1]

§ 60*a*. **Reform Movements on the Eve of the Revolution.** — It does indeed seem, when we study our criminal law of the Old Régime, and compare it with that of the last centuries of the Roman Empire and the first centuries of the Middle Ages, that civilization had made no progress on the subject of penal law, — had in fact remained stationary. Throughout it is marked by the same defects, in each of these epochs. Punishments are unequal; they vary according to the status or rank of the offenders rather than the nature of the crime. Punishments are also cruel and barbarous in their method — the base of the system is the death penalty, and a prodigal use of bodily mutilations. Furthermore, punishments are variable in discretion; crimes are loosely defined; and the individual has no security against excess of severity in the State's repression of crime. Finally, ignorance, prejudice, and emotional violence breed imaginary crimes; and the scope of penal law extends beyond the regulation of social relations and trespasses even upon the domain of conscience.

It is well to recall these shortcomings, so that we may better understand the progress which has taken place and the benefits for which we are here indebted to the French Revolution. In fact, though it is not incorrect to say that the whole of the old French civil law persisted (with some modifications) in the present civil Code,[2] it can be affirmed, nevertheless, that the modern penal law

[1] [§§ 60*a*, 60*b* = §§ 67, 69–74, pp. 118, 122–131, of Vol. I of Professor R. Garraud's "Traité théorique et pratique du droit pénal français" (2° ed., 1898). For this author and work, see the Editorial Preface. These sections replace § 60 of Professor *von Bar's* text. — Ed.]

[2] *Cf. Valette*, "De la persistance de ensemble du droit civil français pendant et après la Révolution de 1789" (Mélanges, Vol. II, p. 250); *Paul Viollet*, "Précis de l'histoire du droit français," p. 206.

has completely broken with the old penal law, and that a comparison between the two consists mainly in contrasts. This idea the eminent Boitard emphasized in his first chapter: [3] "Our new laws are not, as are our civil laws, the reproduction, more or less faithful, more or less exact, of principles accepted in former times. *In the penal law, almost everything is new; almost everything has felt keenly the influence of the times, the customs, and the revolutions.*" [4] To be convinced of this, it would suffice to glance at the passage of Pothier [5] in which the learned author sums up the criminal law of the late 1700 s.

In the 1600 s public opinion had not shown itself hostile to the criminal system of the times. Its cruelty, its inequality, its arbitrariness, are all deemed, by the best minds, to be necessary harshness.[6] In the 1700 s, the point of view begins to change. The Revolution, with its alleviations of the penal law, was only effecting reforms already ripe, because they were demanded by public opinion. How is this change of attitude to be explained? It was due in part to the philosophic movement which marked the

[3] [*Boitard*, "Leçons sur les codes pénals et d'instruction criminelle", 1st ed., Paris, 1836–9; 13th ed., 1896. — ED.]

[4] I am well aware that the eminent criminalist *Faustin-Hélie*, in his notable preface to *Boitard's* "Leçons sur les Codes pénals et d'instruction criminelle" has vigorously disputed this judgment of the professor whose work he was editing. Nonetheless, it is substantially correct. The penal system of our modern law bears no resemblance to the penal system of the ancient law. As for the method of prosecution, it is only the irreducible minimum which has come down through the centuries. But the dross of the old system, the crimes against religion, etc., have been left out of the new law. The comments of Faustin-Hélie are correct only in their application to criminal procedure, which is indeed too greatly saturated even to-day with the spirit of past times.

[5] "Traité de la procédure criminelle," section V, § 6.

[6] We must remember, of course, that the repressive methods of those days corresponded to conditions of criminality altogether different from ours. Studies of the history of criminality have made little headway; but we have here a rich field for the historian and the moralist. From this standpoint, three facts at least seem to stand out, in the light of the information which we possess on the condition of France in the 1400 s, 1500 s, and 1600 s: 1st, Predominance of violent criminality over cunning criminality; 2d, Less criminal individualism than to-day: offenses are more often committed in a band or a group; 3d, As far as we can estimate the importance of the criminality of those times, in the absence of statistics, we may affirm that the number of crimes was greater at that epoch than in our days (*Berriat Saint-Prix*, "Rev. etrang.", 1845, p. 461). On the state of ancient criminality: *Tarde*, "L'archéologie criminelle en Périgord", in "Etudes pénales et sociales", p. 193; *Marty*, "Recherches sur l'archéologie criminelle dans l'Yonne" ("Arch. d'anthr.", 1895, p. 381); *A. Corre* and *P. Aubry*, "Documents de criminologie retrospective" (Arch., 1894, pp. 181, 312, 684). *Cf. Clement*, "La police sous Louis XIV", 1886; *Fléchier*, "Mémoire sur les grands jours d'Auvergne"; *Taine*, "Origines de la France contemporaine, L'ancien régime", Vol. I, *passim.*

second half of the 1700 s, and rested on two new ideas: *reason* and *humanity*. As early as 1721, Montesquieu, in the "Lettres persanes", had discoursed on the nature and the efficacy of punishments; then, in book 6, chap. 12, of the "Esprit des lois", he expounded the true principles of a penal law. But it was reserved for Beccaría, a disciple of Montesquieu, to give to Italy the glory of taking the initiative in the movement of reform. In all epochs Italy has been the classical land of criminal law. Of the works which contributed to make her fame in this period, none has influenced the ideas and usages of Europe to an extent comparable with Beccaría's "Treatise on Crimes and Penalties", which appeared in 1766.[7] Beccaría was the first to formulate precisely the criticisms of the old system and to propose a plan of reform. He drew up, as it were, a declaration of humanity's claims against the criminal law.

Beccaría's doctrines were immediately commented upon and developed in France. Rousseau, to be sure, busy mainly with questions of morals and of politics, gave little attention to criminal law: he devoted to it, in passing, a word or two in his "Contrat social"; but even this much was destined to have a great influence on penal legislation. Villemain has pointed out, as a characteristic trait of the years just preceding the Revolution, "philosophy's invasion of business, of government, of law, — speculative innovation transformed into active and real innovation." At the head of this movement we find Voltaire; he writes "that he is doing nothing but read trials";[8] and he published a commentary on the "Traité des délits et des peines." The learned

[7] *Beccaría*, "Dei delitti e delle pene", Munich, 1766, in octavo. No treatise on criminal law has been reprinted so often. A French edition of this work was published under the title: "Des délits et des peines", new edition, with an introduction and a commentary by *Faustin-Hélie*, 1856. See "Beccaria et le droit pénal, Essai", by *Cesare Cantù*, translated, annotated, and preceded by a preface and an introduction by *Jules Lacointa* and *C. Delpech* (1886, Paris, Firmin-Didot). This treatise on crimes and punishments touches or discusses the most important questions of criminal law, but more particularly it opposes the death penalty and the use of torture. It secures proper limitations for the repressive system by the principle of reducing punishments to the severity necessary for maintaining public safety. It may be said that the classical school of criminal law in the 1800 s was the product of this marvellous little book of Beccaría. Has this school finished its historical cycle, as some now maintain? It is surely true, at all events, that penal law is being transformed, and that the ideas of Beccaría are being abandoned on many points to-day.

[8] See what is said by *Esmein*, "History of Continental Criminal Procedure", p. 362 [Vol. V of this Series] on the ideas and works of the three men who did most among the philosophers for the reform of criminal law, Montesquieu, Beccaría, and Voltaire.

Academies interested themselves in the subject; they assigned for prize-essay competitions "this important subject", as Boucher d'Argis called it;[9] among the prize-winners in these competitions were men who later played an important rôle in the Revolution, — and we note among these names, not without some surprise, Robespierre and Marat.[10] The movement spread to the bench and the bar. Attorney-General Servan reproduced the ideas of Beccaría in his address of 1766 on the "Administration de la justice criminelle", which caused such a great stir.[11] The penal institutions of the time found defenders only among a few jurists who were behind the times.[12]

[9] "Observations sur les lois criminelles, Avant-propos", p. 8.

[10] *Robespierre*, advocate at Arras, was the author of a "Mémoire sur le préjugé qui étend à la famille du coupable la honte des peines infamantes", an essay awarded a prize by the Academy of Metz in 1784. *Marat* was the author of a "Plan de législation criminelle" (1st ed., 1780; 2d ed., 1790).

[11] This address is to be found in Volume IV, p. 332, of the first series of "Barreau français", published by Clair and Clapier. One eloquent and courageous passage in that beautiful address has become classical: "Lift your eyes", said he to his colleagues, "and see above your heads the image of our Lord, himself once an innocent man on trial. You are men, — be human. You are judges, — be just. You are Christians, — be merciful. Men, judges, Christians, whoever you be, show consideration to the unfortunate." *Cf.* in Vol. III, p. 77, of the same work a "Mémoire pour trois hommes condamnés à la roue", published by Chief Justice *Dupaty*, in which the author criticises vigorously the inquisitorial procedure and the system of legal proofs; this memoir was, however, suppressed by a decree of the Paris Parliament, of August 11, 1786, on motion of the then attorney-general, Louis Séguier. *Esmein, op. cit.*, p. 374, gives a summary of this curious argument, delivered on the very eve of the Revolution by a high legal official.

[12] Jousse and Muyart de Vouglans, the two leading criminalists of the epoch, opposed the proposed reforms. The latter even wrote a refutation of the "Traité des délits et des peines" of Beccaria, under the title: "Lettre contenant la réfutation de quelques principes hasardés dans le traité des délits et des peines", Geneva, 1767. To the psychologist this work reveals a strange state of mind in the most distinguished criminalist of his time. Muyart de Vouglans obviously does not understand Beccaria. He regards him as a lunatic (p. 22). What astonishes Muyart most is to find a work on criminal legislation which is not primarily a technical book devoted to positive law (p. 25). As for the proposals which he discovers in the treatise of Beccaria and which he points out with indignation to public opinion as so many social heresies (pp. 6 to 17), they are the very truths which were to become the axioms of criminal justice: equality before the law, exemption of the accused from compulsory oath, and the abolition of torture.

Jousse, in the preface of his "Traité de la justice criminelle", p. 64, expressed himself thus: "The 'Traité des délits et des peines' tends to establish a system of the most dangerous kind. It reveals novel ideas which, if they were to be adopted, would do nothing less than overthrow the laws hitherto accepted by the most civilized nations; they would injure religion, morals, and the sacred maxims of the government." In such terms, however, men have always defended existing institutions, which they considered fundamental, and fought the reform of them. See on this point: *Esmein, op. cit.*, p. 370.

But none of these defenses found favor in public opinion. The legal system, even before the end of the Old Régime, itself had begun to feel the need of reform. In Russia, Catherine II had shown encouragement to the philosophers, and gave instructions for drafting a criminal code. In Germany, Frederick II and Joseph II, influenced by the ideas of the encyclopedists, had introduced some radical reforms in the cruel system then prevailing; the former had begun his reign by the abolition of torture; the latter promulgated a penal Code in which the death penalty was omitted, save for military crimes. In Tuscany, also, the Grand Duke Leopold suppressed the death penalty. In France itself, under the same influence, partial and gradual mitigations were introduced into the criminal law. A royal declaration of August 24, 1780, abolished the preliminary torture. On the eve of the Revolution (May 8, 1788) an edict was issued, announcing a general reform in criminal procedure, and, in the meantime, repealing "several abuses" which pressed for a remedy:[13] 1st, the use of the culprit's kneeling-stool was forbidden; 2d, judgments of conviction must state the reasons therefor; 3d, the abolition of the preliminary torture was confirmed, and torture after judgment was abolished; 4th, sentences involving capital punishment were to be executed, as a rule, only a month after confirmation; 5th, persons acquitted were given the right to reparation for injury to repute. This edict indeed was not carried into effect[14]; but it showed that the reforms were ripening, and that it remained only for the will of the nation to achieve them. Public opinion revealed a unanimity of this sort on no others of the many questions agitated at this period. In the reports made from the various provinces to the States-General, we find already a demand for the reforms which the Constitutional Assembly was to realize,— reforms embodying the ideas of the philosophers of the 1700s: 1st, equality, individuality, and mitigation of the penal system; 2d, suppression of discretionary powers of the judge, both in the definition of criminal acts and of the determination of punishments; 3d, abolition of crimes against religion and morals; 4th, publicity of procedure; 5th, assistance of counsel; 6th, abolition of the accused's compulsory oath; 7th, duty to state the grounds for judgment, and to declare them publicly; 8th, the institution of the jury. Such,

[13] The text will be found in *Isambert*, "Anciennes lois", Vol. XXVIII, p. 527.

[14] See on this point, *Esmein*, *op. cit.*, p. 397.

in their main outlines, were the ideas which were to serve as a basis for the new criminal law.[15]

§ 60*b*. **The Code of 1791, and the Code of Brumaire.** — The work done by the Constitutional Assembly in the domain of penal law was of a double sort. In the first place, it determined to place on record the new principles formulated for the penal system by the philosophy of the 1700 s. In the next place, it set about realizing these principles in the administration of justice, and codifying the law.

The principles were contained in the Declaration of the Rights of Man, of August 26, 1789, and in a few other enactments, especially the decrees of January 21, 1790, and of August 16 to 24, 1790. According to the terms of Art. 2 of the Declaration of Rights, the aim of every political society is " the preservation of the natural and inalienable rights of man." This was a principle borrowed from the theories of the " contrat social " ; its corollary was that the State power ought and can concern itself only in maintaining " good order " in the relations of men among themselves. Hence, the two following consequences: 1st, As to *crimes:* " The law has the right to prohibit only actions harmful to society." Moreover, no person is to be interfered with on account of his opinions, even on the subject of religion, provided their expression does not in any way disturb public order. With the recognition of this sacred principle of liberty of conscience there disappeared all the prosecutions which our early lawyers called " crimes of lèse majesté against God ", such as blasphemy, heresy, sorcery, etc. 2d, As to *penalties:* " The law shall inflict only such punishments as are strictly and clearly necessary." To harmonize the penal system with these principles, the Constitutional Assembly strove to remove all the inconsistent features of our old criminal system. Punishments had been determined according to the judge's discretion; so the Assembly laid down, in Art. 8 of the Declaration, that " *no person shall be punished except by virtue of a law enacted and promulgated previous to the crime and applicable according to its terms.*" Penalties had been unequal; so the Assembly decreed, in Art. 1 of the law of January 21, 1790, " *that offenses of the same nature shall be punished by the same kind of penalties, whatever be the rank and the station of*

[15] *Cf. A. Desjardins*, "Les cahiers des Etats généraux en 1789 et la législation criminelle" (Paris, 1883). See also: *Esmein, op. cit.*, pp. 397 to 402.

the offender "; and Title 1 of the Constitution of September 3, 1790, gave to this principle the status of a constitutional law. Punishments had not always been personal (*i.e.* confined to the offender himself); so the law of January 21, 1790, declared that "*neither the death penalty nor any infamous punishment whatever shall carry with it an imputation upon the offender's family*", since "*the honor of those who belong to his family is in no wise tarnished*", and by the same Article, the relatives of the offender "*shall continue to be eligible to all kinds of professions, employments, and offices.*" The penalty of general confiscation of property was abolished. Punishment was not to outlive the offender's death; not only were there to be no more proceedings against offenders dying before trial, but the corpse of an executed man was to be given back to his family on request. The record of his death was in no wise to mention the mode of death.

Having thus proclaimed the basic principles of penal law, it remained to give effect to them. The ensuing legislation for the system of prosecution and detection was divided into three parts, general (or, municipal), correctional, and detective; corresponding to the three classes of offenses, general (or, municipal) offenses, correctional offenses, and offenses against public security. To mark outwardly this distinction, the Constitutional Assembly enacted two separate Codes, one for crimes in general, the other for misdemeanors; the Penal Code of October 6, 1791, was for crimes; the law of July 22, 1791, for misdemeanors. This system has some disadvantages, to which we shall return.

The Code of October 6, 1791, is exclusively a penal code.[1] It is in two parts, each subdivided into titles and sections. The first part, entitled "Sentences", includes the general penal law, and is divided into seven titles. These titles deal with: 1st, criminal punishments (tit. 1), which are death, labor in chains, reclusion (in a penitentiary), confinement (shutting up the offender in a lighted place without chains or bonds), detention, transportation, civic degradation and the "carcan"; 2d, aggravation of penalties, applicable to second offenders (tit. 2) (the recidivist first suffers the ordinary punishment inflicted for the new crime which he has committed, and is then transferred for the rest of his life to a place appointed for the transportation of criminals); 3d, the manner of enforcing sentences against those who fail to appear for trial (tit. 3); 4th, the legal consequences of sentences (tit. 4);

[1] Such is, moreover, the name under which it has always been known.

5th, age of the offender, as affecting the nature and duration of the punishment (tit. 5); 6th, periods of limitation for crimes (tit. 6); 7th, the rehabilitation of convicted offenders (tit. 7). The second part of this Code, entitled: "Crimes and their punishment", embraces the definitions of specific crimes, and is subdivided into two titles; the first deals with crimes and attempts against public interests, the second, with crimes against individuals. Crimes against public interests include: 1st, crimes against the external safety of the State (section 1); 2d, crimes against the internal safety (section 2); 3d, crimes and attempts against the constitution (section 3); 4th, offenses of individuals against the respect and obedience due to the law and to the authority of officers of the law (section 4); 5th, crimes of public officers in the exercise of powers entrusted to them (section 5); 6th, crimes against public property. Crimes against individuals are subdivided into: 1st, crimes and attempts against persons (section 1); 2d, crimes and misdemeanors against property (section 2). This second part of the Code ends with a third Title (which could better have been placed in the first part) dealing with the rules for accomplices, joint offenders, etc.

The law of July 17 and 22, 1791, deals with jurisdiction and prosecution, but also defines and classifies municipal and correctional misdemeanors and the punishments applicable to them. For these offenses it is both a code of procedure and a penal code. In the penal part, municipal misdemeanors are enumerated, with the punishments applicable. Correctional misdemeanors are grouped under five great divisions. "Misdemeanors punishable by the correctional courts", it provides (tit. II, Art. 7), "shall be: 1st, misdemeanors against good morals; 2d, public disturbances of the exercise of any religious cult; 3d, insults and serious violence to the person; 4th, disturbances of the social welfare and of the public peace, by begging, riots, mobs, or other misdemeanors; 5th, the attempts against the property of individuals, by damage, larceny or ordinary theft, swindling, and the opening of gambling houses where the public is admitted."

To these two laws there was added, four years later, the "Code of misdemeanors and punishments", of the 3d Brumaire, year IV (October 25, 1795). It was drafted by Merlin[2] and, after

[2] A commission of eleven members had been appointed under a decree of 25th Fructidor, year III, to present a draft for a police and safety Code. Although Merlin did not officially belong to this commission, he was, however, entrusted by it with the preparation of this draft. He

two sittings only, the Convention accepted it, with little question. This Code, which is the first to contain a system of Articles in an uninterrupted series (1 to 646), was primarily a code of criminal procedure; penal substantive law occupies only a limited place. Book II, entitled "Administration of justice", contains several provisions for offenses of disrespect to constituted authority (Arts. 555 to 559). In Book III, entitled "Punishments", the only topics are: 1st, a more precise classification of the various kinds of punishments into ordinary police, correctional, afflictive, and infamous punishments (Arts. 599 to 604); 2d, an enumeration of the offenses liable to ordinary police punishments (Arts. 605 to 608); 3d, definition of certain crimes against the internal safety of the State and against the constitution (Arts. 612 to 646). It ends with a confirmation of the law of July 19, 1791, and of the Penal Code of September 25, 1791 (Arts. 609 and 610).

The general system of penal law resulting from this body of legislation had substantial defects, notably in these three respects:

1st, The executive power of pardon and of commutation of sentence were abolished for all offenses tried by juries (P. C. of 1791, tit. VI, Art. 13).[3] This measure was due to the spirit of reaction against the abuses of Letters of pardon, so frequent under the Old Régime. None the less, it was a mistake; for the power of pardon must have a place in any rational system as the necessary complement of social justice.

2d, This first blunder resulted in a second, still more serious: the abolition of penalties involving perpetual loss of liberty. Labor in chains, which was the next highest after the death penalty, was not to exceed a term of twenty-four years. Indeed, in a penal system which does not recognize the power of pardon, there is no place for life penalties, for we take away all hope from the convict; and the most powerful motive for repentance disappears if he is not allowed to feel the possibility of liberation.

presented it to the Convention; and it was adopted upon his mere reading of it, interrupted only by the proposal of some amendments. In his "Notice historique sur la vie et les travaux de Merlin", M. *Mignet* says, of this Code of Brumaire: "A general expression of the most advanced social philosophy, this Code, written with elegant clearness, whose every provision carried, so to speak, its reason within itself, was voted in two sittings by the Convention, which adopted it in reliance upon his sponsorship. Thus the ideas of Merlin remained for nearly fifteen years the legislation of France."

[3] This text runs thus: "The issuance of any document tending to hinder or suspend the exercise of criminal justice or of any Letter of pardon, of discharge, of abrogation, of amnesty, or of commutation of sentence is abolished for all crimes tried by juries."

3d, Finally (and this is the chief defect of this legislation), in the case of offenses punishable with afflictive or infamous punishments, the punishment for each offense was fixed specifically and unalterably, without naming a maximum or minimum, between which the judge might have at least some slight choice. "The Constitutional Assembly," says Treilhard, in the commentary of the Commission accompanying the penal Code of 1810, "was convinced that it could not enclose within too narrow boundaries the powers given to the magistracy: it regulated, therefore, with great precision the duration of the punishment to be applied to each individual case; its aim was that, after the verdict of the jury, the judge's function should be limited to the mechanical application of the text of the law." Thus, through hatred of the discretionary powers which the judges under the old system had so abused, the Assembly went to the other extreme; they abolished the power of pardon, and took from the judge the power of adjusting the punishment to the personal and variable culpability of the offender. The result was that the penalty was frequently disproportioned to the deed which it aimed to repress; and that juries, making a compromise with their consciences, preferred to acquit the offender rather than to bring upon him a punishment which they regarded as exaggerated.

The Code of 1791 held sway over France until it was replaced, in 1810, by the Penal Code still in force to-day.

CHAPTER XIII

THE GERMAN REFORMS OF THE FRENCH REVOLUTIONARY PERIOD

§ 61. **The New Direction to German Criminal Theory in the Late 1700 s.** — While the principle of deterrence was adopted by the French Code as a practical measure, it was in the meantime coming to prevail in German legal science on grounds of principle and in an improved form. The substantial and cogent reasons for this were, indeed, not merely the inherent consistency of the theory itself (the inadequacies of which it is comparatively easy to expose), as the fact that this theory, in the form given it by its champions, was best calculated to eliminate judicial arbitrariness and to demonstrate the necessity of a controlling statute law.

This theory was led up to by a controversy of profound and extensive significance among German jurists over the nature of criminal responsibility. Pufendorf[1] had been the first writer since Aristotle to concern himself with this subject in an independent and scientific manner. Pufendorf's basic theory posited moral responsibility, but was not adequate, starting from that standpoint, to work out a doctrine of legal responsibility. The theory of moral freedom (as we have already remarked) offered one of the best supports for the view that the criminal statute was subject to be overridden by the judge's individual opinion — a view which would undermine the statute. The natural attempt, then, for those who repudiated this view was to find for the criminal statute

[1] "De jure naturæ et gentium", I, c. 9. "De officio hominis", I, c. 1.

a foundation that was completely independent of the assumption of human freedom.[2]

Grolmann and Feuerbach. — For this postulate of freedom of the will, Grolmann substituted the proposition that a human being who has once acted in contravention to the law will again do so in the future in the same or a similar manner. Feuerbach,[3] although himself a noble nature, approached the problem as a cynic; he regarded the human will as a conglomerate or product of purely sensual motives, and believed that in order to reach such motives the law must be as rigid and definite as possible. Both theories were false; but both demanded what suited the progress of the times. At the same time, they were practical theories, in the sense of seeking to make the law as effective as possible. Consequently they were admirably calculated to emphasize the possibilities of constructive legislation and to portray it as capable of rational treatment. Both authors went about their task with such a novel respect for positive law that in their hands it acquired a repute in marked contrast to that which it had suffered at the hands of its disparagers. It so happened (or perhaps was inherent in the very nature of things) that Grolmann and Feuerbach (especially the latter) were men of keen logic and gifted with the highly important talent of exact statement and brilliant exposition. Feuerbach, moreover, was a master of the anatomical dissection of the motives underlying human actions (as is revealed in his "Revision of Criminal Law" and especially in his later and classical work "Notable Criminal Trials narrated from the Records").[4]

Thus the appearance of Grolmann's "Lehrbuch" was an important turning-point in the science of German criminal law.[5] Its proud motto, borrowing the words of Ulrich Zasius: "Communibus uti opinionibus, si vel textus juris vel ratio manifesta repugnat, hoc nos certam veritatis pestem decimus et contesta-

[2] *Cf. Henke*, pp. 334 *et seq.*

[3] Concerning the life of this genial man (born Nov. 14, 1775) who perhaps is the greatest of German writers on criminal law, *cf. Glaser*, "Ges. kleinere Schriften über Strafrecht, Civil- und Strafprocess", I (1868), pp. 19–62; *Geyer*, "Festrede zu Paul Joh. Anselm v. Feuerbach's hundertjährigem Geburtstag"; *Binding*, in "Allgemeine (Augsburger) Zeitung" of Nov. 14th, 1875 (No. 318).

[4] ["Actenmässige Darstellung merkwürdiger Criminalrechtsfälle"; translated into English by Lady *Duff-Gordon*, under the title "Notable German Criminal Trials." — ED.]

[5] "Grundsätze der Criminalrechtswissenschaft nebst einer systematischen Darstellung des Geistes der deutschen Criminalgesetze" (Giessen, 1798).

mur", forecast the destruction of the rubbish which at that time served as authority and the renascence of a constructive system of law. And the turning-point in legal science was further marked by Feuerbach's "Revision of the Criminal Law" (1799), by the vigorous attack of Grolmann and especially of Feuerbach on Klein [6] and others; and ultimately by the learned controversy between these two friendly antagonists themselves, Grolmann and Feuerbach. Once more the distinction was insisted on between general philosophic ideas and a practical system of law. The value of a constructive system of legislation again came to be realized, and with it the possibilities of the judicial administration of such a law. Criminal law and criminal procedure were now cultivated in journals devoted to that field. In 1797, Grolmann, Feuerbach, and von Almendingen began the publication of the "Bibliothek für peinliche Rechtswissenschaft und Gesetzkunde." [7] Klein and Kleinschrod (of Würzburg) in 1798 founded the "Archiv des Criminalrechts", which was for many years the central publication of German criminal law. The false relation between criminal justice and the police authority (embodied in the oft controverted "punishment on suspicion") [8] was completely overthrown by Feuerbach, and the distinction between criminal justice and police measures was clearly demonstrated.

The Movement towards Prison Reform. — During this same period the movement started by the Englishman Howard,[9] for the improvement of prisons and criminal institutions, showed its effects in Germany.[10] The conditions in many of the great

[6] *Klein's* essay, "Ueber Natur und Zweck der Strafe" in the "Archiv des Criminalrechts", Vol. 2 (1800), from the historical viewpoint is far more accurate than Feuerbach's "Revision." *Cf.* also Klein as to Grolmann's "Lehrbuch" in the "Archiv des Criminalrechts", Vol. 1, Portion 4, pp. 128, etc.

[7] Continued to the 3d volume (Giessen, 1804).

[8] As to the treatment at that time of those whose guilt was not absolutely proven, *cf.* especially *Eisenhart*, in the "Archiv des Criminalrechts", 3d ser. (1801), I, pp. 57 *et seq.;* II, pp. 1 *et seq.;* also *Klein, ibid.*, pp. 64 *et seq.*, and *C. S. Zachariä*, IV, pp. 1 *et seq.*

[9] *John Howard*, "The State of the Prisons in England and Wales" (1777); translated in part into German, with notes and additions, by *Köster* (Leipzig, 1780).

[10] *Cf.* especially *Wagnitz*, "Historische Nachrichten und Bemerkungen über die merkwürdigsten Zuchthäuser in Deutschland nebst einem Anhange über die zweckmässigste Einrichtung der Gefängnisse und Irrenanstalten" (2 vols., Halle, 1791, 1792). At that time the "Zuchthaus" denoted an intermediate form of imprisonment. The worst criminals were for the most part sent to the so-called "Stockhäuser" or to fortresses. Thus *e.g.* in Braunschwieg, no one who had committed a crime depriving of civic rights was sent to the "Zuchthaus." *Cf. Wagnitz*, II, p. 25.

criminal institutions in Germany were indeed not so revolting as in most of the English prisons. In many principalities, as a result of reformatories and careful supervision by the local authorities, prison administration observed (at least towards those prisoners not serving the severest sentences) [11] methods of treatment which were based on humanity and even on principles of education. Yet there was no well thought out and systematic scheme of prison-penalties, and even the institutions [12] then regarded as the best were used also as asylums for the insane, the poor, and even the orphans. Ideas of progress, which even yet have not reached their full fruition, were at that time struggling against opinions and conditions [13] which to us to-day are inconceivable.[14]

§ 62. **Feuerbach as Legislator for Bavaria.** — It was natural that a State like Bavaria, which as a result of external circumstances had (for the time) attained such a prominent position and which at the same time inclined so much to follow France, should enter upon a thoroughgoing reform in the province of criminal law as well as in the other branches of governmental activity. This was furthered by the fact that in Maximilian Joseph it possessed an enlightened and liberal-minded ruler. The task of preparing a draft for a penal code was assigned to Kleinschrod, professor at Würzburg. His draft, published in 1802, was in many portions exceedingly ambiguous in both its composition and its underlying purposes. Its general spirit was that of the criminal portion of the "General Prussian Landrecht." It met with an able criticism at the hands of Feuerbach, who was himself a master of style; and the principles he invoked were absolutely correct. Imperfection in a code, he observed, may well consist in the very fact of its excessive detail.[1] "Not only must a code deal with all subjects within its sphere, but it must also govern these subjects by precise exhaustive definitions and by broad rules of universal

[11] *Cf.* the observation of *Wagnitz* (II, pp. 67 *et seq.*) concerning the "Zuchthaus" in Celle.

[12] In many institutions of this character (*e.g.* in Leipzig, Frankfurt a. M., Augsburg, *cf. Wagnitz*, I, pp. 267 *et seq.*; II, pp. 90, 91; II, p. 11) the state of things was bad enough. Brutal treatment — *e.g.* frequent use of wire-braided whips — deadened all sense of honor. An illustration of this brutal treatment was the custom of flogging upon admission to the prison, the so-called "welcome."

[13] Even such a man as *Justus Möser* ("Patriotische Phantasien", IV, p. 157) could approve the sale of criminals for foreign military service (*cf. Wagnitz*, I, pp. 214, 215).

[14] In Stettin, *e.g.* those who were confined in the fortresses were obliged to procure their clothing by begging. *Hälschner*, p. 243.

[1] "Bibl. für peinliche Rechtswissenschaft", Vol. 2, Part 3, p. 10.

application. No code can comprise all cases and examples. . . . If legislation thinks that detail in dealing with the several possible cases and multiplicity of special provisions can make amends for the lack of general definitions and principles, it will be defective and imperfect by the very reason of its prolixity." "The (wise) legislator [2] does not speak in syllogisms, and does not use philosophic and technical words of expression. He displays his philosophic spirit in the depth and breadth of his conceptions and not in the figments of philosophy. He speaks the language of the people with the clear and lofty spirit of wisdom. His simplicity is in harmony with the correctness and precision of his ideas. Capable of being understood by all, his principles furnish the thoughtful with a rich fund of ideas." Feuerbach also justly insisted upon system in a code.[3] "To be sure, a code is not a compendium; it can never aspire to the scholastically artificial and precisely articulated form of a system. But its principles should coördinate in a plain, simple arrangement determined by their association and relationship. Moreover, there are certain negative principles of a system which the legislator should follow. Nothing should be in the wrong place. Laws dealing with extraneous subjects should not be introduced into other laws to the confusion and destruction of their coherence; and laws should not be exposed to mistakes and confusion because of their position or the heading under which they are included or the connection in which . . . they are used. While the work of the legislator is not scientific jurisprudence, yet it is for science and from it science should ensue." All this, to be sure, is but little in harmony with that set conception which many, in their desire to banish all arbitrariness and discretion from the courts, form of the relation of legislation and jurisprudence. Quistorp, for example, in his "Draft of a Code for Penal and Criminal Cases" [4] had proposed to forbid comments on the criminal law by jurists in printed publications.[5]

The result of this criticism [6] of the Bavarian draft was that

[2] Preceding reference, p. 20. [3] Pp. 29, 30.

[4] Part I, Chap. 1, § 5.

[5] To the contrary, *cf. Feuerbach*, "Biblioth.", Vol. II, Part 3, Div. 2, pp. 20 *et seq.*

[6] Feuerbach at the time aspired to the introduction of a new system of criminal procedure, but he did not accomplish it. The portion of the Bavarian Code of that time had become merely an adaptation (with meritorious features however) of the inquisitorial form of procedure. [On this subject, *cf.* Vol. VI of the present Series, *Esmein's* "History of Continental Criminal Procedure", transl. *Simpson*. — TRANSL.]

Feuerbach himself received a commission to prepare a new draft of a code for Bavaria. In 1805 he was appointed Minister of Justice of Bavaria (of which he was a subject), a State which at that time occupied a position of considerable power and was quite disposed towards thoroughgoing reforms in all branches of law.

The Bavarian Code of 1813. — The Bavarian Criminal Code of May 16, 1813, though by no means entirely in accord with Feuerbach's views,[7] was based substantially upon his draft, and was emphatically an epoch-making work in German criminal legislation. It is remarkable for its clearness of expression, worthy in every respect of a legislator, for a completeness in its General Portion [8] and a precision in its definitions thitherto unknown in German law. Naturally, in a work by Feuerbach, nothing is to be found of the doctrine of unlimited judicial discretion; but (as with the French Code Pénal and most of the subsequent legislation) the Code gives the judge the right of fixing the punishment within a certain maximum and minimum. A decided improvement lay in the fact that the rules for aggravation and mitigation of punishment were sharply distinguished from the judicial right to fix the penalty within the customary field for discretion.[9] Like the French Code, the Bavarian Code assumed itself to be complete; and, according to Article I, the resort to analogy, for the purpose of thereby imputing criminality to an act, is forbidden. "For it is upon this principle", says the official Annotation to the Code,[10] "that the security of the State and of every individual depends." It follows the French Code in adopting the triple classification of "Crimes", "Misdemeanors", and "Transgressions."[11] The last mentioned are entrusted to a special Code for Offenses against Police Supervision, and "crimes" are allotted to the "criminal" courts, while "misdemeanors" are allotted to the jurisdiction of the "civic penal" courts, and "transgressions" are left to the jurisdiction of the police officials.[12] The provisions of the General Portion,[13] however, apply both to

[7] Feuerbach did not accomplish his purpose of abolishing flogging. *Cf. Geyer*, p. 15. However, torture yielded in 1806 to Feuerbach's attacks.

[8] "Upon the soundness and completeness of these the fate of all special criminal provisions depends" ("Official Annotations", I, p. 49).

[9] "Official Annotations", pp. 232 *et seq.*

[10] I, p. 66.

[11] *I.e.* "Verbrechen", "Vergehen" and "Uebertretungen."

[12] Art. 3.

[13] Under "crimes" are comprehended all punishable actions which on account of their nature and the extent of their evil are threatened with the death penalty, wearing of chains, imprisonment in a penitentiary,

"misdemeanors" and to "crimes."[14] A well-calculated system of punishment should adjust itself to the character of the individual criminal act, and as stated in the "Annotations" it is the quality and not the quantity of the punishment which should be determined by the character of the act.

Defects. — In contrast to these meritorious features of the Bavarian Code, there were some considerable defects, which for a long time continued to exercise no slight detrimental influence on the legislation of the other German States. Feuerbach certainly was conscious of the distinction between the task of the legislator and that of the scientific jurist. But, as a dialectician, he relied too much upon his own discernment and believed that the fundamental problems of science could receive final solution in definite formulas. For this reason the General Portion of his work contains a long list of perversely unsuitable provisions and definitions. Article 65 and those following, dealing with negligence, are out of place in a code; and the provisions relative to unlawful intent are in large part completely erroneous, and reach their climax in his famous or rather notorious "presumption of malicious intent."[15] This Code of his also originated those unfortunate and subtle provisions as to conspiracy ("Complott"),[16] which infected like disease-germs most of the later German Codes, and were but slowly eliminated. Moreover, as the theory of deterrence, which he sought to follow, required that the greatest possible restrictions be placed upon the exercise of judicial discretion,[17] the Code's details as to penalties lost themselves in trivial distinctions which in many cases were inevitably either incorrect or open to doubt. Another defect, due to the deterrence theory,[18] was the harsh penalties for second

workhouse, or fortress, with forfeiture or declaration of incapacity for all honors or offices under the State or such as are deemed honorable.

[14] "Official Annotations", I, p. 30.

[15] *Cf.* Arts. 41, 43. "Annotations", I, p. 143. As to negligence, *cf.* Arts. 65 *et seq.* Art. 69, while it declares generally that negligence is punishable, includes therein quite a number of new offenses.

[16] Arts. 56 *et seq.* Art 46, Abs. 2, even recognizes unintentional instigation of crime.

[17] Generally speaking, the range between the maximum and minimum of punishment was too narrow. *Cf. Arnold*, in "Archiv d. Criminalr." (1844), p. 196.

[18] The artificial character of the theory of deterrence, at variance with real life, led *e.g.* to giving quite unreasonable consequences to the offenses of theft and defiance of the authorities. The taking of a turnip from a field or of a plum from a tree according to Arts. 218, 220 entailed a penalty of three years' imprisonment in a workhouse (*cf. Arnold*, p. 395), and the Annotations of the Code would not forbid punishment for defiance

offenses;[19] and since the deterrent theory assumes that a penalty which has been announced by way of threat is always justifiable, the Code authorized infliction of severe punishments for acts which only presumably, or even possibly constituted a crime.[20] Moreover, since Feuerbach aimed to separate absolutely law and morality, the Code would in no case regard as crimes grave breaches of morality which did not violate subjective rights.[21] Adultery, for example, is treated, very superficially, merely as the intentional failure to perform a contract[22] and is dealt with in the same division as violation of powers of attorney. It is also peculiar that Article 106 permits of certain species of "punishment on suspicion" ("Verdachtstrafe"), although this is not recognized by the Annotations.

Corporal chastisement appears in the Code only as aggravating the punishment of imprisonment;[23] the legislator however forbade its infliction at the end of the period of punishment. Confiscation of property was abolished by the Bavarian constitution of 1808, and this was confirmed by Art. 33 of the Code. But in accordance with Art. 7, the artificial and unnatural institution of civic death continued in Bavaria until the statute of Nov. 19, 1849. The only aggravation of the death penalty recognized by the Code was preliminary exposure on a pillory.

Soon after the publication of the Code were promulgated the official "Annotations to the Code of the Kingdom of Bavaria according to the Decrees of the Royal Privy Council."[24] But it is worthy of note that the royal patent for its publication[25] forbade the publication of further commentaries on the Code (although it could itself very properly be designated as a work of scientific jurisprudence); and even the lecturers in the Universities cited exclusively to the text of the law and these official "Annotations", although the latter were often at variance with the clear text of the law!

of the authorities in cases where the authorities lack jurisdiction or their order is improper (Annotations, III, p. 52). Even more than the Code, the Bavarian statute of Aug. 9, 1806 concerning the punishment of poaching adheres to the theory of deterrence. *Arnold* (*ante*, p. 402) gives a good description of the effect of this "deterrence" in actual practice.

[19] Arts. 113 *et seq.*

[20] *Cf.* Arts. 149, 160.

[21] Annotations, II, p. 59.

[22] Art. 401. *Cf.* Ann. I, p. 59.

[23] As to the somewhat disproportionate punishment of adultery, *cf.* *Arnold*, pp. 379 *et seq.*

[24] "Anmerkungen zum Strafgesetzbuche für das Königreich Bayern nach den Protokollen des königl. geheimen Raths" (3 vols. München, 1813).

[25] Nov. 13, 1813.

TITLE V. MODERN TIMES

CHAPTER XIV

THE FRENCH CODE OF 1810, AND FRANCE IN THE 1800 s

§ 62*a*. **The Penal Code of 1810.**—French criminal law includes (1) the *general* law, *i.e.* the Penal Code, the Code of Criminal Procedure, and their appurtenant and amending statutes, and (2) the *special* law, *i.e.* special laws covering special offenses and special procedures.

The general criminal law has been several times codified, reformed, and revised since the Revolution of 1789. In fact, we may distinguish, in what concerns criminal and civil law alike, three different legislative processes: codification, which builds on a new plan the whole of a legislation; reform, which modifies the Codes and gives them new life; and revision, which perfects them without altering the fundamental regulations. The provisions of the general criminal law are to-day embraced in two Codes: the Penal Code and the Code of Criminal Procedure, which replace the laws of the intermediary epoch. The history of the original enactment and later changes of these two Codes is as follows:

A commission, appointed under the Consulate (by a decree of 27th Germinal, year IX), and composed of MM. Vieillard, Target, Oudard, Treilhard, and Blondel, had been charged with the drafting of a single Code, to cover both general principles and details. This draft, submitted by this commission and composed of 1169 Articles, was prefaced by some general comments; those prepared by Target dealt with punishments; those of Oudard, with organic provisions and with procedure. This work was immediately

[1] [§§ 62*a*, 62*b*, = §§ 76–82, pp. 132–142, of Vol. I of Professor R. GARRAUD's "Traité théorique et pratique du droit pénal français" (2d ed., 1898). For this author and work, see the Editorial Preface. — ED.]

printed,[2] and sent to the Court of Cassation, the criminal courts, and the courts of appeal, to obtain their opinions. These opinions (not very favorable, on the whole, to the legislation of the Constitutional Assembly and the Convention) showed a tendency toward a return to the old criminal law.[3] On 2d Prairial, year XII, the Emperor ordered the drafting of a series of fundamental questions, to serve as basis for debate in the Council of State.[4] These questions, fourteen in number, were submitted to this numerous body at the meeting of 16th Prairial, year XII. The debate which ensued on these topics was before long postponed, in order first, to reach a settlement upon the question of reorganization of the judiciary. The delay due to this and other reasons[5] suspended action for three years on the code-drafts. When the debate was resumed, in January, 1808, the Council separated the "laws of form" from the substantive law. The former were presented to the Legislative Body[6] as a draft Code of Criminal Procedure, the latter as a draft Penal Code. The former Code was enacted at the end of 1808, the latter at the beginning of 1810. Before promulgating the two Codes, the government waited until the magistracy, reorganized by the law of April 20, 1810, should be regularly in office. Both Codes, therefore, took effect from the 1st of January, 1811.

[2] In an octavo volume, entitled: "Projet de Code criminel avec les observations des rédacteurs, celles du Tribunal de cassation et le compte rendu par le grand juge", Paris, year XIII, pub. Garnery.

[3] "Observations des tribunaux d'appel sur le projet de Code criminel", 4 vol. in 4to, year XIII.

[4] Among these questions, the following were those which concerned more particularly penal law: Question IX: *Shall capital punishment be continued?* — Question X: *Shall there be punishments for life?* — Question XI: *Shall confiscation be permitted in certain cases?* — Question XII: *Shall judges have a certain freedom in the application of punishments? Shall there be a maximum and a minimum which will give them the power of imposing punishment for a longer or shorter period according to circumstances?* — Question XIII: *Shall surveillance be introduced for a particular class of criminals, after the expiration of their punishment, and shall bail be demanded in certain cases for future good conduct?* — Question XIV: *Shall rehabilitation be accorded to convicts whose conduct will have made them worthy of it?*

[5] M. *Cruppi*, attorney-general to the Court of Cassation, in an opening address delivered in 1896, under the title, "Napoléon et le jury", has shown that the principal cause of the delays in criminal legislation was the question of the jury. "Napoleon could not endure a tribunal which, in spite of skilful precautions in its administrative recruiting, would be in constant likelihood of escaping his power: he made repeated attempts to destroy it, but met with sturdy resistance. The jury found energetic defenders among the best jurists of the country."

[6] [For an explanation of the composition of these various legislative bodies under the Empire, see M. *Planiol's* chapter in "General Survey of Continental Legal History," Vol. I of this Series, p. 281. — ED.]

The Penal Code of 1810 was at once reactionary and reconstructive. It took as its basis the principles of the utilitarian school. In essence, it aimed to secure the defense of society, by means of intimidation.[7] The philosophy of penal justice does not seem to have concerned the mind of the legislators any further than a certain attention to the judge's apportionment of the punishment to the offense. The Penal Code was divided under three heads — crimes, punishments, and jurisdiction. In its definitions of crime it is notable mainly for its excessive severity; it also went too far in many points, as in making criminal a failure to reveal a plot and in classing the attempt with the consummated crime, and of the accomplice with the principal.[8] In its system of penalties, the Penal Code concerned itself exclusively with punishment; the idea of reforming the offender through the law was foreign to it. We find the death penalty and life punishments freely applied, excessive chastisements, barbarous mutilations, and penalties unjust in their effects, such as general confiscation and civil death. It inflicted upon the parricide the mutilation of his hand before putting him to death; it employed the brand (for certain convicts) and the "carcan." Its system of imprisonments was only a fiction, for there were no penitentiary establishments appropriate for the various punishments. Such were the chief defects of this legislation. But from other points of view the Penal Code of 1810 did institute or preserve some important advances. First, as a work of codification, it is drawn with much simplicity, clearness, and or-

[7] Upon the philosophic principles which inspired the framers of the Penal Code, we find the following in the "Observations" of *Target*, placed at the beginning of the draft: "Plainly punishment is not vengeance; this wretched satisfaction, the mark of a low and cruel mind, has no place in the theory of the law. The necessity of punishment is alone what makes it lawful. It is not the prime aim of the law that the offender should suffer; the thing of chief importance is that crimes be prevented. If, when a most detestable crime had been committed, we could be sure that no further crime were to be feared, the punishment of this final offender would be useless barbarity; some would not hesitate to assert that it would exceed the power of the law. The gravity of crimes is measured, therefore, not so much by the perversity which they reveal as by the dangers which they entail. The efficacy of punishment is measured less by its harshness than by the fear which it inspires." *Locré*, Vol. XXIX, p. 8. These remarks express with the greatest clearness the doctrines of Bentham; and his doctrines undoubtedly formed the basis of the provisions of the Penal Code of 1810. *Bentham's* treatises on civil and penal legislation had been translated and published in 1802 by *Dumont*. The influence of Kant had not yet made itself felt in France, at least in official spheres.

[8] Its system of criminality, defective though it may be, does not, however, deserve the criticisms which have properly been made upon its system of punishments. *Cf. Chauveau* and *Hélie*, Vol. I, no. 11.

der; crimes and offenses of the same nature, although of different gravity, are no longer separated; these were grouped in Book III, while Book IV was devoted to police misdemeanors. Secondly, the pardoning power, which had already been restored to the Executive by a "senatus-consultum" of 16th Thermidor, year X, and the life punishments, are reëstablished. Thirdly, punishments for a term were no longer absolutely fixed, and the important innovation of a maximum and a minimum was introduced; there was also an embryonic recognition of the principle of extenuating circumstances, the benefit of which was limited to misdemeanors causing damage not exceeding twenty-five francs.

But this Code of 1810 is no longer in force in all its original details; many laws promulgated since 1810 have enlarged or modified its provisions. Throughout these later laws it is easy to recognize the traces of the different régimes which have succeeded one another in our country. In fact, every political revolution necessarily influences criminal law, which is only a branch of the public law of a people.

§ 62b. **Principal Changes during the 1800 s.** — The various measures (suffixed to each of the Articles which they complete or modify) are of two kinds, in respect to legislative method. (1) Some have been incorporated into the text itself of the Code, without alteration of its system. Thus, a general revision of the Penal Code was made by the law of April 28, 1832;[1] and, at that time, a new edition was officially issued. Since then, several very important laws, notably that of May 13, 1863,[2] that of January 23, 1874, and that of November 15, 1892, have again recast a certain number of its provisions. (2) Other statutes so related to the Penal Code as to complete or modify it, have remained outside of the fabric of codification: such are, for example, the law of June 8, 1850, on transportation; that of August 5, 1850, on the education and protection of juvenile offenders; that of May 30, 1854, on the method of punishment by hard labor; that of May 27, 1885, on the banishment of recidivists; and, in part, both that of August 14, 1885, on the means of preventing relapse, and that of March 26, 1891, on the extenuation and aggravation of punishments.

[1] This revision affected 162 Articles of the Penal Code, as also parts of the Code of Criminal Procedure. See *A. Chauveau*, "Code pénal progressif; Commentaire sur la loi modificative du Code pénal" (Paris, 1832).

[2] This revision, less extended than that of 1832, affects 45 Articles of the Penal Code. On this statute, see *G. Dutruc*, "Le Code pénal modifié par la loi du 13 mai, 1863" (Paris, 1863).

The chief reforms, which our penal law has undergone since 1810 may be grouped under the following general principles: *mitigation of penalty;* the *development of the principle of extenuating circumstances; the extension of the application* of the Penal Code; the *reform* of the offender through punishment; the principle of *social defense,* as involving the *distinction between first offenders and recidivists.*

(*a*) The *mitigation* of the penal system inspired three kinds of reforms. (1) A certain number of punishments have been suppressed or lightened. Among other legal provisions having this aim and effect may be cited: Art. 66 of the Constitution of 1814, abolishing general confiscation; the act of April 28, 1832, suppressing branding and amputation of the hand, for a parricide, before his execution; the Constitution of November 4, 1848, abolishing the death penalty for political offenses, and the act of June 8, 1850, substituting for it transportation to a fortress; the act of April 12, 1848, suppressing public exhibition; the act of May 31, 1854, abolishing civic death; the numerous acts modifying the regulations for surveillance by the State police, and the act of May 23, 1885, replacing that method by domiciliary restriction. (2) Some classes of crimes, for which punishment is unjust or useless have been abolished, especially the offense of non-disclosure of plots made or crimes planned against the safety of the State, and of non-disclosure of crimes of counterfeiting, abolished in 1834. (3) A certain number of acts have been taken from the category of crimes and classed as misdemeanors. This legal reclassification began with the act of June 25, 1824, which brought down into the class of misdemeanors thefts committed either in an inn or in a hostelry, by others than the inn-keeper, the landlord, or a manager, or committed in the fields or at sales, — thefts which Arts. 386 and 388 punished by imprisonment; the transfer was completed by the act of April 28, 1832, and that of May 13, 1863. But in this changing of crimes into misdemeanors, the act of 1863 showed more liberality than that of 1832.

(*b*) The extension of the doctrine of *extenuating circumstances,* begun cautiously by the act of June 25, 1824, and completed by the act of April 28, 1832, changed the entire system of the Penal Code. This radical reform gave to the trial tribunal the power to determine, with some discretion, the legal morality of the offense under investigation, and thus to cast a more exact balance between the punishment and the gravity of the particular offense. This power of the judge is almost unlimited for misdemeanors or police offenses, but is limited in the matter of crimes.

(*c*) Penal law has become more and more *extensive;* it has tried to foresee, by new provisions, all anti-social acts, and thus to fill up the gaps which judicial experience had pointed out in the arsenal of social defense. The general scope of the Penal Code, especially of its provisions as to swindling, breach of trust, and theft have been gradually developed since 1810. From this point of view, the act of May 13, 1863 gave to the text of the Penal Code a general and careful revision. For example, the offense of extortion of hush-money (Art. 406, § 2) was then foreseen and penalized. Before that, the law of April 28, 1832, had defined as crimes or misdemeanors: in Arts. 317 and 318, the act of administering substances injurious to health; in Art. 184, § 2, a violation of the domicile by a private individual; in Art. 400, the embezzlement or destruction of confiscated objects; in Art. 408, the conversion of personal property by a gratuitous bailee who was to bestow work upon it. Apart from the Penal Code, important acts have extended the domain of criminal law to public drunkenness (July 26, 1873), and to professional gambling and pandering in the public street (May 27, 1885, Art. 17).

(*d*) The *reformation* of the prisoner through punishment, to which the Code of 1810 gave no thought, has since then become one of the chief objects of penal law. To this end, the legislator has employed two methods: 1st, the method of transportation to penal colonies, regulated by the acts of June 8, 1850 (on deportation), and of May 30, 1854 (on hard labor); 2d, the penitentiary method, of which some interesting applications are found in the acts of August 5, 1850, on the education and the protection of juvenile offenders, in the act of June 5, 1875, of the reform of departmental prisons, and in the act of August 14, 1885, on the means of preventing recidivism.

(*e*) The increasing number of recidivists proved, in spite of these efforts, the inadequacy of the penal and penitentiary régime; and it was concluded that the problem of criminality could be solved only by distinguishing radically between first offenders and recidivists. To avoid prison sentences for the former, and to remove the latter from a social environment where they cannot live without relapsing into their criminal activities, — such seems to have been the attempted program of the act of March 26, 1891, which introduced the suspension of sentence, and of the act of May 27, 1885, on the relegation of recidivists.

To sum up: In appraising the evolution of penal law in France since 1810, it may be said that our legislation has proceeded spontaneously — unconsciously, indeed — towards a realization of the threefold aim above assigned to its efforts: namely to remove from incorrigible offenders the means of doing harm, to improve those who are capable of returning to rectitude, and to intimidate the occasional offender.

As our modern penal law makes its appearance on the stage, the third of these is its feature, viz. intimidation. In the Code of 1810, the penalties seem to have no other purpose. To check the offender, it was thought sufficient to counteract the occasion that tempted him with the threat of the punishment that must fall upon him. Both the prohibitions and the penalties are marked, on the whole, by an excessive severity. But it was soon perceived that this system defeated its own end. The numbers of recidivists showed that the places of detention became hot-beds of mutual corruption. So the second aim, that of improving the offender through punishment (an aim theretofore foreign to the Penal Code) began to attract attention. This idea had its strong partisans, — some of them even fanatics. The law then started timidly on the penitentiary path. We can observe it experimenting and groping for results; we notice first, the favor and then the disfavor accorded to the cellular system. Next, the law passed to the first theory above noted; in the face of the rising wave of recidivism, it resolved to eliminate the incorrigibles by energetic methods. The permanent seclusion of recidivists seemed to be the last goal of this evolution.

But the recidivist (it was perceived) is a direct product of all punishment by imprisonment, as practised in France. So the plan evolved was to avoid sending to prison those who had never yet entered it. Then a distinction took shape and developed, — the attempt to provide a system for first offenders different from that for recidivists. All this, however, was not well reasoned out; no general plan of reform was conceived and executed. From hand to mouth, under the sway of the needs and the ideas of the moment, sundry laws have been drafted and voted. The modern legislator has never squarely faced this problem, the only and the real problem of modern penal law, namely: *Given the various classes of criminals, to systematize the punishments adapted to each of them.*

After all, can he solve it? Unquestionably. The true aim should be to provide *repressive measures* for the occasional offender, *seclusionary measures* for incorrigibles, and *penitentiary measures* for those susceptible to improvement. In spite of the improvements introduced into the Penal Code, it is, incontestably, no longer in harmony with the social environment. Though the enumeration and definition of offenses has been made broader and more flexible, by the Supreme Court's interpretation — an admirable body of judicial law, sagacious and cautiously progressive, which has succeeded in continually rejuvenating our hoary old Code, — yet the penal system has remained very inadequate and very defective, in spite of the successive (and inconsistent) amendments which it has undergone. In some respects, the gradation of punishments has been oddly reversed. Detention in jail is more deterrent than a sentence to hard labor. Deportation, as applied to political offenders, means nothing. Banishment (an inheritance from the former Codes) can no longer be employed as prescribed. Imprisonment, with the promiscuity which now characterizes it, does not intimidate, does not reform, and merely swells the budget. A general recasting of the system of penalties, and especially of the penitentiary system, becomes imperative, therefore, in France.

But after the task of the law comes that of the judge; and for us the latter is the crucial point. The law must leave to the courts the liberty to adapt to the different temperaments of individual offenders the three methods — exclusive, repressive, and penitentiary — the general principles which the law was entitled to lay down. The *individualization of punishment*, therefore, is the imperative need in the scientific Codes of the future. And the general principles of extenuating circumstances, of the suspension of sentence, and of conditional liberation, are only stages in the path along which reforms must be directed.[3]

[3] A commission, charged with preparing a general reform of all our penal legislation, was appointed, in 1887, by the Ministry of Justice. The "Journal officiel" of March 27, 1887 published a report on this subject, addressed to the President of the Republic, by the Keeper of the Great Seal. As a result of this report, a decree was issued, dated March 26, 1887, providing for this commission and appointing its members. The commission was reorganized June 30, 1892, and divided into four sections: crimes and misdemeanors against the public weal, against persons, against property, and special laws. The first commission published a draft in 1889, containing 112 Articles, and entitled: "Book I, of offenses in general, and of penalties." The text is given in: "Bulletin de la société générale des prisons", 1893, p. 757; *Molinier & Vidal*, "Traité théorique et pratique de droit pénal", II, 1–27. For a critique, see *Champcommunal*, "Examen critique et comparé du projet du Code pénal", 1896 ("Journal des parquets", 1895, 1896); *A. Gautier*, in "Revue pénale suisse", 1894, p. 46. As a whole, the draft is of mediocre value, and received only moderate favor.

Chapter XV

GERMANY SINCE 1813

§ 63.[1] **The Criminal Codes of the First Half of the 1800 s.** — The conflict of the various theories of criminal law, aroused by Feuerbach and Grolmann, did not subside throughout the century; but it came to exercise a considerable influence upon the development of even the positive law itself. Alongside this philosophical tendency, there came into play also an historical tendency, originating (in one of its phases) in the researches into Roman law, led by Hugo and Savigny, and (in another) in the researches into Germanic law inspired by Eichhorn and Grimm. In this period, also, the science of criminal law came to be the common field of study for all civilized nations. For in spite of certain national peculiarities, which may be easily accounted for, it is founded upon human and psychological conditions common to all. Comparative criminal law, and also the science of penology (which owes much of its stimulus to the so-called "theory of reformation"), received a lasting service from the numberless essays and minor writings of the indefatigable Mittermaier, an ever-constant and intrepid champion of the cause of freedom and humanity.

Influence of Feuerbach's Bavarian Code. — Feuerbach's advanced Bavarian Code immediately served as a model and as a

[1] [The first paragraph of this section is transferred from § 69, which formed the closing section of Part I in the treatise of Von Bar. — Ed.]

foundation for that series of criminal legislation [2] which was undertaken in most of the German States after the passing of French supremacy. The Oldenburg Criminal Code of September 10, 1814, imitated almost exactly that of Bavaria. The Hanoverian Code of August 8, 1840,[3] although a long time was spent in preliminary drafts and investigation, used the Bavarian Code as its foundation.

The legislation of this period, and the special statutes dealing with criminal procedure [4] which in part preceded it, eliminated a condition of uncertainty and anarchy in the criminal law which to us now seems intolerable, and also abolished a large number of anachronisms [5] which still maintained at least a technical legal existence. In these ways they conferred a genuine benefit upon the people and the courts. As compared with the Bavarian Code many improvements were introduced in particular details, and there was more and more of a tendency to depart from the biased attitude of Feuerbach. A greater field was conceded to judicial discretion; and there was a simplification of definitions and distinctions in the "General" as well as the "Special" portions. Even at the present time one can utilize as a not unprofitable source of instruction the often quite thoroughgoing debates of the legislative assemblies of the various States, as they are preserved in the better commentaries upon the several Codes. Little by little, greater attention came to be given to political offenses (which had theretofore been neglected by jurists), and especially to the question of possible excuses for resistance to the executive power of the State.

[2] *Cf. Stenglein*, "Sammlung der deutschen Strafgesetzbücher" (3 vols. München, 1858). A systematic and comparative presentation is given in *Häberlin*, "Grundsätze des Criminalrechts nach den neuesten deutschen Strafgesetzbüchern" (4 vols. 1845–1849).

[3] *Leonhardt*, "Commentar über das Criminalgesetzbuch für das Königr. Hannover" (2 vols. 1846, 1851). "Magazin für hannoversches Recht" (1850). "Neues Magazin" (1860 *et seq.*; now discontinued).

[4] In Hannover *e.g.* torture was not abolished legally until March 25, 1822.

[5] For example, according to the law obtaining in the Kingdom of Saxony, for every theft of a value of more than 12½ Thaler and for every theft of a value of more than 50 Thaler there must be inflicted a sentence of eight and ten years' penal servitude respectively. For every starting of a fire, by even the slightest negligence, the sentence of death by burning was imposed (this according to a "Mandat" of 1741). Concerning these and other anachronisms in the Kingdom of Saxony, *cf. von Wächter*, "Das königl. sächsische und thüringische Strafrecht" (1857), pp. 22, 23; he says: "These penalties had always been employed by the Saxon courts, even in modern times, until the publication of the Criminal Code, and in such cases it was only by the exercise of pardon that the law could be reconciled with justice."

On the other hand, however, there is a marked absence of that bold legislative spirit by which the end of the 1700 s and even the beginning of the 1800 s were distinguished. There is often manifested a certain timidity, and this is by no means limited to the governing bodies. The punishment of flogging found energetic and effective adherents; and for a long time we encounter examples of useless torment attached in graver cases to the punishment of imprisonment (chains and wooden hobbles on the legs).[6] This phase of development is especially exemplified in the Criminal Code of the Kingdom of Saxony [7] of March 30, 1838,[8] and in the Würtemberg Criminal Code [9] of March 1, 1839.[10] The latter was a more original work than the former and even more dominated by the deterrent theory. With only a few changes the Saxon Code went into effect also in Saxe-Altenberg, in Saxe-Meiningen, and in Schwarzburg-Sondershausen.[11] A quite original and meritorious code of this period in the Criminal Code of Brunswick of 1840,[12] which is remarkable for its comparative brevity and for its preservation of greater freedom of judicial discretion.[13] No provision is made for corporal punishments as part of a judicial sentence; and § 13 contains the following important principles:

"All convicts are to be placed at such work as will be fitted as nearly as possible to their physical capacity and their previous civic position. As far as compatible with this principle, harder labor is to be assigned to those sentenced to severe punishment. . . .

"No one sentenced to imprisonment can be employed against his will either in public work or in work the performance of which

[6] *Cf.* "Königl. sächs. Criminalgesetzbuch", Art. 8, 22. "Commentare" by *Weiss* (2 Parts, 2d ed. 1848) and *Held* and *Siebdrat* (1848). *Cf. von Wächter* (previous note), pp. 35, 36.

[7] "Königl. sächs. Criminalgesetzbuch", Art. 7.

[8] *Cf.* also *Herrmann*, "Zur Beurtheilung des Entwurfs eines Criminalgesetzbuches für das Königreich Sachsen" (1836).

[9] As to this Code, *cf. Mittermaier*, "Archiv des Criminalrechts" (1838), pp. 319 *et seq.* In this Code (which for that period was a relatively mild one) there was capital punishment for most cases of robbery, for extortion, incendiarism, and for one case of perjury. Penal servitude for life was used frequently.

[10] Voluminous "Commentare" by *Hepp* (2 vols. 1839, 1842) and *Hufnagel* (3 vols. 1840–1844).

[11] 1841, 1844, 1845.

[12] "Criminalgesetzbuch für das Herzogthum Braunschweig nebst Motiven" (1840) by *Breymann.*

[13] § 62 confers upon the courts an apparently extensive right of leniency where there is a coincidence of several mitigating circumstances. However, *cf.* the restrictions upon this right of leniency in respect to high treason and most cases of murder, in §§ 81, 145.

would by virtue of his civic status entail for him an aggravation of the sentence.

"Convicts . . . who themselves defray the cost of the execution of the penalty may choose for themselves work compatible with the prison system and may retain the profit." [14]

The Criminal Code of the Grandduchy of Hesse [15] was prepared with greater originality as to individual details. It is upon the whole an excellent work, similar in character to the Brunswick Code, although rather prolix, and, especially in its "General Portion", allowing little range for judicial practice and legal science. This code recognizes three varieties of imprisonment, the penitentiary, the reformatory, and the jail.[16] Imprisonment in a fortress [17] is prescribed for the offense of duelling and also as an alternative to the reformatory.

A marked resemblance [18] to this latter code is shown by the Code of Baden of March 6, 1845. This was similar in length, quite prolix, somewhat minute in all directions and often much given to detail.[19] The so-called Thüringian Code which by agreement went into effect in 1850 in Saxe-Weimar, Saxe-Meiningen, Coburg-Gotha, Schwarzburg-Rudolstadt, and Anhalt-Dessau, may be regarded as a development of the Saxon Criminal Code, although with variations for the respective States. It laid claim to progress in that it abolished the death penalty; [20] but in other respects it was below the standard of the Hessian Code.

The introduction of railroads and telegraphs led also to the enactment at this time of special statutes for the protection of these important institutions against injury and danger. In the later codes the offenses in question were included under the classification: offenses dangerous to the public in general.[21]

[14] The Brunswick Code almost without change was published for Lippe-Detmold on July 18, 1843.

[15] *Breidenbach*, "Commentar über das Grosherzoglich Hessische Strafgesetzbuch", 1st vol., 2d section, 1842, 1844 (including the general portion only).

[16] *I.e.* "Zuchthaus", "Correctionshaus", and "Gefängniss."

[17] Art. 11. "The court may, after a careful investigation of the private position and education of the offender assign the carrying out of the punishment of the reformatory to a fortress or some similar institution." *Cf.* similar provisions in the Code of Baden, §§ 52, 51.

[18] The Code of Nassau of April 14, 1849, was merely a modification of that of Hesse.

[19] As to the Code of Baden, *cf.* the commentaries of *Thilo*, *Brauer*, *Puchelt*, and *Jagemann*. Also *Berner*, "Strafgesetzgebung", p. 207.

[20] Meiningen and Reuss however retained the death penalty. *Cf. Von Wächter*, "Sächsisch-thüring. Strafrecht", p. 182.

[21] *Cf.* the Prussian Ordinance of Nov. 30, 1840, concerning injury to

Influence of the Political Agitation of 1848. — As a result of the political events of the year 1848, and partly in consequence of the "Fundamental Rights of the German People",[22] published December 27, 1848, corporal punishment and the death penalty were abolished in a number of the German States. But many States later reintroduced the death penalty.[23] After the agitation of the spring of 1848 many States mitigated their laws relating to poaching.[24] The abolition of the office of censor led to the enactment of special statutes relative to the press; concerning this a decree of the Confederation [25] on July 6, 1854, established a general standard of a reactionary character. The Criminal Code of the Kingdom of Saxony of 1855, may also be regarded as a revision of an earlier Code (of 1838), although a revision more extensive in character. In spite of many excellent features, it is not of merit, and in many respects exhibits the climax of the reactionary period of 1850 to 1860, *e.g.* in increasing the severity of the punishment of imprisonment by leg irons and wooden hobbles, and even by corporal punishment [26] (the so-called "Willkomen" *i.e.* welcome!).[27]

railroads and the Prussian Ordinance of June 15, 1849, concerning the punishment of offenses against the telegraph.

[22] "Grundrechte", § 9: "Except as provided by martial law and the law of the sea in cases of mutiny, the death penalty is abolished, as is also the pillory, branding, and corporal punishment."

[23] In the Kingdom of Saxony, in accordance with the "Grundrechte", corporal punishment was abolished by an ordinance of April 20, 1849, and in the upper Saxon Chamber the sovereign declared that death penalties not theretofore executed would be remitted. *Cf. v. Wächter*, pp. 34, 178. In Würtemberg, capital punishment was abolished by a statute of Aug. 13, 1849, Art. I, and again introduced by a statute of June 17, 1853.

[24] *Cf. e.g.* the Bavarian statute of July 25, 1850, "dealing with injury to the chase"; also the Hanoverian statute of Aug. 25, 1848 (modifying a special statute of 1840).

[25] This required promulgation as law in the several States and consequently did not everywhere actually go into effect.

[26] *Cf. von Wächter*, pp. 189 *et seq. Cf.* also, for example, the group of unfortunate provisions contained in Cap. V of the "General Portion" having to do with accomplices, or the juristically indefensible Art. 247 concerning self-redress, and Art. 338, which are typical of a State that exercises a meddlesome police control and are models of bad wording. "He who through intentional dissemination of false reports concerning the property or personal relations of another or he who by repeating such reports as facts causes disadvantage to another or hinders his advantage is upon complaint punishable with imprisonment not exceeding four months."

[27] *Krug*, "Commentar zu dem Strafgesetzbuche für das Königreich Sachsen" (1st ed. 1855, 4 divisions), (2d ed. 1861, 3 divisions). Also *Siebdrat*, "Deutsches Strafgesetzbuch für das Königreich Sachsen mit Commentar" (1862). Of importance, also, is "Zeitschrift für Rechtspflege und Verwaltung zunachst für dem Königreich Sachsen" (1838 *et seq.*), and *Schwarze*, "Allgemeine Gerichtszeitung für dem Königreich Sachsen."

§ 64. **Legislation in Prussia.** — There was a peculiar course of development in Prussia, which at the end of the 1700 s began to be the center of reactionary principles in matters of criminal law. Offenses against property, which at that time were increasing in frequency (a thing readily explainable by the disturbed condition of the times), occasioned the "Circularverordnung" of February 26, 1799, dealing with theft and other crimes against the security of property. This was so ambiguously expressed [1] that there was room to doubt whether it really represented a more vigorous repression of the offenses in question, or whether (as viewed by some courts) it introduced milder punishments. Since the Prussian penal institutions [2] were for a large part in a state of utter neglect,[3] the remedy [4] was for a time sought in the expedient of flogging, which was specially recommended and employed (especially for suspects, who were in this way brought to a confession). At the same time, that fear of demagogues and revolutionists so long entertained in Prussia began to bear fruit in provisions against students, secret societies, and acts tending to public disorders. Together with the law of 1799, above mentioned, a number of new ordinances (some of them most extraordinary) directed against libels and insults (in which the legislator met much difficulty in handling the distinction between civil and military persons) so increased the general confusion that as early as 1805 a project to publish a new code was even proposed by the legislative power

[1] *Cf. e.g.* § 2: "He who for the first time is convicted of an ordinary theft shall undergo corporal chastisement, or, if such punishment is not feasible (?) or should be deemed insufficient, shall be sentenced to imprisonment in a reformatory institution, to solitary confinement, or to penal labor." § 7: "More severe (?) chastisement shall be inflicted if, etc." (The amount of ordinary chastisement was not fixed.) § 18 ordered imprisonment until pardon, for repeated thefts accompanied with violence. § 12 in addition to life imprisonment also provided branding and public flogging for repetition of the crime of robbery.

[2] As to the horrible building conditions of many institutions, in which cleanliness was absolutely impossible and the prisoners were consumed by vermin, *cf.* the work of the Prussian Minister of Justice *Von Arnim*, "Bruchstücke über Verbrechen und Strafen" (2 vols. 1803), in which the harmful condition of the Prussian system of criminal justice was portrayed with great candor. *Cf.* especially II, pp. 189 *et seq.* Concerning the pitiful treatment of sick prisoners, *cf.* II, p. 78. But *cf.* also I, p. 235 and II, p. 39 as to the agreeable life in other penal institutions.

[3] The dilemma as to what to do with prisoners led even to a cabinet order of Dec. 28, 1801, which under certain conditions contemplated deportation to Siberia. This was actually done. *Cf. Wagnitz*, "Ideen und Pläne zur Verbesserung der Polizei- und Criminalanstalten" (Halle, 1801), II, pp. 17, 43.

[4] As to the repulsive effects of this flogging in a famous (or rather notorious) trial, *cf. Von Arnim*, I, pp. 38 *et seq.*

itself.[5] Nevertheless, nothing came of this other than a number of separate ordinances against secret societies, disobedience of the censor, crimes against the State, and similar regulations arising from the fear of demagogues.

It was not until 1826 that the preparation of a criminal code was undertaken under the Minister of Justice, Count Dankelmann. Marked progress was shown by the "General Portion" in the draft of 1830, which was substantially the work of the Supreme Court Counsellor, Bode. However, Von Kamptz (who in 1830 succeeded Count Dankelmann as Minister of Justice) sought to warp the legislation towards the standpoint of the police regulation of the "Landrecht," and revised it in an ultra-reactionary spirit. The provisions of the draft appearing in 1836 are almost incredible.[6] Aggravated forms of the death penalty, as well as corporal chastisement (to be administered publicly!), again make their appearance.

It is impossible here to undertake to follow out in detail the complicated history of the long preliminary work for the Prussian Criminal Code. One may attribute the merit of the preliminary draft of 1843 [7] to its subjection to public criticism. But it is astonishing to find in the draft of 1847 (which in other respects shows more of the influence of the law of France and the Rhine countries) provisions by which, in certain graver crimes, the death penalty is aggravated by public exposure of the head of the executed criminal and also by cutting off the guilty right hand after death, and also provisions by which imprisonment in penitentiaries was aggravated by corporal punishment and imprisonment in jails by curtailment of food and by uncomfortable places of repose. There was also imposed confiscation of all the property of those guilty of high and ordinary treason and of evading military service.

The Code of 1851. — The year 1848 marked the end of these vacillations, and the Prussian Criminal Code of April 14, 1851,[8] exhibited in a number of important provisions (although not in all

[5] *Cf.* the publication permit for the "Criminalordnung für die preussischen Staaten" of Dec. 11, 1805.

[6] *Berner*, pp. 224 *et seq.*, gives a selection of examples. For example, the dissemination of principles and opinions which might incite or encourage treasonable plots or sentiments was punished by from two to six years in the penitentiary.

[7] *Cf.* especially *Berner*, pp. 226 *et seq.*

[8] The draft appearing in 1849, based upon the decrees of a commission of the Department of Justice, contained substantially the provisions of the later code.

respects) a most important progress in German legal development.[9] It revealed a step in advance, to which (apart from the Carolina, in its day) perhaps only that made by the Bavarian Code of 1813 may be compared.[10] All this was substantially due to the far-reaching influence of the French Code, which until 1851 had been in effect in the Prussian Rhine Provinces. Like the French Code, the Prussian is remarkable for a brevity of composition, avoiding superfluity and the rejection of all pedantic vagaries, and therefore by the greater freedom which it allows for the scientific regulation of the provisions of the "General Portion." It also resembles the French Code in that (more perhaps than any other of the earlier German Codes) it is adaptable to use under the jury system. It bears a further similarity to the French Code in being free from moralizing and theological tendencies, and generally (but not entirely)[11] free from that meddlesomeness which we encounter in so many provisions of the earlier local legislation. It adopts the triple classification of punishable acts as "Verbrechen", "Vergehen", and "Uebertretungen",[12] and in its "Special Portion" completely separated the last class of offenses from the two other. In an appendix it deals with only some of the offenses against police regulation. On the other hand, while it places limits upon punishment for "Uebertretungen", it extends to them a number of the most important provisions of the "General Portion."

The Code possesses considerable advantages over the French Code. The "General Portion" was conceived in a comprehensive spirit, under the influence of German jurists. The various

[9] *Cf. Goltdammer*, "Materialien zum Strafgesetzbuche für die preussischen Staaten" (1851, 1852); *Beseler*, "Commentar" (1851); *Oppenhoff*, "Das Strafgesetzbuch für die preusslichen Staaten, erläutert aus den Materialien, der Rechtslehre und den Entscheidungen des Obertribunals" (6th ed. 1869); *Temme*, "Lehrbuch des preussl. Strafrechts" (1853); *Hälschner*, "System" (2 Parts, 1855, 1868, not completed; Part I contains the "General Portion"); *Oppenhoff*, "Die Rechtsprechung des königl. Obertribunals in Strafsachen" (1861 *et seq.*). "Archiv für preussisches Strafrecht", established by *Goltdammer* in 1853, in 1871 changed to "Archiv für deutsches und preussisches Strafrecht", and still appearing, ed. *Kohler*, a volume annually.

[10] *Cf. Mittermaier*, "Archiv für preussisches Strafrecht" (1851), pp. 14 *et seq.*

[11] This recalls the well-known "Hatred and Contempt" paragraph (§ 101): "Anyone who through public assertion or dissemination of false or distorted statements of fact, or through public abuse or derision, exposes the institutions of the State or the regulations of the authorities to hate and contempt shall be punished by a fine not exceeding 200 Thaler or by imprisonment not exceeding two months." (*Cf.* also § 101) § 151 of Part II, Tit. 20 of the "General 'Landrecht.'"

[12] *I.e.* approximately "crimes", "misdemeanors", and violations of law not amounting to a misdemeanor.

offenses are more carefully and precisely defined and the Code is uniformly milder than the "Code Pénal" as it appeared originally in 1810. No mention is made of corporal punishment, and imprisonment is simply divided into two kinds:[13] imprisonment in a penitentiary and in a jail.[14] There is also, for certain offenses, confinement in a fortress, which, while very mild in character, might possibly be of long duration. Apart from murder and high treason, the death penalty is provided for grave cases of manslaughter and for crimes endangering the general public; but it is to be inflicted within the prison walls.

In many respects and especially in regard to its theories of participation and attempt, this Code too closely followed the French. Those provisions copied from the French law (in many respects commendable), which permitted the consideration of mitigating circumstances in many cases (but by no means in all), merited censure for this very inconsistency, and subjected the necessary severity and logic of the law to the sentiment of the individual jury. Many of the separate provisions are quite severe, and a punctilious interpretation of the courts, following too much the letter of the law, has rendered certain features the more intolerable.[15] It may be added that the provisions concerning the mode of carrying out imprisonment are inadequate, and in actual practice, apart from the fact that enforced labor of those confined for "Uebertretungen" fell into disuse, the treatment of convicts depended upon the unfettered discretion of the prison authorities, — even to the infliction of solitary confinement.[16] The disciplinary treatment of prisoners was covered neither by the Code itself, nor by any supplementary statutes; and as to a legal protection of, for example, persons of the educated class condemned not for dishonorable offenses but merely for offenses against the press laws

[13] *I.e.* "Zuchthausstrafe" and "Gefängnissstrafe."

[14] This divided also into two classes, for "Vergehen" and for "Uebertretungen."

[15] Thus, for example, § 89 dealing with insubordination was frequently so interpreted that opposition to acts of an official which were of doubtful legality, provided there was no malice on the part of the official, was regarded as punishable. Certain supplementary statutes made this in some respects less severe.

[16] The memorial to the "Landtag" by the Minister of Interior (March 26, 1861) makes this assertion. On the contrary, see *Von Holtzendorff*, "Gesetz oder Verwaltungsmaxime, rechtliche Bedenken gegen die preussische Denkschrift betr. Einzelhaft" (1861). The view of the Prussian government was defended by *Böhlau*, "Die Einzelhaft in Preussen" (1861). Concerning certain tendencies of Prussian prison authorities of this period, *cf.* also *Von Holtzendorff*, "Der Brüderorden des rauhen Hauses und sein Wirken in den Strafanstalten" (1862).

or offenses of a purely political nature, against a treatment in the prisons which in the circumstances in question was absolutely improper, none can be found in this Code.

§ 65. **Influence of the Prussian Code.** — The practical usefulness of the Prussian Criminal Code caused a number of smaller States to take it as a foundation for their own criminal legislation. With minor changes, it was enacted as law in Waldeck and Pyrmont (1855).[1] The Criminal Code of Lübeck, except for a few really significant changes, corresponds almost verbatim with that of Prussia.[2] The Oldenburg Code of January 31, 1858, however, differed from the Prussian in not retaining the death penalty and in substituting imprisonment for life; in a few other cases, the amount of punishment was changed; except in cases of life imprisonment, loss of rights as a citizen was only temporary.[3]

The Bavarian Code of 1861. — The Bavarian Criminal Code of November 10, 1861, which like the Prussian Code was a result of long years of preparation and was the last of the more important local codes, was in many respects similar to the Prussian Code. It resembled the Prussian Code in respect to punishments affecting honor, and in many cases retained the death penalty (although not always the same as in the Prussian Code.) It was defective, however, in having a confused and indefinite system of punishment by imprisonment; and it is difficult to mark the distinction between its jail and prison punishments. In Article 19, it accepts the system of parallel punishments (instead of imprisonment in jail or prison) under certain conditions for persons of the educated classes. In its treatment of attempts and participation, the code assumes a middle position between the French and German law. It differs from the Prussian Code in its " General Portion ", especially in its rejection of a system of extenuating circumstances. However, Article 68 recognized limited mental capacity as an extenuating circumstance; and Article 74 sanctioned voluntary reparation as an extenuating circumstance[4] in certain

[1] Thus, also, in Anhalt (by the statue of Feb. 5, 1852). Here however it was supplanted in 1864 by the Thuringian Code. *Cf. Berner*, p. 257.

[2] Thus the Code of Lübeck did not recognize permanent loss of privileges dependent upon honor, but only a temporary interdiction of these privileges. An attempt was always given a milder punishment than the consummated act. As to details, see *Berner*, p. 257.

[3] A comparison of the Oldenburg and Prussian Code has been made by *Mittermaier*, in "Archiv für preuss. Strafrecht" (1859), pp. 14 *et seq.*

[4] Limitation of the period within which punishment may be inflicted for crime was treated in quite a different manner. In this respect, however, the code is distinctly inferior to that of Prussia.

offenses against property; this latter, however, rested in the discretion of the judge. Upon the whole, the Code is appreciably milder than that of Prussia.[5]

Other States. — It was not until the year 1866 that general codes were enacted in Mecklenburg (two grand duchies), Electoral Hesse,[6] Schleswig-Holstein, Lauenburg, Schaumburg-Lippe, Bremen, and Hamburg. Theoretically the Carolina had still obtained in these countries; but in reality the criminal law had been shaped by the usage of the courts (following the jurists) and by a number of more or less comprehensive special statutes.[7]

§ 66. **Progress towards Greater Legal Unity in Germany.** — The political events of the year 1866 necessarily gave a new and now more effectual incentive to endeavors to establish a general law for Germany. Since the year 1860 this had been specially advocated by the German Bar Association.[1] As a matter of fact, the Prussian government apparently was not planning for the immediate formation of a common North German Code; instead, its first measure was (by Ordinance of June 25th, 1876) to introduce the Prussian Code[2] into its newly acquired territories of Hanover, Electoral Hesse, Schleswig-Holstein, Nassau, Hesse-Homburg, and Frankfurt-on-Main, as well as in the ceded districts of Bavaria.[3]

[5] For literature, see *Berner*, pp. 341 *et seq.* Special mention may be made of the commentaries by *Hocheder* (1862, not finished, only the first volume); *Stenglein* (2 vols. 1861, 1862); *Weis* (2 vols. 1863, 1865); *Dollmann*, (1862, not finished); "Sitzungsberichte der bayer. Strafgerichte" (5 vols. 1850–53); later "Zeitschrift für Gesetzgebung und Rechtspflege in Bayern" (1854 *et seq.*); *Stenglein*, "Zeitschrift für Gerichtspraxis und Rechtswissenschaft in Bayern" (1862; after 1872 appearing as "Zeitschrift f. deutsche Gerichtspraxis und Rechtswissenschaft"; discontinued in 1880).

[6] Published in Electoral Hesse with only a few changes (the so-called "Philippina.") As to Electoral Hesse, *cf. H. Kersting*, "Das Strafrecht in Kurhessen."

[7] For the two Grand duchies of Mecklenburg the following were especially important: a comprehensive ordinance concerning theft of 1839, an ordinance of 1843 concerning offenses against public order, and an ordinance of 1854 as to incendiarism. As to the condition of the law in the above-mentioned countries, *cf.* "Motive zu dem Entwurfe eines Strafgesetzbuchs für den norddeutschen Bund", pp. 6 *et seq.*

[1] *Cf.* "Verhandlungen des 1. deutschen Juristentags", p. 58; *ibid.*, essay by *Von Gross* and *Von Kräwel* dealing with the introduction of uniform German legislation. See also essay by *Wahlberg*, p. 63. As early as 1857, *Krug* had published his "Ideen zu einer gemeinsamen Strafgesetzgebung für Deutschland." [And now see *Banke*, "Der erste Entwurf [1849] eines Deutschen Einheitsstrafrechts" (Berlin, 1912). — ED.]

[2] As to the condition of the law in Hanover, Schleswig-Holstein, Electoral Hesse, Nassau, Hessen-Homburg, Frankfurt-on-Main, at the time of the annexation, *cf. Goltdammer's* "Archiv f. preuss. Strafrecht" (1866), pp. 657–816.

[3] In Lauenburg, which was not really absorbed by the Prussian State until 1876, the common law in the meantime continued in force.

But the Constitution of the North German Confederation of June 26th placed criminal law and criminal procedure [4] among those subjects over which the scope of the legislative power of the North German Confederation should extend. And, in pursuance of a decree of the Reichstag, there was published by the Prussian Minister of Justice [5] towards the end of July, 1869, at the request of the Chancellor of the Confederation, a draft of a Criminal Code for the North German Confederation.[6]

The Draft of 1869 of a Criminal Code for North Germany. — This draft was substantially the work of Friedberg, who at that time was Supreme Counsellor of Justice, and later Prussian Minister of Justice. As declared in its accompanying Report, and as the conditions of the times indeed demanded, it took the Prussian Code as its foundation. It was, however, considerably less severe; *e.g.* it limited capital punishment to a very few cases, and reduced the maximum duration of imprisonment to fifteen years. In numerous respects it had endeavored to comply with the demands of legal science; particularly in its paragraphs dealing with attempts and the criminal capacity of children, it sought to bring itself more into accord with the principles of the German common law instead of the French principles adopted by the Prussian Code. It retained, however, the system of extenuating circumstances, and at the same time considerably expanded its scope. Its important change was: the release on parole of prisoners after they had undergone part of their sentence, — a measure which (following the English model) has been made use of since 1862 in the kingdom of Saxony, by the pardoning of the ruler (but practised in accordance with certain generally received principles). An endeavor was also made to establish a rational rule for the effect of punishable acts upon capacity for holding offices of honor or trust, — a rule looking to the concrete case and having regard not so much to the kind of punishment as to the character of the individual crime.

[4] The authority of the several States to enact criminal laws was obviously not thereby revoked; and so in the Kingdom of Saxony, on October 1st, 1868, a revision of the criminal code was published and Hamburg even published a new criminal code in 1869.

[5] A very serviceable private draft was prepared by *John* ("Entwurf mit Motiven zu einem Strafgesetzbuche für den norddeutschen Bund", 1868).

[6] In addition to the Report there accompanied this draft commentaries on the death penalty and the maximum duration of punishment by imprisonment, and also discussions of problems of criminal law in the province of medical jurisprudence and a comparative collection of criminal provisions from German and foreign legislation.

The draft adopted the only correct and practical attitude in treating in matters of criminal law the entire territory of the Confederation as a single territory,[7] notwithstanding the fact that the Confederation did not constitute a homogeneous State. For as a matter of fact criminal statutes are chiefly influenced by the degree of the civilization of the people and in part by their greater or lesser amount of political freedom, and are but comparatively little influenced by the differences of the civil law. It was recognized, however, that it was possible that both treason and high treason could be committed against the individual States of the Confederation as well as against the Confederation itself, — even where this crime was committed with a view of helping some other one of the confederated States. Obviously, a code complete in the sense that the application of all other criminal statutes was to be precluded was not even to be contemplated. None of the codes of even the larger States were complete in this sense. It was necessary that a certain field of legislation be left to the individual States. Care was to be taken only that the unity of the law should not thereby be destroyed, that the individual States adopt lofty principles of punishment, and that no penalty should be imposed for acts which would be deemed unpunishable under the sense and spirit of the Code of the Confederation by virtue of its silence or the limitations of its definitions.

The draft was quite deficient in respect to imprisonment. There were only a few general provisions which enlarged or restricted the field of local legislation, or (where this was insufficient) of the regulative discretion (especially in Prussia) of administrative boards. However, a uniform and thorough-going regulation was not practicable without providing for numerous incidental details, and particularly for the undertaking of costly and permanent buildings; and this would have meant the postponement of the entire statute.

§ 67. **The Code of the North German Confederation.** — There is perhaps no other example of a code of the importance of the "Norddeutsches Strafgesetzbuch" being prepared in a large State in so short a time. The preliminary draft entrusted to a commission appointed by the Bundesrath on October 1st, 1869, was on the

[7] The ideas and objections brought forward by *Heinze* ("Staats- und strafrechtliche Erortungen zu dem amtlichen Entwurfe eines Strafgesetzbuchs für den norddeutschen Bund", 1870) have proved to be without foundation. In contrast to Heinze, *cf. Bar* in "Archiv f. preussischen Strafrecht" (1870), pp. 83 *et seq.*, and *Rudorff*, "Strafgesetzbuch für d. deutsche Reich" (2d ed. p. 19).

31st day of December, 1869, submitted to the Chancellor. This commission was under the chairmanship of Leonhardt, who at that time was the Prussian Minister of Justice, and among its more prominent members the above-mentioned Friedberg, and Schwarze, the Attorney-General of Saxony. The Bundesrath also promptly gave its approval, and on February 14th, 1870, there was presented to the Reischstag a draft of the law with a draft of its enacting statute ("Einführungsgesetz").

Its Character. — It is not to be expected that, where so great haste was shown, a careful consideration of principles and their application could even be contemplated. The leading political party was dominated by one thought, viz., to produce *something*, — to show that the newly formed Confederation was in a position to produce a new legislative work of general application, and to cement quickly the national unity by means of the criminal law. However, there were numerous and important changes from the first draft, both in matter and form. Thus the provisions of the "General Portion", recommended by the committee of the Bundesrath to be applicable to minor offenses ("Uebertretungen"), were made applicable [1] generally. Offenses (personal) against the princes of the Confederation or members of their families were treated in a different manner, according as there was involved the ruler of the offender's nationality or the ruler of the territory where the act was committed. § 47 of the "General Portion", placing limitations upon capacity for responsibility, was given wider application; and the requirement that a complaint lodged by the injured party precede a prosecution was extended to a larger number of cases. A new treatment was accorded to sentences to prison ("Zuchthaus") "ipso facto" affecting the right to hold positions of trust and honor, in that by § 28 a sentence of this character had as its immediate consequence loss of capacity to serve in the army or navy of the Confederation and permanent loss of capacity for holding public office. This provision of the Code, although chiefly due to the influence of the military element in the Bundesrath, was more in accord with popular opinion than the too idealistic treatment of this subject found in the first draft.

Opposition in the Reichstag. — In the Reichstag the draft was also dealt with in an extremely summary manner. A motion to

[1] Consequently offenses ("Uebertretungen") were no longer dealt with in a third part but were treated in a single (the last) chapter of the "Special Portion" (second) of the Code.

debate the principal questions separately was rejected. The "General Portion", and the first seven chapters of the "Special Portion" dealing chiefly with political offenses, were given immediate discussion in open session. Chapters 9–23 were referred to a committee of twenty-one members. The question of capital punishment nearly brought about the failure of the entire work. At the second debate in open session, on March 1st, 1870, the Reichstag, by a majority of 118 votes to 81, voted for the abolition of the death penalty. (It had in the meantime been abolished in the Kingdom of Saxony.) The Bundesrath, however, by an overwhelming majority, voted to retain the death penalty for murder and for heinous cases of high treason.[2] On the third reading, after the Chancellor, Count von Bismarck, had cast the weight of his authority in favor of the retention of the death penalty, the Reichstag, both in this matter and in a matter touching the procedure for certain political offenses, acceded to the view of the Bundesrath. The Bundesrath was thus enabled, at its session of March 25th, 1870, to give the Code its unanimous approval; and the Code, together with its enacting law, received, on May 31st, the assent of the head of the Confederation, and on June 8th, 1870, was published in Number 16 of the "Bundesgesetzblatt."

Changes made by the Reichstag. — The draft, however, underwent a considerable number of changes as a result of the votes in the Reichstag. Thus, there was abolished all absolutely fixed penalties, with the exception of the two cases of capital punishment. In those cases where life imprisonment had originally been fixed as a penalty, the judge was empowered to inflict imprisonment for a period limited by a fixed maximum. The penalties in a number of cases were reduced. The reduction of sentence for extenuating circumstances was extended to a greater number of offenses. The number of cases in which a prosecution could ensue only upon private initiative was also extended. The changes dealing with political offenses were of marked importance. In this last respect mention should be made of §§ 11 and 12, which extended to members of the legislative assemblies of the separate States and to their proceedings that freedom of speech and immunity from punishment for true assertions which had been sanctioned by the Constitution of the Confederation in respect to the Reichstag. Men-

[2] *I.e.*, attempts against the life of the sovereign, against the life of one's own prince, or the prince of the territory where the act is committed.

tion should also be made of the supplement to § 113 [3] of the Criminal Code, which in fact should be regarded as a guarantee of the freedom of the citizens of the States, and by which punishment for resistance to the acts of an official is limited to cases where the official is acting within his lawful authority.[4]

Criticism of the Code. — The "Norddeutsche Strafgesetzbuch" was *not* a far reaching code in the matter of *reforms*. Its essential merit, and one which must not be too lightly esteemed, consists in laying the foundation for uniformity of criminal legislation in the region included within the Confederation. Moreover, it must be admitted that for a majority of the confederated States, notably *e.g.* for Prussia and Saxony, it entailed a very material step in advance. It must be conceded further that in *all* of the confederated States, while it uniformly gave better expression to the prior law, in many important respects it produced better results in practice.

That the Code had faults and defects is a circumstance which it shares with every other statute. Much could have been given more careful deliberation, and after such deliberation could have been improved. But apart from these faults, the reproach that the Code can be justly criticized for being too mild, or that juristic theory is responsible for its shortcomings, has nothing to substantiate it, — a charge made by many who have scanty acquaintance with the Code or the history of criminal law. There was not sufficient time for the jurists to make a thorough-going and comprehensive criticism of the draft of the Code; and mere theorists, in the narrow sense of the word, had no share in the drafts.[5] The criticism from outside, moreover,[6] was very limited in scope, and no time was given for careful discussion of more than a few individual features.

The Code of the North German Confederation as the Code of the Empire. — Even before the Code went into effect (January 1st, 1871) as that of the North German Confederation, the treaty concluded in 1870 with the Grandduchies of Hesse and Baden and the

[3] *Cf.* also the supplement to § 110 whereby the punishment incidental to summons for contempt is limited to the case where the order is legally valid or the action is within the jurisdiction of the official.

[4] For the history of its origin, *cf.* the brief but excellent exposition in *Rüdorff*, "Commentar."

[5] As to the course of events, *cf.* particularly *Von Wächter*, "Beitrag zur Geschichte und Kritik der Entwürfe eines Strafgesetzbuch für den norddeutschen Bund", 1870.

[6] For list of works and articles dealing with the criticism of the drafts, see *Von Wächter*, p. 18; *Von Holtzendorff*, "Handbuch", I, pp. 131 *et seq.*

Kingdoms of Bavaria and Würtemberg made it certain that it would become the code of the new German Confederation. In Hesse south of the Main the Code went into effect on January 1st, 1871, and in Bavaria, Würtemberg, and Baden it was to go into effect on January 1st, 1872. In the meantime, however, as a result of the North German statute of April 16th, 1871, dealing with the constitution of the German Empire, the Code was proclaimed as a statute of the Empire; at the same time it was provided that the laws of the North German Confederation then enacted or yet to be enacted should prevail as the law of the Empire in territory that was added. Thus the Code obtained as the law of the Empire in Hesse south of the Main from the 1st day of January, 1871, and in Bavaria, Würtemberg, and Baden from the 1st day of January, 1872, and in Alsace-Lorraine by virtue of a special Statute of August 30th, 1871, from October 1st, 1871. The substitution of terms appropriate for the new Empire for terms appropriate for the North German Confederation seemed to render it imperative to prepare a new edition of the Code. The changes incident to this revision were effected for the Code (but not for its enacting law) [7] by the Statute of May 15th, 1871, dealing with the revision of the Criminal Code of the North German Confederation as the Criminal Code of the German Empire.

§ 68. **The Criminal Law Amendment Act of 1876.** — A defect of the Code, which in some of its aspects has been previously criticized and which even at the present time often leads to decisions contrary to the sense of justice, lay in the treatment of extenuating circumstances, for which the only criterion is the attitude of the individual judge. Another obvious defect was in the status which the charge at times might assume, the rule of the so-called "Antragsdelicte" (*i.e.* offenses whose prosecution is based only upon private initiative). The unfortunate features of the last-mentioned principle and the urgent need of their remedy soon became apparent both to the courts and the public. On the one hand, the requirement that a complaint be lodged by the injured person was extended to too large a number of offenses. On the other hand, the right to withdraw the criminal complaint and thereby effect

[7] A new revision of the enacting law was not considered necessary. Here the profession relied upon § 2, Abs. 2 of the Statute of April 16th, 1871: "The . . . laws referred to are laws of the Empire. Where in the same there is mention of the North German Confederation, its constitution, territory, members, or states, rights of natives, institutions of government, officers, officials, flag, etc., the same shall be construed as the German Empire and its corresponding attributes."

a "nolle prosequi" at the arbitrary discretion of the party injured (or his legal representative, as the case might be), had been given too wide a range in criminal procedure (extending even to the time of the final judgment or sentence).[1]

The bill for a statute amending the Criminal Code (*i.e.* "Strafgesetznovelle") which the Bundesrath, in November, 1875,[2] submitted to the Reichstag, went far beyond the elimination of this defect. A case arising in Belgium,[3] involving a frequently uttered threat against the life of Prince Bismarck,[4] led to the proposal that an ineffectual incitement to crime in its widest sense should be subjected to punishment. A special penal provision was also proposed in order to ensure the obedience and fidelity of officials of the Foreign Office.[5] There were also proposed a number of more subordinate special provisions, in part suitable to their purpose and later accepted by the Reichstag. In addition to all this there was proposed a complete alteration of fundamental provisions of the "General Portion" (punishment of offenses committed in foreign countries, punishment of the so-called "completed attempts"). It was furthermore sought by means of broader phrasings and severer penalties to bring about a stricter suppression of the public utterance and circulation of doctrines that seemed dangerous politically.[6]

By the Criminal Law Amendment Act of February 26th, 1876, enacted after a warm debate, a part only of these proposals were enacted. The so-called "ineffectual incitement to crime"[7] in § 49a (the Duchesne case) was made liable to punishment only under certain special conditions, and § 353a (the Arnim case) corresponded to the original proposal in part only. The proposed changes in the method of dealing with attempts, and in the fundamentally different treatment of offenses committed abroad, were

[1] *Cf.* the official "Motive zur Strafgesetznovelle von 1876."

[2] This was less than four years after the Code went into effect as the law of the Empire and less than five years after it went into effect in the territories of the North German Confederation and in Hesse.

[3] *Cf.* the Belgian Statute of July 9th, 1875.

[4] The case of Duchesne.

[5] The case of Count Harry von Arnim. Concerning this, see the opinions given by *von Holtzendorff* (1875), "Vertheidungsreden in der Untersuchungssache wider den Grafen Harry v. Arnim, gehalten von den Rechtsanwälten Dockhorn und Munckel", Berlin (1875).

[6] Another unfortunate proposal of the draft had to do with the introduction for certain cases of the so-called "Friedensbürgschaft" (*i.e.* bonds to keep the peace). *Cf.* in regard to this, *Schierlinger*, "Die Friedensbürgschaft", pp. 76 *et seq.*

[7] *I.e.* "erfolglose Anstiftung."

totally rejected, as were also these for the extension of certain political offenses. On the other hand, the treatment of the so-called "Antragsdelicte" was subjected to a radical change. In a number of offenses the requirement of a complaint by the party injured was completely eliminated; and the rule was adopted that a complaint once lodged could not be withdrawn. This rule, however, was subject to numerous exceptions (so as virtually, in some cases, to amount to a privilege of relationship between the injured party and the offender); and the excessive time limit within which the complaint may be withdrawn was not changed.

Other Criminal Laws. — Previously, by virtue of the statute of December 10th, 1871, and as a result of the controversy with the Church of Rome, the Code had received an additional paragraph (§ 130a) which was directed against inflammatory speeches by the Clergy. The Criminal Law Amendment Act extended this § 130a so as to cover written utterances of the Clergy in the exercise of their vocation or in connection with the exercise of their vocation. Code § 287 had already been supplanted by § 14 of the Statute of November 30th, 1874, for the protection of trademarks; and § 337 had been supplanted by § 67 of the Statute of February 6th, 1875, for the verification of legal status and marriage. With the taking effect of the comprehensive Imperial Justice Act (October 1st, 1879) §§ 281–283 of the Criminal Code, dealing with criminal bankruptcy, were supplanted by §§ 209–214 of the Insolvency Regulations of February 10th, 1877.

That the new institutions of the German Empire and the needs of business rendered necessary a considerable number of special penal provisions in the nature of police regulations is quite obvious. It is also apparent that laws of this character are subject to frequent change. Of a more fundamental and permanent significance (and difficult, moreover, to square with the theory of criminal law) are the statute of May 7th, 1874, dealing with the Press, the statute of May 14th, 1879, dealing with traffic in food supplies, etc., and the statute of May 24th, 1880, dealing with usury. The last-mentioned law gave to the judge (subject however to numerous precautions) a very extensive discretion in respect to the determination of the elements of the offense. And this may become a starting point for further indefinite statutes according to the judge a large amount of discretion in respect to morals; which would harmonize, however, with a socialistic tendency of the State.

§ 69. **The Draft Code of 1909.**[1] — The history of Germany's legislation since 1880 is the reflex of legal science in Germany and its various proposals of reform, and belongs rather in the field of contemporary legal theory. The chief leader, both in science and in proposals for Code revision, has long been Franz von Liszt, professor in the University of Berlin.[2] Among those who entered the arena to support or to oppose his views were notably Birkmeyer,[3] Van Calker,[4] Seuffert,[5] Wach,[6] Kohler,[7] Sichart,[8] Mayer.[9] By 1902 the movement had so far advanced that a so-called "Scientific Commission" was appointed by the government to prepare a draft; it comprised forty-nine members, representing every shade of thought. A first task of this Commission was to prepare and publish the materials for a comparative study of the world's criminal law. This superb undertaking, the "Comparative Exposition of German and Foreign Criminal Law"[10] is a mine of information on the criminal laws of all countries.

In November, 1909, appeared the Commission's Preliminary Draft, with commentary.[11] The preface to the Commission's commentary pointed out that this preliminary draft had no official status as a government measure, and was not to be laid before Parliament. It was meant as a basis for constructive criticism from all quarters.

From the time of its appearance, the Preliminary Draft has been

[1] [This section was prepared by the Editor, from material furnished by Dr. L. VON THÓT. The original § 69 of Von Bar's text is in part omitted and in part transferred to § 63, *ante*. — ED.]

[2] Some of his proposals are set forth in the following places: "XXVI Deutschen Juristentag, Verhandlungen" and "Festschrift", Berlin, 1902.

[3] "Münchener Juristenverein, Verhandlungen", Munich, 1901.

[4] "Vergeltungsidee und Zweckgedanke", Heidelberg, 1899.

[5] "Die Bewegung im Strafrechte während der letzten 30 Jahre", Dresden, 1901.

[6] "Zukunft des deutschen Strafrechts", Leipzig, 1902.

[7] "Reformfragen des Strafrechts", Munich, 1903.

[8] "Beitrag zur Revision des Strafgesetzbuchs für das Deutsche Reich."

[9] "Deutsche Juristen-Zeitung", Vol. VII.

[10] "Vergleichende Darstellung des Deutschen und ausländischen Strafrechts; Vorarbeiten zur Deutschen Strafrechtsreform", edited for the Imperial Department of Justice by *Liszt, Birkmeyer, Calker, Frank, Hippel, Kahl, Lilienthal,* and *Wach;* Berlin, 15 vols., 1906–08.

[11] "Vorentwurf zu einem Deutschen Strafgesetzbuch, bearbeitet von der hierzu bestellten Verständigen-Kommission", Berlin, J. Guttentag, 1909; with a commentary, "Begründung, Allgemeiner Theil" (pp. 1–419) and "Besonderer Theil" (pp. 419–860).

A "counter-draft," proposed by jurists not satisfied with the official draft, has also been published: "Gegenentwurf zum Vorentwurf eines Deutschen Strafgesetzbuchs nebst Begründung", by *Kahl, Liszt, Lilienthal,* and *Goldschmidt* (Berlin, 1910).

the central object of criminalistic discussion in Germany.[12] Its revision has been entrusted to a second Commission, with Lucas at the head. Representing the composite result of extremely opposite views, it has not entirely satisfied any school of thought. Undoubtedly it represents an advance, and a radical advance, in many respects. Its encouraging feature is that it is based on a comprehensive attempt to embody into law the best that criminal science can propose; and its shortcomings are due to the still imperfect agreement among criminal scientists as to the best practical methods for applying a body of scientific principles which as yet is itself in a state of conscious growth.

[12] Out of the library of literature already accumulated may be noted the following critiques: *Aschrott* and *Liszt*, "Kritische Besprechung des Vorentwurfs etc.", 1910; *Mayer*, in "Deutsche Juristenzeitung", XIV, No. 21, pp. 1281–1300; *Lucas*, in "Deutsche Juristenzeitung", XVI, pp. 721, 895, 1022, 1353, 1517, XVII, pp. 299, 423, 653, 825, 1152, 1369; *Lilienthal*, *Liszt*, and *Calker*, in "Zeitschrift für die gesamte Strafrechtswissenschaft", XXX, pp. 224–289; *Langer*, in "Zeitschrift" above cited, XXXI, 2; *Gleispach*, in "Oesterreichische Zeitschrift für Strafrecht", 4, 209; *Michaelis*, in "Blätter für Gefängniskunde"; *K. Meyer*, "Die Postulate der Internationalen Kriminalistischen Vereinigung und die Beschlüsse zweier Strafrechtskommission", in "Mitteilungen der I. K. V.", XXI, p. 224 (1914).

Chapter XVI

OTHER COUNTRIES SINCE 1800

Austria, Netherlands and Belgium, Scandinavia, Switzerland

A. Austria[1]

§ 69*a*. Austrian Legislation since 1848.

§ 69*a*. **Austrian Legislation since** 1848. — Von Schmerling, Minister of Justice in 1851, planned for a new criminal code. But his plan did not mature. The Criminal Code promulgated May 27, 1852, was merely a revision of the Code of 1803. The system of penalties was improved; but the Code could still not be termed in any respect a mild one.[2] Like most of the other newer Codes, it substituted for "serious police-misdemeanors" the term "offense" ("Vergehen"); so that the triple classification became: Crimes ("Verbrechen"), offenses ("Vergehen"), misdemeanors ("Uebertretungen").

The efforts to obtain a really reformed code continued meanwhile; and in 1861–63 a draft was prepared by Hye von Glunek;[3] but it was never enacted. In November, 1867, a supplementary

[1] [This section — except the first paragraph, which is from § 63 of Von Bar's treatise — is compiled by Dr. L. von Thót for this volume; for this author, see the Editorial Preface. — Ed.]

[2] There were two grades of imprisonment, — ordinary, and severe. The former signified close confinement, without chains; no conversation with a visitor except in the presence of a prison officer. The latter signified solitary confinement, with iron shackles; visitors allowed only on extraordinary occasions, and relatives never. Special features for increasing the severity of treatment were: limited food, hard bed, dark cell, flogging.

[In *Silvio Pellico's* "Le Mie Prigioni" will be found a realistic account of the severe kind of imprisonment, as practised in Austria in the 1820 s. — Ed.]

[3] A liberal leader, one of Austria's most celebrated criminalists, then about 55 years of age and professor in the University; afterwards Minister of Justice, member of the House of Lords, and Justice of the Imperial Supreme Court.

law amending some of the penalty provisions did pass. In 1868, another draft was presented, but soon withdrawn. Glaser, now Austria's most distinguished criminalist, was Minister of Justice;[4] and in 1874 he offered a new draft. This in turn failed. And so the story continued through the century; in 1881, the draft of Dr. Prazak's Ministry, and in 1891, that of Count Schonborn's Ministry, equally failed to find acceptance. Thus the Code of 1803–1852 rounded out more than a hundred years of existence.[5]

B. NETHERLANDS AND BELGIUM[1]

§ 69b. Netherlands. | § 69c. Belgium.

§ 69b. **Netherlands.** — The Revolution saw two early but fruitless attempts to reform and codify the criminal law; the work of the Commissions both of 1795 and of 1798 did not obtain legislative sanction. A new Commission — Reuvens, Elout, and Van Musschenbrouk — appointed in 1807, produced a draft which was enacted and went into force February 1, 1809. King Louis Bonaparte's ordinance styled it a "masterpiece of humanity"; its system was, indeed, relatively mild; it gave wide discretion to the judge in applying penalties; and it emphasized the mitigation of sentences for good behavior.

But this Code did not remain long in operation. One of the radical changes resulting from the French annexation of the Netherlands was that by ordinance of December 11, 1813, the French Code went into effect in the Netherlands, — although "provisionally" only. The Code was published in French; there was also a translation in Dutch, but this was not an exact translation, and a royal ordinance provided that in case of doubt the French text should be the guide. Moreover, the reception of the French

[4] Glaser began his professional career in 1849, with an essay on "English-Scotch Criminal Procedure." He became a professor at the University in 1856, and a member of Parliament, and took a zealous and leading part for the reform of criminal law and procedure. His writings on the subject are profuse.

[5] In 1912 a new draft was again prepared: "Regierungs-Entwurf eines Oesterreichischen Strafgesetzbuchs." The text and commentary are officially published as a Supplement to the Proceedings of the House of Peers, in 1912, No. 58, black letter No. 90; the House Commission's Report on the bills, in 1913, as Supplement Nos. 58–63, black letter No. 167. The text and commentary have also been published by Guttentag, Berlin, as Supplement No. 29 to Vol. XX of the "Mittheilungen der Internationalen Kriminalistischen Vereinigung."

[1] [These sections were prepared by Dr. L. VON THÓT; for this author, see the Editorial Preface. — ED.]

Criminal Code was not effected without some changes. Thus, the penalties of general confiscation of property, police oversight, compulsory hard labor, and death upon the scaffold were abolished. The death penalty was inflicted by strangulation or by the sword.

A royal ordinance of April 18, 1814, again appointed a commission to prepare a reformed legislation. This commission was ready on January 17, 1815, with a revision of the Code, and its draft was again revised by a sub-committee, Kemper and Phillipse; but it failed of enactment. In 1827, the government again laid a revision before the Senate, this draft corresponded in its general part with the Criminal Code of 1809, but in its special part (specific crimes) with the French Code. But as it was still based upon the old-fashioned deterrent theory, and its penalties were exceedingly severe, the government was obliged to withdraw it.

The next revision was not proposed until October, 1839; meanwhile ensued a long controversy among the jurists in regard to the abolition of capital punishment and the system of punishments generally. This draft, covering the first or general part of the Code, became a law on June 10, 1840. Successive drafts of the second part in 1842 and 1843, in 1846, in 1847, and in 1859, failed of enactment. Nevertheless, the "provisional" domination of the now antiquated French Code had made various modifications indispensable; and these were accomplished by the statute of June 29, 1864; this law abolished death upon the scaffold and marking with the branding-iron, extended the penalty of solitary confinement, and modified the provisions as to recidivists, and revised the definition of attempts and of specific crimes. Later modifications were effected by the statutes of April 10, 1869, and July 14, 1871.

A royal ordinance of September 28, 1870, again appointed a commission to revise the Code; the members were De Wal, L. Francois, J. Loke, A. De Pinto, M. S. Pols, A. J. Modderman, and Th. Beelaerts Van Blokland. The commission submitted their draft on May 13, 1874; but it was not enacted. In 1878 (under Minister of Justice Smidt) and again in 1880 (under Minister of Justice Moddermann) new drafts were submitted to Parliament; this last draft was enacted on March 3, 1881, to go into effect on Dec. 1, 1886; and, with various subsequent amendments, remains the Code in force.

This Code, the fruit of independent labor of Dutch jurists, has distinctively a national character. Its notable features are its division of criminal acts into two parts; the simplicity of its penal system; the abolition of humiliating penalties; the important part played by solitary confinement; the careful definition of the acts liable to punishment in respect to their subjective elements; and the abolition of special rules of mitigation.[2]

§ 69*c*. **Belgium** became a separate kingdom in 1830–33. The history of Belgian criminal legislation, until the time of its independence and its separation from the Netherlands, is identical with that of the Netherlands. After that date, until 1867, the French Code Pénal was put in force in Belgium. Preparations for a reform of the Criminal law began as early as 1834, when a commission was appointed for the revision of the Code Pénal. In 1848, a new commission was appointed, which submitted the result of their labors to the Parliament in 1855, and this became a law in 1867. This Code is in substance a remodelling of the French Criminal Code. With various amendments, it remains the Code in force.

C. SCANDINAVIA[1]

§ 69*d*. **Denmark.** — Danish codification of criminal law in the 1800s was at first only partial in its scope. The statute of October 4, 1833, punished crimes against corporal security and liberty. The statute of April 11, 1840, punished theft, fraud, forgery, etc. The statutes of April 15, 1840, and March 26, 1841, dealt respectively with perjury and arson. In the year 1850, a commission was assigned the work of preparing a draft of a complete criminal Code. This draft served as a foundation for the work of a new commission appointed in 1859. With this last draft as a basis was prepared the criminal Code in force at the present time, which went into effect on Feb. 10, 1866. The most impor-

[2] Drafts of a new Criminal Code have since been prepared, but without enactment, by the Ministries of Cort van der Linden, in 1900 (pub. Belinfante, entitled "Herziening van het Wetboek van Strafrecht"), and of Loeff, in 1904 ("Handlingen der Staaten-General", 1904–05, Band 80). The subsequent ministries of Nelissen and Regout, in 1911 and 1912, have abandoned the plan of a complete revision, and have sought to revise the Code piecemeal, by separate bills from time to time.

[1] [These sections were prepared by Dr. L. VON THÓT (for this author, see the Editorial Preface); except § 69*g*, on Finland, which was prepared by the translator, Mr. *Walgren*, from Professor *Forsmann's* treatise, cited in the Editorial Preface. — ED.]

tant later modifying statutes are: the statute of May 11, 1897, dealing with the punishment of acts of violence committed against innocent persons, and the statute of April 1, 1894, dealing with explosives.[1]

§ 69e. **Norway.** — In Norway the first movement toward modern criminal codification is found in the criminal statute of 1814, which specified, in its 96th Article, in accordance with the act of the French Declaration of the Rights of Man, that "no one should be convicted or punished except by virtue of a criminal statute." This notable law (Art. 96) further prescribed the immediate preparation of a criminal code, to take the place of the antiquated Code of the King Christian V. A provisional ordinance of 1815 abolished the barbarous methods of punishment in the Code of Christian; and State Councilor Chr. Krogh was intrusted with the preparation of the draft for a new code. On his death in 1828, a new commission was appointed (under J. H. Vogt as president); their draft and commentary appeared in 1832–1835. The Storthing (*i.e.* Parliament) accepted the draft in 1839, and the King approved the statute on August 20, 1842.

This first systematic codification of Norway's criminal law was based upon the revised Hanoverian Code, although influenced by the French Code Pénal.

In January, 1885, a general revision was once more undertaken; the State Council, with Bernhard Getz at its head, was commissioned to prepare a draft. This draft, first, published in 1887,[1] became a law and went into effect on January 1, 1905. Its distinguished author unfortunately did not live to see the fruition of his labors; he died in 1901. The new Code was a notable embodiment in legislation of the most advanced ideas of reform. It contains no death penalty, nor short periods of imprisonment, and it provides for indeterminate sentences of dangerous offenders likely to relapse into crime.

§ 69f. **Sweden.** — In 1809, Parliament appointed a commission, under the presidency of Professor Holmhernsson, to prepare

[1] Parliament now has before it a draft of a new Criminal Code.

[1] "Udkast til almindelig borgerlig Straffelov for Kongeriget Norge, med Motiver", Kristiania, 1896: "Udkast til Lov om Faengselvaesenet om Forbrydelse of Frihedsstraffe, med Motiver", Kristiania, 1896. The former was translated by *Rosenfeld* and *Urbye* in 1902, as Supplement No. 20 to the "Mittheilungen der Internationalen Kriminalistischen Vereinigung" (Gutentag, Berlin).

Numerous critiques of this advanced Code have appeared in the journals of criminal law.

a system of complete codification, both private and criminal. The majority of the commission concluded that an entirely new draft of the criminal code should be worked out, on the foundation of science and of foreign legislation; in consequence of this, Professor Rabenius (to whom the criminal code had been assigned), and also certain of his colleagues, quit the commission. Of the remaining members, Staaff, Richert, and Afzelius prepared the draft of 1815, and laid it before Parliament. The commission busied itself, for the next ten years, exclusively with the codification of private law, and did not return to the preparation of the criminal code until 1826. At that time the commission was working in coöperation with the Norwegian commission. The revision of the criminal code was ready in 1832, and was based upon the Bavarian, Hanoverian, and Austrian codes, and their respective revisions. After considerable criticism by numerous jurists (Boethius, Rabenius, Grubbe, Atterbom, Holmbergsson, Cederschiold), a new commission published in 1839 a revised draft. In the year 1844 the commission (now enlarged by adding Schlyter, Bergfalk and Richert) published its draft and commentary. This revision took the advanced step of recognizing only one kind of punishment, namely, simple imprisonment in seven grades, and was not accepted by Parliament.

For twenty years more, reform took the shape of special separate statutes, — abolition of the death penalty; abolition of whipping and church penance (for theft, pilfering and robbery); punishment of forgery and fraud; punishment of murder, manslaughter, and personal injuries; method of solitary confinement. In 1862 the government presented a new draft code, which was accepted with few changes and went into effect on February 16, 1864.[1]

§ 69*g*. **Finland.** — After the union of Finland with Russia, in 1809, penal legislation there was at a standstill for fifty years. The subject was resumed in 1863, and a bill was introduced in the "Stands" or Estates, declaring the principles on which a new Code should be prepared; the desire being to obtain their assent to the dominant principles before proceeding with the great task. Inasmuch as the Code of 1734 contained penal provisions in conflict with the spirit of the age, and did not prescribe sufficiently severe punishment for many offenses, partial reforms were made in the interim. A provisional code was also prepared,

[1] A new draft criminal code is again before Parliament.

to operate until the new Code should be completed; but it failed to receive the sanction of the government, because it abolished capital punishment. Another provisional law was thereupon enacted in 1867, but its promulgation was postponed because of the defective conditions of the prisons, and by the time this had been remedied, the new Code was almost ready for enactment and hence the law of 1867 was never put in force.

A committee had been appointed in 1865 to draft a code in accord with the principles ratified by the Estates in the Assembly of 1863. This draft was introduced in 1875, was subjected to the criticisms of judges and jurists, and was then recommitted to another commission in 1881. After various vicissitudes, this draft became a law and was finally promulgated on April 14, 1894.

D. SWITZERLAND [1]

§ 69*h*. **First Period: To 1830.** — With the new epoch in Switzerland came great legislative activity. Numerous codes and drafts of codes were produced, in one Canton after another. But on the whole they exhibited in their tenor a cautious conservatism. The legislators realized that neither the French Code of 1810 nor Feuerbach's Bavarian Code of 1813, would be exactly suited in their original form to the genius and traditions of the Swiss people.

In the first place, Switzerland had never possessed a single common law of crimes; nor had it a professionally educated judiciary capable of administering a new and borrowed code. In the second place, the philosophic construction, the abstract principles and generalizations, of the new-style Codes were alien to the traditions of Swiss legislation, — concreteness and simplicity. And in the third place, the rigorous, unbending, and elaborate precision of penalties in these new scientific Codes, and their plenteous use of the prison-penalty, were two features that barred their direct adoption in Switzerland, where there were not many prisons, and the judge's liberal discretion in penalties was a car-

[1] [These three sections are by the Editor; their authority is the treatise of Dr. L. PFENNINGER; for this writer and work, see the Editorial Preface. — ED.]

dinal tradition of criminal justice. — And, indeed, in the earliest of the Swiss Codes now framed could be seen emerging these same traditional traits of its people, — a repudiation of philosophic and doctrinal formalism; a refusal to attempt to solve all cases in the Code without leaving wide discretion to the judge; and an avoidance of elaborate definition and systematization.

The first but short-lived effort for a national code was the Criminal Code of the Helvetian Republic (May 4, 1799), founded on the French Code of 1791. But in 1803 the Helvetian Republic came to an end; each Canton became once more independent in its legislation, and only five preserved the Helvetian Code. Nevertheless its influence had been important and useful. Its provisions represented a fusion of German and French ideas, and were much better adapted to Swiss needs than either the French or the German Code itself.

In the other Cantons, the materials serving as authorities in criminal law were now varied enough, — the old customary law; the old statutes; the Carolina; Feuerbach's treatise; the Helvetian Code; and the French and the German Codes of 1810 and 1813. Gradually this complex of authorities was superseded by codification. Between 1805 and 1830 five more Cantons adopted Codes (in St. Gall, indeed, twice over, 1807 and 1819). During the same period and until 1838, in Germany, only one Code — Feuerbach's, for Bavaria — was enacted; though numerous drafts were worked upon.

This long interval of legislative uncertainty and inactivity was due partly to political conditions, partly to the tedious methods of preparation. In Hanover twenty-five years elapsed between the resolution calling for a code and the final Act of its adoption. The struggle between governmental absolutism and popular demands made it almost impossible to construct a criminal code which would satisfy both ministry and representative assembly. In Switzerland, the methods of legislation were not thus hampered, and the result was a large progress towards needed clarification of the law.

It is frequent to speak of the Swiss Codes of this period as mere imitations of either the French or the Austrian or the Bavarian Code. But they should rather be regarded as the natural product of the indigenous law, revised to suit the times. In one important feature they notably showed their native trait, by avoiding the faults which Mittermaier never ceased to criticize in the German codes; namely, over-generalization, over-systematization, and the passion for fixing into law the logical consequences of abstract principles in all their details, regardless of practical needs or historic traditions.

§ 69*i*. **Second Period: 1830–1848.** — In this period ten Cantons adopted criminal codes. Most of them were enacted before 1838, when the long-delayed legislation came to pass in the German States (seven codes within a few years). The July Revolution of 1830 at Paris had found a quick response in Switzerland; within six years of that European event sixteen Cantons had adopted new constitutions. The new spirit showed itself, however, most notably in the field of procedure rather than of substantive law; for Mittermaier and his school of jurists were now emphasizing measures of reform of criminal procedure throughout Europe.

Basel's Code was based on its own earlier one; it was the simplest and clearest of all; giving wide discretion to the judge, it still preserved its local tradition of severity. Zürich's Code was its first, and followed German models, but was marked by lenity of rule and by simplicity and brevity of expression. Vaud's Code combined German and French features, while avoiding the severity of the former; it was mildest of all in its spirit, and broadest in the discretion given to the judge. Luzern followed German models, but without accepting their severity. Thurgau kept closest of all to the German type.

Common characteristics of all the Swiss Codes, in relative contrast to the other European legislation, were simplicity, lenity, and judicial discretion. The topics of criminal intent, negligence, attempt, accomplices, conspiracy, etc., notably exhibit this. Offenses against public law were not so emphasized as in the German codes. Treason received the death penalty in Zürich and Thurgau only; the whole subject was a minor one in the Swiss legislation, while in Germany it received elaborate attention.

§ 69*j*. **Third Period: since 1848.** — From 1848 to 1870 there were sixteen codes (new or revised) enacted in the Swiss Cantons; and since that time a dozen more. Some still looked to France as a model; some looked to Germany; a few sought independently to adapt their own traditions to their own needs.

As in other countries, the political events of Europe in 1848 showed their influence here. Political offenses were handed over in part to the Federal Government in 1853. Another notable feature was the abandonment of minimum penalties, as well of numerous petty distinctions fixed in the text of the law, *i.e.* by enlargement of the judicial discretion. Freiburg stands out as one of the most progressive Cantons; it was the first to abolish the death penalty and imprisonment in chains. In the Swiss Codes, as in the German ones of the same period, is seen a more or less groping uncertainty in the use of penalties. Imprisonment with hard labor was applied with the greatest diversity of terms, varying from a few months to a life-time; ordinary imprisonment was used with equal variety; imprisonment in chains was abolished in all but three codes; the death penalty was retained in all but three; flogging found a place in almost all of the codes, — though after 1865 it was never used; honor-penalties — loss of all civic rights, or of specific ones — were widely employed. The doctrines of intent, attempt, accomplices, and the like, show (as in the earlier codes) a marked simplicity and liberality in contrast with the German legislation. The traditional duty of the citizen to give information of a known crime, *i.e.* the crime of failing to do so or failing to hinder the offender — an offense universally preserved in the German legislation, and punished *e.g.* in Saxony's Code by four years' imprisonment — was almost ignored in the Swiss codes.

Political crimes showed the most notable contrast. A totally different spirit from that of Germany was visible in the Swiss pages. In the first place, the death-penalty for treason, freely used in the four great German codes, was abandoned in all those of Switzerland, and in many of them not even a minimum penalty was prescribed by law. Again, the kinds of acts defined as political offenses were relatively few; the very chapters on this subject were (in the phrase of a German jurist) "idyllic in their simplicity"; their brief provisions took no more than from four to twenty-four sections, while the German chapters extended into sixty and seventy sections. The contrast was visible in the elaborate definitions of the various criminal acts of assistance, connivance, and preparation, by which the German legislators sought to draw into the shadow of political crime all possible conduct. The truth was (as Mittermaier pointed out), the German Governments lived under the obsession that political unrest was to be ascribed to the mildness of the deterrent criminal law; and thus, in spite of the jurists' protests, the spirit of official terrorism gained ground more and more. The most innocent and well-disposed citizen might now come into the grasp of the law for acts and utterances which a suspicious government and a facile judiciary chose to interpret as offenses under the new definitions. As late as 1866, Professor Holtzendorff's "Journal of Criminal Law" reported the case of Zachariae, an eminent professor, who came in danger of criminal proceedings for contempt, because of a critical comment on a Supreme Court decision. — In this field the Swiss Codes showed a thoroughly different attitude.

And, lastly, the traditional simplicity of the Swiss legislation is again in this period notable, in contrast with the German elaborate particularity. The length alone of the codes suffices to show; for the four chief German Codes ranged between three hundred and fifty and five hundred and thirty sections, while the Swiss Codes ranged between one hundred and fifteen and two hundred and ninety sections, except for three which reached three hundred and fifty.

Meanwhile, *unification of law* was becoming a principal problem. The German political unification of 1870, and the consequent movement there towards unification and centralization of law, gave an impetus to a similar movement in Switzerland, as well as a tendency to imitate the German imperial legislation in cantonal law. Ten new or revised cantonal codes were enacted between 1870 and 1889. A general feature was the elaboration of the definitions of offenses and the lenity of the penalties. The Federal Constitution of 1874 abolished the death-penalty and flogging; and though the Amendment of 1879 restored liberty of cantonal action, only a few Cantons took advantage of it, and capital punishment has never since been inflicted. Imprisonment and fines became the principal penalties. Reformation as the avowed objective led to many changes in the method of applying penalties. In form, the newer Codes (in spite of German influence) preserved the traditional Swiss traits of simplicity, concreteness, and avoidance of theorizing.

The tendency towards unification gradually matured. Since the early intercantonal treaty of 1291 (which concerned murder, arson, robbery, and wrongful distress) there had been no efforts of the kind until the short-lived Helvetic Criminal Code of 1797. Then the question slumbered again, while the new ideas were being assimilated in cantonal experiments, until 1865. In that year a notorious case of the flogging penalty moved national feeling to shame. From then onwards the subject was steadily before the public. The draft Constitution of 1872 contained an Article granting to the Federal Government legislative power over criminal law and procedure; but this Constitution was rejected at the polls, and the new draft, accepted by the people in 1874, lacked that Article. In 1887, the Swiss National Bar Association declared in favor of exclusive Federal jurisdiction and unification. The Federal Council authorized the preparation of an exhaustive report on the cantonal criminal law; this report, by Carl Stooss, professor at Bern, took the form of his well-known treatise on Swiss Criminal Law.[1] In 1888, with other leaders, he founded the "Swiss Journal of Criminal Law", which has since been the useful organ for the historical and critical discussion of the subject. Since that time, three drafts have been prepared by Professor Stooss; but thus far, none has had the fortune to be enacted.[2]

1 "Grundzüge des schweizerischen Strafrechts" (2 vols., 1892–93).
2 "Schweizerisches Strafgesetzbuch, Protokoll der zweiten Expertenkommission" (Luzern, Vols. 1–4, 1912–13); "Vorentwurf zu einem Schweizerischen Strafgesetzbuch nach den Beschlüssen der Expertenkommission" (Berlin, J. Guttentag, 1908, Beilage zu M. I. K. V.).

PART II

HISTORY OF THE THEORIES OF CRIMINAL LAW

Chapter I

ANCIENT GREECE AND ROME [1]

§ 70. **Practical Importance of Theories of Criminal Law.** — Indubitably from time immemorial, the criminal law has been found an absolute necessity for the public order and for human society in general.[2] Among the multitude of questions concerning

[1] Concerning the matter contained in this Part the following writers may be consulted: *Henke*, "Handbuch des Criminalrechts und der Criminalpolitik", I (1823), pp. 52–129; *Bauer*, "Die Warnungstheorie nebst einer Darstellung und Beurtheilung sämmtlicher Strafrechtstheorien" (1830); *Hepp*, *"Ueber die Gerechtigkeits- und Nutzungstheorien des Auslandes und den Werth einer Philosophie des Strafrechts" (1834); *Hepp*,* "Darstellung und Beurtheilung der deutschen Strafrechtssysteme", 2d Part (2d ed. 1843, 1844); *A. Freytag*, "Die Concessionalgerechtigkeitstheorie des Strafrechts, nebst einer kurzen Darstellung und Beurtheilung der übrigen neueren Theorien des Strafrechts" (1846); *Köstlin*, "Neue Revision der Grundbegriffe des Criminalrechts" (1845), pp. 764–850; *A. Franck*, "Philosophie du droit pénal", (1864); *Röder*, "Die herrschenden Grundlehren von Verbrechen und Strafen in ihren inneren Widersprüchen" (1867); *Heinze*,* in *Von Holtzendorff's* "Handbuch des deutschen Strafrechts", I (1871), pp. 239–344; *Laistner*, *"Das Recht in der Strafe" (1872); *Wharton*, "Philosophy of Criminal Law" in the eighth edition of his "Criminal Law of the United States" (Philadelphia), pp. 1–29. — The works marked with an asterisk [*] contain the most complete presentation of the subject as a whole. Hepp pays the most attention to the jurists and Laistner deals more with the philosophers. *Cf.* also *P. Janet*, "Histoire de la philosophie morale et politique" (2 vols., Paris, 1868).

[2] The theories of criminal law are usually classified as "Absolute" and "Relative." By the former it is maintained that punishment is something inherent in the very nature of the crime, — a necessary consequence of the crime. The latter seek to justify punishment by showing that it has an effect which is in harmony with some purpose whose attainment is, on other grounds, desirable. Since this purpose can be found only in the conditions imposed by the social life of human beings, these relative theories regard punishment as coming into existence only with the State which governs these conditions. The absolute theories, however, regard punishment as possible without the State, and as having

the right to inflict punishment, there is one which constantly arises: How is it possible that the *public* power enforcing morality (and as such must criminal law after all be regarded) may require an injury of the wrongdoer, while in *private* morals, rules such as: "Love your enemies", "Do good to them which hate you", "Pray for them which despitefully use you" find (not always practically, but at least theoretically) absolute acceptance? Even the purely practical individual, who is not affected by doubts of this character, will at times be confronted with the question whether the State, when it punishes one act and not another, or remodels its legislation in accordance with this or that tendency, is pursuing the proper course. He will have occasion to consider whether the axe and guillotine should be regarded as relics of former barbarism and persistent error, or as exemplifications of the supreme and ultimate law of human or even divine justice.

Now these questions are of immediate practical importance, at least for the legislator, and their determination will also be indirectly reflected in the practice of the courts. For example,

been adopted by the State for the sake of accomplishing certain purposes. The so-called "mixed" theories ("Coalitionstheorien") seek to reconcile the various theories of criminal law, and especially the absolute and the relative theories of the foundation of punishment. A reconciliation of the kind last mentioned is conceivable in various ways. Thus, for example, one may give punishment an absolute foundation but modify or limit its exercise in accordance with purposes of expediency in attaining certain results. It may also be undertaken to prove that the absolute foundation of criminal law is not prohibitive of a regard for attaining certain purposes (*i.e.* beneficial purposes), but rather that it contemplates such. Those classifications are of a more superficial character which make a distinction between theories of right and theories of utility (interest), according as the theories taken up assume a special legal right on the part of the punishing State (*e.g.* acceptance of a contractual submission of the crime to punishment, outlawry of the criminal as a result of the crime), or are simply satisfied with reasons of utility or the empirical indispensability of things. The same can be said of the "Contractual" theories ("Vertragstheorien"), the "Compensation" theories ("Vergütungstheorien"), and the "Restitution" theories ("Erstattungstheorien") which found punishment upon a requisite restoration or removal of the social injury caused by the crime, etc. Heinze (p. 243) would insert an intermediate class between the division of theories into "Absolute" and "Relative", *i.e.* those absolute theories which, without regarding punishment as of absolute necessity, yet find the legal justification of punishment solely in the crime that has been committed, and which treat punishment as an absolute *right* and not as an absolute *duty* of the State, and also as a privilege of which use may possibly not be made. However, it is difficult to definitely fix the limits of this intermediate division, and Laistner (p. 180) has therefore declared himself opposed to it. More detailed and minutely classified surveys may be found in *Bauer*, "Abhandlungen aus dem Strafrechte und Strafprocesse", I (1840), pp. 28 *et seq.*; *Hepp*, I, pp. xiv *et seq.* They have the fault however of presenting the theories only in part or strained to suit their methods of classification.

the courts will have occasion to consider whether or not at certain times they have the right, although keeping within the statutory limitations upon punishment, to make a public example of some individual. Questions arise such as : 1. What acts are to be punished by the State? 2. What methods of punishment shall the State employ? 3. What are the considerations which should influence the State in varying the degree of punishment? Apart from adherence to habit and a blind following of tradition, these questions are not to be answered until the fundamental principles underlying criminal law itself are first established. For it is by these principles that the scope and form of criminal law are to be determined.

§ 71. **The Beginnings of Speculation.** — Just as to-day the purely practical instinct of many individuals finds nothing objectionable in the numerous and (to say the least) but thinly veiled inconsistencies of the criminal law, so was it, at the beginning of the historical development of criminal law, with those who first contemplated the nature and effect of punishment. Their thought simply reflected (*i.e.* gave back like a mirror) the effect of punishment from one or the other viewpoint or perhaps a variety of viewpoints. Retaliation [1] tending to restore the universal harmony; purification of the land from the effects of the evil deed and from the presence of the offender; the appeasing of the wrath of the gods [2] (*i.e.* the idea of divine justice); reformation of the offender; and deterrence of others, — all these appear upon the screen in variegated succession. The early peoples seem all unconscious of the warring consequences of such contradictory principles.

The Sophists. — As a matter of fact, the first thoroughgoing investigation deserving the name of scientific attempt began with the Sophists. Protagoras [3] definitely abandons the idea of retaliation. "He who desires to inflict punishment in a rational manner," says he, according to Plato,[4] "chastises not on account of the wrong that has been committed — for that which is done

[1] The Pythagoreans advanced as the principle of criminal law, the "*αντιπεπονθὸς τε καὶ ἴσον*." *Cf. Laistner*, p. 8: "Leidet er, was er gethan. so ist es der geradeste Rechtsweg", "*τὸ Ῥαδαμάνθυος δίκαιον*." *Aristotle*, "Eth. Nicom.", V, 5, 3. *Cf. Hermann*, p. 6.

[2] *Cf.* the passages from the Greek authors in *C. F. Hermann*, "Ueber Grundsätze und Anwendung des Strafrechts im griechischen Alterthume", 1855, pp. 10, 27, 28.

[3] Taught about 480 B.C.

[4] *Cf. Plato's* "Protagoras", 324.

cannot be undone — but rather, having in mind the future, that neither the party punished shall again commit a crime nor he who witnesses the punishment." Improvement of the criminal and deterrence of others are the ends of punishment. The justification, when we inflict the penalty of death on an individual who has lost the sense of right or wrong, is the same as if he were a disease (diseased limb) of the State (" νόσος πόλεως "). In every infliction of punishment, one has to consider only whether or not the offender can be improved. Law and order, however, for whose maintenance the State is a means, must be preserved, since without them human society is impossible. To be sure, a superficial connection is still maintained with the old religious beliefs of the people; in so far as the sense of right and wrong is acknowledged as an instinct given by Zeus, and the law, in accordance with which the unhealthy member of the State is condemned to death, is regarded as ordained by Zeus. These connecting threads were severed by the later Sophists. As a result of the fundamental maxim of the Sophists: " The measure of all things is man "[5] (and not man with a nature assumed to be unchangeable, but rather man with his changing aspects and needs) the laws appear as artificial rules of convenience and calculated, as Kritias maintained, to protect the weak against the strong and opulent. While the criminal law was allowed to receive such additional effectiveness as it might from the belief in all-powerful and omniscient deities, so that secret as well as known offenses would be prevented, yet (as in modern times by Feuerbach) the emphasis was laid upon the threat of punishment rather than its fulfilment.

§ 72. **Socrates.** — The philosophy of Socrates had this in common with the Sophists, viz., that both founded ethics upon utility. Socrates, however, had a predilection for the principle that ultimately the virtuous man attains the greatest benefit from his virtue itself. But in doubtful cases he sought to ascertain what course of action was productive of the greatest possible degree of benefit. Moreover, this reference to the acquisition of benefit served merely as an " a posteriori " demonstration of an assumed divine regulation of things.

Plato. — In Plato's philosophy this ideal of a divine regulation of things is definitely assumed as actual and existing, and the empirical manifestation of individual objects is regarded as its

[5] *Cf. Zeller*, "Geschichte der griechischen Philosophie", I, p. 921.

imperfect reflection. This ideal of a divine regulation thus becomes of prime importance. To this divine regulation, there were forthwith attributed, as some of its individual features, those institutions which by philosophy were customarily regarded as necessary and by the world at large as sacred. Such was the case with the institution of punishment. It was contemplated as being, in an ideal and perfect manner, in unison with the divine regulation of things. In this conception it was not something which disturbed the harmony of the universe, but rather something by which this harmony, which had been disturbed by the crime, was restored, *i.e.* internally for the criminal himself, as well as externally. The criminal, in undergoing the punishment, renders to the order of the universe that which is called the "δίκη" (*i.e.* the just, customary, proper, or due) and at the same time receives it himself.[1] He receives a benefit, since justice itself is something of a benefit. He is restored to a right condition. Thus the judge is likened to the physician, to whose knives and cauterizing irons one submits and endures the pain. The criminal who fears punishment is likened to the foolish boy who out of fear of the knives and irons would remain ill.

As a matter of fact Plato does not enter into a discussion of those individual details which are so important in practical life. He goes no farther than to show the divine background of things, or, speaking more correctly, to paint it with artistic lights. He meets the argument drawn from actual life, in the case of a cruel execution, with the brief words: "You paint a terrifying picture, but you refute nothing."[2] The questions concerning the death penalty are never carefully discussed. Capital punishment is merely mentioned incidentally along with the other punishments. It is taken up in such a way as to lead one to infer that the philosopher felt that it also had to do with the restoration of the universal harmony of things, that it could be deserved, and that it was a great evil if anyone, especially great wrongdoers such as kings and tyrants, escaped the punishment deserved in this life, *i.e.*, avoided the restoration of harmony in this life.

As a matter of fact (as Laistner, differing from others, very correctly infers), this is an absolute foundation for punishment, — derived from that universal harmony of things which with irresistible power renders itself complete in this or the future life. The foundation of punishment is not, though this in certain pas-

[1] "Gorgias", 472*e*.

[2] "Gorgias", 473*c*. *Müller*, I, p. 431.

sages appears to be of prime importance, its curing and beneficial effect upon the individual. It is even conceived as possible that the individual may be permanently sacrificed for the sake of this harmony. While the effect of punishment in reaching out to and deterring others is not ignored, yet this deterrence is not a principle from which a human legislator may derive conclusions. It is merely an incident of punishment, and while it may, in accordance with the laws of harmony, come about spontaneously, it is not an object for human calculation.[3]

Plato's "Politics" and "Republic" take us from the realm of the general harmony of the universe into that of the harmony of the State. As against this latter no more than the former is the individual ascribed an independent position. If he disturbs this harmony of the State, he can be eliminated and destroyed, and the State may be purified by the death or banishment of those who do not conform to its requirements. While upon the whole the idea of paternalism prevails, yet the individual can make no complaint; for suffering, as such, even if it is not deserved, is regarded as having in it for every one something of a curative nature. Here again there is certainly reference to a transcendental divine background which should be a solace to the individual in case he falls a victim to the State. In the uncertain outlines in which punishment here appears as an extreme and artificial agency not used in the ideal State,[4] the philosopher loses sight of that contradiction which upon a more careful treatment is bound to appear between the employment of punishment for mere purposes of expediency (and often such as are merely temporary) and the idea of harmony, as well as the idea of retaliation which shimmers through from the background.

In the "Laws" this concession, made by Plato in his old age to the imperfect visible world, recedes into the background, and the viewpoints of security and deterrence assume importance. The "Laws" take human imperfection as a basis for calculation. With deep insight Plato realized that that form of legislation is best which, through the punishment,[5] also tends to arouse in the criminal

[3] "Gorgias", 525*a*, *b*.

[4] "Republic", III, 405*b*.

[5] In addition there are other means mentioned (*e.g.* by giving of privileges). "Whether the end is to be attained by word or action, with pleasure or pain, by giving or taking away of privileges, by means of penalties or gifts, or in whatsoever way the law shall make a man hate injustice and love or not hate the nature of the just, this is the noblest work of law" ("Laws", IX, 862). [Jowett's rendering substituted for German rendering. — TRANSL.]

himself inclinations in harmony with the law. Consequently the effect of imprisonment in a reformatory ("σωφρονιστήριον")[6] is first tried upon those who cherish and disseminate principles destructive of belief in the gods. But if other punishments prove to be of no avail, the "Laws", in pursuance of the purposes of security and deterrence, justify the infliction of the death penalty. They make the comment (which later was frequently repeated by others) that it is better for the incorrigible himself to die than to live.[7] This practical attitude of the State, which may not arrogate to administer divine justice, explains his abandonment of the principle of retaliation. It constantly recurred in the ideal State of the "Republic", and in the "world harmony" of the "Gorgias" it made the punishment appear as a good deed, whereby the effect of the wrong, reversing itself, falls upon the wrong itself[8] and its author. But it is expressly repudiated in the "Laws."[9] The practical State has no right to retaliation, but merely the right to strive to attain rational results in the future. That which is done cannot be undone.

Thus Plato's philosophy of criminal law ends in obvious contradictions. While, in the earlier works, the reader believes that an absolute foundation must be found for punishment, yet the dialogue of the "Laws" leaves no doubt that this attitude has been abandoned. And yet this contradiction is more apparent than real. The State, contemplated in the "Laws", is merely the State contemplated by the modern jurist, and one in which a well-considered law should erect a barrier against wrong and suffering. The State of the "Republic" was an ideal one having no practical existence. Here, not as in a real State, Plato might maintain a kind of retaliatory justice in the place of the divine justice, and, in the universal "world harmony", regard every punishment as either a benefit or a retaliation.

The dualism, upon which Plato's philosophy is ultimately

[6] *Cf.* p. 909.

[7] "Laws", IX, 862. "But if the legislator sees any one who is incurable, for him he will make a law and fix a penalty. He knows quite well that to such men themselves there is no profit in the continuance of their lives, and that they would do a double good to the rest of mankind if they would take their departure, inasmuch as they would be an example to other men not to offend, and they would relieve the city of bad citizens." [Jowett.]

[8] The passage in the "Laws", V, 728, which designates association with the wicked as the greatest of penalties does not, as Laistner (p. 27) has it, refer to punishment inflicted by the State.

[9] "Laws", IX, 934: "οὐ γὰρ τὸ γεγονὸς ἀγένητον ἔσται ποτέ."

based, is also manifest in his conception of punishment. It is often difficult to ascertain whether the discussion has to do with real and existing conditions, or whether it has as its basis an ideal that is never to be attained. Plato offered absolutely no solution to the question concerning relation of the ideal and the actual. Consequently a reconciliation by him of the relative and absolute foundations of punishment is not to be expected.

§ 73. **Aristotle.** — Aristotle's theory of criminal law is unique; it stands quite by itself in ancient times. All other ancient philosophy vouchsafed no independent rights to the individual as against the State, and rather, when necessary, allowed the individual to be absolutely sacrificed to the harmony of the whole without further thought or justification. But Aristotle regarded criminal law not only from the viewpoint of the State inflicting the punishment, but also from the viewpoint of the criminal who has to suffer the punishment. He does not arbitrarily adopt the position (of which Plato availed himself in his discussion of ideals) that punishment is a benefit to the criminal.

Aristotle makes a distinction between *justification* in punishing and *obligation* to punish. He bases the former upon a contract entered into by the offender. The offender has encroached too far, since justice consists in no one having too much and no one having too little. The offender, by the commission of the crime, makes an involuntary contract whereby his undue proportion shall be reduced by the judge.[1] This undue proportion, however, which he has taken, does not consist in the advantage which he has obtained, but rather in the encroachment which he has made upon justice; and so the punishment must often be greater than the (external) injury caused by the crime. Accordingly, Aristotle derives punishment not from a justice equalizing matters in accordance with a geometric proportion, but rather from a justice equalizing matters in accordance with an arithmetic proportion. In other words, criminal justice is merely a lateral branch of civil justice and has to do with the reparation of injury. But as the example used by Aristotle — an insult to a magistrate[2] — shows, it is an ideal injury which is contemplated. While the question, whence the State receives the right of criminally punishing, is not directly answered by Aristotle, yet from his treatment of suicide, we perceive that he regarded the injury suffered by the

[1] "Eth. Nicom.", V, 5 and 7.
[2] *Ibid.*, 5, § 1.

individual as also suffered by the State, and from this must have been inclined to derive the right of the State to inflict punishment.

The relation between *justification* in punishing and *obligation* to punish is not clearly marked by Aristotle. When he considers punishment from the latter viewpoint, it has for him an entirely different significance. Here in Aristotle, as in Plato, punishment signifies a healing of the offender.[3] So sharply marked is this meaning that, in his opinion, vengeance is regarded as the best method of punishment,[4] because of the special satisfaction of the party exercising vengeance. However, this idea is later not uniformly adhered to. It becomes associated with the idea of deterrence. Punishment counteracts the prevalent desire of the masses for profit at the expense of others,[5] and opposes the prospect of pleasure with one of unhappiness and sorrow.[6] It is not clear whether the mere deterrence of the party punished is contemplated, — a thing reconcilable with the idea of his reformation, — or whether the deterrence of others is meant — a thing which, at least in its intended results, is not reconcilable with the idea of the offender's reformation. The banishment of incorrigibles as a last resort is merely advanced as a viewpoint favored by others, and Aristotle himself does not express an opinion.[7]

§ 74. **Influence of Aristotle.** — Aristotle had certainly obtained a deeper comprehension of the problems of criminal law than any of the other philosophers of antiquity. For the theory of responsibility, which even to-day is considered meritorious, we are indebted to his opinion (found in the Nicomachean Ethics [1]) that the right to punish is derived from the will of the party punished. This view, however, is imperfectly set forth in the theory of an involuntary contract. In this respect, Aristotle attained no following in ancient times, and the manner in which he sought to solve the problem strikes us as being artificial and unsatisfactory. An open mind will regard punishment (in its ordinary sense) and reward as correlative, and both are derived from a distributive justice, and not from an equalizing justice governing the field of private rights.

An important factor was that, with Greece's decline, Grecian philosophy gave less and less attention to the regulation of the

[3] "Eth. Nicom.", II, 3, § 1.
[4] "Rhet.", I, 10.
[5] *I.e.* "αὔξησις."
[6] "Eth. Nicom.", X, 9, §§ 3, 8, 9.
[7] *Ibid.*, 9, § 9.
[1] *Ibid.*, V, 8.

State, and found the principle of ethics in the individual and his self-sufficiency, — either (as with the Epicureans) in an unbroken rest and cheerfulness of spirit, or (as with the Stoics) in the lonely and rugged virtue of the wise.

The Stoics. — To the Stoic philosophy punishment and criminal law could be nothing more than matters of secondary importance, the ascertainment of whose basis was not worth the necessary trouble. The wicked were simply left to be dealt with by the world, in whatever way it might happen. The legislator, in inflicting punishment (of whatever sort he pleased) upon the wicked, did them no injustice. As a matter of fact he always treated them too gently and never "*παρὰ τὴν ἀξίαν.*" Pity for the wrongdoer is only weakness. This in fact was based upon the idea of the non-reality of all evil, *i.e.*, the fact that evil merited destruction. The author of evil was directly identified with evil itself, insofar as the evil and the good were regarded as diametrically opposite. The power of punishment as a means of better training (illustrated by Protagoras by the gradual bending straight of crooked sticks) was discarded, with the remark that between the good and the evil there is no middle ground, and consequently no transition from one to the other.[2]

The Epicureans. — While the Stoic abandoned crimes and punishment to the course of events, since his firm and positive attitude assumed the worthlessness of the offender without further thought, the Epicurean relegated the entire matter of the regulation of States and arrangement of laws to maxims of convenience and expediency. If the Epicurean conceded the existence of guilt, it was not so much the crime he regarded as an evil but rather the being punished [3] and the fear of the consequences of the crime. Accordingly it was self-evident that punishment could be merely an instrument in the hands of the lawgiver for the discipline or deterrence or perhaps the reformation of the individual, in order to make him serve the purposes of the lawgiver. According to this conception there is no need of a basis for punishment which shall justify it from the viewpoint of the party punished. To undergo punishment is merely a species of misfortune. And the most that can be said against him whose actions entail punishment is

[2] *Cf.* the collection of passages from the writings of the Stoics in *Laistner*, pp. 34 *et seq.*

[3] "*τὸ γὰρ κλέψαι οὐδὲ αὐτό ὁ Ἐπίκουρος ἀποφαίνει κακόν, ἀλλὰ τὸ ἐμπεσεῖν*", *Epictetus*, "Diss.", III, 7, 12. *Cf. Hildenbrand*, "Geschichte und System der Rechts- und Staatsphilosophie", I (1860), p. 516.

that he, in his attitude and inclinations, did not happen to be in harmony with the law, or that he was not clever enough to avoid the evil resulting from his act.

Scepticism. — The Sceptic philosophy (the school of Pyrrho), while it renounces all explanation, substitutes authority and that which exists positively for the conventional ideals. It regarded theoretic certainty as impossible, but since there must be some compass by which to guide practical existence, it acknowledged as such simply tradition and that which exists.

Roman Philosophy. — The Roman philosophy, while it did not attain to a system of its own, rested essentially upon the foundation of Stoicism. But (as was in keeping with its tendency to Eclecticism and a characteristically practical bent) it softened the harsher conclusions of Stoicism through broad humanitarian ideas, which were then paving the way for Christianity. Thus Cicero [4] is solicitous that punishment shall not exceed its proper degree. He would have punishment fall upon only a few, but fear hold all in check.[5] Seneca [6] repeats with approval the words of Plato concerning the healing power of punishment, and even with rhetorical pathos justifies capital punishment as a benefit which, in extreme cases, must be conferred upon the criminal. While, by the Roman jurists, the purposes of deterrence, of security against the individual offender, and sometimes also of retaliation with no ulterior motives, were introduced merely for the justification of individual practical observations and decisions, there is an almost Christian sound to their words. According to Epictetus, the wise man should regard even the greatest criminal as one unfortunate and confused, and should not be angry with

[4] "De Off.", I, 25 (89).

[5] "Pro Cluentio", c. 46 (128): "Statuerunt enim majores nostri . . . ut metus videlicet ad omnes, pœna ad paucos perveniret." *Cf.* also "De Off.", I, 11 (33): "Atque haud scio an satis sit, eum qui lacessierit, injuriæ suæ pœnitere, ut et ipse ne quid tale posthac (faciat), et ceteri sint ad injuriam tardiores."

[6] "De Clement.", I, 21. "De Ira", I, 5, 14–16; II, 31. Cf. Ulpian in L. 6 § 1 D. "De pœnis", 48, 19: ". . . ut exemplo deterriti minus delinquant." L. 16 § 10 (Saturninus): "Nonnumquam evenit, ut aliquorum maleficiorum supplicia exacerbentur, quoties nimium multis personis grassantibus exemplo opus est." L. 20, D. "De pœnis": "Si pœna alicui irrogatur, receptum est commenticio jure, ne ad heredes transeat. Cujus rei illa ratio videtur, quod pœna constituitur in emendationem hominum quæ mortuo eo, in quem constitui videtur, desinit." *Cf.* also, L. 6 § i. f. "De custod. reor.", 48, 3; L. 9 § 3 D. "De off. proc.", 1, 16; L. 1 § 1 D "De J. et J."; L. 131 D. "De V. S.": ". . . Pœna est noxæ vindicta." *Cf.* also, *e.g.* L. 55 C. "De episc.", 1, 3; Nov. 12, c. 1. *Heinze* in *Von Holtzendorff's* "Handbuch", I, pp. 247, 248, and especially *Abegg*, "Die verschiedenen Strafrechtstheorien", pp. 78 *et seq.*

him; furthermore, he enjoins every one to work for the improvement of others. If we may draw conclusions from other utterances of that estimable philosopher and pupil of Epictetus, Marcus Aurelius, who sat upon the imperial throne, he may have regarded the cardinal idea of punishment as merely the reformation of the individual, since he considered it a mandate of morals [7] to love and assist those who have fallen and who do wrong.

Hierocles. — In spite of numerous artificial expressions, Stoicism really devoted to the province of ethics only a superficial attention. There was, however, in ancient times, an adherent of the Neoplatonic philosophy, who had a deeper comprehension of the problem of criminal law than was shown in these last outcroppings of Stoicism. Neoplatonism sought to bring the subjective tendency of Stoicism into alliance with the objective general ideas of the universe of Plato; as a result, it reproduced in part Plato's views regarding punishment. Hierocles' [8] explanation of punishment was to the effect that the law, which did not want evil to be done, maintained itself by means of punishment. The good could not be indifferent to a breach of the law, and respect for the law must be restored in the offender himself. In accordance with this opinion, punishment was aimed at the act. The *person* of the offender was unimportant, for, as observed by Hierocles, the object was to save the Deity from the reproach that it was inflicting punishment upon the individual, and, on the other hand, to preserve the idea of human freedom, without resorting to a fictitious contract made by the criminal in respect to his own punishment. But how, then, does the punishment come to attach itself to the person of the wrongdoer and impose upon him an evil? This, said Hierocles, might appear to human notions as being a merely coincidental result. But, in truth, the offender thus satisfies the conditions of the law, and the purpose of the Deity can be nothing other than to improve the offender through suffering, which in its true nature is not suffering but something which ultimately shows itself as a good, since its origin is in God. Hierocles, like Plato, believed that it was better to be punished than to remain unpunished, and that the offender, by having undergone punishment, attains a kind of restoration. After having undergone punishment he should be regarded as having again attained a certain average of worthiness and virtue.

[7] *Cf. Zeller*, III, 1, p. 683.

[8] Concerning Hierocles *cf.* especially *Laistner*, pp. 45 *et seq.*

Since Hierocles believed that the only purpose that could be ascribed to the Deity was that of reformation, and appears to reject those ideas of retaliation allied with the prominence given to the freedom of the will in Neoplatonism, it can be said that his theory failed to demonstrate the justice of punishment from the human viewpoint. Mankind, since it must live and act in accordance with divine will, thus has the right to repudiate the *deed* as a thing not to be condoned; but (we ask) how does it come about that it can lay hands on its *author?* The appeal here made by Hierocles to divine law [9] is merely a confession that the philosopher has failed to find the truth which to us seems so evident. There is a very mystical sound (which reminds one of the modern "Soirées de St. Petersbourg" of Count J. de Demaistre) in Hierocles' observation that the peculiar benefit (the ultimate purpose) of the law was to bring together the criminal and the judge inflicting the penalty. As Laistner properly points out, it sounds almost as if the crime were a thing to be desired, in order to display the majesty of the law in offering up the offender as a victim. In reality, like Plato, he avoids the entire problem. Since the philosopher proceeds upon the basis that punishment, in accordance with its very nature, cannot be an evil, and it is only the wickedness within the individual that is an evil, there yet remains the problem how the civil community can be justified in inflicting an evil, in the form of punishment, upon any one. In other words, it amounts to nothing other than the fallacy already committed by Plato, — a confusing of an absolute, divine, and mystical viewpoint with that human viewpoint which is the only one of which we can conceive and which alone is practical.

All these theoretical dissertations had no effect in ancient times upon the practical shaping of the criminal law. The most influence it could have had was when a philosopher such as Marcus Aurelius was emperor and judge. To be sure, it did render less harsh a number of criminal sentences. Yet the stress and the confusion of the times were too great to have been influenced by mere contemplative study. As has already been pointed out in Part I of this work (the history of criminal law), a remarkable influence was exercised by Christianity. It still remains for us to ascertain how Christianity theoretically adjusted itself to criminal law.

[9] *Συνάγει οὖν ὁ νόμος ὡς εἴρηται τοὺς πεφυκότας κρίνειν καὶ τοὺς πεφυκότας κακύνεσθαι δι' αμφοτέρων τὸ οἰκεῖον ἀπεργαζόμενος ἀγαθόν . . .*" *Mullach*, p. 75.

CHAPTER II

THE PHILOSOPHY OF CRIMINAL LAW IN THE MIDDLE AGES

§ 75. **Attitude of the Early Christians towards the Law.** — In the beginning, the Christians were merely a sect, at best only tolerated and often persecuted. In their doctrine such institutions as the State and the legal system found no part. Christianity at first recognized only a Christian system of *morality* and knew nothing of a Christian system of *law*. Law was regarded as superfluous, — brotherly love alone was sufficient.[1] If all obey the precepts of Christian love, no one would fear injury from another, nor would any compel another to give redress. Since too high a degree of self-denial will seldom be found, Christian morality could afford to lay down the precept: "Whosoever shall smite thee on thy right cheek, turn to him the other also."[2] The heathen might have his State and its legal system; but between Christians brotherly love was all in all.

The Christian doctrine, the doctrine of a sect at first oppressed, concerned itself with the State only in so far as it enjoined its own followers not to come into conflict with the laws of the State. "Render therefore unto Cæsar the things which are Cæsar's" are the words of Christ himself. With this end in view, and for no other purpose, and certainly not in the sense of giving divine sanction to institutions at the time existing, Christ also said: "Put up again thy sword into his place: for all they that take the sword shall perish with the sword."[3] In a doctrine based upon

[1] *Cf. P. Janet,* "Histoire de la philosophie morale et politique" (2 vols., Paris, 1868), I, p. 216.

[2] Matthew, v, 39.

[3] *Ibid.*, xxvi, 52.

the principle: "My kingdom is not of this world," these sayings could have no other meaning. The aid of a more exact translation was not required (although it was thereby verified), in order to ascertain that this did not contain a sanction of the death penalty.[4] Moreover, the well-known words of the Apostle Paul [5] did not mean that the civil authority, as it then existed, satisfied the requirements of the Christian doctrine; but only that the Christian should perceive in this civil authority merely a manifestation of a divine providence. It was not the part of Christian duty to oppose it, even though it was not at that time a Christian institution.

Changed Position of Christianity as a State Religion. — When Christianity was raised from its position of an insignificant sect to that of a State religion, its earlier conception of law and the State necessarily underwent a change. This was furthered by the fact that the Church at first permitted, and indeed later required, an active persecution of unbelievers. Moreover, when the State came under the influence of the Christian ideal of morality, it became necessary to find a way to bring into harmony with this ideal the barbarous system of criminal law which then prevailed in the State, and also to justify the cruel persecutions of heresy. This end was easily attained by ascribing the State and its system of law to a divine origin, thereby apparently withdrawing them from human direction and interference.

Responsibility for all the atrocities committed in the name of justice was thus lifted from the shoulders of humanity; it was no longer encumbent upon the human mind to find a way to harmonize the State and law as human creations with the Christian system of morality. The problem to be solved was rather this: to find a way to bring the presence of war, pestilence, and other destructive phenomena of nature into harmony with the eternal goodness of God.

§ 76. **Views of Medieval Philosophy as Exemplified by Thomas Aquinas.** — Thomas Aquinas,[1] whom it is proper to regard as the

[4] *Cf. Hetzel*, "Die Todesstrafe in ihrer culturgeschichtlichen Entwicklung" (1870), pp. 49 *et seq.*

[5] The passage referred to is: Romans, xiii, 1–6. "Let every soul be subject to the higher powers. For there is no power but of God; the powers that be are ordained of God. Etc."

[1] B. 1125– (?) d. 1274. The best modern edition of his works is that prepared at the expense of Leo XIII (Rome, 1882–1903). Most of the passages referred to in this chapter can be found in English translation in *Rickaby*, "Aquinas Ethicus" (London, 1896).

central figure in the philosophy of the Middle Ages, did not disguise from himself the fact that the penalties inflicted by human agencies went far beyond the "medicina" (as required by Christian morality) of the offender. But he satisfied himself with the reflection that the same could be said of the eternal damnation ordained by God. Thus there appeared to be divine authority for the maxim: "Pestilente flagellato stultus sapientior fit,"[2] especially if the "vindicatio" (as distinguished from the "medicina") was justified on the ground that it was directed towards a "coercitio malorum" (deterrence). He, however, was not of the opinion that, since deterrence is the purpose of punishment, the basis of punishment is the wickedness of those whose deterrence is intended, rather than the wickedness of the offender. Moreover, he was far from believing that such a principle, laid down in so positive a manner, was in harmony with the principles of divine justice. On the contrary, he clearly announced, as Augustine had done before him,[3] that temporal justice should be merely an imitation of divine justice.

However, this brilliant and exact philosopher did not overlook a distinction which Plato had allowed to pass unnoticed. The "lex humana" — the human reason — is parcel of the divine reason, and has the mission of searching out the "lex æterna," *i.e.* that ultimate destiny of all being, ordained of God.[4] It has the duty of deducing from the "lex æterna" definite conclusions, but it cannot punish each and every sin in accordance with divine justice, — "quia dum aufferre vellet omnia mala, sequeretur quod etiam multa bona tollerentur et impedirentur."[5] This was the first attempt, founded on a correct basis, to distinguish between law and morality, — since it assumed that the entire province of morality was comprehended by the term "divine justice." As a result of this idea his entire discussion is based upon consideration of utility; and it comes to appear as if the principle of retaliation, which together with "medicina" and "coercitio malorum"

[2] "Summa Theologiæ", 2, 1, qu. 87, n. 3, 4. Old Testament, Proverbs, xix, 25 ("Smite a scorner, and the simple will beware.")

[3] "Summa Theologiæ", II, 2, qu. 108, art. 3, n. 5: "Dicendum quod sicut Augustinus dicit judicium humanum debet imitari divinum judicium in manifestis Dei judiciis, quibus homines spiritualiter damnat pro proprio peccato. Occulta vero Dei judicia quibus temporaliter aliquos punit absque culpa (*e.g.* the children for the sins of the father) non potest humanum judicium imitari, quia homo non potest comprendere horum judiciorum rationem."

[4] Aquinas, like Aristotle, treats of man according to his "τέλος."

[5] "L. theol.", II, 1, qu. 90, 91, 95 a, 1.

(deterrence) was regarded as an imitation of divine justice, is completely abandoned.

It must not be forgotten, however, that it is characteristic of the philosophy of the Middle Ages, with all its freedom of discussion, to adhere to the belief in *authority*, and it is in accord herewith that Thomas Aquinas suggested that the " lex humana " needs to be supplemented by divine (*i.e.* revealed) law.[6] Consequently, it came about that since the Mosaic law was also regarded as revealed law, the principle of retaliation in its widest sense was justified, — even if one should overlook the fact that the maxim borrowed from Aristotle: " Per pœnam reparatur æqualitas," which Thomas Aquinas advances in another passage, is also an invocation of this same principle.[7] But, with a more searching view than many of the modern writers, this philosopher of the Middle Ages saw that, although he made a distinction between law and morality, he was regarding law as merely a modified and limited form of morality; thus *e.g.* he saw that the rule: " Thou shalt not kill " is merely a single consequence of the general principle: " Do harm to no one." [8] Are there not many much-argued modern questions in which we discuss whether a criminal law (or perhaps a police regulation) concerns a violation of this or that principle, — whether it involves an independent or subordinate, a compound or simple principle — that savor more of scholasticism than this simple but comprehensive observation of the great scholastic of the Middle Ages?

The Lack of Interest of the Medieval Philosophers in Criminal Law. — Since the greatest of the medieval philosophers devotes only a meager and cursory discussion to the question of the temporal power of punishment, in which he merely suggests a well-founded doubt as to the justice of punishment inflicted by human agencies, is it to be wondered that the rest of the philosophy of the Middle Ages (apart from the real controversy as to the relation of the spiritual and the temporal powers) passes over, as it were with closed eyes, social conditions of the most evil character? One need not be surprised to find that it loses itself in a vain display of definitions, or in mysticism touching upon the relation of man and God. It has no sense of those vagaries of criminal justice which are the shame of the later Middle Ages; and it

[6] L. c., art. 4.
[7] II, 2 qu. 108, art. 4.
[8] L. c. qu. 91, art. 2, qu. 95, art. 2.

received from them no inspiration to investigate the doctrinal problems of criminal law.

It was certainly possible to have made progress, if there had been a development of the line of thought suggested by the " Doctor Universalis " as to the bearing of the " lex humana " upon the criminal law. But nothing of this sort was done. Those supporting the worldly power of the Pope had no greater interest than the champions of the independence of the temporal power, in discussing or criticizing criminal justice as it then existed. The former were satisfied with the criminal law, since it granted (at least in theory) the greatest possible protection to the Church, and treated those of another faith as criminals. The latter also, since they argued that the independence of the temporal power was ordained of God, were obliged to uphold the divine origin of criminal law in its existing condition.[9] At any rate, they had no special motive to subject it to criticism and examination. Casual observations as to the application of punishment can interest us little, when they consist solely of repetitions of passages from the Bible, from Aristotle, and from the Corpus Juris.

The question naturally suggests itself: Whether, if the power of the Papacy had been undisputed and the prosecution of heresy had not been necessary, the philosophy of the Middle Ages might not have attained to a critical examination of the fundamental elements of criminal law? The origin of the theory of the Law of Nature is to be sought in the darkness of the Middle Ages. This, together with the theory of the sovereignty of the people,[10] which based the power of the ruler upon the consent of the governed and was not unknown to medieval Europe, constituted a sufficient foundation upon which the fundamentals of criminal law could be developed through the operations of the human will seeking to attain rational purposes. Immediately after the Reformation, the Catholic philosophers, in their discussion of the State and the legal system, exercised the utmost freedom. This is especially true of Molina and Suarez.[11] But at this point we encounter the narrowing and retrogressive influence of the Reforma-

[9] This is especially noticeable in, *e.g. Dante*, "De Monarchia" [English translation by *A. Henry*, Houghton, Mifflin and Co., 1904], where in a peculiar manner it is argued that the temporal power is given divine sanction through the fact that Christ underwent punishment for all the sins of humanity by means of the temporal power.

[10] *Cf. Janet*, I, p. 403. *Gierke*, "Johannes Althusius und die Entwicklung der naturrechtlichen Staatstheorien" (Breslau, 1880), pp. 63, 64.

[11] *Cf. Gierke*, p. 65.

tion. There could not be further open-minded discussion (except the cynical utilitarianism of Macchiavelli) [12] until it was perceived that the modern legal system was independent of the orthodoxy of either the Catholic or the Protestant. It was only by slow degrees that the mass of the people could attain this attitude. The Reformers were apparently far removed from the opinion that it is possible for people to live in proximity to one another in a legal and moral manner, without a definite and fixed confession of faith. This truth first became apparent in the practice of those States which, although Catholic or Protestant, were located near one another and obliged to have mutual intercourse.

Consequently, it was not entirely an accident that the writer who is regarded as the founder of modern international law was also the propounder of the first modern theory of criminal jurisprudence, — Hugo Grotius.

[12] *Cf.* especially the seventeenth chapter of "The Prince."

CHAPTER III

CRIMINAL THEORIES FROM GROTIUS TO ROUSSEAU

§ 77. **Grotius.** — Hugo Grotius (while not felicitous in his conception of the right of war as the right of the offended or injured State to punish) undertakes, in the 20th chapter of the second volume of his famous work "De Jure Belli et Pacis", a complete discussion of the principle, scope, and enforcement of criminal law. In that comprehensive and profound spirit, which is characteristic of his work, he takes up the problem in such breadth and thoroughness, that his theory (which in certain aspects even attempts to portray the historical development of the subject) remained for a long time essentially undisturbed by his successors, although they may have surpassed him in their treatment of some particulars.

It is still the idea of *retribution* which forms the foundation of Grotius' theory, and this idea is left without further support. The most there is to say for it is that it does not conflict with that ideal of fairness ("æquitas") which was to Grotius the essential element of the positive law. In other words, this idea of retribution does not conflict with those conditions which, for the affairs of man, are to be inferred from his nature and his inherent social instinct ("appetitus socialis"). Punishment is something which results directly from the nature of crime: "Crimen grave non potest non esse punibile."[1] The assertion of this retribution was forced upon Grotius by his empirical (to say the least) definition of punishment: "Malum passionis quod infligitur ob malum actionis",[2] — a definition often repeated but more appropriate to his time than now.

[1] II, 20, § 2, n. 3.

[2] II, 20, § 1.

But retribution was by Grotius conceived in a sense different from that previously prevailing. The question whether punishment must necessarily consist in some evil for the party punished had not yet been raised. In the Middle Ages and in ancient times, retribution was deemed both a *duty* and a *right;* to Grotius it was a *privilege.* Just as every right as Grotius asserted [3] is to be exercised only in pursuance of some rational purpose, so it was with criminal law.[4] Therefore, says Grotius, even vengeance is not to be repudiated, provided it has a rational purpose, *e.g.*, the purpose of preventing, in the future, injuries similar to those received. Grotius, indeed, correctly recognized vengeance as the historic root of criminal law. He posited the right to take vengeance [5] as originally belonging to every one; it was only for reasons of expediency, notably because vengeance is so apt to transgress the limits imposed by reason, that the criminal law was placed in the hands of the judge (the State).[6]

Range of Punishable Acts. — The question as to what crimes should be punished was left as completely untouched by Grotius as were the questions concerning the amount of punishment. In this regard, since he considers law and morality to be in their very essence identical, he proceeds upon the principle that sin ("peccatum") and punishable acts (in their essence and apart from the requirements of a concrete system of law) are likewise identical. Thus, it was *e.g.*, with the ancient Greeks, who recognized no principal distinction in this respect and regarded extravagance and arrogance ("ὕβρις") as acts and attitudes possibly amenable to criminal punishment. The principle that punishment is merely a right and not a duty made it possible for him to reach the correct conclusion that the range of punishable acts is narrower than that of immoral acts. No punishment should be inflicted for acts which neither directly nor indirectly touch human society (acts the injurious effects of which do not extend to others). Since the State is not bound to punish but is merely entitled to punish, there also, according to Grotius, exists the possibility of foregoing punishment by pardon, and as reasons for

[3] Thus also *e.g.* the right of property (II, 20, § 5).
[4] II, 20, § 22, n. 1: "Naturalitur qui deliquit, in eo statu est, ut puniri licite possit; sed ideo non sequitur eum debere puniri."
[5] Hence, under extraordinary circumstances, the right of individuals to punish can even now find a place. *Cf.* II, 20, § 9, n. 2.
[6] II, 20, § 8, n. 4. *Cf.* also II, 20, § 40, n. 1. The "Summa potestas" in the State does not by virtue of its nature possess the exclusive right to punish: "Subjectio aliis id jus abstulit."

this pardon, considerations of utility are acknowledged as sufficient.

Amount of Punishment. — In respect to the amount of punishment, we indeed find in Grotius considerable uncertainty and inconsistency. On one hand, he has recourse to the Aristotelian argument which ascribes punishment [7] not to a "Justitia assignatrix" but rather to a "Justitia expletrix." Accordingly, he regards punishment as an adjustment of the injury (although surpassing the exact amount).[8] Yet, in another passage, in the discussion of self-defense, he reaches the correct ideas that (logically speaking) there is no such thing as commensurability of guilt and punishment, and that it is merely a conscientious obligation ("caritas") [9] on the part of legislation to exercise moderation in the warding off of wrong. In connection herewith it is well if the legislator be given a free hand in fixing the punishment in accordance with reasons of utility, although there must be no punishment "ultra meritum"; [10] but how define "meritum"?

Justification of Punishment from the Standpoint of the Criminal. — The punishment was also justified from the standpoint of the criminal by a reference to his own will, to a voluntary acquiescence: "qui deliquit sua voluntate se videtur obligasse pœnæ, quia crimen grave non potest esse non punibile, ut qui directe vult peccare per consequentiam et pœnam mereri voluerit." However, this standpoint of voluntary acquiescence does not lead him to give to the statute law such preëminent importance as later is found in Feuerbach. It does not appear in Grotius as a foundation but rather a limitation of the criminal power. This is apparent in the sense that he considered it ill-advised not to give full enforcement to any statute that has once been enacted,[11] since, in any case, an act which is in violation of a special criminal statute through this alone is dangerous and deserving of punishment: "Lex prohibens omnia peccata geminat; non enim sim-

[7] II, 20, §§ 2 *et seq.*, and in regard to this, *Hartenstein*, "Darstellung der Rechtsphilosophie des Hugo Grotius" in "Abhandlungen d. Königl. Sächs. Gesellschaft der Wissenschaften, histor-philosoph. Klasse" (1850), pp. 529, 530.

[8] "Nec enim æquum est, ut par sit periculum nocentis et innocentis", II, 20, § 32, n. 2. *Cf.* in regard to this *Laistner*, "Das Recht in der Strafe" (1872), p. 64. On these grounds Grotius under some circumstances approved also of the modified death penalties.

[9] II, 1, § 10, n. 1; III, 1, § 4, n. 2.

[10] II, 20, § 28.

[11] II, 20, § 2, n. 3. — § 24, n. 1–3. Here indeed Grotius has in mind a new criminal statute.

plex est peccatum, sed etiam vetitum committere", as Augustine had previously stated.[12]

Defects and Merits of Grotius. — The weakness of this famous legal philosopher's theory of criminal law consisted chiefly in his having, from the outset, regarded punishment as an evil. Punishment as reaction against immorality and relatively as reaction against wrong permits of an ethical and logical foundation; but as an evil it can only be founded empirically. Thus the idea of retribution has to be invoked as an aid, and presumed without proof. But the idea of retribution necessarily implies that its exercise is not primarily a right but is essentially a duty and only incidentally a right. It has also the consequence that, whatever treatment is required by retribution, nothing can be deducted from it for considerations of utility and humanity. Yet Grotius with accurate insight perceived that in the hands of the State punishment in every case is not an unconditional duty.

But, apart from all this, the criminal theory of Hugo Grotius is remarkably superior to the attempts which, for almost two hundred years thereafter, were made by others towards solving the problem. The possibility that historic development may be justified, a point which is indisputable in the view of Grotius, but which is utterly repellent to dull and narrow minds, prevented its general acceptance. It often happens that one-sided theories have the greater following, if the consequences imported in the theories serve definite temporary needs or are capable of easier comprehension. The successors of Hugo Grotius are especially illustrative of this phenomenon.

§ 78. **Hobbes.** — While Grotius derived the legal system and the State from a compact of individuals, yet the impulse which led to this compact was a moral one based upon the general arrangement of the universe. He regarded (not always consistently, however) the State as bound by this general moral arrangement, just as the individual. The adherents of the doctrine of the Law of Nature little by little allowed the element of arbitrary or discretional power to appear in this compact. Influenced by the turmoil and confusion of the English Revolution, Thomas Hobbes

[12] The passage II, 20, § 35, is not correctly construed by *Laistner*, p. 66 Anm. 4. Here Grotius does not say that the judge should not apply a severe criminal statute if there is a general custom of committing the offense in question. He says merely that such a custom may be for the judge a mitigating circumstance, while the legislator may find herein a ground for increasing the penalty.

founded the State and the legal system upon a pessimistic view of human nature. The evil natural attributes of individuals should be held in check by the State and the law. Unlimited selfishness, or to speak more accurately, desire to injure others, appears to him to be the fundamental characteristic of human nature. The State, accordingly, is merely an institution for coercion calculated to put an end to "war of all on all" arising from such selfishness and to the general insecurity therewith connected. Before everything else in law, punishment is necessary. A mere contract would soon be broken by passion, "ut aperte majus sit periculum fecisse quam non fecisse. Omnes enim homines necessitate naturæ id eligunt quod sibimet ipsis apparentur bonum est." [1] Punishment has no purpose other than that of deterrence by the threat contained in the statute.

Since Hobbes was not capable of any deep historical comprehension he failed to discover the relation [2] between revenge and punishment, and he considered that punishment did not originate or become possible until the existence of the State. He thus stands primarily upon a purely relative theory to which the later theory of Feuerbach exhibits a marked kinship, — although Feuerbach, as is well known, wrote in opposition to Hobbes.[3] The relation between a punishable wrong and a civil wrong on one hand, and on the other the relation between criminal law and morality, is almost completely abandoned.[4] To Hobbes, torts and the payment of damages have nothing in common with crime and punishment. While he also recognizes that, for example, theft, adultery, and manslaughter are forbidden by the "Lex naturalis", and that the power of the State can not be at variance with the "Lex naturalis", yet in Hobbes this observation of the "Lex naturalis" is explained away by the statement that the power of the State is obliged to create the regulation and to maintain a regulation that has once been prepared, but the kind and the manner of the form of this regulation should depend entirely upon the pleasure of the holder of the sovereign power: "Furtum homicidium adulterium atque injuriæ omnes legibus naturæ

[1] "De Cive", c. 6, § 4. *Cf.* also "Leviathan", c. 28: "Pœna malum est transgressori legis auctoritate publica inflicta eo fine, ut terrore ejus voluntates civium ad obedientiam conformentur." "De Cive" was first published in 1646.

[2] "Leviathan", l.c.

[3] "Anti-Hobbes, oder über die Grenzen der bürgerlichen Gewalt" (1798).

[4] "De Cive", c. 3, § 4.

prohibentur, cæterum quid in cive furtum, quid homicidium, quid adulterium, quid denique injuriæ appellandum sit, id non naturali, sed civili lege determinandum est." [5]

From which it follows further, that the amount of punishment absolutely depends upon the discretion of the " summa potestas " in the State, acting in pursuance of the " utilitas publica." The reference of the punishment to something that is past is expressly repudiated as absurd.[6] A penalty fixed by statute must not be exceeded, although it is not at all necessary that there be a special threat of punishment, a mere prohibition being sufficient for the punishment of its transgressor. For that would be nothing other than to allow another to make amends for a fault committed by the legislator.[7]

Justification of Punishment from Standpoint of Criminal. — The justification of punishment from the standpoint of the party punished is not entirely disregarded by Hobbes, — but his argument is almost inconceivably weak. Hobbes, to be sure, realized the inadequacy of the fiction that the offender in the commission of the crime voluntarily acquiesced in the punishment. As the later more detailed arguments of Pufendorf have shown, this recognition is not entirely unimportant in the appraisement of acts based upon the natural impulse of self-preservation, and is also in contrast with the extreme consequences of the inquisitorial principle in criminal procedure. Hobbes, however, believed that he had done enough in this respect, since as part of the contents of the contract (upon which according to his theory the State was based) he had adopted the principle that no one should render assistance to those whom the holder of the " summa potestas " deemed it well to punish.[8] But the right to punish, he believed, did not need to be specially transferred to the highest power in the State. It was originally possessed by " all against all." Hereby Hobbes (unconscious of the contradiction) comes back to an absolute basis for criminal law. It is not a basis resting upon an ethical idea, but merely upon a reference to that general position of warfare which is allowed to each against every one else. It is thus a founding of criminal law upon a power not controlled

[5] "De Cive", 6, § 16. Here moreover Hobbes confuses the civil law question as to how ownership, etc., arises with the criminal law question as to what violations of once existing property constitutes theft, etc.
[6] *Ibid.*, 3, § 11.
[7] *Ibid.*, 13, § 16.
[8] *Ibid.*, 6, § 5; "Leviathan", c. 28, init.

by an ethical regulation. In the case of those crimes whose essence consists in an attack upon the authority of the State as such, and so in crimes of "lèse majesté", Hobbes believed this pure condition of warfare to exist. This principle justified such abnormal rules as the extension of certain punishments to the descendants of those guilty of high treason. Yet, as a principle, it is illuminated by one correct idea, *viz.*, that (as later maintained by Fichte) the criminal law and penal statutes may to a certain extent be conceived as limitations upon vengeance and the right of war.

§ 79. **Spinoza.** — It is a peculiar phenomenon, to which Ahrens [1] has properly called attention, that opinions, such as those emanating from Hobbes — the unrestrainable power of the individual uncurbed by ethical motives — and Pantheism — ascribing no independence to personality and rather regarding it merely as a transitory manifestation of the whole — are in accord in many of their results. This is especially the case, we may add, in respect to criminal law. Thus we find in the famous "Tractatus theologico-politicus" [2] of Spinoza, the founder of modern Pantheism, almost the same foundation of criminal law as in Hobbes. According to Spinoza, law in its origin and essential nature is nothing other than force, — and naturally so, since ethical ideals presuppose freedom. But if the activities of the individual being are of necessity determined by the universal being, then these activities are incapable of any valuation in pursuance of an idea which presupposes a "should" and not an absolute "must." The large fish have the right to swallow the small fish; and in the condition of nature every one has the right to take and do that to which his desire prompts him.[3] He acts in accordance with his nature, in accordance with the law of the universe in him obtaining. With Spinoza, as with Hobbes, it is only the consequent general insecurity which leads to the compact of the State and therewith to criminal law (*i.e.* that criminal law imposed by the State). This latter, properly speaking, did not come into existence until the State. In nature, every one has all that his power is sufficient to obtain; in the State, the power of the State acts only because individuals have irrevocably acquiesced therein. The aim of the punishing power and of the criminal law is to secure obedience, as disobedience constitutes the essence of crime. Therefore, the

[1] "Naturrecht", Bd. I, p. 100 (6th ed.).
[2] First published in 1670.
[3] "Tract.", c. 16: "Jus itaque naturale unius cujusque hominis non sana ratione, sed cupiditate et potentia determinatur."

direct purpose of the criminal statute is *fear*, which should be felt by the masses, who are inclined to act in pursuance of their baser sensual desires and contrary to the true laws of nature: "terret vulgus nisi metuat." In other words, criminal law is based on deterrence and determinism. It is left undecided whether the effect is to be attributed to the statute or to the execution of the punishment.[4] But in one respect, Spinoza, the more profound thinker, differs very materially from Hobbes. He gives to the "lex naturalis", from which the State may not completely separate itself, a far more definite meaning than had been given by Hobbes. His philosophy of law betrays a democratic tendency in the remark (reminding one of Aristotle) that a great body of people who, united, exercise the criminal power will not readily do anything that is absolutely perverse; and so he suggests the conditions of lasting sovereignty to be the satisfaction of the true needs of the people: not a formal contract but rather rational agreement binds the subjects.[5] From this there arises a far wider limitation of the power of the State in respect to what acts may possibly be punished (a matter, however, argued by Spinoza merely in regard to freedom of thought and religious belief).

Influences of Spinoza's Life upon his Work. — Upon the whole, Spinoza's philosophy of the State and of law reflect in clear outlines the peculiar circumstances of the philosopher's life. Spinoza belonged to the Jewish race, which was at that time almost universally persecuted. This circumstance excluded him from active participation in public life; and he therefore found in quiet meditation and investigation of the relations of things the highest pleasure and calling of humanity. For this reason he does not expect much from the power of the State; but he does demand at least a certain guarantee of quiet and the enjoyment of the natural essentials of life and above everything else freedom of investigation. With the possible exception of the province of freedom of thought and religious faith, there was hardly an opportunity for such a sensitive and retiring disposition to have any conflict with the criminal law, — a conflict experienced by even noble natures who come into real participation and active share in public life. He regarded criminal law as essentially intended only for the rabble, and therefore views it from its baser side as a

[4] The evil entailed by the punishment must be greater than the advantage obtained by the crime.

[5] "Ex quibus concludimus, pactum nullam vim habere."

means of deterrence intended to hold in check evil passions and thus he overlooks its general and higher ethical significance.[6] This is in history a constantly recurring conception and attitude. Especially is this the case among the ranks of the fairly comfortably situated and blasé middle class, who, to be sure, pay taxes but in other respects are inclined to follow their own special interests, until some unexpected case reminds them that it is not always the common people who come into contact with the criminal law and that the correct limitation of the criminal power of the State is an ideal and at the same time a substantial benefit to all.

§ 80. **Pufendorf.** — Samuel von Pufendorf,[1] in that part of his work which deals with criminal law, was fully in accord with the point of view accepted by Hobbes,[2] and he often expressly appealed thereto.[3] Like Hobbes, he denied the originally ethical character of the relationship between man and man; and, like Hobbes, he considered a man in the natural state as entitled to all which his individual power enables him to attain. He derived the criminal law, belonging exclusively to the State, from a simple waiver of the right originally belonging to each individual, in pursuance of his own interest, to cause harm to any one who in his view, opposed this interest or stood in his way.[4] Punishment, in the true sense, according to Pufendorf, exists only in the State, and is inflicted "al imperante." Of retribution as a principle of punishment, he would have nothing, — "non est homo propter

[6] In accordance with this conception little attention can be paid to the criminal. Spinoza entertains no doubt as to the expediency and legal propriety of the death penalty. Where he deals specially with punishment, he almost always speaks of the scaffold as "formido malorum." *Cf. Laistner*, "Das Recht in der Strafe" (1872), p. 78.

[1] *Cf.* especially the third chapter of the eighth volume of his comprehensive work, "De jure naturæ et gentium", first published in 1672. The chapter referred to is entitled: "De potestate summi imperantis in vitam ac bona civium in causa delicti."

[2] I am unable to concur in the statement of *Heinze* ("Staats- und strafrechtliche Erörterungen"), p. 254, that Pufendorf holds essentially the same conception as Grotius.

[3] *Cf.* particularly, *l.c.*, § 5, where in opposition to Grotius, it is argued that criminal justice belongs to "justitia expletrix."

[4] Pufendorf, like Hobbes, contemplates the right of punishing as ultimately merely a question of might. No attention is given to founding punishment from the viewpoint of the party punished. The idea of voluntary subjection to punishment is very correctly and effectively criticized: "quum nemo delictum admittat quin simul speret, sese latendo aut alia ratione pœnam declinaturum." However, in § 23, it is stated that no one can complain about the severity of a punishment which has been made public previous to the commission of the offense.

pœnam, sed pœna propter hominem,"[5] and consequently the principle of the "lex talionis" in criminal law, according to his view, is both practically and theoretically impossible. The true character of punishment exists rather in a security against future injuries, — *i.e.* deterrence of others, or reformation (or relatively a "making harmless") of the criminal himself. In consequence of this (and in accord with a fallacy of Pufendorf and of many others), as applied to intentional homicide, the death penalty under certain circumstances appears justified.

Comparison with his Predecessors. — Pufendorf, as perhaps no other, spread abroad through Germany those fundamental maxims of the absolute power of the State, which eliminated the State of the Middle Ages and its social system. Yet his theory of the absolute power of the State does not have the one-sided, harsh, yet essentially logical character, which distinguishes the theory of the State and law propounded by Thomas Hobbes. As with Spinoza, the "lex naturæ" and the "lex divina" had with Pufendorf a definite meaning, and the "publica utilitas", the "salus reipublicæ", is the foundation and at the same time a limitation of the absolute power of the State. Nevertheless, the dangerous point of this principle, which otherwise would so readily lead to the theory of the sovereignty of the people, was blunted by Pufendorf, in that he set forth a presumption, by virtue of which the acts of the power of the State correspond to the "salus reipublicæ."

This is his point of resemblance to Hugo Grotius. But unlike Grotius, instead of having the State and law proceed from the inner and ethical nature of man, Pufendorf laid its foundation merely upon the aspiration and need for external advantage and security, or at any rate for a certain improvement. Thus he substantially divested law of its ethical character. On the other hand, he considered man, in the condition of nature, merely from the moral standpoint; and so it came about, that while, to the law, as it was to obtain in the State, an ethical character was denied, the law which existed before the State, or was contemporaneous therewith, was regarded as prevailing from the moral point of view.[6] Thus the result obtained from regarding law as a moral duty was partially carried over to the State and to the law

[5] VIII, 3, § 17.

[6] *Cf. e.g.* the investigation "De defensione sui" (Lib. II, c. 5) and "De jure necessitatis" (II, c. 6).

in the State. So law and morality, in spite of the fact that Pufendorf seemed to deny their common source and original unity, are confused. It was a mistaken attitude on the part of Hobbes and Spinoza to conceive the criminal law as a means of chastisement (discipline), and not primarily as a protection, or (as it were) an outer covering of the otherwise existing right, turned toward an aggressor. This aided the omnipotence of the State, but departed farther and farther from the original starting point of Germanic law, which alone was able to give stability to the criminal law.

Value of his Work. — Nevertheless, that Pufendorf was of eminent service for the advancement of law, and especially of criminal law, cannot be denied. Although he was referred to by Leibnitz as " homo parum jure consultus et minime philosophus ", and although his didactic and dialectic manner [7] at times proved quite barren, yet, on the other hand, he knew the law applicable in particular cases, and had an interest in practical questions, — both of which elements are often lacking in a philosopher. His discussions of responsibility,[8] self-defense, necessity and measure of punishment,[9] must have brought new life to a judicial practice that was ossified and clinging steadfastly to authority. And in one important respect, as contrasted with Grotius, one can observe the progress of the times. Pufendorf rarely regarded it as necessary, in his investigations of criminal law, to have recourse to theology or biblical history; while the extensive investigations of Grotius as to whether his conclusions harmonize with the practice of Moses and the Hebrew judges and kings, make a strange impression to-day.

For a long time after Grotius, Hobbes, and Pufendorf, criminal theories made no remarkable progress, and, in the 1700 s there were even attempts to revert from the emancipation from theology, which these men had accomplished. Yet, during this period, there were certain of the more important authors whose opinions and points of view seem worthy of mention.

[7] Perhaps it may be of interest to the adherents of the "Normentheorie" ("rule theory"), which is now so popular, to learn that this theory is suggested in *Pufendorf*, VIII, c. 3, §§ 2, 4. He also says that the penal clause of the statute is intended for the magistrate, not for the criminal. *Cf.* also *Hobbes*, "De cive", XIV, § 7, § 23, who is almost more explicit. However it arises only incidentally.

[8] *Cf.* I, cc. 4 and 5.

[9] VIII, c. 3, §§ 18 *et seq.* Little attention is given to the varieties of punishment.

§ 81. **Other Writers. Locke.** — Locke,[1] like Hobbes, proceeded upon the theory of a right belonging originally to the individual to revenge real or fancied wrongs according to his discretion, — a right which, through relinquishment, passed over to the State. Fundamentally regarded, criminal law and the right of self-preservation appear to him to be identical; therefore the purpose of punishment is security, through the reformation of the criminal, if it can be so obtained, — if it cannot, then through the death penalty. To inflict the latter is in no way different from the killing of lions and tigers, whom every one has a right to hunt. The criminal (and this reminds one of the later theory of Fichte) has no reason to complain of the punishment. He has declared, through his crime, that with law and equity he is not concerned, and also that every restriction is removed which protected him from violence and injustice.[2] For this reason, the amount of punishment is determined merely by the conscience of the party inflicting the same. However, there is no absolute obligation to punish; a penalty can, if it seems expedient, be remitted.

The ideas, from which an actual advance of criminal law could arise, lay in the different utilitarian purposes of punishment, which, however, portray in proper order and in a correct relationship, the absolute principle of justice regarded, as it were, from the other side. The absolute theory (which does not include relative theories) stands essentially for continuity of purpose, — at any rate it operates as a warning to change, in case criminal law and its theories start upon a false path or are led astray in following out a relative theory.

Leibnitz. — Historically speaking, little influence has been exercised by the ideas of Leibnitz, which appear scattered throughout his "Théodicée." Leibnitz,[3] in his fundamental idea, reminds one of Plato. To Leibnitz, as to Plato, reward and punishment seem to be part of a principle of harmony governing the entire world, and, as externally, so internally in the criminal himself, the punishment restores the obscured predominance of ideas

[1] "On Government" (London, 1690), II, especially § 87. *Cf. Laistner*, pp. 72 *et seq.*

[2] § 8.

[3] "Nouveaux essais de théodicée", I, c. 2 (ed. *Erdmann*, I, p. 215 *b*), I, 70, 71, 73, 74 (Werke, ed. *Erdmann*, I, pp. 521 *et seq.*). I, 73 says as to punishment: "un rapport de convenance qui contente non seulement l'offensé, mais encore les Sages qui la voient comme une belle musique on bien une bonne architecture contente les esprit bien faits." 74: ". . . Dieu a établi dans l'Univers une connexion entre la peine ou la récompense et entre la mauvaise ou la bonne action."

divinely implanted. Naturally this leads to the purpose of reformation. But Leibnitz does not entirely abandon the principle of deterrence. He says, however, that it must be harmonized with the purpose of reformation. As with Plato, however, everything is subjected to an absolute theory. Satisfaction ("Genugthuung"), which is dependent for its meaning upon the acceptance of freedom of the will, is the primary element;[4] and justice, according to Leibnitz, does not rest upon the possibly changing needs and opinions of mankind. A deeper insight is shown by that passage in which Leibnitz points out, as one of the most effective means of punishment, the general scorn of the community towards the criminal, and he compares this especially with excommunication among the early Christians.[5] This is not far removed from the principle that punishment may conceivably be something other than an external evil.

Cocceji. — Samuel von Cocceji's "Theory of Indemnity"[6] (which likewise exercised little influence), based upon the opinion that a wrong, in addition to a material injury, also created an ideal injury, and that this must be rectified by the penalty,[7] was founded upon a divine dispensation of things. Yet it is quite peculiar in this, viz.: that punishment is regarded as necessary for the preservation of the right ordained for the individual and the authorities of the State (including the right to obedience), and that the absolute theory was practically debased into the old and oft-repeated consideration of expediency.[8] Simple indemnity, in case of an offense, does not suffice, since, in that case no one would suffer from having committed an offense, and there would thus be incitement towards the commission of wrongful acts.

The "lex talionis" appeared to Cocceji essentially the correct form of punishment,[9] and the existence of a wrong presupposes the violation of a right. But the jurist felt obliged to modify the idea of the "lex talionis" into the idea of an evil of equal impor-

[4] *Cf. l.c.*, I. 74.

[5] "Nouveaux essais sur l'entendement humain", II, c. 28.

[6] "Introductio ad Henrici de Cocceji Grotium illustratum" (1751), diss. XII.

[7] L.c., § 555.

[8] This was conformed to by Cocceji from the very beginning.

[9] § 554: "Sane talio non intelligi potest de retribuendo ejusdem generis modo. . . . Sed tantundem illud æstimationem recipit, vi cujus aliquid pensamus cum aliis rebus vel factis quæ sunt vel ejusdem quantitatis vel qualitatis." *Cf.* § 561, n. 8; The death penalty is also justified (according to the principle of the "talio"): "si tanta est malitia ut spes eum meliorem fieri posse nulla supersit." "Arbitrio judicantis definitio talionis reservata est."

tance.[10] Thus it becomes as pliant as wax and as elastic as rubber; and by the maxim that every act that is contrary to a statute or the command of a superior is also a violation of a right (namely, the right to obedience[11]), everything can be justified. The distinction between law and morality is often confused, since the violation of a right is presumed, unless the law expressly gives to a person the privilege of acting in the manner in question.

Thomasius and Wolff. — The legal philosophers and jurists who preceded Beccaria, and sought to found criminal law upon a relative theory, contributed just as little to the advancement of the cause.[12]

Thomasius reproduced, in the short remarks which appear in his "Fundamentes juris naturæ et gentium", the theories of Pufendorf. Expiation, insofar as it is undertaken by men, he designates as "crudelitas." "Assecuratio" and "emendatio" appear to him to be the goal of punishment; but he chiefly emphasizes the latter, and compares punishment especially with medicine, which must be differently applied according to the time and circumstances. Nevertheless, and in spite of the fact that Thomasius had striven so often against the theologians, he has recourse, in some passages, to the ban of theology, since he is of the opinion that, for certain offenses, the punishment is fixed through "jus divinum."

Christopher Wolff proceeded consistently.[13] He believed that no act deserves punishment as a consequence of its own nature. The only purpose of punishment should be the warding off of injury from the individual and from the legal community ("Salus reipublicæ suprema lex esto!"). It is worthy of mention that, in Wolff, there is clearly apparent the relation of punishment to the protection afforded by law. There should be no punishment on account of an act that is only meditated ("actus internus"); punishment may be based only upon an injury ("læsio"). The

[10] § 521. Thus, especially, the punishment of suicide was justified, since no one had a right over himself, except for his own maintenance. *Cf.* also XI, § 27: "Principium juris naturalis est voluntas Creatoris . . . Omnis autem illa voluntas hac generali propositione continetur, ut creaturæ ratione præditæ 'Jus suum cuique' tribuat."

[11] *Cf.* § 513, c. 4.

[12] The enumeration in *Leyser*, "Medit. Sp." 649, n. 1, of the six different purposes of punishment sounds almost comical: "1. satisfactio læsi, 2. pensatio mali cum malo, 3. emendatio malifici, 4. detractio virium nocendi, 5. terror aliorum, 6. incrementum rei publicæ, aut alia rei publicæ utilitas . . . perfectissima . . . pœna est, per quam omnes istæ fines simul obtinentur."

[13] "Institutiones juris naturæ et gentium" (1754), §§ 93, 157, 410, 758, 809, 1043 *et seq.*

justification of punishment as toward the criminal is thus based upon the violated right, and, from the point of view of the State, is based upon the " Salus reipublicæ."

Rousseau. — One cannot call what little is found in Rousseau [14] a real theory of the basis of criminal law. Rousseau merely endeavored to reconcile that punishment which, whether good or evil, he was obliged to regard as practically indispensable, with his theory of the absolute freedom of the individual, — a freedom upon which not even the State might infringe. He accomplished it in this way, namely, that he considered the crime as a breach of a contract which gave to the State the right of war and defense against the individual. Yet there was connected herewith another fundamental principle which bases punishment upon the will of the criminal; and it is in connection with this second fundamental principle that Rousseau, under certain circumstances, would require that the individual be sacrificed for the State. According to Rousseau's view, every one assumes the risk that the State may say to him, that it is necessary that he die for the sake of the State. It is certainly true, that Rousseau abandoned the purpose of deterrence in punishment; — also that he observed something of worth even in the basest individual, — yet the maxim that one has the right to kill any one who cannot be allowed to live without danger, entirely releases the conception of punishment from its historical and ethical bases, and makes it expansive as rubber. It has been seen how the fairest theories of humanity and nobility were able to justify themselves in the French Revolution under the plea of necessity. Necessity, measured solely by concrete circumstances, gave rise to the theory of extraordinary legislation and despotism.[15] And yet it is still more questionable, if one proceeds (as Rousseau certainly did not do with any degree of precision) upon the basis that crime consists not so much in the violation of a right as in disobedience. In the case of violations of a right, one is traditionally rather accustomed to fixed degrees of punishment, — yet a fervid imagination is able to deduce, from every act of intentional or actual disobedience, the overthrow of the State, and therewith the need for repression " à outrance " by means of the criminal law.

[14] "Contrat social" (1762), II, ch. 5.

[15] Along with this there are occasionally profound and correct observations. Thus, in the "Discours sur l'origine de l'inégalité" ("Œuvres", ed. *Musset-Pathay*, Paris, 1823, I, p. 281), he states that in the initial stages of legal development every violation of a right was conceived as a personal injury.

Chapter IV

CRIMINAL THEORIES FROM BECCARÍA TO FEUERBACH

§ 82. **Beccaría.** — The famous book of Cesare Beccaría "Dei delitti e delle pene",[1] in its day so influential, is in these times often rather unfavorably criticized.[2] And if one applies to its theoretic basis the criterion of absolute consistency and exactitude, many objections can be raised, — even if one ignores the lack of historical attitude, and also that superficial and perverted opinion (yet shared by so many in the past century) that criminal law could and must be without a scientific interpretation. The theory of Beccaría founded the State and law upon a contract. It reminds one of Hobbes in that it assumes the establishment of security as the motive for the making of the contract. His position, however, differs from that of Hobbes in this, — that while Hobbes offered the entire freedom of the individual as a sacrifice to the sovereign power, Beccaría proceeded upon the principle that there was but a small portion of the individual freedom which needed to be paid as a price for the security offered by the law. In addition to this, according to Beccaría, in order that the individual, yielding to his selfishness, may not enjoy both his own freedom and encroach upon that of others, a larger part of his freedom is, as it were, placed in pledge, — to be confiscated by the State, if an attack is made upon

[1] First published in 1764.

[2] *Cf. Janet*, II, p. 412. *Laistner*, pp. 92 *et seq. Faustin Hélie* in his (faulty) French translation of the writings of Beccaría (2d ed., Paris, 1870, with introduction and notes), overestimates the services of Beccaría. Beccaría's ideas are almost entirely not original. A correct appraisement is given by *Glaser* in the preface to his excellent German translation (2d ed., 1876).

that portion of freedom guaranteed to others. This pledge lays the basis for punishment, — the purpose of which is security obtained by deterrence, since a crime either violates or endangers the rights of others. In other words, it is the fiction of the consent of the criminal on one side and on the other the principle of the necessity or inevitableness of punishment, to which Beccaría has recourse. But the lack of truth in the fiction that the individual has agreed to have himself offered up as a victim for the purpose of deterring others is to-day apparent, — and the more so, since, both in Beccaría (as well as later in Feuerbach), the deterring element rests not so much in the threat contained in the statute, as in the carrying into effect of the punishment.

Defects and Merits of Beccaría's Work. — The weakness of the argument [3] is especially apparent in its theoretical objections to the death penalty [4] (Beccaría, however, availed himself of other and more correct bases, learned from experience). Beccaría was of the opinion that the individual could not have conceded to the community the right to put him to death, — since this right was not his to concede. This argument obtains equally against all punishment, except possibly mere confiscations of property by virtue of a fine,[5] — and the terrible punishments by way of imprisonment, which he would substitute for the death penalty, and which presently found practical expression in the Austrian Code of Joseph II, were in reality worse than death.

Nevertheless, his theoretical foundation was well suited to establish a truth upon which the reform of criminal procedure, at that time, must turn, — and this explains the extraordinary consequences of the book and its opinions. The method of dealing out criminal justice in the middle of the 1700 s was naturally open to the reproach that it exhibited a revolting prodigality in its punishments, — in other words, in its dispensation of human misery, — and that these penalties by no means achieved adequate results. What Beccaría did was not so much to lay a foundation of criminal

[3] *Cf. Glaser*, pp. 10, 11.

[4] C. 16. He would, however, under exceptional conditions, not entirely reject the death penalty as an extreme means for attaining safety. He regarded the death penalty as a kind of relapse into the condition of warfare.

[5] *Cf. Glaser*, pp. 69, 70. Beccaría, however, believed that imprisonment of long duration had more effect upon the one observing it than upon the convict himself (?). Thus there are in him traces of the idea of an *appearance* of punishment. The idea that imprisonment should be made as terrifying as possible in external aspects (*e.g.* through the appearance of prisons) recurs in others.

law as to emphasize its limitations. According to his argument, only those acts should be punished which were dangerous to the State and relatively to others. Only so much punishment should be inflicted as was absolutely indispensable for deterrence.[6] The State has the duty to prevent crimes [7] by means other than punishment, and has to consider whether or not some other means would serve this end better, and, accordingly, whether or not it would be better in many cases if punishment were given up. These principles are undoubtedly correct; and Beccaría used them to assail a countless number of grave abuses in the criminal law and the criminal procedure, — abuses such as torture, the disgraceful conditions of the prisons in which suspects were detained, the long duration of the trials, the lavish infliction of the death penalty, the cruel punishments tending to harden the sensibilities, the infliction of severe penalties for offenses entailing little danger, confiscation, etc. In this consisted his indisputable and never to be forgotten service, — as all concede. He also recommended the greatest possible celerity of punishment.

It is self-evident that such a theory was opposed to the conception of punishment inflicted by the State as a pouring out of divine justice, and to the conception of crime as sin.[8] In this respect, to be sure, his writings contributed nothing new. But the subject had never been so popularly presented. Although Beccaría made no attempt to harmonize his relative theory with an absolute basis of criminal law, yet the noble enthusiasm of its author and the masterly language in which the book was written, permits the reader to assume, as it were, that an absolute principle could be found, behind his principle of the general utility, of the greatest possible happiness of the many.[9]

Later Writers. Filangieri. — As a result of Beccaría's writings, there arose the view that punishment by the State and divine justice are not identical, and this apparently became the general view of the educated classes, of legislators, and of prominent ju-

[6] The punishment must, however, exceed in value the benefit which the criminal anticipates from the crime (c. 15).

[7] This principle to be sure is rather crudely expressed in c. 13. But Beccaría does not openly accept it in the sense so sharply criticized by Laistner, p. 98, that the State may punish only if it has previously exhausted all means to anticipate the crime, — a principle which, scientifically considered, would necessarily lead to the suppression of criminal justice.

[8] However, in c. 25, Beccaría would maintain the connection between criminal law and morality in the determination of punishable acts.

[9] c. 1.

rists.[10] The theory of retribution was virtually abandoned, until it was again habilitated by Kant. The Austrian jurist, Von Sonnenfels,[11] a jurist of great merit, speaks as follows: "Through a kind of tradition, an explanation of punishment has intruded into jurisprudence, which is more ingenious than correct: an injury to the feelings because of the wickedness of the act." He also [12] rejects the definition of Hugo Grotius.

Filangieri [13] considers it no longer necessary to refute the basis of criminal justice as resting upon divine or human retribution.[14] To him, punishment is reparation for the breach of contract implied by the crime,[15] and this reparation can only consist in security from the individual offender and a destruction of the influence which the bad example can have upon others. Thus Filangieri's theory consists of an uncertain and vague commingling of the so-called "special prevention" theory and the theory of "deterrence" (deterrence by the infliction of the punishment).[16] There is no mention of a justification of criminal law from the viewpoint of the criminal. The extravagant results of deterrence are rejected only by appeal to the necessary observance of humanity. It deserves mention, however, that Filangieri has more of the historical sense than *e.g.* Beccaría and others,[17] and that he by no means represents the unlimited omnipotence of the State. His arguments concerning the range of punishable acts have even to-day a claim to recognition. He is as far removed from confusing law and morality, as he is from denying that they have any relation, and in this

[10] The theory of divine and relatively moral retribution was yet maintained, *e.g.* in 1744 by the Professor of theology and philosophy, *Crusius* in his "Anweisung vernünftig zu leben" (3d ed., 1766), and by the philosopher *Baumgarten* ("Metaphysik", Halle, 1757). As to this *cf.* *Hepp*, I, pp. 15–21.

[11] "Grundsätze der Polizei-, Handlungs- und Finanzwissenschaft", Part I (3d ed., 1777), p. 335.

[12] Von Sonnenfels' own ideas as to the basis of criminal law are unimportant. He represents an inconsistent and vague theory of deterrence and at the same time the idea of humanity in criminal law.

[13] In his famous work "Scienza della legislazione", first published in Naples, 1780–1785.

[14] *Cf.* "Introduzione za Libro III" (Vol. I, p. 86 of the Florentine edition of 1820), and III, cc. 25 *et seq.*

[15] "Il delitto non è altro che la violazione d'un patto."

[16] How far should the principle of security and how far should the principle of making an example extend? There are many cases in which the former principle would be satisfied when the latter would require something additional, and vice versa.

[17] Filangieri had *e.g.* apparently correct conceptions of the historic origin of criminal law. According to his view, it was only after the lapse of some time that criminal law was transferred to the State. To this extent his theory can not be designated a relative one.

respect he assumes a higher and more correct attitude than Feuerbach.

§ 83. **Globig and Huster.** — Of far more superficial and (from to-day's viewpoint) almost intolerable character is that abortive treatment which the views of Beccaría received in the treatise of Globig and Huster, "Uber die Criminalgesetzgebung" (1783), — a treatise famed in its time and awarded a prize for merit. The book deserves mention, however, because its authors for the first time worked out a theory of criminal law as a preliminary to legislative action. While both authors evinced their hostility towards "visionary appeals to a divine law" for justification, yet they themselves grouped together a number of theories for punishment (compensation, retribution, deterrence, reformation) without any attempt whatsoever to determine which should be given precedence. They were, however, chiefly influenced by the ideal of deterrence (although at times this was obscurely combined with the ideal of retribution).[1] And they even went so far in this as to recommend, in spite of the improving practice of the times, steps manifestly contrary to progress. Thus, for example, they recommended insulting treatment of the offender's dead body, if he could not be caught alive, and even mutilation by the cutting off of the tongue,[2] although only in exceptional circumstances. Naturally nothing is said of a foundation of criminal law from the viewpoint of the offender. The book, indeed, expounds many correct views; it asserted that a punishment that is necessary is also justifiable; that the legislator should not confuse offenses that are criminal and those which are merely violations of police regulations; that punishment is not to be founded upon a contract with the criminal (and that for this reason the propriety of capital punishment cannot be contested). But it also contains pernicious juristic blunders. Thus, for example, there is a complete confusion of the conception of "dolus" and "culpa" (*i.e.* malicious intent and negligence). There are also principles which only the most shallow understanding could admit,[3] and throughout there is an absolutely unrestrained and arbitrary application of the maxim: "Salus reipublicæ suprema lex esto."[4] One would be inclined to

[1] *Cf. e.g.* pp. 73, 85.

[2] *Cf.* p. 73.

[3] *E.g.* should the notion of honor be merely subjective? p. 124.

[4] Thus the severest penalties were recommended for persons who preached new religions in the State (p. 254). The authors also expressed themselves in favor of punishments by imprisonment that were truly barbarous (p. 168).

wonder at the influence exercised by this writing, if there had not been such frequent repetitions of such things in scientific writings. Acknowledgment should be made, however, of the suggestion as to the need of making the criminal law more definite and more suited to the times.[5]

§ 84. **Servin.** — Beccaría's ideas as to the necessity of punishment were transformed, in the treatise of Servin, into a formal theory of self-defense. This treatise[1] was originally written, in competition with that of Globig and Huster, for the prize offered by the Society of Economics at Berne. Servin regarded criminal law merely as the individual's natural right of self-defense transferred to the State. Just as the individual, in the state of nature, can render himself secure against a repetition of an attack by slaying his aggressor, so, later, the State may do the same thing by means of punishment. According to this, by virtue of the presumption (incorrect, however) that the criminal would repeat the crime he had perpetrated, one would necessarily expect security against the individual criminal to be the purpose of punishment. But, regardless of the fact that self-defense can have reference only to the aggressor and not to third parties, the author gives especial prominence to the deterrence of others. The logical deduction from the theory of deterrence, viz., that the degree of the punishment should depend, not upon the importance of the punishable act but rather upon the strength of the inducement to commit the act, which is often stronger in minor offenses (*e.g.* thefts when opportunity presents itself), is avoided (as later by Feuerbach) by a second infringement of logic; for, while quite openly recognizing this deduction,[2] he says it is not in accord with experience. There is absolutely nothing to be said in defense of the logic of this once-renowned commentator. While, for example, like Beccaría, he approves the greatest possible restriction of punishment and makes the pathetic appeal, "Spare the liberty of the citizen",[3] he has not the slightest scruple against asserting an extensive duty to inform on others, and advocating punishment of the party in-

[5] The principle of deterrence in accordance with the maxim: "Salus reipublicæ suprema lex esto" appears in a more moderate manner in *Gmelin*, "Grundsätze der Gesetzgebung über Verbrechen und Strafen", 1785.

[1] "De la législation criminelle, mémoire fini en 1778, envoyé à la société Economique de Berne 1778 et rétiré du concours 1782. Avec des considérations . . . par Iselin, Sécrétaire d'Etat de la république de Bâsle" (Basel, 1782).

[2] *Cf.* pp. 27, 28.

[3] *Cf.* I, 4 and p. 265.

jured by the crime, in case of his failure to lodge complaint of the crime,[4] and urging the punishment of emigration.[5] While he rejects the death penalty (but primarily for the reason that it does not sufficiently deter), he favors the widest range of corporal punishment, and even those punishments by mutilation which the practice of his time had abandoned. The application made by Servin of the distinction between "droit naturel" and "droit conventionnel" is also remarkable. Infringements of the former he regards as "crimes" (*i.e.* offenses of a graver character), while infringements of the latter are merely "délits" (*i.e.* offenses of less grave character).

Here, for the first time,[6] we meet this classification of punishable acts, which later became so important, — but he is unfortunate in the application of his classification. Life, health, and freedom belong to natural law; the "droit conventionnel" consists of that which results from the "contrat social", and herein is also included property, since the State apportions property(!);[7] consequently theft is never a "crime", but only a "délit."[8] As to punishment, he derived from the conception of the "droit conventionnel" the principle that a death penalty or a sentence to life imprisonment should never be inflicted for a "délit", since no one can enter into a contract extending to another the right of slaying him or depriving him, for life, of his freedom.[9] Together with these useful, although mistaken, attempts to distinguish the various kinds of punishable acts, there appears a considerable confusion of law and morality. Servin quite correctly recognized that grave crimes are always also violations of the laws of morality.[10] But he committed the error of deducing legal maxims directly from the moral law. And as a result of the interchanging of law and morality, he characterized "dolus" as "intent to injure" ("envie de nuire"), — a conception which later became seriously harmful, in many respects, for French administration of justice.

Wieland. — The extent to which the maxim "Salus reipublicæ suprema lex esto" can lead to a disregard of the experiences of

[4] P. 24; *cf.* p. 367.
[5] P. 275.
[6] The words "crime" and "délit" were used interchangeably prior to the legislation of the period of the French Revolution. *Cf. Schäffner*, "Geschichte der Rechtsverfassung Frankreichs", III, p. 440.
[7] However, this argument was used primarily for the purpose of opposing the death penalties which then were so often inflicted for simple theft.
[8] P. 298. [9] P. 179. [10] P. 91.

history, is remarkably well illustrated in the work of the Leipzig professor of philosophy, E. C. Wieland, " Geist der peinlichen Gesetze." Even to-day it is of interest. Although its author was not a jurist, he was not without knowledge of juristic writings, and (perhaps as none other) he reflects the spirit of the enlightened judicial practice of his time, though as a matter of fact his work often gives us the impression of being a caricature.

Proceeding from natural laws (which he identifies unquestioningly with the mandates of morality),[11] Wieland, like Servin, regards criminal statutes as a means to compel the observance of natural laws, and of those laws the only purpose of which is to promote the welfare of the individual citizen. Nevertheless, the criminal law is based upon the natural right of protection [12] which is transferred from the individual to the State; and from this principle of safety against the individual criminal, most of his deductions for the treatment of crimes and offenses are derived. A refutation of the theory of Wieland on this point need not be made here, since the so-called " special prevention " [13] theory, advanced in a more complete form by Grolmann, succumbed under the attacks of Feuerbach.

It is worthy of notice that Wieland had completely failed to comprehend that the nature of the right requires complete freedom of action within the right to be conferred upon those acting justly; and that, in violation of this fundamental maxim, he directly limited the range of the positive right in accordance with the ultimate purpose of the progress of the human race; and that, on this basis, a general intermixture of law and morality is a characteristic of his work.[14] This intermixture of law and morality took especially the following course. The essence of crime, according to Wieland, is its " wickedness " (" Bösheit "), *i.e.* an intent of the criminal which is diametrically opposite to the laws of nature. Where the criminal appears to have followed a certain natural impulse, he has not acted with complete " wickedness " and the highest penalties of the law can not be inflicted upon him. In other words, the principle of moral freedom is maintained as a condition precedent to regular punishment.[15] Where any plausible

[11] I, pp. 5 *et seq.;* p. 102.

[12] I, p. 393.

[13] *I.e.* "Specialpräventionstheorie."

[14] This is especially prominent in the discussion of self-defense (II, p. 136) and also in the discussion of suicide and neglect of one's own health (I, p. 335).

[15] I, pp. 275, 276. "He only can make himself guilty of a crime, who has knowledge not only of the violated statute, but also is conscious of

reason can be found which induced the criminal to commit the crime, there the regular punishment can not be applied, and the criminal must be treated more leniently. So it is, for example, with a robber who murders his victim because he fears discovery. Also, as a further illustration, a false witness who by his false testimony merely desires to obtain an advantage for another or even for himself is not actually a criminal. Consequently the State and the judge (in pursuance of most unsafe presumptions and of fundamental principles which in their practical application conflict with each other every moment) are obliged to fix (arbitrarily) the punishment, *i.e.* to mitigate it. But the State and the judge, if they are sufficiently convinced of the " wickedness " [16] of the criminal, may also punish very severely. The author who, in the beginning, seems so much concerned that the State should not punish where no useful purpose would be served, and who, in the beginning, argues that only a violation of the so-called natural right should be a crime, is ready later to designate as an actual crime " wicked disobedience" to any law of the State whatsoever; for,[17] of course, such disobedience towards the State will ultimately be availed of to violate natural rights.

This is the argument of despotism,—an argument, indeed, which is not scorned by a certain stupid liberalism of to-day (one has only to substitute the word " principiell ", which here has but little different meaning, in the place of the word " wicked ", which is no longer in favor). Since every act whatever *can* be " wicked " and every act *can* be dangerous, mere persuasion leading to discontent in the State can also be a crime; and since the perfecting of the individual is an unconditional duty of the State, so the individual may be coerced by means of punishment.[18] Thus we find preached the greatest conceivable interference of the police (with privilege of punishing) in the affairs of the individual and of the family; and with such omnipotence in the power of the State, is inherently associated the doctrine of the limited intelligence of the

the fundamental motives which are connected with its observance, and in the moment of transgression has sufficient strength to suppress every motive and by means of this suppression to fix for himself an entirely opposite application of his powers." *Cf.* also I, p. 336, where it is argued that violent passion may preclude the action of the real self.

[16] "The deliberate choice of detrimental acts is wickedness and every wicked violation of a statute is a crime." I, p. 275; II, p. 109 and other places.

[17] I, p. 306.

[18] I, pp. 177 *et seq.;* I, pp. 250 *et seq.* At times even prizes and rewards for good behavior are recommended. I, p. 165.

subjects.[19] One is forcibly reminded of the methods of the General Code of Prussia, promulgated a few years after the appearance of Wieland's work. That his views were those of many of his time is also apparent from a comparison with the "Draft of the Bavarian Criminal Code" by Kleinschrod, which was so ably criticized by Feuerbach.[20]

§ 85. **Kant.** — When such errors were prevalent, it became a matter of practical importance, on one hand, to mark the distinction between law and morality, and on the other hand to save the law from being completely reduced into mere considerations of expediency in the individual case. A theory which could undertake this successfully must necessarily create a remarkable impression upon contemporary thought, however striking may be its defects in other respects. This primarily explains the remarkable influence of Kant's theory of criminal law.[1]

Kant absolutely denied to man the possibility of knowledge of "things in themselves" (truth in the objective sense); but (as is well known) by a rather daring mental leap he saved the possibility of an ethics based upon the free will of the individual. This he did by the acceptance of a standard for practical action which presupposed freedom, God, and immortality, and was capable of being directly known, and was inviolable. This "categorical imperative" meant for him, in criminal law, *retribution*. Unconditional retribution must come upon the criminal. In this retri-

[19] I, p. 147. "The citizens are usually too light-minded and unintelligent." "There must be aroused in them a realization of these restrictions (*i.e.* of natural freedom) in order to make of them good citizens."

[20] Compare the account of this Code, *ante*, Part I, § 58. Wieland (I, p. 406) says: "Men who are so steeped in wickedness that they cannot live without either actually undertaking injurious acts or with restless vigilance await the first favorable moment for the execution of an already planned injurious act, are beneath all reformation and nothing but death is able to effectively put a check to their crime." The Bavarian draft (§ 129) says: "Capital punishment shall be inflicted only upon those guilty of high treason, murder, manslaughter, rebellion and incendiarism, since criminals of this character can not be so guarded in prisons and jails that immediate danger is avoided: they might regain their liberty and again commit such crimes." § 130. "Cases of this character are deemed to exist, if such criminals have so strong a following that there is reason to fear that their adherents may set them free from the place of punishment to which they are brought or if the number of such criminals is very large or especially if an offender is of such a character that any other punishment does not suffice to render the state and our other true subjects secure against him." As to this, *cf.* *Feuerbach*, "Bibliothek für peinl. Rechtswissenschaft" (1804), vol. II, part 3, pp. 166 *et seq.* The death penalty is also incidentally justified by Wieland (I, p. 419) because it made it no longer necessary to feed incorrigible men (among whom the murderer is not always included).

[1] "Metaphysische Anfangsgründe der Rechtslehre", 1797, pp. 195–206.

bution commanded by justice, no place is left for additions or for modifications on grounds of expediency. Upon it depended the dignity and value of all human institutions. "If justice ceases, then no longer is it worth while for man to live upon the earth." "Even if civil society should dissolve with the consent of its members . . . the last murderer found in prison must first have been executed, so that each may receive what his deeds are worth."[2] From this standpoint the justice and necessity of the death penalty are especially asserted.

Criticism of Kant's Theory. — It is easy to refute Kant. If one will be self-respecting and not permit himself to be dazzled by a famous name, Kant's theory hardly deserves the status of a scientific attempt. It is nothing other than an appeal to pure sentiment, — a sentiment which, even in Kant's time, varies greatly with the individual. It would be very difficult to-day for a man of scientific training to maintain that there is a uniform categorical imperative, in the way that Kant accepted it. Ethics has its historical phases of development; and this fact, as well as legal history in general, relentlessly militates against the acceptance of capital punishment for murder as a principle valid from the very beginning. Kant was correct merely in this, that the fate of the individual criminal should not (as in his time was so often maintained) be made to depend upon indefinite considerations of expediency. For this purpose, his emotional appeal to the "categorical imperative" superior to time and space was admirably adapted.

Since, however, it is impossible to carry out a theory of retribution, so Kant (although it was not his task really to carry out any theory) was actually obliged to give up his theory, which did not proceed further than aphoristic statements; for, in many cases, he substituted for the real retribution of like with like a retribution according to effect or feeling.[3] However, his "categorical imperative" involved him in some serious entanglements. *E.g.* an illegitimate child, being a child contrary to law, should, strictly speaking, not exist, and consequently it is difficult to declare the murder of such a child as punishable. The demands of honor appear as "categorical imperative" (is there anything that may not at some time and under some circumstances appear as "categorical imperative"!);[4] as a result, on the question of duelling, he

[2] P. 199.

[3] P. 198.

[4] The guillotine and radical action by the State had also in their time been moral duties.

finds no proper avenue of escape. Here the "categorical imperatives" contend with each other and, although they should stake their life on the issue, they form here an exception.

However Kant's theory very properly criticized and refuted that sophistry that the criminal himself wills the punishment as a consequence, and that it is for this reason justified.[5] The same exposure, indeed, in a somewhat more decisive manner, had already been made by Hobbes and Rousseau. That it so soon afterwards could have been set up by Feuerbach, is indeed proof of the vitality of such legerdemain of logic, with which, the solving of the weightiest problems is so lightly attempted, and ever anew.

§ 86. **Fichte.** — Like Kant, Fichte made a complete separation of law and morality,[1] and based law upon the correct, although in itself meaningless, conception of freedom.[2]

As Fichte based the right of property upon an arbitrarily conceived contract of abandonment by non-owners to the owners, and as he bases the State merely upon contract, so he regards crime simply as a breach of contract, *i.e.* of the rights guaranteed by contract. This breach on the part of the criminal, strictly regarded, results in a severance of all legal relations between the State and the criminal, *i.e.* the loss of rights on the part of the criminal. He who is without rights is an outlaw.[3] Still the State

[5] P. 203: "If then I enact a criminal law against myself as a criminal, it is in me the pure Reason, legislatively giving a right (homo noumenon) which subjects myself to the criminal law as a person capable of crime, *i.e.* as another person (homo phænomenon), together with all others in the compact of the citizens. In other words, not the people (each individual among them) but rather the court (the public justice), *i.e.* some one other than the criminal, establishes the capital punishment, and certainly the social contract does not contain the promise to allow oneself to be punished and thus to dispose of one's self and one's life."

[1] This was characteristic of the period, which again is closely related to Hobbes. *Abicht*, "Ueber Belohnung und Strafe" (2 Parts, Erlangen, 1796), would also completely separate moral retribution (divine retribution) from civic retribution (criminal justice). (As to this, see *Hepp*, I, pp. 61–64.) *Carl Chr. Erhard Schmid*, "Versuch einer Moralphilosophie" (Jena, 1790), distinguished (*cf.* especially § 397): *coercive evil* — this can be applied by any injured individual and by the State in his name, *chastisement* — this is an affair of the educator, *making an example* — the authorities are entitled to do this by virtue of the social contract. Schmid believes that only the Infinite can punish, *i.e.* fix a lesser degree of happiness in accordance with deserts of character. Kant even had previously in his "Kritik der praktischen Vernunft" portrayed punishment simply as moral retribution. As to this see *Hepp*, I, pp. 24, 25.

[2] "Grundlage des Naturrecht nach den Principien der Wissenschaftslehre" (Jena and Leipzig, 1796), 2 parts. Nothing relative to criminal law was offered by Fichte's later and mystical "Staatslehre, oder über das Verhältniss des Urstaates zum Vernunftreiche."

[3] II, pp. 113–130.

does not take complete advantage of these harsh results. It can, as a general rule, satisfy itself with a guarantee that, in the future, the criminal will better observe the contract; and it finds this guarantee in the so-called "Abbüssungsvertrag" (*i.e.* contract of expiation), from which the criminal derives "the important right" that he is not declared absolutely without rights but is to be punished.[4] Thereupon, by virtue of this "Abbüssungsvertrag", the criminal is subjected to a reformatory punishment.

But, as above stated, the "Abbüssungsvertrag" merely constitutes the general rule. There are crimes of such a character that the criminal does not appear to be able to give a satisfactory guarantee of his future observance of the contract. In these cases "Abbüssung" ("atonement", *i.e.* punishment in its proper sense) does not take place; there still continues the total deprivation of rights. As a result of this deprivation of rights, the State is justified, for its own security (and, if need be, for the security of the rest of the citizens), in taking the criminal's life. But, as Fichte expressly emphasizes, this is not punishment, but rather a police measure. A purely judicial sentence of death is, according to Fichte, an impossibility.[5] And since, if the "Abbüssungsvertrag" did not exist, *any* action would be permissible against the criminal, who, in the abstract, has absolutely no rights, he believes that it is not only right but also expedient for the law, which necessarily regards the "Abbüssungsvertrag" as a benefit to the criminal,[6] to also assume the purpose of deterrence.[7]

Fichte, indeed, had but little conception of the specific consequences upon the individual criminal of the theory of deterrence and the theory of security. The controversy between Grolmann and Feuerbach soon enough revealed that these theories did not harmonize. Fichte made absolutely no attempt to specify what acts are punishable (deserving of punishment). The most he

[4] II, pp. 97, 98.

[5] II, p. 124. Upon the whole Fichte is *opposed* to the death penalty. He justified it only as Cato, according to Sallust's account, justified the throttling of the followers of Catiline. *Cf.* II, pp. 124, 125. The strange presumption that a murderer is incorrigible is merely an attempt to harmonize the advanced theory with a principle of the positive law which is considered indispensable.

[6] In Fichte, the principle of deterrence at times assumes the coloring of the principle of the "talio." *Cf.* II, p. 100. "Every one must necessarily stake as much of his own rights and freedom as equals the rights of others . . . which he seeks to injure (the punishment of equal disadvantage, 'lex talionis')."

[7] II, pp. 99 *et seq.*

proposes, by way of allotting the objective amount (degree) of punishment, is indemnification in the form of a certain punishment, obscurely defined, by imprisonment in a workhouse.[8]

According to Fichte, the law in general, and obviously criminal law also (as Stahl [9] has very correctly demonstrated), is nothing other than an external arrangement for coercion, bereft of all moral ideas, with but one exception — the maintenance of a certain abstract freedom. Fichte's ideal [10] is that of an "arrangement working with mechanical necessity, whereby, from every illegal act, there results the opposite of its purpose." [11] Consequently a conception such as this, in which the sentiment of the members of the State amounts to nothing, amounts to nothing other than holding that the ultimate security for the maintenance of the legal system is found in unlimited police supervision and red tape (with permits and passports). This is remarkable enough in a philosopher who had so ardently defended the German nationality against the French. It is nevertheless instructive to that pedantic and false liberalism which seeks primarily for security against wrongdoing and in no manner trusts to natural sentiments. Fichte is also absolutely lacking in a true historical sense. Otherwise he certainly would have realized that that basis for the outlawry of the criminal which he everywhere ascribes to criminal law is merely in conformance with the first stages of legal development.

However, some things may be learned from Fichte. In the first place, there is involved in this assumption of the outlawry of the criminal a relative truth well worthy of consideration; it leads to a valuation of criminal statutes which is much more correct than *e.g.* in the later theory of Feuerbach.[12] In the second place, the philosopher has a better perception than many of the jurists soon to be mentioned, in that he sought a basis for criminal law from the viewpoint of the criminal also.

[8] II, p. 112.

[9] "Die Philosophie des Rechtes", I (3d ed.), pp. 230 *et seq.*

[10] I, p. 169.

[11] The purpose of reformation is in inextricable contradiction to this mechanical manner of conception; for according to Fichte the law has nothing to do with the understanding. But how there can be reformation without a change of the understanding, it is difficult to conceive — since even mere habit certainly changes the understanding. Fichte here (II, p. 114, cf. pp. 118, 119), just as is done later by Grolmann, avails himself of the statement that it is political (?) reformation that is aimed at rather than moral reformation.

[12] The criminal statute (if it would rest upon historical necessity and not upon despotism) should be the limitation rather than the basis of the punishment.

§ 87. **Grolmann. The "Special Prevention" Theory.** — Grolmann's theory (that of special prevention),[1] like that of Fichte, found the basis of punishment, as against the criminal, in this, viz.: that, against him who opposes government by law, there may be a right of coercion, which may go even so far as to include his destruction. In his search for a moderation of this coercion,[2] he finds it in the use of a means whereby the one threatening danger (*i.e.* the criminal) can, for the future, no longer be regarded as such. This means is punishment.[3]

The criticism of Grolmann, made by Feuerbach especially and by others, that he would make the mere possibility (apparently the evil intent) of an act rather than its actual commission the reason for punishment, is, upon closer investigation, not well-founded. Grolmann, indeed, would prevent future wrongful acts of the criminal, but the punishment is to be directed in reality against the character of the criminal as revealed by the act he has committed, from which the commission of future crimes seems indicated as likely. An evidence of this[4] (although Grolmann himself does not bring it out in his definition of punishment) is the fact that he takes the unlawful disposition,[5] *i.e.* the permanent character of the criminal, as the determining factor in the fixing of the punishment to be applied, and advances the rule[6] that the greater the wrongful tendency of the criminal, and thus the more dangerous he is for the future, the greater must be his punishment. The extent of the wrongful tendency, he sees reflected in the nature of the right violated by the illegal act.[7]

Herein the untenability of his entire theory becomes openly manifest. Criminal law and morals, according to Grolmann's conception, have nothing to do with each other. He formally protests against the assumption that a man should be improved morally by his punishment.[8] Punishment should be directed not against the wrongful tendency of the heart, but rather against the

[1] "Grundsätze der Criminalrechtswissenschaft nebst einer systematischen Darstellung des Geistes der deutschen Criminalgesetze" (Giessen, 1798); "Ueber die Begründung des Strafrechts und der Strafgesetzgebung" (Giessen, 1799).

[2] *Cf.* "Begründung", p. 157. The State would itself become degraded if without further reason it killed the banished criminal.

[3] P. 32.

[4] P. 54.

[5] *Cf.* especially pp. 120 *et seq.*

[6] P. 121.

[7] "The more irreparable and important the violated right, then the more urgently does the interest of humanity demand the 'not doing' of the act, and the greater the wrongful tendency."

[8] P. 125.

will. But how shall one distinguish them? There can be no doubt that under Grolmann's theory attention must be chiefly given to the individuality of the criminal in the fixing of his punishment. The answer to the question whether or not he who has once committed a crime will presumably repeat it or later commit some other crime, depends more than anything else upon the individuality of the criminal and the special circumstances of the case. While Feuerbach often avails himself of sophistry in his attacks upon Grolmann, yet he is quite correct in maintaining that a code which can only decide as to men and their crimes in pursuance with broad lines and general principles adapted to the majority of cases, presupposes the impossibility of determining punishability in accordance with the character of the offender. The fixing of punishment in accordance with the importance of the right violated by the crime is a radical departure from the original principle. The theory of reformation acts more logically, since it absolutely abandons all fixed punishments, and makes the amount of the punishment dependent upon the reformation of the criminal, which can not be determined until later.

Grolmann's " special prevention " theory necessarily succumbed to Feuerbach's method of attack. It could not serve as the foundation for real progress in criminal law. The most it could have done would be to introduce a more lenient enactment and administration of the criminal law in cases where the criminal, punishable in accordance with a presumed divine justice, might be regarded as harmless for the future. During the time when the life of the State is in the process of development, the consideration given to making the individual criminal harmless is very subordinate, and one to which the judge who comes into contact with the individual criminal can even with a wide discretion as to punishment scarcely do justice. And so even Grolmann himself realized that he was being driven into a corner by the attacks of his friend and opponent Feuerbach. In his later work dealing with the foundation of criminal law, he is considerably influenced by Feuerbach's ideas of deterrence.

§ 88. **Feuerbach.** — In contrast with the foregoing theories, Feuerbach's theory [1] was calculated to serve as a foundation for

[1] "Revision der Grundsätze und Grundbegriffe des positiven peinlichen Rechts" (1799), 2 parts; also the article in the "Bibliothek der peinl. Rechtswissenschaft" (1798), part I, division 2, No. 2; also the work "Ueber die Strafe als Sicherungsmittel" (1800); and "Lehrbuch des gemeinen in Deutschland geltenden peinlichen Rechts" (1801).

that positive legislation of which there was at that period urgent need.

His efforts are directed primarily towards freeing the criminal law from the prevailing theories, which regarded the positive criminal law merely as an imperfect attempt to give expression to an ultimate criminal law corresponding to the nature of things. These theories declared a judge to be justified in setting aside a rule of positive law where it did not seem to be in harmony with that law derived from general principles. The speculation upon and the discussion of the purposes of criminal law, and the theory connected therewith that moral freedom was a prerequisite to the complete amenability of the criminal to the law, were especially well suited to justify the above-mentioned method of procedure, and at the same time to give the judge the necessary *appearance* of being bound by the statute. This resulted in that arbitrary discretion of the judges which has been described in Part I. This arbitrary judicial power even extended to an increasing of the penalties; since it was considered that, as the judge in some cases dispensed with the statutory penalties, so in other cases he was entitled to increase the penalties in pursuance of general principles.

As opposed to all this, the issue now was how to strengthen the authority of the positive law of the statute, and also (since the Carolina, the codification of the common law, had in many respects become impractical) to show how much might be accomplished by a precise and up to date code. Feuerbach indeed, primarily, had only the first purpose in view. But the second was a logical and natural result; consequently it was not merely an accident that Feuerbach was soon entrusted with the composition of an important code.

His Theory. — Feuerbach's theory (he also vigorously opposed the intermixture of theology and criminal law) [2] is in substance as follows: It is a function of the State to prevent wrongs. Not being sufficiently able to attain this object by direct physical compulsion, it is therefore entitled to use psychological compulsion by threatening an evil to those who would commit a wrong (a crime). This *threatening*, in itself, is permissible; it violates the right of no one. But without *fulfilment* the threat would become ineffectual. Therefore the fulfilment of the threat is justified. This is so even from the standpoint of the party punished. Since he had knowledge of the threat of punishment prescribed for

[2] *Cf.* also the criticism of *Grolmann's* "Criminalrechtswissenschaft" in the "Bibliothek für peinl. Rechtswissenschaft", Vol. 2, St. 1, p. 366.

the wrong, which he, even apart from this, was bound to avoid, he has voluntarily subjected himself to the fulfilment of the threatened punishment.

Feuerbach's theory accordingly is called the "theory of psychological coercion" or the "theory of deterrence through threat of law," and it is proper so to designate it. But perhaps it would be more correct to call it the "theory of the positive law." The punishment is justified by the positive law. It extends so far and only so far as can be expected from the operations of a positive statute, *i.e.* a published statute, made known to everyone. This is the true essence of his theory; deterrence played a more subordinate part.

As may easily be seen, this theory was not entirely original. In its fundamentals it frequently reminds one of Pufendorf. But in its thorough treatment of details it is new and original. Originality is also a fit word with which to describe Feuerbach's polemic against the theory of moral freedom, and his ability to formulate laws. In certain respects Feuerbach and Kant form a parallel. Both seek a permanent support for criminal law. Kant, however, in his idealistic fashion, derives our knowledge of criminal law, as it were, from Heaven, by means of apodeictic maxims of eternal justice, which are without proof or further foundation, — axiomatic facts, as he believes. Feuerbach bases criminal law upon the power of an earthly legislator over the baser impulses of human nature. Herein there lies a great, although limited, truth. The power of an earthly legislator and the baser impulses of human nature permit of a certain calculation, and consequently Feuerbach's theory accomplished a greater step in advance than the grandiloquent emotionalism of the philosopher of Königsberg.

Above everything else, Feuerbach denies that punishment, as inflicted by the State, is moral (retributive) punishment based upon a pretended and, to us incomprehensible, moral freedom; the assumption of this moral freedom entailing for criminal law the most absolute contradictions, as Feuerbach ably demonstrated. Punishment is *civic* punishment (*i.e.* temporal, inflicted for purposes of State as distinguished from morality). It is based upon the clear pronouncements of the statute, which finds its justification, from the viewpoint of the criminal, in the latter's voluntary submission, brought about by means of the threat of punishment, and from the viewpoint of the State, in the possibility of deterring from crime and thus preventing crime by means of the threat.

This threat of punishment has, essentially, nothing to do with the individual. With him, only the fulfilment of the threat is concerned; and this, according to Feuerbach, is somewhat of a secondary matter, and is requisite only that the threat may be effective in the future.

In this way, Feuerbach was able to increase the authority of the statute law, and also to effectively demonstrate the subordinance of the judge to the statute law.[3] For now the issue no longer rests upon the nature of the individual, which is so difficult to ascertain, but upon whether or not there is included in the act those characteristic elements which the legislator has established for every case; since it is only these that can be the criterion, in the abstract threat contained in the statute. That which lies in the heart of the criminal and that which is external, coming from attendant circumstances, are equally unimportant. There must be but one exception, and that is where the threat of punishment *could* not be effective in advance, — where an intelligent decision of the author of the act in accordance with the baser impulses against which the legislator has interposed the threat (itself a mental impulse) was not possible.

Thus Feuerbach acquired a firm position for answering the question as to criminal capacity.[4] Moreover, since he found the ultimate purpose of the threat of punishment to be security from violations of right, *i.e.* the subjective right of the State and of individuals, he, at the same time, acquired a criterion [5] for determining the punishability of a crime in relation to its objective or subjective dangerous character. Objectively, its dangerous character is appraised according to the importance of the jeopardized or injured right, and subjectively according to the dangerous nature and intensity of the baser impulse.

It is apparent that all these principles are easily grasped and are adaptable to legislative enactment. In their presence, illumined by Feuerbach's polemic, the doctrines of moral freedom and of indeterminism vanished into thin air. Against all the other relative theories with their special purposes of punishment (security against the individual offender, reformation, etc.), Feuer-

[3] *Cf.* especially the chief principles in the "Revision" (I, p. 147) concerning the importance of the criminal law.

[4] "Revision", II, pp. 131 *et seq.*

[5] Herein Feuerbach is governed by the conception of criminal law at that time prevailing, viz. that the only purpose of law was the protection of external freedom.

bach invoked that undeniable truth which alone corresponds to the dignity of criminal law, yet properly restricts it, viz. that criminal law has its effect not so much through its execution in the individual case but rather by applying itself to the generality of affairs, and by establishing certain fundamental principles of conduct as inviolable,[6] — and for these reasons, proceeding dispassionately and in accordance with broad considerations. No restrictions, on the other hand, are recognized by the theories of deterrence by punishment, or of security against the individual offender, or even of that of reformation.

Criticism of his Theory. — Feuerbach was far removed from that which the great majority usually conceive as the theory of deterrence, and especially from that brutal theory of punishment which, in moments of social unrest or danger, would inflict a severer punishment upon a man because others as well as himself have committed crime. His gradation of punishment is primarily based upon the importance of the violated right, and only gives secondary regard to the impression it will make upon the minds of the public at large. Therefore Feuerbach's meaning is completely misunderstood if we assert (as Hepp does, II, pp. 260 *et seq.*) that according to Feuerbach the statute law is superfluous. As a pure matter of logic it is certainly correct that according to Feuerbach the legal basis of punishment on the part of the State lies in the fact that the State regards the punishment as necessary, and that accordingly the propriety of the threat of punishment rests upon the propriety of the fulfilment of the threat (but not the latter upon the former). It is also true that Feuerbach himself later had to abandon the view of the acquiescence of the criminal in the punishment which he had earlier adopted.[7] In this latter [8]

[6] There is absolutely no merit in the criticism often made of Feuerbach that the threat of the statute (more properly of the criminal law) has no effect upon the criminal, since the criminal is governed by his hope of evading the punishment and thus of the statute being ineffective. (*Cf. e.g. Ziegler*, in "Gerichtssaal", 1862, p. 15.) He who actually commits a crime may indeed cherish this hope. But how many beside him would not commit the crime, if they were assured of immunity from punishment? Feuerbach has often stated that he did not regard the criminal law as the only means to prevent crime, although he regarded it as an indispensable means.

[7] *Cf.* "Ueber die Strafe als Sicherungsmittel", pp. 92 *et seq.;* "Lehrbuch", § 17, II, § 16, II, and as to this *Hepp*, II, p. 222.

[8] This especially weak point was capably controverted by *Grolmann*, "Begründung", pp. 10 *et seq.* He who steals bread, does not enter into a contract to purchase it. A private individual cannot assume that he who enters his room will pay him ten thaler if he fixes this as the condition of entry.

alteration of Feuerbach's theory, it is apparent that, abandoning a justification of punishment from the standpoint of the criminal, it used the criminal chiefly as a means for other ends, — as did the theory of deterrence by the infliction of punishment, which Feuerbach had opposed, and the " special prevention " theory. It is also clear that it did not escape many of the vagaries of these last-mentioned theories, and that it dealt with the criminal, not according to his individuality but according to a certain *average of humanity* — since the *law* does not know anything about the individuals.

If Feuerbach had arrived at a full comprehension of this, he would necessarily have discovered that there was not as much opposition between moral judgment and the criminal judgment of the State as he believed. (Nevertheless he was obliged to confess that everywhere in the criminal law,[9] moral conceptions and judgments " intrude.") He would also have come to realize that these two kinds of judgments differ merely in this, that the judgment of the criminal judge tests the morality of the act only to a point that is certain and easy to establish, and also that criminal law presents in broad and general lines the morality of the community. In that case he would not have been led, as he was, to separate the law from the popular conscience, nor to justify punishment merely upon the ground of an alleged utility in threatening punishment or upon the dangerous character of the act. Nor would he have been led to base criminal law exclusively upon the violation of rights in the subjective sense. He would not have needed [10] to resort to his discredited presumption of " dolus " (malicious intention), in order to avoid the result that a person ignorant of the criminal statute and its penalties or mistaken in thinking his act did not come under the statute, could not be punished on account of " dolus " (malicious intention) — since deterrence is possible only where there is knowledge of the penalties. And, finally, he would not have been obliged to regard man as committing crime only for baser motives, nor the legislator as operating solely upon these motives.

The short work of Thibaut: " Beiträge zur Kritik der Feuerbachischen Theorie über die Grundbegriffe des peinlichen Rechts "[11]

[9] "Revision", I, p. 161.

[10] Offenses against morality which do not at the same time violate a subjective right, are, according to Feuerbach, only offenses subject to police regulation. *Cf.* "Kritik des Kleinschrod'schen Entwurfs", I, p. 16.

[11] 1802.

(which in many respects is excellent, although it seeks to establish deterrence as the correct theory in criminal law) [12] lays down the following sound principle: No criminal legislation is more successful in attaining its ultimate purpose than that which takes as its criterion the ordinary conceptions of moral retribution, while the principle of deterrence, in its consequences (since that evil must always be threatened which is fitted to deter, and thus as far as possible to overcome the impulse to crime) necessarily leads constantly to more terrifying punishments and therewith to impoverishment and animosity.[13] Thibaut herewith openly repudiated the logical results of the principle of deterrence; Feuerbach had already unconsciously done so, since he desired primarily to appraise punishability in accordance with the importance of the jeopardized or injured right.[14] The importance of the injured or jeopardized right can be fixed only in accordance with the moral valuation of the public conscience. Deterrence on the contrary is obliged to take into consideration primarily the greatness of the impulse to the commission of the crime, and this is often very strong in the minor offenses. The practical weakness of Feuerbach's theory lies in this, viz. that it leads the legislator at certain times and under certain circumstances to confuse the former standard with the latter, and also convinces him that if only the punishment has been threatened by the statute, he himself can not be blamed for its injustice. Feuerbach's theory also leads to a frequent confusion of legislation and right.

[12] P. 58.

[13] P. 98; pp. 82 *et seq.*

[14] This had already been correctly brought out by *Schulze*, "Leitfaden der Entwicklung der philosophischen Principien des bürgerlichen und peinlichen Rechts" (1813), p. 326.

Chapter V

CRIMINAL THEORIES FROM BENTHAM TO HERBART

§ 89. **Bentham.** — An interesting parallel and, in many respects, a valuable completion of Feuerbach's theory is to be found in the theory of the famous Englishman, Jeremy Bentham.[1] Bentham completely abandons any attempt to justify criminal law from the viewpoint of the criminal. He simply declares it as an axiom that crimes must be prevented by punishments; and that since the law is founded simply upon general utility, it seems sufficient to describe the punishment as advantageous for the maintenance of the general legal system, this being obvious. Therefore the only endeavor of the legislator should be, on one hand not to punish acts whose punishment would not serve a useful purpose, or would in fact be harmful, and also not to apply those kinds of punishment

[1] As to *Bentham*, *cf.* especially *Mohl*, "Geschichte und Literatur der Staatswissenschaften", Vol. 3 (1858), pp. 595 *et seq.* Concerning his theories of punishment, *cf. Hepp*, "Gerechtigkeits- und Nutzungstheorien", p. 50. The matters considered in the text can be found, apart from the original editions of Bentham's collected writings, readably and cleverly collected in the "Traité de législation civile et pénale, ouvrage extrait des manuscrits du M. Jérémie Bentham, par *Et. Dumont*" (Paris, 1820), 3 vols. Feuerbach himself declared ("Lehrbuch", § 18, Note 11) that Bentham's theory substantially corresponded with his own. [The learned author's account of Bentham's theories, here given, does not do justice either to the scientific importance of his position or to its actual influence on the Continent. See more fully the Critique of Bentham by *John M. Zane*, in Vol. II of the present Series, "Great Jurists of the World." — Ed.]

which would attain such a result, and on the other hand to threaten harmful acts with sufficient and effective punishments. Accordingly Bentham, in masterly fashion, analyzes to their extreme ramifications the actual or presumed evil which arises or could arise from acts actually or possibly coming into consideration as offenses. He also investigates the effects of the punishments which might possibly be applied. The question of the degree of punishment herein assumes a subordinate position. Thus, less than in Feuerbach, is there to be noticed the contradiction which lies in attributing more or less of a punishable character to acts in accordance with the greater or less importance of the injured or jeopardized relation of life, and in the theory of the subduing of impulses to crime by threat of evil. But, as everywhere in Bentham, one is obliged to accept much that is erroneous and distorted along with his numerous ideas that are truly profitable.

Romagnosi's Theory of Necessary Defense. — Romagnosi's theory in many of its aspects agrees with that of Feuerbach, but in others it is quite different. This is the theory of "necessary defense"[2] and was first advanced in 1791, though it did not acquire influence in Germany until later.[3]

[2] "Genesi del diritto penale." Translated into German by *Luden*, "*Romagnosi*, Genesis des Strafrechts" (2 vols. 1833).

[3] Among the adherents of this theory are: *Martin*, "Lehrbuch des deutschen gemeinen Criminalrechts" (first published in 1812); *Carmignani*, "Teoria delle leggi della sicurezza sociale" (3d ed. 1832, Pisa), pp. 47 *et seq.;* furthermore, *A. Franck*, "Philosophie du droit pénal", *cf.* especially pp. 115 *et seq.* Necessary defense of the community, since it need not be completely analogous to that of the individual, is reducible to a coercion to repair an intended moral injury. In reality, Franck's theory of necessary defense is identical with the "restitution theory" of Welcker. But in addition there is present in Franck (p. 120) the foundation laid by Fichte. *Carrara*, "Programma del diritto criminale" (ed. 5, Lucca, 1877, II, §§ 608 *et seq.*) may also be called an adherent of the theory of necessary defense: However, he deduces criminal law not as a right of the State but rather as a right founded upon "Necessita della umana natura" (§ 608). The State has the right to punish merely so far as it accomplishes that legal protection ("Tutela giuridica") which is entrusted to it. Carrara stands upon the basis of the old law of nature and the logical consequences of his view would accord therewith, to the extent that criminal law (which it is stated in § 612 is to maintain human freedom) may not be applied merely to promote the welfare of the State. The difficulties inherent to this theory of "difesa" or of "tutela giuridica" are too easily dismissed by this famous and useful writer, whose theory, since it fixes as the goal of punishment the attainment of peace (of the party wronged and of the citizens), is completely reversed in the "restitution theory" of Welcker. From defense calculated to operate in the future, there does not necessarily follow (as Carrara, p. 614, postulates) the justification of any admeasurement of punishment whatsoever. We would gladly express our approval of the several excellent statements of Carrara, but a separate volume would be requisite for this purpose.

Romagnosi separates himself from Feuerbach by very properly refusing to give recognition to the doctrine of a voluntary submission by the criminal to the punishment. Such agreements he characterises as figments of the imagination. In his conception, punishment is simply defense against future injuries, which might be committed either by the criminal himself or by others. The right of defense, as he undertakes to explain it, is merely one element of the right to life and all other rights. When man was in his natural solitary condition, the right of self-defense, indeed, would cease at the same moment as the attack. But when human society came to exist, there arose from the impunity of the individual making the attack a new danger both for the party attacked and for all others,[4] — a danger for which, as the natural consequence of his attack,[5] the criminal is liable. In other words, there arose the right of punishment, which of course has no purpose other than that of deterrence.[6] This last-mentioned line of thought brings Romagnosi to the same conclusions as those reached by the theory of Feuerbach. Moreover, like Feuerbach, Romagnosi falls into the error of assuming that it is in accord with the principle of deterrence to establish more severe penalties where rights of greater importance[7] are attacked; whereas the principle of necessary defense, as a matter of fact, would require the same penalty for each and every aggression, if it could not in some other way be prevented. This last deduction is recognized even by Romagnosi himself, since, according to his conception, there really arises only *one* right, which appears in its sundry phases along with the various other so-called rights.

Difference between Romagnosi and Feuerbach. — Romagnosi's conception, however, is to be distinguished from that of Feuerbach by the fact that while he, like Feuerbach, makes a distinction between law and morality,[8] he does not regard them as absolutely separate. Yet, on the other hand, for this very reason he fell into a fatal error which Feuerbach was able quite easily to avoid, and against which, as we have seen, he very emphatically and effectively undertook to warn his contemporaries. Romagnosi regarded the

[4] §§ 221, 251 *et seq.* The conception of punishment as atonement is expressly repudiated. § 1345.

[5] §§ 46, 47.

[6] *Cf.* especially § 395.

[7] These attacks should show a stronger criminal tendency. § 1367. Romagnosi, just as Feuerbach, takes the average human being as the basis of calculation for his punishments. § 1386.

[8] §§ 922, 1385.

so-called moral freedom of the criminal as a prerequisite for his liability to the full penalty of the law. His "malvagita"[9] is nothing other than this moral freedom; and closely connected with it is his error of ascribing the basis of the crime, not to the self-love of the criminal, but rather to unnatural impulses. Here Romagnosi's theory goes absolutely astray.

Defects of the Theory of Necessary Defense. — There are other respects also in which the theory of necessary defense is not satisfactory. Its falsity does not lie so much in the fact that the necessary defense ends as soon as the attack does; since this, if one consider it closely, holds good only under conditions where the administration of justice is very certain, and where this is not the case, the party attacked can so extend his defense that the aggressor will be rendered harmless in the future. The falsity of the theory lies rather in the fact[10] that the criminal in reality is not always punished because of his own baseness but because of that of others. If these others were morally perfect, they would not allow the baseness of the criminal to lead them astray. Thus the criminal must suffer for the others; thus the theory of necessary defense is no more just than that of deterrence.[11] Moreover, it has the evil of gravitating towards the theory of security against the *individual* criminal, — a theory which in its strong personal tendency necessarily leads to despotism. Proof of this is given by Romagnosi's arbitrary and false provisions relative to the degree of punishment.[12]

Oersted. — There came about necessarily a reaction against Feuerbach's theory, and especially against his absolute separation of law and morality (which Romagnosi had already repudiated). To every unbiased observer the relation between criminal law and morality is too manifest. The adherents of Feuerbach's theory were in this respect obliged to make some revisions. Thus the Danish jurist Oersted, at the very beginning of his valuable and famous work "Ueber die Grundregeln der Strafgesetzgebung",[13]

[9] *Cf.* especially § 473.

[10] Thus particularly *Hepp*, II, pp. 716 *et seq.*

[11] The founding of punishment upon the disadvantageous results of absence of punishment is, as a matter of fact, a "petitio principii." It is as if one designated the absence of a dam as the cause of a flood, and thereby hypothecated that there should have been a dam at the place in question, "id quod erat demonstrandum."

[12] In Romagnosi's work, which is a maze of dialectical argument, and is often quite tedious, there may also be found many excellent principles of permanent value. [See *Borettini's* critique of Romagnosi in "Rivista Penale", Feb. 1914. — ED.]

[13] Translated from the Danish (Kopenhagen, 1818).

declares that, according to his view, criminal laws are rooted in the moral laws.[14] He thus casts overboard the erroneous view of Feuerbach which regarded a criminal statute as a necessary prerequisite for a punishment,[15] and also Feuerbach's doctrine of a voluntary submission of the criminal to the punishment. But, as already remarked, the abandonment of this last-mentioned doctrine destroyed the scientific unity of Feuerbach's system, and the defense undertaken by Oersted against the reproach of having the characteristics of a Draco which was cast upon the system of Feuerbach as being its ultimate result,[16] is just as little effective as that by which Feuerbach himself sought to avoid this same result. Where Oersted breaks away from the logical deductions of the theory and accepts milder punishments because popular sentiment does not desire the harsh penalties required by pure deterrence, he is saying nothing other than that popular sentiment repudiates the results of the theory of deterrence, and thereby repudiates the theory itself.[17]

§ 90. **Bauer. The " Admonition " Theory.** — The " admonition " theory of Bauer is also regarded as a modification of Feuerbach's theory of deterrence.[1] Yet Bauer, by proceeding on the course on which he began, might have accomplished more than a mere attenuation of Feuerbach's principles, as his theory is designated. It was the severity and the erroneous conclusions of Feuerbach's theory which led Bauer to his attempt to modify it. Bauer, like Feuerbach, made a distinction between the purpose of the criminal statute and the purpose of the infliction of the punishment; and, like Feuerbach, he justified the latter not upon some relation already existing between the individual and the State, but rather solely upon the existence of the criminal statute or the positive legal rule.[2] Still, the difference between Bauer and Feuerbach is one deeper and more far-reaching than even Bauer himself perceived. The " admonition " of Bauer[3] is not an effect

[14] *Cf.* especially p. 5.
[15] Especially p. 109.
[16] Pp. 149 *et seq.*
[17] Oersted's attempt to unite the "special prevention theory" with Feuerbach's "theory of deterrence" is a complete failure. *Cf. Hepp*, II, pp. 590 *et seq.*

[1] *Cf.* "Die Warnungstheorie nebst einer Darstellung und Beurtheilung sämmtlicher Strafrechtstheorien" (1830). Also an article published by Bauer in 1827, in the "Archiv des Criminalrechts", pp. 429–472 ("Versuch einer Berichtigung der Theorie des psychologischen Zwanges").
[2] "Warnungstheorie", p. 44.
[3] "Moneat lex priusquam feriat" p. 130.

upon the baser impulses (or, more correctly, a paralysis of the same) produced by the threat of the punishment. For (as Bauer very correctly remarks) by no means all crimes have their origin in the baser impulses. Crimes can also arise from political or religious fanaticism, *i.e.* from an erroneous comprehension of moral duties.[4] The "admonition" in the conception of Bauer affects the moral as well as the baser nature of man,[5] and is rather the reflected image of the value of the legal system. The legislator holds up before the citizens a picture of the liability to punishment of the criminal acts; and the measure of the punishableness he derives from the importance of the individual legal institution or legal interests which are jeopardized or attacked by the act of the criminal.[6]

From this point of view, Bauer, unlike Feuerbach, concedes the criminal punishment of acts which violate no subjective rights but which indirectly undermine the legal system.[7] Yet, although Bauer (as above mentioned) repeatedly maintained that the "admonition" of the criminal statute also affected the moral element of man, he was unable to discover a relationship between law and morality.[8] Since he repudiated Feuerbach's view of the voluntary submission of the criminal to the punishment,[9] his theory ended in a renunciation of a philosophical justification of punishment, and thus in a justification merely by reference to the positive law (*i.e.* ultimately again shifting towards the viewpoint of Feuerbach), which is at least open to question.[10] In strict analysis, the legislator can threaten *any* evil by way of punishment, and if the threatened evil is inflicted, the criminal upon whom it is inflicted may not complain as to its injustice. This freedom of the legislator, according to Bauer's presentation, is not limited by regard for historical tradition, and is, indeed, limited only by the consideration that possibly too severe penalties are less effective. This reliance upon the positive law is something totally different from the "admonition", the operation of which is to be seen only in the voice of conscience. In spite of its fair promise to find a better principle, the conclusion of the admonition theory is merely a reproduction in paler colors of the theory of Feuerbach, or, as Heinze puts it,[11] a rechristened theory of deterrence.

[4] P. 169.
[5] P. 38.
[6] Pp. 126 *et seq.*
[7] Pp. 106 *et seq.*
[8] Pp. 50, 56.
[9] P. 83.
[10] *Cf.* pp. 226 *et seq.*; p. 233.
[11] In *Von Holtzendorff's* "Handbuch", I, p. 268.

§ 91. **The Reaction against Feuerbach's Theory of Deterrence. Schulze.** — Of those writings which were published in opposition to Feuerbach and Grolmann and sought to establish again the relation between law and morals, the most important and the most valuable in criticism of principles, is that of the philosopher, G. Ernst Schulze: "Leitfaden der Entwickelung der philosophischen Principien des bürgerlichen und peinlichen Rechts", published in 1813. Schulze's combination of his ideas with the formal theory of necessary defense has unfortunately led to his theory being regarded as merely a slight modification of the other, and for this reason it has not received the attention it deserves.

Schulze regarded morals as the principal criterion in determining the range of punishable actions. Consequently, he does not make a specific distinction between juristic guilt and moral guilt; he regards the punishable character of an act as existing independently of the statute law.[1] Without any special predilection for dealing with definite varieties of punishment, he exhibits as the chief purpose of punishment,[2] not the evil which may be inflicted upon the criminal, but rather the express designation of the crime as an act prejudicial to the progress of humanity.[3] But instead of proceeding from this basis to determine how the morality exercised generally by the State, and which must coerce the individual, is to be distinguished from the morality of the individual, and thus founding the specific character of law as opposed to morals in the ordinary sense, Schulze suddenly substitutes the principle of necessary defense (or protection of the legal system). The criminal is punished because punishment is a means to restrain both him and others from doing further damage. This opened the door to critical objections. That punishment is not necessary defense in the ordinary sense is, as already remarked, easy to demonstrate. For this reason Schulze's other and more thoroughgoing ideas were overlooked, and consequently his book actually had little effect.

Steltzer. — In the meantime, in Steltzer's "Kritik" of Freiherr *v.* Egger's draft of a penal code for the Grandduchies of Schleswig and Holstein,[4] the Fichte-Grolmann doctrine is found, with a fundamental change, viz. punishment was to be regarded as a means of reformation. According to Steltzer, punishment did away with the

[1] Pp. 378 *et seq.*
[2] P. 52; p. 353 *note.*
[3] Schulze also gives an excellent criticism of the theories of deterrence, reformation, and retribution.
[4] 1811, 2 Parts.

otherwise existing necessity of excluding the criminal from the legal community; since by reformation of the offender it secured immunity from him for the future.[5] But a presumption of reformation should be determinative in the fixing of the amount of punishment. Since the uncertainty of a moral reform [6] by means of the State and its agencies is self-evident, Steltzer speaks of effecting a juristically reformed attitude [7] on the part of the party punished; he seems not to have realized that this is an impossible conception. Punishment, according to Steltzer, is essentially a continuing suffering by deprivation of liberty.[8] Steltzer did not attempt to designate precisely the acts which are punishable in accordance with his principle; but generally speaking, he regarded all acts as punishable which imperiled the rights of others.[9]

Apart from the objections to be noticed later, which could be urged against any punishment having as its principal and primary purpose the reformation of the individual, Steltzer's theory of reformation lacks a foundation, in so far as he was unable to establish punishment against the criminal as a right. He conceived it rather as a rule imposed upon the State by necessity. There is no need of such a basis if the punishment is contemplated not as an evil but rather as a means of education.

§ 92. **Theory of Reformation Founded upon Determinism. Groos.** — The theory of reformation was taken up also from the standpoint of medicine and natural science by Groos, and from a general philosophic standpoint by Krause and the adherents of Krause's philosophy, notably Ahrens and Röder.

Groos [1] regarded the criminal as a grown-up man in need of further training. A crime he regards as a piece of roguish mischief ("Bubenstück").[2] His investigation of guilt was, on the one hand, influenced by an understanding, due to his experience as a physician of the insane, that crime and insanity border upon each other and are at times hard to distinguish. Also (in accord with the Greek philosophy) he sought for guilt not so much in the will as in a defective understanding of the good. Thus, his theory rested upon a clearly defined determinism. Man acts necessarily and only according to motives, although these motives are often

[5] Pp. 8, 13. [6] P. 129. [7] P. 37.
[8] P. 11. The death penalty is justified as an extreme method of obtaining security.
[9] Pp. 8, 26.
[1] "Der Skepticismus in der Freiheitslehre" 1830.
[2] *Cf.* p. 140.

quite obscure. But these motives are not moral.[3] Man's decisions are based on his intellectual conceptions. He desires the good and can desire nothing else. Only he has often a false conception of the good, as when he deems it good to purchase his own advantage with another's disadvantage. He makes a false calculation. Consequently the question is simply, through education, to bring about in the criminal a different conception, or, as we may say, a different standard for his course of action.

To be sure, there thus disappear, as Groos himself points out,[4] the conceptions of merit and guilt. But since the former owes its origin to our pride, and the latter to our desire for vengeance, their disappearance is not to be regretted. Nevertheless, according to Groos, criminal law and morality in no way lose their fundamental principles. On the contrary, in accordance with the deterministic doctrine these principles are more sure in their operation, while the usual doctrine of freedom of will openly admits the possibility of even the trained and educated man continuing to revolt against law and morals. Groos' conception allowed determinism to exercise a very effective influence over criminal law. The extent of the offender's capacity for ideas, as exhibited in his mental operations, should be studied and taken account of by the legislator and jurists, in order that, through chastisements and deprivations, the offender may perhaps be transformed.

There is, however, no foundation for the charge that Groos confuses crime and insanity. He expressly says that the responsible transgressor of the law is amenable to the influences of improvement of his understanding and of deterrence, while for the lunatic such influences are unavailable and he must be subjected to medical cure. But the fallacy and error of his doctrine consist in its absolute exclusion of the idea of merit and guilt, without which practical life and the law (which represents one side of life) cannot

[3] Pp. 53, 77, 78, 90, 128. Groos designates his determinism (p. 53) in contrast to the mechanical baser determinism as a higher and religious determinism which, by him as the original source of good, is derived from a divine intelligent impulse born in man. According to Groos every human being of necessity strives for the good. Related with the idea of Groos and the "Phrenology" of Gall, but far more crude than the former is the foundation of criminal law in *Dankwardt*, "Psychologie und Criminalrecht" (1863). Dankwardt proceeds from the acceptance of an absolute lack of freedom in human beings and conceives criminal law as a means, (1) to satisfy the undeniable natural impulse of the injured party for vengeance; (2) to eliminate danger for the community. He explains the mitigation of punishment in advancing culture as a softening of the natural impulse to revenge (destroy).

[4] P. 25.

exist. Even conceding that there generally dwells within man an impulse towards the good and rational (a point contested by Theology), there still arises the question whether this is not, perhaps, for the reason that the individual's belief in his own responsibility can never be entirely extinguished. The weakening of this thought[5] will undoubtedly lead to the spread of evil. Moreover, let no one think that, from highly developed determinism a humane criminal law will readily arise. From the remark made by Groos that, under some circumstances, even capital punishment is justifiable, it is evident that a different method of estimating the efficacy of the means of educating the offender might lead to harsh penalties and the.frequent application of the death penalty. But Groos had never made an attempt to define the limits of criminal actions and to demonstrate the possibility of a sufficiently definite criminal law based upon his theory. Here his theory was subject to all the charges which Feuerbach had justly made against the theory of Grolmann.[6]

Krause. — Krause,[7] who in other respects was not an adherent of determinism, regarded punishment as a means of education (*i.e.* not in its nature and purpose as an evil). He who was undergoing punishment, was under guardianship like the immature. The State has the right to interest itself in the development of the immature, in the reformation of the morally depraved will. According to Krause,[8] there can be no such thing as a legal authority to inflict evil, as such, and thereby cause suffering. These theories have their deeper foundation, on the one hand, in that absolute value placed upon the individual by the philosophy of Krause, which forbids an employment of the individual solely as an instru-

[5] *Cf.* also Jarcke's polemic in *Hitzig's* "Zeitschrift für die Criminalrechtspflege in den preuss. Staaten" (1829, Vols. 21–23).

[6] It will not be necessary to take up carefully those erroneous doctrines which are indispensable as a basis for exact observation in the sense of natural science, — doctrines which regard crime as a consequence of a mental prefiguration of the criminal (George Combe). Concerning this, and especially in opposition to the results of the mental doctrines of Gall, *cf. Mittermaier*, in "Neues Archiv des Criminalrechts" (1820), pp. 412 *et seq.; Hepp*, II, pp. 646 *et seq.; Franck*, "Philosophie du droit pénal", pp. 64 *et seq.* A new attempt at a founding of criminal law upon the foundations laid by Groos is that of *Karel J. Rohan*, "Ein Versuch über die Entstehung und Strafbarkeit der menschlichen Handlungen" (Wien, 1881). But here determinism is made use of in the sense of Feuerbach's "theory of deterrence."

[See § 102*a*, *post*, for this group of theories. — ED.]

[7] *Cf.* especially *Karl Christ. Friedr. Krause*, "Das System der Rechtsphilosophie", ed. *Röder* (1874).

[8] Pp. 457, 532.

ment of the civil community; and, on the other hand, in that solidarity of interests of members of the community, which Krause so frequently emphasizes, and in accordance with which the community must interest itself in the training and culture of its individual members.

Ahrens. — Ahrens [9] gives to this theory a coloring which touches even its absolute foundation; for he regards the purpose of the punishment as the restoration of the violated legal order of things. But he found this restoration of the legal order only in the personality of the criminal and not in an effect upon others. Consequently, rejecting all absolute theories (which he regards as amounting more or less to retribution), he designates his theory as the theory of reformation, and effectively defends himself against numerous obvious objections.

The first of these objections consists in the criticism made against theories of reformation in general, viz. that they confuse the standpoints of legality and morality. Attention to reformation involves solely the latter, — reformation has no place in a legal decision. In opposition to this, Ahrens justly observes that a decision as to guilt presupposes a certain moral consideration.

The second objection is that, under the theory of reformation, crimes committed in a rebellion must remain unpunished, since it is certain that their author will never again commit them. To this Ahrens in a sense answers with justice: "Where a man's proper power of will has shown itself so weak that, through emotion or passion, it gives way to a crime, *e.g.* homicide, can certainty exist that he will not again, through his passions or emotions, yield to further or similar crimes? This must be answered in the negative, and for his reformation a full period of time will certainly be necessary."

However, the theory of reformation can never defend itself against the objection that the execution of penalties, even when done in the most humane and advanced manner, must necessarily differ specifically from the training of the immature. The teacher must deal with the pupil solely with the viewpoint of advancing him. If this were done by the State in respect to the criminal, then, for those classes among which crime especially arises, the punishment would be something to be welcomed. The State would improve the individual, but would encourage the masses

[9] *Cf.* "Naturrecht oder Rechtsphilosophie" (6th ed., 1871), II, pp. 448 *et seq.*

to the commission of crime. This is impossible to contemplate. Punishment can never be completely relieved of its character of disgrace, which (however leniently yet positively) must manifest itself in the treatment of persons given a significant sentence of imprisonment. There is no substantial merit in the reply that we are yet far enough removed from such an enticing arrangement of our penal institutions, and that there is for financial reasons little to be feared in this respect. According to the theory of reformation, such hindrances to a better treatment of convicts must, as far as possible, be eliminated; even these efforts, for that matter, if carried through regardlessly, would, little by little, remove from popular usage the idea of guilt, and substitute the notion of "defective training" for which the offender is not to blame.

If the theory of reformation is carried to its logical results, as, in fact, was done by Ahrens, this elimination of the conception of guilt involves further that the decision of the judge must almost entirely lose its significance; for the duration of the punishment (and even its kind) would be fixed not by the statute and the judge, but rather by the observation and discretion of the prison officials. Such a system of punishment would undoubtedly result in hypocrisy and arbitrary action, and would necessarily seem odious to a people who still cherished freedom in its ideal sense. It would deprive the people of the satisfaction of seeing a base, contemptible act sufficiently branded as such by the State. The consistent theory of reformation is merely the theory of advanced despotism; can any one deny that such a theory can be excessively cruel? Moreover, it is not apparent why punishment should be limited essentially to wrongs. Perhaps, from the moral standpoint, everyone is susceptible of improvement, and since punishment is no evil but rather a benefit, then better punish too much than too little.

Röder. — Röder[10] sought to give greater definiteness to the theory of reformation by his statement that the purpose of punishment lies in the elimination of the actually proven immoral will; wherefore, everyone may be placed under supervision (*i.e.* criminal supervision) exactly to the extent that he has manifested a will

[10] *Cf. Röder*, "Zur Rechtsbegründung der Besserungsstrafe" (1846); "Grundzüge des Natturrecht" (2d ed. 1860–1863), II, pp. 163 *et seq.*; "Der Strafvollzug im Geiste des Rechtes" (1863); "Besserungsstrafe und Besserungsanstalten als Rechtsforderung" (1864); "Die herrschenden Grundlehren", pp. 97 *et seq.*; "Kritische Vierteljahrsschrift für Gesetzgebung und Rechtswissenschaft" (1869), pp. 375 *et seq.*

inclined to wrongdoing.[11] But there is no identity between the extent of the wrong and the duration of the unlawful or immoral will, and they in no way run parallel. A reformatory punishment, to be consistent, can and must be pursued only so far as an improvement (presumptive at least) is obtained; it can never, at least only occasionally, be generally and certainly fixed by statute or judicial decree. The above-stated principle is, therefore, only a sophistry with which Röder (who is really of value in the problem of prison systems) deceived himself; the possibility of shortening a sentence that has been pronounced because of the subsequent improvement of the convict can never have more than a relative justification. While Röder, in order to maintain the character of actual punishment for his educative penalties, speaks of the "untaught simpletons" [12] who are to be thus educated, he thus conceals the further obnoxious logic of the theory of reformation, viz. that the desirable things in life must be conferred upon the delinquents, if we can manage to raise the needed funds, whenever these good things would help to reform the said delinquents, and although the great mass of honest people in the world have to get along without them. The theory of reformation [13] can never free itself from the reproach of raising an exclusive cult of the individual.[14]

§ 93. **The "Restitution" or "Compensation" Theory.** — The so-called "restitution theory" or "compensation theory" which has been worked out in an interesting manner especially by Welcker,[1] is in reality merely a collection of the various relative theories, especially of the theories of reformation and of deterrence. However, the theory of deterrence appears in such a mild shape and form that it is similar to those theories which would merely designate, by means of punishment, certain limits which a man's course of action must not violate. In order to justify the

[11] *Cf.* especially "Grundlehren", p. 99. [12] P. 107.

[13] *Carrara*, "Programma del diritto criminale", II, 619 very aptly states that the uncertain duration of the punishment resulting from the principle of reformation completely destroys its moral effect "forza morale."

[14] Incidentally the reformatory punishment can also be pushed in the contrary direction, if one argues that the convict must *not* be set free *until* he has reformed and there is no danger from him for human society. The legal system in the State does not need to secure absolute safety from violations of law and injuries, and it is not able to do so. That dangerous men must be set free is no reproach against the other criminal theories.

[1] "Die letzen Gründe von Recht, Staat und Strafe" (1813). *Cf.* also *Welcker*, "Die Universal- und die juristisch-politische Encyclopädie und Methodologie" (1829), pp. 573 *et seq.* The citations refer to the former work.

punishment from the standpoint of the criminal, he joins to this theory the contract theory of Fichte, although in a more moderate form and not designated as such. The violation of a right contained in the crime creates an obligation to make indemnification. The criminal does not (as Fichte would have it) become completely without rights, but only to the extent that the community possesses an absolute right over him, since it can hold him to compensation.[2] The damage occasioned by the crime may be either material or ideal (or both at the same time). The material damage was the object of the civil law, while the ideal damage was the object of the criminal law, and its indemnification is the punishment. This latter is accomplished in the individual.[3] Through the commission of the crime the criminal exhibits: (1) an evident absence of lawful intent and of its principle, a lack of consideration of moral values and of the statute law, a lack of that predominance of reason necessary for legal relations (the legal system); (2) especially, a superabundance or too great strength of baser impulses and an absence of harmony between these impulses and the requirements of justice. In the other citizens the crime produced (without any fault of theirs): (1) a lack of respect and confidence in the criminal, who through the crime has become disqualified as a member of the civil community; (2) a violation and destruction of their lawful will. The non-observance of the statute encourages the baser impulses of the others to the like commission of wrongs. Especially is harm done to the mental attitude of respect for the law on the part of the party wronged, who feels that the crime is a disgrace in so far as it is not avenged or expiated. Accordingly there are seven proper purposes of criminal punishment:[4] (1) Moral, (2) Political improvement of the criminal, (3) Restoration of the respect and confidence of his fellow-citizens towards the criminal, (4) Restoration of the proper mental attitude of regard for the law on the part of the citizens, of their moral and political respect for the law, (5) Restoration of the honor and esteem of the party injured, (6) Restoration of his mental attitude of

[2] P. 249. "If a member of the social union . . . in contradiction to himself and his deliberate avowal" (Welcker bases the State and law upon a contractual declaration of individuals) "violates the legal relation and inflicts injury upon it, then it is the first condition of his legal existence, his foremost legal duty . . . to make the greatest possible reparation."

[3] *Cf.* p. 262. "In so far as the criminal for his part has contributed to the lessening of respect for the law and to the incitement of base impulses, a punishment for arousing abhorrence of the crime and deterring from its commission is legally permissible and necessary."

[4] P. 265.

regard for the law, (7) Purification of the State from the completely pernicious member.

There is no merit in the objection raised against this theory that ideal injury can not always be shown, and does not invariably exist, and that, for this reason, it is improper for Welcker to place this ideal damage on an equality with civil law damage, which is invariably only indemnified when it is proven in the individual case.[5] The law can, and to a certain extent must be, satisfied with that which holds good in the majority of cases; a further search as to whether the result in question holds good in each individual case would be too difficult, and indeed would often fail in its purpose. Moreover, purely civil law methods of reckoning damage are derived from fundamental principles of custom and expediency; it is certainly not to be denied that unpunished commission of offenses (as well pointed out by Welcker) would gradually result in the dissolution of law, morality, and the State. The civil law tolerates inexact calculation of damage only because it is an evil which is difficult to avoid. In criminal law, however, justice would go completely astray as a result of a too exact discussion of the consequences of the individual crime.

But, despite this answer, Welcker's doctrine contains a fallacy. For, although he maintained a moral basis for the law, and (though perhaps not with sufficient clearness) designated the law as morality practiced by the community and enforced upon the individual, yet he conceives punishment not as a necessary reaction of morality against the immoral act, but rather as based upon the effect upon the criminal himself, upon the injured parties, and upon others. Now this unfortunate effect of crime upon others and upon the injured parties does not come about, as Welcker believes, without their own fault. It is rather the sign of a morally imperfect condition, of a condition not yet relatively well advanced, if the commission of a crime or the wrong done by the crime constitutes an incitement to the commission of a crime. The ideal damage can not in every case be charged exclusively to the account of the criminal, and consequently, according to Welcker, the criminal is really punished to make an impression upon others. The attempt made by Welcker to base the punishment directly upon the wrong is also

[5] Thus particularly *Heinze*, pp. 279, 280. If the statement in answer to this objection, given in the text, is correct, then Welcker is relieved from the deductions made by Heinze, viz. that according to Welcker's theory the criminal statute may not contain definite penalties but rather the ascertainment of the harm must be left to the judge.

unfortunate. Reformatory punishment, even less than deterrent punishment, is not to be derived from a violation of a right (as Welcker would in part derive his punishment). How the State, if it may not directly enforce morality upon the individual,[6] acquires by the wrong of the criminal the right of reformation, of compulsorily restoring confidence in the criminal, is not clear. Moreover, the results of the principle of reformation necessarily come into conflict with the principle of producing the necessary effect upon others. And finally, the indemnification of the so-called ideal damage furnishes a perverted criterion of the punishable character of an act. As Heinze correctly points out: "The disgust of the citizens at the act, the general disapproval of the crime, if it existed also for the punishment (which in the worst crimes will seldom be the case), would bring about not an increase but rather a lessening of the punishment."

Nevertheless, only a slight modification was necessary, in order to attain a simple and true path for the foundation of criminal law. Welcker himself (p. 262) says: "At the most" (this is the chief point) "through general disapprobation directed towards the crime [7] and contempt of the criminal there must be aroused and restored . . . the sense of the inviolability and sacredness of the law"; and it is also quite proper to recognize the punishment and compulsory payment of damages as functions of the power of civilization, which can supplement and defend itself. It is quite proper to call attention to the fact that, in public punishment, there is always contained a remnant of satisfaction for the party injured, and therefore punishment and pardoning are not entirely unconnected with the party injured. But the inclusion of punishment under the conception of indemnity is not clear. One generally thinks of indemnity in a case where the party bound to indemnify has an advantage or has enjoyed an advantage; and here, at any rate, is involved the simple idea that the law can not tolerate an illegal condition, in order that it may compel the criminal to make restitution or to give an equivalent. On the contrary, the foundation of a duty to indemnify, in many cases in which the party bound to indemnify has not derived the slightest benefit from the guilty act, and never even intended to derive any benefit,

[6] P. 31.

[7] One may merely say "of the criminal" and not "of the crime." In opposition to the statement of Welcker are well founded the objections of *Hepp*, II, p. 766, that the infamy and disgrace of the criminal are little in harmony with the idea of his reformation.

is just as difficult as the foundation of a punishment. For, in concrete cases, the rendering of indemnification can actually constitute a very mortifying punishment, and it is very possible that in such cases one law is satisfied with the indemnity, while another inflicts punishment. Here, at least, the chief considerations for excluding punishment do not govern.

Hepp. — Hepp's "Theory of Civil Justice"[8] ("Theorie der bürgerlichen Gerechtigkeit") is, in principle, only a repetition of Welcker's theory under another name. The offender has to repair the moral damage arising from certain actions. But it is not clear how it comes about that this compensation consists of the evil inflicted as punishment, which must be undergone by the offender. It must therefore be that the strength of the evil example (which in any case is not to be denied,[9] and which in reality rests upon the defective moral sense of those who are, as it were, led astray) is regarded as a reason for this. This influence of the example is indeed broken by evil undergone by the offender as a punishment. In individual matters, many correct statements of Hepp deserve appreciation, particularly those concerning the distinction of a wrong criminally punishable from a mere breach of morality and a tort.

§ 94. **Changes in the Absolute Principle of Criminal Law. C. S. Zachariä.** — We may now revert to a consideration of the evolution of the *absolute* principle for the basis of punishment.

The mistaken attempt of C. S. Zachariä,[1] to give to the absolute theory of retribution an interpretation more in harmony with the sentiment of his time, deserves little attention. He regards the crime as an encroachment upon the freedom of others, and accordingly would have the retribution consist of punishment by deprivation of freedom.[2] This deduction rests upon a simple confusion of conceptions: in the crime, the encroachment upon freedom is conceived as a wrong; in the punishment, freedom is regarded as the opposite of imprisonment. With such manifest faults there is no profit in taking up the unsatisfactory and artificial provisions relating to the amount of punishment and, in part, to the kind of punishment, which Zachariä believed must be deduced from this fallacy.

[8] *Hepp*, II, pp. 770–852.

[9] *Cf.* p. 779.

[1] *Carl Solomon Zachariä*, "Anfangsgründe des philosophischen Criminalrechts" (1805); "Strafgesetzbuchsentwurf" (1826). *Cf.* especially "Anfangsgründe", § 42.

[2] But from the law of necessity of the State other punishments are allowed.

Henke. — The modification given to the theory of retribution by Henke,[3] according to which it appears practically as a theory of reformation, is more attractive. Punishment is to him the necessary reaction against every attempt of the individual to tear himself away from the unity of the community and to avoid the law whereby the community orders its life. There exists no further proof of the necessity of this reaction; it proclaims itself in convincing tones to every one in whom there is developed the instincts of humanity. The punishment is based upon a moral impulse, and the criminal must sooner or later bring it upon himself. It represents the cure of the State, which again attains its health through the civil or physical death of its diseased member (*i.e.* the criminal), or through his undergoing some other punishment. It also frees the criminal from internal discord, since it improves him by a retribution which corresponds to the inner guilt and is in its effects not entirely external. This reminds us of Plato. Henke is also in accord with Plato's course of ideas in requiring the punishment to bring about an actual moral improvement of the criminal. And he abandons (justly) the idea of a mere so-called political reformation as an empty abstraction. But Henke was no more able than Plato to bring into actual harmony the retribution, in the sense of a restoration of the "majesty of the State" (the law), and the reformation of the criminal. It is an undeniable truth that the evil is eliminated in the most complete sense if the offender, because of a change of heart, recognizes the supremacy of the good (and of law). But, while the general ideas of retribution and reformation seem to dwell in such peace and harmony, their logical results are in violent discord. Punishment meted out up to the time of reformation is not retribution if even a severe offense is quickly followed by the reformation of the criminal, and it is more than retribution if the stubbornness of the criminal, even in a minor transgression, causes the reformation to be long delayed.

§ 95. **Combination of the Absolute and Relative Purposes.** — More approval has been given to the combinations of the theory of

[3] *H. W. E. Henke*, "Ueber den Streit der Strafrechtstheorien" (1811); "Lehrbuch" (1815); "Handbuch des Criminalrechts und der Criminalpolitik", I (1823), especially pp. 9, 10, 146 *et seq.* In his "Geschichte des peinlichen Rechts in Deutschland", II, pp. 362 *et seq.*, Henke had originally declared himself against every absolute theory, and in the work "Ueber den gegenwärtigen Zustand der Criminalrechtswissenschaft in Deutschland" (1810), he substantially embraced the theory of Fichte (pp. 15 *et seq.*).

retribution with a theory that is relative. This combination takes place in the view that punishment is given its legal basis in necessary retribution; while the consequent justification for penalties may be used only in so far as it serves to attain rational future purposes, or, if the attainment of the single purpose is not allowed to prevail exclusively, only in so far as it is necessary for the maintenance of the legal system. This coalition of the theory of retribution with a certain indefinite theory of necessary defense has found favor, especially in France and among those commentators who are strongly influenced by the French spirit. It has also been, in truth, equally the predominating influence in legislative commissions and legislative assemblies. The judicial practice of Germany, however, dominated by trained jurists, has almost universally condemned such a coalition. There is good reason for both positions. While the form in which it is advanced is theoretically untenable, this coalition in practice furnishes the most correct results; results which actually harmonize with those of a theory which professes to find its practical, direct, and evident conclusions only as the reverse side of a principle absolute in itself.

Rossi. — The first and ablest of the supporters of this coalition was Rossi.[1] He regarded the retribution of evil with evil as an unqualified and firmly established mandate of justice.[2] But since the duty of the civil community consisted merely in maintaining the legal system, it was not incumbent upon it to give complete and absolute effect to this mandate. It gave effect to it only in so far as seemed necessary for the maintenance of the legal system. Thus the consideration of utility restricted the exercise of justice, but it was not its basis.[3] And so, quite correctly, the propriety or impropriety of the punishment for acts contrary to morality was discussed with a view to the fact that while human justice claims the right to punish such acts, it has to reckon with the possibility of error and the difficulty of certainty.[4]

[1] *Rossi*, "Traité du droit pénal" (Paris et Genève, 1829), I, pp. 125–289.
[2] This statement is axiomatic: "elle est, parce qu'elle est", p. 289.
[3] "Le but de la justice humaine est extérieur et borné. C'est encore la justice absolue, mais la justice absolue appliqué seulement aux violations de nos devoirs envers les tiers, en tant que ces violations troublent d'une manière sensible l'ordre social." p. 290: "La répression des délits par la peine n'est donc légitime qu'à la condition que la peine s'appliquera aux coupables, et aux coupables seulement . . . Dès qu'on dépasse d'un atome le mal mérité, il n'y a plus justice: on retombe dans le système de l'intérêt."
[4] *Cf.* I, pp. 297, 303.

Haus,[5] **Ortolan,**[6] and **Gabba**[7] merely adopted this theory in different language. The same holds true of **Von Preuschen,**[8] **Mohl,**[9] **Mittermaier,**[10] and **Henrici.**[11] But these writers made the theory less clear, since they placed primary stress upon the utility of the punishment and secondary stress upon justice, which they desire to be the preliminary condition of punishment. Mittermaier had perhaps specially in view the numerous punishments for offenses against the police measures and other coercive penalties, which are practically indispensable but which are not readily justifiable from the standpoint of absolute and eternal justice; hence he shows traces of the thought that, under some circumstances, a punishment can be justified by the fact of having been threatened. Henrici[12] assumes at the outset an independent position for the principle of the right of punishment, since he begins with the relative theory of defense or maintenance of the legal order, and as opposed to this principle he regards absolute justice as a restricting principle. As a matter of fact, it all amounts to one and the same thing,—if one goes only so far as the two principles are in harmony, one may consider an individual question either by principle A or by principle B.

In the case of Rossi, as will be conceded, there is the danger of transferring punishment primarily and perhaps too much to the realm of pure morality; in the case of Mittermaier and Henrici, there is especially the danger that punishment as a measure of expediency will be extended to many things which in fact do not deserve punishment, and that it will be difficult for justice to

[5] "Principes généraux du droit pénal Belge" (1869), pp. 26 *et seq.*; p. 29: "La peine est un mal qui est rendu pour un mal; elle retombe sur le coupable parce qu'il a enfreint la loi, et parce que cette infraction mérite la souffrance qu'on lui fait éprouver. Le pouvoir social a-t-il le droit de punir? Pour qu'il ait ce droit, il faut que la peine soit un moyen propre à réaliser le but qui lui est assigné. Il faut ensuite qu'elle soit un moyen de protection nécessaire."

[6] *Ortolan*, "Elements du droit pénal", I, pp. 176 *et seq.* According to page 187, society says to the one whom it punishes and who raises a question concerning the evil inflicted upon him: "Tu le mérites", and as to the further question how this concerns the society, it answers: "It has to do with my maintenance."

[7] "Il pro ed il contro nella questione della pena di morte" (1866), p. 52.

[8] "Versuch über die Begründung des Strafrechts" (1835), especially pp. 37 *et seq.*

[9] "Ueber den Zweck der Strafe" (1837), especially pp. 36 *et seq.*

[10] "Neues Archiv des Criminalrechts" (1836), pp. 403 *et seq.* *Mittermaier* in the 14th edition of *Feuerbach's* "Lehrbuch" prepared by him, § 20 *b*.

[11] "Ueber die Unzulänglichkeit eines einfachen Strafrechtsprincips" (1839).

[12] P. 78.

cause the legislator to desist from using such measures of expediency. But there is little importance in this distinction. However, the matter is completely confused by Henrici's observation that justice (*i.e.* absolute justice) [13] must also guard the legislator against doing too little and against giving way to unseasonable pity in respect to crimes deserving the death penalty. Here, according to Henrici's conception, absolute justice is also advanced simply as a constitutive principle, without being limited by ideals of utility and humanity. If this is permissible, then the choice between the punishments of absolute justice (sentiment) and punishments based on considerations of utility or relative necessity becomes merely a matter of sentiment.

This criticism is manifestly applicable to the views of von Wieck,[14] who substitutes for the general purpose of maintenance of the legal system, the special purposes of deterrence and reformation, and, indeed, would give attention to these only in so far as they do not do injury to the chief purpose of the punishment: retribution through the infliction of suffering. It should be noticed that von Wieck, who uniformly adopts a positive Christian attitude, seems to have a sense of the irreconcilability of the infliction of suffering and Christian ethics. The uncertain assertion that the State in its existing condition, where evil is not overdone, may exercise mercy and charity only in so far as it may be done without material prejudice to punishment, confirms rather than abolishes this contradiction.

§ 96. **Herbart's Retribution Theory of Æsthetic Judgment.** — Herbart [1] sought to give to the absolute theory of retribution a modification which was really new although certainly not fortunate. In many respects he reminds one of Plato and Leibnitz. Retribution is contemplated and demanded as an æsthetic judgment. As law is only the means to eliminate the æsthetically offensive conflict of numerous individual wills, so punishment rests on the axiom: an act for which there has been no retribution is offensive. In Plato the punishment, merely as an ideal, assists in completing the harmony of the universe, and therefore, apart from a few extreme cases, is also regarded as a benefit for the party punished, who thereby is reinstated in the universal harmony, thus becoming

[13] P. 85.
[14] "Ueber Strafe und Besserung" (1853).
[1] *Cf.* his "Werke", ed. by *Hartenstein*, 8, p. 318, 9, pp. 387 *et seq.* *Cf.* also *Geyer*, "Geschichte und System der Rechtsphilosophie" (1863), pp. 127 *et seq.*

better. But in the æsthetic judgment of Herbart, we find ourselves immediately upon the real and practical ground of the present criminal law, and hence it is especially noteworthy that Herbart has but little knowledge or interest in the reformation of the criminal.[2] And Herbart's idea of punishment (which may quite properly include death and life-long imprisonment) is opposed, even from his æsthetic standpoint, to that lofty idea which does not desire the death of the sinner, but rather the suppression of evil by means of good. It is at least a "petitio principii" to maintain that the former is æsthetically more agreeable than the latter.

Herbart was himself sensible of this. He concedes that the retribution of evil with an evil merely for its own sake falls within the sphere of malevolence ("Uebelwollen") and therefore punishment requires a motive.[3] Such motive is furnished it by the ethical ideas of perfection, benevolence, and justice, and especially the ideas of the improvement, advancement, and security of the entire people. Thus ultimately Herbart's theory becomes merely a reproduction, only under another name, of Rossi's "coalition theory"; *i. e.* as against the criminal, punishment is based upon the idea of retribution, but the community may make use of this retribution only in so far as its purposes require it, or (speaking rather in the sense of Herbart) in so far as its purposes make it seem desirable. For a strong legal system with as free development of the individual as possible was not the object of Herbart's State. An administrative system, a system of rewards and a system of mutual benevolence, could necessarily make a far more extensive coercion of the individual than the legal system would require. "It is possible to exercise discipline wherever it advances welfare, and wherever the general recognition that the punishment produces no strife can be presumed"; and "the legislator may discipline where the judge may not."[4] In other words, where general sentiment would not be injured by the punishment, there may punishment be inflicted, and at all events, in this case where the positive law so desires.

Ultimately this leads to pure positivism. It is in accordance with the æsthetic feeling that the laws be obeyed, and therefore, in

[2] "Aphorismen zur praktischen Philosophie", "Werke", 9. p. 418. "Legal reformation of the party punished? No! Rather, since unfortunately this is often impossible: legal reformation of the community."

[3] "Praktische Philosophie" (I), "Werke", 8, pp. 44, 45.

[4] "Werke", 8, p. 87.

accordance with them, if they so desire, punishment be inflicted.[5] This is the standpoint of the most absolute modern liberalism, which is no longer able to distinguish justice and law. There is no doubt that Herbart was far removed from this adoration of the law as such. A law may have just come into being, upon the vote of a bare majority, but afterwards we tend to regard it as an idol secure from criticism. But the outcome of the theory very clearly revealed the impracticability of the æsthetic judgment as a means of reaching sure ground for criminal law. Essentially corresponding with the categorical imperative, Herbart's so-called æsthetic judgment exceeds it in indefiniteness. According to the categorical imperative, punishment can be inflicted only if our conscience unconditionally demands it; according to the æsthetic judgment, punishment may be inflicted if our conscience is not expressly opposed to it.

It is impossible here to take up the aphorisms concerning criminal law [6] which are more or less closely connected with Herbart's fundamental conceptions. But though they include some well thought out statements, as a whole, they demonstrate that the philosopher knew little about criminal law, the subject upon which he was philosophizing.[7]

Geyer. — Herbart's philosophy of criminal law has found few followers. It is best and most skillfully defended by Geyer. But even this defense, remarkable as it is for its many excellent and apt statements,[8] shows that an effective defense of Herbart's principle is not possible for any one who does not possess a complete knowledge of the subject. In Geyer, the maxim: [9] "The act for which no retribution is made is offensive", again changed over completely to the idea of simple retribution. But this retribution, although it is fundamentally contrary to its nature, according to Geyer admits of the limitation: "The giving of pain is offen-

[5] P. 85: "To sum up, the foregoing gives rise to a sharp distinction between the *possibility of being punished* and the *possibility of punishing*. That any one should be punished is only possible because he has previously done something from which the punishment recoils upon him. . . . Whether any one can punish depends upon a new condition, whether or not there is present a motive, that the punishment be merely a means and not an end."

[6] "Werke", 8, pp. 415–418.

[7] Thus *e.g.* the erroneous statements concerning "dolus" and "culpa."

[8] *Cf.* especially the article: "Ueber den Begriff des Verbrechens" in *Haimerl's* "Oesterreich. Vierteljahrsschrift für Rechts- und Staatswissenschaft" (Vol. 9, 1862), pp. 215–253, and *Geyer* in *Von Holtzendorff's* "Rechtsencyclopädie", Vol. I.

[9] *Cf.* the article above cited, p. 219.

sive."[10] Therefore the State must punish, as such, all intentional giving of pain, and even, as Geyer later sets forth, every giving of pain caused by negligence. However, the æsthetic judgment is a categorical imperative which permits of treatment. Consequently the maxim "Minima non curat prætor" takes root; a too extensive criminal power results in numerous evil conditions; accordingly the spirit of the people and the force of existing circumstances must be recognized.[11] Under some circumstances the obligation to indemnify can arise in the place of punishment.[12] Since indemnification under some circumstances is also required of those to whom there is attached no guilt, this is indeed a complete rejection of the idea of retribution, of æsthetic judgment. It is impossible for it to be otherwise. As soon as one comes to the consideration of individual details, it is only by a rejection of the ideas of retribution that Kant's absurdities may be avoided.

According to Herbart's and Geyer's conception, the evil act is a discord. Would one be less sensitive to one discord, by having a second one result from it? Punishment, however, should furnish evil or pain to the criminal. If one schoolboy whom another has struck cries, this cry does not become a pleasant sound because the second boy whom the schoolmaster has chastised for his offense also cries. Of course, for one who takes an interest in pedagogical discipline, it may be a pleasant sensation to know that discipline was applied in this case. This is exactly the case with punishment. If we conceive punishment chiefly as an infliction of pain, as an evil, then this evil can lose its repulsive character only if it becomes a means of attaining some benefit. And if it must be retribution, would it not be the best retribution, and also one to be recognized as such by the State, if the criminal in the commission of the act brought down upon himself a mortifying pain or damage, without obtaining an advantage[13] at all? Geyer[14] meets this objection

[10] *Cf.* pp. 225 *et seq.*, especially p. 228.

[11] P. 231.

[12] *Binding's* arguments ("Die Normen und ihre Uebertretung", I, pp. 207 *et seq.*) concerning the diametrical opposition of indemnification and punishment are properly opposed to a theory which would found punishment upon retribution or unconditional æsthetic approval. But it is different if the punishment is not founded upon retribution, or if the matter is not viewed from the standpoint of the positive law but rather historically and politically.

[13] Common opinion will always regard this as retribution in its eminent sense.

[14] P. 223.

with the statement that the evil must come about as "retribution." But is it not in accord with the essential idea of retribution, that it is more perfect the less it requires artificial preparation? Every well-constructed tragedy gives evidence of the correctness of this refutation of Geyer. Careful consideration certainly shows that these conceptions of retribution and punishment are not satisfactory.

Chapter VI

CRIMINAL THEORIES IN GERMANY FROM HEGEL TO BINDING

§ 97. **Theory of the Negation of Wrong. Hegel.** — In contrast to the foregoing theories, the theory of Hegel reveals a distinct step in advance.[1] To Hegel, punishment is simply a negation of wrong, and wrong is the negation of right. Of course, wrong as opposed to right (*i.e.* as opposed to the general system of right, which abstractly regarded, cannot be harmed) is in itself a nullity; but punishment has to bring about this non-reality of wrong in the individual will of the criminal and also to restore therein the right. This gives rise to a distinction of reactions corresponding to the various kinds of wrong, — simple wrong (*i.e.* "unbefangene Unrecht"), fraud and crime. The first of these (*i.e.* "unbefangene Unrecht") is not that which exists in the will of those who oppose the right, — it refers rather to cases in which the right, in abstract, is desired, but in the concrete case is confused with the wrong. This is the case in civil wrongs. In fraud ("Betrug") the appearance of right is maintained, but under this appearance the wrong is desired. In crime, the right is both objectively and subjectively repudiated by the offender. Here it is also necessary to exhibit externally the non-reality of the wrong by means

[1] "Grundlinien der Philosophie des Rechts", ed. by *Gans* (3d ed., 1854), §§ 82 *et seq.*

of punishment. Therefore punishment from its very nature can not be termed an evil. As Hegel expressly states, the infliction of one evil merely because another exists is irrational. "The undoing of crime is retaliation to the extent that it is conceived as an injury, and, conformably to its being, crime has a definite quantitative and qualitative extent, and the same thing also holds true of its negation. But this contemplated identity is not parity in the specific character of the injury, but rather in its abstract character; it is sameness in accordance to value." "In crime, when the infinity of the deed is the fundamental issue, the mere specific external elements tend to vanish, and the parity remains merely the fundamental rule for the essential, *i.e.* for what the criminal deserves, but not for the specific external form of this which is deserved. It is only according to their specific form that theft, robbery, fines, imprisonment, etc., are absolutely unlike, but, according to their value, to their general capacity to be simply injuries they are *capable of comparison*." In other words, the essence of crime is rebellion against the general principle of right; and therefore the question by what external means, conformably to quality and quantity, should this rebellion become expressed as a non-reality is not decided by the principle. First the "idea as to value" fixes the ratio of comparison between the act and the means of its elimination. Accordingly (as is not developed however by Hegel) the dimension and the form of the punishment depend upon the "*idea as to value*", *i.e.* upon the valuation in a certain State and at a certain time. These elements of dimension and form would not be governed by the principle.[2] Furthermore, it is quite conceivable that the declaration of the non-reality of the wrong may not be an affair of the State. It can take place in the form of the vengeance of the party injured. This, however, is imperfect and easily becomes pernicious, since the negation of wrong easily becomes confused with wrong or can degenerate into wrong, when in the form of vengeance.[3]

[2] *Cf.* the statement in § 63 concerning the conception of "value." Supplement to § 96: "How any crime may be punished is not to be determined by these ideas (*i.e.* as to value), but positive provisions are necessary." Only in the case of murder, according to § 101, a different condition exists. "Since the entire range of existence is comprehended in life, therefore punishment cannot consist in a valuation which cannot exist, but can consist only in deprivation of life." Here is seen an effect of the traditional view, and the "retribution" view, the idea of which has not entirely disappeared.

[3] §§ 102, 220.

This theory which, because of its frequently abstruse method of expression,[4] is not sufficiently appreciated by many, has, at any rate, one merit. As appears from the deduction given above, it can be reconciled to history. It is able to recognize in revenge the preliminary step towards punishment inflicted by the State. It is able to regard the numerous forms of positive definite punishment as phenomena in which its principle manifests itself without becoming inconsistent. But its most important service is that it does not conceive punishment as an evil, *i.e.* as something which has, as its chief purpose, the creation of an evil for the criminal. Here, for the first time, from the standpoint of the absolute theories, there is actually eliminated the contradiction between morality (especially Christian morality) and punishment inflicted by the State (not merely pedagogical discipline).

The attempt is also made not merely to justify punishment as a necessary standard for people as a whole, for the community, but also to show that punishment is also required by the individual characteristics of the offender himself. Punishment is even a right of the criminal. In him there exists that universal reason which controls the punishment. Thus in the punishment "the criminal is respected as a rational being."[5]

This last statement, indeed, sounds almost like mockery, and seems calculated to bring Hegel's theory into ridicule. As advanced, it is, moreover, incorrect. The criminal does not recognize that universal reason which obtains in right and in positive law. At least this is the case with that hardened class of criminals who, as it were, engage in war with the rest of humanity. But the principle approaches the truth. Even with hardened criminals an enlightened criminal law proceeds differently than with a beast which threatens our life or property, or with the animal which we sacrifice, perhaps in a painful manner, for purposes of humanity. Compared with these last-mentioned methods of procedure, punishment always honors the reason in the criminal. It ought not to be said that the reason in the criminal demands the punishment. It must be said that, strictly taken, the criminal severs himself from lawful society. Therefore he can be dealt with without consideration, and so it was done in the initial steps of legal development. The criminal lost all rights. The moderate

[4] In the foregoing presentation this has in part been translated into ordinary language so as to be more easily understood.

[5] P. 136.

punishment of later times is thus a benefit to him. The bond of legal society is still regarded as existing in respect to the criminal, and thus, as a matter of fact, he is respected as a rational being. Here again we have Fichte's ideas, viz., that to be punished and not to be treated as one absolutely without rights is an important right.

Hegel's distinction between civil wrong and punishable wrong also approaches the truth. In the first place, however, the intermediate grade of wrong, Hegel's fraud ("Betrug"), must be rejected. This is apparently the result on one hand of his well-known dialectical division into threes, and the result on the other hand of the observation that in social intercourse the maxim "Invicem sese circumscribere licet" can apply and therefore cunning fraud be immune from punishment. This latter, however, is so only to a limited extent and not generally. In the second place, it can only be conceded that punishment *generally* limits itself to intentional wrong. But by no means every intentional wrong is punished. There are also cases of civil wrong where malicious intention is present and cases of punishable wrong where it is not present. There can, however, be no punishable wrong without there being some will (although perhaps only indirectly) responsible therefor. The starting point for the question, which is still, in our times, so much discussed as to the distinction between wrong that is punishable and wrong that is not punishable, is contained in Hegel's remarks.

The dialectical transformation of right in punishment is more unsatisfactory. Right is not an active principle. A right does not say: you *must* do this; it says merely: you *may* do this. If the injured party (or the State) has the right to punish, yet he is not obliged to punish. The duty to punish, which, according to Hegel, apparently must be received along with the right to punish (at least where the State is concerned), requires a special demonstration. It does not follow from the necessity of self-preservation of the law. From this the mere deduction may be made that, if one entitled thereto desires, a condition actually contradictory to law shall yield to a lawful condition. It necessarily entails nothing more than a compulsory restoration dependent upon the pleasure of the one entitled — as far as such a thing is possible. A duty can be derived only by seeking out a moral basis in the right. A right in itself is not active, but morality under some circumstances must become active or cease to be morality. Thus there is a flaw in Hegel's deduction, which also involves an uncertainty. Punishment is not a *purely logical* outcome of the conception of wrong. If this were so, as Hegel indeed believed, it would not be permissible for the State to refrain from punishment. There could not exist that pardoning power [6] permitted by Hegel; for a result conformable to the principle is inevitable.

§ 98. **Modern Theological Tendencies. Stahl.** — The effects of Hegel's philosophy of criminal law have been far-reaching. Many of the most eminent students of the subject have been and still remain under its influence. As the modifications of Hegel's theory are represented chiefly by theorists who are now living, it is appropriate to turn our attention first to that theological character which this theory assumed at the hands of F. J. Stahl.[1] Among the students of the subject this has found comparatively few followers.

Here the idea of retributive *divine* justice as a basis for the criminal law of the State is again entertained. The latter is nothing other than a limited divine justice, or (as Stahl also portrays it), a *moral* punishment, with the peculiar characteristic of being applied only to external manifestations and therefore effective only upon external manifestations. Thus, from that dialectical or logical effect which, according to Hegel, the law, through the punishment, should have upon the wrong, there arises an act of authority emanating from divine omnipotence. But at the same time Stahl keeps one foot upon the relative theory. Perhaps, on one hand, this is indicative of the feeling that it is little in harmony with enlightened opinion, and particularly Christian opinion, to attribute to the Deity an unlimited desire for vengeance and retribution; while, on the other hand, it shows that this able and experienced statesman and jurist has been unable to deny

[6] § 282.

[1] "Die Philosophie des Rechts" (3d ed. 1856), Vol. II, pt. 1, pp. 160 *et seq.;* pt. 2, pp. 681 *et seq.* The fundamental outlines of this theory are also to be found in *Jarcke*, "Handbuch des gem. deutschen Strafrechts", I (1827), pp. 240 *et seq.*, and in the otherwise unimportant work of *Linck's*, "Ueber das Naturrecht unserer Zeit als Grundlage der Strafrechtstheorien" (1829). It should be noted that Jarcke (pp. 244, 245) perceives the advantage of a philosophy of criminal law only in the fact that "thereby the course of practice is closed to false and one-sided theories, and to that laxness which at times even intentionally allows guilty offenders to escape." Philosophy should have no influence upon the detail of criminal law, which is purely a matter of historical development, nor should it ever be allowed to specify punishments as irrational. The purely retrograde tendency of the absolute theory, in so far as it regarded punishment as a harm or suffering of the offender, is here very well illustrated.

that punishment is also obliged to adjust itself to purposes other than that of retribution.

It is not the legislative statute (Stahl says) which should be maintained by the punishment, but rather its majesty (or supremacy). "Every (criminal) act involves an assertion of authority; there is contained in it a permanent actual power, an absolute effect." This authority (rebellion) of the individual will should be suppressed by the punishment, should be eliminated.[2] In other words: "By means of the punishment . . . the State is preserved and secured against the danger to it which is contained in the crime; and if the State does not perform its moral duties of administering justice and of punishing, it must externally and automatically fall to pieces (self-preservation). The punishment does not merely render permanently or temporarily incapable of doing harm that worst portion of the people who through actual crime make a test of the punishment (prevention). But, what is far more important, it also restrains the entire people from crime (deterrence) by fear of punishment. With the predominance of evil in our present earthly condition, nothing but fear is able to preserve order and security for the individual and for all. — In the same way, morality is aided by punishment and the dealing out of justice. First, the morality of the criminal (reformation); since the external suffering which deservedly falls upon him must bring him to his senses and to reform, unless he resists through stubbornness. Secondly, the morality of the people; since the punishment not only psychologically deters from crime through fear of the contemplated evils of the punishment, but also morally supplements both the consciousness of the utter perdition of crime and the abhorrence of baser motives which lead to crime."[3] This attribution of the origin of the State and of punishment to a divine will may indeed be accepted. Every one, who will at all recognize a higher relation of things, is also obliged to recognize it in respect to the State and to punishment; and through the reference of punishment to a law higher than that of human despotism or of calculated utility, there may perhaps be secured for criminal justice a certain wise moderation.

Stahl's criticism of Hegel's purely dialectical derivation of punishment is also appropriate. "The question, how the injury of the criminal in person may constitute an elimination or even a logical negation of his preëxisting criminal influence and deed is

[2] II. 1, p. 166.

[3] II. 2, p. 684.

not answered, nor is it at all explained how a repentant criminal in whom the crime no longer has existence must or merely may be punished."[4] But Stahl, according as it suits him and his tendencies, picks out certain maxims of the Bible as *legal* maxims; and, in spite of his protest,[5] he succumbs to the danger of confusing the divine sanction of the institution in general with the divine sanction of a certain development of the institution, and relatively, of the institution in certain of its operations.[6] Furthermore, the derivation of punishment directly from divine justice (although from modified divine justice exercised by a representative) is not to be reconciled with the founding of punishment upon the necessity of maintaining the law and the State. As an illustration, from the latter there can be deduced the necessity of some punishment which the former does not require. Such a punishment is not, as Stahl [7] believes, excused as a law of necessity. It is simply without any justification; since divine justice admits no more of being supplemented than of being curtailed. Also, the conception of punishment as a manifestation of divine justice, and of the State as an external representation of the Kingdom of God, must ultimately lead to the tendency to make the punishments of the State coincide as nearly as possible with divine punishments, and also as far as possible to identify sins (immorality) and crimes. The suggestion, often made by Stahl, that the State is only an external kingdom places but a feeble restriction upon this tendency. For, according to such a conception,[8] the very fact of "externality" must appear merely as an imperfection [9] to be overcome as completely as possible.[10]

[4] II. 1, p. 174. [5] II. 2, p. 683.

[6] *Cf.* especially II, 2, pp. 701, 702, the discussion of the death penalty. "Authority does not carry the sword in vain."

[7] II, 2, p. 702.

[8] *Cf.* II, p. 691. According to this, sin and lack of piety should also be punished, although only by the police jurisdiction, for the promotion of morality and reprobation of offensiveness. The qualification of the punishment as being one proper for police regulation, could not actually be changed. That no one may be beheaded or imprisoned for life for lack of piety or for sin is obvious.

[9] This tendency is manifest especially in *E. J. Bekker*, "Theorie des heutigen deutschen Strafrechts", I (1857), pp. 28 *et seq.*, who for this reason designated as the ideal standpoint the abolition of all fixed rules of law so that the judge could punish all deserving punishment. Bekker regarded crime as rebellion against the (Christian) will of State. *Walter*, "Natturrecht und Politik im Lichte der Gegenwart" (1863), § 409 simply adopts Stahl's theory.

[10] At the beginning of the 1800s the principle of retribution was advanced in a peculiarly mystical way by that representative of the Legitimists and the Papacy, Count *Joseph de Maistre*. This theory, however,

Schleiermacher. — As a matter of fact, the alliance between Christian theology and the criminal law of the State, with its indispensable attribute, the headsman's axe, is neither original in Stahl nor is it given a new foundation. It is simply a repetition of the viewpoint of the leaders of the Reformation. More profound and interesting is that adjustment of the differences between Christianity and the punishment of the State which was attempted by the famous theologian Schleiermacher.[11] The passages of the Bible which make it a Christian duty not to appeal to the civil authorities are quite correctly explained by Schleiermacher as being a result of the conditions existing at a time in which there were no Christian authorities. Consequently, since without the function exercised by the criminal courts the power of evil would be invincible, he finds no obstacle to assuming that the Christian can support the authorities in the exercise of criminal jurisdiction, and can himself even occupy a post of authority.[12] The death penalty, however, appears to him as being absolutely contrary to the spirit of Christianity, and he assails it in vigorous terms as a relic of ancient barbarity. Nor will he countenance the idea of retribution; he feels that the suffering entailed by punishment, where it does not prompt the criminal to repentance, is at variance with the highest Christian sentiment. Consequently, he would acquiesce in a threat of punishment, preferably where the threat without the fulfilment would not be ineffective;

while not dealt with in detail, will serve as an illustration of the results that may ultimately be obtained from the theory of divine retribution, or even from retribution generally — since the idea of retribution always leads ultimately to a deification of existing institutions. According to de Maistre, human victims are required because of universal sin. They fall in numbers in war and singly under the axe of the executioner, and there is no reason for concern in their increased or diminished number. The executioner is the mysterious correlate of earthly authority, without which earthly majesty, the representative of God, cannot exist. The executioner inspires horror and aversion, and one cannot perceive how any one can be found for this fearful office. But because of a mysterious dispensation of Providence there is no lack of executioners, and as a matter of fact the executioner does nothing different from the soldier (!) who is seized by rage and the enthusiasm of the battle and desire for victims. There is no need to be disturbed if perhaps some innocent party *is* executed. There are far more grievous evils, and every one merits it because of his sins. — And yet all this exposition is not as absurd as it seems. In reality, the idea of retribution in criminal law is always a confusion of the human and practical standpoint with the divine but (for us) unattainable and impractical standpoint. ("Soirées de St. Petersbourg", I, pp. 14 *et seq.*, pp. 34 *et seq.;* II, p. 4, p. 23; I, pp. 182 *et seq.*, pp. 214 *et seq.*).

[11] *Cf. Schleiermacher*, "Die christliche Sitte, herausgegeben von Jonas", pp. 241 *et seq.*

[12] Pp. 247 *et seq.*

indeed, it almost seems to be his idea that no punishment should be inflicted upon the sinner who is really repentant; although, if punishment is inflicted upon the repentant Christian, he should submit to it with obedience.[13]

Thus Schleiermacher, while correctly expressing the thought that if all — or, as we would state more exactly, if the vast majority — were true Christians, punishment would have to be discarded,[14] is forced into Feuerbach's theory of psychological coercion.[15] He even lays down the principle that, where the threat is preëxisting and known to the criminal, it is not essentially the authority who inflicts the evil, but rather it is the criminal who brings the evil upon himself.[16] He avails himself of this principle to exonerate completely those Christians who take part in the complaint, the prosecution, and the punishment; herein failing to realize that responsibility for the necessity of the punishment must be attributed not only to the criminal but also to a certain extent to every one else, even to those imperfect Christians of whom he is speaking.

But, in all this, Schleiermacher does not appear to have attained complete satisfaction of mind. He even resuscitates the ancient principle that the punishment is also something of a benefit,[17] and in connection with this idea he repudiates those punishments bearing the characteristic of pure vindictiveness. Consequently he wavers between the conception of punishment as a "pœna vindicativa" and as a "pœna medicinalis", — just as had previously been done by the Church, before the time when orthodoxy had completely established the direct justification of the punishments of the State upon divine precepts. Schleiermacher reveals his status as a theologian in regarding the crime not (with Feuerbach) as a violation of a right, but as disobedience

[13] This, however, is not perfectly clear, since the passages in question speak only of self-accusation and of the right or duty to call in the authorities. *Cf.* pp. 254, 257 *note.* In the first passage it says: "The moral law does not require that one give himself up as a transgressor of the law. . . . If any one . . . has actually come to recognize his sin, then he is even upon the path that should lead to a revocation of the punishment."

[14] P. 260.

[15] He is not certain however as to its results.

[16] P. 248.

[17] P. 251 *note.* In connection with this idea there is found also that false principle, reminding one of the contract theory of the law of nature, that the death penalty is allowable, since the Christian can be satisfied in that it inflicts no greater evil upon the offender than each may bring upon himself.

of the orders of the State,[18] and also in not being able to conceive that vengeance is not always positively immoral. Thus, the State again appears, after all, not as the work and creation of man, but rather as "Deus ex machina", which confers upon man the favor of inflicting evil (punishment) upon the wicked, so that the Christian in his innocence may wash clean his hands.[19]

Daub. — The Protestant theologian Daub[20] allies the Platonic conception of punishment with Hegel's conception of punishment as a negation of wrong. He portrays the blotting out of the wrong in the will of the criminal by means of the punishment as something necessary, but at the same time he denies that punishment bears the character of evil. Since the source of law is "love", punishment is a kindness, a benefit. Mere sins which concern only the individual and his God may be blotted out by remorse and penitence, but crimes which also affect others can be done away with only by the punishment of the offender. Thus, even the death penalty appears as a benefit. The blood-guilt of the murderer can be removed from him only with his own blood. However, if one consider it closely, this is so only if the criminal can be brought to pronounce his own sentence, so that he be convinced that justice is being done him. If this be not the case, the criminal merely succumbs to the unavoidable and the execution assumes somewhat the character of murder.[21]

A special criticism of this view is not necessary. The criticism of Plato's views and those of Hegel also contain a criticism of this combination of both. It is, however, interesting to observe that Daub vigorously assails the idea of retribution, which is at variance with Christianity (retribution, not through God, but through men !), and protests against the misuse of the offender for arbitrary purposes of deterrence or of reformation according to the dictates[22] of a class privileged to impose reform.[23]

[18] P. 258.

[19] Occasionally, however, this clear thinker has not failed to recognize that a different condition exists. Thus on p. 251, he says: "The criminal law can be nothing other than an expression of the general will inspired by the Christian spirit", and on p. 252 (*note*): "The Christian authorities cannot justify themselves by saying that they found the law (*i.e.* of capital punishment) already in existence, because every law can be changed."

[20] "System der theologischen Moral", II, 1, especially pp. 347 *et seq.*

[21] P. 285.

[22] I. pp. 342 *et seq., note.*

[23] The statements concerning punishment and criminal jurisdiction of *Rothe,* "Theologische Ethik", III, pp. 874 *et seq.* (1st ed.), have no original significance. They amount substantially to an uncertain repetition of Hegel and Stahl, except that the negation of wrong is taken rather in the sense of Kant's retribution. (*Cf. e.g.* pp. 877, 886: "The justi-

§ 99. **Later Developments of Hegel's Theory. Trendelenburg.** — The purest conception of Hegel's theory was held by Trendelenburg,[1] who at the same time rewrote it in very plastic style. A crime is to him essentially a wrong done intentionally, and right is restored by the punishment — in an ideal way at least (since a wrong that is done can not be undone). "In its innermost purpose, punishment is the force of law over the criminal, — the force of law for the party who has been injured, and the force of law in the community."[2] While attention is called to the fact that historical development and higher conceptions have caused the satisfaction[3] of the injured party to be merged in the idea of general restoration; punishment, as the force of law over the criminal and as force in the society of men, is the subject of special amplification. Punishment, the reaction against wrong, is aimed to enable the offender who has maliciously violated the law to perceive that the punishment is a necessary consequence of his guilt and that it is *deserved*, and to enable him, in so far as his rebellion against the law is broken by the power of the law, to feel that the punishment is atonement for his wrong, and, as regards the divine government of affairs, expiation. In this relation, punishment is the right of the offender. It is a recognition rather than a violation of his individuality.

To be sure, this aspect of punishment depends upon the conception of the criminal as something that is free and can not be

fication of punishment consists in its actually being retribution.") They also contain other manifestly retrograde ideas. Differing from Hegel, Rothe believes it is possible upon the whole to fix gradations in punishment by retribution and that the death penalty is justified by the usual references to certain passages of the Bible (which passages historically considered have another meaning), p. 887. On pages 876 and 877, referring to Nitzsch, he says: "And indeed as a *Christian* State, the State must punish; for even upon a basis of a complete conciliation of the conflict between the interests of holiness and those of grace arising from the redemption (Would that this conciliation were already accomplished !), Christian love can not stay the arm of criminal justice, but rather it must in its own interests expressly urge it to activity"(!). For the judge indeed, the two-soul theory which he advances is correct; — but how the state may be Christian love and yet — not from love for or interest in its innocent subjects — because of blind retribution assign the criminal to the executioner, is not readily comprehensible. The criminal law of the 1500s and 1600s which arose from these opinions furnishes a criticism of such theories. It is natural that the fact is overlooked that criminal law historically had its origin in vengeance, which is everywhere condemned (*cf.* p. 877, *note*). In all these matters Schleiermacher has shown greater depth of thought.

[1] "Naturrecht auf dem Grunde der Ethik" (2d ed., 1868), §§ 50, 56–62.

[2] "Natturrecht, etc.", § 58.

[3] Apart from external indemnification.

moulded at will; but if punishment were the abolition of one wrong by the infliction of another, this punishment would be impossible. Only that punishment will appear just to the criminal which, on one hand, necessarily springs from the nature of his own act, and on the other, from the provisions of the law he has violated. First, the wrong is plucked at its root in the mind of the criminal. His reformation is the victory of the law over the hostile will; hence, that it may the more readily be perceived by the criminal, the purpose of reformation is included in the punishment. Furthermore:[4] "Successful crime incites greed and the evil will of others for secret enjoyment. The evil example loses its power of incitement only when, destroyed by the punishment, it leads to the opposite of incitement, or when, in the psychological process of the usual association of ideas, the illusion of pleasure associated with the example is counterbalanced by the influence of fear and unhappiness. Intentional wrong seldom arises of its own accord and without association with something else. Rather it has its conditions in the various social notions favorable to its production; there is in every man a germ of malicious wrong in all its forms." Upon this necessary effect of civil punishment upon the community, there also rests, as Trendelenburg further remarks, its distinction from pedagogical punishment.

Trendelenburg's conception has but slight resemblance to the old view which regards punishment specifically as suffering, as evil for the criminal. The idea is not quite so clearly present as in Hegel that crime and punishment are not commensurable, and that it can only be established historically and not in principle that a definite punishment is merited.

Abegg. — Hegel's dialectic reaction against wrong assumes, on the other hand, more and more of the character of *retribution* in certain jurists who in principle stand or seem to stand on the same ground as Hegel. If, on one hand, one can not free himself from the old remnant of the maxim: "Malum passionis ob malum actionis", and, hence, is involved in new difficulties, so, on the other hand, a proper effort is made to show that the purposes of the punishment recognizable as meeting temporary requirements are directly the reverse of the absolute principle, and to portray punishment as having a Janus head, — one face, turned towards the past, permits the absolute principle of punishment to be recognized, and another face, turned towards the future, reveals the

[4] § 61.

relative purposes of punishment. And at the same time, an attempt is made, as must be the case in a correct theory, to adjust the theory to historical development.

This last-mentioned attempt is made by Abegg.[5] He portrays how the elimination of wrong passed from the form of vengeance to that of composition, and from this changed to punishment inflicted by the State with relative purposes (deterrence of others, safety from the criminal, reformation), and ultimately finds its completion in the principle of justice, which, however, adopts these relative purposes but in proper measure and relation. Hegel's method of dialectical contrast — the direct expression of feeling in vengeance, accepted purposes of punishment, and the treatment of the criminal in accordance therewith, and ultimately remission and expiation in the higher sense — is here followed, but quite foreign elements are injected into his opinions. Hegel's reaction against wrong [6] is, as it were, meaningless in itself; it is only in the sphere of finiteness (*i.e.* in history) that it assumes the coloring of a definite evil inflicted upon the criminal, in accordance, also, with the prevailing tendencies of thought. In Abegg there again prevails the illusion that, in accordance with an eternal and immutable rule of justice, the kind and degree of the punishment (or more correctly and in Abegg's sense, the evil contained in the punishment) can be definitely fixed.[7] Under this conception, the alliance of the purposes of deterrence, security from the offender, and reformation, with the absolute principle, is only an appearance. Such an alliance is impossible, — for those very reasons which of necessity prevail against Rossi's theory. If absolute justice and a relative purpose of punishment are two

[5] "Die verschiedenen Strafrechtstheorien in ihrem Verhältniss zu einander" (1835), pp. 8 *et seq.*

[6] In *Abegg's* "Lehrbuch der Strafwissenschaft", § 48, punishment is conceived as the bowing of the criminal to the will of the law.

[7] *Cf.* especially page 28: "Punishment is allowed only to serve the ends of *justice*, and this furnishes the rule for its application, and its conditions, its kind and amount." However, in § 49 of his "Lehrbuch", mention is again made of a relation between guilt and punishment determined by considerations of the nation and morality, and the resulting retribution. But in the "Archiv des Criminalrechts" (1845), p. 262, Abegg formally defends himself against Hepp's criticism that he, Abegg, had said in the sense of Hegel that punishment is not an evil. Abegg would merely say that punishment which is primarily and directly an evil for the criminal, *could and should* (?) be also a benefit for him. Here may be observed that "could and should" which are so easily said in the same breath. But what if these premises do not apply? There is no doubt about the "could", but the "should" gives punishment an entirely different meaning, and, when logically thought out, under some circumstances a quite different form.

different aspects of the same thing, then both are consistent. The acceptance of them as consistent is Rossi's theory. But in Abegg's theory, also, there is no possibility of these two conceptions being reconciled, as is revealed by a contemplation of the results. He who takes the trouble to follow up closely the results of the various theories (as was done by Feuerbach) thus pragmatically united, will necessarily agree with Feuerbach's criticism, that the two garments are so badly torn that it is impossible to patch up a decent covering for the State.

Heffter. — The defect of such a combination of theories [8] is especially manifest in the clear and concise expression given it by Heffter, one of its supporters, in § 109 of his valuable treatise. "Punishment," says Heffter, "in its absolute character, as an elimination of the guilt in the offender, is in and of itself not dependent upon the attainment of any specific purposes. It is rather a purpose in itself, and in accordance with its nature has the effect of curing. In the sphere of the State and its rights, as in finite affairs generally, punishment assumes certain peculiar relations. While here it may be inflicted solely in the general legal interest ('for the general utility'), it becomes a satisfaction which the State requires and takes from those guilty of a violation of the general legal system, for the purpose of the restoration and maintenance of the same." It is, indeed, not apparent how in the sphere of finite affairs the absolute purpose of eliminating guilt can change itself into the purposes of deterrence, reformation, etc., and at the same time remain true to itself. Nor is it apparent how it is just that the criminal must submit to these purposes. The solution of the problem is presumed, but it is not given. The contradiction is merely concealed by distinguishing between the sphere of principle (idea) and the sphere of finite affairs.

Köstlin, Merkel. — Köstlin [9] and Merkel, in spite of the many excellent statements concerning individual points of criminal phi-

[8] *Freytag's* attempt ("Die Concessionalgerechtigkeitstheorie", *cf.* especially p. 46) is particularly an alliance of the absolute theory (fundamentally the theory of Hegel) with the contract theory, the theory of voluntary submission. He regards the principle of criminal law as a right acquired by agreement or concession to realize the idea of law in all those cases in which an act is done contrary to the laws representing it. This realization is attained by means of an evil inflicted as a punishment upon the doer of the act. According to Freytag, every one responsible for his acts, by living in the State proclaims his submission to its criminal law. A criticism of this view is not necessary.

[9] "Neue Revision der Grundbegriffe des Criminalrechts" (1845), pp. 1–53, pp. 764–850; "System des deutschen Strafrechts" (1855), §§ 1–8, 114–124.

losophy for which we are indebted to them, do not carry their ideas substantially farther than the foregoing. Köstlin, in part adhering more closely than Heffter to Hegel, merely adds an examination into the possible kinds of wrong. He classifies unconscious wrong as the object of civil justice, possible wrong as the object of the police system, and known antagonism of the will of the individual towards the general law as crime. He designates punishment as coercion brought to bear on the will of the criminal. According to Köstlin, punishment may not consist of a general reaction against the personality of the criminal, but it may be such only to that degree to which the criminal himself has thwarted the general will. Consequently, as Köstlin himself says, he regards punishment externally as retribution and as an evil.

The theory of retribution here again becomes very prominent; and the statement that this is the case only "externally" does not suppress the truth. It merely conceals the difficulty of proving that the punishment should also inwardly be a benefit to the criminal, — a thing which in empirical conditions is by no means uniformly the case. If, without giving that necessary attention to an injury to the public, one could, in the case of many a repentant criminal, forego the punishment, he would certainly thereupon reform. And if we consider how defective the means of punishment have been and still remain (how difficult, for example, is the erection of a penal institution corresponding to all requirements), we shall, as it appears, perceive that here a single phrase has bridged over the chasm between good and evil. Moreover, Köstlin's classification of the three kinds of wrong is not satisfactory, — the distinction between civil wrong and criminal wrong for the reasons previously dealt with. As to the intermediate classification favored by the dialectical method of Hegel, the penalties inflicted by the police power are, as a rule, not juristically preventive, but rather, as it were, remedial; the action contravening a police regulation is not merely a possible wrong but an actual wrong, although it is not necessary that it directly violate a subjective right or work a real external injury. This is exactly the case with quite a number of criminal offenses; and the fact is merely that police regulations concern themselves chiefly with acts which are not aimed at a violation of a right but which nevertheless place a right in jeopardy. — The justification of punishment as a right of the criminal is only incidentally treated by Köstlin. He believes that punishment reaches the criminal only in accordance with laws which the latter himself has established.

Merkel involves himself in a peculiar difficulty.[10] He capably demonstrated that the distinction favored by Hegel between the circumstances of punishable and non-punishable wrong acts is not tenable. But this demonstration carried with it the assumption that no distinction exists at all between criminal wrongs and civil wrongs, and that civil and criminal sanction are identical in nature. Both do away with wrong, — criminal sanction in the ideal inner sphere and civil sanction in the external sphere. This is fundamentally connected with Merkel's assumption that wrong is conceivable only as blameworthy, and that law consists merely of commands (rules) and prohibitions addressed to persons who are responsible for their acts. However plausible[11] this assumption may be made through the observation that the contrary view would logically compel us to regard an unreasoning character as a possible author of a legal injury, yet fundamentally it rests upon the long-since repudiated foundation of law by contract. I have a right only because a rule of law forbids other responsible beings to take the object from me. That is, I have a right merely by virtue of a forbearance on the part of others which is either voluntary or compelled by the legal system. I do not have it by virtue of a reason inherent in the nature of things. Not because my family and I have possessed and cultivated a field for one hundred years is it my property; but the legal system can give effective orders to others that they leave it alone. If Merkel's assumption were correct, the State would have no right to protect itself and its subjects against predatory attacks of barbaric hordes and nations. It would only protect a "factum." Yet the spontaneous feeling of every one leads to a different conception, viz., that there exists a right to protect peaceable possession and culture against barbaric destruction, whether the invader had the capacity to understand this or not. Not for a moment can we concede that humanity at large has no right to protect itself against wild beasts

[10] "Criminalistische Abhandlungen", I ("Zur Lehre von den Grundeintheilungen des Rechts und der Rechtsfolgen"), 1867, p. 41, pp. 104 *et seq.* *Cf.* also *Merkel*, "Zum Reform der Strafgesetze, ein Vortrag" (Prag, 1869), and more recently in the "Zeitschrift für die gesammte Strafrechtswissenschaft" (1881), pp. 553 *et seq.*

[11] For the contrary view, and especially concerning the controversy as to the possibility of wrong without guilt, *cf.* the numerous discussions by *Thon*, "Rechtsnorm und subjectives Recht" (1879), pp. 71 *et seq.* However, for an adherent of the "Norm" theory this matter has its special difficulties.

and unreasoning nature. It has this right. It merely uses it and avails itself of it in a different form than as man against man; wild beasts and lifeless objects are not possessors of rights.

The logic of Merkel's view would also compel the judge of the civil court, before ordering a debtor to pay or a detainer to deliver, to ascertain whether these parties had realized their wrong; for without this preliminary condition no legal obligation exists, and the judgment is not intended to create legal obligations but merely to declare those already existing. From this standpoint, also, it becomes impossible to construe the differences between the civil sanction (*i.e.*, payment of damages) and punishment which exist in the positive law and are uniformly recognized as reasonable. If the civil sanction pursues exactly the same object as the criminal sanction, why is punishment in its positive development governed by laws quite different from those of the civil sanction? Why, *e.g.*, does not the punishment pass, as does generally the obligation to indemnify, to the heirs of the party originally obligated? [12] In this complete disintegration of the conception of punishment it is no longer, as a matter of fact, possible to arrive at the conception of retribution which Merkel on the other hand finds realized in criminal justice. Private law and civil justice have essentially nothing to do with the conception of retribution, but nevertheless punishment according to its nature should not be different from the criminal sanction.

The postulate [13] of a comprehensive foundation of criminal law is contained in the following principles: [14] "To each and every living being there is conceded the right to maintain and preserve himself and the conditions upon which depend his being and his existence. To the struggle for the latter belongs the reaction which in social life responds to the crime, whether individuals or the community take part in the same. For the crime which is not followed by retribution jeopardizes all of those conditions." Pun-

[12] In respect to this, *cf. Binding*, "Die Normen und ihre Uebertretung." In spite of which, the principle so excellently developed by Merkel is sound, viz., that to a certain extent and under certain conditions the civil sanction may represent punishment and take its place and that the State should inflict punishment for an act only in so far as the civil sanction does not suffice. *Cf. Merkel* also in the "Zeitschrift für die gesammte Strafrechtswissenschaft" (1881), pp. 582, 583.

[13] "Criminalistische Abhandlungen", I, pp. 113, 114.

[14] I do not believe that Merkel, if he would maintain the principles quoted, can avoid having Hegel as the basis for his fundamental views of criminal law, as he curiously enough appears (?) to desire. *Cf.* "Zeitschrift, etc.", p. 555.

ishment is, indeed, the reaction against acts hostile to the conditions upon which the life of society depends, — a reaction which necessarily takes place where society as a whole would still express itself as being moral. Moreover, the way and manner in which Merkel rejects a retribution which should sever itself from social interests and which at the same time would not be in a position to adopt the relative theories of punishment, must command our entire accord. But one cannot perceive the bridges which on one hand connect these interests with that retribution, and on the other lead from that retribution to that vague residue of simple coercion (sanction) into which punishment is reduced.

Hälschner. — Hälschner [15] also uses Hegel's ideas as his foundation. But he is not satisfied with the mere dialectic necessity of punishment, and consequently (more even in his latest works than in his earlier) he is under the influence of the idea, which sees in the law merely rules for the will of those who, in the concrete case, are without rights. Thus, the right is merely the vacuum which is left to those entitled to something when it is appropriated by those not entitled. This is a view which we have already seen in Merkel, but which has since found its clearest expression in the "Norm theory" of Binding. Hälschner [16] quite properly asserts that the legal rule should be a moral one; and he is also quite correct in maintaining that law should not be merely the compass, or at any rate, a skilled adviser of power, but rather that law and morality be in themselves a power. But, peculiarly enough, he is unable to assert for law in itself either activity or coercive power (sanction). This activity and coercive power, apart from cases of self-defense, first arise through the State "in which the organism of law acquires its finite existence",[17] and in which "every exercise of vengeance is designated as not merely formal, on account of the danger of its getting beyond control, but also as material, as unlawful, because morally unlawful, and improper." [18] Punishment is that coercion which is used against an active opposition of the will to the law, or against a force done to the law, or against a power which has intruded into those spheres over which the State alone predominates, and which is therefore designed to repel

[15] *Cf.* "System des preussischen Strafrechts", I (1858), pp. 11–17, pp. 435–443; "Die Lehre vom Unrecht und seinen Formen", in "Gerichtssaal" (1869), pp. 11–36 and pp. 81–114 (also published separately), also "Gerichtssaal" (1876), pp. 401–440. But especially see "Das gemeine deutsche Strafrecht", Vol. I (1881), pp. 3–36, pp. 558–574. The citations following are from the work last mentioned.

[16] Pp. 13, 14.

[17] P. 12.

[18] Pp. 26, 27, 30.

the despotic encroachment of the individual will upon the legal power of the State. Its purpose is: "to administer justice by the elimination of wrong, by the restoration of the legal condition and the undiminished power of the State. In this sense and not for the sake of a limited utilitarian purpose, to punish is a moral necessity."[19] However, the sanction should not be unrestrained, nor should the criminal be seized by the power of the State "as something absolutely without a right." Justice should be satisfied by a punishment which completely corresponds in kind and amount to the guilt in respect to all elements under consideration.[20] And yet the various possible purposes of punishment (security, etc.) should be attained. A conflict of these various purposes, Hälschner feels, is possible only when exclusive predominance is given to some one of these purposes, or if there is assigned to punishment some purpose foreign to its ideal nature (?).

We have already frequently pointed out that a combination of the relative criminal theories, either singly or collectively, with a theory which believes that an absolute standard of justice must be established for punishment, is impossible. The so-called inner agreement of such an absolute theory and a relative theory is and remains simply a pious wish, which will not bear up under examination in the individual cases. For example, suppose, in the light of that theory, we try to answer the simple question whether or not the legislative power in a case of special temporary danger, *e.g.*, in a time of special excitement, has the right to materially increase the severity of the punishment for certain offenses,—as it were, to make an example. But apart from this, the doctrine cannot free itself from numerous inconsistencies. It is asserted that coercion is in no way an element of law, and yet it is immediately stated that coercion is, on other grounds, not only morally possible but even necessary for the law.[21] But if a thing is necessary for law, then it is also included in the nature of law. The point of view which lies at the basis of this is incorrect. It is assumed that law can be completely separated from the other relations of human life. As such it requires no coercion. But as soon as law is considered and asserted as existing among these relations of life and dealing with them, then coercion becomes necessary. But this last-mentioned point of view is alone permissible. A law which floats in the air, withdrawn from all relations of life, is a will-o'-the-wisp.

[19] P. 32. [20] P. 565. [21] P. 11.

As to Hälschner's comment that the rules of law applicable to monarchs do not cease to be legal rules because no coercion sanction can be applied to monarchs, he overlooks the fact that coercion may exist without a civil or a criminal procedure. A very effective coercion may exist by virtue of the pressure of the united conditions of things, without there being an especially organized machinery for giving effect to the same. The coercion might very well *e.g.*, consist in this, viz., that the monarch, by the disavowal of such a legal duty, might encounter opposition to legal rules otherwise intended by him, and in glaring cases could not avoid a breach of the constitution which would be prejudicial to his position. The coercion exercised by the law can also very well consist in this, viz., that the law deny to him who violates its provisions any assistance, or that it recognize the right of self-defense on the part of those offering opposition, etc.[22] Coercion is absolutely necessary, because the law must be valid generally; and the law, as opposed to the individual will, must, because of this very generality, not yield but must compel. Consequently it is not apparent wherein vengeance specifically differs from punishment. Historically, as Hälschner admits, it is the root from which the criminal law sprang. Therefore theory requires identity with it in its fundamental essence; and has not the State often given its assent to the exercise of vengeance? Moreover, in the initial stages it is certainly not necessarily immoral, and the less so since it can then hardly be distinguished from self-defense. If in those times a bold aggressor had merely encountered opposition as limited as is our modern self-defense, and never had to fear anything further, then certainly (*e.g.*, as with the early Germans) there would never have existed a sure legal protection. And the same thing can be asserted if the range of self-defense had been limited merely to the protection of one's own rights. It is not so limited even to-day. In the initial stages of development, when there is no strong governmental power, such egoism would destroy all further development of the law and of the State; yet, in times of danger, when another's right is boldly attacked, we recognize the correctness of the principle: "Tua res agitur." And it is not apparent how punishment should

[22] There are also rules which make up a border province between law and morality, rules which may equally be regarded as moral or as legal (accompanied by legal prosecution) or in which it is doubtful whether legal prosecution can be considered.

be a necessary consequence of wrong deserving punishment, if it did not exist prior to the State.

All this is but a result of our knowledge of the ideas which Herbart first promulgated (cleverly but incorrectly): that the sanction for the law did not originate with the law. Thus the sanction must first have been introduced from without the law, and the same would hold true of punishment, which should be a sanction. But since punishment should also be distinguished from that which we customarily term as sanction in the administration of private law, Hälschner does this by denying that the administration of private law contains a sanction (although this is contrary to the simple and natural way of viewing the matter), and ascribes the private law duty to indemnify to the injured person's power over the property of the one doing the damage.[23] Finally, it is not an improvement upon Hegel's classification of civil wrong and criminal wrong, to conceive the latter as a wrong in which the criminal essentially places himself in opposition to the general legal system. We shall revert to this point later.

Berner. — In spite of many excellent comments for which we are indebted to Hälschner's discussions, his involved theory does not leave a satisfying impression and is in many respects a very difficult one for precise examination. Much more satisfactory is the simple theory of Berner.[24] Following mainly the speculative system of ethics of J. U. Wirth,[25] he clearly and definitely changes Hegel's idea of elimination of the wrong to one of retribution (measured according to the intention[26] as evidenced by the external injury). Moreover — and this is a special feature of Berner's view, wherein, in our judgment, he is quite correct — he maintains that retributive justice leaves a certain province for free discretion as to the quantum of the punishment (which however is again conceived as suffering inflicted through the senses).[27]

[23] P. 21. The private law duty of compensation in torts is hereby based upon quasi-contract, as it was also by *Binding* ("Normen", I, pp. 222, 223). It is a species of "negotiorum gestio." In opposition to Hälschner, *cf.* especially *Merkel* in the "Zeitschrift für die gesammte Strafrechtswissenschaft" (1881), pp. 580 *et seq.*

[24] "Lehrbuch des deutschen Strafrechts", §§ 28–32.

[25] Concerning this, see *Laistner*, "Das Recht in der Strafe" (1872), pp. 153 *et seq.*

[26] "Lehrbuch", § 31.

[27] "To ascertain that which is deserved herein is the province of empiricism rather than of formal calculation. In this attention is to be given especially to the existing conditions of society and also to national morals and opinions conditioned as they are by relations of time and space. In the place of comparison in kind ('talio') we retain merely the idea of proportion and the criterion of experience." § 28 (*cf. ante*).

Within this province the purposes of deterrence and reformation can and should exercise an influence upon the amount of the punishment. "Here are the limits within which justice allows the realization of these purposes." And within these limits (as had already been demonstrated by Abegg and Wirth) both these purposes are simultaneously achieved with the retributory punishments. Thus, according to Berner, the relative theories of criminal law ultimately acquire an extensive influence upon determining the amount of the punishment.

Kitz. — Hegel's theory receives from Kitz a new tendency which is deserving of notice.[28] It deals, we may say, more with inner and subjective matters, thus practically veering around towards the theory of reformation. The immoral act is declared not so much to become "nil" as to be undone, rescinded ("Rescission theory"). The intention which has not yet become an act, which has not manifested itself to the external world, may be rescinded by being given up, by simply being withdrawn.[29] But where the intention has become an act, its rescission requires a positive contrary act, an opposite treatment of the will; and since the offender has acted in order to furnish gratification to his baser nature and desires, it requires his receiving pain inflicted through the senses, receiving punishment. As it had already been stated in the Decretum of Gratian:[30] "Qui peccator est, et quem remordet propria conscientia, cilicio accingatur et plangat . . . propria delicta . . . et cubat et dormiat in sacco, ut præteritas delicias, per quas offenderat Deum, vitæ austeritate compenset."[31]

Kitz has very correctly combated certain objections which could be raised against this theory. Thus, there is the objection that in actual life an equalization of the pleasure of the crime and the suffering of the punishment cannot be established. A principle, however, is not valueless, because in its application to concrete life a certain province for the exercise of discretion cannot be avoided. Moreover, it cannot be asserted that, according to Kitz's theory, an action that had no effect must remain unpunished, since the essence of the intention as manifested does not lie in its consequences; an absolute rascal, in whom a slight sensual enticement furnished a motive for the commission of a grave offense,

[28] "Das Princip der Strafe in seinem Ursprunge aus der Sittlichkeit" (Oldenburg, 1874).

[29] *Cf.* p. 25: "In my heart, my deed was not my own."

[30] Causa 33 qu. 3, 1, "De pœnitentia."

[31] Thus p. 35.

does not for this reason get off with a slight punishment. That desire for sensual gratification, existing prior to the act and become habitual, is to be considered as the motive, and thus the punishment rather increased. The distinction between punishable crime and mere immorality is marked by the fact that the function of the State is limited to counteracting encroachments upon moral freedom, and that within this province the State fixes and controls the suffering afflicting the senses which seems necessary for the rescission of the immoral intention. It is perfectly manifest that herein the State has to aim at the conversion of the intention of the criminal (and also his reformation). For this reason, imprisonment seems an especially commendable form of punishment, while the death penalty, on the contrary, is objectionable.

However, as the reference to the penance of the Canon law shows, the character of temporal punishment (*i.e.*, inflicted by the State) is not preserved in Kitz's rescission theory. This temporal punishment attains greater perfection, the more it is calculated to bring about the inner reformation of the criminal; but first and foremost, it has in view as its object not the criminal but the purposes of the community. The logical outcome of Kitz's rescission theory is a theory of reformation, on one hand limited by a consideration that means of reformation may never be a pleasure for the condemned, but rather suffering, and on the other hand materially restricted because the means of reformation must be suffering. According to Kitz, the State has no further right to punish, if the offender has already voluntarily undergone the evil which (according to the view of the State and also according to the statute) must be inflicted upon him. This would be the perfect punishment. In this the *official* character of the punishment vanishes. And finally, it is a fiction that a deed which has been done can be undone by the contrary desire of its author; for this, as the ancients said, could not even be accomplished by the gods. Even an evil intention and desire cherished and nourished in the inner recesses of the soul leaves its trace. The reality of criminal law cannot be founded upon a fiction.

§ 100. **Combination of the Theories of Hegel and Fichte. — Heinze.** — The theory of Heinze,[1] which in part at least stands upon the basis of Hegel, is complicated and perhaps difficult to comprehend in the sense in which it was intended. One cannot

[1] In *Von Holtzendorff's* "Handbuch des deutschen Strafrechts", I, pp. 321–344.

deny its searching glance into the nature of wrong, of law, and of punishment; but on the other hand (as Laistner's criticism [2] has revealed and manifested) it exhibits a certain wavering back and forth between various principles and a certain obscurity.

Heinze very correctly perceives that a proper theory of criminal law must also be adapted [3] to historical development and to the various, and perhaps also imperfect, manifestations of punishment. He also perceives that a correct theory of criminal law has to consider principally, although not exclusively, punishment inflicted by the State. From this point of view, Heinze very correctly observes that punishment does not need to be an " evil " or a " suffering." It is regarded as the specific substance of civic punishment that it be *something done* by the criminal, which should be the guiding principle in the fixing of imprisonment, along with which the punishment of banishment (complete or partial banishment from the legal·community) is recognized. Both of these punishments are diminutions (" Minderung ") of rights (*i.e.*, of the criminal). The undergoing of the punishment by performance of something and the fulfilment of an obligation frees from the diminution of right in the future, yet it directly asserts the diminution of right in the most direct and actual manner; [4] and it follows from this conception, as Heinze argues, that it is an error to assume that punishment cannot attain realization until the beginning of physical atonement. No one can deny that a criminal sentence, in itself, fulfils a part of the function of punishment; [5] a portion of its activity takes place, even though it was certain from the beginning that the punishment would not be inflicted. Even before the commission of the crime, the punishment has an independent existence. In the criminal statute or in the rule of criminal law founded upon custom two aspects may be distinguished; the ideal one lies in the judgment that the punishment is the legal equivalent of the crime; the practical one, in the order that this punishment shall be inflicted upon the author of the crime. The punishment is also a manifestation of the criminal's unworthiness.

These two ways of conceiving punishment, as they are advanced, cannot be reconciled. It is possible, if one regard the manifestation of the unworthiness of the criminal as the cardinal element,

[2] Pp. 169–178. [3] P. 329. [4] P. 327.

[5] The author of this book had already expressed these thoughts in "Grundlagen des Strafrechts", pp. 3, 84: There can be no punishment without public disapproval of the act, but the punishment may possibly consist merely in public disapproval.

to proceed from this to an accompanying diminution of right or performance of punishment, and also even to banishment. But the reverse cannot be accomplished. The community has no further interest in him who is expelled,[6] and there is no special need to proclaim the unworthiness of him who has paid what he owes.[7] It is also clear that if there can still be an effect to punishment when a real diminution of rights in individual cases is impractical, real diminution of rights cannot be the essence of punishment.[8] Moreover, if banishment, according to Heinze's conception, is the prototype of public punishment and is little by little mitigated by public punishment, then would not the criminal have the right to choose banishment from the society of the State instead of undergoing public punishment? Heinze is able to avoid this result, which would be quite acceptable to our modern criminal world, only by appealing to the civilizing mission of the State. Suddenly the State appears as the one formally injured. "The crime within the State is the violation of that law of life operative in civil society and in the State and indispensable to its progress. . . . Through the crime the criminal formally becomes, in respect to the State, a wanton violator and despiser of the legal system of the State and materially a renegade of that civilization which furnishes the basis for rights." For this reason "there cannot be ascribed to the individual criminal the right of choosing a voluntary withdrawal [9] from the State and the association of civilized mankind in preference to undergoing the punishment which will rehabilitate him in the State. This would be directly to allow him that which constitutes the essence of the worst crime, viz., a complete lapse from civilization expressed and accomplished by a withdrawal of one's self from the State and from civilized humanity." According to this, any one, who, as a hermit, betook himself to a desert island would thereby commit the worst

[6] Considering it practically, what would be thought if a society first expelled one of its members and afterwards punished him under its by-laws? But the reverse is quite conceivable.

[7] And yet a certain effect of grave crimes that have been atoned for, an effect which would apply to honor, although perhaps no longer to be fixed by law can never be eliminated. Such a thing is also not to be desired.

[8] There is hereby manifested the correctness of the course of thought pursued by me in a reverse fashion in the "Grundlagen des Strafrechts", which Heinze however has scarcely noticed.

[9] The individual State does not, however, completely represent this general union, particularly since every State is not equally civilized. For the contrary view, see Laistner, p. 173 and Heinze's own statements in opposition to Stahl, Heinze, p. 300.

crime conceivable. The doctrine involves the following simple fallacy: One may regard grave crimes as being also a lapse from civilization, but not every withdrawal from civilization is a grave crime. If the punishment rehabilitates, then it is a right and not a duty of the criminal. "Beneficia non obtruduntur." If one desires to insist strongly on the philosophic attitude, a moral duty does not always give rise to a right,[10] and the civilizing duty of the State does not carry with it the right to punish. Otherwise there could be inferred from the civilizing duty of the State the right to improve (all) individuals through punishment as far as it might seem desirable to the State.

As a matter of fact, Heinze's theory, as supported later by Laistner, reveals two distinct circles of thought. To the system of Hegel [11] belongs the idea of the declaration of nullity or baseness of the crime; to Fichte belongs the thought that crime breaks the legal union between the criminal and the State, and that this is reunited by punishment.[12] "If we inquire after the embodiment of the penal power, on both sides we are told it is the State; the one State as the defender of rights, the other State as the party injured, which relies not upon its criminal law but rather upon its missionary duty." However, we do not subscribe to that severe judgment which Laistner [13] later passes upon Hegel's theory, after he had in the beginning praised that "Janus head" which Heinze in a somewhat mysterious manner had set up as the only correct starting-point. We are rather of the opinion that the ideas of Hegel and Fichte may quite well be joined in a certain unity; and we can express to Heinze the appreciation of science for his suggestion in this respect. But the way in which it is sought to bring about this unity is in our opinion misleading.

And misleading also is the way in which the relative purposes

[10] From the moral duty *e.g.* to feed children, there does not arise the right to do so at another's expense, — indeed there arises no definite right against others.

[11] *Cf. e.g.* p. 327: "Punishment is the right inherent in the crime."

[12] "Not punishment, but crime and punishment together must be regarded as the Janus head, — the face with the features of wrong is the crime and the face with the features of justice is the punishment." Heinze, p. 327. Such a figure can be made use of at the end of a deduction in order to make it more clear and impressive; but at the beginning of the deduction it leads to the error of confusing the figure and the deduction and thereby even itself to become uncertain.

[13] P. 175. "And the web is so loosely woven that the warp and woof can be distinguished without effort. We also have here before us one of the so-called mixed theories to which the criticism of its own author as to such mixtures may be applied."

are finally inserted in Heinze's theory. They are designated simply as "accidental purposes of punishment." But in a theory there can be nothing accidental. One can not thus accidentally adhere to an absolute principle, nor cherish the pious thought that these relative purposes are so peaceably reconciled to each other or to the principle of rehabilitation or of banishment or to the principle of pronouncing the unworthiness of the criminal or his crime. Heinze refers here to the operation of the statute. The statute may indeed reassure the judge but not the legislator or the theories and their philosophers. And since (on p. 333) the justice of mere police penalties, which may be felt as keenly as criminal punishment, is founded simply upon the fact [14] that the State has the right for the sake of the public welfare to gain its end by means of threatening with punishment, what need was there, for expounding together crime, wrong, and punishment, of "the right inherent in the crime" and the "Janus-head"? Would not the theories of Bentham and Feuerbach have been more simple and logical?

Since it seems to be a natural right of authors to place their own theories at the end of their investigations, although chronologically regarded this may have preceded some other theory, so, with Heinze's "combination theory", we will take leave of the description of the evolution of Hegel's principle and turn to the other most recent theories. Upon the whole, either they amount to a renunciation of any philosophic explanation (except in so far as they are content in the belief that the description of a phenomenon or its process constitutes its explanation) or else they contain simple reproductions of former theories. A special position can perhaps be assigned to Binding's theory, which will be mentioned at the close.

§ 101. **Von Kirchmann.** — The doctrine of Von Kirchmann [1] in reality entails a renunciation of every theory of criminal law. This renunciation, in a peculiar manner, reminds one of Kant. But closer consideration reveals that here we have to deal merely with the shell of Kant's philosophy, and not with its true kernel. According to Kant, morality consists in an unquestioning obedience to the categorical imperative, in this direct fact of our perception. Kant understands by this the unconditional submission

[14] As to the relation of criminal punishments and those of the police, see *infra*.

[1] "Die Grundbegriffe des Rechts und der Moral" (2d ed., 1873).

to the transcendental principle, existing in God of development or being. But Von Kirchmann derives from this an unquestioning obedience towards any authority whatsoever, *i.e.*, obedience to every authority which appears absolute to the individual.[2] For this power (of God, but also of the ruler, of the nation as a whole, and of the father over the child of tender years) there is no morality, since it considers itself sovereign and actually exercises sovereign prerogatives.[3] Now law in the subjective sense, in its very nature, consists of physical power, which, on one hand, is strengthened and protected by means of the authorities, and on the other by means of a coercion called by the authorities to their assistance, and especially by means of threatening with evil for any case of injury done to this power.[4]

Criminal law is thus degraded into a mere means of deterrence. We do not need worry our heads to ascertain whether or not such a conception violates the sense of justice and morality or stands in contradiction with other known facts. For the settlement of the controversy between absolute and relative theories, Von Kirchmann has, as a result of the foregoing, a ready and simple expedient. "Both utility and morality are the foundations of punishment; the former for the authorities, the latter for their subjects."[5] In other words, the individual must accept all that the authority ordains, but the authority may do what it pleases. There is justice only within the sphere of the statute, but to the statute itself the standard of justice cannot be applied.[6]

Schopenhauer. — Schopenhauer's conception of law and of criminal law is an almost perfect reproduction of Feuerbach's theory on a metaphysical (Spinoza) basis, but without Feuerbach's exact presentation in detail. In accordance with his general philosophic doctrines, Schopenhauer does not require a special justification for punishment, in the sense that no injustice be done to the party punished. For, according to Schopenhauer, the existence of the individual being is only an appearance; since the

[2] "Grundbegriffe", pp. 62 *et seq.*, and especially p. 65.

[3] P. 113.

[4] "Grundbegriffe", pp. 107 *et seq.*, p. 111.

[5] "Grundbegriffe", pp. 165 *et seq.*

[6] A broader theory of the law of might and morality can scarcely be conceived. Also *cf.* especially p. 178. "It has already been shown that the substance of morality is based upon the accidental, disconnected, and often doubtful commands of various authorities. Von Kirchmann also in 1848 published a pamphlet which was intended to demonstrate the worthlessness of all judicial practice." ("Die Werthlosigkeit der Jurisprudenz, ein Vortrag".)

veil of the "Maja" does not permit the individual to see the entire truth, the individual believes himself distinct from the rest. Also, if the individual being inflicts suffering upon another, this in reality brings harm to himself, and as a result every evil act carries in itself its own retribution; a further retribution, such as vengeance, is absolutely senseless and without purpose.[7] Law, the State, and criminal law are consequently merely external means whereby, in the world of appearance, there may be reduced to the narrowest possible limits, with a certain sacrifice, the doing of harm, which is the result of the irrepressible "egoism" with which every living being is imbued. Law and the State therefore have nothing to do with true morality, which is only in the common feeling, in the recognition that one is merely part of a whole, although law has its origin in morality to the extent that it marks the point to which the will of the individual can go, in its own assertion, without denying the existence of another will, which is in any case a violation of morality. The State is based upon well-calculated "egoism" because no one desires to *suffer* wrong. Morality, on the contrary, desires no one to *do* wrong. Up to a certain point the result of both can be the same. "A Wolf with a muzzle is as harmless as a lamb." The criminal statute, *i.e.*, the threat contained in the criminal statute, is nothing other than the "muzzle" for the egoism.[8] If this "muzzle" required victims in the enforcement of the punishment, then, in Schopenhauer's sense, one could simply find consolation; to meet the criticism that the criminal must have been sacrificed for others, one could say that in reality the punishment was not inflicted upon one but upon all. And also, for other reasons, it would be permissible to behead as many as one might choose, since the beheaded would all be dispatched to that happy land of indefinite nothing or everything, the "Nirvana."

However, Schopenhauer seems to have an indefinite feeling that

[7] *Cf.* particularly: "Welt als Wille und Vorstellung" (2d ed. of complete works by *Frauenstädt*, Vol. II, 1877), I, p. 418. Moreover it deserves notice that the theory of deterrence has been gaining adherents, recently. Doubtless this has been furthered by the exaggerations and extravagances of the theory of reformation, and also by the apparent simplicity of the theory of deterrence, the defects and contradictions of which are not visible to the purely philosophical view of those who are not jurists. This also holds true in respect to the indefinite "Fear and Discipline Theory" of *Ulrici* ("Gott und der Mensch", II, 1, esp. pp. 411 *et seq.*), who in opposition to Schopenhauer proceeds from the freedom of the will (*cf.* pp. 12 *et seq.*).

[8] See citation above; p. 408.

since all are as one and hence all are equal, it will not do to leave the world of appearance to its own brutality.[9] He accordingly remarked — herein reminding one of Rousseau — that, for the security of his life, the individual has pledged his life, his freedom, etc.; but at the same time he acknowledges, since a pledge [10] has meaning only if it possesses value, that a certain value is as a matter of fact attached to the individual.

And so Schopenhauer's philosophy varies back and forth between the world as it actually is (the " thing or things in themselves ") and the world of appearance. Schopenhauer embarked upon a voyage into the world of " things in themselves ", which Kant had declared to be impossible and of which he believed only a fragment could be acknowledged in the " practical reason " under the domain of ethics. In a subjective mood (and so frequently that the reader finds difficulty in observing it) he shifts the scenery between the world of appearance and the world in abstract. Principles which according to Schopenhauer can have application only in the world in abstract are suddenly applied to the world of appearance. Practically regarded, it is the philosophy of the " blasé." If things become disagreeable, the sensitive philosopher retires to the world in abstract; then suddenly the world of appearance has no further meaning. Strictly examined, the State and law have only those meanings which protect the comfortably located philosopher from unpleasant disturbances. In criminal law particularly he can be little interested. He himself will not commit a crime. For character is unchanging and he acts or fails to act as necessity dictates, and the philosopher knows his character. So, criminal law is, in reality, only for the brutal masses, or, at any rate, for those who have charge of their discipline and prisons. It is merely sympathy that connects the philosopher with the criminal.

This sympathy, however, does indeed lead to a noble suggestion, which can be turned to good account in the criminal law: We are made of the same material as the criminal whom we condemn; we all share his guilt with him; therefore we may not use him solely as a means for accomplishing other purposes. There

[9] II, p. 687: "A criminal code should be nothing other than a list of motives in opposition to criminal acts."

[10] The theory of pledge, under which the theory of retribution crept in, is introduced by *Schopenhauer* (II, p. 686) in commendation of the death penalty for murder. But why is it not also in commendation of the death penalty for manslaughter caused by negligence?

are many evidences of deep insight on Schopenhauer's part which one must admire. And even if one regard his fundamental principles as absolutely wrong, one can only agree with him in his considering the criminal dispassionately and in a certain sense as a product of nature, and in his application of the punishment (like Hierokles) primarily to the act rather than to its author.[11] His specific statements concerning law and criminal law, where they are not limited by his philosophic principle, will always maintain their value. In conclusion, he rises above Feuerbach in that he does not explain crime merely by sensual motives, and that he does not make so complete a separation between law and morality as Feuerbach would have done.[12]

Dühring, E. von Hartmann, von Liszt. — The theory of criminal law in Dühring,[13] E. von Hartmann [14] and von Liszt [15] amounts to a mere description of the origin of criminial law, with, however, a repudiation of the negative tendency of ideas of retribution. According to these writers, criminal law developed from the natural impulse for revenge, the active return of an injury received. This impulse towards retaliation, according (especially) to E. von Hartmann, while directly related to the impulse of self-preservation and of necessary defense, unconsciously serves the end of creating and supporting the legal system. Later, however, it becomes more moderate, and, since it comes to be exercised by the State and no longer by individuals, it consciously assumes various purposes, — the purpose of giving security to the community and the purpose of bringing about a reformation of the criminal.

[11] *Cf.* "Welt als Wille und Vorstellung", II, p. 685: "According to my view, there lies at the basis of criminal law the principle that not particularly the man but rather the act is punished, from which it does not follow that the criminal is merely the material substance in which the act is punished."

[12] A philosophy such as that of Schopenhauer, which completely denies the freedom of any one and which nevertheless maintains the unity of all, necessarily wanders back and forth between refined sentiment and gross brutality. In this respect compare the discussion in "Die beiden Grundprobleme der Ethik" (pp. 238 *et seq.*), concerning the torture of beasts and the statements in "Welt als Wille", II, p. 687: "The damage to be avoided gives the proper standard for the punishment to be threatened, but it does not give the moral value (lack of value) of the forbidden act. Therefore the law can justly cause penal servitude to be inflicted for allowing a flower-pot to fall from a window, or can impose labor with a wheelbarrow for smoking tobacco in a forest in the summer, although this be allowed in the winter."

[13] "Kursus der Philosophie" (1875), pp. 219–243.

[14] "Phänomenologie die sittlichen Bewusstseins" (1879), pp. 196–212.

[15] "Das deutsche Reichsstrafrecht systematisch dargestellt" (1881), §§ 2–6, pp. 2–24.

Abegg had previously suggested that this transformation of the natural impulse was the last step, but was not the realization of the purpose aiming solely at human welfare. He designated it as the realization of justice. Von Liszt [16] positively rejects this last step: everywhere progress lies in making this natural impulse, as a power of nature, serviceable to the purpose to be attained. Definiteness of aim and choice of means suited to its purpose are the criteria of all progress. E. von Hartmann [17] expressly asserts: "Every concession to the demand for the 'talio' (*i.e.*, retribution in kind) for its own sake we must regard as immoral. We certainly no longer inflict punishment because sin has been committed, but rather that sin may not be committed." This view does not need to consider justification of punishment as being justice in respect to the individual criminal. The natural impulse is there and as such has its justification.

However, E. von Hartmann's remarks concerning the possibility of making wrong cease to be harmful, not by means of punishment but by means of forgiveness, show that here a certain remnant of contradiction still prevails (even that which is natural is regarded as justified "per se") and that the views of the writers mentioned do not contain a theory but merely a description. It is quite evident that we may derive from them neither the slightest information as to the function of legislation nor a criterion for the criticism of the historical and positive.

Von Liszt, however, desires, by emphasis upon the purpose of punishment, to introduce new progress, and so long as his theory keeps time with a certain indefinite "music of the future", it prospers exceedingly.[18] Thus he says: "Punishment in its substance and range must be one thing if it would prevent, another if it would reform, and still another if it would furnish security. However, it is only seldom and for the most part unconsciously that modern legislation cherishes this thought. It deals in the same manner with both the incorrigible habitual thief and the criminal of opportunity who is crushed with repentance. But the sharp emphasis upon the element of purpose, both in law generally and especially in punishment, is constantly finding countless and more important adherents. And it is to be hoped that in the not too

[16] *Cf. ibid.*, p. 24 (§ 6).

[17] P. 210.

[18] *Von Liszt*, "Das deutsche Reichsstrafrecht", p. 4. [Since the learned critic wrote the above text, von Liszt's views have enlarged; he now stands as the leader of a modern school of thought in Germany. Compare § 102*a*, *post*. — ED.]

distant future the time will have passed by when the demand that the State's power shall not without aim or purpose destroy the legal rights of members of the State, can be dismissed merely as a piece of rationalistic determinism." But as soon as he begins to proceed from such generalities to practical details, it becomes manifest that the various purposes of expediency which apparently are reclining so harmoniously together commence a hard conflict with each other.[19] Such are the results of neglecting that principle of justice inherent in the historical aspect of the subject. Ultimately this entire tendency, rejecting every absolute principle (as even von Liszt [20] cannot deny) rests and is even expressly placed upon the doctrine that law is only a product of the State will. The controversy between these relative theories and an absolute principle of criminal law is thus a continuance of the old controversy concerning the δίκαιον νόμῳ and the δίκαιον φύσει.

§ 102. **Binding's Theory of the Effect of Disobedience to a Rule.** — And here, too, is the point of connection with the theory of Binding, who regards the right to punish "as a related right to obedience on the part of offenders." [1] Binding regards the entire law as merely the sum total of rules, commands, and prohibitions, and the State enacts and makes use of these rules.[2] For disobedience to a rule it demands satisfaction in the punishment.[3] Yet this corporal satisfaction should be neither revenge nor retaliation.[4] It is somewhat like payment of damages in private law, merely, a right of the State, not a duty. Whether or not there arises this duty, which the State claims for itself in its criminal legislation, is determined by the consideration whether the evil of not punishing is greater for the State than the evil of punishing, — since the

[19] Von Hartmann *e.g.* (p. 210) says: "Since society as a whole is more important than the individual criminal, so the protection of society is more important than the moral discipline of the criminal. Therefore the latter can be followed only as a subsidiary purpose when allowed by the chief purpose, the protection of society."

[20] § 2.

[1] *Cf.* "Das Problem der Strafe in der heutigen Wissenschaft" in *Grünhut's* "Zeitschrift für das Privat- und öffentl. Recht" (1877), pp. 417–437. Especially *cf.* "Grundriss zur Vorlesung über gemeines deutsches Strafrecht" (1879), § 70, pp. 108–115.

[2] "Grundriss, etc.", p. 109.

[3] In so far as the State is considered as acting absolutely without restraint, it is not clear. Moreover, in the very first principles of the "Grundriss" right and law are confused with each other. "Punishment is the loss of legal rights which the State imposes . . . for satisfaction for an (of the offender) (his) irreparable breach of right, in order to maintain the authority of the violated law."

[4] "Grundriss", p. 110.

punishment is also an evil, and certainly not only for those upon whom it is inflicted.

Von Liszt, himself an adherent of Binding's "norm" theory ("Normentheorie"), "without which a deeper understanding of the criminal law . . . is scarcely possible",[5] is certainly not hostile in his criticism. We may therefore, while we ourselves abstain from criticism, give here as our own the criticism of Liszt,[6] to which, perhaps, something could be added: "Binding's view is not a solution; it is rather a shifting of the problem. Whence the State obtains the right to establish rules and to require obedience, and why the State's right to obedience is transformed into punishment, we are not told."

Laistner. — If we correctly comprehend the meaning of the above, Laistner's work has exercised some influence upon Binding's theory. Laistner aims especially to distinguish sharply the right of the State to punish and the *duty* to punish; so that, while the right is based upon justice, the duty can be fixed and especially can be limited in accordance with considerations of expediency. We are not of the opinion that law and duty are traceable to actually different origins for the *State* (as is hereinafter shown). Laistner's own attempt to establish a theory of criminal law is indeed quite extraordinary. It reminds one of Schopenhauer's theory of right and wrong, although not of Schopenhauer's theory of criminal law. "The criminal, while intruding upon another's sphere of will and right, is in his own view the master thereof; the injured party, however, accepts only the single fact that each one belongs in the realm of his own will and regards the intruder as being placed at his disposal. The true punishment, as a direct consequence of the crime, does not consist in the execution (*i.e.*, of the punishment), but rather in detention under the will of the party injured . . . The above described condition being inevitable, it is equally true that the necessity for the execution does not arise from the formal character of the act, as is maintained by the absolute theories; what we find is not a right, it is a privilege. Whether and how far and in what manner use is to be made of this right, — these are no longer legal questions, but are rather practical questions, questions of morality." [7]

[5] "Das deutsche Reichsstrafrecht systematisch dargestellt", p. 6.
[6] "Das deutsche Reichsstrafrecht", p. 23.
[7] *Laistner*, "Das Recht in der Strafe", pp. 196, 197.

This theory can be illustrated in the following manner: The (subjective) right is a spider's web; the violator of this right conducts himself as a fly in the net; apparently master therein, he merely falls into the power of the spider, the owner, lurking in the background. The spider does not need to suck the blood from the fly, but he has the power so to do. Whether or not he does so depends upon considerations of expediency, *i.e.*, his hunger, etc. Now if Laistner does not limit the "right" so exclusively to the subjective right of the individual, and if Laistner *e.g.* does and must conceive, as also violations of right, grave violations of general morality or even the violation of such of the commands and prohibitions of the State as he may choose, then what does the entire theory mean other than that one may legally do anything he pleases with the criminal, the transgressor of a rule? The only restrictions imposed are those of expediency and morality. In other words, law is that which the omnipotent State desires. The limitations which it herein imposes upon itself concern neither the law nor relatively the philosophy of law. Or, expressed in another way, there is no philosophy of law. And indeed there can be no philosophy of law at all, if it is true, as Binding maintains,[8] that the science of law is obliged to build only upon the squared cornerstones of the legal maxims of the State, instead of upon the waves of moral opinion which constantly advance and recede in the State and also in the individual. Does not philosophy signify the contemplation of things and of science in their relations, one with the other?

§ 102*a*. **Modern Theories of Criminality outside of Germany.** — [At this point the learned author's historical outline of criminal theory comes to an end. But at the very time of his writing (1882) a movement in another country was giving new directions on a grand scale to criminal theory; and in the succeeding generation entirely novel vistas were broadly opened and the older general theories took on a new content and new applications.

Von Bar's history ends in Germany with 1880 and in other other countries with 1850. But the story of the rest of the century has been fully told by another author, in a treatise which (with slight overlapping) begins where Von Bar left off, and traces the progress of criminal theory in chapters which exactly complement Von Bar's work and render unnecessary any supplement here. C. Bernaldo de Quirós' "Modern Theories of

[8] "Die Normen und ihre Uebertretung", I, p. 184.

Criminality"[1] serves the purpose as if it had been composed therefor.

De Quirós divides his account under two heads, Criminology, and Criminal Law and Penal Science.

I. Criminology. Under this head, he groups the various theories as follows, in chronological order:

(I). Origins. (1) Occult Sciences (Physiognomy, Phrenology): Lavergne, Carns, Casper. (2) Psychiatry: Morel, Despine, Maudsley. (3) Statistics: Quételet.

(II). The Three Innovators: Lombroso, Ferri, Garofalo.

(III). Development: A. Anthropological theories: (*a*) Atavistic theories: from Bordier to Ferrero; (*b*) Theories of degeneration: from Magnan to Dallemagne; (*c*) Pathologic theories: Roncoroni, Ottolenghi, Perrone, Capano, Lewis, Benedikt, Ingegnieros. B. Sociologic theories: (*a*) Anthropo-sociologic theories: Laccassagne, Aubry, Dubuisson; (*b*) Social theories: Vaccaro, Aubert, Nordau, Salillas; (*c*) Socialistic theories: Turati, Loria, Colajanni.

II. Criminal Law and Penal Science.

(I). Origins: Beccaría, Howard, the International Prison Congresses.

(II). Tendencies: (1) Traditional: Makarewicz. (2) Reformers: Liszt, Prins, Van Hamel, Stoos, Zucker, Lucchini, Ferri, Alimena, Carnevale, Manzini, Pozzolini, Berner. (3) Radicals: Vargha, Dorado, Tolstoy, Solovieff.

(III). Applications: Garraud, Tarde, Poletti, Gross, etc.

This imperfect outline of the progress of theory described in De Quirós' chapters indicates their service as complementing Von Bar's history for the 1800 s and completing the account to the present day. — ED.]

[1] Modern Criminal Science Series, Vol. I (Boston, Little, Brown, & Co., 1911; published under the auspices of the American Institute of Criminal Law and Criminology).

APPENDIX

A CRITIQUE OF THE THEORIES, AND AN EXPOSITION OF THE THEORY OF MORAL DISAPPROBATION (REPROBATION)

By C. L. Von Bar[1]

[1] [This Chapter forms the final Chapter (D) of the author's Part II. But as it is not historical in treatment, but critical, it is here placed as an

§ 103. **Defects of the Absolute and Relative Theories.** — Consideration of all the theories of criminal law heretofore advanced reveals that none of either the absolute or the relative theories has been satisfactory. The absolute theories lack purpose and also preclude the possibility of the criminal law being sufficiently used to serve the well-being of the public at large. The relative theories are in overwhelming majority,[2] but these are unable to satisfy the conscience of the people, because (as they are expounded) they renounce the principle of justice. An impartial mind will always require that it be the crime, and not some purpose disconnected with the crime, which brings down the punishment upon the offender.

The combinations of these two theories must also be characterized as erroneous; for an absolute foundation of criminal law, taken unrestrictedly, admits of no compromise with relative theories. That in this respect such combinations, and the so-called "pragmatic coalition," suffer the same fault of inconsistency, we have previously undertaken to demonstrate.

Merit of Hegel's Theory. — Of the previous absolute theories, there is only one which, if logically carried out and freed from erroneous additions so as to be properly understood, is reconcilable both with utilitarian purposes and the course of history. This is the theory of Hegel.[3] It is, in addition, entitled to a certain presumption of correctness, because of the fact that it has been adopted with more or less modifications by a considerable number of the most eminent criminalists in Germany. There remains, however, in Hegel a remnant of the old theory of retribution, and punishment cannot be deduced from the conception of right as he has attempted it. The chasm between wrong and punishment cannot be bridged over by defining the latter as a negation of wrong and consequently an assertion of right. It is conceivable that wrong could be removed from the world by some means other than by that which we call punishment, *e.g.* by the forgiveness of the wrong or the doing of kindnesses to the offender. E. von

Appendix. It belongs more naturally in the "Modern Criminal Science Series," already cited.

Von Bar's own theory is on the whole the most complete, correct, and well-balanced of any contributions to the subject. — Ed.]

[2] *Cf.* also *Sontag*, in *Dochow's* and *Von Liszt's* "Zeitschrift für die gesammte Rechtswissenschaft" (1881), pp. 486 *et seq.*

[3] In this respect, *Hälschner*, "Das gemeine deutsche Strafrecht", p. 4, carried his point as against *Merkel*, "Zeitschrift für die ges. Rechtswissenschaft" (1881), p. 555.

Hartmann[4] makes the apt statement that forgiveness corresponds to the former moral balance, *i.e.* that existing before the wrong, but that the payment of an evil with an evil presses down further one end of the scales. Moreover, as we have previously stated, there is nothing in the conception of right which requires an active prosecution of the criminal.[5]

Morality as the Basis of Law. — On the other hand, morality is an *active* principle — at least to a certain extent. The law can give to one the right to kill another, *e.g.* can give the master the right to kill the slave. That which determines whether or not we exercise this right is not the law, but rather a morality, correctly or incorrectly understood, in accordance with which (whether we will it or not) we measure all our acts of which we are clearly conscious. Now it is not the meaning of an absolute principle that a right is given to any one to punish or not punish the criminal, and certainly not a right to be exercised at pleasure. It is rather the meaning that the right is also essentially (although there are conceivable exceptions) a duty. Consequently the absolute principle of criminal law can be found only if we discover a moral basis in the law. The proof that law is nothing other than the morality of the *community* which is conclusive in respect to the individual is not to be expected here.[6] There are, however, a great number of legal rules which have no direct relation with morality, but rather rest upon historical tradition or upon purposes of expediency. These also are of service to morality, since they preserve to the individual a sure province for the exercise of choice and thus of ethical action.[7] Regulation, therefore, whether it

[4] "Phänomenologie des sittlichen Bewusstseins", p. 208.

[5] The objection that Hegel gives to *conceptions* a reality which they do not possess (*Von Liszt*, "Reichsstrafrecht", § 6, p. 22) is based upon a misconception. Hegel does not think that the conception can shut the criminal in jail or bring him to his death, but he thinks that the power of the conception over men can have this effect.

[6] *Schopenhauer* even says ("Die beiden Grundprobleme der Ethik", p. 218) that legal doctrine is a part of morality which establishes what are the acts which one may not commit if he would not harm others. In "Der Welt als Wille und Vorstellung" (I, p. 407), legal science is called "transformed morality." *Cf.* the meritorious but little-known work of *Felix Eberty*, "Versuche auf dem Gebiete des Naturrechts", 1852, and the able work of *Jellinek*, "Die socialistische Bedeutung von Recht, Staat und Strafe" (Wein, 1878), especially p. 42: "The law is the ethical minimum."

[7] Therefore to a certain extent law even protects unethical conduct, *e.g.* the unethical use of a right for one's own advantage and the disadvantage of another. If all morality were included within the law, freedom would be destroyed and with it ethical conduct.

take one form or another, may merely as such lay claim to ethical value. It follows therefore that an act which violates the legal system is, as such, more or less immoral, either directly or indirectly.

§ 104. **Ethical Judgment, Especially Ethical Disapprobation, as a Necessary Element of Morality.** — Now the nature of ethics is such that from the ethical or unethical character of each act it forms or seeks to form an opinion of others. In the language of Herbart, it could be said that one involuntarily seeks to determine whether the act furnishes a basis for approval or disapproval. However, a thinking man, who has learned that the motives leading to human action are often very complicated and that the circumstances under which these acts are done are often very difficult to comprehend, will frequently be reticent about forming this opinion. The familiar "Judge not that ye be not judged" of Christian morality stands opposed to that spiteful condemnation of the faults of others in which the individual egoism loves to exhibit itself as a shining contrast to the supposed shortcomings of others. But in itself there is nothing immoral in the forming of opinions as to the actions of others; it may even be considered an essential for the development of moral character. From the acts of others and their consequences one acquires his own morality and the lesson for his own life. Where the actions of another display an aspect either strikingly in harmony or at variance with morality, moral judgment takes place uncontrollably, with the power of a natural impulse. The discovery of some especially grave crime, *e.g.* an attempt to take the life of a highly revered ruler, causes this judgment to come into being with the irresistible force of a natural instinct; no hairsplitting distinctions [1] are able

[1] *Binding,* "Die Normen und ihre Uebertretung", I, p. 184, says that we may not derive law from morality and as proof of this he argues, first, that in the province of morality an unconditionally binding rule cannot exist — "unquestioning obedience to the so-called moral views of public opinion represents a very low degree of moral value" — since the ethical character of an act consists in its harmony with the conscience of its author; and, secondly, that the rules of morality are too changeable. To which the answer may be made that no intelligent man can confound public opinion, *i.e.* in Binding's sense, "the fashionable opinion of the great majority" with established morality, *e.g.* Christian morality as it is generally recognized. Such a shifting of the expression and the idea has no place in scientific investigation, and is a questionable method of polemic.

Taking up the last point, it is not true that moral opinions change so rapidly, "go up and down as waves", as Binding believes. On the contrary, they are far more stable than principles of law. The taking of excessive advantage of another's necessity, for example, has been long considered as morally reprehensible, while as is well known the law

to limit or deprive the individual or the public at large of this moral judgment. Dühring and Von Hartmann recognize this in their theory of resentment, or moral antipathy, but they pay too much attention to the egoistic aspect of the question. In natural man this moral judgment is most strongly manifested if he himself be the party suffering from the immoral act. But this restriction of the idea to one's own injury is not necessary. On the contrary, where man is changed from his natural state (*i.e.* of isolation) into that of membership in a certain association, where he becomes a *Ζῶον πολιτικόν*, this judgment, although with less spontaneity, is likewise provoked and occasioned by the malicious injury of others.

Disapproval of an Act Entails Disapproval of its Author. — This diapproving judgment prevails primarily against the act. But of necessity it extends also to its author; for an act cannot be contemplated independently of its author. If the author is not known individually, there appears always in the act, although in hazy and indistinct outlines, a mental picture of the author. Whether we may start from the acceptance of extensive freedom in human action, or from the assumption of complete determinism (the "operari sequitur esse" of the Scholastics and Schopenhauer), the deed appears as the product of the nature or character of its author. In our disapprobation of the act we also always express our disapproval of the personality of its author.[2]

The Possible and Proper Methods of Expressing this Disapproval. — But this disapprobation in the abstract [3] does not reveal the

relative to usury has undergone many changes. Binding even confuses the moral rule with the comprehension by the same of the individual case. This inclusion of the act with those coming under the rule is frequently more difficult and is subject to more changes in "fashionable opinion" than in principles of law. Why this is so, appears later.

But as far as the sovereignty of the individual conscience is concerned, a thing disputed by Binding, this reproduction of Fichte's theory of morality is untenable according to the modern researches. The conscience of the individual is a product of history and of the morality of the entire nation. *Cf. Hegel*, "Philosophie des Rechts" (3d Ed.), pp. 192 *et seq.; Lotze*, "Mikrokosmos" (3d Ed.), II, pp. 308 *et seq.; Alaux*, "Ueber die Wandlungen des Moral im Menschengeschlechte" ("Vortrag", Basel, 1879); *Baumann*, "Handbuch der Moral und Abriss der Rechtsphilosophie" (1879); *Von Ihering* in *Schmoller's* "Jahrbuch für Gesetzgebung", etc. (N. S. Vol. 6, 1882), pp. 1 *et seq.;* and especially in contradiction to Binding, see *Jellinek*, p. 123.

[2] This answers the objection made by Hugo Meyer to the reprobation theory that disapprobation of the person of the author of the act yet remains. On the other hand, that punishment is *primarily* applied against the act and not against its author has been maintained ever since antiquity by many of the most profound thinkers.

[3] *Seber*, "Gründe und Zwecke der Strafe" (1876), p. 11, regards the principle of disapprobation as not sufficient. Although it can be conceded

manner of its concrete expression. It could possibly confine itself to the mere mental processes of the one disapproving; or on the other hand it could manifest itself in a destruction of the author, which except for this would be without purpose. For the destruction of an object without ulterior purpose is of necessity the strongest expression that there is nothing for which it should exist, — that it is of no moment, and is thus the strongest expression of absolute disapproval. Reserving the various methods for the expression of this disapproval, we will seek first to establish the extent of the justification of this possibility of expression.[4]

The more doubt involved in the moral judgment of an act, the more reserved and the less manifest must be its disapproval. But, vice versa, in the case of obviously grave violations of morality, wherever there exists a moral community this judgment necessarily becomes a public one. For (as even Kant believes), morality is not a thing prepared for all times and exclusive of everything else; it is a product of the history of humanity and thus a product of the community. The moral judgment of the individual is founded upon tradition, upon the moral judgment of others. This necessarily presupposes a certain communication of the moral judgment, without which tradition would be impossible — in other words, it presupposes a certain *publicity* of the moral judgment. Here again logic is in accord with the actual facts. In the case of grave violations of morality, in the case of serious crimes, public disapproval, as already remarked, manifests itself irresistibly. *Public disapproval* therefore, in a manner more or less formal or informal, is within certain limits and in certain cases

that the inviolability of certain fundamental maxims of morality must be continually emphasized, he believes proof was yet needed that this emphasis can be made *only* by punishment. However, this proof is lacking in Seber's own arguments, which (p. 19) amount to a paraphrase of my own, yet (*cf.* especially p. 29) with the elements of uncertainty that with the fundamental principle of criminal law — emphasis of certain fundamental moral principles — there are coördinated the principles of deterrence and reformation. The result is that in reality the asserted principle loses its true meaning and can with difficulty be distinguished from a moderate principle of deterrence. The proof desired by Seber is already furnished, if it is proven that in general punishment is requisite. There is no need to show that punishment is absolutely necessary in each individual case, since the law must as a rule ignore the special features of the individual case. And this is certain, that if criminal justice should at the present time suspend its functions, morality would thereby receive its deathblow.

[4] According to our view, that which we are accustomed to call punishment (*e.g.* deprivation of freedom or property) is only the *amount of punishment*. *Cf.* the derivation and earlier meaning of the word "Strafe" ("punishment").

the necessary attribute of morality; and since without morality (as will be at once conceded), a human community could not exist and the progress of humanity would be altogether impossible, the public disapproval of certain acts contrary to morality is an unconditional right.

Every disapprobation of an act, or (what amounts to the same thing) of its author, has for the latter at least the consequence that he is lowered in the moral estimation of those who disapprove. One cannot treat him entirely as if he had not given reason for disapprobation. If it were desired to do this, then the disapprobation should be removed by some "factum contrarium." If disapproval of an evil act did not find some real expression (this may consist merely in the withdrawal of the confidence previously reposed in its author), complete forgiveness applied *universally* would abolish morality; for this would render necessary the assumption that an act contrary to morality was not prejudicial to the moral standing of its author. If the precepts of the Founder of Christianity commend something different, it must be remembered that in part they are expressed in the excessively emphatic manner characteristic of oral statements. When directed towards an individual case, this stronger method of statement can seem justifiable; and these precepts were primarily intended to govern the private intercourse of a small circle who called themselves the "Children of God." The application of the moral principles of Christianity to the Christian State was left to the future. But even in case of the most complete forgiveness (forgiveness in the sense that not the slightest intentional evil accrue to the wrongdoer as the result of his act), yet there always remains a certain shadow as a result of the evil deed, which entails for him a disadvantage if he lay claim to full fellowship with us. This is something we cannot avoid, even if we so desire.

Now if the violation of morality is a very grave one, so that the wrongdoer assumes the rôle of an antagonist to that moral system which deals out rules of conduct to individuals as conditions of their existence and further development, it comes to pass that the moral community regards the wrongdoer as no longer a part of itself. Every association has the right of expulsion as against the individual who does not observe the rules which it regards as the conditions of its existence. Christ himself said in such a case: "Let him be unto thee as a heathen and a publican."[5] Since

[5] N. T., Matthew, xviii, 17.

in the early periods of the human race, law and morality are the same, it is quite logical that a serious violation of law, of morality, brings upon the wrongdoer exclusion from the legal association, *i.e.* outlawry. For this reason (as Fichte has correctly observed), everywhere the original punishment was outlawry. This outlawry, as was naturally the case in the rather loose association of the old German " Edelhöfe " and " Freihöfe," might affect only the party injured, who thereby obtained an unlimited right of revenge. It might, as was the case in the city of Rome with its closely crowded population, entail an immediate outlawry in respect to all (as " sacer ").

Accordingly *every* expression of disapproval, even where it involves complete destruction of the offender, or any other conceivable injury to him as an expression of this disapproval,[6] is justice in respect to the offender: "Jus læsi infinitum." The latter cannot complain, since he it was who first severed the bonds of morality and law. This is the true and correct meaning of the principle (which Hegel indeed did not fully comprehend) that the method and measure of punishment belong to the realm of chance. Hegel herein overlooked the fact that history also gives prominence to a certain principle of justice. A remnant of the original conception always continued to exist. Even the strongest adherent of the principle of justice in its ordinary sense, which would measure the justice of punishment in accordance with its method and amount, cannot to-day fail to perceive that *to a certain* extent the criminal and his sphere of rights are placed at the *disposition* of society. Otherwise it would be impossible to in any way account for the purpose of reforming the criminal, etc. Any recognition of a relative purpose in punishment necessarily carries with it the principle that the criminal may to a certain extent be placed at the discretionary disposition of society.

Disapproval is Not Retribution. — The history of criminal law exemplifies the foregoing idea in its course of gradual

[6] *Cf.* also *C. L. Von Haller*, "Restauration der Staatswissenschaften", II, c. 34. On this point I modify my earlier view. I had found a justification for the violation of the sphere of rights of the individual in this, viz.: that in other cases (*e.g.* in war) the individual may be sacrificed for the sake of the community ("Grundlagen des Strafrechts", p. 76). But such cases are different. The individual and his property may be sacrificed only in so far as voluntary acquiescence would be of *service*. Punishment is essentially coercion. This applies especially against the attempt at a justification of punishment in *Ed. Hertz*, "Das Unrecht und seine Formen" (1880), p. 48.

advancement.[7] In the beginning, vengeance knew of no restraint. Retaliation in kind ("lex talionis") furnished something akin to a fixing of the amount for certain cases (but by no means for all). It was a very imperfect measure, but nevertheless a measure which is characterized by a certain ideal symmetry. But, as history shows, this is not a fundamental principle, but rather a principle limiting the application of the dominant principle of destruction. A readily conceivable change has been able to raise the idea of retaliation to an independent principle. It is absolutely impossible for any one who has given close consideration to the history of criminal law even to speak still of the possibility of a principle of retaliation. There is sense in saying that evil things and persons must be destroyed. It is possible only for one who considers himself an administrator of divine justice to say: "I do an injury, — because evil must be requited with evil." This idea is of later origin, and was long ago proven to be inapplicable for the criminal law of the State.

It is only if one cease to regard retaliation as the causing of evil or sorrow, and regard it merely as tending to lessen progress and hinder development, that it has a rational meaning, and furthermore a meaning in harmony with the idea of disapprobation. If to live and act morally is in accordance with the general rule of existence, then the opposite must impede and hinder the author of the immoral act,[8] just as he who lives contrary to the laws of health suffers injury for so doing. The moral system abandons the evil doer or, what amounts to the same thing, it turns against him; but to find its principle in causing pain to the evil doer, is logically impossible and is the opposite of morality.

The more firmly the moral system is established, the less vigorous need be its expression of diapproval — for in many respects this is supplanted by the natural reaction of the moral system. If

[7] *Ulrici*, "Gott und der Mensch", II, 1 (1873), p. 393, although he acknowledges that the one element common to all punishments is disapproval, rejects my argument because pure disapproval, historically speaking, did not arise until relatively later and public punishment was chiefly introduced for the suppression of private vengeance. The first point, however, merely corresponds to the law of development; and as far as the second point is concerned, it may well be asked whether vengeance also does not contain the element of disapprobation. Ulrici would regard vengeance merely as retribution and absolutely repudiates both. Then punishment inflicted by the State would be a completely new principle not in harmony with history, a thing which is historically false.

[8] This opinion is expressed by *Merkel*. See *ante*, § 99.

the thief has difficulty in finding some one to receive the stolen goods, because general honesty subjects the title of a vendor to a scrupulous test, theft hereby comes to be something which in most cases does not profit the thief but is only to his detriment. If to the cheat, the swindler and the conscienceless speculator, the doors of the homes of honorable people (who form by far the great majority) are closed, then in many cases the expression of formal disapproval is perhaps superfluous. Consequently punishments become milder as civilization increases,[9] *i.e.* a civilization which signifies an advance not only in knowledge and refinement of enjoyment but also in morality. It is possible that in an ideal state of society the individual criminal might be left simply to the consequences of his own crime; or there might be applied the principle: Overcome evil not with evil but with good. Thus punishment, regarded as disapprobation, may be reconciled with Christianity, but regarded as retribution through human agencies, it is fundamentally the opposite of Christianity. For (as even Kant has fairly and candidly shown) the principle of retribution never permits forgiveness.

Various Phases of Disapprobation as Punishment. — In order that the disapproval of an act (and consequently of its author) may have that ideal effect of confirming the morality of those disapproving, it is necessary that the determination of the act and of its author be as exact as possible. Therefore a punishment inflicted upon a man innocent (or generally believed to be innocent) does not have the moral effect of punishment. Fear can be spread through the venting of rage against innocent people. But where a people is not completely enervated the ultimate effect of this fear will be directed against its author. A *just* punishment, however, strengthens the position of the legal system.

Moreover, it is in harmony with the character of punishment as disapprobation that in countries where there is a high degree of culture and refinement of feeling the trial and condemnation of the criminal constitute a part, and often a very important part,

[9] There is even recognized in the German Criminal Code a punishment (frequently used in England) which consists entirely in public disapproval, — *reprimand.* Hugo Meyer, § 5, maintains that the essence of reprimand is not disapproval of the act but rather of its author (*i.e.* thus a mild form of suffering). However, this assertion is in itself a "petitio principii", and if reprimand is not a "humiliation of the offender" only secondarily, then why are all the special forms of humiliation therein eliminated? Why is the pillory not to-day a desirable form of punishment?

of the punishment.[10] If punishment were necessarily an external evil, there would be no explanation of the fact that in concrete cases the punishment may consist merely of a money fine or a few weeks' imprisonment.

The character of punishment, regarded primarily as disapprobation of the criminal act (and only secondarily as disapprobation of its author), makes it necessary that the expression of disapprobation be directly attached to the act itself as portrayed by the trial, — in other words, makes it necessary that the judicial sentence, which is nothing other than the fixing of the act in the minds of the public, substantially specify the punishment. It is contrary to the nature of criminal law to attempt in general to determine the punishment later, after observation of the character of the convict. We would say nothing here of the hypocrisy of prisoners, their unmanly actions, and their deceit of the prison officials. These are unfortunate conditions to which rise is given by the foolish modern movement (so totally at variance with history) to eliminate from the judicial sentence the fixing of the amount of the punishment, and to allow the duration of the punishment to be fixed later, after observation in the prison, or to remain for a time undetermined. As previously stated, the sentence of the criminal court *could* contain an abstract significance, without having an actual result of a penal nature; but in this case the actual result of the evil act should be affixed publicly and be of general application,—at least it should be fixed independently of anything else. The judicial sentence loses its influence upon the mass of the people when the actual result of the act is connected with something else, *i.e.* when it depends upon the discretion of prison officials which is not manifest to the public and which cannot be publicly verified. The individual criminal may be reformed, to the heart's desire, but among the masses of the people crime will continue to flourish. However, if the punishment were actually retribution of evil, *i.e.* of the wickedness of the criminal, then no objection could be raised to first making a long observation of this wickedness, since the deed of the criminal does not afford an adequate criterion for its accurate measurement.

Furthermore, the punishment of disapprobation can never be supplanted by suffering which comes upon the criminal as a matter of chance, even if this is a result of the crime and reveals (as they

[10] This opinion expressed by me in the "Grundlage des Strafrechts" p. 4, had been advanced by *Heinze*, p. 326, as stated above.

say) the "hand of God." If a thief breaking into a house falls from a ladder and as a result of the fall becomes a cripple for life, we would not for this reason spare him from punishment any more than we would the highwayman who lost an arm or his sight as a result of the vigorous defense of his opponent. If temporal punishment were merely the representative of divine punishment, then in such cases it would be presumptuous to desire further punishment. If it were the retribution of evil with evil, then in such cases, to punish would be senseless.

The True Purposes of Punishment. — The essential matter is *active disapproval* rather than the pain of the criminal. Therefore, whether or not the criminal in the individual case finds the punishment an evil makes no difference. He may even regard it as a benefit, — as *e.g.* perhaps in these times a criminal, who is not completely pernicious, regards with favor the prison which keeps him from further wrongdoing and furnishes him instruction. We should not for this reason change the punishment, so as to cause him suffering. According to Plato's ideal conception, the offender *should always* regard the punishment as a benefit. If pain were the essential element, why should we to-day be so violently opposed to torment and torture of convicts? This would be nothing other than a mistaken feeling of humanity, and there would still arise the question whether a short punishment entailing severe physical suffering or even mutilation, where this does not affect the capacity to earn a living (*e.g.* cutting off the ears) is not preferable to imprisonment lasting for years. The fact that we find nothing repulsive in the physical destruction of the criminal in capital punishment, but are offended with torture and suffering commanded for any other purposes, has as a matter of fact its deep reason, which none of the previous criminal theories has explained.

However, the treatment of the offender must always be expressive of disapproval; and so far, but only so far, it is proper that the punishment should contain a disadvantage for the condemned. Criminals should not constitute a favored and pampered class (this is a consideration which obviously opposes the extreme deductions of the theory of reformation), although other praiseworthy purposes might be better attained through such good treatment. The distinction must always remain, that as a general thing it is preferable *not to be punished.* A penal institution must never assume the character of an institution for instruction. However great may be the attention given to purposes of reformation, and consequently to the individual criminal, this attention is only a secondary one. The primary element is attention to the necessity of public disapproval (or if one prefers so to term it, repression). Thus Krohne[11] states, in regard to the last international Congress for the Improvement of Prisons and the tendencies there observed: "With all the compassion which is aroused by every human failure, be it moral, mental or physical, the men who to-day are concerned in prison reform are primarily governed by the opinion that the vital question is the *defense of society*."

As Hälschner and others have correctly stated, punishment is primarily to be conceived as a *suffering* of the criminal, — as coercion brought to bear upon him, to the extent that the criminal is involuntarily subjected thereto, but not in the sense that he should be tortured. In disapprobation there is an active manifestation of the one disapproving. Punishment cannot, as Heinze would have it,[12] be conceived chiefly as a *payment* by the criminal to the community. If this were so, then voluntary acceptance of the external method of punishment fixed by the State for the case in question would be the most perfect penal atonement. The suicide of a person condemned to death, instead of being prevented as is now done, would necessarily be encouraged. Only when the criminal regards himself as a means for furthering the purposes of humanity, and only when he has learned to regard the punishment as rational, can the punishment be conceived as a payment. It is only in this sense that I have previously expressed the opinion that the criminal must undergo retribution. It is with this just as with reformation; the ideal punishment will reform in fact the offender, but nevertheless the chief purpose of punishment is not reformation.[13]

§ 105. **Private Vengeance as an Expression of Disapprobation.** — We have already remarked that the earliest punishment consisted of a dissolution of the legal tie existing between the injured party (or as the case may be, the community) and the criminal. Accord-

11. *Krohne*, "Der gegenwartige Stand der Gefängnisswissenschaft" in *Dochow's* and *Liszt's* "Zeitschrift" (I), 1881, p. 58.

12 *Heinze*, pp. 322 *et seq.*

13 For the reasons mentioned, voluntary submission to a punishment inflicted by the State is not sufficient. Public disapproval cannot arrive at expression without a judgment. Therefore, only a very subordinate importance can be assumed by waiver in criminal procedure.

ingly, if every punishment substituted for this dissolution were a benefit, or as a matter of history the earliest right afforded the criminal, then the statement of Fichte in regard to the citizen's important right to be punished would not be so paradoxical as it seems. The development of punishment by compositions, which we are able to trace in Germanic law, confirms this absolutely. There is an apparent contradiction in the fact that later, and especially to-day, the criminal may not escape punishment by going into exile. But exile later and also to-day has no longer the significance of the old "Rechtlosigkeit" (deprivation of all rights, outlawry) or (to use the language of the old Norse or Germanic law) "Friedlosigkeit" (being without the "peace"). This was an entirely different matter.

Disapprobation as a punishment, when inflicted by the individual, lacks not only (as is obvious) a definite objective amount, but it also lacks a general recognition that the occasion of its infliction is a just one. Such a punishment is often very hard to distinguish from a mere unlawful attack; and it is very easy for the criminal, in order to avail himself of the assistance of others in his own defense, to set up the pretext that the attack upon him is unlawful. Thus private vengeance becomes a standing feud between various families, and the community or the king finds it well to intervene, and out of this intervention there later arises the taking over of this private vengeance by the State. This is furthered by the increasing realization that the legal security or insecurity of one individual involves that of the others. Vengeance becomes punishment. From disapproval subjectively manifested there arises one of more general recognition. It becomes liberated from its egoistic character, — a liberation that is not merely accidental but which is in accord with the laws of development.[1]

Punishment a Right of Society Rather than of the State. — Upon this transfer of the criminal law to the State, there arises, from the right to punish, a duty. That which the individual has heretofore possessed as a right is taken over by the State, as it were, with trustworthy hands — for careful administration and not for arbitrary exercise or neglect. In the hands of the State, this right becomes a duty — a duty not only of the State but also

[1] This process of transfer is excellently described and explained by *C. L. Von Haller*, "Restauration des Staatswissenschaften", II, pp. 241 *et seq.* (c. 34).

of *society*. It necessarily follows that the State cannot forego punishment at its discretion, as can the individual.[2] As far as it is able, the State must prosecute actively. It is in the same position as the individual whom custom will not allow to permit the murderer of his kinsman to escape if he has him in his power or to leave to chance or a third party the work of vengeance. Exile is not a right,[3] but a mere " de facto " possibility for the individual. With the passing from memory of that original condition in which criminal law was a right of the individual or possibly of all, the State becomes less able to consider or assume that the mere privilege of harming the criminal entails for the latter a real consequence, even apart from the fact that this involves a possibility of degenerating into the old barbarous custom of vengeance.

Desirability of Prosecutions Initiated by Private Parties. — There always remains, however, a certain recollection of the fact that criminal justice was merely *transferred*[4] to the State, and did not belong to it originally. In a case in which popular opinion regards a private person as primarily concerned in the punishment and the public right of the State as only secondarily concerned, a pardon or dismissal of the case is considered a wrong; *e.g.* in case of an insult, if some satisfaction has not been privately rendered the injured party or his forgiveness or his consent to the pardon has not been obtained. It is also well for the State authorities to bear in mind that the criminal law, although in a rather crude form, is older than the State itself, and that it must not be used to further temporary purposes, *e.g.* that it must not be used or misused perhaps to punish those having one tendency and to spare those having another. If criminal law were in all respects an original attribute of the State, such a course would not be so injurious and demoralizing. The preservation to the public or to the injured party of a possibility of a supplementary prosecution, even against the will of the sovereign or the State, is a very wholesome corrective to that opinion (which may easily arise) that the excellence of the

[2] The individual is often also under the not less actual coercion of morality.

[3] That for a long time a different condition obtained among the Romans has been stated above; but this is not evidence against the argument in the text, since it was *not until later* that this right of exile arose, when the pride of the Roman citizen no longer allowed an *active* exercise of the criminal power.

[4] *E. Von Hartmann*, "Phänomenologie", p. 202, justly calls attention to the fact that this process of transfer has by no means completely ended. It is in part upon this that there depends the continued existence of duelling in spite of the criminal laws.

party in power can offset minor breaches of the criminal law which become intolerable when repeated. As the eminent French jurist, Faustin Hélie,[5] has stated: criminal prosecution rests partly with the community and not exclusively with the State. The supplementary complaint instituted by a private citizen is (if guarded with sufficient precautions) a proposition justifiable from the viewpoints both of history and of logic.

In the case of grave violations of the duty to punish crime, the idea that this despotic power of the criminal authorities injures society manifests itself in an elementary way in lynch law and acts of violence. This also has a bearing upon the fact that legislation in criminal matters must not depart too far from popular sentiment, and that in criminal legislation there may be seen a direct reflection of the civilization of the people.

The objection can always be raised — and in fact has been raised — that disapprobation contains nothing that makes its *practical* application necessary — at least not in the form of criminal procedure, and even less in the actual infliction of the punishment. If only disapprobation were involved, one might in legislation go no farther than to set up general principles which would disapprove of one act or another. However, in this objection it has been overlooked that there would be no recognizable inclusion of the act under these general conceptions or principles. It is the vengeance of the injured party, the punishment inflicted by the State, which first declares that this *concrete* act deserves disapproval and is absolutely reprehensible. This immediately becomes clear if one considers that there may be various grounds of extenuation for acts which possess the external elements of crime. A concrete act does not actually become a crime until this character is, as it were, stamped upon it by judicial decision. The reason why one at the present time is able to conceive that a judicial decree is not necessary in order for certain acts (*e.g.* aggravated cases of murder, etc.) to be regarded as crimes by the public at large, is that one forgets the long tradition of judicial decrees which obtains as a decision for the individual case in advance of the actual decision. It would soon become otherwise if the giving of judicial decisions concerning individual criminal cases should be generally discontinued. To become convinced of

[5] "Traité de l'instruction criminelle", II, n. 473. The French Court of Cassation has also stated: "L'action publique appartient à la société et non au fonctionnaire public chargé par la loi de l'exercer."

this, it is only necessary to consider how falsely in the absence of established rules and regulations, the general public would decide as to the questions of responsibility and the special circumstances of extenuation (coercion, error, necessity, etc.).

§ 106. **Summary.** — Summing up the foregoing statements, the purpose of criminal law is as follows: "Certain fundamental principles of morality should be publicly and notoriously characterized by the civil community as inviolable by attaching to actions which are contrary to these principles an impressive mark of disapprobation. This mark also necessarily affects the author of the action, since a deed and its author cannot be contemplated separately. This is simply a result of the fact that the civil community is obliged to give practical recognition to the fundamental maxims of morality."

The Idea of Disapprobation Expressed by Other Writers. — The foregoing is not very different from the recent statement of my honored friend, Hugo Meyer. He, however, is unable to free himself completely from the traditional view that the scope of criminal law and the amount of the punishment should *also* be derived to a certain extent from absolute justice. For this reason he often speaks of retribution and conceives punishment in the sense of Hugo Grotius as "malum passionis ob malum actionis."[1] His words are as follows: "The legal basis of punishment consists simply in this: It results from the very nature of the State that in cases of necessity it give expression to the inadmissibility of actions prejudicial to the civil community by the infliction of punishment." The statement of Montesquieu[2] also amounts to the idea of disapprobation, where he says that in the State which corresponds to his ideal, "La plus grande peine d'une mauvaise action sera d'en être convaincu." The statement of the great Leibnitz (given above) also expresses the idea that exclusion from the community, a thing resulting from disapprobation, is the ideal essence of punishment.[3]

[1] "Lehrbuch des deutschen Strafrechts" (3d Ed., 1881), § 2, p. 9.

[2] "Esprit des lois", VI. Ch. 9. *Cf.* also ch. 21: ". . . les formalités des jugements y sont des punitions." That disapprobation and an artificial "infamie" are something different, scarcely needs to be asserted.

[3] The profound and eminently practical *Francis Lieber* (Franz Lieber) also says (in his article "On Penal Law", printed in his "Miscellaneous Writings" (Philadelphia, 1881), II, pp. 464–494, esp. p. 478): "A society in which every sort of wrong might be permitted with impunity would necessarily lose its ethical character. . . . The expression of *public disapproval* would be missing." *Cf.* also the very recent system of "Rechts-

As soon as the purpose of punishment is no longer directed towards the person of the criminal, but rather society or the community is regarded as that which is aided or protected by the punishment, and the criminal is regarded merely as something incidental — which he certainly is, as contrasted to the community — this theory necessarily gains favor. The theory of reformation treats the criminal as the chief goal towards which the purpose of punishment is aimed. It is the same with the theory of retribution. According to the latter, the *criminal* should receive the desert of his acts in the punishment.

The deterrence theory is the only one which harmonizes with our view in regarding society, and not the criminal, as the chief issue. But, on one hand, it takes too mechanical and base a view of the relation between the criminal and society, and on the other hand it pays too little attention to history. It is quite proper, however, (as Hugo Meyer also maintains) to ascribe the first place among the relative theories to the purpose of deterrence (or, as we prefer to say, of *turning away*) the public from crime. Criminal legislation which, in respect to its means of punishment, is based upon the deterrent theory, is at any rate, as history shows, capable of existing; but legislation which is based exclusively and consistently upon the theory of reformation would soon render itself impossible.

Moreover, credence may not be given (as is done by the theory of deterrence in its too base conception of the purpose of criminal law) to the belief that the criminal law has its chief effect upon the criminal world or those who are irresistibly disposed to crime because of evil training, degeneracy, etc.; or that passion which has become strong and overwhelming can be held in check through the existence and operation of a criminal statute. In this respect the objections to the deterrent theory are rather well taken. Fear of an indefinite although severe future evil can but seldom counteract the impulse to crime. Therefore, it is a great mistake, in times when grave crimes are prevalent, to expect any very important result from liberal use of capital punishment, flogging, etc. The history of the 1700 s illustrates the result of a harsh

philosophie" by *Lasson*, 1881 (especially p. 533, § 46), where punishment is designated as the victory of reason over its opposite. Yet in Lasson, punishment rather uncertainly shifts to retribution, since apparently the amount of punishment is to be derived from absolute justice. Lasson, moreover, as is usual with most philosophers, treats the subject at long distance and with only a bird's-eye view.

criminal system destructive of sentiment. The truth is rather as correctly pointed out by Schopenhauer, with that clearness of vision which he displays in so many particulars. He says that perhaps the chief effect of criminal legislation is that, upon the whole, it preserves the morality of the better elements of the people; that true criminal punishment is that which brings about "exclusion from the great freemasonry of honorable people,"[4] and that public opinion judges a single misstep with great and perhaps too relentless severity.[5]

Kinds and Methods of Punishment. — For these reasons, as the criminal statistics of various countries show, it makes no very considerable difference, in respect to the more heinous crimes, whether, *within certain limits*, the penalties are administered in one manner or in another.

But on the other hand, in respect to the less heinous cases, blunders of legislation are far more important. If here the proper distinction between honorable actions and dishonorable actions is not drawn, and if *e.g.* persons who are generally respected but who have failed to comply with some mere regulation of the State, — perhaps even from considerations of conscience — are treated as common criminals, one cannot help wondering if in such a case an axe is not laid at the root of morality and the legal system, and if the echo of its stroke is interpreted in the criminal world as showing that no very essential difference exists between honorable people and itself.[6] Therefore, legislation in dealing with offenses against mere police regulations should be more sparing with those penalties of imprisonment with which it is now so liberal, at least as alternative punishments (at the discretion of the judge).[7] As quite correctly stated by Von Ihering, "It is not disobedience but rather attack upon the conditions of the life of society which constitutes the essence of crime. Therefore, where the question

[4] Punishment for violation of police regulation is taken up later.

[5] "Grundprobleme der Ethik" (2 Ed., pp. 190, 187). Lieber (p. 479) says that *insecurity* is not the worst evil resulting from frequent non-punishment of grave crimes, or as we would add, actions deserving punishment, but rather the general lowering of the moral standard. For this reason, although not for this reason exclusively, the certainty of punishment is more important than its amount. The fact that a thing *will* be punished is more important than *how* it will be punished. Naturally this principle must be taken "cum grano salis."

[6] For this reason that system of tutelage which is now so popular and which requires coercion, *i.e.* requires punishment, is ultimately demoralizing.

[7] "Der Zweck im Rechte", I (1879), p. 481. *Cf.* also *Schulze*, "Leitfaden der Entwicklung der philosophischen Principien des bürgerlichen und peinlichen Rechts" (1813), p. 259.

is merely to overcome disobedience, only those punishments should be employed which, to the greatest degree, render impossible the confusion of such a case with cases of punishment for crime." Lieber [8] directly opposes this conception of disobedience. "One should avoid any appearance of punishing as if for the reason that the transgression or offender has ventured to be disobedient. In other words, punishment is inflicted because the authorities represent the purpose of the common good, and *therefore* disobedience to the authorities is an offense, *i.e.* is immoral."

According to the foregoing argument, anything which entails a disadvantage for the party to be punished is "in abstracto" applicable as a means of punishment. For every disadvantage done to the author of an act, *on account of the act,* expresses a disapprobation of the same, and that which is taken or diminished is merely something which is generally regarded as a gift of the legal system, — since the right, in case of extremity, extends even to destruction of the criminal. However, the most perfect kind of punishment is that by which the criminal himself is brought to disapprove of the act that has been done, inwardly renounces it, and is reformed. Here the objective disapprobation of the act becomes a subjective one. But it always remains as the essential element,[9] on account of the primarily objective character of disapprobation, that public opinion should regard the action usually taken as a sufficient disapprobation, and that not too much consideration be paid to the personality of the individual criminal. By the last mentioned consideration, justice incurs the danger of losing its supremacy, certainty and dignity, and of degenerating into a system of physical suffering and breaking of the will, which serves as a basis for numerous blunders. Punishments involving physical suffering which bear the stamp of a seeking after individual vengeance are at variance with quiet and deliberate disapprobation through the public authorities. The same is the case with punishments which are usually applied to animals, since disapprobation has meaning only as against the acts of rational beings and it is necessary that the expression of such disapprobation be retained.

The same objections may be raised to punishments which are so

[8] *Lieber* (Note 27, *ante*), p. 493.

[9] Therefore it is no objection to a method of punishment that certain individuals of a type still existing do not regard it as a punishment, as a murderer must be sentenced to death, if the law prescribes capital punishment for murder, although he committed the murder from weariness of life so as to die on the scaffold. The State in punishing may not accommodate itself too much to the criminal.

excessive as to immediately arouse pity, because pity dispels disapprobation. This also applies to punishments which are appropriate only under quite exceptional circumstances. This last objection, together with others, may be raised to punishment by flogging which is now so popular. On the other hand punishment by deprivation of property is not objectionable merely because one individual feels it but little or because, in the case of others who have no means of paying, it must be changed into some other penalty. For both reasons, however, it cannot represent the higher and sharper degree of disapprobation. That capital punishment is not *absolutely* improper follows directly from the original right of destruction. But whether it is relatively improper, *i.e.* improper for a given period of time and a certain stage of culture, is quite a different question, for it is by no means an absolute requirement of ethics. The *means* of punishment is, as we have already remarked, a part of the question of the *amount* of the punishment, and that this is dependent upon time and circumstances is obviously manifest.

§ 107. **The Degree of Punishment.** — But if, as according to our view, the criminal is placed at the absolute disposal of the community, so far as concerns the expression of its disapprobation, what becomes of that *justice* which we feel is requisite in the fixing of the degree or amount of the punishment?

The answer to this question is simple. This justice appears only by considering the *historical element* in criminal law. It has nothing to do with the *basis* of criminal law. Punishment and crime (*i.e.* immoral acts detrimental to the conditions upon which depend the life of society and therewith the life of the State) are not commensurable. If they were commensurable, then the theory of retribution would be tenable, at any rate theoretically, if not practically. For example, how can one balance the larcenous taking of a purse with a year's imprisonment? And even in the death penalty — the favorite example to adduce — the balance is very imperfect, at least in many cases. If a murderer lies in wait for his victim and by a single well-directed blow strikes him dead, is such a death physically equal to the death on the scaffold with the mental tortures of a long period of expectation? We must cease to speak of the justice of punishments, unless we either cease to punish many cases now punished or unconsciously measure out the punishment in accordance with historical tradition. Criminal law is no more able to estimate crimes than the governmental authorities are able to place an absolute value on property and industry. But there is always a justness in treating like matters in a similar manner or in like matters producing a like result. And so in criminal punishments it is tradition which furnishes the justness.

While the valuation of the degree of criminality is primarily arbitrary, yet tradition allows considerable room for the exercise of discretion. No one can say (unless he refers to the very detailed provisions of a definite statute) whether, for a certain crime, two and one half or three years in prison should be the proper penalty. Nothing can be said as to absolute justice or injustice in regard to the question of solitary confinement or ordinary confinement for a prisoner or his employment at one task or another. Within this rather extensive province the State is given a free hand, since the administration of justice should be made to serve the welfare of the public and to pursue freely purposes beneficial to the community. Herein good results may be obtained from the purpose of turning the criminal into a useful member of society.

§ 108. **What Acts should be Punished.** — From the principle of disapprobation which we have adopted, it follows that it is only in certain grave violations of morality that the voice of public disapproval is given general manifestation; it does not follow that this disapproval extends to *every* violation of morality. The State is not the blind instrument of an absolute principle. It does not adopt the maxim: "Fiat justitia pereat mundus", but rather the principle that justice prevails that thereby the world may continue to exist.[1] Our principle is absolute only in the sense first mentioned.

As the individual may have reasons to be sparing of his moral judgments, so is it even to a greater degree with the State. The disapproval of the State is an authoritative one. On one hand it presupposes the utmost precision and certainty in the judgment of the act, and on the other hand it is conclusive as against the individual. For this latter reason this disapproval must extend only

[1] Herein the principle adopted differs very essentially from all the absolute principles heretofore advanced, in which it is quite impossible to preserve room for a discussion of purposes of expediency without a breach of logic. Even Hegel does not seem to have understood this point. It is in this sense that I have stated that punishment is a designed and artificial measure for the individual case ("Grundlagen", p. 9). Heinze (p. 298, note), who indeed recognizes a reprobation theory as a logical development of Hegel's principle, has therefore misunderstood me, since he seems to regard this "designed and artificial measure" as a deviation from the absolute principle of punishment.

to a relatively small number of acts. Otherwise it will eliminate the freedom of the individual, and in so doing destroy the source of morality and of voluntary devotion. At the same time it would destroy that moderate and proper egoism which ultimately operates for the good of all and is a mighty impetus towards human progress.

Naturally this disapproval should extend preferably towards acts which violate the rights of others, — this is in accordance with the historical origin of the criminal law of the State in the vengeance of the individual. Acts whose disadvantageous results almost exclusively or even generally fall upon the author of the act are not the objects of the disapproval of the State, although they have a remote effect upon the interest of others and of the public at large. This is also in accord with many practical reasons, such as difficulty of determining the questions of fact, of guilt, the imperfect equipment of the public for the discovery of the act, etc.

Since the disapprobation of the State entails a disadvantage for the party toward whom it is directed, and since it always (in criminal procedure) operates by virtue of numerous means of coercion and entails much expense, or at least loss of time to the parties concerned, and since it imposes a very severe temporary evil even upon innocent suspects — *e.g.* imprisonment, temporary loss of reputation, — it is always an evil in itself. Where unlawful or immoral acts find a sufficient disapproval in some other way or fail to attain the intended result (particularly because of the milder remedies of private law), it is reasonable and indeed necessary that the punishments of the State be dispensed with.

The Principle of Parsimony in Punishment. — The aspect of criminal law from the viewpoint of national economy is important. In former times human unhappiness and pain were squandered lavishly. Beccaria is entitled to credit for having first brought to attention comprehensively [2] the principle of the greatest possible parsimony with penalties and the superfluity of many punishments. Where other means are effective for the realization of the law the use of punishment is inexcusable, since, as correctly stated by Von Ihering,[3] it recoils upon society. Thibaut [4] indeed

[2] This phase of the subject finds obvious application to the means and the amount of punishment. *Cf. Wahlberg*, "Criminalistische und nationalökonomische Gesichtspunkte mit Rücksicht auf das deutsche Reichsstrafrecht" (1872), pp. 96 *et seq.*

[3] "Der Zweck im Rechte", I, p. 477; *cf.* p. 362.

[4] "Beiträge zur Kritik der Feuerbach'schen Theorie" (1802), p. 103.

called the criminal law a " testimonium paupertatis " which the authorities of the State exhibit. We would at least assert that every new criminal statute is a certificate of poverty for the moral condition of society. The disapprobation of the State is the artificial and organized disapproval of an act and is necessary only when there is not sufficient spontaneous disapproval on the part of unorganized society.[5]

Consideration should also be given to tradition or history. There is no more an absolute principle of justice for the choice of the acts for which punishment is to be inflicted, than there is for determining the means of punishment. There exists, however, a *relative* principle of justice, in the sense that acts which possess the same elements of immoral or detrimental significance may not be given different treatment, and that the State may not act inconsistently with the history of the people in respect to the choice of acts to be punished. Inconsistent action of this character creates the opinion that criminal justice is not the result of an inevitable necessity but rather of despotic action and possibly of error, and that it is not the expression of moral disapprobation, since moral opinions change very slowly. There are, to be sure, perverse traditions, just as there are perverted formations of physical being. But they can be recognized, if one survey long periods of the life of the people, and of their history, or if one is sufficiently unprejudiced to study closely the instructive example of the legal life of other peoples. Moreover, the significance of an act can vary with time and circumstances. And with individuals who are advanced in years, so with peoples having an old and well-established culture, general theories have but little influence upon practical action, which is already governed by detailed provisions regarded as fixed and inviolable. Perverted philosophical doctrines, pessimism, or extreme religious principles (*e.g.* the infallibility of the Pope), are not nearly so dangerous to-day as they would have been a few centuries ago or during the Middle Ages.

Punishments which do not possess a certain connection with tradition are somewhat odious, even when emanating from the spirit of well-intended moral reform. This is quite natural, as the people regard punishment as merely an echo of their own disapproval. Such acts appear to be merely acts of despotism and

[5] *Von Ihering*, pp. 478, 479, pertinently points out that *e.g.* in business, dishonesty may become so great that it cannot be counteracted by civil remedies without great injury to the community.

undermine the effectiveness of criminal justice in other cases. Too many punishments create indifference. One must not imagine that every coarse or vulgar act, every little violation of right, may demand suppression by punishment. The State, like the individual, must learn to endure many minor iniquities; it must remember that the world will not immediately come to an end and that Nature has guarded against the trees growing up to the sky, and it must have confidence in the firmness of its own position and in the natural effective power of moral opinions. Where there is a progressive increase of penal statutes, or where upon every occasion the public raises a general cry to help something by penal statutes or to increase the severity of the penal statutes, it is not well for freedom. For every penal statute is really one more inroad upon freedom. And the ultimate results may well be felt most keenly by those who have been the most noisy in demanding it. One may well ponder the maxim of Tacitus: "Pessima respublica, plurimæ leges."[6]

Expediency and Justice in Punishment. — While, upon our theory, the choice of acts to be punished by the State is determined by numerous reasons of expediency, yet there is here no antagonism between expediency and justice. It is rather that, from the standpoint of the State, expediency *is* at the same time justice. However, an act of which the moral sense of the people does not disapprove should not be punished. *Practically* speaking, this is an acceptance of the viewpoint adopted by Rossi and Mittermaier, where they seek to limit absolute justice by reasons of expediency, a correct standpoint and therefore a favorite of legislative proposals and legislative assemblies. But *theoretically* it is erroneous to weld together in such a manner absolute justice or retribution

[6] *Thibaut*, "Beiträge zur Kritik der Feuerbach'schen Theorie" (p. 100), says that the ruler does not stand so high and is not the representative of God upon the earth in the sense that he can enact criminal statutes in conflict with the sentiments of his subjects. To punish in violation of prevailing opinion is not conferring a benefit but rather is inflicting a punishment upon the nation. This matter is no longer an issue in constitutional States, but nevertheless temporary opinions and disturbances can be utilized to extort the approval of the representatives of the people to perverted criminal statutes in violation of the spirit of history and the entire legal system. A notable example of the opposite kind — resistance of temporary opinion — was furnished on Oct. 26, 1880, by the Minister of Justice of Holland, Moddermann, when in a long argument he undertook to disprove the alleged reasons for the reëstablishment of the death penalty. *Cf.* the translation of this argument in the "Münchener kritische Vierteljahrsschrift für Gesetzgebung und Rechtswissenschaft" (1881), Vol. 23, pp. 96 *et seq.*

and expediency. The State does *not* exercise *absolute* justice;[7] it exercises merely relative justice, and such it does when it defines the various cases to which the rigid principle of organized public disapprobation shall apply or shall not apply, in pursuance of purposes of expediency which for all of these cases are the same. It is not a departure from justice for purposes of expediency, but rather genuine and exact justice, when the State inflicts a lesser degree of punishment for an attempt at a crime than for the consummated crime, or when it pays so much attention to the outcome in a question of punishment, or when it does not punish a shameful seduction but does punish an act of violence which is possibly not so immoral, or when much refined dishonesty in business matters is ignored but he who steals a sausage from the market is haled before the criminal judge.

The fact is simply that the State (the law) measures illegal or immoral intention to a certain extent by external result. This same principle leads to the ignoring of that will which does not manifest itself in some external action that may be definitely recognized ("Cogitationis poenam nemo patitur!"); and it ultimately orders that less punishment be inflicted for the attempt than for the consummated act. Furthermore, this regard for a safe criterion of application, and one excluding despotism and purely individual opinion, also leads to the use of a somewhat rigid moral criterion, which is not sufficiently pliant to permit of its being applied to many relations which the individual at least *believes* can be passed upon judicially. The morality applied by the State in criminal law is somewhat crude. However, its gradual refinement in the course of time is not precluded. In-

[7] I am unable to concur in the attempts recently made by *Hugo Meyer* ("Die Gerechtigkeit im Strafrecht", "Gerichtssaal", 1881, pp. 101–153 and pp. 161–188; also published separately) to separate justice and utility or expediency in criminal law. This merely is a result of Meyer's conception of punishment as an act of retribution. A consistent use of the process of separation employed by Meyer would show that ultimately practically nothing is left for justice (even the justice of the "Cogitationis poenam nemo cogitur" tends to disappear), or that the just provisions proposed by Meyer rest just as much on grounds of expediency as those which he places in the division of expediency. The practical result of Hugo Meyer's view would be a tendency to extend the criminal law to many acts not now punishable. For the justice — *i.e.* according to Meyer, if one closely consider the inner immorality — is upon first glance the same in many acts not now punishable or only lightly punished as in many which are punishable and punished severely. This questionable tendency is also very prominent in Hugo Meyer's treatise. In opposition to Meyer, *cf. Merkel*, "Zeitschrift für die ges. Strafrechtswissenschaft", 1881, pp. 556–558.

deed, this appears decidedly possible if we compare the early Germanic criminal law with that of the present time. But morality in its narrower sense also advances and becomes more and more refined, at the same time that the coercive morality of the State progresses; and so, for immeasurable ages, the difference between them continues, and the application of principles to matters of detail in the fixing of the boundaries between them must always be attended with doubt and controversy.

Criminal Law and Morality in its Narrower Sense. — The fact that the morality of the State in its form and operation as criminal law is, as it were, a net of coarse mesh, has indeed one advantage, viz. that it can be relied upon with more certainty than that more discriminating moral judgment which the individual is in a position to pass (or believes that he is). But this character of the State's morality, together with the fact that the State, not being infallible, sometimes enacts radically erroneous penal measures, makes it possible for a criminal law to come into conflict with the moral sense of the individual and even of the entire population.[8] For these reasons, furthermore, it is possible that an act which is contrary to the criminal law may appear to be permissible (or even commanded) by a free moral judgment which is independent of the rule expressed in positive law.[9]

[8] But such conflicts are frequently based upon an illusion. Egoism, which will not bring itself into accord with general morality, flatters itself with the idea that its condition or its case requires an extraordinary decision.

[9] With this and with his statements previously referred to, *Hugo Meyer's* ("Lehrbuch", § 4) objection that in regard to no act could it be said in advance that it is immoral is refuted. I believe if this cannot be said in advance, it cannot be said afterwards. The only reason for which a judgment according to the fundamental principles of morality must be omitted is that the exact circumstances of the act, subjective and objective, are not known. It cannot be perceived why the imagination is not sufficiently able to portray the act in advance. For example, did there not take place in Rome many acts which are in conflict with the moral sentiments of one reading of them? Morality is not such an individual matter, as Hugo Meyer believes. If so, it would be unfortunate for the social life of mankind and for human development.

The question may also be asked, what basis can there be, other than morality, upon which Meyer founds his retributing justice. He rejects the derivation of criminal law solely from purposes of expediency. Perhaps Meyer's view has been influenced by the ingenious essay of Rümelin which he cites ("Ueber die Idee der Gerechtigkeit") in *Rümelin*, "Reden und Aufsätze", II, 1881, pp. 176–202). Here retribution is expressly made the basis of the criminal law, but in a peculiar manner, for this conclusion is not derived from the premise of moral retribution, but from the idea of equality. According to this the most rigorous retaliation in kind ("talio") would constitute the spirit of the criminal law. But even this principle of justification cannot be completely separated

But all this is merely an exception due to the general imperfection of human affairs. It is by no means a ground of objection to the doctrine which sees the crime as immoral action. Furthermore, when considered closely, it comes to the same thing, whether we say (as above): "Crime is an action at variance with morality — an action which the State, since the act seems especially burdensome (or disadvantageous) to the general welfare, feels itself obliged to subject to special disapproval", or whether we say (with Von Ihering) [10]: "Crime is an endangering of the conditions upon which depend the life of society, declared to be such by the State", or whether we say (with Hugo Meyer): "Crimes are acts threatened with punishment by the State and which are at variance with the conditions upon which the community and its progress depend." The apparent difference rests only in that error which has long since been laid to rest by modern philosophy, but which frequently stalks forth among the jurists, viz.: that morality is something purely individual and that each one makes for himself his own conscience. Morality and conscience are products of the development of the human race for a thousand years, — products which, like law, show different phases of development at different periods. The act that is contrary to morality is simply an act which, according to the opinions at the time prevailing among the people in question, is more or less out of harmony with or in contradiction to the ultimate goal of man, his progress and the conditions of his existence.

§ 109. **Tort and Crime.** — The distinction between civil wrongs (*i.e.* torts) and wrongs punishable criminally is now apparent. A civil wrong represents a condition at variance with a right regardless of whether it is founded upon an action contrary to morality. Wrong punishable criminally is an act specially characterized as being contrary to morality; and it is generally

from morality, as Rümelin admits (p. 192). ("Forgiveness of injuries suffered may be favored by religion and morality, but it can never be a principle of a legal system since it would make wrongdoers the lords of society.") But Rümelin's principle is completely untenable, from the historical standpoint. The "talio" has never been a fundamental principle of the criminal law, but only a principle tending towards moderation. It may also be asked whether this idea of equality, which closely regarded, is merely an idea of relative evils, has any claim to preservation. In the statement of Rümelin above quoted, the idea of deterrence, otherwise only incidentally observed, creeps in, since punishment, *i.e.* not forgiving, is justified by the remark that otherwise the wrongdoers would become the lords of society.

[10] "Der Zweck im Rechte", I, pp. 480, 481.

but not necessarily a violation or at least a jeopardizing of a subjective right.[1] It is not possible " a priori " to go further in fixing the distinction between civil wrongs and wrongs punishable criminally, since, according to the premises, the conception of crime can not " a priori " be completely determined for a definite positive law and a definite period of time.

Hegel's Distinction. — Especially is it incorrect to hold with Hegel that the distinction consists in crime being intentional wrong and in tort being unintentional or innocent wrong. The positive law shows us that there are acts of negligence which are punished criminally, and that on the other hand there are cases of wrong committed quite intentionally which nevertheless remain merely torts; for example, when a person, openly and with knowledge of its illegality, but without other violence to person or thing occupies a piece of ground belonging to another, or when one shamelessly refuses to discharge an obligation of debt unequivocally entered into. It is not proper to regard these instances as errors of the law; nor to maintain, that negligence should be completely eliminated from the province of criminal law and that every intentional wrong should incur the reaction of the criminal law. The importance for the civil community of an intentional act of the individual is not to be measured solely by whether or not it is the direct cause of an action, of a result which the State disapproves. Rather (and most essentially) it is to be measured in accordance with the rights and interests which it objectively violates or jeopardizes. There is no impropriety in speaking of " minor

[1] The applicability of the idea of damages is, in spite of all positive law, denied by *Ed. Hertz*, "Das Unrecht und seinen Formen", I, pp. 72 *et seq.* But Hertz's argument is defective. It is based upon a confusion of the absolute standpoint with the standpoint of the limited human understanding, which is the only possible one for the criminal law. Regarded from the absolute standpoint, there is not danger but only necessity. If we in one moment knew the relation of everything, then no offenses or attempt at crime could deserve blame. But from the practical human standpoint we can never give up the attitude of regarding things according to their physical manifestations. However, in this manifestation of our thought, which from the abstract standpoint may be termed lack of precision, there rests also the possibility of general conceptions which is the condition of all progress. If one apply the abstract standard, animals think with more precision than men, since they substantially consider only individual physical manifestation, — and for this reason they make no progress. This objection can be advanced against Hertz more fittingly than against Binding and his theory of interdependence of causes. Hertz's criticism of Binding, who rejects the idea of being guided by physical manifestation and therefore speaks of the "equality in importance of the conditions of a manifestation of a result", is in every respect correct.

transgressions." "Trivial" and "malicious" are not terms which in the concrete case are mutually exclusive. But if something is objectively quite trivial and entirely without danger, then it would be absolutely improper to put into motion the clumsy machinery of criminal justice which entails such heavy expense for the country. This is apparent from what has been stated in regard to the determination by the State of what acts are punishable. On the other hand, when the individual is dealing with especially important rights or interests of others or of the community, this very fact in its purely moral aspect should serve to warn him not to injure unintentionally such rights and interests and also to exercise caution. As a matter of fact, the punishment of injuries caused by negligence is thus *to a certain extent* justified.

But only to a *certain* and *limited* extent. On the one hand, the rights and interests which are concerned must be of especial importance, and on the other, these rights and interests must be such that the fact of their being jeopardized must be easy to perceive in concrete cases. By way of illustration, the general interests of the State are certainly important, but the fact of their being actually jeopardized is not easily recognizable, or in concrete cases may give rise to very diverse opinions. Therefore the offense of high treason or State treason by negligent action would be a juristic monstrosity, though it is quite natural and proper to punish homicide caused by negligence. However, one can assent to Hegel's view that intentional acts, in which the result in question is intended, are those which constitute the major portion of crimes, and that in private law the question of guilt occupies a very subordinate position. Private law is the law as external regulation; criminal law is the law as morality. But as criminal law does not limit itself to the intention, but also takes into consideration the external effect of the act, so to a certain extent the private law proceeds more leniently with him who is innocent than with him whose guilt or malice can be proven. Criminal justice *must* use guilty intention as a foundation, but private law does not require it.[2]

Hälschner's Distinction. — Hälschner's distinction is even less tenable than that of Hegel.[3] According to Hälschner, crime should be an attack upon the general legal system, a violation of law in

[2] *Cf. Von Bar*, "Grundlagen des Strafrechts", p. 44.

[3] "Die Lehre vom Unrechte und seinen verschiedenen Formen" in "Gerichtssaal" (1869), pp. 1–36, 81–114 (also published separately). To the contrary *cf. Merkel*, "Zeitschrift" (1881), pp. 586 *et seq.*

principle, while a tort is merely a violation of a concrete right, the law as a principle being recognized.[4] But this conception is undoubtedly incorrect in the vast majority of cases, from the standpoint of the one committing the act. The thief in stealing does not absolutely reject the right of property; [5] on the contrary, he desires to be the owner or at least to actually occupy the position of the owner. What he rejects, from his standpoint, is merely the concrete right of the party whose property is stolen. To be sure, the *objective* law regards the theft as in principle irreconcilable with the theory of ownership. Yet as a matter of fact this also applies to other violations of property which are not punished.

Hälschner in the beginning had a conception different from his later one as to this antagonism of the intention towards the law in crimes and the absence of this antagonism in torts.[6] In the beginning he laid emphasis upon torts having to do only with property rights that might be renounced, and only becoming punishable wrong if the will of the injured party has expressed itself against the act; later he laid emphasis upon the intention of the wrongdoer in cases of private wrong not being *permanently* at variance with the law. But this coloring does not add to the correctness of this shadowy distinction. As Binding [7] has correctly shown, a tort is not changed into a crime by the declaration of the party injured. The assumption that the criminal is permanently opposed to the law is no better than the false presumption of Grolmann's "special prevention" theory.

Hälschner's distinction is neither in harmony with the positive law nor capable of serving a useful purpose. By way of illustration, suppose that a legislative assembly desired to decide, in accordance with Hälschner's theory, some concrete question of legislation, *e.g.* the punishment of usury or of breach of contract. Nothing definite would be furnished. Of greater practical value is that version of his view which Hälschner gives as something incidental, to wit: that private wrong represents merely a negative relation,

[4] *Stahl*, "Die Philosophie des Rechts", II, 2, § 185, had already advanced a similar view, — acts which violate the legal system are crimes only if they challenge the authority and respect due to the State. However, Stahl's conception is more true to life and its results are more readily perceived. In the emphasis which he lays upon the *positive* nature of crime, his insistence that the act must manifest itself "in thesi" (thus under all circumstances) as contrary to law, there lies the principle that crimes must be readily distinguishable from acts that are not punishable.

[5] *Cf.* also "Das gemeine deutsche Strafrecht", I, pp. 33 *et seq.*

[6] "Gerichtssaal" (1876), pp. 401 *et seq.*, especially p. 417.

[7] "Normen", I, pp. 154 *et seq.*

while crime represents a positive attack upon the law. But taken in a strict and precise sense this principle is also incorrect; for mere absence of action may well constitute a crime. But it is admissible in the sense that an act which is to be punished must be distinguishable by definite, readily determined and comprehensible characteristics from those acts which the law does not punish; and it must, as it were, be given "positive" expression in contrast to the permissible acts of every day life. It is only as thus conceived that this criterion leads to expedient and realistic results.[8] Yet Hälschner[9] rejected it with the statement that its results were not sufficiently solid and perceptible.

Merkel's Distinction. — Merkel[10] is certainly correct when he asserts that criminal punishment is necessary only where the civil sanction is not sufficient for the repression of wrong. But, as shown above, the premises upon which he argues are defective in that he declares the sanctions of the civil and criminal law to be similar in character and different only in degree or intensity. On the other hand, Binding[11] is correct in his statement that the positive law deals with civil damages and with criminal punishment in accordance with totally distinct principles. Punishment would affect the guilty and only the guilty; civil damages would restore to the injured party that of which he has been deprived. It is possible only by the most artificial reasoning to maintain that the obligation to pay damages should never affect any but actually guilty parties. The so-called "Liability Law" ("Haftpflichtgesetz") of June 7, 1871, for the German Empire, was a complete contravention of this theory. In English law there is given wide recognition to a liability (at least a secondary liability) for obligations (*i.e.* in tort) incurred by agents (*e.g.* the master for his servants, etc.). Merely to raise one further point, how does Merkel's theory explain that punishment does not, but obligation to pay damages does, pass to one's heirs?

Relation of Tort and Crime. — Moreover, one may not, as Binding has done, draw the general conclusion that the distinction between tort and crime is purely a creation of positive law, —

[8] *Von Bar*, "Grundlagen des Strafrechts", pp. 50 *et seq.* In respect to the real grounds of distinction for law and legislation, it is with pleasure that I find myself in harmony with the frequently cited recent articles of Meyer and Merkel. *Cf.* especially the annotation, *Hugo Meyer* in "Gerichtssaal", Vol. 33, p. 105.

[9] "Das gemeine deutsche Strafrecht", p. 15.

[10] "Criminalistische Abhandlungen", I, pp. 57 *et seq.*

[11] "Normen", I, pp. 166 *et seq.*

that there is no fixed principle nor even a general basis for this distinction, and that every crime contains the essential element of tort. However, every wrong, even the most insignificant, entailing only a civil sanction, contains *one* element which might possibly qualify it as a crime, although often only one: and Merkel is really correct to the extent that *in certain cases* the obligation to pay damages can tend towards the repression of wrong, just as punishment.[12] The legislator who would subject every wrong to criminal punishment would work a hardship upon humanity and do violence to his own authority. Such freedom of action and omnipotence do not belong to him. Where gentler means would accomplish the same end, the legislator commits a grave wrong by inflicting punishment. Therefore it is absolutely correct to say that where the civil sanction is sufficient, there is no meaning in punishment.

This is the only occasion where from our standpoint it is necessary to investigate the relation of tort and crime. We have not derived punishment from the law but directly from the principle of morality. The problem why at one time the legal principle assumes the form of punishment and later assumes the form of the civil sanction is for us not a real problem. The condition is simply this. Because of the existence of surer civil justice, many wrongful and therefore immoral acts lose much of their dangerous character. This explains why in the earlier stages of legal development many acts and also especially many omissions are punished, for which later civil sanctions alone are found sufficient. Such, for example, in the development of the Germanic law, was the case with simple breach of contract.[13] "As the idea of law grows, punishments decrease; profusion of methods of punishment stands in an inverse ratio to the perfection of the legal system and the maturity of the people." [14] But the sanction of civil justice is by no means uni-

[12] It must be admitted, however, that a strict obligation to make indemnity can exercise a deterring and disciplinary influence. *Cf. Zink*, "Die Ermittlung des Sachverhalts im französischen Civilprocesse", I (1860), pp. 591 *et seq.; Von Bar,* "Recht und Beweis im Civilprocesse" (1867), pp. 24 *et seq.*

[13] *Cf. R. Löning,* "Der Vertragsbruch und seine Rechtsfolgen", Vol. I (1876), and *W. Sickel,* "Die Bestrafung des Vertragsbruch und analoger Rechtsverletzunger in Deutschland" (1876). These writers, however, with the characteristic predilection of authors for the object of their investigations, seem to regard the reintroduction of such legal rules as desirable.

[14] *Von Ihering,* "Das Schuldmoment im römischen Privatrechte", p. 67.

versally sufficient as moral reprobation, although perhaps it is so at various times and in certain cases. For, as we have seen, this sanction also takes place where there is a violation of rights that are purely objective and devoid of guilt. With this assumption, (which harmonizes with the customary method of expression,[15]) of a possibly guiltless violation of right it must be noted by way of contrast civil sanction must also occur for the acts of irrational beings. Merkel expresses this radically in the following manner: According to this conception, it is only their insolvency which prevents us from declaring that the very mice who waste our crop are bound to render indemnity. But we do not exercise civil justice against the mice because they, as contrasted to ourselves, are not possessors of rights and they cannot be said to be under the protection enjoyed by the possessor of rights. Therefore we maintain our right to use such methods as may seem agreeable to us, without any judicial decree. On the other hand, if we were dealing with a possessor of rights who was incapable of intention, *e.g.* with one who is irresponsible for his actions, it is the respect for this possessor of rights (or, otherwise expressed, the possibility of an injury of this possessor, and thus of his sphere of rights, being contrary to law), which is the basis of the prohibition of unlimited self-redress.

It is more in accord with actual relations, if one place the nature and purpose of private justice simply in the adjustment and arrangement of the actual or alleged confusion of the spheres of rights of two or more possessors of rights. While the element of guilt is of very considerable importance in private law, yet it plays only a secondary part. It is only by an artificial and therefore defective argument that the duty to indemnify is based upon guilt. Especially is this true of the Roman Law. Even less does this hold good in other positive laws, *e.g.* the French or the English.[16] It is at least not an absolute injustice for the law to make one, who is legally and financially responsible, pay for material damage which he has caused,[17] and the

[15] *Thon*, "Rechtsnorm", pp. 84 *et seq.*, in this respect pronounces himself in accord with *Von Ihering*, pp. 5 and 6.

[16] As to this, *cf. Von Bar* in *Grünhut's* "Zeitschrift für das Privat- und öffentliche Recht der Gegenwart" (1877), pp. 74 *et seq.*, and *e.g.* "Code civil.", § 1385: "Le propriétaire d'un animal ou celui qui s'en sert pendant qu'il est à son usage, est responsable du dommage que l'animal a causé, soit que l'animal fût sous sa garde, soit qu'il fût égaré ou echappé", and *Pfaff*, "Zur Lehre vom Schadenersatz ... nach osterr. R." (1880).

[17] Concerning this, *cf. Thon*, "Rechtsnorm", p. 106. *Cf.* also *Unger*, in *Grünhut's* "Zeitschrift" (1881), pp. 209 *et seq.*

older Germanic law,[18] as is well known, attached liability in this manner.

Since the element of guilt takes a subordinate position in private law, the latter by itself is not suited to preserve the requisite moral character of the law. A relation which, upon the whole, is morally indifferent (although there may be important modifications in individual cases conditional *e.g.* upon "bona fides" or "mala fides") is treated the same as an act contrary to morality. He who unlawfully detains must surrender the object, whether he possess it "mala fides" or "bona fides." It is not the object of the civil sanction to strike at that which is morally reprehensible, or to reprove it. It is rather that its primary object is to eliminate the objective illegality, be its source what it may. It is merely a secondary matter that the civil sanction deals more gently with him who has done nothing immoral, *e.g.* where one bona fide has acquired an object belonging to another. The reaction of the civil law against wrong which contains the element of guilt is one which in many cases can be perceived with difficulty and is exceedingly obscure.

Crime distinguished from Tort. — In conclusion, our view avoids the difficulty arising on one hand from the fact that the same act, *e.g.* injury to a person or thing, may under some circumstances entail results both in private and in criminal law, and on the other from there being acts which are punishable criminally but for which no result in private law ensues, *e.g.* criminal acts for which a civil remedy is excluded by the maxim: "Volenti non fit injuria." According to our conception, an act is in principle punishable not because it violates a subjective right, but rather because it is contrary to morality. It maintains a relationship to subjective right only through the fact that the State for the most part prosecutes or subjects to moral reprobation only those acts which are immoral because they violate or jeopardize subjective right. Heyssler[19]

[18] *Cf.* "Sächsisches Landrecht", II, 65, § 1, III, 3.

[19] "Das Civilunrecht und seine Folgen" (Wien, 1870). *Heyssler*, p. 15, correctly says: "The essential element in tort is the material injury to a material legal condition. Without this there is no tort. Intention has according to this conception merely an incidental (qualifying) significance. The essential element in crime is guilt, — the tracing of the act to the will as its original source. Without this there is no crime." This had previously ("Grundlagen", p. 44) been stated by me, and furthermore I maintained that criminal justice must use the guilty will as a foundation, while civil justice does not require it (but under some circumstances it may). The criticism made by *Heyssler*, p. 11, note 6 upon my "Grundlagen des Strafrechts" that it was to be distinguished from

and Binding[20] are thus quite correct in seeking to eliminate guilt from the private law based on the obligation to indemnify, so as to treat this excluded element of unlawful action as the foundation of amenability to punishment. Both writers have the possibility of the correct view. This is so in respect to Heyssler, since he will not acknowledge for the distinction between private wrong and punishable wrong the basis of expediency but rather prefers aprioristic and abstract distinguishing characteristics.[21] Binding believes that guilt may be established exclusively as an element of an offense and not as a possible basis of a duty to indemnify. On one hand, the aprioristic basis advanced by Heyssler is not satisfactory, and on the other hand private wrong is too narrowly conceived as a consequence of human action. But in respect to its effect the conception of *action* (*i.e.* as of operation in the external world) can not be separated from the conception of guilt. So Heyssler finally becomes involved in the contradictory and completely incomprehensible maxim: "Guilt for which one is responsible is an offense, guilty private wrong is wrong possessing guilt, but not guilt for which one is responsible."[22]

Binding, on the contrary, while he maintains that private law has nothing to do with guilt, arrives at the strange principle that the private law duty of indemnification has its basis in a quasi-contract, a negligent or fraudulent "negotiorum gestio."[23] A simple, unartificial and correct opinion would say that the duty to indemnify in a private wrong, *e.g.* in a personal injury caused by negligence[24] that is perhaps not punishable, arises without regard

that quoted above only upon close observation because it belongs to those theories, which "merely furnish personal satisfaction to their author", does not seem to have been avoided by Heyssler himself. A more recent attack by Heyssler upon Binding's theory (*Grünhut's* "Zeitschrift für das Privat- und öffentliche Recht" (1879), pp. 357 *et seq.*) may upon the whole be concurred in.

[20] "Normen", I, pp. 142 *et seq.*, 172 *et seq.*

[21] This was done for the civil law in a very artificial manner in "Bestreitbarkeit der rechtlichen Qualification der That und Negativität des rechtswidrigen Thatbestandes", pp. 22 *et seq.*, and thereby (without any proof) it was asserted that all development of civilization of the present time rested upon this basis.

[22] *Cf.* in opposition to this complete contradiction, *Binding*, "Normen", I, p. 233, and *Hälschner*, p. 418.

[23] "Normen", I, pp. 222, 223. Incidentally *Binding* desires to show that what I stated in my "Grundlagen des Strafrechts" pp. 41, 42 as to "Schadensersatz" and "Schadenstragung", which he so haltingly condemned, corresponds with what he on page 227 said as to "Schadenstragung." Here even the words are identical.

[24] Hälschner, in opposition to Binding, observes that the latter's quasi-contract theory contains a contradiction scarcely less marked than

to the concrete intention or generally against the concrete intention of the party bound to indemnify, just as punishment attaches itself in punishable wrong without regard to the intention of him who commits the wrong. But this last problem, the derivation of the duty to indemnify from guilt, exists, as previously stated, only for a theory which rejects the direct derivation of criminal law from morality and therefore, for good or evil, must found the civil sanction at the beginning of the investigation, since it conceives punishable wrong as "injury of legal rights." In a theory which founds criminal law directly upon morality, the civil sanction receives attention simply as a[1] "factum", a "factum" which may have the possible consequence that the State may omit punishment.

§ 110. **Violations of Police Regulations. The Three Types.** — It yet remains to explain from our standpoint the so-called "police offenses" (*i.e.* violations of police regulations). This is a simple matter. We previously stated that not only the actual damaging but also even the placing in jeopardy of an object of a right or of a legal relation, could constitute an immoral act amenable to the criminal law. Now it is quite possible that this placing in jeopardy of a right is not that which is foremost in the mind of the party committing the act. He may be aiming at some ulterior result or course of action. Nevertheless in most or many of the cases his conduct involves danger, *e.g.* smoking a cigar in the vicinity of explosives entails danger of an explosion. This must be realized by the individual himself upon more careful consideration. Therefore it involves an endangering (of others or their rights) by negligence; and this can always be characterized as an immoral act (although of minor degree), and thus with complete justice subjected to punishment. To be sure, as a general rule, in such

does Heyssler's principle stated above, since according to Binding the same act is viewed by the civil judge as a lawful act giving rise to a legal obligation and is viewed by the criminal judge as an act contrary to law and subject to punishment. But Hälschner, whose latest treatise is very decidedly influenced by the "Normentheorie" ("Gem. deutsches Strafrecht", p. 21), founds the obligation to pay damages in a manner not differing widely from a quasi-contract, since he sees in the injury of another (*i.e.* of his property) a "permit to make use of one's own property." Naturally Hälschner provides that the one doing the injury is not required to have this intention "in concreto." But the law attributes to his act the "equivalent" of such an intention. More simply stated the principle is that the law, since it does not pay attention to the actual intention, compulsorily attaches to the act the result that compensation must be rendered. Hälschner here simply repeats the old error that the thing which (on other grounds) is reasonable is always desired by the party suffering thereby. According to this logic, the individual condemned to death always desires to be executed.

cases the *authorities* should have *designated* the act in question as possessing this dangerous character. The immoral nature of the act is so remote that it should be expressly so declared to the individual.

Furthermore, it is necessary to a certain extent and under certain conditions that the individual make some sacrifices in the interests of the public at large, *i.e.* that there be some positive contribution on his part. If this performance is not rendered as due, then this constitutes an immoral act, provided however, that the necessity of such a special performance should have been clearly announced, *i.e.* that it be determined by the authorities to whom the community has entrusted the maintenance of such general interests.

In conclusion, it is possible that, because of their very insignificance, actual violations of right assume a different character. There is something different in unlawfully picking up an apple and eating it and in stealing a gold coin. The smallest violation of a right is also an immoral act; but to a certain extent it can be placed on a plane with those acts whose immorality, as shown above, only becomes manifest in some more indirect manner.

The circle of the so-called "violations of police regulations" ("Polizeivergehen") may be closed with these three varieties, viz.: actions that involve danger; the not doing of that which one is bound to do (*e.g.* giving information or a report to the authorities is such a duty, although perhaps not one upon which there can be placed a money value); and violations of right that are quite insignificant.

The true basis of the propriety of punishment here lies in the immoral character of the act. For this to become obvious, one has only to consider that the preservation of a certain *external good order*,[1] because of its substantial importance, may be regarded as the *equivalent* of a moral principle. For it is upon this external order that well-ordered human intercourse depends, and thus it contributes to the progress and development of humanity. It may indeed appear to have nothing to do with morality whether one goes to the left or to the right on a bridge. Yet on account of

[1] Many excellent remarks as to this are contained in *E. Von Hartmann's* "Phänomenologie des sittlichen Bewusstseins", pp. 485 *et seq.*; "Das Moralprincip der Ordnung." *L. Von Stein*, "Verwaltungslehre" (1867), IV, p. 36, says: "If that which the police regulation provides is an actual essential for the development of the public at large, then non-compliance with the same by the individual is an offense against the public at large."

traffic it may be necessary to arrange that those going over the bridge from either end keep to their right, and the violation of such a provision may result in great disaster. Thus it is improper, immoral, not to comply with such a rule. It may even be said that to a *certain extent* the authority, as such, must be respected, even if its commands and prohibitions are materially injudicious. For disobedience, as such, readily becomes contagious, and the external order and therefore authority itself rests upon the principle of subordination. Therefore it is *possible* that disobedience as such can justly be punishable.

Relation of "Violations of Police Regulations" to Crime. — From the foregoing it is apparent that "a priori" there is no distinction in principle between criminal offenses and "violations of police regulations," just as historically this distinction is uncertain and flexible. It reduces itself to this, viz.: that the so-called "Polizeidelicte" bear far less of an immoral and therefore far less of a punishable character. It certainly can not be asserted that mere disobedience to commands *always* constitutes merely a "violation of police regulation"; it is not so in an oriental despotism and even with ourselves, disobedience in military matters is quite a grave offense. The degree of immorality varies with time and circumstance. There are many actions in which it can be very doubtful whether they should be treated as crimes or as "violations of police regulations."[2]

Since the propriety of punishment for "violation of police regulations", just as in crimes, is based upon the immorality of the act, it furthermore comes about that in such punishment, just as in punishment for crimes, there must be guilt. Purely arbitrary punishment of individuals[3] is here precluded, and when it does take place operates just as in criminal offenses. Consequently it is a decided step in advance that the modern development of law establishes fundamental general principles essentially the same for "violations of police regulations" as for crimes,[4] and that

[2] Among other things, § 322 of the German Criminal Code punishes the kindling of fires on beach-cliffs, when likely to endanger navigation, with penal imprisonment not exceeding ten years, thus with special criminal punishments. *Cf.* also *e.g.* the German imperial statute of May 21st, 1878, dealing with violations of prohibitions enacted for the prevention of cattle disease.

[3] *E.g.* the punishment of a man who is innocent in order to inspire the public with terror.

[4] Thus especially the German Criminal Code, of which the first or general part generally has reference to all offenses against police regulations that may be created.

the former are committed to the courts and to those officials to whom the legal protection of individuals is, for the most part, entrusted. Yet the individual often feels a punishment is of equal severity whether it be inflicted upon him as a criminal punishment or as a sanction of the police system. And so it is often mere sophistry to seek an exit from a worn-out theory or a view which does not have the courage to pronounce itself openly upon the liability to or immunity of an act and to regard a judicious sanction of the police system as acceptable.

An act which is not amenable to the criminal law because it is very difficult to ascertain or because its injurious effects are substantially limited to its own author is no more punishable as a "violation of police regulation" than as a crime.

It must however be admitted that the distinction between "violations of police regulations" and criminal offenses which is not "a priori" admissible, has a very great importance from the standpoint of the positive law, since public opinion has difficulty in a large number of offenses in recognizing their immorality. It does not refer these offenses to a defect in character, but rather regards them as something which can now and then happen to any one without in any way disturbing his social or legal position. The legislator who, in general, should give expression only to the moral convictions of the people must observe this distinction; and doubtless it is substantially upon this that there exists, in positive law, the distinction of crime and "violation of police regulations."[5]

General Characteristics of "Violations of Police Regulations." — The only result of combining crimes and "violations of police regulations" would be to create confusion. It is a mistake which modern legislation very properly avoids. This is the more so since acts whose immorality is recognized only after considerable reflection, and possibly known only because of the pronouncement of the authorities, are not in a class with those which attack the *permanent* foundations of human society. The permitting or

[5] Thus, offenses in this classification do not exactly correspond with the so-called "Polizeidelicte" (violations of police regulations), because the objective severity of the punishment *e.g.* the amount of the fine, also exercises an influence upon the form of the *procedure*. It is possible also that the punishment of an act which is in itself so little or only indirectly immoral must be rigorous because *e.g.* the profit derived from the offense or its likelihood of repetition have to be considered, or because the offense is *e.g.* as a rule committed only by well-to-do persons. There may be yet another reason, an act, *e.g.* duelling, which public opinion does not regard as dishonorable, must be punished with really significant punishments.

prohibiting of such acts is far more dependent upon transitory circumstances and possibly upon purely local needs and conditions. These are facts which involve quick changes in the law. The more indispensable and stable portion of the criminal law must be separated from that which is less requisite and more subject to change. Since the immorality of "violations of police regulations" is only an indirect one, the repression in such cases must be milder. Severe penalties must not be applied, and especially not penalties which affect honor. Such penalties would confuse the minds of the people and especially would readily give the impression that law rests a great deal upon changing and even arbitrary commands and prohibitions. The lightness of the penalties also leads to the propriety and indeed the practical necessity of a simpler procedure. Procedure as a means must always maintain a certain relation to its end, punishment. A trial which could have as its conclusion nothing more than a sentence to pay a few marks as a fine, but which had all the machinery which is occasioned by a trial for murder, would be a monstrosity, which could only tend to lessen the effect of criminal proceedings that are actually important. The fact that the procedure is less thorough makes it more possible for an innocent man to be convicted in trials for "violations of police regulations" than in trials for crime. The lesser importance of the cases also makes it conceivable that each and every minor "violation of police regulations" is not investigated with the utmost rigor. The legislator even finds that he is impelled to make no distinction between transgressions that are intentional and those occasioned by negligence, since the result would not justify a very precise investigation. He may also possibly feel impelled to allow the punishment to be imposed upon a party only *presumed* to be guilty, *e.g.* the owner or possessor of a piece of land.

It is therefore not difficult to criticize the variant views as to the nature of "violations against police regulations."

There is hardly a material difference between the view of Hugo Meyer and the view here represented. He says: "The true distinction between the two kinds of punishable wrong lies in this. The 'violation of police regulations' injures the useful elements of the legal system, while crime injures the necessary elements. But as the conceptions of usefulness and necessity overlap, so there are many kinds of offenses as to which one can only conjecture whether they belong to the province of crimes or should be included among 'violations of police regulations.'" The permanent and more unchanging fundamental rules of human society are also the necessary rules and the temporary or less permanent or those exhibiting greater local differences are merely the useful rules.[6]

On the other hand, other opinions incorrectly emphasize some element as being exclusively the distinguishing one. Thus, the older view, represented especially by Feuerbach, regarded a crime as being only that which violates a subjective right. This distinguishes, as it were, the core of the matter, but a very considerable margin extends on each side. This also applies to the view[7] which regards crime as a violation of a right and "violation of police regulations" as an endangering of a right. And the same may be said of the view which conceives a crime as a *substantial* and a "violation of police regulations" as merely a *formal* wrong.[8] This last view gives too much prominence to that element of obedience to an external formal order, to the authorities. To this element we also have given some consideration.

But we must absolutely dissent from the distinction of that later view which finds in "violations of police regulation", not punishment in its proper sense, but rather "discipline."[9] The individual should be disciplined by the punishment for the violation just as little (or just as much, if one prefers this last expression)

[6] I would remark that I do not entirely believe that legislation should exclusively distinguish offenses according to their gravity, *i.e.* according to the gravity of their punishments. At least the jurisdiction of those administering the criminal law should not be determined solely by the amount of the penalty, but also with consideration for the moral significance of the offense. *Cf.* "Grundlagen", p. 31.

[7] Thus *Grolmann*, "Lehrbuch", § 365. *Cf.* also *Seeger* in *Goltdammer*, "Archiv" (1870), p. 245. *Köstlin's* view ("System des deutschen strafrechts," 1855, § 18) that a criminal offense is an actual wrong, and a "polizeidelict" is a possible wrong, is only an inapt expression of this view. It would at all events be more correct, as *Fichte* says ("Naturrecht", p. 294), for police laws to prohibit possible violations of the rights of others and for the civil laws to prohibit actual violations.

[8] Thus *e.g.* *Merkel*, "Abhandlungen", I, pp. 95 *et seq.*; *Binding*, "Normen", I, pp. 179 *et seq.*, pp. 205 *et seq.* (who designates an offense punishable by the police authorities as *purely* disobedience). In agreement with Binding is also *Hälschner*, "Das gemeine deutsche Strafrecht", I, p. 35, and earlier "System des preuss. Strafrechts", I, p. 2; "Gerichtssaal", (1876), p. 429.

[9] Thus in a peculiar manner *Hälschner*, "Gem. deutsches Strafrecht", I. p. 37, where it is said that punishment inflicted by the police authorities should serve as a warning to the party punished. Should this not also be the case with *criminal* punishments? Admonition to discretion and obedience are certainly not the exclusive province of punishments inflicted by the police authorities. It is sufficient to consider on one hand offenses occasioned by negligence, and on the other hand resistance of officials.

as by the criminal punishment; less perhaps, if one considers the real nature of the punishments actually inflicted for the violations (fines, short imprisonment). Certainly punishment for "violations of police regulations" cannot be placed on the same plane as discipline (school punishment, or even parental punishment). Real disciplinary punishment, while possibly not excluding the purpose of reformation and the well-being of the one punished, has as its first purpose his correction. This is not the case with punishment inflicted by the State, and most certainly not the case with punishment for "violation of police regulations." It is of more importance that this idea should be repudiated, since it is calculated to introduce a certain element of despotism into the infliction or non-infliction of punishment in the police courts on purely individual considerations. When it is considered how closely these punishments for "violation of police regulations" touch the individual's sphere of rights, such despotism appears intolerable and at total variance with the conception of "government based on rights" ("Rechtsstaat").

§ 111. **Disciplinary Punishments.** — That theory of that class of punishments known as "Disciplinary punishments" ("Disciplinarstrafe")[1] while at the present time of the utmost importance, can not be exhaustively treated here. Its relation to ordinary punishment inflicted by the State should however be expounded. It must first be distinguished from the so-called "Public Order" penalties ("Ordnungsstrafe") in the proper sense,[2] *i.e.* punishment specially threatened in individual cases for compelling one or more specific acts. "Disciplinary punishment" is essentially a means of coercion. If the purpose aimed at by the appropriate officials or the government in the threatening of this punishment is in some way or other achieved, the exaction of the punishment may frequently be foregone, without disadvantageous results. For in these punishments a very subordinate position is taken by moral reprobation of the act, although

[1] *Cf.* especially *Heffter*, in "Neues Archiv des Criminalrechts" (Vol. 13, 1832), pp. 48 *et seq.; Mittermaier, Feuerbach's* "Lehrbuch" (14th ed.), § 477, Notes I and IV; *Bülau* in *Bluntschli's* and *Brater's* "Staatslexicon", Vol. III, p. 140; *Pözl* in the same, Vol. IX, pp. 696 *et seq.; Meves* in *Von Holtzendorff's* "Handbuch des deutschen Strafrechts", III, pp. 939 *et seq.; Laband*, "Das Staatsrecht des deutschen Reiches", I, pp. 447–459. The work of Heffter is of especial importance and also the exposition of Laband.

[2] Inappropriately insignificant punishments prescribed especially for the non-observance of merely formal provisions are also called "Ordnungsstrafen."

some thought of the same, which is reflected in the principle of guilt herein prevailing, is not entirely lacking. Consequently, it is generally conceded, in these coercive punishments, the officials who inflict these punishments, whether they be against subordinates or private persons, have the right, if the object is realized, to dismiss or remit the same.

Lack of Definiteness. — The law imposing "disciplinary punishment" is an imitation of the criminal law for a limited circle of persons within the State united by a special course of life. There is however the modification that the special purpose of the association must also have its influence upon this special criminal law. For example, where education is the purpose of the association, consideration of the individual receives more attention than can be the case in public punishment, or in the disciplinary punishment of State officials, where, at the most, *reformation* is but an incidental feature.[3] The minimum of morality required is in excess of that minimum which finds its expression in the criminal statutes of the State. From officials of the State, those who attend higher public institutions of learning, possibly from military persons, etc., more is demanded than from the general public at large.[4] Along with their very special duties, they have the duty to conduct themselves in harmony with their position, conspicuous as it is in one way or other. To a certain extent, it is possible for the requirements of this conduct to be precisely fixed by custom and statute. But a general provision is useful which provides that he who is subject to disciplinary punishment should not show himself unworthy[5] of that special position which he holds, or that he should so conduct himself (as it was expressed in the old oaths of allegiance) as "becomes a man of good standing, etc."

[3] Therefore in disciplinary punishments in institutions of learning, the punishment may *to a certain extent* be foregone, if it would be especially injurious to the education, or the advancement of the one punished. The smaller the institution, the more attention can be given to considerations of the individual.

[4] This position may indeed be termed "disadvantageous", a "privilegium odiosum", just as *e.g.* the position of convicts in penal institutions. The convict as a matter of fact has more compulsory duties than one at liberty. He has the duty of industry, or order, of respect and of obedience to the prison officials.

[5] *Cf.* the Prussian Statute of July 21, 1852, concerning breach of duties by non-judicial officials: "An official who (1) violates a duty incumbent upon him, or (2) in his conduct in or out of his office shows himself unworthy of the esteem, respect, or confidence which his calling demands, is liable to the provisions of this statute." *Cf.* also §§ 72 and 10 of the German Imperial Statute of March 31st, 1873, concerning the legal status of imperial officials.

This lack of definiteness is explained by the fact that the range of these duties is nearly coextensive with that of the purely moral duties, which latter it is very difficult to comprehend within single principles. Therefore it is never possible to completely eliminate this defect of lack of definiteness, and for this reason in this disciplinary law, much depends upon the composition of the disciplinary tribunals, — a matter in which we in our present discussion have no interest.

Relation of Disciplinary Punishment to the Public Criminal Law. — There are various relations which may be held by this disciplinary law towards the public criminal law.[6] The attitude may be taken that *every* public offense in which a person subject to this disciplinary law is concerned, shall be regarded only as an offense subject to the disciplinary law, although the rules for decision are substantially those of the public criminal law. For the discipline derived from the general statutes of the States is also binding upon the individual within the special disciplinary circle. This conception of the relation of the disciplinary law and public criminal law more readily obtains, where the individual is regarded, as it were, as merged in the disciplinary circle, where belonging to the disciplinary circle is considered of overshadowing importance. Such was the case in the law of the Middle Ages (the Canon law) in respect to crimes of the clergy, and such is the case to-day in the law of the German Empire,[7] and Continental Europe generally, in respect to offenses of military persons.

It is possible to proceed from the opposite side, and to regard the breach of the general criminal law and the breach of the disciplinary law comprehended within the same act, as matters to be quite separately considered. The common law adopts this attitude in respect to offenses of public servants, and (of late years, since the abolition of the so-called "academic" jurisdiction by the introduction of the legislation of the Empire [8]) in respect to offenses of students in the German Universities. According to

[6] Moreover it is possible that a breach of a duty as a public servant may because of the special importance of the office, constitute a *criminal* offense, thus particularly violation of a duty as a judicial officer.

[7] Although the non-military offenses of military persons are according to § 3 of the "Militar-Strafgesetzbuch" for the German Empire of June 20, 1872, to be judged according to the general criminal laws, yet the jurisdiction in such cases belongs to the military officials, *i.e.* thus to the disciplinary officials.

[8] "Deutsches Gerichtsverfassungsgesetz", § 13, Prussian Statute of May 29, 1879, dealing with the legal status of students, etc.

this view, the disciplinary law is in principle something entirely independent of the general criminal law. There is nothing to prevent the same act from being punished according to both laws. For it is possible for an act to entail a very slight punishment, or indeed no punishment at all, according to the general criminal law, and at the same time when considered from the disciplinary viewpoint, *i.e.* from the standpoint of maintaining the honor and morality of a class to merit the severest repression. For example, an injury, under § 199 of the German Criminal Code, might because of some compensation or set-off, or of extra-judicial redress, go unpunished by the ordinary judge, while the same act — *e.g.* a public brawl among students or officials — might from the disciplinary standpoint deserve a very sharp penalty.

However, the disciplinary punishment should not be made too independent of the ordinary punishment. Unless one would, as it were, constitute the class in question a State within the State, there must be adopted the general attitude that the ordinary punishment constitutes a sufficient repression for the members of *all* the classes in the State, but that the judge, as far as his range for the exercise of discretion extends, is not prevented from taking into consideration the rank of the accused and his corresponding duties. One would have a sense of injustice if in the *same* case a public officer or a student, for example, should be subjected to *double* punishment, although an effective appeal could not be made to the rule of procedure "Ne bis in idem", since judgment is only passed on that for which the judge in question is competent.[9] (The purely disciplinary phase of the matter cannot be passed upon by the ordinary judge.) Frequently the party to whose hands the disciplinary punishment has been entrusted has no incentive to inflict a special penalty, since the public punishment *at the same time* serves the ends of discipline. This is of importance where there is an *acquittal* by the ordinary judge. If the judge acquits the accused because that which is proven against him does contain the facts necessary for a public offense,[10] it may well be that a state of facts exists which would

[9] I am unable to perceive how the rule "Ne bis in idem" causes difficulties which can be obviated only in the most formal manner, as Laband believes (p. 448).

[10] *Cf.* also *e.g.* § 5 of the Prussian Statute of July 21, 1852: "If there is an acquittal in the ordinary courts, then there can be a disciplinary procedure in respect to those facts which have come under discussion in the trial in the courts only in so far as these facts in themselves con-

justify the infliction of even a very severe disciplinary penalty. For example, the criminal judge may be of the opinion that an injury in the legal sense, a fraud, etc., has not occurred,[11] and yet there may exist facts constituting a lack of the respect due to a superior, sharp practice, etc. In this case the acquittal does not form the slightest obstacle to disciplinary punishment. But quite a different condition obtains if the criminal judge denies the existence, as far as the accused is concerned, of that state of facts which could render the accused amenable to even the disciplinary penalty — if for example, the judge found it not proven that the accused took part in the act, *e.g.* the brawl, with which he is charged. In such a case it is natural that those to whom the infliction of disciplinary penalties is entrusted should respect the acquittal. If the criminal judge, to whom the State has granted means of investigation at least as effective (and in most cases more effective), as those of the disciplinary officials, could not arrive at a conviction, the disciplinary officials may not advance the claim that they have greater powers of discernment. It is in no sense the function of the disciplinary procedure to make amends, in a manner more or less arbitrary, for the failure of the ordinary criminal administration to obtain results.

Effect of Conviction by the Public Criminal Law. — A conviction by the ordinary criminal judge is not conclusive for the disciplinary judge as indicating the guilt of the accused. If the statutory law does not make special provision to the contrary, the arriving at a positive opinion as to guilt must be unhampered, and an accused is entitled to this also before the disciplinary judge. And why should a man who is possibly innocent undergo a double penalty because he has once been formally convicted? On the other hand, in regard to its actual results the conviction is very often conclusive. For example, where a man has been convicted of a dishonorable crime or sentenced to severe punishment, it will be said immediately that we can no longer tolerate him in the circle to which we belong.[12] There can also be the penalty of exclusion (expulsion from the public institutions of learning or dis-

stitute a breach of a duty of public service, without regard for the elements of fact fixed by statute as constituting the violation, misdemeanor or crime."

[11] In this respect, *cf.* also *Leyser*, "Spec." 650, n. 50.

[12] *Cf. e.g.* § 7 of the Prussian statute just referred to. For the reasons given in the text, if a *judicial* investigation is begun, its results will often be awaited. *Cf.* § 4 Abs. 2 of the quoted Prussian Statute; § 78 Abs. 2

missal from employment or from public service.) Logically this should be the only punishment.

Difference of the Public Criminal Law and Disciplinary Law in Attitude towards the Offender. — This brings us to a point where the difference between the disciplinary law and the public criminal law is very marked. It is true that in their *fundamental* idea public criminal law and disciplinary law are not distinguished, and particularly that, as is confirmed by the practice of every disciplinary tribunal, the element of *guilt* is as vital in the disciplinary law as in the public criminal law. However, *incidentally* the uselessness of the individual or his unworthiness may be given consideration in the disciplinary law, and hereby the law is extended or (as the case may be) limited. At least, this is so in all those cases in which the inclusion within the disciplinary circle in question presupposes a special capacity or merit. In this respect there is an element of private law in disciplinary law.[13] The State can not be bound to retain an official in its service and to give him all the advantages of his position, when the State can not use him because he is mentally or physically incompetent to attend to his duties,[14] or because by his actions he has lost the necessary confidence of others and their respect. The institution of learning can not be bound to retain as its fellow or student one who has committed a dishonorable act. This private law aspect comes more into prominence where entrance into the circle in question appears to be either a privilege or else a voluntary act of the individual.

of the Imperial Statute of 1873. It all depends however upon the character of the group subject to the discipline in question. In suspending the previously mentioned statutes of disciplinary investigation, § 14 of the Prussian Statute of May 29, 1871, dealing with the legal status of students says: "The disciplinary action of university authorities is independent of any investigation in regard to the same act conducted in the law courts."

[13] This aspect of the question, which *Heffter* also considered ("Lehrbuch des gemeinen deutschen Strafrechts", p. 178), is argued too one-sidedly by *Laband*, pp. 449 *et seq*. He regards the disciplinary power of the State over its officials as an indemnification in an action in contract. But the question of merit upon which, according to Laband, the possibility of the fulfillment of the contract should depend, necessarily involves a moral decision akin to one of the criminal law. *Hugo Meyer*, "Strafrecht", § 1, note 3, expresses himself as opposed to Laband's too biassed conception. *Pözl* in *Bluntschli-Brater's* "Staatslexicon", IX, p. 696, however, goes too far, since in cases of doubt he favors the analogous application of the fundamental principles of the public criminal law.

[14] This phase of the subject — incapacity to perform official duties because of mental or physical defects — in respect to members of the German Imperial Court is *exclusively* dealt with in § 130 of the German "Gerichtsverfassungsgesetz."

This is especially so in the case of public servants.[15] It would be possible to refer the question of expulsion or of unfitness to a civil tribunal.[16] If for other reasons this were not done, and even where a disciplinary official rendered the decision, nevertheless the actual question remains the same.[17] There exists here by force of a positive legal provision a connection between the disciplinary law, peculiar to itself, and a portion of the law which, while related to it, is not of the same character.

From this viewpoint disciplinary punishment can in the cases mentioned become subject to a certain limitation. If the individual renounces his adherence to the favored class in question and also renounces all the special advantages resulting therefrom, *e.g.* the title, etc., then any infliction upon him of disciplinary punishment seems useless and irrational. Since he has departed from the special class, it knows him no more. Punishment of a *prior* act in violation of the disciplinary law would cause this act to assume the character of a public crime.[18] Such a punishment can be justified only where a money fine fixed prior to the offender's departure is thereafter enforced on the ground that it constitutes a "jus quæsitum", a property right, of the holder of the disciplinary power. This latter could be based upon the consent of the parties interested to the rules laid down for their government.

[15] Together with the question of lack of merit, consideration must also be given to whether the conduct of the official has created an impression on the public. The State is not concerned in things which are not publicly commented upon. A stringent investigation of the morality of its officials would be more injurious than beneficial. The "infamia", upon which the earlier Canon procedure laid so much stress, always had its significance in this respect. For this reason the transfer to the disciplinary procedure of *all* the compulsory methods of the public criminal procedure is not proper, and it can not be admitted that the disciplinary officials apart from special statutory provision possess the rights of a public criminal judge.

[16] As to this, *Heffter*, p. 178, and *Pfeiffer*, "Prakt. Ausführungen", III, pp. 411 *et seq.*

[17] However, in many cases in which a man, without having committed a grave crime, shall have been deprived of his office as a matter of discipline, he must retain a portion of his compensation. As to this, *cf.* also *Herm. Schulze*, "Das preussische Staatsrecht", I, p. 344, and *Leyser*, "Spec." 650, n. 31.

[18] However, an offense previously committed can constitute an exclusion from the group in question. For this reason, § 64 of the German Ordinance of July 1, 1878, dealing with solicitors, very properly provides: "There can be an investigation as to the fitness of a solicitor on account of acts committed before he became such, only when the acts are such as would exclude him from his profession."

For example, the officials of a German university can expel such persons as have obtained admission by fraud and *e.g.* have previously committed a common crime.

Other Varieties of Disciplinary Punishment. — In conclusion, it is possible that a kind of disciplinary law can be founded in private relations through contract, *e.g.* if the workers in a factory subject themselves to factory rules established by the owner and to definite penalties for the breach of these rules. Such a disciplinary law juristically falls *entirely* under the conception of contract. If the factory worker is not satisfied, *e.g.* with the reduction of wages established by the owner of the factory as a penalty, then in the absence of other provisions, recourse may be taken to the civil courts. There is therefore precluded from this punishment every disadvantage which can not be specifically determined in the contract in advance. Therefore all imprisonment is precluded, — at least deprivation of freedom would become illegal and criminally punishable from the moment the prisoner would declare that he desired to no longer be deprived of his freedom.

Where Church and State are actually separated, this also is applicable to those punishments which the clerical power inflicts upon its adherents.[19] The privilege of using imprisonment as an actual punishment is thus obviously always a concession from the State to the Church.

It is not possible to advance a universal and sufficiently definite theory of disciplinary punishment. It all depends upon the purpose of the group to which the disciplinary law applies. Merely its general outlines may be given and its relation to the general criminal authority of the State.

§ 112. **Summary.** — In conclusion, we desire to reduce our theory of criminal law to the following brief principles:

Criminal law is founded upon that moral disapprobation, to a certain extent inevitable, of actions which are immoral, *i.e.* which are detrimental (or dangerous) to those conditions upon which depend the existence and progress of human society. This disapprobation is inevitable to the extent that morality is generally founded and built upon a certain concurrence in the moral opinions of all. This general principle, however, furnishes no answer to the question as to what individual acts should be subject to the organized disapprobation *of the State*. This is determined by numerous considerations of utility. These are identical with justice (which in criminal law can only be relative, *i.e.* historical)

[19] *Cf. Richter,* "*Lehrbuch* des katholischen u. evangelischen Kirchenrechts", edited by *Dove* (7th ed.), p. 690.

only in so far as they are in harmony. That which we usually call punishment is only an external means of emphasizing moral disapprobation: the *method* of punishment is in reality the *amount* of punishment.

Confirmation of our view that punishment ("Strafe") is nothing other than moral disapprobation is furnished by the German language itself.

The word "Strafe" as signifying public punishment is of comparatively recent origin. It does not occur until the time when, on the one hand, the old private vengeance and composition and, on the other, the more despotic treatment of those who were not free had completely disappeared. Originally it had no meaning other than that of censure, or disapprobation.

The original meaning of the word "strafen" most certainly was not to inflict pain or to torment.[1] When criminal law abandoned the old characteristics of private law, and its moral idea acquired a clearer expression, the language with rare discrimination retained the original word.

[1] *Cf. Grimm*, "Deutsche Rechtsalterthümer", pp. 680, 681; *Weigand*, "Deutsches Wörterbuch"; *Lexer*, "Mittelhochdeutsches Wörterbuch"; *Schiller* and *Lübben*, "Mittelniederdeutsches Wörterbuch"; *Schmeller*, "Bayerisches Wörterbuch", under "Strafe" and "Strafen." The original and true meaning of "strafen" is: "To compare something with a rule, an object for measuring, and either to approve of it, or to bring it to its proper condition. Thus the carpenter 'strafft' the wood. 'Straffen' a copy with its original. To hold in good 'Straff.'"

INDEX

www.ingramcontent.com/pod-product-compliance
Lightning Source LLC
La Vergne TN
LVHW092116300926
849161LV00002B/143